7511575985
AF744583
WITHDRAWN FROM
UNIVERSITY OF LEIC
LIBR

REMEDIES FOR BREACH OF PRIVACY

Over the last 15 years, privacy actions have been recognised at common law or in equity across common law jurisdictions, and statutory privacy protections have proliferated. Apex courts are now being called upon to articulate the law governing remedies, including in high-profile litigation concerning phone hacking, covert filming and release of personal information. Yet despite the practical significance of the courts' approach to damages, injunctions and other remedies for breach of privacy, very little has been written on the topic. This book comprehensively analyses these developments from a comparative perspective and provides solutions to issues which are coming to light as higher courts forge this remedial jurisprudence and practitioners look for guidance. Significantly, the essays are important not only for what they say about remedies, but also for the attention they give to the nature of the new privacy actions, providing deep insights into substantive law. The book includes contributions by academics, practitioners and judges from Australia, Canada, England, New Zealand and the United States, who are expert in the legal disciplines implicated by privacy remedies, including torts, equity, public law and conflict of laws. By bringing together this range of perspectives, the book offers authoritative insights into this cutting-edge topic. It will be essential reading for all those seeking to understand and resolve the new issues associated with privacy remedies.

Remedies for Breach of Privacy

Edited by
Jason N E Varuhas
and
N A Moreham

WITHDRAWN FROM
UNIVERSITY OF LEIC
LIBR

•HART•
OXFORD • LONDON • NEW YORK • NEW DELHI • SYDNEY

HART PUBLISHING

Bloomsbury Publishing Plc

Kemp House, Chawley Park, Cumnor Hill, Oxford, OX2 9PH, UK

HART PUBLISHING, the Hart/Stag logo, BLOOMSBURY and the Diana logo are trademarks of Bloomsbury Publishing Plc

First published in Great Britain 2018

Copyright © The editors and contributors severally 2018

The editors and contributors have asserted their right under the Copyright, Designs and Patents Act 1988 to be identified as Authors of this work.

All rights reserved. No part of this publication may be reproduced or transmitted in any form or by any means, electronic or mechanical, including photocopying, recording, or any information storage or retrieval system, without prior permission in writing from the publishers.

While every care has been taken to ensure the accuracy of this work, no responsibility for loss or damage occasioned to any person acting or refraining from action as a result of any statement in it can be accepted by the authors, editors or publishers.

All UK Government legislation and other public sector information used in the work is Crown Copyright ©. All House of Lords and House of Commons information used in the work is Parliamentary Copyright ©. This information is reused under the terms of the Open Government Licence v3.0 (http://www.nationalarchives.gov.uk/doc/open-government-licence/version/3) except where otherwise stated.

All Eur-lex material used in the work is © European Union, http://eur-lex.europa.eu/, 1998–2018.

A catalogue record for this book is available from the British Library.

Library of Congress Cataloging-in-Publication data

Names: Varuhas, Jason, editor. | Moreham, Nicole, editor.

Title: Remedies for breach of privacy / edited by Jason NE Varuhas and Nicole Moreham.

Description: Portland, Oregon : Hart Publishing, 2018. | Includes index.

Identifiers: LCCN 2018021855 (print) | LCCN 2018022079 (ebook) | ISBN 9781509915620 (Epub) | ISBN 9781509915606 (hardback : alk. paper)

Subjects: LCSH: Privacy, Right of. | Privacy, Right of—Criminal provisions.

Classification: LCC K3263 (ebook) | LCC K3263 . R43 2018 (print) | DDC 345/.0256—dc23

LC record available at https://lccn.loc.gov/2018021855

ISBN: HB: 978-1-50991-560-6
ePDF: 978-1-50991-561-3
ePub: 978-1-50991-562-0

Typeset by Compuscript Ltd, Shannon
Printed and bound in Great Britain by TJ International Ltd, Padstow, Cornwall

To find out more about our authors and books visit www.hartpublishing.co.uk. Here you will find extracts, author information, details of forthcoming events and the option to sign up for our newsletters.

UNIVERSITY OF LEICESTER LIBRARY

7511575985

PREFACE

The law of privacy has been developing with extraordinary speed since the turn of the present century, in response to equally rapid developments in technology and social practices. Throughout the course of human history, until the very recent past, the knowledge we could obtain about each other was confined to what could be remembered, or what could be accessed by research in documentary sources. If we wanted to communicate information, we had to speak directly or on the telephone, or send the information through the post. If we wanted to share an image, we had to show it to others in person, or send it through the post to each individual recipient. Few of us had the equipment to enable us to film the activities of others or to record what they said. None of us could surreptitiously examine other people's documents or communications without breaking into or bugging their homes or offices.

Now, search engines provide instant access to most if not all of the information about any individual which has ever entered the public domain. Other information is held on official and private databases, and may be disclosed in a variety of damaging ways. E-mail and social media have enabled individuals to make private information and images available as widely as they please. Changing social practices have led to people sharing intimate communications and images. Portable devices enable them to film and photograph every aspect of their lives, and to share them with the rest of the world. Everyone who uses search engines or social media has their private activities treated as a marketable commodity, as information about their browsing habits and interests is automatically collected and sold to advertisers. Private information held on computers, and private conversations on mobile phones, are liable to be hacked. Passwords and encryption, until recently the preserve of the intelligence services, have become a familiar aspect of everyday life.

Most of these developments have been greeted with more enthusiasm than dismay, as people spend large amounts of time posting images of their activities and checking the images posted by others. The downsides are usually shrugged off. But even the most blasé learn the potentially devastating impact of a loss of privacy when embarrassing information about them is published to the world on social media, or when the intimate photographs they shared with a former partner are posted as 'revenge porn'.

The development of the Internet is not the only reason why privacy has become an increasingly important legal issue. Other changes in social practices have also contributed. Examples in Britain include the development in the media of what might be described as mass voyeurism, the use by the media of new technologies in order to intrude on the private lives of celebrities, and the greater readiness of public servants to share confidential information with the media and to facilitate their intrusions into private life.[1]

These cultural and technological developments raise issues going beyond the law. But the law should in principle be able to address the most serious problems arising from them, even in the absence of statutory regulation. It has long been understood that respect for other people involves respect for their privacy, for all that is intimate and of no true public concern. Examples long pre-date the Internet age: for example, the grant of injunctions to prevent private etchings made by Queen Victoria and Prince Albert from being publicly exhibited,[2] and to prevent the marital confidences of the Duchess of Argyll from being published by the Duke.[3]

As those examples illustrate, there is nothing new about the legal protection of privacy. But the new technology presents new problems of kind as well as of scale. For example, proceedings concerning violations of privacy used to be the concern primarily of celebrities and the media. In the somewhat niche area of practice known as media or entertainment law, advance warning of publication was commonly given, and the remedy usually sought was an interlocutory injunction. Now, every user of the Internet can be his or her own publisher, and the person whose privacy is violated can be anyone he or she has encountered. Notice of publication is not usually given. Once publication has occurred, the information or image is likely to be accessible worldwide. The circumstances in which injunctive relief is sought are therefore different, and the availability of damages becomes an important consideration.

The developments described have resulted in a dramatic increase in the number of cases in which claimants have sought to prevent violations of their privacy, or to obtain redress after violations have taken place. Each jurisdiction has had to respond, by identifying an appropriate legal basis for the protection of privacy and by developing appropriate remedies. Some have extended the equitable protection of confidences. Others have developed a tort of infringement of privacy, or a group of related torts, such as intrusion upon seclusion and the public disclosure of private facts. Others again have relied on statutory protections of privacy or statutory guarantees of human rights. The legal basis of protection may affect a number of aspects of that protection, including the availability of remedies. Arguably, much turns in particular on whether the cause of action is tortious or equitable.

[1] See, eg, *Gulati v MGN Ltd* [2015] EWCA Civ 1291, [2017] QB 149; *R (Ingenious Media Holdings plc) v Revenue and Customs Commissioners* [2016] UKSC 54, [2016] 1 WLR 4164; and *Richard v BBC* [2017] EWHC 1648 (Ch), [2017] EMLR 25.

[2] *Prince Albert v Strange* (1849) 1 H &Tw 1.

[3] *Duchess of Argyll v Duke of Argyll* [1967] Ch 302.

One consequence of these developments is that a number of fundamental issues in the law of remedies have assumed considerable practical significance. For example, if breach of privacy is a tort, can damages be awarded in the absence of loss? What, in law, is loss? Can an interference with a right to privacy be categorised as being in itself a form of loss or damage? If not, what are the relevant heads of damages? Is damage a presumed consequence of the interference? Or are damages for breach of privacy a solatium for distress? Are they designed to vindicate a right? If the law addresses breach of privacy through the equitable route of breach of confidence, are damages an available remedy? Is the measure of damages the same in equity as at common law? Can aggravated, exemplary or punitive damages be awarded? In what circumstances is it appropriate to grant injunctive relief? What is a super-injunction, and when should it be granted? What practical considerations affect the grant of injunctive relief? Can an account of profits be ordered? When can class actions be brought? What is the legal significance of apologies and corrections? How does the classification of the cause of action as tortious or equitable affect the choice of law? How does it affect vicarious liability? What are the cross-border implications of remedies in this area of the law, given the location of Internet users, servers, and the operators of search engines and social media platforms, in a variety of different jurisdictions? Surprisingly little has been written on these topics, despite their practical importance.

The *International Workshop on Remedies for Breach of Privacy*, held in Melbourne in December 2016, from which this book arises, brought together leading scholars, judges and practitioners from Australia, Canada, New Zealand, the United Kingdom and the United States to examine these and other questions. The participants combined expertise in the different areas of the law relevant to this subject, including equity, tort and human rights law, with experience of a range of common law jurisdictions that have adopted different approaches to the subject. The result was a rich and stimulating discussion, the fruits of which are contained in this collection of essays.

The essays are unusually interesting and thoughtful, and also timely. They demonstrate the extent to which a shared language and a shared legal tradition provide the basis for a cross-fertilisation of ideas. They are not only of value to scholars, but provide a fruitful source of ideas for practitioners and judges. They are also, at a time when lawyers in this country are contemplating the prospect of withdrawal from the European Union and possibly also the European Convention on Human Rights, a valuable reminder of the degree of unity of the common law around the world and, above all, of the continuing strength and vitality of the common law tradition.

The Rt Hon Lord Reed
18 December 2017

ACKNOWLEDGEMENTS

This book has its origins in the *International Workshop on Remedies for Breach of Privacy*, held at Melbourne Law School from 12 to 13 December 2016. The coming together of leading academics, practitioners and judges from across the common law world led to two days of rich and stimulating discussion, which produced new thinking on the difficult questions raised by the emergent law of remedies for breach of privacy. We thank the participants for their time, energy and intellectual generosity. The workshop was a collaborative project between Melbourne Law School and Victoria University of Wellington. We are grateful to Melbourne Law School for hosting the event, and to the Law School's Centre for Media and Communications Law for its support of the workshop. We wish to thank the Centre Administrator, Hamish Carr, who provided exceptional administrative support, always with good humour. The workshop would not have been possible without substantial financial support provided by the Melbourne Law School International Collaboration Fund and the Royal Society of New Zealand, for which we are grateful. Thank you also to Etienne Wain and Rosa Laugesen of Victoria University of Wellington for their careful assistance with proofreading. Lastly, we wish to thank Hart Publishing, and in particular Bill Asquith, who originally commissioned this book, and Catherine Minahan for her meticulous copy-editing. As ever, it has been a great pleasure to work with the team at Hart.

Jason NE Varuhas and Nicole Moreham
Melbourne and Wellington
12 March 2018

CONTENTS

LIST OF CONTRIBUTORS

Katy Barnett is Associate Professor of Law at the University of Melbourne.

Jeff Berryman is Distinguished University Professor and Professor of Law at the University of Windsor.

Robyn Carroll is Professor of Law at the University of Western Australia.

Eric Descheemaeker is Professor of Law at the University of Melbourne.

Richard Garnett is Professor of Law at the University of Melbourne.

Rodger Haines QC is Chairperson of the Human Rights Review Tribunal of New Zealand.

Barbara McDonald is Professor of Law at the University of Sydney.

NA Moreham is Associate Professor of Law at Victoria University of Wellington.

Hon Marcia Neave AO is a former Judge of the Victoria Court of Appeal.

David Partlett is the Asa Griggs Candler Professor of Law at Emory University.

Lord Reed is Deputy President of the Supreme Court of the United Kingdom.

Michael Rivette is a barrister at the Victoria Bar.

Megan Richardson is Professor of Law at the University of Melbourne.

David Rolph is Professor of Law at the University of Sydney.

Robert Stevens is the Herbert Smith Freehills Professor of English Private Law at the University of Oxford.

Sir Michael Tugendhat is a former Judge of the High Court of England and Wales.

PG Turner is a University Lecturer and Fellow of St Catharine's College in the University of Cambridge.

Jason NE Varuhas is Associate Professor of Law at the University of Melbourne.

Normann Witzleb is Associate Professor of Law at Monash University.

1

Remedies for Breach of Privacy

JASON NE VARUHAS AND NA MOREHAM

Since the turn of the century, privacy actions have been recognised at common law and in equity across the common law world, while statutory privacy protections have simultaneously proliferated. With the emergence of these actions courts are being called upon to determine which civil remedies are available for breaches of privacy and to enunciate the rules and principles that govern their award, often in the context of high-profile litigation concerning phone hacking, revenge porn, covert filming or the disclosure of sensitive medical, relationship or financial information. The remedial questions thrown up by these cases are among the most important and complex facing common law jurisdictions today. They raise profound issues of principle and classification, which have ramifications that extend well beyond the field of privacy and which implicate fundamental principles such as *ubi ius, ibi remedium*, freedom of expression and the rule of law. The law of remedies is also of great practical importance for plaintiff and defendant alike, for practitioners advising clients, and for courts which are increasingly being called upon to grant relief for serious invasions of privacy.

This book comprehensively analyses the emerging remedial jurisprudence and provides solutions to the doctrinal and theoretical problems that are coming to light as higher courts forge the new law of privacy remedies. Importantly, the essays herein not only make significant headway towards resolving the most challenging questions in the law of privacy remedies, they also provide deep insights into both the law of remedies more generally and the nature and normative underpinnings of the substantive law of privacy.

Three preliminary points can be made about the book's contributors and our aims in bringing them together. First, we have brought together scholars from common law jurisdictions that all face similar questions about the way in which privacy should be protected through remedies. Examination of the differences between these various jurisdictions deepens our understanding of each of those systems. A comparative understanding of privacy developments is also necessary because these developments are inherently interconnected; it is simply not possible fully to understand developments in one system without understanding the comparative context in which they have occurred. Second, we have solicited chapters from academics, practitioners and judges, the last of these having been involved in some of the leading privacy decisions in common law jurisdictions. All legal analysis can be enriched by the different perspectives brought to bear by these groups of legal thinkers. However, nowhere is such an exchange of ideas more valuable than in a field such as the law of remedies, a highly practical field that also raises fundamental issues of principle, coherence and theory. Third, privacy is not an island: the field lies at the intersection of several areas of law, including torts, equity and human rights. We have therefore brought together leading legal thinkers with specialisms in these different fields. As a result the chapters provide rich and varied insights into the core questions at the heart of the emergent law of privacy remedies, debates about privacy remedies are situated within the wider legal landscape, and the implications of these debates for other areas of law are brought squarely into focus.

In this introductory chapter we discuss the emergence of the privacy actions, the importance of addressing the law of remedies, and a core theme that connects the chapters herein: the connection between right and remedy. The chapter then explains our motivations for examining the law of remedies in comparative perspective; in so doing we provide background to the legal developments in each jurisdiction under consideration. In the final section we sketch the core issues in the law of privacy remedies which are the focus of this collection, and introduce the chapters.

I. Beginnings

Just over 20 years ago, the late Professor Peter Birks convened a seminar at All Souls College to examine the topics of privacy and loyalty, which at that time were of emerging practical significance and scholarly interest. The papers presented were ultimately published in a collection edited by Birks, entitled *Privacy and Loyalty*.[1] In his editor's preface, Birks observed that the law's protection of privacy had developed too timidly, contending that privacy needed a fresh start.[2] Whereas privacy had been protected obliquely via pre-existing torts and the equitable action for breach of confidence, there were increasing signs of a judicial willingness to make a 'more honest and direct beginning'.[3] Birks's call for change was echoed by many other scholars, law reformers and judges across the common law world.

Twenty years on the legal landscape has changed fundamentally. The formerly timorous approach to the direct judicial protection of privacy has been superseded by a new boldness of spirit. A wave of judicial activity has swept the common law world. In many jurisdictions judicial innovation over the last 10 to 15 years has resulted in recognition of dedicated actions either at common law or in equity,

[1] P Birks (ed), *Privacy and Loyalty* (Oxford, Clarendon Press, 1997).
[2] P Birks, 'Preface', ibid vii.
[3] ibid vi.

which afford direct protection to privacy. Privacy has therefore been a core site of common law development. It provides this century's best example yet of the common law's capacity to adapt to changed technological, social and economic conditions, and to new societal understandings of fundamental human interests. It is also a paradigmatic modern example of the bottom-up nature of legal development in common law systems. Although lawyers typically focus on apex courts' articulation of the nature and requirements of these new actions, such decisions are often the end-point of incremental legal development at lower court level, as trial judges respond to facts which cry out for a legal remedy. It is these streams of jurisprudence that crystallise into the fully-formed actions we now know so well. The privacy actions are new; the path of the law familiar.

Given the emergence of dedicated privacy actions in most jurisdictions, the focus of scholarly and judicial attention has shifted away from the question of whether privacy ought to be afforded direct judicial protection. While that question remains of theoretical interest, in most jurisdictions the courts have given their answer. Privacy has been given the fresh start that Birks and many others argued for. It is no longer a question of whether to protect the privacy interest but how.

II. Why Remedies Matter

This collection is concerned with the principles that govern relief in these new privacy actions. The essays examine which remedies should be available, their nature, and the legal principles governing their grant and terms. The remedial principles in the new field of privacy are not well-established and in general have not been the subject of extended treatment either in intermediate or apex courts or in scholarly work. The relative paucity of deep thinking about privacy remedies is obviously a function of the novelty of such claims. But the gap also reflects a general propensity of both judges and commentators to focus on substantive law at the expense of remedies (though as we shall see, the extent to which substantive and remedial law can sensibly be considered in isolation is highly questionable).

The amount of attention paid to privacy remedies is, however, inversely proportional to the importance of remedies principles. The legal principles governing remedies for breach of privacy are of acute practical significance. For example, whether a plaintiff can obtain an injunction to prevent a breach of his or her privacy can have a fundamental impact on that plaintiff's wellbeing; consider, for example, an application for interim relief to restrain publication of a news story that, if published, could destroy the plaintiff's home life and seriously affect his or her family, or an application for a prohibitory injunction to restrain ongoing repeated intrusions upon the plaintiff's solitude, which are causing serious distress, anxiety and upset. Damages rules, governing recovery and quantum, have a significant impact on the life of a plaintiff who is facing the cost of psychological counselling or days off work because of stress caused by a privacy intrusion. Remedies make rights real in practice for plaintiffs. They can provide redress and solace, punish and condemn outrageous violations, potentially deter future harmful conduct, and vindicate interests that are of importance to individuals and society as a whole. On the flipside, they can impose heavy burdens on defendants, including heavy financial loss, reputational damage and potentially serious incursions upon liberty.

Remedies also raise core questions of principle, most prominently the balance to be struck between free expression and open justice on the one hand, and protection of privacy and vindication of the rule of law on the other, especially in the context of specific relief. Privacy is a core location – if not *the* core location – of current debates over cutting-edge issues of principle within the field of remedies. As the restitution debates of the 1990s showed, new fields often stimulate new thinking. This in turn has ramifications for established legal principle and modes of analysis. Privacy remedies raise numerous fundamental questions that have the potential to have this kind of impact. Can breach of a privacy right in itself constitute a compensable harm, and when should such 'normative' damages be available? Are heads such as mental harm or loss of dignity recoverable in equity? Ought an account of profits to be available exceptionally for breach of a common law privacy right? Are Lord Cairns' Act damages recoverable where the privacy action is an equitable one? Should the novel head of vindicatory damages be adopted in the field of privacy? Should court-ordered apologies form part of the arsenal of judicial remedies? How do remedial principles at common law or in equity interrelate with remedial principles developed in the context of statutory privacy protections? What are the conflict-of-laws implications of legal classification of privacy actions as equitable or common law, and in what forum does one sue for breaches of privacy that transcend national borders?

The recent establishment of privacy actions, the growing incidence of claims, the importance of remedial issues as a matter of practice and principle, and the relative paucity of serious thinking about remedial issues in the field of privacy, provide the prompt, and illustrate the pressing need for this collection. Importantly, while the immediate focus of these essays is privacy, the significance of the insights they offer extends well beyond this immediate field.

III. The Connection Between Right and Remedy

Consideration of remedial principles is important in itself. But it is also important because it sheds light upon core questions about the nature and proper categorisation of the emergent privacy actions, including – in jurisdictions where the issue is in doubt – whether the action is or ought to be properly categorised as a creature of equity or tort (and which type of tort). Indeed, the essays in this book – often working from questions about remedies to questions about rights – provide some of the most striking insights into the nature of the substantive law of privacy. This is because remedial issues cannot be properly understood and resolved in principled fashion without a sound appreciation of the nature of the primary obligations (and protected interests), breach of which gives rise to remedial liabilities. That the common law has been marked by an unbreakable bond between right and remedy flows from the historical nature of the common law as a law of *remedies*: primary norms and substantive law were secreted in the interstices of remedial forms.[4] The law worked from remedies to rights. Whilst the forms of action may be dead, they continue (as Maitland observed[5]) to influence both scholarly thinking and judicial adjudication from the grave.

But the importance of linking primary norm and remedy is not simply a matter of history, and it would be an error to dismiss such modes of thinking and analysis as anachronistic – though this has not stopped some from maintaining this perspective. The common law continues to observe the connection between right and remedy for fundamental reasons of principle and pragmatism. If remedies were informed by policies with no connection to the normative concerns underpinning the creation of primary rights, the law would be incoherent. Practically speaking, if remedies were untethered from the primary norms to which they relate, there would be a significant risk of remedies cutting across and undermining the motivations underpinning recognition of a law of privacy in the first place; the law's goals would be frustrated. More generally, if remedies are analysed in isolation of rights, it is not apparent why a given remedy ought to issue for breach of a given right; there would be no necessary or logical connection between right and remedy. Furthermore, to cast off the normative framework provided by the nature of primary rights in considering remedies would leave scholars, practitioners and judges mid-ocean, bereft of the equipment needed for navigation;[6] we would have no framework by reference to which we could resolve issues relating to remedies in a principled fashion, or at least it would not be clear why we should choose one framework over any other.

All this reinforces the fundamental importance of considering the substantive law of any cause of action alongside remedies, and vice versa. Exploration of the bond between right and remedy therefore forms a core theme of this collection.

IV. Comparison and Context

This collection, in common with the *International Workshop on Remedies for Breach of Privacy* from which the collection derives, considers remedial questions

[4] Paraphrasing HS Maine, *Dissertations on Early Law and Custom* (London, J Murray, 1891) 389.

[5] FW Maitland, *Equity; also, The Forms of Action at Common Law* (Cambridge, Cambridge UP, 1909) 1.

[6] Paraphrasing P Birks, 'Preface' in P Birks (ed), *The Classification of Obligations* (Oxford, Clarendon Press, 1997) vi.

both within different jurisdictions and from a cross-jurisdictional perspective. There are at least three reasons for considering this range of perspectives: commonality, interconnectedness, difference.

First, the jurisdictions considered herein – Australia, New Zealand, Canada, the United States and England – share a bedrock of commonality that makes comparison feasible. As common law systems they have a common legal heritage. Each jurisdiction has also had to grapple with a common set of questions about whether and how to afford direct legal protection to privacy and, now that dedicated privacy actions have been recognised, how to approach judicial remedies for breach. These commonalities mean that these jurisdictions can usefully learn from each other, regardless of whether the solutions they devise for given remedial problems are different or the same. Comparative experiences may suggest a range of potential solutions to given questions, reveal unexpected practical difficulties with certain approaches, or stimulate new thinking and novel solutions.

Second, apart from the United States, each of these jurisdictions has witnessed significant legal development in the field of privacy over the same 15-year period, with most recognising new dedicated privacy actions during this time. In fashioning this new field the courts of each jurisdiction have considered comparative common law developments. The phenomenon of transnational judicial 'conversations' has therefore been pronounced in this field:[7] privacy has been a core site of rich and fruitful cross-jurisdictional discourse and learning. The longer experience of the United States, with its privacy torts, has heavily influenced legal change across other common law jurisdictions, either explicitly or obliquely; the American model thus provides a useful common frame of reference for considering privacy developments across the different jurisdictions examined in this collection. The developments are thus interconnected; comparative legal development provides a fundamental aspect of the wider context of legal change in single jurisdictions. It is likely that courts will continue to look abroad when fashioning the law of remedies, in turn reinforcing the importance of a comparative understanding of remedial principles.

If the first reason for a comparative understanding of remedial privacy principles is commonality, the third is difference. Different jurisdictions have developed different types of action to protect privacy. Also, the law of each jurisdiction has been shaped by local conditions and contextual features, meaning that, for example, common labels, such as 'loss' or 'vindication', may upon closer examination refer to quite distinct concepts or operate differently from one jurisdiction to the next. Comparative analysis can bring these variables and their influence sharply into focus, and thus deepen our understanding of given legal principles and the forces that have shaped them, and therefore shed light on the reasons for similarities and differences in remedial responses across jurisdictions. Importantly, in considering normative questions over what principles ought to govern remedies,

[7] Borrowing the phrase from C McCrudden, 'Common Law of Human Rights? Transnational Judicial Conversations on Constitutional Rights' (2000) 20 *OJLS* 499.

one must understand the overarching model of privacy protection that prevails in a given jurisdiction – as remedies must cohere with that model – as well as wider contextual features. This helps to ensure that remedial principles 'fit' within local conditions and properly serve local needs. Understanding such phenomena is critical in gauging the appropriateness of cross-jurisdictional transplants and the borrowing of ideas.[8] The 'right' answer to a given remedial question will depend on the context in which the question arises.

It is important, then, that this introductory chapter sketches some of the key variations among the jurisdictions considered in this book – Australia, New Zealand, Canada, the United States, England.

A. Different Models

Different models of privacy protection prevail in different jurisdictions. In Australia, the High Court has left open the possibility of developing a privacy tort.[9] A number of lower courts have supported such a development, but there is as yet no explicit endorsement by a higher court. In the absence of a recognised action at common law, and in light of the Commonwealth Government's lack of action on the Law Reform Commission's recommendation of creation of a statutory privacy tort,[10] lower courts have used the breach of confidence action to afford privacy protection where possible (without reorienting the substantive law to the degree that English courts have). The two most important cases – *Giller v Procopets*[11] and *Wilson v Ferguson*[12] – both concerned what is known colloquially as 'revenge porn', where the defendant discloses intimate videos or images of the plaintiff, a former partner, to third parties. The deployment of breach of confidence in these types of cases has led to some controversy, however. The action's two key requirements – that the information have the necessary quality of confidence about it and that it was imparted in circumstances importing an obligation of confidence – are flexible enough. But courts, concerned to give a remedy in cases that clearly demand one, have stretched the remedial parameters of the confidence action by suggesting awards may be available for mental distress and pain and suffering, and that damages may be awarded under the local equivalent of the Lord Cairns' Act jurisdiction where the action is in equity as opposed to common law. There may, at some point, be a limit to how much further these extensions can continue.

[8] See further on this point, C Saunders, 'Transplants in Public Law' in M Elliott, JNE Varuhas and SW Stark (eds), *The Unity of Public Law? Doctrinal, Theoretical and Comparative Perspectives* (Oxford, Hart Publishing, 2018).

[9] See *Australian Broadcasting Corporation v Lenah Game Meats Pty Ltd* (2001) 208 CLR 199.

[10] See Australian Law Reform Commission, *Serious Invasions of Privacy in the Digital Era: Final Report*, Report No 123 (2014).

[11] *Giller v Procopets* [2008] VSCA 236.

[12] *Wilson v Ferguson* [2015] WASC 15.

In the United States, dedicated privacy torts have long been recognised in the common law of individual States. According to the prevailing description of the torts in the *Restatement (Second) of Torts*[13] (for which William Prosser was Chief Reporter, and which draws heavily on his seminal 1960 article on privacy),[14] there are four such privacy actions: intrusion upon the plaintiff's seclusion or solitude into his or her private affairs; public disclosure of embarrassing private facts about the plaintiff; publicity which places the plaintiff in a false light in the public eye; and appropriation, for the defendant's advantage, of the plaintiff's name or likeness. The first two of these torts have heavily influenced the development of privacy protection across common law jurisdictions.

Courts in New Zealand and Ontario have, following the United States model, recognised both the intrusion and disclosure privacy torts. Unlike in England, there was little contention in these jurisdictions about recognising these new actions and situating them in the law of torts. Breach of confidence, which as discussed below was the vehicle for developing privacy rights in English law, was expressly dismissed by the New Zealand Court of Appeal in *Hosking v Runting* as unfit for purpose.[15] The uncoupling of privacy protection from breach of confidence in these jurisdictions has made extending privacy protection to cases of intrusion upon seclusion, such as spying by government or phone hacking absent any disclosure of the obtained information, much easier. For example, the Judge in New Zealand's leading intrusion case had little hesitation in treating the tort of intrusion into seclusion as 'a logical adjunct to [the] tort of wrongful publication of private facts'.[16] Indeed in Ontario the intrusion tort was recognised first, with the disclosure tort developing subsequently.[17] In contrast, it is difficult to see how breach of confidence can do the business in cases that do not involve disclosure without fundamentally changing the action beyond recognition. Breach of confidence may, however, continue to play a role in protecting privacy in disclosure-type cases even where tortious liability exists (though the touchstone of that action remains conscience rather than protection of privacy).

In England, the classification of the action for misuse of private information has evolved over time. Breach of confidence was originally the vehicle for developing the privacy action. Courts, including the House of Lords in the leading decision of *Campbell*, held that the horizontal effect of the Human Rights Act 1998 meant that they were obliged to develop that action consistently with the right to respect for private life in Article 8 of the European Convention on Human Rights (ECHR) (although even in *Campbell*, Lord Nicholls referred to the action as a 'tort').[18] Strategically, development of breach of confidence provided a more incremental

[13] American Law Institute, *Restatement (Second) of Torts* (Philadelphia, PA, ALI, 1977) §§652A–652E.
[14] WL Prosser, 'Privacy' (1960) 48 *California Law Review* 383.
[15] *Hosking v Runting* [2005] 1 NZLR 1, [23]–[53].
[16] *C v Holland* [2012] 3 NZLR 672, [75].
[17] *Jones v Tsige* 2012 ONCA 32 (intrusion tort); *Jane Doe 464533* 2016 ONSC 541 (disclosure tort).
[18] *Campbell v MGN Ltd* [2004] 2 AC 457.

and less radical way to introduce the privacy action than creating a novel action in tort, and enabled the House of Lords to draw support from prior authority. As Sir Robert Megarry V-C observed in a much earlier privacy case, '[t]he extension of the existing laws and principles is one thing, the creation of an altogether new right is another'.[19] Further, confining legal development to the confidence action enabled the House to dodge the contentious issue of whether a general privacy action should be developed, the confidence action being narrowly focused on cases of disclosure of confidential – or now private – information. Subsequent case law indicated that even though the action of misuse of private information was of the confidence genus, it ought to be considered distinct from the 'traditional' confidence action.[20] Indeed, in the 2015 case of *Vidal-Hall*, the English Court of Appeal held that the misuse of private information action was properly classified as a tort for the purposes of conflict of laws doctrine.[21] Since the Supreme Court has not yet expressly ruled on this question, classification of the action could still be said to be open to debate, but there is a strong argument that the action has cast off its equitable origins (not least as the Supreme Court declined leave to appeal in *Vidal-Hall*). Further, Article 8 of the ECHR demands horizontal protection not just of informational privacy, but also of the bundle of privacy interests protected by that Article, including physical privacy, and an 'intrusion' variant of the privacy action has been recognised at lower court level in England.[22] Although such developments can be reconciled with precedent, they cannot be housed within breach of confidence without doing violence to the coherence of that action.[23] All that said, the courts have stressed the need for breach of confidence and privacy to develop consistently where possible, and it is clear that the former will continue to be relied on in cases where the parties are in a traditional relationship of trust and confidence.

These jurisdictional differences are important, because variation in an action's history and in the model of protection ultimately adopted will affect decisions about remedies. Most importantly, different ramifications will follow, and different remedial issues will arise, depending on whether the action is one in equity or at common law. For example, the availability of damages for mental distress would be relatively uncontroversial in the context of a privacy tort that was actionable per se and conceptualised as protecting interests which were dignitary in character. However, the availability of awards for mental distress is more controversial in the context of the equitable action of breach of confidence in light of, for example, the traditional focus on proprietary as opposed to personal interests in the field of equity; indeed, compensation is itself an emergent remedy in equity.[24] On the

[19] *Malone v Metropolitan Commissioner of Police* [1979] Ch 344, 372.

[20] See *Imerman v Tchenguiz* [2011] 2 WLR 592.

[21] *Vidal-Hall v Google Inc* [2015] 3 WLR 409.

[22] *Goodwin v News Groups Newspapers* [2011] EMLR 27.

[23] NA Moreham, 'Beyond Information: Physical Privacy in English Law' (2014) 73 *CLJ* 350.

[24] See further, S Degeling and JNE Varuhas (eds), *Equitable Compensation and Disgorgement of Profit* (Oxford, Hart Publishing, 2017).

other hand, the availability of an account of profits for a profit-driven disclosure of private information would be relatively uncontroversial in the field of equity, whereas the availability of such awards in the field of torts, outside of intellectual property torts, is highly controversial given the traditional focus upon compensation and the historical separation of law and equity. If the action is a tort, the type of tort might also affect the approach to damages. For example, in torts for which loss is the gist of the action, such as negligence, damages are generally limited to 'factual' losses, such as physical injury, mental harm or economic loss. For torts for which breach of a basic right is the gist of the action, such as battery or defamation, on the other hand, damages have included damages for the interference with the right itself, irrespective of whether factual loss is suffered.[25] New Zealand is a curious example in this regard, as the lead judgment in *Hosking* made clear that the action for disclosure of private facts is analogous to other rights-based torts, and is actionable per se, but on the other hand included several statements[26] suggesting a focus on recovery of factual losses such as distress, though the matter remains to be worked out in future case law. The types of privacy action recognised may also affect the development of remedies. For example, it might be plausibly argued that if protection is limited to disclosure cases, adequate protection is provided by the availability of injunctive relief to prevent disclosure and delivery up of the private information so that it can no longer be distributed, coupled with the availability of an account of profits to deter profit-making disclosures. However, in intrusion upon seclusion cases, one might consider the remedial arsenal incomplete if there is no provision for compensation for distress caused by such intrusions, especially as monetary remedies such as an account will be of less relevance given there may be no disclosure.

B. Different Contexts

Beyond the model of privacy protection, wider contextual features may also affect both the operation of the legal rules in a given system and normative questions concerning remedies. Such contextual features have clearly shaped, and explain core differences between, the privacy actions in different jurisdictions, and are likely also to affect – explicitly or obliquely – the development of the law of remedies in each jurisdiction. For example in the United States the First Amendment has had an extraordinary effect on the development (or more accurately, retardation) of the protection of privacy. Any consideration of privacy protection and remedies in that jurisdiction would therefore be incomplete without consideration of the extraordinary weight placed on free expression.

[25] See JNE Varuhas, *Damages and Human Rights* (Oxford, Hart Publishing, 2016) ch 2.
[26] *Hosking* (n 15) [126], [128], [138].

In England, Article 8 of the ECHR has been a central driver of legal development and operated as a counterbalance to the pull of freedom of expression; in contrast to the United States, under the European Convention, and hence under English law, privacy and freedom of expression are, *ceteris paribus*, of equal weight. This difference plays out in different ways, including in a much more liberal approach to the grant of prior restraint in England, and more restrictive liability rules in the United States. Further, in England there has been persistent public concern about press conduct[27] and political inaction in its wake, leaving the courts to 'sort out the mess'.[28] It is notable in this regard that the most significant damages judgment[29] in England resulted from endemic phone-hacking practices by tabloid newspapers, and that many major cases, including the landmark decision in *Campbell*, concerned press intrusion.

In both Canada and New Zealand the courts, in developing privacy actions, have drawn inspiration from the respective sections of the Canadian Charter and New Zealand Bill of Rights that protect against search and seizure, and the inclusion of privacy as a fundamental human right in multilateral international treaties such as the International Convention on Civil and Political Rights and the United Nations Convention on the Rights of the Child. This is despite the lack of an enumerated right to privacy – and explicit recognition of a right to free expression – in each country's domestic rights instrument. Canadian and New Zealand courts have also been influenced by the evolving statutory protection of privacy in their respective jurisdictions, which has been interpreted as evidence of the importance placed on privacy by contemporary society. The privacy actions recognised in the United States have also been highly influential, though the Canadian and New Zealand jurisprudence has been largely shorn of the sort of free speech fundamentalism that characterises the United States jurisprudence, meaning that the influence of United States doctrine is largely confined to the formulation of the elements and general structure of the actions. What appear at first sight to be the same actions may therefore operate quite differently in different jurisdictions because of varying background assumptions about the relative importance of given values. Though in New Zealand certain of the judgments in *Hosking* suggest that free expression may yet cast a shadow over the development of privacy law,[30] not least in the light of a human rights tradition that favours proceduralism over substantive entitlements[31] (albeit the lead judgment[32] did stress that in developing the disclosure tort it would be necessary to consider the differences in the

[27] See, eg, *An Inquiry into the Culture, Practices and Ethics of the Press: Report*, HC 780-I (2012).

[28] D Feldman, 'Privacy-related Rights and their Social Value' in Birks (ed) (n 1) 50.

[29] *Gulati v MGN Ltd* [2016] FSR 12 (Ch), affirmed [2016] 2 WLR 1217 (CA).

[30] Note in particular the strong emphasis on free expression in the dissenting judgments of Keith and Anderson JJ.

[31] As observed in *Hosking* (n 15) [92]. The proceduralist underpinnings of the New Zealand Bill of Rights Act 1990 reflect in particular the intellectual influence at the time of drafting of JH Ely, *Democracy and Distrust* (Cambridge, MA, Harvard UP, 1980).

[32] *Hosking* (n 15) [76].

constitutional frameworks of New Zealand and the United States). The differing relative weight given to privacy versus free expression in New Zealand compared to, say, England may help to explain why the New Zealand Court of Appeal did not, when importing the disclosure tort from the United States, eschew the high threshold for breach while English courts rejected it: in New Zealand, for liability to be established, the plaintiff must show both that he or she had a reasonable expectation of privacy and that disclosure would be highly offensive to a reasonable person, whereas in England the courts simply ask whether the claimant had a reasonable expectation of privacy which, if breached, establishes prima facie liability.[33] These differences may feed through to remedies: for example in *Hosking*, Tipping J indicated that, in general, there would be very limited scope for interim relief that impinged upon free expression.[34] Further, in contrast to English jurisprudence,[35] the judgments in *Hosking* do not seem to contemplate damages for the infringement in itself (though the issue of damages was not examined in great detail).[36] It is worth noting in this regard that jurisdictions such as New Zealand and Canada have not experienced many of the intrusive media practices that prevail in England, at least not with the same prevalence.

In respect of Australia, regard must be had to, inter alia, the implied freedom of political communication under the Constitution (and the lack of any right to privacy or rights against search and seizure therein), the Federal Government's lack of action on recent Law Reform Commission recommendations to enact a statutory privacy action,[37] greater opposition to any fusion of law and equity than in other common law jurisdictions (especially in New South Wales) and, more generally, the lack of any federal bill of rights and the comparatively narrow conception of the judicial role under the Australian separation of powers. All of these factors could militate against bold judicial steps towards recognition of a free-standing privacy action and the muscular approach to remedies that has been taken in other jurisdictions.[38]

V. Core Issues

The chapters in this collection interrogate core issues in the emergent law of remedies for breach of privacy. This section will outline each issue in turn and introduce the chapters.

[33] Tipping J explicitly referred to protection of free speech in formulating the relevant legal tests: ibid [255]–[256].

[34] ibid [258].

[35] See *Gulati* (n 29).

[36] *Hosking* (n 15) [126], [128], [138] (indicating a focus on factual harms).

[37] Australian Law Reform Commission (n 10).

[38] Albeit note that various of the judgments in *Lenah Game Meats* (n 9) indicate openness to further legal development (see, eg, [132], [328]–[336]).

A. Injunctions

The decision whether to grant an injunction to protect privacy implicates a complex web of interests and requires courts to strike a sometimes difficult balance between competing interests. The question of how to strike this balance is perhaps most difficult where plaintiffs seek to restrain the publication of information which they allege violates their privacy rights, especially where a so-called super-injunction is claimed; that is an injunction, a term of which is that the existence of the injunction and proceedings cannot be disclosed. Courts must, in making decisions about whether to grant such relief, consider not only the importance of protecting privacy, but also other fundamental interests including freedom of expression and open justice. Sir Michael Tugendhat's chapter squarely addresses these issues, his analysis being informed by his long experience at the coalface, Sir Michael being one of the leading judges who forged the English law of privacy. His chapter offers a careful analysis of the law and practice of privacy injunctions in England, in particular pre-publication interim non-disclosure orders – including consideration of the leading case of *PJS*[39] – examining the circumstances in which such orders may be necessary and justified. The chapter explores the origins of super-injunctions, the evolution of the law and practice of such relief over time, and the controversy that has sometimes attended grant of such orders; Sir Michael discusses and responds to misreporting and misinformed criticism of the use of such injunctions to protect privacy rights. Importantly, in addition to those interests already mentioned, he places emphasis on the maintenance of the rule of law as a fundamental value that ought to inform consideration of injunctive relief, specifically in the context of the relationship between the courts and Parliament.

The issue of injunctions, and particularly prior restraint, is one that demonstrates the importance of local factors in shaping the law. In this regard the law as it has developed in England and other common law jurisdictions such as Australia, discussed in Sir Michael's chapter, and Canada, discussed in Jeff Berryman's chapter, stands in contrast to the approach in the United States. As David Partlett elaborates in his chapter on the approach to privacy remedies in the United States, prior restraint is frowned upon and rarely granted because of the privileged position of the First Amendment within the legal system. Injunctive relief is available, but only in a narrow band of cases where property rights and harm to dignity combine with minimal impingement upon free speech.

Particular challenges in respect of compliance with, and thus the efficacy of, injunctions can arise within the field of privacy. A number of these challenges are considered in the chapters. For example, Sir Michael considers the use that has been made of parliamentary privilege by Members of Parliament to defy non-disclosure orders, and the case of *PJS*, in which an order was maintained despite the wide availability of the relevant information on the Internet. Jeff Berryman, in

[39] *PJS v News Group Newspapers Ltd* [2016] AC 1081.

considering the Canadian position, examines the challenges posed in cases where the plaintiff seeks removal of information from the Internet, including the extra-territorial reach of court orders.

Other chapters consider important questions of general principle as they apply in the field of privacy. The chapter by Barbara McDonald and David Rolph and that by Peter Turner set out the various ways in which the law governing injunctions is affected by whether the privacy action is classified as breach of confidence, for which injunctions have historically been a core remedy in equity's exclusive jurisdiction, or a tort, in which case injunctions will be granted in equity's auxiliary jurisdiction. Those two chapters, as well as that by Megan Richardson, Hon Marcia Neave and Michael Rivette, consider the potential for so-called Lord Cairns' Act damages to be awarded for a past breach of confidence in cases where the court would have had jurisdiction to entertain an application for an injunction to prevent disclosure. They focus on the important Victoria Court of Appeal decision in *Giller* – in which Neave delivered the lead judgment and Rivette was counsel.[40] The chapters reach different views on the acceptability in principle of such awards. In the context of English law, the chapter by Jason Varuhas considers in detail when, if the privacy action is classified as a tort, damages in lieu of an injunction ought to be awarded and how such damages should be assessed. The chapter by Robert Stevens also discusses such damages.

In addition to analysis of injunctions, the chapter by Turner examines the availability and role of a range of other forms of specific relief in equity, such as delivery up and the cancellation or destruction of documents or chattels, while the chapters by Rodger Haines QC and Normann Witzleb consider various orders available under data protection statutes.

B. Money Remedies

The question of what principles should govern money remedies for breach of privacy, including rules of quantification, is perhaps the most pressing issue in the emerging law of privacy across common law jurisdictions. Many questions of basic principle remain unresolved, including the types of available damages, the nature of compensatory awards and the heads of recoverable loss that ought to be recognised. Deeper scholarly work on the theoretical underpinnings of damages for breach of privacy has also been in short supply.

This section will set out the various aspects of money remedies discussed in this collection. It should be noted that in addition to the chapters discussed in this section, which focus on specific issues relating to money awards, the chapters by Berryman and Partlett (discussed in section V.E below) provide a general analysis of the law and practice of damages for breach of privacy in each of Canada and the

[40] *Giller* (n 11).

United States, while the chapters by Witzleb and Haines (discussed in section V.F) consider the law and practice of money awards under privacy statutes.

i. Loss

One of the core issues, which forms the key focus of four chapters in this collection, is the availability of damages for breach of privacy in the absence of consequential or factual losses such as negative physical, emotional or economic effects. Consideration of this issue is spurred by contemporary academic writing, which has argued that damages for breach of a right in itself are and ought to be available in certain tort contexts. In the field of privacy, consideration of the issue is prompted by the seminal English judgment of Mann J, upheld by the Court of Appeal, in the phone-hacking case of *Gulati*, in which he held that substantial – ie more than nominal – compensatory damages could be awarded for the interference with privacy in itself and that such damages, while compensatory in nature, should be distinguished from damages for factual losses such as emotional distress.[41] Such damages may be recovered for the wrong regardless of whether the claimant suffers any negative factual effects, such as physical or psychological harm, mental distress or economic loss.

There is much terminological and conceptual confusion that attends discussion of damages absent factual loss. For this reason it is important at this stage to distinguish the type of award in *Gulati* from two other types of awards. First, so-called 'vindicatory damages' have been awarded in a number of Privy Council appeals from the Caribbean.[42] These types of awards (discussed further below) are not compensatory, whereas the award in *Gulati* is. Second, as discussed in the chapter by Berryman on Canadian privacy remedies, in the important case of *Jones v Tsige* the Ontario Court of Appeal recognised a type of damages for intrusion upon seclusion that appears to be available absent factual loss, but the exact conceptual nature of which is not clear.[43] Later jurisprudence may well reveal that such awards are similar to those recognised in *Gulati*. But given the 'functional' conception of damages for non-pecuniary loss in Canada – which contrasts with the 'conceptual' approach in *Gulati* – it may be that such awards do not purport to restore through a money award the right that has been invaded but are rather a solatium designed to bring comfort or happiness to the plaintiff for the violation of his or her rights.[44]

[41] See *Gulati* (n 29).

[42] See, eg, *Merson v Cartwright* [2005] UKPC 38; *Attorney General of Trinidad and Tobago v Ramanoop* [2006] 1 AC 328.

[43] *Jones* (n 17).

[44] On the functional approach to non-pecuniary loss, and competing approaches more generally, see A Ogus, *The Law of Damages* (London, Butterworths, 1973) 194–96, 206–18. See also, on the Canadian functional tradition: J Berryman, 'Non-Pecuniary Damages for Personal Injury: A Reflection on the Canadian Experience' in E Quill and RJ Friel (eds), *Damages and Compensation Culture Comparative Perspectives* (Oxford, Hart Publishing, 2016).

Returning to the awards made in *Gulati*, many questions arise in respect of such damages, ranging from their conceptual nature and normative justification to more practical questions about how judges ought to quantify such losses. The chapters offer a plurality of perspectives on this issue. Jason Varuhas and Nicole Moreham support the availability of compensatory awards absent factual loss, while Robert Stevens and Eric Descheemaeker oppose their availability for breach of privacy, each on different grounds.

In his chapter, Varuhas argues that such damages are best conceptualised as 'normative' damages for the wrongful interference with the privacy interest in itself. They are normative in the sense that they do not respond to a factual loss but rather compensate for a loss constructed by the law so as to give effect to the protective and vindicatory policies that underpin the creation of fundamental rights. Such damages have long been available in the context of other actions that protect basic rights, principally torts actionable per se, such as trespass to land, false imprisonment and defamation. Varuhas argues that such damages ought also to be available for breach of privacy, as the privacy action in English law shares all of the fundamental features of torts actionable per se, is underpinned by similar protective and vindicatory policies, and protects an interest which is similarly basic. Put simply, such damages give effect at the remedial stage to those policies that underpin creation of the primary rights. The chapter goes on to explain in detail how such awards can be quantified in a principled fashion, which is distinct from the method by which compensatory damages for consequential factual losses such as distress are quantified, and distinguishes such damages from exemplary damages, restitutionary damages, vindicatory damages and damages in lieu of an injunction. For good measure, Varuhas also argues that the English Court of Appeal was, with respect, right to reject an argument that damages for breach of privacy should follow the remedial practices of the European Court of Human Rights.

Consistently with these ideas, Moreham's chapter explores the conceptual nature of damages for the loss of privacy in itself. She argues that the availability of such damages is consistent both with widely held philosophical, sociological and psychological understandings of the nature of privacy harms and, as a result, with the reasons why English courts developed the misuse of private information action in the first place. Indeed, the availability of such damages follows from the action being per se actionable, that is actionable absent any proof of actual harm such as distress. She contends such damages should be understood as compensating for the loss of dignity and autonomy inherent in all breaches of privacy, and connects right and remedy by explaining that the need to protect these interests also provides the justification for the legal right to privacy itself. Damages for distress and other harms are distinct from damages for loss of autonomy and dignity, and should also be recoverable.

Stevens and Descheemaeker are more sceptical about recent developments. Stevens' important book, *Torts and Rights*, was among the first pieces of scholarship to recognise and systematically analyse the availability of damages absent loss in the law of torts.[45] He has argued that such damages are best explained as substitutive; that is, they are a second-best substitute for performance of a primary obligation, and are distinct from compensatory damages. However, in his chapter in this collection he argues such damages should not be available for breach of privacy. He offers sceptical reflections on the development of a privacy action in English law, questioning the justifications for affording legal protection to privacy through the imposition of liability. He argues that the justification for the rights that we have in the law of torts is that those rights maintain equal freedom; rights ought not to be recognised simply to secure virtuous behaviour, or to protect people from misery or distress. However, he argues that protection of privacy cannot be justified on the basis of equal freedom, and considers other alternative rationales such as autonomy and human rights to be similarly unconvincing. Given his conclusion that the normative underpinnings of the privacy action are questionable and that privacy is not of the same order as other basic rights protected by the common law, he argues that if such an action is to be recognised then damages should only be available for consequential factual harm and substitutive damages should be ruled out.

Descheemaeker argues against recent privacy developments for a different reason. In his view, it is incoherent, within the emerging law of privacy, to allow recovery of compensatory damages for both the violation of the right in itself and the intangible consequential harms that flow from the wrong, such as mental distress. He argues these are alternative, not cumulative, bases for damages; in other words, the law can either select a model in which the interference is a loss in itself or it can elect a model in which recoverable losses are those consequential upon the interference, but not both. The availability of both types of damages within the emergent law of privacy therefore melds what Desheemaeker considers to be two distinct analytical models of conceptualising loss. This, he says, leads to incoherence and double recovery. He argues that this melding of analytical frameworks is at variance with what he considers to be tort 'orthodoxy', and that a clear justification is therefore required if damages for breach of privacy are to diverge from the approach within the rest of tort.

While the foregoing chapters focus on damages for a breach of privacy in itself, the chapter by Richardson, Neave and Rivette focuses on money awards for the consequences of a breach of privacy, specifically mental distress. The authors argue that mental harm is and ought to be a recoverable head of loss in privacy actions, whether those actions are in equity or common law, since a large part of the point of such actions is the avoidance or alleviation of such harms. The chapter begins with a valuable exegesis of recent and older English and Australian cases, which the authors argue recognise either implicitly or explicitly that mental distress is a recoverable head of loss in cases of breach of privacy, whether the action is in equity or at common law. The chapter then reinforces the conclusions derived from

[45] R Stevens, *Torts and Rights* (Oxford, Oxford UP, 2007) ch 4.

doctrinal analysis by arguing that awards for mental distress ought to be available for reasons of policy and logic, focusing on the contentious question of whether such awards should be available if protection is situated within the equitable action for breach of confidence. It should be noted that the authors, in their conclusion, make clear that their support for awards for mental harm should not be taken to rule out awards for the breach of the right in itself; indeed they consider that the two types of award are both of importance and should be understood as conceptually distinct.

The specific issue of whether compensation for mental distress is recoverable for breach of confidence in cases concerning privacy is also addressed in the chapter by McDonald and Rolph, who are sympathetic to arguments that compensation should be available, and by Turner, who – in an extended treatment of the issue – considers equity to be ill-equipped to protect against the kinds of personal harms, like distress, that infringement of privacy tends to involve. In Turner's view, it would be more rational and coherent to house protection of privacy within the law of torts.

It is pertinent to note at this stage that damages for breach of privacy under data protection statutes have tended to focus on compensation for mental harm. Such awards under statute are a focus of the chapters by Haines and Witzleb (see section V.E). As Berryman's chapter shows, focusing on the British Columbia Privacy Act 1996, where the statute creates a freestanding privacy tort, damages beyond mental distress may be recognised (depending, of course, on the terms of the particular Act).

ii. Gain

Moving from money remedies that compensate for loss to those which reverse wrongful gains, Katy Barnett's chapter considers the contentious question of what role gain-based remedies do and should play within the developing privacy actions, focusing on Australian and English law. The question ties into wider debates over the fusion of law and equity, and over the proper classification of certain types of damages as loss- or gain-based. Barnett argues that whether gain-based relief ought to be available for breach of privacy should depend not so much upon the historical division between equity and common law but more upon the normative reasons for recognising a privacy action. She argues that it is preferable for privacy to be protected as a standalone tort rather than via breach of confidence, but that this should not bar the availability of gain-based relief, specifically an account of profits, which has its origin in equity. Coherence and a concern for deterring profit-driven breaches support the availability of a disgorgement remedy for privacy torts, although such awards should only be available where an injunction is unavailable, compensatory damages are inadequate, and the defendant has acted in conscious and advertent disregard of the claimant's rights with a view to making a profit. In contrast, reasonable fee damages, which Barnett would classify as restitutionary in nature, should not be available in privacy cases as they are at odds with the fundamental nature of privacy. The Lord Cairns' Act jurisdiction should not be used as a mechanism for awarding gain-based relief, as this is to obscure what is really happening and avoids consideration of the normative basis of the cause of action.

Varuhas propounds a different set of views. He argues that the remedy of an account of profits should not be available in the context of the English privacy action, or at least that it should only be available exceptionally. Having argued that the action is closely analogous to vindicatory actions in tort, he highlights a number of crucial ways in which the tort context differs from the equitable context in which disgorgement awards have traditionally been made, and which in turn render it inappropriate as a matter of principle to read the remedy across from equity to tort. He also argues that exemplary damages have many advantages over an account of profits as a response to profit-driven wrongs, a view which Barnett debates in her chapter. He maintains that user or reasonable fee damages are not restitutionary in nature, contrary to the claims of restitution theorists, and further argues that such a market measure would be inappropriate in the privacy context as it would treat a basic dignitary interest as a tradeable commodity.

Turner similarly contends that if a tortious privacy action is recognised, an account should not in general be available, such remedies being associated with voluntary, facilitative relationships which protect proprietary entitlements, a paradigm removed from an obligation imposed by law to protect an interest that is not conceptualised as proprietary in nature. Similarly, when it comes to the potential for waiving a tort and seeking money had and received in a claim for breach of privacy, he considers that much depends on whether the privacy interest is properly conceptualised as proprietary in nature. In Turner's view, so much uncertainty surrounds the concept of restitutionary damages that it is difficult to reach a conclusion as to what role, if any, such awards ought to play in privacy cases.

iii. Exemplary and Vindicatory Damages

Several chapters consider the availability of other types of awards. In his chapter, Varuhas argues that, by analogy with other actions that protect basic rights, exemplary damages should be available for the English privacy tort, and he responds to arguments that such awards are impermissible as contrary to the practice of the European Court of Human Rights. Such awards could play a crucial role in response to profit-driven privacy invasions by the media. The chapters by Turner and McDonald and Rolph both observe that the availability of exemplary damages has depended and is likely to depend on whether privacy is protected by the development of a privacy tort or through breach of confidence, as punishment as a goal is traditionally unknown in equity, though the extent to which equity and punishment are strangers varies across jurisdictions. The chapters by Berryman and Partlett discuss the availability of exemplary damages for breach of privacy in Canada and the United States respectively. As they record, significant awards have been made in both countries, including in the Gawker sex tape case in the

United States and the 'revenge porn' case of *Jane Doe* in Canada. Such awards have not in general been recognised under statutory privacy protections, as discussed by Witzleb and Haines in their respective chapters, marking a potential area of divergence between common law and statutory protection. However, the nature of statutory protection may vary, and this may in turn affect the approach to remedies: as Berryman discusses in his chapter, the British Columbia Privacy Act 1996 creates a tortious action for breach of privacy – in contrast to the New Zealand and Australian statutes, which are in the nature of data protection statutes – and exemplary damages are available.

Important questions arise over the availability of the novel head of 'vindicatory damages', especially since the idea of vindication is often invoked in the privacy context. Such damages have been recognised in several Privy Council appeals from the Caribbean concerning constitutional violations,[46] and considered – and rejected – by the UK Supreme Court in the *Lumba* case in the context of the tort of false imprisonment.[47] In his chapter, Varuhas argues such damages should not be available for breach of privacy principally because they are unnecessary, given that other orthodox remedies can provide sufficient protection and vindication of privacy, a position Moreham agrees with in her chapter. Importantly, Varuhas maintains that such damages should not be confused with normative damages, which compensate for an interference with privacy interests. The vindicatory damages recognised in Caribbean appeals are *not compensatory* but either perform a function akin to exemplary damages or operate as an enhanced form of nominal damages. Stevens also considers it important to maintain this distinction, lest different types of award with different aims become confused. Descheemaeker also considers vindicatory damages, albeit his definition is wider than those awards made in the Caribbean cases, examining their coherence in the light of the availability of nominal damages and compensatory damages for factual harm. Witzleb considers the potential for the award of vindicatory damages under Australian privacy legislation, observing that their availability may depend on whether the primary obligations under statute are conceptualised as rights. This analysis dovetails with Berryman's analysis of the British Columbia Privacy Act 1996, which does create a statutory tort, and for which damages absent loss do seem to be available.

C. Apologies

Apologies and corrections have emerged both as potentially important considerations in a court's assessment of damages awards and as freestanding, novel remedies in common law jurisdictions, adding new strings to the courts' remedial

[46] See, eg, those cases cited in n 42.

[47] *R (Lumba) v Secretary of State for the Home Department* [2012] 1 AC 245.

bow and supplementing existing remedies. Robyn Carroll's chapter explores the role and effectiveness of apologies and corrections in privacy cases. She takes as her starting point the Australian Law Reform Commission's unimplemented proposal for the enactment of a statutory tort of serious invasion of privacy and recommendations for incorporating apologies and corrections within the proposed legislation.[48] Two key elements of the Commission's proposal are assessed: the requirement that courts consider apologies and corrections when quantifying damages, and provision for court-ordered apologies and corrections. The chapter explores the place of apologies and corrections in the legal context, appreciating the inherent subjectivity of both their purpose and effect. In so doing, the author argues that any legislative incorporation of either remedy must allow sufficient scope for the courts to take account of individual circumstances. For example, when assessing how an apology or correction may affect damages, consideration of individual circumstances is vital, as factors such as the timing and fullness of an apology may affect the degree of emotional distress suffered by a plaintiff. In terms of a court-ordered apology or correction, the remedy remains rare and will only be appropriate in limited circumstances. However, if legislated for, courts must still account for specific factors in deciding whether such order is appropriate. Ultimately, Carroll argues that apologies and corrections have a valid place as remedies for serious invasions of privacy.

Although his predominant focus is money awards, Witzleb considers apologies as a means of providing relief for breaches of the Australian Privacy Act 1988. In that context, the remedy has been regularly ordered by the Privacy Commissioner. Apologies voluntarily given may be considered in assessing compensation under the Act – which is also the case in respect of awards under the New Zealand Privacy Act 1993, as discussed by Haines in his chapter.

D. Classification: Equity and Torts

The issue of legal classification is a golden thread that runs through all of the chapters in this collection. However, two chapters have this topic as their focus, specifically the remedial ramifications of classifying the privacy action as equitable or tortious. Both focus on England and Australia. These jurisdictions have both protected privacy via the equitable action of breach of confidence, at least initially in the case of England. The protection of a dignitary interest, which one might typically associate with the functions of tort, via an equitable action in turn raises questions of classification and coherence. The issue does not arise in the same way in jurisdictions such as New Zealand and Canada, which have explicitly recognised the new forms of privacy action as torts rather than variants of breach of confidence.

[48] Australian Law Reform Commission (n 10).

The chapter by Barbara McDonald and David Rolph considers a number of legal ramifications that flow from the classification of the English action for misuse of private information as a claim in tort by Tugendhat J in *Vidal Hall v Google Inc*, a decision upheld by the Court of Appeal.[49] Such a classification had been hinted at in previous decisions but only in obiter dicta, and it raises, without a clear answer, the question of when and how this tort was created by the courts. While the classification was for the purposes of the Civil Procedure Rules, the Court of Appeal seemed to accept that the classification would apply more broadly and recognised that the ramifications for issues of vicarious liability and remedies would need to be worked through in future cases. The chapter contrasts principles of remedies applicable to claims based in equity and those based in tort, looking particularly at money remedies and injunctions, also considering the implications of the Human Rights Act 1998 for the latter. The chapter considers several further issues of great practical significance that have so far been underexplored in the literature: the implications of classifying the action as equitable or tortious for choice of law – a matter which is the focus of Richard Garnett's chapter (see section V.G) – and cutting-edge issues of attribution of conduct and vicarious liability.

In his chapter, Turner considers the remedial implications of protecting privacy through breach of confidence or through development of a dedicated action in tort. He considers the implications for injunctions, compensation, account of profits, restitution, aggravated awards, exemplary awards and proprietary relief. He concludes that the law of remedies would differ fundamentally depending on whether a legal entitlement to privacy was established in equity or at common law. He argues that equity is ill-equipped to develop an equitable law of torts, so that liability for invasions of privacy should be developed at common law; outside of cases of voluntarily assumed obligations of confidentiality, and except where equity may act in aid of common law rights, interests protected by a privacy entitlement make no call on equity to correct the conscience of the defendant who violates the plaintiff's privacy. However, if privacy is protected via tort, equity could still intervene in appropriate cases in its auxiliary jurisdiction. For example, injunctions, delivery up and destruction of chattels would be commonly available, although equitable accounting and proprietary relief would most likely be unavailable.

Several other chapters squarely address the topic of classification. Richardson, Neave and Rivette consider how classification of the action would affect availability of compensation for mental distress. Similarly, Barnett considers how classification would affect the availability of gain-based relief. Moreham's analysis is predicated on the view that privacy is a tort, and Varuhas mounts a sustained argument that the English privacy action is and ought to be properly classified as a vindicatory action, alongside other such tortious actions, including trespass, false imprisonment and defamation. Varuhas's argument proceeds by demonstrating

[49] *Vidal-Hall v Google Inc* [2014] 1 WLR 4155 (QB), affirmed *Vidal-Hall* (n 21).

that the privacy action and other vindicatory actions protect similar interests, perform similar functions and share nearly identical internal legal structures. The law of remedies in privacy has gradually come into line with the law of remedies that prevails within vindicatory actions, and so, Varuhas argues, it ought to. The ramifications are that compensatory damages ought to be available for the infraction of the privacy right in itself as well as for proven consequential losses; that exemplary damages ought to be available; that gain-based remedies should not in general be available; and that damages should rarely if ever be awarded in lieu of an injunction for an ongoing infringement of privacy – an injunction should in general be granted. It also follows from classification of the action as analogous to vindicatory torts that the approach to damages should not follow the European Court of Human Rights' approach to 'just satisfaction' under Article 41 of the ECHR.[50]

E. Comparison

As already discussed, one of the core themes of the collection is the importance of considering remedial questions in their jurisdictional context. The majority of the chapters in the collection, introduced in the preceding and following sections, focus on English and/or Australian law, while also integrating comparative insights, while Richard Garnett's chapter (see section V.G) considers the legal principles governing cross-border litigation in Australia, Canada, England and New Zealand.

Two chapters seek to provide a systematic analysis of the law of privacy remedies as they have developed in single jurisdictions, reflecting not only on legal doctrine but also the context in which doctrine has evolved. These chapters perhaps more than any others bring into focus the importance of local context in shaping remedial law, including national and subnational – Province or State – context. Jeff Berryman's chapter considers the laws of Canada, with a particular focus on Ontario, the common law jurisdiction among those considered herein which has most recently developed common law protection of privacy. David Partlett's chapter considers remedies for privacy actions in the United States, the jurisdiction whose laws have most strongly influenced the development of privacy actions across the common law world (since the United States was the first, among those countries considered herein, to develop a worked out set of common law privacy actions).

Berryman considers the emergence of privacy actions in the laws of several Canadian Provinces, in particular the emergence of common law privacy torts in Ontario, the approach to damages for these actions, the law and practice of class actions, and issues relating to injunctions. He charts the emergence, first,

[50] See further Varuhas (n 25) especially chs 2–3.

of an intrusion upon seclusion tort in *Jones* and then of a disclosure of private facts tort in *Jane Doe*, including the role played by the wider statutory context in Canada.[51] He examines the approach to damages in regard to each, observing that only modest conventional awards were contemplated in *Jones*, while an approach akin to damages for sexual assault was adopted in *Jane Doe* resulting in awards far exceeding the range indicated in *Jones*. These decisions and their progeny are compared with the approach to damages under the British Columbia Privacy Act 1996, which creates a statutory privacy tort, courts in that Province notably adopting a higher level of awards. Berryman also notes wider contextual differences between England and Canada, which may account for the relative underdevelopment of the public disclosure tort and remedial principles in Canada and help to place the trajectory of Canadian legal development in perspective. He goes on to consider the law and practice of class actions in the privacy context (which have played a particularly important role in cases concerning accessing and disclosure of bank and health records). Given the modest range of damages indicated in *Jones*, such actions may be necessary to render litigation viable but there may be doubts over whether such claims are the most effective and efficient way to encourage good data management within defendant organisations, especially given the disruptive potential of damages litigation. Lastly, Berryman considers injunctions, discussing inter alia the challenges posed by ordering the removal of information from the Internet and the balance between protecting privacy and other important rights and principles.

Partlett's chapter examines the law of remedies in relation to the privacy torts recognised by the common law of the individual American States. The heart of the chapter is a detailed doctrinal exegesis of the law of remedies in the context of each of the four privacy actions recognised in State laws, with different issues arising in relation to each as well as common themes. One important theme, among several, is that courts subscribe to the American realist tradition of loosely tying remedy to primary right, the law reflecting a 'dualist' position, and that a wide range of remedies is available to perform a variety of functions. Another core theme that is brought out squarely by Partlett's discussion of the American context is the way in which the common law of torts is rooted in the local and national community of a jurisdiction. A fundamental aspect of the American context is the tension between the private privacy rights of individuals and the public imperative of free speech; the First Amendment 'juggernaut' has fundamentally shaped and enfeebled both liability rules within the privacy actions and the courts' approach to remedies, and led to adoption of prescriptive rules to constrain juries. The effect of the free speech imperative varies across the four torts and the different remedies awarded, its effect on the latter being most pronounced in (but by no means limited to) prior restraint. Thus despite its early acceptance and influential endorsement by Prosser, privacy law remains fragile, with no sign of change of direction in respect

[51] *Jones* (n 17); *Jane Doe* (n 17).

of the First Amendment on the horizon. Other important contextual factors are discussed, including a relatively greater distrust of government action compared to other common law jurisdictions – with the grant of judicial remedies to constrain free speech viewed as government action – and a deep suspicion of local (State) norms on which protection of privacy rests. Thus, while the American model will always be of interest abroad, has shaped the development of privacy law in other common law jurisdictions and is elegant in its own way, it should be recognised as an unreliable model to be applied elsewhere. Context matters.

F. Statute

While many of the chapters in this collection focus on developments at common law or in equity, statute is of fundamental importance in any consideration of the protection of privacy through the imposition of civil liability. There are several reasons for this. First, over the last few decades common law jurisdictions have witnessed not only the recognition of judicially-created privacy actions, but also the passing of statutes dedicated to the protection of privacy. These protections may take different forms, but the two most important types are considered herein: data protection statutes and statutes that create privacy torts. No consideration of the remedies available for breach of privacy would be complete without discussion of the remedies available to victims of privacy violations under these statutes. Furthermore, consideration of statutory remedies would be incomplete without consideration of common law/equitable remedies and vice versa, as each provides the context in which the other operates and develops. Second, statute not only creates direct privacy protections and associated remedial powers, it may also directly or indirectly alter common law or equitable doctrine. For example, statutes, originally the Lord Cairns' Act and now its modern equivalents, provide jurisdiction for equitable damages to be awarded, for example in lieu of an injunction. The power to award such damages in a privacy claim is a core issue discussed in many of the chapters in this collection. We have also seen how rights protected in constitutions or under statutory rights charters may fundamentally shape the trajectory of legal development at common law or in equity. For example, the First Amendment has radically shaped common law privacy protection in the United States; Article 8 was a core driver of the development of the privacy action in English law, while the Article 10 right to freedom of expression affects defences and remedies; and the proliferation of statutory privacy protections was held to reinforce the need to develop privacy torts at common law in both New Zealand and Canada.

Two chapters consider the approach to remedies under what may loosely be described as data protection statutes. These statutes seek to regulate the collection, use and disclosure of personal data and information relating to individuals by public and private sector organisations, requiring relevant organisations to comply with an enumerated set of privacy principles and/or privacy codes, and providing for remedies in cases of non-compliance. Claims for remedies under such statutes are typically to a privacy commissioner and/or tribunal in the first instance. The chapter by Rodger Haines QC considers the remedial jurisprudence under the New Zealand Privacy Act 1993, and the chapter by Normann Witzleb considers remedies under the Australian Privacy Act 1988. The chapters are path breaking. As far as the editors are aware, these are the first two detailed scholarly treatments of remedial law and practice under these statutes. Given the proliferation of similar statutes across the common law world, they will be of great interest not only in New Zealand and Australia, but in other jurisdictions as well.

Haines's chapter provides an overview of the New Zealand Privacy Act 1993, setting out its objectives, scope of application, the relevant privacy principles, criteria for actionability and the procedure governing claims. He makes the important preliminary point that while the statute has a human rights dimension, one of its purposes is the facilitation of data flows to enhance government and private sector efficiency. In the first instance, claims are to the Privacy Commissioner and then to the Human Rights Review Tribunal, of which Haines is Chairperson. There is a right of appeal to the High Court, though as Haines observes, the ordinary courts have played a limited role in shaping the remedial jurisprudence. A core criterion of actionability, which distinguishes the statutory claim from the privacy action at common law, is that the plaintiff must show a breach of a privacy principle *and* that this has caused an enumerated type of harm or negative consequence (albeit in certain instances causation of harm is deemed upon proof of breach). Interestingly the harms relevant to actionability do not exactly overlap with the types of harm for which damages may be awarded. The bulk of Haines's chapter is dedicated to doctrinal exegesis of the Tribunal's burgeoning jurisprudence and the High Court's smaller body of case law. He considers each available remedy in turn, including declarations, restraining and remedial orders and damages, with a particular focus on damages. In contrast to the orthodox position at common law, damages are not available as of right. Haines explains how the damages jurisprudence has developed over time and the respective roles of the Tribunal and the High Court in doctrinal development, how the defendant's conduct may affect damages, and the Tribunal's capacity to award damages greater in quantum than those sought by the plaintiff. He provides a valuable account of the heads of loss which are recoverable, the heads including pecuniary loss, loss of a benefit, and humiliation, loss of dignity and injury to feelings. In terms of quantum, significant awards have increasingly been made, and the Tribunal has articulated damages guidance, adopting bands, to facilitate consistency in assessment of damages for emotional harm – whilst also emphasising that each case must be assessed on its own facts.

In the absence of a common law right to privacy in Australia, other private law actions and regulatory mechanisms have been relied upon to provide relief for invasions of privacy. Witzleb's chapter examines one regulatory mechanism that is of growing practical importance. The Australian Privacy Commissioner has the power, pursuant to the Privacy Act 1988, to investigate individual complaints of breach of informational privacy principles by organisations and to issue determinations. Although successive Privacy Commissioners have made sparing use of their powers, the current Commissioner has adopted a more pro-active approach so that there are now over 30 published determinations. The chapter begins by outlining the core substantive and procedural features of the Privacy Act and the determinations that can be made under it. Notably, determinations by the Privacy Commissioner, including those declaring that compensation should be paid, are not binding, although the Commissioner or applicant can seek court enforcement. Determinations are subject to merits review in the Administrative Appeals Tribunal, and a small number of Tribunal decisions have set the parameters of the Commissioner's remedial approach. The chapter goes on to provide detailed analysis of this emergent body of determinations and case law. It reviews the range and quantum of monetary awards made under the determinations power. A particular focus is assessment practices in relation to non-economic losses, which include aggravated damages. The chapter explores the standards that guide the making of awards, including quantum – which has generally been modest – and interrogates the relationship between such awards and common law damages. It establishes that the principles governing statutory redress are aligned with those from related areas such as anti-discrimination law, and that the principles applying to equivalent remedies in the ordinary law of torts have been highly influential. Witzleb observes that whether awards are or ought to be conceptualised as vindicatory in nature is a complex matter, especially as the norms under the Privacy Act are not rights as such, though he notes the idea of vindication is evident in a number of determinations. The chapter goes on to discuss the Commissioner's approach to the availability of non-compensatory remedies, such as apologies and orders to review or change existing privacy practices.

Berryman's chapter also warrants mention in relation to the role of statute in the law of privacy remedies. In the course of his chapter on Canadian privacy law he considers remedial practice under statutes creating torts of privacy in several provinces, and compares the approach to damages under these statutes to remedial Practice in Ontario, where privacy torts have been recognised at common law. He also examines how the approach to remedies under privacy statutes in other Provinces, in particular the Manitoba Privacy Act 1987, influenced the development of common law remedies principles in Ontario.

G. Cross-border Issues

The collection ends on a high with Richard Garnett's comprehensive analysis of the cross-border issues that arise in connection with breaches of privacy. The rules of private international law are of crucial importance in considering remedies for breach of privacy, as they will affect, inter alia, access to remedies and which country's laws will be applied to a given claim. Technological advances, as well as other phenomena such as the increased mobility of natural and legal persons, have increased the scope for infringements of privacy that transcend national borders, including the capacity for simultaneous and multi-territorial infringements, and for breaches which result from acts in different countries. As such, conflict-of-laws doctrine will be of increasing importance in claims for remedies for breach of privacy. Garnett examines the law of Australia, Canada, England (and by association the EU) and New Zealand. In respect of each jurisdiction he considers three key matters. First, the laws governing whether the court of a given country has jurisdiction to hear a claim, including consideration of common law and statutory jurisdiction, and will exercise that jurisdiction. Second, the rules governing what law – local or foreign – the court will apply to the merits of the case, including liability rules and remedial law. Third, the circumstances in which a court will recognise and enforce the judgment of a court in another jurisdiction, including the grounds on which a foreign judgment may be impeached. McDonald and Rolph also consider cross-border issues in their chapter, focusing on the implications of classification of a privacy action as a tort or variant of breach of confidence, a matter also examined in detail by Garnett.

2

Privacy Injunctions and the Rule of Law

MICHAEL TUGENDHAT*

I. Introduction

The *International Workshop on Remedies for Breach of Privacy* in Melbourne provided a most appropriate place to reflect on what are now called 'interim non-disclosure orders' (INDOs, or orders prohibiting the disclosure of information, usually because it is confidential or private). It was in Australia that there took place both the disclosure and much of the litigation concerning Peter Wright's book, *Spycatcher*.[1] Wright retired to Tasmania, and disclosed in his book information about his work in the UK for the British Security Service. In 1985, the United Kingdom (UK) Government claimed that the disclosure would constitute a breach of his duty of confidentiality under the terms of his employment. While the English and Strasbourg courts each upheld the claim to confidentiality (and the remedy by way of an account of profits), the claims for an INDO failed. It was in practice impossible to obtain any injunction against Wright and his Australian and American publishers, with the result that the information became public. Enforcement against the UK-based newspapers would thereafter have afforded no practical benefit to the UK Government.

Now is also a most appropriate time to reflect on INDOs, because the UK Supreme Court has recently reconsidered the law in *PJS v News Group Newspapers Ltd*.[2] PJS and his partner were in the entertainment business and had two young children. He sought an INDO, to restrain the defendant from publishing in one of its national newspapers a story about his alleged extra-marital sexual activities. He contended that the proposed publication would be a breach of confidence and a violation of his right to respect for his private life. The information and the

* I wish to acknowledge my indebtedness to Tom Blackburn SC for his assistance in the preparation of this chapter.

[1] *Attorney-General v Observer Ltd (Spycatcher)* [1990] 1 AC 109. The book dealt with the operational organisation, methods and personnel of MI5. It included an account of alleged illegal activities by the Security Service. The history of the litigation in both Australia and the UK is summarised by the European Court of Human Rights in *Observer and Guardian v United Kingdom* (1992) 14 EHRR 153.

[2] *PJS v News Group Newspapers Ltd* [2016] UKSC 26, [2016] AC 1081.

identity of PJS were widely available on the Internet. The Court distinguished a claim in confidentiality for information that was not private (in the sense of personal) from a claim in respect of private and personal information. Claims based on respect for private and personal information did not depend on confidentiality (or secrecy) alone, since the right to respect for private life also embraced the right to prevent unwanted intrusion into one's personal space.[3] And even though no injunction could be enforced against publishers posting the information from abroad, an injunction could be enforced against the UK-based newspaper publishers, whose publications in hard copy would be much more intrusive than publications on the Internet. While *PJS* was an interim order, it is common for such orders to become permanent in practice. Indeed, *PJS* has in fact been settled on the basis of a permanent restraint on disclosure.[4]

Spycatcher also established that in cases of government secrets, the Crown must establish not only that the information is confidential, but also that publication would be to its 'detriment', in the sense that the public interest requires that it should not be published. This is because of the nature of the public interest served by the right of freedom of expression: 'in a free society there is a continuing public interest that the workings of government should be open to scrutiny and criticism'.[5] Claims relating to personal information can also be defeated, if disclosure is, or would be, in the public interest. But it is the defendant who must establish that public interest, and in *PJS*, as in many cases about sex, the defendant could not do that.

Both these cases are best known for what they say on the right of freedom of expression. But *Spycatcher* is also authority for the general principle of limited government: government must be for the benefit of the people, and the Government has only such powers as the law allows it. And both cases illustrate the practical limits of state sovereignty. Sovereignty is a topical subject today. These two cases are a reminder that sovereignty is in practice territorial. If a wrongdoer is not personally present within the territory of a state, and if he or she has no substantial assets in that state, there is little that the sovereign can do to enforce the sovereign's law. If sovereigns are to enforce their law, they must make treaties for mutual enforcement with other sovereigns. The problem today is that such treaties may be seen by the public as undemocratic surrenders of sovereignty, rather than as beneficial exercises of sovereignty. This raises questions about the rule of law, and how it is in practice to be upheld.

[3] ibid [58]. In *Spycatcher* ((n 1) 260), Lord Goff said that 'if in the *Argyll* case the Duke had secured the revelation of the marital secrets in an American newspaper … [t]he publication in England would be more harmful to her than publication in America' (referring to *Argyll v Argyll* [1967] 1 Ch 301).

[4] *PJS v News Group Newspapers Ltd* [2016] EWHC 2770; and see the news report 'Celebrity Injunction: Sun on Sunday Publisher Makes Payment' (4 November 2016) *BBC News Online*, available at www.bbc.co.uk/news/uk-37869801 (last accessed 2 May 2017).

[5] *Spycatcher* (n 1) 282–83.

II. Prior Restraint

These two cases raise a further issue about the rule of law. Should the courts grant such interim injunctions at all? These injunctions may be referred to as prior (or previous) restraints. Writing in the mid-eighteenth century, Blackstone considered that liberty of the press is 'essential to the nature of a free state'. But he made clear that that freedom, properly understood, was not infringed by post-publication criminal sanctions, because freedom of the press

> consists in laying no *previous* restraints upon publications, and not in freedom from censure for criminal matter when published … the will of individuals is still left free; the abuse only of that free will hereby laid upon freedom, of thought or enquiry: liberty of private sentiment is still left; the disseminating, or making public, of bad sentiments, destructive of the ends of society, is the crime which society corrects.[6]

For Blackstone (as for Locke in the seventeenth century and Fortescue in the fifteenth century), the ends of society are to protect people's rights.[7] Blackstone gave a further reason for condemning licensing or censorship, which had ceased in England in 1694 when Parliament refused to renew the Licensing Act. It was that 'To subject the press to the restrictive power of a licenser … is to subject all freedom of sentiment to the prejudices of one man, and make him the arbitrary and infallible judge of all controverted points in learning, religion, and government'. But this reason has little application to INDOs (which did not exist in Blackstone's day), because they are interim orders, pending a public trial (in some jurisdictions before a jury).

In *Prince Albert v Strange*, the court continued an injunction restraining disclosure of the royal family's etchings, because that alone would be an effective remedy.[8] The Lord Chancellor made no mention of Blackstone, prior restraint or freedom of expression. He said:

> I have always held, that it was for the discretion of the court to consider whether the defendant might not sustain greater injury from an improper injunction, than the plaintiff from delay in granting it. In the present case, where privacy is the right invaded, the postponing of the injunction would be the equivalent to denying it altogether. The interposition of this court in these cases … to be effectual … must be immediate.

[6] 4 Bl Comm ch 9, 151–52.

[7] 1 Bl Comm ch 1, 124 ('to protect individuals in the enjoyment of those absolute rights, which were vested in them by the immutable laws of nature'); J Locke, *Two Treatises of Government*, P Laslett (ed), 3rd edn (Cambridge, Cambridge UP, 1988 [1689]) Second Treatise 355, para 134 (Lord Camden had quoted the same passage from Locke in *Entick v Carrington* (1765) 19 State Trials 1029, 1066); J Fortescue, *On the Laws and Governance of England*, S Lockwood (ed) (Cambridge, Cambridge UP, 1997 [1471]) ch XIV, 23 ('no people ever incorporated themselves into a kingdom by their own agreement and will, unless in order to possess safer than before both themselves and their own, which they feared to lose').

[8] *Prince Albert v Strange* (1849) 47 ER 1302, 1312; see also *Francome v Mirror Group Newspapers Ltd* [1984] 1 WLR 892, 898, 900, 902.

In *Attorney-General v Newspaper Publishing Plc*,[9] Sir John Donaldson MR also referred to the need for an effective remedy:

> [I]f, pending the trial, the court allows publication, there is no point in having a trial, since the cloak of confidentiality can never be restored. Confidential information is like an ice cube … Give it to the party who has no refrigerator or will not agree to keep it in one, and by the time of the trial you just have a pool of water.[10]

As the Supreme Court noted in *PJS*,[11] on the final appeal in *Douglas v Hello! Ltd*[12] the Court found that the claimants had a virtually unanswerable case that their privacy was infringed. The infringement was by publication of wedding photographs taken surreptitiously, and an INDO had been discharged on the first appeal in 2000. The Court in 2005 stressed the need for an effective remedy:

> [D]amages, particularly in that sum [£24,500], cannot fairly be regarded as an adequate remedy … [B]earing in mind the nature of the injury they suffered, namely mental distress, a modest sum by way of damages does not represent an adequate remedy.
>
> The sum is also small in the sense that it could not represent any real deterrent to a newspaper or magazine, with a large circulation, contemplating the publication of photographs which infringed an individual's privacy. Accordingly … the refusal of an interlocutory injunction in a case such as this [as had in fact happened in that case] represents a strong potential disincentive to respect for aspects of private life, which the Convention intends should be respected.
>
> … Only by the grant of an interlocutory injunction could the [claimant]s' rights have been satisfactorily protected.[13]

By contrast, when the courts first started to grant injunctions to restrain the publication of libels, they cited the principle of freedom of expression, making no mention of the need for an effective remedy other than damages. In *Bonnard v Perryman*[14] it was said that

> the subject-matter of an action for defamation is so special as to require exceptional caution in exercising the jurisdiction to interfere by injunction before the trial of an action to prevent an anticipated wrong. *The right of free speech is one which it is for the public interest that individuals should possess*, and, indeed, that they should exercise without impediment, so long as no wrongful act is done; and, unless an alleged libel is untrue, there is no wrong committed; but, on the contrary, often a very wholesome act is performed in the publication and repetition of an alleged libel.

[9] *Attorney-General v Newspaper Publishing* [1988] Ch 333, 358.

[10] A similar point was made by Lord Nicholls in *Cream Holdings Ltd v Banerjee* [2005] 1 AC 253, [18], and by the Court of Appeal in *Greene v Associated Newspapers* [2004] EWCA Civ 1462, [2005] QB 972, [78].

[11] *PJS* (n 2) [41].

[12] *Douglas v Hello! Ltd (No 3)* [2005] EWCA Civ 595, [2006] QB 125. For the first appeals, see below (n 64).

[13] *Douglas* (n 12) [256]–[257], [259].

[14] *Bonnard v Perryman* [1891] 2 Ch 269, 284 (emphasis added).

INDOs have been granted to protect personal confidential information with some regularity, at least for the nearly 50 years since *Argyll v Argyll.*[15] The question whether the rule against INDOs in defamation claims can be reconciled with the rule in confidentiality and privacy cases could have been raised at any time since *Bonnard v Perryman*. In fact, it seems only to have been raised in England since the Human Rights Act (HRA) 1998.[16]

In his dissenting judgment in *Australian Broadcasting Corporation v O'Neill*,[17] Heydon J gave a comprehensive survey of the history, and criticised the reasoning in *Bonnard v Perryman*. In that case, the defendant was serving a prison sentence for murder. He sought an INDO restraining publication of allegations of his involvement in other unsolved deaths of children, which were thought to be murders. The application failed at both first instance and on appeal.

In Australia, the rule in *Bonnard v Perryman* has been qualified. In *O'Neill*, the majority upheld the grant of an INDO, referring both to the need for an effective remedy and to the principle of freedom of expression:[18]

> The principles were discussed, for example, in *Chappell v TCN Channel Nine Pty Ltd*[19] …, *National Mutual Life Association of Australasia Ltd v GTV Corporation Pty Ltd*,[20] and *Jakudo Pty Ltd v South Australian Telecasters Ltd*.[21] As Doyle CJ said in the last-mentioned case, in all applications for an interlocutory injunction, a court will ask whether the plaintiff has shown that there is a serious question to be tried as to the plaintiff's entitlement to relief, has shown that the plaintiff is likely to suffer injury for which damages will not be an adequate remedy, and has shown that the balance of convenience favours the granting of an injunction. These are the organising principles, to be applied having regard to the nature and circumstances of the case, under which issues of justice and convenience are addressed. We agree with the explanation of these organising principles in the reasons of Gummow and Hayne JJ,[22] and their reiteration that the doctrine of the Court established in *Beecham Group Ltd v Bristol Laboratories Pty Ltd*[23] should be followed.[24] In the context of a defamation case, the application of those organising principles will require particular attention to the considerations which courts have identified as dictating caution. Foremost among those considerations is the public interest in free speech. A further consideration is that, in the defamation context, the outcome of a trial is especially likely to turn upon issues that are, by hypothesis,

[15] *Argyll* (n 3).

[16] See P Milmo et al, *Gatley on Libel and Slander*, 10th edn (London, Sweet & Maxwell, 1997) para 25.19, cited in *Coys Ltd v Autocherish Ltd* [2004] EWHC 1334, [2004] EMLR 25, [56]; *Greene* (n 10) [67]–[81].

[17] *Australian Broadcasting Corporation v O'Neill* [2006] HCA 46, (2006) 227 CLR 57.

[18] ibid [19].

[19] *Chappell v TCN Channel Nine Pty Ltd* (1988) 14 NSWLR 153.

[20] *National Mutual Life Association of Australasia Ltd v GTV Corporation Pty Ltd* [1989] VR 747.

[21] *Jakudo Pty Ltd v South Australian Telecasters Ltd* (1997) 69 SASR 440, 442–43.

[22] See *O'Neill* (n 17) [65]–[72].

[23] *Beecham Group Ltd v Bristol Laboratories Pty Ltd* (1968) 118 CLR 618.

[24] See also *Firth Industries Ltd v Polyglas Engineering Pty Ltd* (1975) 132 CLR 489, 492 (per Stephen J); *Winthrop Investments Ltd v Winns Ltd* [1975] 2 NSWLR 666, 708 (per Mahoney JA); *World Series Cricket v Parish* (1977) 16 ALR 181, 186 (per Bowen CJ).

> unresolved. Where one such issue is justification, it is commonly an issue for jury decision. In addition, the plaintiff's general character may be found to be such that, even if the publication is defamatory, only nominal damages will be awarded.

Heydon J argued convincingly that the damage to a claimant can be just as irreparable, and damages just as inadequate a remedy, in a case of libel as it is in a case of confidentiality or privacy.[25] But he understated the extent to which the damage to the public, and to the defendant, is irreparable if an INDO is granted. If news is not published soon, it will in practice be unlikely to be published at all, since later news will assume priority over it. INDOs usually are in practice final, as has happened in *PJS*.[26]

Information can be, at the same time, both confidential and defamatory. That was the case in *Chappell*, which was a kiss-and-tell allegation. It seems that at least some aspects of the threatened publication in *PJS* might also have been defamatory, albeit that they might have been true. In such cases in England, it is generally open to a claimant to decide whether to rely on defamation or on confidentiality/privacy.

The rule in *Bonnard v Perryman* may be challenged again in England as incompatible with Article 10 of the European Convention on Human Rights (ECHR). If it were challenged, one possible outcome might be that the court would replace that rule with the Australian principle explained in *O'Neill*: that is, to apply in defamation cases the same test as in privacy and confidentiality cases, while giving 'particular attention to … the public interest in free speech'. Even if that test were to be applied, the actual result in any given case might well be the same.

A third major consideration (in addition to the adequacy of non-injunctive remedies and freedom of expression) is the enforceability of any remedy. Even if damages, or criminal sanctions, might in principle be considered an adequate remedy, those wishing to publish libels and confidential information in England could always put themselves beyond the reach of English criminal law, damages and INDOs by secretly importing books, or by publishing from abroad. Tom Paine famously fled to Paris to escape a conviction for sedition on the publication of his *The Rights of Man* during the French Revolution. In the sixteenth to eighteenth centuries, books prohibited in England, Scotland and France were often smuggled into those countries from The Netherlands. The problem of enforcing English law, whether by awards of damages, criminal law such as the Official Secrets Acts or by INDOs, became increasingly acute in the 1960s, when international travel made emigration and importing books and papers cheap and easy. It became even more acute in the 1990s, when the Internet became generally available to the public.

[25] *O'Neill* (n 17) 280 ('attention would have to be directed to whether in modern conditions the mass media are more able to inflict harm which is not also grave but irreparable, and if so, whether it ought to be less difficult for plaintiffs to obtain urgent interlocutory relief to prevent such harm').

[26] Above (n 4).

III. The Rule of Law

A principled approach to justifying the grant of INDOs should come through arguments based on the rule of law, such as that advanced in *PJS* by Desmond Browne QC.[27] The Court did not use the words 'rule of law' in the judgments, but it clearly had Mr Browne's submission in mind. The court also had the rule of law in mind in *Spycatcher*, although it is only in the Court of Appeal that there was an express reference to the rule of law.[28]

The idea of the rule of law was made famous by Dicey, writing in 1885. But the principle had been established in English law for centuries. It is one of the two principles of the British constitution,[29] and is best summarised by Lord Bingham:

> [A]ll persons and authorities within the state, whether public or private, should be bound by and entitled to the benefit of laws publicly made, taking effect (generally) in the future and publicly administered in the courts.[30]

Lord Bingham's definition of the rule of law embraced the protection of human rights. Even the narrowest definitions of the rule of law necessarily embraces at least one human right, namely the right of access to justice. But Lord Bingham, like Dicey, expressly included the guarantee of other human rights in his definition.[31]

That everyone should be equally 'bound by and entitled to the benefit of laws' requires that law should, within the bounds of possibility, be enforced. It is not enforced if there is no adequate remedy for a person whose rights are infringed, or threatened with serious infringement. An effective remedy is required by the common law, and is also provided by the HRA 1998.[32]

[27] *PJS* (n 2) 1085–86 ('The Supreme Court needs to consider the practical ramifications of the Court of Appeal's reasoning and whether it is acceptable in a country where the rule of law prevails').

[28] *Spycatcher* (n 1) 192 ('What [the editor] must not do is to seek to place himself above and beyond the reach of the law and the rule of law').

[29] J Jowell, 'The Rule of Law' in J Jowell, D Oliver and C O'Cinneide (eds), *The Changing Constitution*, 8th edn (Oxford, Oxford UP, 2015) (where there is a discussion of the modern constitutional principle); AV Dicey, *Introduction to the Study of the Law of the Constitution*, 8th edn (London, Macmillan, 1915) 178–79. The other main principle of the constitution is the supremacy, or sovereignty, of Parliament.

[30] T Bingham, *The Rule of Law* (London, Penguin, 2010) 8.

[31] ibid 67–83. Dicey referred to human rights as principles of the constitution: 'the constitution is pervaded by the rule of law on the ground that the general principles of the constitution (as for example the right to personal liberty, or the right of public meeting)' (Dicey (n 29) 188, cited by Bingham (n 30) 4). The principles are also referred to as rules of legal policy: *Halsbury's Laws of England*, 5th edn (2012) 96 *Statutes and Legislative Process* [1133]–[1145].

[32] European Commission for Democracy through Law, *Report on the Rule of Law*, CDL-AD(2011)003, para 42 (Report adopted by the Commission at its 86th Plenary Session on 25–26 March 2011); *AXA General Insurance Ltd v Lord Advocate* [2011] UKSC 46, [2012] 1 AC 868, [118]. That is one of the principles in the Bill of Rights 1688 ('the pretended power of suspending of laws or the execution of laws') and *Ashby v White* (1703) 2 Lord Raymond 938, 953; 92 ER 126 ('If the plaintiff has a right, he must of necessity have a means to vindicate and maintain it, and a remedy if he is injured in the exercise or enjoyment of it; and indeed it is a vain thing to imagine a right without a remedy; for want of right and want of remedy are reciprocal'). In regard to the HRA and ECHR, see, eg, *Re W (A Child)* [2016] EWCA Civ 1140, [72] ('the Court will examine whether the procedural protection enjoyed by the applicant at the domestic level in respect of his right to respect for his private life under Art 8 of the

In *PJS* the Court argued primarily from the ECHR, rather than from the common law. But the ECHR and the common law are the same. The Preamble to the ECHR refers to the rule of law both directly and by its reference back to the Universal Declaration of Human Rights (UDHR). It expressly includes requirements of the rule of law, although not in words that identify them as such. The requirements that everyone should be equally 'bound by and entitled to the benefit of laws', and that law should, within the bounds of possibility, be enforced, underlie Article 1 of the ECHR ('The High Contracting Parties shall secure to everyone within their jurisdiction the rights and freedoms defined in Section I of this Convention') and Article 13 ('Everyone whose rights and freedoms as set forth in this Convention are violated shall have an effective remedy before a national authority notwithstanding that the violation has been committed by persons acting in an official capacity').

In *PJS* the Court accepted Mr Browne's submission that

> [b]y exercising its discretion so as to discharge the injunction, the Court of Appeal failed to ensure that the claimant's privacy rights were 'practical and effective': *Von Hannover v Germany* 40 EHRR 1, para 71,[33] *Armoniene v Lithuania* [2009] EMLR 7, para 38 …[34]

IV. Defamation

In *Bonnard v Perryman* the court also argued from the rule of law: 'The right of free speech is one which it is for the public interest that individuals should possess, and, indeed, that they should exercise without impediment, so long as no wrongful act is done'.[35] There is, of course, a sense in which all human rights are ones which it is in the public interest that individuals should possess. That is why they are human rights in the first place. But the point being made in *Bonnard v Perryman* is that the law should protect not only (or even primarily) the speaker's right to speak, but also (or rather) the listener's or reader's right to receive the information. As Hunt J expressed it,

> the right of the community in general to discuss in public matters of public interest and concern and to be informed of the different view held by others … It was that factor which led the Full Court of Appeal in *Bonnard v Perryman* … to say that the subject matter of an action for defamation is so special as to require exceptional caution in exercising the jurisdiction to interfere by injunction before trial of an action to prevent an anticipated wrong.

Convention was practical and effective and consequently compatible with that Article' (quoting *Turek v Slovakia* (2006) 44 EHRR 861, [113])), [111]–[113] ('the right to an "effective remedy" enshrined in ECHR, Art 13 and to the Human Rights Act 1998, ss 7 and 8').

[33] The cited passage from *Von Hannover* reads 'the Convention is intended to guarantee not rights that are theoretical or illusory but rights that are practical and effective'.

[34] *PJS* (n 2) [38]–[43].

[35] *Bonnard* (n 14) 284.

Hunt J's use of the word 'discuss' echoes both Blackstone's and Dicey's use of 'freedom of discussion' to refer to what is today known as freedom of expression.[36]

The right of freedom of expression informs the law of defamation at every stage. The common law gives a restricted meaning to what counts as defamatory: the definition does not include allegations that lower the reputation of the claimant in the estimation of only a section of the population, nor allegations which are below a threshold of seriousness,[37] nor mere insults. It is, in part, to uphold the principle of freedom of expression that actions will be struck out if they are abusive (when the game is not worth the candle).[38]

The defences to defamation are also framed to uphold the right of freedom of expression. The earliest defences to defamation included absolute privilege in respect of words spoken in court and qualified privilege in respect of references for prospective employees, tenants and the like. In each of these defences the interest of the recipient(s) of the information in receiving the communication is likely to be much stronger than the interest (if any) of the speaker in communicating it. The recent extension of qualified privilege to matters of public interest[39] is primarily justified by the interest of the public in receiving information which the speaker believes to be true, rather than the interest of the speaker in communicating it. The defence of truth is also predominantly to advance the interests of the public in knowing the truth (unless there is a strong reason why they should not know it, such as because it is confidential or private, or would interfere with the right to a fair trial, or endanger national security or someone's life, or infringe another person's right to confidentiality or privacy[40]).

It is also to uphold the principle of freedom of expression that the law in England has limited the remedies available to a claimant – both the maximum amount of any damages that may be awarded[41] and the circumstances in which an interim injunction may be granted.

In this respect, Heydon J's criticism of *Bonnard v Perryman* does not address the full extent of the public interest engaged. It is not the case that 'the role of free speech is neither greater nor less than its reflection in the substantive defences to the tort of defamation'.[42] This is illustrated by Heydon J's interesting comparison

[36] *Chappell* (n 19) 164; 1 Bl Comm ch 7, 230; Dicey (n 29) 238.

[37] *Thornton v Telegraph Media Group Ltd* [2010] EWHC 1414, [2011] 1 WLR 1985; Defamation Act 2013, s 1.

[38] *Jameel v Dow Jones* [2005] QB 946; *Kaschke v Osla* [2010] EWHC 1075, [22]; *King v Grundon* [2012] EWHC 2719, [28] (the fact of being sued at all may be such an interference with freedom of expression as to justify striking out a claim that is disproportionate).

[39] *Reynolds v Times Newspapers* [2001] 2 AC 127; Defamation Act 2013, s 4.

[40] Such limitations were enshrined in the common law before they were included in the qualifications to Art 10 of the ECHR.

[41] *Rantzen v Mirror Group Newspapers Ltd* [1994] 1 QB 670, 696.

[42] *O'Neill* (n 17) [275].

with the right to work (the public policy against restraint of trade). By abandoning *Bonnard v Perryman*, he argued,

> freedom to speak as one wishes is not given greater weight in relation to interlocutory injunctions against defamation than, for example, freedom to work as one wishes is given in hearings relating to interlocutory injunctions against breach of covenants in restraint of trade.[43]

It is true that the right to work is a human right protected by the common law (albeit not one that is protected by the ECHR),[44] and it is true (although Heydon J does not say so) that that right is for the benefit of the public at large, and not just for the individual seeking to work or to compete freely. The public at large benefit as consumers from freedom to work, both in increased choice of suppliers and in lower prices. Freedom to work, or competition law, underlies the economies of the whole of the modern Western democratic world. But important as it is, the right to work is not as important for the public as freedom of expression. Freedom of expression has been recognised as essential to liberty in the sense of the right of a people to consent to, and to participate in the making of, the laws that govern them. Today the right to consent to government is guaranteed in the UK and Australia by democracy, in the sense of the right of almost every adult man or woman to vote in elections. But the right to consent to government was recognised by Blackstone, and indeed in the medieval concept of limited kingship and in the emergence of Parliament as a representative body in the same period. This was long before the idea of universal suffrage. Democracy in the sense of universal suffrage emerged to carry that idea to its logical conclusion.

As Laws LJ has said, 'The balance to be struck between public interest and private right is … to be seen as a function of our constitution; and the law of defamation is … to be seen as an aspect of it.'[45] That idea was crucial to the decision in *PJS*. In saying that there was 'no public interest in the publication of the material, however interesting it might be to some members of the public',[46] the Court was focusing on the interest of the public in receiving the information, not on the (essentially commercial) private interest of the newspaper defendant in communicating it. That was also the reasoning of Hunt J in *Chappell*, where (at that time) the Australian law of justification required a defendant to prove both that the words complained were true and that the imputations in question related to a matter of public interest.[47]

It follows that there need be no inconsistency between the different principles applied to INDOs in cases of defamation, on the one hand, and privacy or confidentiality, on the other. The differences between the public interest at stake in each

[43] *O'Neill* (n 17) [248], [275].
[44] It is recognised in Art 23 of the UDHR.
[45] *Lait v Evening Standard Ltd* [2011] EWCA Civ 859, [45] (a case in which the principle of freedom of expression informed the Court's generous interpretation of the defence of honest comment).
[46] *PJS* (n 2) [84].
[47] *Chappell* (n 19) 165.

cause of action can lead to the different approaches being consistent with the rule of law.

Nevertheless, in England there has been acute controversy over INDOs granted in privacy claims. It is to be hoped that this controversy has been finally laid to rest by the Supreme Court in *PJS*, and by the developments in law and practice in relation to so-called super-injunctions.

V. What is a Super-injunction?

A super-injunction is a popular term invented to refer to an INDO with a particular ancillary provision. The definition given in the Report of the Committee on Super-Injunctions ('the Neuberger Report')[48] is:

> The feature which transforms an interim injunction into a super-injunction – the 'super' element … is a prohibition on the disclosure or communication of the existence of the order and the proceedings.

It was probably in the late 1970s, and certainly before 1992, when I first saw a super-injunction. The prohibition that characterises a super-injunction is a provision commonly inserted into interim injunctions issued either to preserve assets, or to preserve evidence of wrongdoing. These were formerly known as *Mareva*[49] and *Anton Piller*[50] orders, and are now known as freezing and search orders.

VI. *Anton Piller* and Search Orders

The earliest reported decision granting a search order is *EMI Ltd v Pandit*.[51] This was a claim for injunctions and delivery up of copies of sound recordings that infringed the plaintiff's copyright. The defendant had been ordered to swear an affidavit identifying those who had supplied him with infringing copies. The defendant had been found to have sworn a dishonest affidavit, and the judge was satisfied that 'if notice were given to the defendant, that would almost certainly result in the immediate destruction of the articles and information to which the plaintiffs are entitled'.[52]

[48] Committee on Super-Injunctions, *Super-Injunctions, Anonymised Injunctions and Open Justice*, Report (20 May 2011) paras 2.13–2.14, available at www.judiciary.gov.uk/wp-content/uploads/JCO/Documents/Reports/super-injunction-report-20052011.pdf (last accessed 2 May 2017).

[49] *Mareva Compania Naviera SA v International Bulk Carriers SA* [1975] 2 Lloyds Reports 509; *AJ Bekhor & Company Ltd v Bilton* [1981] QB 923.

[50] *Anton Piller KG v Manufacturing Processes Ltd* [1976] Ch 55.

[51] *EMI Ltd v Pandit* [1975] 1 WLR 302.

[52] ibid 305H–306A. There was no mention of any prohibition on the disclosure of the existence of the order in the Law Report. Today the Civil Procedure Act 1997, s 7 empowers the court to make what is now known as a search order.

The need for the prohibition on the disclosure of the existence of the order generally arises in two classes of case. The first class is where there are two or more defendants, and the plaintiff demonstrates an entitlement to a 'without notice', or ex parte, order against more than one. Since the defendants would be likely to be served at different times, the benefit of proceeding ex parte would be lost as soon as any one of the defendants had been served. This was because he or she could give notice by telephone to another defendant, thus ensuring the destruction of the articles or information to which the plaintiff is entitled.

The second class of case is where there is a risk that the defendant might be keeping the infringing articles, or the evidence of wrongdoing, at a location other than the address identified in the order (or the first of the addresses to which a search party gains entry). If the defendant can tip off the person controlling the infringing articles or documents at a remote location, then the claimant will lose the benefit of having proceeded without notice.

Counsel have from time to time submitted there is a third class of case in which a super-injunction may be granted, although there is no reported case of a super-injunction being granted on this ground. These are cases where claimants would be deterred from exercising the right of access to the court by fear of the publicity that they might attract, which might amount to an interference with the course of justice of the kind alleged in the Thalidomide litigation in *Sunday Times v UK*.[53] This concern is usually obviated by the grant of anonymity, which is often necessary in any event, to prevent the public from inferring the nature of the private or confidential information.

When a super-injunction is granted, it is an added measure adopted by the court to ensure that the order is effective in circumstances where an order without notice is necessary.

The Civil Procedure Rules (CPR) contain detailed provisions as to what such an order may provide for.[54] There is also an example of such an order attached to the relevant Practice Direction. It includes:[55]

> PROHIBITED ACTS – 20. Except for the purpose of obtaining legal advice, the Respondent must not directly or indirectly inform anyone of these proceedings or of the contents of this order, or warn anyone that proceedings have been or may be brought against him by the Applicant until 4.30 pm on the return date or further order of the court.

In 1992, the late Professor Martin Dockray wrote a monograph on *Anton Piller* Orders.[56] By that time, *Anton Piller* Orders had been made for some 16 years. Professor Dockray set out a form of order that included (at para 4(b) and (c)) a prohibition very similar to the prohibition in the CPR form. He included no

[53] *Sunday Times v UK* (1979) 2 EHRR 245.
[54] CPR, r 25.1(h); Practice Direction 25A, para 7.
[55] Practice Direction 25A, Annex.
[56] M Dockray, *Anton Piller Orders* (London, Watson Hill, 1992).

commentary upon that paragraph, and there is none in the White Book. Professor Dockray records an estimate that 500 orders a year were made in the period 1975–80. I infer that the 'super' element of the injunction was thought not to need any comment or explanation.

Until 2010 there was not, so far as I am aware, any discussion of the 'super' element of the orders. The need for that provision was obvious, and as uncontroversial as the need for ex parte injunctions generally.

In 2010 Professor Zuckerman published 'Super-Injunctions – Curiosity-Suppressant Orders Undermine the Rule of Law'.[57] He wrote that there was nothing of concern in the use of super-injunctions in freezing and search orders to prevent tipping off. The situation that Professor Zuckerman regarded as giving rise to public concern and alarm was when such orders remained in force indefinitely, instead of expiring as soon as the purpose of the substantive part of the order had been achieved. It was the derogation from open justice (a requirement of the rule of law) that was the basis of his concern.

The standard forms of orders referred to above do both specify a time of expiry ('until 4.30 pm on the return date or further order of the court'). But the orders are not made in public, and the inclusion of a return date does not mean that these orders necessarily become public. It is common in those cases for the first step in the action to be the obtaining of a freezing or search order (often before the issue of a claim form). Those cases are commonly settled before any return date that may be set. If that happens, there is no further hearing. If assets, property or evidence of wrongdoing have been found on a search, it might be obvious to a defendant that he or she has no choice but to settle. And if no assets, property or evidence have been found, the claimant might not wish to pursue the case.

Freezing orders are still made frequently, whereas search orders are made less frequently than in the past. There is no record of how many are made in relation to commercial disputes, and judges do not normally give public judgments when they make these orders. Public judgments are likely to be made only where there is a dispute on the return date, or an application to commit for contempt of court for breach of the order. A search on Westlaw of the keyword 'search order' reveals only one or two transcripts of judgments in each of the few years up to 2016.

Search orders, freezing orders and super-injunctions have also been used in claims for breach of commercial confidence. Employees may seek to set up in business in competition with their employers, and they may remove their employers' confidential papers and information for that purpose. Employers may seek delivery up of their customer lists, or technical secrets, and disclosure of the names of the customers whom the defendants had solicited.

[57] A Zuckerman, 'Super-Injunctions – Curiosity-Suppressant Orders Undermine the Rule of Law' (2010) 29 *Civil Justice Quarterly* 131.

In *Aspect Capital Limited v Hugh Christensen*,[58] the claimant had dismissed the defendant. Following his dismissal a forensic examination of his work computer revealed that he had uploaded large quantities of confidential data and information to Internet sites under his control. The claimant obtained a search and seizure order. This included the 'super' prohibition on disclosure of the existence of the proceedings.[59] The judgment of Lewison J was on the application to commit the defendant for contempt of court for breaches of the order. These included a breach of the 'super' provision prohibiting disclosure of the fact of the search order. The defendant had made a secret phone call to a friend to ask him to access an e-mail account and delete e-mails on it.[60]

VII. Breaches of Confidence other than in Personal or Private Information

Prince Albert v Strange[61] related to private family sketches, but, for the next hundred years, most breach of confidence cases related to commercial information and information communicated to lawyers subject to legal professional privilege.[62]

In the 1970s the law of confidentiality came to be used to protect official secrets.[63] The primary means by which official secrets are protected is the criminal law, the Official Secrets Acts. But the criminal law has limitations. One is that it may seem inappropriate as a procedure to determine the legality of a proposed publication, as in the case of the memoirs of a former Cabinet Minister. Once a court has decided that disclosure would be unlawful, that may well affect the decisions of the person intending to make the disclosure, and of newspaper publishers and others. They may decide not to carry out their intention to publish. In cases such as those of Tom Paine (who fled to France) or Mr Wright (who went to Tasmania), where the criminal law was, or might otherwise have been, thought to provide the appropriate procedure, it may be impossible to arrest a person before, or even after, that person discloses official information (the person may, for example, be abroad but intending to make disclosure of the information within the jurisdiction). It is for similar reasons that in blackmail cases (where the demand and menaces may be sent to or from abroad) a claimant may apply for injunction rather than complaining to the police.

[58] *Aspect Capital Limited v Hugh Christensen* [2010] EWHC 744.
[59] ibid [5](13).
[60] ibid [33].
[61] Above (n 8).
[62] eg, *Ashburton v Pape* [1913] 2 Ch 469.
[63] *Attorney-General v Jonathan Cape Ltd* [1976] 1 QB 752 (the diaries of Richard Crossman written while he was a member of the Cabinet).

Spycatcher is the most famous case, or series of cases, on official secrets and injunctions, but it was not the first. I recall being instructed in the 1970s in relation to a manuscript prepared by a former member of the Security Service, in which no public judgment was delivered. The first occasion on which I recall seeing a super-injunction in a claim for breach of confidence was in a later claim relating to an official secret. Not long before the HRA 1998 came into force, the case appeared on the Daily Cause List at the Royal Courts of Justice as 'In Private', with each party identified only by a single initial. I was instructed by a newspaper that was not a party to the main proceedings, but which wished to be present at, or at least to be given further information about, the proceedings.

The defendant had been a public servant. The claimant was the relevant department of state. The claimant alleged that the defendant was threatening to disclose information in breach both of a duty of confidence and of the terms of his engagement. But what was most important, the claimant alleged that disclosure of the information would expose former colleagues of the defendant to the risk of torture, or even death, at the hands of terrorists. The claimant had difficulty in serving the defendant, although this was eventually achieved. The case was then settled, on the defendant's giving of undertakings to the court. All the proceedings were heard in private.

At the start of the proceedings the claimant had applied ex parte in the Queen's Bench Division (QBD) for an INDO. This included a super-injunction. This order had been limited as to its duration. But before the defendant could be located for service, the claimant had had to apply on several further occasions to judges in the QBD for extensions of the orders, always on similar terms.

The newspaper came to hear rumours about the case, but could find no record of the case on the court files. The newspaper considered that this was a breach of the rights of the public. The claimant brought a second action against the newspaper. If the orders in that case have ever been made public, or discharged, I am not aware of that fact. The defendant's undertakings were permanent, and it may be that the last super-injunction was unlimited in time (I do not know). If so, that may be an example of a case where a super-injunction was justified without any restriction of time, to preserve an official secret and to save life.

VIII. Privacy Cases

Claims to protect information that was personal and private were brought in the early 1970s. They became increasingly common in the 1980s and 1990s. The list of cases cited in the first appeal in *Douglas v Hello!*[64] shows the extent to which the common law had developed to protect personal information before the HRA.[65]

[64] *Douglas v Hello!* [2001] QB 967.

[65] That case was heard only days after the HRA 1998 came into force in October 2000.

The cases on personal confidential information cited in that case included some where the claimants had succeeded[66] and others where they had failed.[67]

Where personal private or confidential information is at risk of disclosure, there can often be found a defendant who has been in a confidential relationship with the claimant. The weakness in the law before 2000, from the point of view of claimants, was in cases where there was no pre-existing confidential relationship, typically where a photographer had taken an image in a public place, sometimes surreptitiously.[68] Many of the privacy cases that have been brought since 2000 could have been brought before that date as claims for breach of confidence. *PJS* appears to be one such case (notwithstanding that the judgments are framed in terms of the HRA). In many cases the defendants were the claimants' employees or agents. In other cases, the defendants were former spouses or lovers.

IX. Open Justice

The pre-2000 reported cases on personal or private information are for the most part in the Court of Appeal, or in the Chancery Division. The reason for that is that interim applications in the Chancery Division were generally heard in open court, unless the court decided to sit in private. But until *Hodgson v Imperial Tobacco Ltd*,[69] similar applications in the QBD were heard in chambers as a matter of course. And a hearing in chambers was at that time understood (mistakenly) to be a hearing in private. Accordingly, where the claim was for an injunction to restrain the disclosure of confidential information, and there was not also a claim in copyright (which had to be brought in the Chancery Division), the claimant would commonly proceed in the QBD.

The reported cases therefore represent a small proportion of the total number of such cases. In my professional experience of years before 1998, it was not uncommon for people prominent in public life to apply for INDOs in respect of

[66] *Albert* (n 8) (drawings made by the Prince of the Royal Family); *Pollard v Photographic Co* (1888) 40 ChD 345 (photograph used without consent); *Argyll* (n 3) (communication between husband and wife); *Stephens v Avery* [1988] Ch 449 (communication of information about a lesbian relationship); *Attorney-General v Barker* [1990] 3 All ER 257 (information learnt in employment with the royal household); *Francome* (n 8) (tape recordings which had been obtained by illegal telephone tapping); *Shelley Films Ltd v Rex Features Ltd* [1994] EMLR 134 (photos on a film set); *Hellewell v Chief Constable of Derbyshire* [1995] 1 WLR 804 (photographs taken without consent); *Barrymore v News Group Newspapers Ltd* [1997] FSR 600 (an intimate homosexual relationship).

[67] *Woodward v Hutchins* [1977] 1 WLR 760 (information obtained in employment); *Bernstein of Leigh v Skyviews and General Ltd* [1978] QB 479 (aerial photos); *Malone v Metropolitan Police Commissioner* [1979] Ch 344 (telephone tapping by the police); *Khashoggi v Smith* (1980) 124 SJ 149 (information learnt in employment – an order granted out of hours in the QBD was discharged on appeal (the transcript is available through Westlaw)); *M and N v MacKenzie and News Group Newspapers Ltd* (QBD, 18 January 1988) (referred to in *Stephens v Avery* (n 66); *Spencer v United Kingdom* (1998) 25 EHRR CD 105; *Kaye v Robertson* [1991] FSR 62 (both *Spencer* and *Kaye* concerned photographs taken in hospital).

[68] In *Kaye* (n 67), the photograph had been taken in a public hospital.

[69] *Hodgson v Imperial Tobacco Ltd* [1998] 1 WLR 1056. See further below at n 75.

personal confidential information. When applications succeeded, the cases were often settled, or the interim injunction was allowed to continue without either party seeking a trial. So the public would not hear of the case.

Until word processors became common in the 1990s, very few judgments were transcribed; and when they were transcribed, they could be distributed only in the form of photocopies. Unless practitioners heard of an unreported case from a colleague or an opponent, they would be unlikely to hear of it at all. The media might never hear.

So even where civil cases were held in public, in practice there might never be any report of the proceedings. Judgments were usually given *ex tempore*, and rarely transcribed. If there was no reporter in court, even applications in the Chancery Division would in practice remain unknown to the public.

The consequence of all these conditions was that there were many cases that might have given rise to the concerns about secret justice which Lord Woolf raised in *Hodgson*. Only a small number of cases attracted publicity in the news pages of the tabloid press. The most notable of these were where one of the persons concerned was associated with a celebrity. But the parties were not always celebrities, as appears from *Stephens v Avery*.[70]

X. Orders Made Without a Return Date

That injunctions in the QBD did not have a return date was in part due to the pressures under which judges have long been working. In *R (on the application of Casey) v Restormel Borough Council*[71] Munby J explained this. That case concerned an ex parte mandatory injunction granted out of hours by a judge in the QBD. It was not a disclosure case. On 20 July 2007, the judge ordered the defendant local authority to provide the claimant with accommodation to avoid her being street homeless. But the practice and conditions in the QBD which Munby J described applied generally to injunctions. He said:

> 29. It is no secret that the Administrative Court is having great difficulty coping with its present workload. … So there are delays in listing cases for hearing in court. …
>
> 30. In the present case the defendant was initially expected to wait … – a period of almost three months – for the hearing of an application … for the discharge of an *ex parte* injunction. Moreover, the judge who had granted that injunction had specified that the defendant was to be entitled to apply to discharge it on 48 hours' notice. The court was not even able to offer a date within 48 days, let alone 48 hours; by my calculation the date offered was 82 days hence. No wonder the defendant was dismayed. This was wholly unacceptable delay, even allowing for the fact that the defendant's application was not made until a month after the grant of the injunction …

[70] Above (n 66).
[71] *R (on the application of Casey) v Restormel Borough Council* [2007] EWHC 2554 (Admin).

> 38. I do not know what the modern practice is in either the Queen's Bench Division or the Chancery Division but in my days as a junior … one of the great differences in practice was that *ex parte* injunctions were often granted until further order in the Queen's Bench Division whilst the rigorous practice in the Chancery Division was always to express *ex parte* injunctions as lasting for a defined – and usually fairly short – time. It seemed to me then, and more mature reflection has not caused me to change my opinion, that the Chancery practice was plainly preferable: not merely was it right in principle but it avoided everyone falling into the trap of thinking that it is for the injuncted defendant to demonstrate that the injunction ought to be discharged when it is surely for the applicant to demonstrate that an injunction granted *ex parte* should be extended.
>
> 39. Given the current state of business in the Administrative Court it might be thought that there is also a very practical reason why all *ex parte* injunctions should initially be granted only for a defined and usually fairly short time: this will ensure that the case comes back to court for an *inter partes* hearing within the period before the injunction expires. So the delays in obtaining *inter partes* hearings will be minimised.

The workload in the ordinary QBD list fluctuates, and is not always as bad as that. One of the reasons why there grew up the practice of granting ex parte injunctions without a defined time limit (a 'return date') was because of the difficulty and costs involved in listing cases for a further hearing. In most cases a return date was in practice unnecessary in any event, because the parties would reach a settlement, as parties almost always do in all litigation. But the difficulty in finding time for a hearing is one of the explanations for the most famous of all super-injunctions, the one in the *Trafigura* case.[72] The Neuberger Report describes some of the circumstances as follows:[73]

> The facts of that case were as follows: on 11 September 2009 Maddison J granted an injunction against *The Guardian* newspaper and a person or persons unknown. The basis of the injunction was not personal privacy, but rather related to a confidential document which was subject to legal privilege. The applicants' names were anonymised as RJW and SJW and a prohibition on reporting the fact of the proceedings was included in the order. The order was subsequently extended by Sweeney J on 18 September 2009 who also ordered that an application by the claimants be heard on a date to be fixed in the week commencing 12 October 2009. On 12 October 2009, at a time when the injunction was still in force (and when the application was due to be heard), Paul Farrelly MP tabled the following question in Parliament, 'To ask the Secretary of State for Justice, what assessment he has made of the effectiveness of legislation to protect (a) whistle-blowers and (b) press freedom following the injunctions obtained in the High Court by (i) Barclays and Freshfields solicitors on 19 March 2009 on the publication of internal Barclays reports documenting alleged tax avoidance schemes[74] and

[72] *RJW and SJW v Guardian News and Media Ltd and Person or Persons Unknown* (QBD, 11 September 2009), claim no HQ09.

[73] Committee on Super-Injunctions (n 48) para 5.10.

[74] *Barclays Bank Plc v Guardian News Media Ltd* [2009] EWHC 591 (this case was not about personal privacy either).

(ii) Trafigura and Carter-Ruck solicitors on 11 September 2009 on the publication of the Minton report on the alleged dumping of toxic waste in the Ivory Coast, commissioned by Trafigura.

September was part of the legal vacation. Both parties to the action were represented by very experienced specialist counsel, but neither of the judges was a specialist in the field. There has been no publication of the reason why a super-injunction was applied for and granted in that case: it is unusual to grant them against a generally law-abiding defendant such as a national newspaper. If it had been possible to fix a return date within a week or so, it may well be that the super-injunction would have been discharged at that hearing, and that there would have been no debate in Parliament and the press. But the pressure of the court's work may be the reason why that was impossible.

XI. Super-injunctions after 1998

Before 1998, when all hearings in the QBD prior to trial were heard in private, there was rarely an occasion to ask for a super-injunction in cases of personal information. I do not recall a personal confidentiality case where a super-injunction was ever asked for.

The practice of private hearings in the QBD changed with *Hodgson*.[75] In *Hodgson* a hearing for directions was heard 'in chambers', and an issue arose as to what the parties could say about that hearing. The judge had not delivered a judgment, and had said that a copy of his directions could be released to the public, but that the parties and their advisers were not to make any comment to the media in relation to the litigation without the leave of the court. In the Court of Appeal Lord Woolf recognised that there are practical advantages in holding hearings in private.[76] But he said that it would have been preferable to have given all the directions in open court, together with a judgment explaining why they were made, so that it would not have been necessary for the legal advisers to communicate with the media in order to explain what had happened.[77]

It is in accordance with this guidance that it is now common for judges sitting in the QBD to give formal judgments explaining their reasons for decisions on contested interim applications, just as they had always done after a trial (and just as judges in the Chancery Division had always done in interim applications).

[75] Above (n 69).

[76] He said: 'Hearings in private in chambers already make an important contribution to the administration of justice. They allow issues to be determined informally and expeditiously. They allow less strict rules as to representation to apply. They allow matters to be discussed which the parties might not wish to discuss in open court. They encourage openness. They are less intimidating to litigants which is particularly important in the case of the small claims jurisdiction. With the movement which is now taking place in relation to case management chambers hearings are likely in the future to make a greater contribution to the administration of justice than they do already.' (*Hodgson* (n 69) 1070H).

[77] ibid 1073G.

They sometimes now also give judgments explaining why they have made orders by consent.

It was, of course, always understood that an application for an interim injunction made ex parte was a derogation from one of the most fundamental of all principles of justice, namely that both parties have a right to be heard before a court makes an order (*audi alterem partem*). It follows that, in so far as a super-injunction is designed to achieve the same aim as an ex parte injunction (as argued above), a super-injunction is also a derogation from that same principle of justice. So such orders may only be made if there is a sufficient risk that the rights of the claimant will be defeated if the order is not made ex parte.

XII. The Numbers

In his 2010 article, Professor Zuckerman stated of super-injunctions that '[i]t is said that newspapers have been made subject to some 200 such orders in recent years, though given the secrecy shrouding such procedures it is difficult to have reliable information'.[78]

The suggestion (that there had been some 200 cases) upon which he is commenting is regrettable. There would be reliable information, if newspapers chose to disclose it. The court does not know upon whom a claimant has served its orders. But newspapers who are served with an order do know that fact. And if the newspapers thought the orders had been wrongly granted, it was always open to them to apply to the court to vary or discharge them (as the newspaper instructing me had done in the official secrets case I have described).

The only evidence in the Neuberger Report of an unlimited super-injunction is one example of an order made in 2008 that was not brought back before the court until 2011.[79] But there are few, if any, other old cases that have been brought before the court.

Professor Mullis and Mr Doley (a partner in a firm specialising in this field), as editors of *Carter-Ruck on Libel and Privacy*, describe the estimate of hundreds as 'fanciful'. I have never seen evidence to support such a figure. A comparison with the number of confidentiality and privacy injunctions granted as recorded in reported judgments and government statistics suggests that the figure is improbable. Although I have referred to the cases of orders granted in the QBD before 2000 in which there is a transcript or other public record as representing only a small proportion of the orders actually made, I have no evidence that such injunctions have ever been granted in numbers approaching a total of 200.

[78] Zuckerman (n 57) 131.

[79] *Goldsmith v BCD* [2011] EWHC 674. The Report referred to this case and reminded the press that they were free to apply to discharge orders.

One explanation for the figure of 200 may be that it includes anonymity orders, which do not contain super-injunctions within the definition used by the Neuberger Report.[80] Anonymity orders are regularly granted in the criminal courts and the Family Division.[81] Anonymity orders, and pseudonymity orders, are granted in all common law jurisdictions, including the USA.[82] For example, the real name of the plaintiff in *Roe v Wade* was not Ms Roe.[83] Anonymity orders are not super-injunctions. But they have sometimes been misreported as such. Two examples of such reporting are discussed in *ZAM v CFW*.[84]

In most cases in which a super-injunction has been granted (eg search and freezing orders in commercial disputes), no newspaper will have been notified of the order. Claimants do not give notice to third parties that they have obtained a non-disclosure order, unless there is a risk that that third party might disclose the information. But cases where the newspapers were not notified would obviously not be included within the figure of 200 to which, it is said, newspapers have been made subject.

In granting super-injunctions in cases of privacy or breach of personal confidence, the courts have not sought to introduce any new procedures. They have applied to such cases the same procedures that they developed in cases involving commercial confidential information and official secrets. As in those cases, so in privacy cases, INDOs could properly include a prohibition on disclosing the fact that they had been made, to prevent tipping off, as was referred to in the Neuberger Report.[85] In very rare cases there may be reasons why the order may be made for another reason.

Recent experience shows that in privacy cases there is often evidence that the defendant's motive is revenge or extortion.[86] This sometimes carries a risk of a pre-emptive disclosure, if the defendant is tipped off about the order before the claimant can notify him or her. There may also be a risk that e-mails and other evidence of wrongdoing will be destroyed because, if there is more than one defendant, they cannot all be served at once, or where, if served or given formal notice of the order, the defendant would be free to call friends to ask them to

[80] That is, the definition to which I have referred in this chapter: see Committee on Super-Injunctions (n 48) paras 2.1, 2.16.

[81] In the QBD, anonymity orders are granted in accordance with the guidance of the Court of Appeal given in *JIH v News Group Newspapers Ltd* [2011] 1 WLR 1645, [2011] EWCA Civ 42. Although (as they did in that case) the media are free to make representations on anonymity, they very rarely do so in privacy cases.

[82] See L Strahilevitz, 'Pseudonymous Litigation' (2010) 77 *University of Chicago Law Review* 1239; and see the recent privacy case *Plaintiff B v Joseph R Francis*, No 10-10664 DC Docket No 5:08-cv-00079-RS-AK (11th Circuit, 1 February 2011).

[83] 'Roe v Wade: Woman in US Abortion Legal Test Case Dies' (18 February 2017) *BBC News Online*, available at www.bbc.co.uk/news/world-us-canada-39016181 (last accessed 2 May 2017).

[84] *ZAM v CFW* [2013] EWHC 662, [99], [111].

[85] Committee on Super-Injunctions (n 48) para 2.29.

[86] Recent cases include *EWQ v GFD* [2012] EWHC 2182; *SKA v CRH* [2012] EWHC 2236; *London Borough of Lambeth v Pead* [2013] EWHC 212; and *ZAM* (n 84). Although none of these involved a super-injunction.

destroy the evidence. The *Aspect Capital* case illustrates how the destruction of evidence has become easier in the Internet age.[87] So a super-injunction may be both necessary and proportionate to protect a claimant's right to privacy.

However, as in cases involving commercial confidential information and official secrets, so in privacy cases, some orders were in the past made without a return date, when there should have been a return date, and some orders were made (particularly those made out of hours) that included provisions which either should not have been included, or should have been included only subject to specified expiry dates.

Some of the reasons why orders were made that were not necessary arise out of the circumstances described by Munby J in 2007. Judges commonly granted these orders out of hours, on urgent applications.[88] For the judge, an out-of-hours application may be one of several to be heard that night, following a whole day sitting in court. In such circumstances, neither the applicant nor the judge may have the time to give to the drafting of the order the attention that would be desirable. In out-of-hours applications the pressure of time can be extreme. For the applicant's lawyers, instructions have to be sought and recorded in writing. The intended claimants have to be advised of their duties to the court. They also have to be advised of the implications (which are sometimes enormous) of any decision to take proceedings, and of the need to give a cross-undertaking in damages. Investigations have to be made as to the extent of any disclosure to date, of whether there might be a defence and as to how one or more defendants are to be served. Judges and lawyers have been anxious to avoid the expense of a return date.

Those matters explain, if they do not justify, why some unnecessary super-injunctions may have been granted.

Since 2010 judges have adopted the exceptional practice of giving judgments in uncontested cases (posted on to the website of the British and Irish Legal Information Institute (Bailii.org)) for every non-disclosure order made where the subject matter was personal information said to be private or confidential.[89] And it is now also the practice in such cases to require claimants who have obtained interim orders to proceed to trial or to a final order arrived at by agreement.[90] The increased burdens that these practices place upon the court are significant. The Ministry of Justice statistics on privacy injunctions show that privacy injunctions continue to be granted, but in small numbers.[91]

[87] Above (n 58).

[88] eg, *AB v Barristers Benevolent Association Ltd* [2011] EWHC 3413, which did include a super-injunction when that was not necessary (at [2]) and was soon discharged.

[89] See Committee on Super-Injunctions (n 48) para 2.27.

[90] *JIH v News Group Newspapers Ltd* [2012] EWHC 2179, [32]–[37]; *Giggs (previously CTB) v News Group Newspapers Ltd* [2012] EWHC 431, [2013] EMLR 5, [20]. It was the failure of the claimant to comply with this requirement (not the actions of the third parties who disclosed his name in spite of the injunction) that led to the discharge of the INDO.

[91] Statistics on privacy injunctions are now included in the Ministry's Civil Justice Statistics Quarterly bulletins, available at <www.gov.uk/government/collections/civil-justice-statistics-quarterly>.

I am not aware of any super-injunction in a privacy case since the one mistakenly granted on 5 December 2011 in *AB v BBA*. There have been few injunctions granted against the media in the years since 2011.[92] As Lord Woolf said in *Hodgson*,[93] 'the great majority of matters dealt with in chambers are of no interest to anyone except the parties involved'. It is rare in the extreme for representatives of the media, or anyone else, to apply to vary or discharge a non-disclosure injunction where not themselves a defendant.

There may be a number reasons for the apparent decline in the number of privacy injunctions. One reason is that the law has become clearer in recent years. Cases of photographs taken surreptitiously were relatively common. They are not now, because the newspapers know that they will be acting unlawfully if they publish them in most circumstances.

In 2011, Professor Zuckerman wrote to the effect that the concerns he expressed in 2010 had since been assuaged.[94]

XIII. Parliament and the Rule of Law

The rule of law precludes arbitrary government. So it requires the separation of powers. The legislature and the executive should refrain from interfering with the administration of justice. As the *Trafigura* case illustrates, the controversy about super-injunctions, and about privacy injunctions generally, has led to breaches of this principle. The *PJS* judgment records that a breach of the principle in that case was only avoided by the Speaker of the House of Commons intervening to prevent the claimant's being named in Parliament.[95]

The Neuberger Report records how this constitutional principle is expressed by the House of Parliament's *sub judice* rules, to ensure that each refrains from trespassing on the other's province, and explains that '[t]heir proper application ensures that the rule of law is not undermined and that a citizen's right to fair trial is not compromised'.[96] The Neuberger Report also records that '[t]he *Trafigura* case demonstrated that where a super-injunction or an anonymised injunction exists, there is no adequate mechanism to enable the relevant Parliamentary authorities (the House authorities) to ascertain whether there are active proceedings in place'.[97] It recommended that '[t]he [Minister of Justice], [Her Majesty's

[92] *Spelman v Express Newspapers* [2012] EWHC 355 and *Rocknroll v News Group Newspapers Ltd* [2013] EWHC 24 are examples on Bailii since 2011. Neither included a super-injunction or an anonymity order.

[93] Above (n 69) 1071A.

[94] A Zuckerman, 'Common Law Repelling Super Injunctions, Limiting Anonymity and Banning Trial by Stealth' (2011) 30 *Civil Justice Quarterly* 223.

[95] *PJS* (n 2) [8].

[96] Committee on Super-Injunctions (n 48) vi, ch 5.

[97] ibid vi.

Courts and Tribunals Service] and the House [of Commons] authorities should consider the feasibility of a streamlined system for answering *sub judice* queries from the Speakers' offices'.[98]

This breakdown in the relationship between Parliament and the courts led to discussions between the Lord Chief Justice, Lord Judge, and Sir Robert Rogers, the Clerk of the House. Sir Robert Rogers was both the principal constitutional adviser to the House, and the principal adviser on its procedure and business. He recounted what happened in a lecture published later. Sir Robert Rogers states that the two Houses of Parliament set up a Joint Committee on Privacy and Injunctions. He suggested to the Committee that what was needed was a rule on court orders that would both formalise a rule against breaking them and arm the Chair with disciplinary powers if the rule were broken. But 'the Joint Committee decided not to go down this road because – interestingly – they did not see it as a sufficiently frequent problem. And there, at least for the moment, matters rest.'[99]

Cases cited in *PJS* explain the effect of these breaches of court orders in Parliament. The news media defendants returned to court to apply for the INDOs to be discharged, arguing that the information was no longer secret. These arguments failed (as they did in *PJS*). By seeking to frustrate the orders of the Court, those who have instigated these disclosures by MPs in Parliament in breach of the separation of powers, and the MPs who named claimants in Parliament, were undermining the rule of law.

The breaching of court orders in Parliament is not the only means by which the rule of law has been undermined, whether intentionally or unintentionally. Another means has been misreporting. Examples of misreporting, both in Parliament and in the press, are discussed in some cases.[100]

Unfortunately, the misreporting persists, and has extended even to the *PJS* case itself. In its online report of *PJS*, the BBC includes the statement that 'Before [the HRA changed the law in 2000] newspapers could publish whatever they liked about a person. As long as it wasn't defamatory, it could be as private as they liked.'[101] This is, of course, incorrect. News publishers have known since the *Prince Albert* case in 1849,[102] or at least since *Argyll* in 1967,[103] that they could not lawfully publish private information disclosed in breach of confidence, unless they could establish a public interest in their doing so. This inaccurate report appeared (as it still appeared in May 2017) notwithstanding the citation in *PJS* of the pre-HRA

[98] ibid.

[99] Lord Lisvane, 'The Courts and Parliament' [2016] PL 272, 274.

[100] *Goodwin v News Group Newspapers Ltd* [2011] EWHC 1309, [10]–[11]; *Goodwin v News Group Newspapers Ltd* [2011] EWHC 1437, [2011] EMLR 27, [28].

[101] 'Celebrity Injunction Déjà vu All Over Again' (19 May 2016) *BBC News Online*, available at www.bbc.com/news/uk-36084207 (last accessed 1 May 2017).

[102] Above (n 8).

[103] Above (n 3).

confidentiality cases *Spycatcher* and *Blair v Associated Newspapers Ltd*,[104] and the statement in the Neuberger Report that

> [i]n cases of confidentiality … the information which such injunctions seek to protect has long been capable of protection in English law. Confidential information, which is sometimes but not necessarily sexual information, passing between individuals in certain types of relationship, where the source of the information is a party to that relationship, has long been held to be capable of protection by court order: *Prince Albert v Strange* (1849) 41 ER 1171, where Lord Cottenham LC observed that the real issue in the case was privacy; 1 Mac & G 25, *Argyll v Argyll* [1967] Ch 302, *Stephens v Avery* [1988] Ch 449.[105]

The effect of such misreporting is to give to the public the impression that the HRA has had a greater impact on the freedom of the press to disclose private information than in fact it has. In reality, few privacy injunctions granted since 2000 would not have been granted under the law of confidentiality as it was understood to be before the HRA came into force in October 2000. Perhaps the most notable development of the law since the HRA has been to discourage newspapers from publishing photographs taken without consent in, or from, public places, such as in a hospital (*Kaye v Robinson*),[106] or by telephoto lens (as in *Spencer v United Kingdom*).[107]

Human rights include government under the rule of law, privacy and freedom of expression. Undermining one undermines them all. David Feldman has repeated a view expressed by many:

> Ordinary citizens … must internalize the values of individual and group rights, because democracy can be reconciled with respect for rights only if the people who participate in political decision-making, however remotely, exercise their powers in the light of people's rights.[108]

If the people are encouraged by misinformation to despise rights and the rule of law, democratic decision-making will suffer. It is remarkable that, in what the news media claim to have been a fight for freedom of expression, they have undermined that very principle. By the misreporting of privacy cases they undermine one of the main arguments in support of freedom of expression: that it leads to discovery of the truth.

[104] *Blair v Associated Newspapers* (QBD, 10 March 2000).
[105] Committee on Super-Injunctions (n 48) para 1.3.
[106] Above (n 67).
[107] Above (n 67).
[108] D Feldman, *Civil Liberties and Human Rights in England and Wales*, 2nd edn (Oxford, Oxford UP, 2002) 1089.

3

Varieties of Damages for Breach of Privacy

JASON NE VARUHAS*

I. Introduction

This chapter interrogates which types of damages are and ought to be available for the action of misuse of private information in English law, and which types of damages are not and ought not to be available. The chapter first considers compensatory damages, arguing that a vindicatory model does and ought to characterise the approach to compensatory damages. According to this approach, damages are available as of right for the wrongful invasion of privacy in itself, as well as for proven consequential losses. The chapter then examines non-compensatory damages. The courts are yet to authoritatively determine the availability of such damages for breach of privacy, and the principles governing their award. The chapter argues that exemplary damages ought to be available but that disgorgement and 'vindicatory damages' ought to be rejected. Reasonable fee or user damages should not be recognised. Lastly, the chapter considers damages in lieu of an injunction, arguing that these damages are equivalent to a fee for the loss of a liberty to enforce primary rights. Such damages ought very rarely to be awarded in the place of an injunction in a case of ongoing, unjustified invasion of privacy.

All in all, the remedial approach to breaches of privacy ought to, and increasingly does, follow that which has characterised vindicatory torts such as trespass to land, false imprisonment and battery. These actions have long performed a constitutional role in protecting those interests fundamental to English civil society.

* I am grateful to participants at the *International Workshop on Remedies for Breach of Privacy*, Melbourne Law School, 12–13 December 2016 for comments on an earlier draft of this chapter and for two days of stimulating discussion on the law of remedies for breach of privacy. An earlier draft of this chapter was also presented at a 'Judges and the Academy' seminar held at the Supreme Court of Victoria on 17 February 2017. I am grateful to participants for their very helpful comments, and in particular to fellow panellist, Hon Marcia Neave, and to Hon Chris Maxwell, President of the Victoria Court of Appeal.

II. Compensatory Damages

This section will first sketch the outlines of a 'vindicatory' model of compensatory damages that has long pertained within, and indeed is a defining feature of the English law of torts. The section then advances a normative claim that this model of compensatory damages ought to be adopted within the action for misuse of private information, and an allied expository claim that the law of privacy, as it has evolved, has embraced the vindicatory model. The law is thus on the right course.

A preliminary point requires to be made. I consider that only limited insight can be gained from debating whether the action for misuse of private information is or is not 'a tort'. This is because there are many torts, they perform different functions and they may have radically different characteristics from one another, including – importantly for present purposes – quite different approaches to causation and damages. Of greater value is to identify the normative concerns that underpin creation of the primary privacy rights, and a remedial model which gives effect to and carries forward these concerns at the remedial stage. This will ensure that, as a practical matter, remedies help the law to achieve its normative ends, rather than stymieing fulfilment of those goals. As a matter of principle, connecting rights and remedies ensures that the field of privacy is coherent. As Lord Reed observed in *AIB*, 'the loss resulting from a breach of duty has to be measured according to legal rules, and different rules apply to the breach of different obligations', these rules in turn reflecting the distinctive 'nature' and 'rationale' of the obligations breached.[1]

A. Preliminaries: Factual and Normative Losses

Let us begin our examination of compensatory damages by distinguishing two different types of compensatory damages.[2]

The first type of compensatory damages is damages for material or factual loss. Such damages compensate for the negative physical, emotional, psychological or economic effects actually suffered by the claimant in consequence of a wrong, such as costs of repairing a machine, pain and suffering or distress. These types of loss are subjective in the sense that whether they are suffered and their extent will vary from one claimant to the next, according to the actual consequences they experience

[1] *AIB Group Plc v Mark Redler & Co Solicitors* [2014] 3 WLR 1367, [92]. See also, to similar effect, Lord Reed's judgment in *Morris-Garner v One Step (Support) Ltd* [2018] UKSC 20, [31] et seq. Please note that *Morris-Garner* was handed down by the Supreme Court as this chapter was going to press. I have done my best to incorporate reference to the case where appropriate.

[2] See further JNE Varuhas, *Damages and Human Rights* (Oxford, Hart Publishing, 2016) chs 2–3; JNE Varuhas, 'The Concept of "Vindication" in the Law of Torts: Rights, Interests and Damages' (2014) 34 *OJLS* 253.

as a result of the wrong. Recovery of this type of loss is at least subject to ordinary 'but for' analysis and to remoteness rules, albeit those rules may vary from one type of wrong to the other. This type of material or factual loss is recoverable across the law of torts, although specific heads of damage vary across different actions.

The second type of compensatory damages is radically different in nature, and the availability of these damages is, within the law of torts, in general limited to those torts, like trespass to land, battery, false imprisonment and defamation, which are actionable per se and constituted to afford strong protection from outside interference to basic interests. Within these torts a claimant may recover damages for the injury to those of his or her interests directly protected by the tort. So traditionally one recovers in false imprisonment for the damage to one's interest in liberty inherent in the wrongful imprisonment under the head of loss of liberty. In battery one may recover for the damage to one's interest in physical integrity inherent in unwanted physical contact, whether or not the battery caused the claimant any injury, distress or medical expenses. One may recover in defamation for the damage to one's interest in one's reputation, regardless of whether the libel causes any distress or loss of income. In trespass to land the landowner recovers damages for the wrongful interference with his or her interest in exclusive possession of land, notwithstanding whether the wrong left the landowner no worse off.

Unlike damages for factual losses, which correspond with real-world effects, these damages compensate for a damage that is constructed by and only exists on the plane of the law. In this way they are akin to expectation damages in the law of contract; there is no such thing as an expectation loss outside of the law, but without construction of this head promises would be rendered hollow. I refer to these types of damages as 'normative damages'. In constructing these heads of damage the law is seeking an end or a goal – that is to give effect to the policies which underpin creation of the primary rights. As we shall see, torts such as false imprisonment and trespass are characterised by a primary function of affording strong protection to basic interests from outside interference, and vindicating these interests, in the sense of affirming and reinforcing their importance within a hierarchy of legally protected interests and that they ought to be respected. The law, by responding to every wrongful infringement with a substantial award of damages for the interference with the interest in itself, and regardless of the happenstance of whether factual losses are suffered, affords strong protection to the interest, which is the very object of the law's protection, and sends a signal that these are interests of the utmost importance, which ought to be maintained inviolate.

For normative damages factual causation is irrelevant. Normative damage is inherent in the wrongful interference. This is often captured in the idea of a presumption of damage within torts actionable per se. In the leading authority of *Ratcliffe*, the Court observed that the law 'implies' general damage 'in every breach of contract and every infringement of an absolute right'; '[i]n all such cases the law presumes that *some* damage will flow in the ordinary course of things from the mere invasion of the plaintiff's rights'.[3] In contrast within torts actionable only upon proof of loss, 'it is the damage done that is the wrong; and the expression "special damage," when used of this damage denotes the actual and temporal loss which has, in fact, occurred'.[4] Similarly in *Forster*, Stephenson LJ observed, '[w]hereas damage is presumed in trespass and libel, it is not presumed in negligence and has to be proved'.[5]

Thus, if someone camps on my land for two weeks without my consent, I may recover substantial damages in trespass regardless of the fact that I would not have leased the land but for the trespasser's use, and regardless of the fact that I myself, for whatever reason, could not and would not have made use of the land. So I am left no worse off in any material sense but I still recover.[6] Similarly in conversion, I can recover against you for converting my airplanes, even though it was inevitable that if you had not converted them someone else would have.[7] So your conversion leaves me materially no worse off as I would not have had the planes anyway. Nonetheless, I can recover substantial damages. In defamation the claimant 'gets damages because he was injured in his reputation, that is simply because he was publically defamed'.[8] In respect of battery it has been said at the highest level that the 'most trifling and transient physical assault' will give the claimant an action 'sounding in damages (and if appropriate aggravated or exemplary damages)'.[9] There is no appeal here to but for counterfactual analysis; one gets damages simply because one's basic interests were wrongfully interfered with. Similarly, if one is falsely imprisoned it ought not to matter that one could have been lawfully imprisoned in exactly the same way in any case, albeit this orthodoxy has come under threat in recent times.[10]

How do we explain this approach to factual causation? Why does it not matter that, for example, the claimant would have suffered an interference in any case? To answer this we need to go back to the nature of torts such as defamation or battery as being torts concerned with protecting interests *from outside interference*. The law's starting assumption in these actions is that the position each person ought to be in is one in which his or her basic interests are inviolate and maintained in pristine form. Wherever there is an interference with those interests that cannot be justified, the law takes the view that the claimant has been subject to an interference to which he or she ought not to have been subjected. Normative damages redress the imbalance between the position the claimant is entitled to be in – one in which the claimant's interests are in pristine form – and the claimant's

[3] *Ratcliffe v Evans* [1892] 2 QB 524, 528 (emphasis in original).

[4] ibid.

[5] *Forster v Outred & Co* [1982] 1 WLR 86, 94.

[6] Varuhas, *Damages and Human Rights* (n 2) 55–59; Varuhas, 'Concept of Vindication' (n 2) 284–89.

[7] *Kuwait Airways Corp v Iraqi Airways Co* [2002] 2 AC 883.

[8] *Uren v John Fairfax & Sons Pty Ltd* (1966) 117 CLR 118, 150.

[9] *Watkins v Secretary of State for the Home Department* [2006] 2 AC 395, [68].

[10] Compare *Christie v Leachinsky* [1947] AC 573 (especially the speech of Lord du Parcq) and *R (Lumba) v Secretary of State for the Home Department* [2012] 1 AC 245. See Varuhas, *Damages and Human Rights* (n 2) 61–67.

position given the wrongful interference, where his or her interests are subject to an encumbrance to which they ought not to have been subject. This approach is most explicit in conversion, where the courts assess damages by reference to 'the owner's position had he retained his goods' – that is, the position the owner ought to have been in – as opposed to the position the owner actually would have been in but for the defendant's wrongful actions.[11] Thus, 'there may be no actual loss' but 'the law takes the view as a matter of policy that the claimants … are entitled to substantial compensation for the mere invasion of their rights';[12] in such circumstances, 'damages do not necessarily depend upon precisely what would have occurred but for the wrong'.[13]

As Lord Hoffmann said in *Kuwait Airways*, 'causal requirements follow from the nature of the tort'.[14] How we frame the damages inquiry depends on the normative concerns of the law, and in vindicatory, protective torts the counterfactual is constructed in such a way as to give maximal protection to basic interests.

Remoteness is irrelevant for normative damage. A head of damage that responds to the wrongful interference in itself can never be too remote from the wrongful interference.

B. Connecting Rights and Remedies

i. Vindicatory Torts: Fundamental Features

Within the law of torts, normative damages have been confined to a set of torts which I refer to as vindicatory torts and which protect those rights that Blackstone described as absolute rights, and which – within the common law system – have been regarded as constitutional in nature. The paradigm vindicatory torts are trespassory torts, such as trespass to land, false imprisonment and battery. However, other torts in this category include defamation, conversion and nuisance by interference.

The reason normative damages have traditionally been confined to these torts lies in their primary functions. These torts are concerned to protect the most fundamental of human and proprietary interests from outside interference, creating zones of protection, and to vindicate these interests in the sense of affirming and reinforcing their importance and that they ought to be maintained inviolate. Normative damages give direct effect to these protective and vindicatory policies at the remedies stage. In this light it is unsurprising that newer contexts in which such damages have been recognised or contemplated include anti-discrimination torts and human rights damages actions, these fields

[11] *Kuwait* (n 7) [80]–[83].
[12] *Devenish Nutrition Ltd v Sanofi-Aventis SA* [2009] Ch 390, [36].
[13] *Experience Hendrix LLC v PPX Enterprises Inc* [2003] EMLR 25, [26].
[14] *Kuwait* (n 7) [127]–[129].

similarly being underpinned by a policy of strong protection and vindication of basic interests.[15]

We see the primary protective and vindicatory concerns of these actions in their core features. They are all actionable per se; loss is *not* the gist of the action. That an individual may prove a wrong and access remedies for a mere interference with their interests, even if it leaves him or her no worse off, attests to and reinforces the fundamental importance of the interests as well as their inherent value, while affording those interests strong protection. Thus in false imprisonment it has been said that '[w]hen the liberty of the subject is at stake questions as to the damage sustained become of little importance'.[16] Of defamation, Lord Hoffmann explained that reputation is a part of a person's 'personality, the "immortal part" of himself and it is right that he should be entitled to vindicate his reputation and receive compensation for a slur upon it without proof of financial loss'.[17] In regard to battery, Lord Goff in *Re F* recalled the fundamental principle that every person's body is inviolate, and that one is protected not only against injury but also against any physical molestation.[18]

Within these torts liability is not fault-based but strict or relatively strict.[19] The focus is firmly on the claimant's interests and whether they were interfered with, rather than whether the defendant's conduct was blameworthy or not. Such strict approach to liability signals the importance of the protected interests, and that it is inexcusable to trespass upon these interests whether one is acting benevolently, reasonably or innocently. Liability is strictest in trespass to land, where voluntarily walking onto another's land is sufficient to generate liability, whether the defendant knew it was someone else's land or not. In defamation the defendant may be liable even if he or she had no reason to know the material published was defamatory, his or her belief as to the truth of the statement was reasonably held or the defamation was the product of an innocent mistake. Liability is less strict in battery and false imprisonment, but still relatively strict. Intention to cause harm is not required, nor necessarily an intention to, for example, touch in the knowledge that the claimant did not consent. However, in battery an intention to touch is required, or at least reckless touching. In false imprisonment it may be that only an intention to do the act that causes the imprisonment is required, albeit some authorities suggest an intention to imprison or recklessness is necessary. Either way, it does not matter that the claimant did not know that he or she was imprisoned and would have had no occasion to leave the

[15] eg, in Australia under anti-discrimination law (*Wotton v State of Queensland (No 5)* [2016] FCA 1457, [1619]–[1629]) and in New Zealand for breach of the New Zealand Bill of Rights Act 1990 (*Dunlea v Attorney-General* [2000] 3 NZLR 136).

[16] *John Lewis v Tims* [1952] AC 676, 680.

[17] *Jameel v The Wall Street Journal Europe Sprl* [2007] 1 AC 359, [91]. But note the Defamation Act 2013, s 1 and certain procedural restrictions: *Tamiz v Google Inc* [2013] EWCA Civ 68, [48]–[52].

[18] *In re F* [1990] 2 AC 1, 72.

[19] See further Varuhas, *Damages and Human Rights* (n 2) ch 2.

place of confinement, while the defendant's blameless, good faith or benevolent acts or acts based on a genuine misunderstanding may generate liability.[20]

If the claimant proves an interference with his or her protected interests, the onus is on the defendant to justify his or her act. Whereas it is relatively easy for the claimant to make out a prima facie case, the defendant may face an uphill task; this reflects the importance placed on the protected interests – the cards are stacked in the claimant's favour, as the law's preference is for basic interests to be maintained inviolate. Defences protect only the most important of countervailing interests and will be construed narrowly. Something of great importance is required to justify interference with fundamental interests.

Thus the basic features of these torts reflect and give effect to the underlying normative concerns of these actions – to afford strong protection to fundamental interests and to affirm and reinforce their importance and the fact that they ought to be maintained inviolate and respected.

ii. The Evolving Privacy Action: Fundamental Features

The action for misuse of private information – or perhaps more appropriately, the action for breach of privacy[21] – as it has evolved over time, shares the basic features of these vindicatory torts. That protection of privacy belongs to the genus of vindicatory, rights-based actions has likewise been recognised explicitly in comparative jurisprudence.[22]

Actionable Per Se. Such claims are actionable per se. It is not a prerequisite for bringing a claim for misuse of private information that one is able to demonstrate actionable or special damage, as is the case for loss-based actions such as negligence or misfeasance in public office. For example, in *AAA* the claimant, a child, did not even know the relevant photos were taken. The child suffered no physical injury to person or property, nor any financial losses, in consequence of the breach of privacy.[23] Indeed there was no evidence of distress before the court. Yet a claim was successfully brought and damages awarded. Similarly, two of the child claimants in the case of *Weller* successfully bought privacy claims and recovered damages, despite apparently suffering no distress or other actual loss.[24] In *Imerman* it was held that simply accessing or retaining private information could be wrongful in itself.[25] In similar vein, in *Gulati*, it was confirmed that phone hacking constituted an actionable breach of privacy, regardless of whether the

[20] See, eg, *R v Governor of Brockhill Prison, ex parte Evans (No 2)* [2001] 2 AC 19.

[21] See the discussion below in this section regarding the expanding scope of the action to encompass protection of privacy interests beyond those in information.

[22] eg, *C v Holland* [2012] 3 NZLR 672, [75]; *Hosking v Runting* [2005] 1 NZLR 1, [2], [42].

[23] *AAA v Associated Newspapers Ltd* [2013] EMLR 2; *Weller v Associated Newspapers Ltd* [2014] EMLR 7 (QB), [2016] 1 WLR 1541 (CA).

[24] *Weller* (QB) (n 23) [189]–[197]; *Weller* (CA) (n 23) [64]–[65].

[25] *Imerman v Tchenguiz* [2011] 2 WLR 592, [68].

claimant was aware of the phone hacking and whether the information garnered was ever published (see, eg, Yentob's case).[26] Again, claims were actionable regardless of the fact there was no physical injury to person or property or special losses: wrongful interference with privacy is the gist of the action, not the suffering of loss. This is also made clear by the fact that causation is not a formal element of the privacy cause of action, as it is for torts for which loss is the gist of the action, such as negligence. That causation is a core feature of such actions follows from the fact that proof of loss is also a core element; if loss is a core element then one must also show that it was the defendant who caused that loss.

It has been suggested that the impact of the defendant's actions on the claimant is a factor relevant to whether an expectation of privacy arises.[27] However, it has not been suggested that a serious impact on the claimant is a *prerequisite* to an expectation of privacy. And more generally the proposition that whether an expectation exists in the first place depends on an *ex post facto* analysis of the impacts of the defendant's actions on the claimant seems a dubious proposition: how can the determination of whether a right existed or not depend on events subsequent to the conduct giving rise to the (putative) wrong? Such proposition also seems out of step with the dicta in *Campbell* that it is not a necessary precondition for a privacy claim that disclosure of the relevant information would be 'highly offensive'; indeed the information in *Campbell* itself was held to be obviously private absent any inquiry into whether disclosure would be highly offensive or had had any actual impact on Campbell.[28] In any case, the 'highly offensive' test – which barely features in the post-*Campbell* jurisprudence – does not implicate an inquiry into whether the claimant in fact was offended or suffered mental distress. Rather the court asks, as one indicium of whether the claimant had a reasonable expectation of privacy in the relevant material, whether a reasonable person in the claimant's position would likely be highly offended by disclosure of the relevant information.[29] As such, as Lord Nicholls said in *Campbell*, if relevant, questions over actual degree of harm or impact more properly go to questions

[26] *Gulati v MGN Ltd* [2016] FSR 12 (Ch), [2016] 2 WLR 1217 (CA).

[27] eg, *Murray v Express Newspapers* [2009] Ch 481, [36]; *Weller* (CA) (n 23) [36]–[38].

[28] It is important to record that the high threshold of 'highly offensive' derives from the United States, where the tests governing the privacy torts have been heavily influenced by the a priori weight given to free expression. The context is very different in the UK, where – following jurisprudence of the European Court of Human Rights (ECtHR) – free expression and privacy are, *ceteris paribus*, accorded equal normative weight (*Campbell v MGN Ltd* [2004] 2 AC 457, [12], [55]). To adopt a 'highly offensive' test would afford privacy insufficient protection and strike the law's balance systematically in favour of free expression. See further JNE Varuhas and NA Moreham, 'Remedies for Breach of Privacy', ch 1 of this book, in relation to the importance of local context in analysing the law of privacy.

[29] Similarly one might ask how certain conduct would make a reasonable person in the claimant's position feel in determining whether a reasonable expectation of privacy should be recognised: eg *Campbell* (n 28) [99]; *Murray* (n 27) [35]. This differs from inquiring into actual subsequent effects on a given claimant, as such an inquiry can only be answered retrospectively whereas an objective inquiry can be answered prospectively. Further, the objective inquiry controls for overly-sensitive reactions of particular claimants. Of course, it may be that the actual impact on a given claimant carries *evidential weight* in determining how a reasonable person would be impacted by the disclosure.

of proportionality, and thus defences, than to the existence of an expectation of privacy in the first place.[30]

It is right that the privacy action is and ought to be actionable per se: privacy is a dignitary interest of such importance that one ought to be able to bring a claim in respect of a wrongful interference regardless of whether the interference leaves one worse off. This is one reason why breach of confidence would not be an appropriate vehicle for the protection of privacy. Albeit the condition is contested, and has arguably been so watered down that it is meaningless,[31] it is the case, as a matter of principle, that the suffering of detriment is a precondition for such a claim.[32]

Strictness of Liability. Albeit the principles are still being worked out, liability for misuse of private information seems to be towards the stricter end of the spectrum, in common with other vindicatory actions. However, this is not immediately obvious. The reason is because every such claim begins with an inquiry into whether a reasonable expectation of privacy exists, and this inquiry can implicate a range of considerations, including the type of information obtained by the defendant, the place in which the defendant's challenged conduct occurred, characteristics of the claimant, such as whether he or she is a child, and actions taken by the claimant, such as steps taken to keep out prying eyes. This indicates that there may be significant hurdles over which a claimant may have to leap before establishing a prima facie breach of his or her legal right. This stands in contrast to, for example, a claim in trespass to land, where as soon as the claimant can show that the defendant entered the claimant's land through a not involuntary act, the defendant is prima facie liable.

However, this difference does not necessarily demonstrate that liability in misuse of private information is not strict, or at least relatively strict. The reason is that the inquiry into whether there is a reasonable expectation of privacy in the relevant information is an inquiry into whether the claimant had a right that that information be maintained as private. In other words, the reasonable expectation inquiry is an inquiry into whether the claimant had a privacy right *in the first place*, and the scope and extent of that right. Once the court concludes that there was a reasonable expectation of privacy then the defendant may be liable for simply acting inconsistently with that expectation, even if there was no malice or disclosure was the result of a simple error; the defendant did not grasp that the information was sensitive; the defendant acted out of a genuine concern for the claimant's best interests and/or in good faith;[33] the claimant had no idea his or

[30] *Campbell* (n 28) [22].

[31] See the suggestion in *Attorney-General v Guardian Newspapers (No 2)* [1990] 1 AC 109, 270 (and see 281–82) that a loss of friends may suffice to fulfil this requirement.

[32] *Coco v AN Clark (Engineers) Ltd* [1968] FSR 415, 421.

[33] eg, *Campbell* (n 28) [166] ('the motives of the respondents in publishing the information, which they claim to have done to give a sympathetic treatment to the subject do not constitute a defence, if the publication … revealed confidential material').

her privacy interests were being interfered with;[34] the defendant simply repeated known facts;[35] or the defendant strove to ensure that the claimant's privacy was protected but failed (eg digitalising someone's face in an image but not doing it well enough). In this way a 'misuse' of private information does not necessarily connote a blameworthy act (in the same way that the concept of 'wilful default' in equity does not necessarily connote blame, despite first appearances).

The case law is not entirely clear on the mens rea element required – the law is still in a developmental phase – though the law of privacy in this regard does not appear to be any less strict than the approach taken in other vindicatory actions.

It is clear that there is no need for the claimant to prove that the defendant intended to inflict loss or harm upon the claimant through the disclosure of information or other invasion of privacy, in common with other vindicatory actions. It also seems relatively clear that a defendant may be liable even if he or she did not intend a disclosure. In the case of *TLT*, the Court held disclosure of private information by mere error or carelessness to be wrongful.[36] In that case the Home Office, by mistake and unintentionally, uploaded private information concerning applicants for asylum and leave to remain to the UK Border Agency website. Claims for misuse of private information were proven and substantial damages awarded. Lord Mance's statements of principle in *PJS* reinforce this approach: 'any … disclosure' of sexual information 'will on the face of it constitute the tort of invasion of privacy'.[37] Such strict approach is consonant with a protective conception of the privacy action: what matters is the fact of invasion of basic interests, not whether the defendant can really be said to be to blame. Where basic rights are at stake the onus ought to be on the defendant to organise his or her conduct and take steps so as to avoid trespassing upon those rights, especially where he or she controls sensitive information relating to the claimant.

Some cases suggest that the defendant's knowledge is relevant, specifically whether the defendant knew the information accessed or disclosed was private or not. For example, in *Imerman* a key step in the Court's reasoning in finding that the defendant had breached the claimant's privacy by accessing the claimant's electronic documents, was that the defendant knew that the claimant reasonably expected his documents to be private.[38] However, even if knowledge is an element, it would seem from the emergent jurisprudence that the law will not typically insist on actual knowledge.[39] To insist on subjective knowledge would seriously weaken the protection of privacy (as well as raise potentially serious difficulties of proof for the claimant). Thus, many important categories of private information,

[34] As may be the case with phone hacking (*Gulati* (n 26)) or covert photos of a young child (*AAA* (n 23)).

[35] *PJS v News Group Newspapers Ltd* [2016] AC 1081, [26], [32]; *JIH v NGN Ltd* [2011] EMLR 9, [59].

[36] *TLT v Secretary of State for the Home Department* [2016] EWHC 2217.

[37] *PJS* (n 35) [32].

[38] *Imerman* (n 25) [68].

[39] See, eg, *Campbell* (n 28) [134].

such as medical, financial and sexual information, are in general considered to be 'obviously' private – as was clearly established in *Campbell* – so that any claim in respect of such information would not depend on what the defendant actually knew. Thus, if knowledge is indeed an element of the action then in this class of case the defendant shall be fixed with knowledge, and if the defendant discloses he or she shall be liable, even if the disclosure was the result of simple error.[40] As such, liability in these cases is very strict, as is apt where interests in highly sensitive information are at stake, and consonant with the approach in other vindicatory actions: the focus is on maintaining the claimant's basic interests inviolate, not on the defendant's blameworthiness.

Further, it would seem that even outside categories of case in which the information is 'obviously' private, the courts may find liability where the defendant did not subjectively believe or recognise that the information was private, on the basis that the court nonetheless considers there was, following an all-things-considered analysis, a reasonable expectation of privacy in the information disclosed by the defendant. It may be that knowledge is an element in such cases, but that the courts readily fix the defendant with constructive knowledge – that is, where a reasonable expectation of privacy is held to arise, the defendant will be assumed to have recognised the private quality of the information (albeit it is then difficult to distinguish such cases from the 'obvious' category of cases, the only difference being that in the 'obvious' cases no detailed multi-factor inquiry into the existence of a reasonable expectation of privacy is conducted). It is worth noting, however, that such approach does not necessarily render the defendant's actual knowledge irrelevant. What the defendant knew, and especially whether he or she knew that the claimant would not consent to the capture of the relevant information, may be one factor (among many) that goes to whether there was a reasonable expectation of privacy in the information in the first place. Thus, if the defendant subjectively knew the claimant would not consent to the taking of given photos, this may make it more likely that a court will conclude that the claimant had a reasonable expectation of privacy in the photos.[41] Importantly, such approach is conceptually distinct from requiring, as a *prerequisite* to liability, that the claimant prove that the defendant subjectively recognised the private quality of the information.

Thus, even if knowledge is an independent element – which is not entirely clear from the jurisprudence – it will often be assumed, and certainly where sensitive information is at stake. In combination with a strict approach to disclosure of information, overall the liability criteria for breach of privacy are relatively strict, in common with other protective, vindicatory actions constituted to protect basic interests.

Defences. Once the claimant has established a reasonable expectation of privacy and a breach of that expectation, the onus lies on the defendant to justify

[40] See *TLT* (n 36).
[41] *Murray* (n 27) [57]; *Weller* (CA) (n 23) [35], [63].

his or her act. In this way the basic structure of the privacy action matches that for the vindicatory torts; any interference calls for justification given the importance of the claimant's interests, and if the defendant has no good reason for his or her actions then he or she shall be liable. Only the most important concerns will be sufficient to justify an invasion of privacy, such as prevention and investigation of crime or national security. Commercial interests of newspapers, for example, do not carry much currency.[42] Consonant with the approach in human rights law, which has inspired the privacy action, justifications will be construed narrowly. Further, public interest justifications will be subject to the strict conditions of the proportionality test;[43] for example, even if the defendant can show that the interference with the claimant's privacy was genuinely motivated by a legitimate public interest in protecting national security, the defendant will need to show in addition that the interference was the least necessary to safeguard that public interest and that there was more general proportionality between means and ends. Again in common with human rights law, where purported justifications advanced by the defendant are premised on factual claims, evidence will be required to substantiate those claims, and the defendant's failure to establish relevant facts will lead to the defence failing.[44] Another justification often raised, especially in cases of press intrusion, is preservation of the basic rights of another, specifically freedom of expression. Of course even assertion of another fundamental right, freedom of expression, is insufficient in itself. In general there will need to be a real public interest in giving publicity to the private information before a disclosure can be justified. And for information of a particularly personal nature, such as medical information, financial information, information about sexual activity or information about a child,[45] it would seem that only an exceptionally strong real and legitimate public interest in release of the information could justify accessing or disclosure of such information.[46] For example, in *PJS* it was observed that 'there is not, without more, any public interest in a legal sense in the disclosure or publication of purely private sexual encounters, even though they involve adultery or more than one person at the same time'.[47] And even if it is legitimate to disclose such sensitive information, because there is a real public interest, it will only be justifiable to publish the least information necessary so as to satisfy the public interests at stake; for example, even where publication of the fact of a sexual affair is in principle justified, publication of the salacious details of the affair or the identity of the other party to the affair may well not be.[48]

[42] *McKennitt v Ash* [2008] QB 73, [66]. Albeit they may be relevant: eg *Campbell* (n 28) [77], [143].

[43] eg, *Campbell* (n 28) [138]–[141].

[44] See, eg, *Goodwin v News Groups Newspapers* [2011] EMLR 27, [134], [135], [137], [139].

[45] *PJS* (n 35) [36]; *AAA* (n 23); *Weller* (n 23).

[46] In this regard early statements, made at a time when the law of privacy was in its developmental phase, that countervailing rights of publishers will very often be expected to prevail, were too broad and have been superseded by subsequent developments: *Campbell* (n 28) [137].

[47] *PJS* (n 35) [32].

[48] See *Goodwin* (n 44); *Campbell* (n 28) [60].

From Breach of Confidence to a Vindicatory Action. Other features of the jurisprudence reinforce the protectionist concern that underpins the recognition of privacy rights. In particular, whereas breach of confidence was the original vehicle for developing the action for misuse of private information, as the jurisprudence has evolved the courts have gradually uncoupled the action from breach of confidence, and in doing so recalibrated features of the action to more closely resemble those of vindicatory torts. This process is of some importance, as it goes to proper classification of the action, but also because core features of the equitable action for breach of confidence, which have now been shed, would otherwise operate to impede full protection of privacy.

As the courts have emphasised, the privacy claim affords wider protection than the classic action for breach of confidence, in that information that is in the public domain may still remain private whereas confidence in it may be lost.[49] Importantly, as the courts have again emphasised, the privacy action is not, unlike breach of confidence, concerned only with maintaining secrets, while confidence has more generally developed principally in a commercial context – that of trade secrets – which in turn has fundamentally shaped its character. The concern within the privacy action is a wider one, which encompasses protection of individual dignity and autonomy from interference, something against which breach of confidence is not set up to protect given its narrower focus on information and its disclosure;[50] 'the concepts of confidence and privacy are not the same and protect different interests'.[51] This recognition as the jurisprudence has matured also reinforces that the privacy claim increasingly resembles the vindicatory torts, in that the concern is to protect basic interests from outside interference:

> What a concept of privacy does … is accord recognition to the fact that the law has to protect not only those people whose trust has been abused but those who simply find themselves subjected to an unwanted intrusion into their personal lives.[52]

Furthermore, obligations of confidence have often depended on a pre-existing relationship, whereas privacy, as a recognised human right, is of such importance that its protection ought not to depend on whether such a relationship can be demonstrated; to inquire into the existence of a relationship would 'distort' outcomes,[53] while the damage done by giving publicity to intimate facts may be no less because information has been sourced in the absence of a pre-existing relationship.[54] On the other hand, to continue to stretch breach of confidence so

[49] *OBG Ltd v Allan* [2008] 1 AC 1, [255] (noting also that, eg, a trade secret may be confidential but not private); *PJS* (n 35) [25], [57].

[50] *CTB v NGN Ltd* [2011] EWHC 1326, [23]; [2011] EWHC 1334, [3]; *PJS* (n 35).

[51] *Vidal-Hall v Google Inc* [2015] 3 WLR 409, [21]; *OBG* (n 49) [255] ('two distinct causes of action, protecting two different interests: privacy, and secret ("confidential") information'). See also *Hosking* (n 22) [48], [246].

[52] *Douglas v Hello! Ltd* [2001] QB 967, [126].

[53] *McKennitt* (n 42) [8], [15]; *Campbell* (n 28) [12]–[14].

[54] *Hosking* (n 22) [109].

as to afford sufficient protection to privacy will be to introduce incoherence into that action and warp its application in traditional fields, including trade secrets and employment.[55]

As long as the privacy action remained hitched to breach of confidence it could not evolve to protect types of privacy other than informational privacy. But in order to comply fully with the European Convention on Human Rights (ECHR), it seems inevitable that the action will have to evolve to embrace all types of privacy protected by Article 8, these types of privacy going well beyond informational privacy.[56] Indeed, the courts have routinely observed that the action has absorbed Article 8;[57] and it follows naturally from this that courts have explicitly begun to hold that intrusion upon privacy, absent any misuse of information, is actionable under the domestic privacy action. In *Goodwin*, Tugendhat J explicitly recognised that '[t]he right to respect for private life embraces more than one concept', ruling in that case that while the relevant disclosure would not constitute a misuse of private information, it would constitute wrongful intrusion upon private life more generally.[58] In *Imerman* it was held that merely accessing or retaining information may be wrongful.[59] This was reinforced by the decision in *Gulati*, which held that accessing phone messages was in itself wrongful, notwithstanding whether the information obtained was disclosed.[60] However, in *Imerman*, the Court nonetheless maintained that the privacy action remained of the confidence 'genus'.[61] But as the breadth of protection invariably expands to ensure compliance with Article 8, the conceptual integrity of this categorisation will be stretched to breaking point, or the categorisation will simply be rendered meaningless.[62] As such, it is unsurprising that since the decision in *Imerman* in 2011, the overwhelming trend has been for courts to classify the action as a tort.[63]

Lastly, whereas in breach of confidence the focus is upon the obligations of confidence owed by the defendant and considerations of conscience, within a vindicatory action the focus is upon the interests of the claimant and their protection from outside interference. As Lord Hoffmann said in *Campbell*, the focus is not on duties of good faith applicable to confidential information but on protection of human autonomy and dignity; thus the starting point is whether the claimant had

[55] ibid [46], [49].

[56] *Campbell* (n 28) [15] ('An individual's privacy can be invaded in ways not involving publication of information. Strip searches are an example. The extent to which the common law as developed thus far in this country protects other forms of invasion of privacy is not a matter arising in the present case'). Cf *Wainwright v Home Office* [2004] 2 AC 406.

[57] eg, *Imerman* (n 25) [65]; *A v B Plc* [2003] QB 195, [4]; *McKennitt* (n 42) [11]; *Campbell* (n 28) [17].

[58] *Goodwin* (n 44) [85] et seq. And see also *PJS* (n 35) [58]–[60].

[59] *Imerman* (n 25).

[60] *Gulati* (n 26).

[61] *Imerman* (n 25) [67].

[62] As Gault P and Blanchard J observed in the New Zealand Court of Appeal decision in *Hosking*, as long as protection of privacy is tied to breach of confidence, 'the United Kingdom courts will increasingly have difficulty reconciling decisions with Human Rights Act obligations' (*Hosking* (n 22) [40]).

[63] eg, *Vidal-Hall* (n 51); *Burrell v Clifford* [2017] EMLR 2, [149]. And see *Campbell* (n 28) [14]; *McKennitt* (n 42) [8].

a right to privacy in relevant information rather than an inquiry into whether the defendant ought to be held to have owed duties of confidence or the character of the defendant's conduct.[64] It follows from this, for example, that while actual knowledge has been an important aspect of the law of confidence (especially in cases outside those involving a pre-existing relationship) – as it marks the engagement of the defendant's conscience and justifies imposition of equitable duties – the defendant's actual state of mind is likely to be of less prominence within the developing law of privacy, which seeks to mark out a zone of protection within which basic interests ought to be maintained inviolate, regardless of considerations of conscience. The logic of this proposition is evidenced by a ready willingness to impute knowledge in the developing law of privacy, and the less prominent role of knowledge within privacy cases more generally.[65]

Thus the trajectory of legal development suggests the action is one concerned to protect and vindicate basic interests. This is reinforced by judicial statements to this effect. The courts have emphasised that '[p]rivacy is a fundamental right'[66] and that it 'lies at the heart of liberty in a modern state. A proper degree of privacy is essential for the well-being and development of an individual'.[67] The law of privacy is concerned 'to protect such matters as personal dignity, autonomy and integrity'.[68] Privacy is a recognised human right, and the emergence of the action for misuse of private information was a direct response to the requirement in human rights law that respect for privacy requires that privacy interests be protected from interference by private parties.[69] Vindication or the reinforcement of the importance of the interest in the face of interference has similarly been emphasised by courts, especially – as we shall see – in determinations as to remedies.[70]

C. Compensatory Damages for Breach of Privacy

There are thus strong similarities between the privacy action and longer-established vindicatory torts. In this regard the emergence of the privacy action might be accurately explained as an updating of the vindicatory torts, the new cause of action emerging so as to protect an interest that society today recognises as being of fundamental importance. Given that vindicatory torts and the action for misuse of private information protect similarly basic interests and perform

[64] *Hosking* (n 22) [2], [42], [246].

[65] See discussion at nn 38 et seq above. Of course there are increasingly indications that in at least some classes of case, an objective approach may be taken within breach of confidence itself. See the discussion in B McDonald, 'Privacy Claims: Transformation, Fault, and the Public Interest Defence' in A Dyson et al (eds), *Defences in Tort* (Oxford, Hart Publishing, 2015) 297–303.

[66] *Gulati* (CA) (n 26) [46].

[67] *Campbell* (n 28) [12].

[68] *Mosley v NGN Ltd* [2008] EMLR 20, [214].

[69] eg, *Von Hannover v Germany* (2006) 43 EHRR 7.

[70] *Mosley* (n 68) [216]–[217].

similar functions, as evidenced by their very similar legal structures, there is a powerful argument that the approach to damages ought to be analogous. Such a vindicatory approach to damages would give effect to the action's underlying policies at the remedial stage.

i. Damages for Interference with Privacy

It is therefore unsurprising that the damages jurisprudence has over time come to embrace an approach to compensatory damages identical to the vindicatory approach within torts actionable per se. We can trace the seeds of this approach back to Lord Hoffmann's speech in *Campbell*: 'An infringement of privacy is an affront to the personality, which is damaged both by the violation and by the demonstration that the personal space is not inviolate'.[71] In other words, the claimant suffers damage by the fact of interference with an interest that ought to be maintained inviolate. In the 2008 decision of *Mosley*, Eady J invoked an idea of vindication similar to that elaborated herein.[72] He indicated that damages could be awarded for the interference in itself, arguing that to award only nominal damages for breach of so basic a right would be inadequate. Put another way, damages ought to be awarded for the rights-violation, in part so as to reflect and reinforce the importance of the right. This idea, that quantum is a symbolic marker of the importance of the protected interest, is arguably evidenced in the more general and deliberate uplift in damages awarded for breach of privacy, which can be traced through the case law and which has brought sums more into line with other vindicatory actions such as defamation. In the 2011 decision of *Cooper*, Tugendhat J awarded £30,000 for a breach of privacy, this sum not apparently including any portion for consequential loss; he said that the sum would have been £40,000 if distress had been taken into account (distress had been compensated by a separate award for defamation).[73] In *AAA*, £15,000 was awarded to a very young child who had been covertly photographed. The child had no appreciation of the breach, and thus could not be said to have suffered any consequential losses such as distress. The award could only therefore be for the privacy interference in itself, and this is reinforced by the Judge's express statements that the award should reflect that the claimant's rights were breached 'and serve as notice, both as to the present and the future as to how seriously the court regards infringement of a child's rights'.[74] Put another way, the award vindicates the right, in the sense of reinforcing and affirming that privacy rights ought to be respected and maintained inviolate. In *Weller*, awards were made to three children, whose pictures had been

[71] *Campbell* (n 28) [75], quoting *R v Broadcasting Standards Commission, ex parte BBC* [2001] QB 885, 900.
[72] *Mosley* (n 68) [216]–[217].
[73] *Cooper v Turrell* [2011] EWHC 3269, [107] (QB).
[74] *AAA* (n 23) [127]. See similarly *Burrell* (n 63) [163].

published by a newspaper in breach of their privacy.[75] Two of the children received substantial awards of £2,500 each, despite not having suffered any distress – in contrast to the third child, whose award was explicitly uplifted as he had experienced feelings of embarrassment – suggesting the awards were for the breach of privacy *in itself*. This is further reinforced by the 'objective' nature of the factors that guided the Court in setting awards, which go more to assessing the seriousness of the wrong rather than gauging actual losses suffered. These included the degree of intrusion, what the photos showed, the extent of publication and how long the article was online.

The explicit embrace of the vindicatory model came in Justice Mann's magisterial judgment in *Gulati*, upheld by the Court of Appeal (permission to appeal to the Supreme Court refused). Justice Mann held that damages may be awarded to 'reflect infringements of the right itself', regardless of the suffering of consequential loss: 'The absence of distress does not mean that there was any less an invasion of privacy … If there was an invasion of a right then prima facie there ought to be a remedy.'[76] Mann J employs similar reasoning to that of Eady J in *Mosley*, saying that a failure to award damages simply because distress was not suffered would render the rights 'illusory', at least to a significant degree.[77] He makes a point of the utmost importance when he says:[78]

> The tort is not a right to be prevented from upset in a particular way. It is a right to have one's privacy respected. Misappropriating (misuing) private information without causing 'upset' is still a wrong. I fail to see why it should not, of itself, attract damages. Otherwise the right becomes empty.

The law of privacy is first and foremost constituted to protect the interest in privacy. It is therefore damages for damage to that interest that ought to be the first head of loss recognised by the law. It would make little sense for the law to afford compensation for consequential losses parasitic on the wrong, but not damage to the interest that is the very object of the law's protection. If the law's principal concern was to prevent consequential loss then consequential loss would be a prerequisite to bringing the claim, as it is in negligence. The right would not be a right in respect of privacy but a right not to be caused harm through interference with privacy. That is not the law: the action is actionable per se.

Justice Mann explicitly stated that such damages are compensatory in nature, confirming the normative loss thesis. These normative damages are, as in vindicatory torts, to be assessed objectively, with quantum varying with the seriousness or extent of the interference with privacy and not with the subjective effects suffered by the claimant, which are the province of consequential loss. This helps to explain why it was defensible *as a matter of principle* for Mann J to adopt a

[75] *Weller* (QB) (n 23) [189]–[197]. Appeal dismissed: *Weller* (CA) (n 23).
[76] *Gulati* (Ch) (n 26) [115].
[77] ibid [113].
[78] ibid [143].

tariff of £10,000 per year for serious violations by phone hacking (the approach makes sense *as a matter of practice* as it will facilitate settlements). *Ceteris paribus*, every victim of phone hacking suffers a basic level of interference with his or her privacy interest of the same extent or seriousness. The extent of the interference can of course be aggravated, so that the seriousness of the interference may be worse in one case relative to others; for example, where the information accessed is highly sensitive medical information, damages will rise significantly above the tariff, in contrast to a case where the phone messages contained fairly anodyne information.[79] One might respond that this is unfair on the defendant, who may have no idea in advance what type of information he or she will find. But this is the wrong perspective: damages compensate for the degree of interference with *the claimant's* privacy interests, and it is simply the case that a greater infringement is suffered when a defendant accesses information that is highly sensitive. Furthermore, it hardly lies in the mouth of someone who engages in phone hacking to complain.

Thus, quantum is assessed objectively. In cases of false imprisonment, damages for the interference with liberty in itself vary according to, inter alia, the duration of the imprisonment and the extent of the confinement. In trespass to land, user damages, for the interference with the interest in exclusive possession of land, are assessed according to, inter alia, the duration of the use and amount of land used. These considerations are indicia of the extent or seriousness of the violation. Damages for normative damage to privacy interests will vary according to similar considerations; as the Court put it in the post-*Gulati* case of *Burrell*, damages for normative damage respond to the 'degree of intrusion'.[80] I suggest that such damages should vary according to considerations similar to those that go to the existence of an expectation of privacy in the first place:[81]

> Where the violation entails the taking of information, the nature of that information will be material: *ceteris paribus* damages should be higher where the violation entails unauthorised taking of intimate pictures versus unauthorised accessing of the claimant's order history on the Star Wars online store. Extent of publication will be relevant: if the defendant publishes the information in a national newspaper, the interference shall be far more serious than if they publish it to no one. Location may be pertinent: installing a camera in the claimant's family home, and recording them, is likely to entail a far more serious interference with privacy, than recording someone on a public street. Duration shall also bear on quantum: *ceteris paribus*, damages should be higher where the defendant bugs my house for four months relative to where they bug my house for two weeks. The more times a violation is repeated – for example if there have been multiple instances of wrongful accessing of private information – the greater the award should be.

[79] ibid [229].
[80] *Burrell* (n 63) [162].
[81] Varuhas, *Damages and Human Rights* (n 2) 132.

Mann J took an approach on all fours with this. In setting quantum he considered, for example, the nature of the information accessed, whether it was disclosed, and the length, degree and frequency of the interferences by hacking. In other cases the extent of the disclosure has also been considered as one factor indicating a more or less serious breach, as well as how long the information was made available.[82] In *Burrell*, Spearman QC, sitting as a Deputy Judge of the High Court, explicitly stated that those factors relevant to determining the existence of an expectation of privacy could be relevant to damages.[83]

In setting quantum of normative damages (and also consequential non-pecuniary loss) courts have, so as to facilitate consistency and coherence of awards, sought guidance from: (1) awards made in past privacy cases, while making due allowance for the different facts of each case and the fact that the general level of awards have increased over time, so awards made early in the development of the jurisprudence may not be a safe guide today; and (2) scales applied in other fields of tortious liability, using scales applied in defamation, personal injury and anti-discrimination law as a rough sanity check, while always being aware that there is no precise correlation between awards made in different fields, and that privacy awards have their own character (for example awards for non-pecuniary loss in anti-discrimination torts do not include a component for normative damage for the wrong in itself, being limited to factual losses).[84]

ii. Damages for Consequential Loss

In contrast to the objective approach to normative damages, consequential losses depend on the subjective effects of the wrong on the individual claimant: '[a] thinner-skinned individual may be caused more upset, and therefore receive more compensation, than a thicker-skinned individual'.[85] These losses have to be proven, and factual causation established. In contrast to the position in respect of normative damage, which is inherent in and inseparable from a violation, rules of remoteness will likely apply to limit recovery of consequential losses for breach of privacy. The courts have not so far given detailed consideration to the remoteness rules that apply to the emergent privacy action. However, given the action's

[82] *Burrell* (n 63) [138] ('the extent of the misuse should be a relevant factor when assessing compensation for the wrong itself – because disclosure to the world at large involves a greater loss of control than a disclosure to, for example, a small number of journalists'); *Weller* (QB) (n 23) [196].

[83] *Burrell* (n 63) [139].

[84] See ibid [162]; *Gulati* (Ch) (n 26) [185]–[202]; *Gulati* (CA) (n 26) [60] et seq. Note also that while the *Simmons v Castle* [2013] 1 WLR 1239 10% uplift was not applied in *Gulati*, it seems from the reasoning therein that the uplift may apply to awards for non-pecuniary loss in future privacy cases: see *Gulati* (Ch) (n 26) [160]–[166]. For examples of courts considering scales in other fields in assessing privacy damages see eg *Mosley* (n 68) [212]–[231]; *Cooper* (n 73) [102]–[107]; *WXY v Gewanter* [2013] EWHC 589, [25] et seq; *TLT* (n 36) [11].

[85] *Gulati* (Ch) (n 26) [229](viii); *Burrell* (n 63) [140], [159].

evolving nature courts are likely to follow the approach within other vindicatory actions. In contrast to actions for which loss is the gist, such as negligence, recovery is not limited to those losses that are reasonably foreseeable. Rather, within vindicatory torts the defendant is liable for all factual losses that are a direct and natural consequence of his or her wrongful actions, at least where the wrong is intentional and arguably more generally.[86] Holding the defendent liable for all losses that flow directly from his or her violation of a basic right, regardless of foreseeability, carries forward the protective policies that underpin vindicatory actions, ensuring that the plaintiff does not have to internalise losses caused directly by the defendant's wrong. That courts have regularly awarded damages for various types of factual loss for breach of privacy without any inquiry into or mention of reasonable foreseeability in itself strongly suggests the absence of such a limit.

The vast majority of awards for consequential loss have been for distress, but awards have also for example been made for recognised psychiatric illness.[87] One would expect damages for consequential pecuniary losses to be recoverable on an analogy with other vindicatory actions; in contrast to non-pecuniary losses, which are 'at large', economic losses would need to be specifically pleaded. Aggravated damages are available for breach of privacy, in common with other vindicatory actions, and have been regularly awarded where the defendant's conduct is such as to injure the claimant's proper feelings of dignity and pride, including the defendant's conduct of proceedings.[88]

It is worth noting that in *Burrell*, Spearman DHCJ indicated his concern that the application of the egg-shell skull rule in regard to non-pecuniary loss may result in claimant A, who is unusually sensitive, receiving a higher award for an objectively less serious infringement of privacy than claimant B, who is not unusually sensitive but suffers a more serious infringement.[89] That there could be such disparity would seem unlikely (as Spearman DHCJ appears to acknowledge) given that awards for mere distress – which would comprise the majority of A's award – are typically modest, whereas one would expect claimant B to receive a significant award for a serious invasion of his privacy, whether or not he suffers distress, as the awards in cases of serious violation, such as *Gulati*, indicate. Indeed, the outcome in *Burrell* itself illustrates this point. A relatively modest award of £5,000 was made for an objectively less serious invasion of privacy but which caused significant distress to the claimant, who was particularly sensitive; as was noted in the decision, this was well below the £10,000 starting-point set by Mann J for serious cases of phone

[86] Varuhas, *Damages and Human Rights* (n 2) 72; J Edelman, *McGregor on Damages*, 20th edn (London, Sweet & Maxwell, 2018) [8-012]–[8-013], [8-050], [8-062]. See *Harnett v Bond* [1925] AC 669, 681–682; *Kuwait* (n 7) [99]–[104]; *Quinn v Leathem* [1901] AC 495, 537; *Jones v Ruth* [2012] 1 WLR 1495, especially [32]; *Essa v Laing* [2004] ICR 746, especially [38]–[39], [48] et seq.

[87] See, eg, *TLT* (n 36).

[88] See, eg, *Campbell* (n 28); *Gulati* (Ch) (n 26). Albeit a separate award of aggravated damages was not made in *Burrell*, interestingly Spearman DHCJ considered the fact that the breach had occurred in the context of a relationship of trust was a factor that would aggravate distress: (n 63) [160].

[89] *Burrell* (n 63) [142].

hacking, and far below any of the awards made in *Gulati*, which involved objectively very serious and sustained invasions of privacy. In any case, even if the type of disparity identified by Spearman DHCJ did arise, this simply follows from a compensatory approach: one receives damages in proportion to one's losses, otherwise one will be undercompensated. But perhaps what we ought to take from Spearman DHCJ's judgment is a reinforcement of the point made in section II.C.i, that it is the fundamental interest in privacy which the action is principally constituted to protect, rather than insulation from mere upset, and it is right that awards for the interference itself ought to be afforded primacy at the remedies stage, through awards on a higher scale than will be applied to consequential mental distress.

iii. Compensatory Damages Available as of Right

Importantly, in all of the major damages decisions discussed, damages followed as of course from the wrongful interference. There was no suggestion that awards were, for example, discretionary. There was no suggestion that, as some hangover of the action's origins in breach of confidence, equitable bars to relief applied. Rather, damages appear to be available as of right. This is the correct approach, especially for normative damages. Normative damage is a reflex of the wrong. If an individual suffers a trespass to land, that person ipso facto suffers damage to his or her interest in exclusive possession of land. If an individual is the subject of defamation, that person ipso facto is injured in his or her reputation. Similarly, if an individual suffers a wrongful invasion of privacy, that person ipso facto suffers damage to his or her privacy interests and ought to be compensated for that loss. This has been the general approach to damages for breach of basic interests in English law. It is difficult to see a basis for deviating from such approach specifically in the case of privacy. Indeed to do so would be to suggest that privacy is an interest of lesser importance, contrary to judicial statements reiterating its fundamental importance; rather than vindicating the normative importance of privacy interests, this would be to treat privacy rights as second-class rights. Furthermore, it would cut down protection of the right, again contrary to the policy of strong protection that pervades this field. Even in equity, where it is an available remedy, equitable compensation is generally awarded as of course where a claimant proves loss suffered pursuant to an equitable wrong (such as breach of a fiduciary duty of skill and care), albeit equitable bars are potentially applicable in theory at least.

iv. Vindicatory Approach to Other Relief

It is worth observing that the law's vindicatory policy in this area is also evident in the approach to other remedies. For example, in *PJS* the Supreme Court maintained an injunction restraining disclosure of private information even though the information was widely available. It is specifically where privacy has been egregiously violated that the courts ought to send a strong message that privacy is a right of fundamental importance and which ought to be respected. As Lord Neuberger said, 'The courts exist to protect legal rights, even when their protection is difficult or unpopular in some quarters.'[90] Consideration of the view of the minority Justice, Lord Toulson, sheds further light on the vindicatory dimensions of the majority's decision. Lord Toulson, in dissent, would have discharged the injunction on the basis that 'Once [the information] has become readily available to anyone who wants to know it, it has lost the essence of confidentiality. The court must live in the world as it is and not as it would like it to be.'[91] If Lord Toulson's judgment is based on an acceptance of facts as they are, one might say the majority judgments are based in a commitment to a normative view of how things ought to be. Whereas Lord Toulson's approach was to face up to the fact that PJS's privacy had been and was going to continue to be seriously infringed on a large scale, the majority's approach is consonant with a view that maintains that these are the very circumstances in which, despite the practical limits of the court's powers, the court can at least send the signal that these are rights of the utmost importance, which ought to be maintained inviolate and for which individuals ought to be able to enlist the aid of the courts.

D. Irrelevance of Strasbourg Practice under Article 41 ECHR

In the *Gulati* case in the Court of Appeal, Lord Pannick QC, for the defendant, argued that the approach to damages for misuse of private information ought to follow that of the ECtHR in making awards of just satisfaction under Article 41 of the Convention. This submission, if accepted, would have several key implications.[92] Awards would be set at scales far lower than domestic tort scales. Awards could be denied in the discretion of the court even where loss had been suffered,[93] a finding of violation being just satisfaction.[94] Normative damages would be unavailable, as the ECtHR only awards compensation for consequential losses such as distress. Further, as discussed below, the ECtHR does not award aggravated and exemplary damages.

[90] *PJS* (n 35) [71].

[91] ibid [86].

[92] See further JNE Varuhas, 'Damages under the Human Rights Act' in Edelman (n 86) pt V.

[93] Notably, discretionary factors applied under the HRA to deny damages have not affected claimants' entitlement to damages for the action of misuse of private information. For example, under the HRA, disproportion between the costs of litigation and the amount that could be awarded in damages has been a basis for denying awards. However, in *Burrell*, a privacy claim at common law rather than under the HRA, such factor was held to be irrelevant to the claimant's 'entitlement to compensation' ((n 63) [158]).

[94] Albeit a de minimus rule has been recognised within the action for misuse of private information, it would seem the threshold is exceptionally low and easily passed (*TLT* (n 36) [15]), whereas the ECtHR, and domestic courts under the HRA, have been willing to deny money awards in their discretion for relatively substantial losses on the basis that the loss is not considered 'sufficiently serious'.

The Court of Appeal rejected this argument and upheld Mann J's approach. With respect, the Court was right to do so. Elsewhere I have argued in detail why the ECtHR's approach to just satisfaction is inappropriate for transposition into domestic law.[95] Only a brief summary of those arguments is possible here. First, the Article 41 jurisdiction is that of a supranational court that performs a secondary, subsidiary and supervisory role in monitoring member states' compliance with an international treaty. The jurisprudence of such a court is not a model and is not intended as a model for the remedial practices of domestic courts, which have *primary* responsibility for remedying rights violations. Rather, remedial practices in domestic law are governed by Article 13, the right to an effective remedy. In contrast, Article 41 is not an article directed to or binding on member states; it is directed inwards to the ECtHR's own subsidiary remedial jurisdiction. Mann J in *Gulati* recognised this point, and rejected an approach that focused solely on consequential loss as one that would fail to provide an effective remedy in all cases: 'a regime in which damages were confined to damages for distress would render the rights (to a degree) "illusory" (to use the word used by the ECtHR) and would, to a degree, fail to provide an effective remedy [as required by Article 13]'.[96] Furthermore the ECtHR has itself, in laying down the requirements of Article 13, articulated an approach for domestic courts to follow that envisions something akin to damages for normative loss:[97]

> [T]he Court is of the opinion that the domestic courts, as the custodians of individual rights and freedoms, should have felt it their duty to mark their disapproval of the State's wrongful conduct to the extent of awarding an adequate and sufficient quantum of damages to the applicant, taking into account the fundamental importance of the right of which they had found a breach in the present case, even if they considered that breach to have been an inadvertent rather than an intended consequence of the State's conduct. As a corollary this would have conveyed the message that the State may not set individual rights and freedoms at nought or circumvent them with impunity.

Second, the ECtHR has itself said that domestic courts are free to and ought to follow their own remedial traditions.[98] Thus there is no imperative from Strasbourg that domestic courts follow the Article 41 jurisprudence.

Third, the Strasbourg jurisprudence is riddled with problems: the jurisprudence under Article 41 is characterised by parsimonious and opaque reasoning, and a lack of coherence, consistency, principle and predictability. Under the HRA, where this jurisprudence has been followed domestically, lower court judgments are replete with statements that the court has been unable to divine any tariff or meaningful principles or guidance from the ECtHR jurisprudence. As a result, the

[95] Varuhas, *Damages and Human Rights* (n 2) ch 5.
[96] *Gulati* (Ch) (n 26) [113].
[97] *Shilbergs v Russia* App no 20075/03 (ECtHR First Section, 17 December 2009) [78].
[98] *Scordino v Italy (No 1)* (2007) 45 EHRR 7, [188]–[189].

domestic case law on damages under the HRA has come to be characterised by many of the problems associated with the supranational jurisprudence.[99]

In addition to these points, the direction in section 8(4) of the HRA for domestic courts to have regard to the principles applied under Article 41 (to the extent any can be discerned) only applies to damages under the HRA; there is no such requirement to have regard to Article 41 jurisprudence applicable to the action for misuse of private information, which is an action sourced at common law.[100] As Arden LJ said in *Gulati*:

> English law has only recently recognised a civil wrong for intrusions of privacy. Initially the law of confidence was expanded by reference to the values to be found in articles 8 and 10 of the Convention. However, an action for breach of confidence did not completely coincide with a right of action for pursuing private information in violation of article 8 … The court, when making an award for misuse of private information is not proceeding under either section 8 of the Human Rights Act 1998 or article 41 of the Convention.[101]

The new action may have been inspired by the European Convention jurisprudence under Article 8 but the action is one for breach of duties sourced at common law. As such, the remedial approach must be one that coheres with the approach to damages for similar types of actions in English law, and quantum must be matched to domestic conditions: 'national courts are intrinsically better able to assess the adequacy of an award in their jurisdiction than an international body … the conditions of the tort are governed by English law and not the Convention'.[102] In subsequent privacy cases courts have cross-checked awards for losses such as mental distress and recognised psychiatric illness against domestic tort comparators in the personal injury context, and stated: 'damages are to be assessed under English domestic law and not the approach adopted by the Strasbourg court'.[103]

III. Non-Compensatory Damages

A. Exemplary Damages

On a vindicatory model of remedies, exemplary damages ought to be available for misuse of private information. In *Mosley*, Eady J ruled them out.[104] But in *PJS*, both Lord Mance and Lord Toulson suggested that Eady J's decision may not be

[99] See Varuhas, *Damages and Human Rights* (n 2) ch 5; Varuhas (n 92).
[100] In any case, even under the HRA recent lower-court decisions have, notwithstanding s 8(4), indicated a move towards domestic tort principles: *Alseran v Ministry of Defence* [2017] EWHC 3289, [871] et seq (QB).
[101] *Gulati* (CA) (n 26) [88]–[89].
[102] ibid [89].
[103] *TLT* (n 36) [19] and see [11]. See also text to n 84 above.
[104] *Mosley* (n 68) [172]–[197].

the last word on the matter.[105] Lord Toulson observed that such damages might play a useful role in 'deter[ring] flagrant breaches of privacy and provid[ing] adequate protection for the person concerned'.[106]

For some actions, such as the loss-based torts of negligence and misfeasance in public office, exemplary damages have traditionally not been available in principle. As a practical matter, such damages have never been awarded for negligence in England, and the House of Lords observed that exemplary damages will very rarely be available for misfeasance in public office.[107] In contrast, for vindicatory actions, exemplary damages have long been available and regularly awarded in cases of egregious wrongdoing. Their availability for such actions reflects the vindicatory and protective functions of these actions. The 'micro' goal of exemplary damages is punishment, such damages responding to and sanctioning outrageous wrongdoing. However, on a 'macro' level such damages give effect to the law's vindicatory and protective purposes. First, that significant awards may be made against defendants who egregiously interfere with very basic interests serves to enhance protection of those interests against such conduct. Second, that the civil law takes the exceptional step of punishing such interferences, and in so doing marking the law's 'vigorous disapproval'[108] of such conduct, signals the importance of the protected interests and reinforces that they must be afforded the utmost respect. Third, that such damages have traditionally been available, and indeed played a significant role within vindicatory actions, but have traditionally not been available for other actions reinforces the importance the law attaches to those interests protected by vindicatory actions.

In principle such awards ought to be available for the privacy action, as that action is informed by the same vindicatory and protective policies that underpin other vindicatory actions for which exemplary damages have long been a recognised remedy. Such awards would afford enhanced protection and a strong reinforcement of the importance of the protected interests and that they ought to be maintained inviolate in the face of an egregious violation, sending a signal that the law will not tolerate such disregard for the most basic of interests. As we shall see in section III.B.i, such damages can play a particularly important role in cases where the defendant deliberately breaches the claimant's privacy so as to make a profit.

One of Eady J's reasons for ruling out exemplary damages in *Mosley* was that it was questionable whether the privacy action is a tort. This issue has now been resolved in the case law in favour of the view that the action is a tort,[109] while, as discussed in section II, the key to making decisions as to remedies is to consider whether particular remedies are consonant with the policies underlying

[105] *PJS* (n 35) [42], [92].
[106] ibid [92].
[107] *Watkins* (n 9) [26], [32], [81].
[108] *Rowlands v Chief Constable of Merseyside* [2007] 1 WLR 1065, [42].
[109] *Vidal-Hall* (n 51).

creation of the primary rights. Another core reason given by Eady J for ruling out exemplary damages was that this would be inconsistent with the Article 41 jurisprudence of the ECtHR, which does not recognise exemplary damages.[110] With respect, this argument is not persuasive. First, the action for misuse of private information is a creation of domestic law. It has been informed by Strasbourg jurisprudence but it has been woven into domestic legal traditions. It would be inconsistent for compensatory damages to be approached on the basis of domestic legal thinking, as they have been, but for exemplary damages to be ruled out on the basis of Strasbourg jurisprudence. Similarly, that the Strasbourg jurisprudence does not recognise aggravated damages has not prevented those damages becoming a core aspect of the damages jurisprudence for breach of privacy. Second, as we saw in section II.D, the Article 41 jurisprudence is not a remedial model intended for adoption by domestic courts. As Starmer has argued, the Strasbourg Court's reluctance to award exemplary damages 'is in keeping with its role as an international supervisory body' – 'domestic courts have a different role'.[111] There are further reasons linked to this that explain why the Strasbourg Court has not embraced such damages but which are irrelevant to the domestic context; for example, the Court is cautious not to threaten its own legitimacy by making huge awards against member states and risking a significant political backlash. Third, as already noted, it is Article 13 that governs member states' remedial responsibilities – not Article 41. Under Article 13, the Strasbourg Court has made clear that domestic courts are free to develop remedial jurisprudence according to domestic traditions, and exemplary damages have long been an important aspect of the English law of damages. The one important limit that Strasbourg jurisprudence does impose on exemplary damages is that quantum should not be so large as to constitute a disproportionate interference with freedom of expression.[112] But this principle that exemplary damages should not be disproportionate in itself involves an acceptance by the Strasbourg court that it is permissible for domestic courts to award exemplary damages. This tells against Eady J's view that adoption of exemplary damages at all would be disproportionate and at odds with the Convention framework.[113]

B. Gain-Based Relief

Let us first consider a truly gain-based remedy, an account of profits, and then go on to consider reasonable fee damages, which restitution theorists claim are restitutionary, but which are properly analysed as compensatory for normative damage.

[110] *Mosley* (n 68) [196].
[111] K Starmer, *European Human Rights Law* (London, LAG, 1999) [2.46]–[2.47].
[112] *Tolstoy Miloslavsky v UK* (1995) 20 EHRR 442; *Steel and Morris v UK* (2005) 41 EHRR 22.
[113] *Mosley* (n 68) [197].

i. Account of Profits

In *PJS*, Lord Mance left open the question of whether an account of profits is available for the action for misuse of private information.[114] In my view such an award should not be available, or if it is to be made available, it ought to be available only exceptionally.[115] Such awards have been made in equity specifically in the context of pre-existing legal relationships. For example, such awards are available for breach of fiduciary duties. It makes sense that awards are available in the context of a fiduciary relationship. The fiduciary is required to act for the principal's interests, so the law holds that if the fiduciary deviates from this course, abusing his or her position to make a personal profit, the fiduciary ought to be required to put the beneficiary or the fund in a position as if the fiduciary had acted as he or she ought to have acted. If the fiduciary had acted as he or she ought to have, the monies ought to have been earned for the beneficiary's benefit. Of course such awards may be made for breach of confidence too, and breach of confidence is perhaps more analogous to the action for misuse of private information than a claim that a fiduciary breached the no-conflict rule. However, breach of confidence, at least traditionally, is also commonly based in a pre-existing relationship of confidence, and often one arising in the context of a fiduciary relationship.[116] For example where an employee or agent misuses the relevant information, such as trade secrets, for his or her own, rather than the principal's, purposes.[117] Again, logically one can understand why profits made by such misuse should be disgorged to the principal.

Some seek to sever the link between account of profits and equity, and argue that an account of profits – now, reframed in common law terms, 'disgorgement damages' – ought to be available for a more diverse range of wrongs, often arguing that there is no reason why the remedy should not be more widely available or could not play a useful role in other fields.[118] However, a weakness of such arguments is that they often ignore or place too little weight on the distinctiveness of different types of obligations and different doctrinal contexts. That compensation is the general remedy for vindicatory torts follows from the nature of the obligations, which are quite different from those in fiduciary relationships or relationships of confidence. The obligation in vindicatory torts is a negative one of non-interference with basic interests, and this applies regardless of any pre-existing relationship, being a general obligation imposed by law. It is consonant with a concern for non-interference that awards compensate for the extent

[114] *PJS* (n 35) [41].

[115] See also K Barnett, 'Gain-Based Relief for Breach of Privacy', ch 8 in this book.

[116] See also Turner's discussion of the nature of facilitative institutions: PG Turner, 'Privacy Remedies Viewed Through an Equitable Lens', ch 11 in this book.

[117] *Imerman* (n 25) [54].

[118] See, eg, A Burrows, 'We Do This at Common Law But That at Equity' (2002) 22 *OJLS* 1; *Attorney-General v Blake* [2001] 1 AC 268, 283–84. See also J Edelman, *Gain-Based Damages* (Oxford, Hart Publishing, 2001).

of a wrongful interference, and it is consonant with a concern to protect and vindicate the claimant's interests that normative damages respond directly to the invasion of those interests. There is a rational connection between the nature of the wrong and the remedial response. An account of profits could potentially go further, resulting in an award well beyond one required to compensate for the interference. In this way it invites the windfall objection: an award beyond that required to make the claimant whole represents a windfall gain for the claimant.

The common premise of arguments for an account is that compensatory damages may not be available or adequate on certain facts, for example where no loss is suffered in a case of a serious wrong. These were the circumstances in the case of *Blake*, where the House of Lords recognised that an account could be ordered exceptionally for breach of contract.[119] But the problem for this argument is that on a vindicatory approach to remedies, it is wholly unlikely that there would ever be a case where compensatory damages were inadequate (in combination with other remedies) or unavailable, given that such damages are granted as of course for normative damage, regardless of whether the claimant incurred any consequential, material losses. Even in contract the profit-based remedy recognised in *Blake* is effectively a dead letter, and even on amenable facts the courts have shied away from making such an award.[120]

These arguments suggest that an account of profits, if it were to be available for vindicatory torts, should be an exceptional remedy, limited to cases where other remedies would be unavailable or inadequate. In other words, it would have a gap-filling role (albeit it is wholly unlikely, or indeed impossible, that a gap could arise). Thus in contract the remedy is available exceptionally and where other remedies are inadequate.[121] In tort such an award has not – outside the intellectual property context – been recognised, although the courts have suggested that if it were to be available, it would be so only exceptionally outside of property cases.[122]

However, as has been observed many times, there is a lack of clarity over when a case will be exceptional, which in turn reflects a lack of clarity over the rationale for an account of profits outside of its traditional context of equity. The most common rationale given is that of deterrence. But this rationale is deeply problematic. First, if deterrence is to be the rationale we would need to know whether such awards in fact deter, yet there is little evidence on this, and in any case courts are not well placed to judge when such awards are necessary to alter incentives. Second, because the argument is an instrumentalist one, we would need to know that the benefits of making such remedies available would outweigh any costs.

[119] *Blake* (n 118).

[120] eg, *Experience Hendrix* (n 13).

[121] *Blake* (n 118) 285–86. Note that the continued force of *Blake* may well be open to question given core aspects of the reasoning in that decision were questioned recently by Lord Reed, in his lead judgment in *Morris-Garner* (n 1).

[122] *Forsyth-Grant v Allen* [2008] EWCA Civ 505, [31], [33]; *Devenish* (n 12) [88]; *Lawrence v Fen Tigers Ltd* [2014] AC 822, [131], [248].

Third, this rationale is completely removed from any doctrinal context, and there is little sensitivity to the discrete normative concerns of distinct fields of law such as contract or vindicatory torts. Protagonists of the wider availability of disgorgement typically offer deterrence as a general justification across torts and contract.

If a rationale is to be identified for the exceptional availability of such relief for misuse of private information, it must lie in the field's normative concerns and not rest on questionable speculations as to behavioural effects. Elsewhere I have suggested that one possible rationale, in the context of vindicatory actions, is that such awards could afford *added* protection and serve to *strongly* vindicate the importance of protected interests and that they ought to be respected, in exceptional circumstances where such added protection and vindication is warranted, and the factual circumstances make stripping profits a rational way of achieving these objectives.[123] On this rationale, one exceptional circumstance where such remedy might potentially be made available for vindicatory actions is where fundamental interests are particularly vulnerable to wrongful interference because there are acute financial incentives to commit the wrong, the claimant is a member of a class particularly vulnerable to exploitation and the defendant acted on those incentives thus earning a profit.

However, albeit this rationale might be a principled and defensible one, the practical reality is that such awards are unlikely to be necessary because we already have an established remedy to offer enhanced vindication and protection in such situations: that is, exemplary damages in the second category of *Rookes*.[124] Furthermore, exemplary damages have many advantages over the remedy of an account of profits as a tool for affording heightened protection and vindication in the case of a profit-driven wrongdoer.

Lord Devlin in *Rookes* explained that exemplary damages may be available in the following circumstances:[125]

> Where a defendant with a cynical disregard for a plaintiff's rights has calculated that money to be made out of his wrongdoing will probably exceed the damages at risk, it is necessary for the law to show that it cannot be broken with impunity.

Exemplary damages in this category have several advantages over the remedy of an account of profits. First, these damages can be awarded in response to a cynical profit-motivated wrong even though the defendant does not end up making a profit or makes a very small profit. This is because quantum is not necessarily hitched to the amount of profit in fact made. Second, an account will only offer added protection where the gain sought and made is financial. However, the conception of gain for the purposes of the second category of *Rookes* is wider than financial profits: 'This category is not confined to moneymaking in the strict sense.'[126]

[123] Varuhas, *Damages and Human Rights* (n 2) 120–21.
[124] *Rookes v Barnard* [1964] AC 1129, 1226–27.
[125] ibid 1226–27.
[126] ibid 1227.

Third, the claimant who suffers a cynical, profit-driven wrong can recover both compensatory and exemplary damages, whereas they would need to elect between compensatory and disgorgement damages. Fourth, gain can be very difficult to calculate, and causation can be hard to prove, especially if profits derived from the wrong are intermingled with other profits. Fifth, in calculating profits a court would make an allowance for the defendant's skill and expenses, whereas no such discount need be made from exemplary damages.

In addition to exemplary damages other forms of relief may also be utilised to address gains. An injunction may issue to prevent a defendant from using private information to continue to make a profit from distribution of that information. The court could order the defendant to deliver up the information, thus preventing its use.[127] In *Spelman*, Tugendhat J also contemplated the making of an order akin to that made in *Blake*, preventing the defendant from receiving money in relation to the relevant information.[128]

Thus, all in all, disgorgement damages do not add anything to orthodox remedies available for vindicatory actions, and they ought not to be available. If they are to be made available, they ought to be an exceptional remedy, and the criteria for their award should be formulated by reference to the normative concerns underpinning creation of privacy rights.

ii. Reasonable Fee or User Damages

Where a defendant uses the claimant's land without the claimant's consent the defendant shall be liable in trespass for user damages, calculated according to the market rate for the use of the land. For nearly their entire history these damages were conceptualised by the courts as compensatory. However, more recently restitution theorists have preyed on the characterisation of such damages as loss-based. They have argued that these damages cannot be compensatory because they are available whether or not the claimant would have, or even could have, leased out his or her land to another person but for the trespass. On this premise they argue that a gain-based analysis – such damages reverse a transfer of value from the claimant to the defendant – should be preferred. It is correct that 'but for' analysis does not apply to such damages. But it does not follow from this that they must be characterised as gain-based.[129] Rather, the absence of 'but for' analysis shows that such damages are not factual damages but normative damages for the wrongful interference with exclusive possession and use of land in and of itself. The courts have explained them as such. In the leading authority of *Morris-Garner*, Lord Reed, giving the lead judgment in the Supreme Court, said that user damages provide

[127] See the discussion of the line of confidence cases in *Imerman*, which demonstrate that delivery-up has been an important remedy in this area: (n 25) [54] et seq.

[128] *Spelman v Express Newspapers* [2012] EWHC 355, [118] (QB).

[129] See further Varuhas, 'Concept of Vindication' (n 2) 284–89.

compensation for the loss of the right to control use of one's property that goes with proprietary rights of exclusive possession, this ability to control use of one's land being conceptualised as a valuable asset in itself; such losses are conceptually distinct from financial losses of a 'conventional kind', such as the cost of repair.[130] Lord Sumption, in the same case, said the availability of user damages follows from the nature of the right infringed: the law treats the 'exclusive dominion' conferred by property rights as having an independent pecuniary value – one might say, a normative value constructed by the law – which is assessed according to the user measure where those rights, and thus one's interest in exclusive possession, are infringed.[131] *Morris-Garner* built on earlier authority to similar effect. The Privy Council had previously observed that damages are 'readily awarded at common law for the invasion of rights to tangible moveable or immoveable property', and acknowledged the availability of 'compensatory damages which exceed the actual financial loss caused to the claimant by an actionable breach of duty'.[132] In trespass loss has a wider meaning than simply being left materially worse off:[133]

> It is an established principle concerning the assessment of damages that a person who has wrongfully used another's property without causing the latter any pecuniary loss may still be liable to that other for more than nominal damages. In general, he is liable to pay, as damages, a reasonable sum for the wrongful use he has made of the other's property. The law has reached this conclusion by giving to the concept of loss or damage in such a case a wider meaning than merely financial loss calculated by comparing the property owner's financial position after the wrongdoing with what it would have been had the wrongdoing never occurred. Furthermore, in such a case it is no answer for the wrongdoer to show that the property owner would probably not have used the property himself had the wrongdoer not done so. In *The Mediana* [1900] AC 11, 117, Earl of Halsbury LC made the famous observation that a defendant who had deprived the plaintiff of one of the chairs in his room for 12 months could not diminish the damages by showing that the plaintiff did not usually sit upon that chair or that there were plenty of other chairs in the room.

This modern authority follows on from the line of wayleave cases decided in the latter part of the nineteenth century, and which explicitly conceptualise user damages as compensatory – and explicitly reject gain-based analysis.[134] In *Morris-Garner*, Lord Reed, in his leading judgment, authoritatively reasserted this orthodoxy: 'The courts did not … adopt a benefits-based approach, but conceived of awards as compensating for loss.'[135]

In the important High Court of Australia case of *Plenty* it was held, as a more general proposition applicable beyond user cases, that substantial damages

[130] *Morris-Garner* (n 1) [25]–[30], [66], [79], [95](1).
[131] Ibid [110].
[132] *Pell Frischmann Engineering Ltd v Bow Valley Iran Ltd* [2011] 1 WLR 2370, [46], [48].
[133] *Stoke-on-Trent City Council v W & J Wass Ltd* [1988] 1 WLR 1406, 1416. The passage was quoted with approval in *Morris-Garner* (n 1) [29], [110].
[134] Varuhas, *Damages and Human Rights* (n 2) 55–59.
[135] *Morris-Garner* (n 1) [79].

follow a wrongful interference with land, whether or not that interference causes material loss:[136]

> True it is that the entry itself caused no damage to the appellant's land. But the purpose of the action for trespass to land is not merely to compensate the plaintiff for the damage to the land. That action also serves the purpose of vindicating the plaintiff's right to the exclusive use and occupation of his or her land … The appellant is entitled to have his right to property vindicated by a substantial award of damages.

Such approach reflects the 'policy of the law', which is 'to protect the possession of property and the privacy and security of the occupier'.[137] As Arden LJ says in *Devenish*, 'there may be no actual loss' but 'the law takes the view as a matter of policy that the claimants if they prove their claims are entitled to substantial compensation for the mere invasion of their rights'.[138] As the analysis in *Morris-Garner* shows, this policy aim is effectuated by the law conceptualising exclusive possession and use of land as a thing of value in itself, with the corollary that its infringement involves the suffering of a compensable detriment.

If loss-based explanations are open we need not have recourse to heterodox gain-based analysis.[139] Furthermore, the normative damages thesis provides an explanation that coheres with the nature of the cause of action. The concern of trespass is to protect and vindicate the protected interests. It therefore makes sense that the focus of damages would be upon the extent of the interference with those protected interests, rather than on the defendant's gain.[140] There are further problems with gain-based accounts, albeit they cannot be explored here given space constraints.[141]

Should reasonable fee damages be available for the action for misuse of private information? For example, a reasonable fee could conceivably be applied to assess the normative loss suffered by a claimant where a defendant newspaper makes use of the claimant's personal information without the claimant's permission, for instance by publishing the claimant's private photographs. The fee might be assessed on the basis of the market fee that could have been charged by the claimant for use of those photos. In my view the courts should be reluctant to apply such a measure. Reasonable fee measures are usually applied to assess normative loss where the interests interfered with are proprietary in nature, as we routinely value property interests in market terms. However, where damage is to interests such as those in liberty and physical integrity, not typically measured in market

[136] *Plenty v Dillon* (1991) 171 CLR 635, 654–55.
[137] ibid 647.
[138] *Devenish* (n 12) [36].
[139] A point also made by Lord Reed in *Morris-Garner* (n 1) [66].
[140] Contrast unjust enrichment claims, such as a claim for money had and received, where restitution is the logical remedy given that the 'not-wrong' (to borrow from Birks) is that the defendant was unjustly enriched at the claimant's expense: enrichment is the very gist of the action, so that restitution (reversal of a gain) is the apt remedial response.
[141] See Varuhas, 'Concept of Vindication' (n 2) 284–89.

terms, a reasonable fee is not applied. This must partly be because it is unnatural to describe imprisoning someone as involving a *use* of that person's liberty.[142] But more fundamentally it would be inappropriate to assess damage inherent in being deprived of one's liberty or pictured at a personal moment according to market value, given that this involves treating basic dignitary interests as interests in tradeable commodities. In this regard it must be recalled that the interest in the photos protected by the privacy action is the claimant's privacy interest in the photos, not, for example, their intellectual property interests or their commercial interests in confidentiality.[143]

C. Vindicatory Damages

'Vindicatory damages' are a novel head of damages awarded for violations of constitutional or human rights in some jurisdictions. The principles governing such awards 'are not greatly developed'.[144] However, some broad principles are discernible. Such damages are generally awarded only where compensatory damages are considered insufficient to vindicate the right, and an additional award is necessary to mark the sense of public outrage at the violation, the importance of the right and gravity of the violation, and to deter future violations.[145] In terms of assessment it has been suggested that awards are 'conventional', '[a]llowance must be made for the importance of the right and the gravity of the breach', account taken of the possible deterrence effects of the award[146] and quantum no more than necessary to recognise the wrong but not derisory.[147]

Going by their name, one might expect such damages to be available for vindicatory actions such as the action for misuse of private information. Indeed, in *Jones v Tsige* the Ontario Court of Appeal recognised a type of 'symbolic' award, designed to 'mark the wrong' and 'vindicate rights or symbolize recognition of their infringement', within cases of breach of privacy by intrusion upon seclusion.[148] Nevertheless, the exact conceptual nature of the awards recognised in *Jones* is not clear,[149] and such awards must be understood in the light of the distinctive

[142] Though this has not prevented Kantian torts theorists from attempting to explain false imprisonment on the basis of 'use': eg A Ripstein, *Private Wrongs* (Cambridge, MA, Harvard UP, 2016) ch 2. The idea is perplexing.

[143] See Lord Hoffmann's discussion in *OBG* (n 49) [118]–[124] differentiating the privacy claim from interference with commercial interests. See also *Douglas v Hello! Ltd (No 3)* [2006] QB 125, [246].

[144] *Lumba* (n 10) [177].

[145] *Attorney-General of Trinidad and Tobago v Ramanoop* [2006] 1 AC 328, [19]; *Subiah v Attorney-General of Trinidad and Tobago* [2008] UKPC 47, [11].

[146] *Lumba* (n 10) [178]–[180].

[147] Ibid [180].

[148] *Jones v Tsige* 2012 ONCA 32, [75], [87]–[90]. Contrast the approach in *Jane Doe 464533* 2016 ONSC 541, in the context of the misuse of private information tort, where damages were approached on an orthodox compensatory basis, on an analogy with sexual assault cases.

[149] Oddly, the factors identified in *Jones* ((n 148) [87]) as being relevant to assessment of such awards include factors that would be relevant to damages for the wrong in itself (eg the nature and incidence

'functionalist' approach to damages for non-pecuniary loss that prevails in Canada (and which does not characterise English law).[150] However, notwithstanding the approach in Ontario, in the English case of *Lumba* the UK Supreme Court held, in the context of a false imprisonment claim, that vindicatory damages are not generally available in tort. With one caveat, the Court was, with respect, right to do so. Two interrelated reasons given by the majority for rejecting such awards are particularly convincing: the purpose of vindication is met by established remedies,[151] and vindicatory damages perform similar functions to exemplary damages.[152]

We have seen that damages are generally available across vindicatory torts for damage to the protected interest, which are proportionate to the seriousness of the interference and take account of the normative importance of the interest. This means no additional award is necessary to address the seriousness/extent of the interference. It is also of the utmost importance to observe here that vindicatory damages are super-compensatory in nature whereas normative damages are compensatory in nature, compensating for the interference with protected interests. Mann J articulated this distinction in *Gulati*: 'Damages awarded to reflect the infringement [of the right in itself] are not vindicatory in the sense of *Lumba*. They are truly compensatory.'[153] The Court of Appeal agreed.[154]

The only remaining functions that a 'vindicatory' award could perform would be to express public outrage at the *manner* of the interference, or deterrence. Indeed, in those constitutional cases where an award has been made, it has been in response to the outrageous *manner* of the violation.[155] The making of such awards for the privacy action would serve to attest to and reinforce the importance of the protected interests, and therefore give effect to the law's vindicatory function. However, given that exemplary damages would be available on a vindicatory remedial model, respond to and express outrage at the manner of the violation by punishing the defendant, reinforce the normative importance of protected interests and may theoretically deter future interferences, vindicatory

of the wrong), damages for consequential loss (eg effect on the plaintiff's health and financial position, and any distress suffered), and aggravated and punitive damages (eg conduct of the defendant). As such the award recognised in *Jones* is not easily classified and does not appear coherent, seemingly being a fusion of conceptually different types of award. It is also unclear why such awards should be capped at C$20,000 for intrusion upon seclusion, as indicated in *Jones*, when much higher awards are available for other torts and indeed for the public disclosure tort.

[150] Though there are questions over the extent to which Canadian law continues to adhere to the functionalist approach: J Berryman, 'Non-Pecuniary Damages for Personal Injury: A Reflection on the Canadian Experience' in E Quill and RJ Friel (eds), *Damages and Compensation Culture Comparative Perspectives* (Oxford, Hart Publishing, 2016).

[151] *Lumba* (n 10) [101], [236], [237].

[152] ibid [100], [233], [255].

[153] *Gulati* (Ch) (n 26) [132].

[154] *Gulati* (CA) (n 26) [48]. Similarly the Court of Appeal in *Shaw v Kovacs* [2017] EWCA Civ 1028 seems to have, with respect, correctly distinguished vindicatory damages from compensatory damages for the infringement of a right (albeit such damages were refused in that case, in the very different context of negligence).

[155] *Merson v Cartwright* [2005] UKPC 38; *Ramanoop* (n 145); see also *Graham v Police Service Commission* [2011] UKPC 46, [17].

damages are otiose.[156] The degree of overlap is recognised in the Caribbean cases on vindicatory damages. Vindicatory and exemplary awards cannot be recovered concurrently for the same wrong; where a vindicatory award is made, 'the purpose of exemplary damages has largely been achieved' given the element of deterrence '[t]hat a substantial award carries'.[157] The overlap was evident in *Lumba*, where those aspects of the case that convinced the minority that a vindicatory award was warranted were the same features that came close to convincing other Justices to make an exemplary award.[158]

Thus it is unnecessary to recognise this novel head of damages. However, one important caveat ought to be entered. If the Supreme Court, for example, overrules *Gulati* and holds that normative damages are not available and only consequential loss is recoverable for breach of privacy, there would be a strong argument for recognising vindicatory damages to fill the gap left by the absence of normative damages, especially in a case where no consequential loss was suffered and thus no damages otherwise payable. The possibility that *Gulati* might be overruled is not fanciful, given that in *Lumba* itself the Supreme Court, with respect, mislaid the orthodoxy that substantial damages ought to follow breach of a fundamental right in the context of the paradigm vindicatory tort of false imprisonment.[159] However, overall it would be nonsensical to deviate from the orthodox approach to damages for vindicatory actions by rejecting the availability of normative damages, only to have to then again deviate from orthodoxy to correct for the original departure by recognising the novel head of vindicatory damages.

Furthermore, vindicatory damages are far from a perfect substitute for normative damages. First, such damages are exceptional and discretionary. Second, in most cases where they have been awarded, especially in the Caribbean cases, vindicatory damages have served as a surrogate form of exemplary damages; they do not perform the same function as normative damages, which are available as of course and specifically respond to the damage to the claimant's interests.

Third, very modest awards of vindicatory damages have been contemplated outside of cases of egregious wrongdoing (the exemplary damages type of case), for example where compensatory damages were not available but it was thought important to mark the wrong with an award. Used in this way, are vindicatory damages a substitute for normative damages? No. First, in these cases vindicatory damages remain an exceptional and discretionary remedy. Second, quantum in such cases is exceptionally modest, so that the awards effectively operate as a

[156] One might argue that vindicatory damages would be more freely available than exemplary damages, which are limited by the *Rookes* categories. However, vindicatory damages have been developed within constitutional claims against public actors. This category of case roughly maps onto the first category in *Rookes*; *Lumba* itself involved claims against officials.

[157] *Takitota v Attorney-General of The Bahamas* [2009] UKPC 11, [15]; *Webster v Attorney-General of Trinidad & Tobago* [2011] UKPC 22, [16]; *Lumba* (n 10) [233]; *Ramanoop* (n 145) [19].

[158] Compare *Lumba* (n 10) [176], [194] with [165]–[168].

[159] For a critique of that judgment and an explanation for why this misturning in the law of damages occurred, see Varuhas, *Damages and Human Rights* (n 2) 61–67.

form of nominal damages. For example in *Lumba*, minority Justices would have awarded sums of between £500 and £1,000 in vindicatory damages to mark a two-year period of false imprisonment. If orthodox principles had been followed, a *compensatory* award for two years of false imprisonment would have been in the tens of thousands of pounds: £500 is a poor substitute. Despite their name, such awards do not vindicate basic interests; they achieve the inverse. Such a measly award trivialises an important interest long afforded strong protection at common law through routine imposition of damages liability. Lords Brown and Rodger, who would have maintained that substantial damages ought to follow wrongful imprisonment, said that to do otherwise would 'devalue the whole concept of false imprisonment'.[160] There is, with respect, inconsonance between Lord Hope's statements in *Lumba* that the breach was 'deplorable', 'the right is a valuable one', vindicatory awards should register the 'gravity of the breach of the fundamental right', any award should not be 'nominal' or 'derisory', and his conclusion that an award of vindicatory damages on the facts should be 'modest' and 'substantially lower' than £1,000.[161] Also problematic is the suggestion that such paltry awards could encourage 'all concerned to avoid anything like it happening again'.[162] If anything is likely to affect a defendant's behaviour it is unlikely to be such a small sum, especially in a case like *Lumba*, where there were powerful political incentives to commit the wrong (those falsely imprisoned were foreign national prisoners) and the evidence tended to suggest that the defendant officials had maintained their course of conduct despite a full appreciation of liability risks.[163]

IV. Damages in Lieu of an Injunction

Another form of damages that may possibly be awarded in a claim for breach of privacy is damages in lieu of an injunction. Here I am going to consider specifically a situation where (i) there is an ongoing breach of privacy or pattern of breaches; and (ii) a court has jurisdiction to grant an injunction and there are no discretionary bars to granting the injunction. In such a case, albeit the court could and would ordinarily grant an injunction, the court may nonetheless grant damages in substitution of the injunction under the Lord Cairns' Act jurisdiction. In this section I argue such damages should very rarely be awarded in a case of breach of privacy: the claimant should have an injunction as of course to restrain an ongoing wrong. To understand why this is, it is important to first consider the nature of damages in lieu. Their nature has not always been clear, and clarity has been further muddied

[160] *Lumba* (n 10) [343].
[161] ibid [176], [178], [180].
[162] ibid [217].
[163] ibid [154]–[164].

by attempts by restitution theorists to explain such damages as gain-based. At this point it will suffice to record Millett LJ's view that restitutionary explanations are 'puzzling', and that courts consistently have analysed such damages as compensatory, including the Supreme Court in its recent decision in *Morris-Garner*.[164] It is to be hoped that in this area at least we may avoid the instability and commercial uncertainty that has been generated in other fields, such as user damages, by restitutionary theories.

Cases concerning damages in lieu have often involved situations where an injunction is sought by the claimant to enforce a restrictive covenant, or to restrain a continuing nuisance or trespass. The defendant argues that damages should be awarded in lieu of the injunction so that the defendant can continue with his or her wrongful activity, albeit for a price. What do damages address in such situations?

The *practical effect* of granting damages in lieu of an injunction is that the claimant will not be able to enjoy his or her rights, as the courts will refuse to coerce the defendant to discontinue the infringement.[165] Thus it has sometimes been said that damages represent compensation for an appropriation of the claimant's rights. In a case of nuisance this would be the claimant's right against the defendant that the defendant shall not interfere with the enjoyment value of the claimant's property, or in trespass the right of the claimant against the defendant that the defendant shall not interfere with the claimant's interest in exclusive possession of land. However, while it is true that the award of damages and concomitant refusal to grant an injunction broadly have similar effects for the claimant as if his or her primary rights had been appropriated, damages do not as *a matter of principle* involve the defendant in appropriating the claimant's primary rights.[166] For example, in trespass the claimant remains the owner of the land, continues to have a right in exclusive possession and can sue others who trespass – there is, for example, no transfer of title to the defendant, nor is the defendant granted some sort of proprietary interest such as an easement, which the defendant can then sue upon against others. This is why I consider that it is also inaccurate to refer to damages in lieu as 'release fee' damages – the defendant is never released from his or her primary duties to the claimant.

All of this is not to say that the practical consequences of refusing an injunction and granting damages in lieu should not be taken seriously – below I argue that these practical effects ought to weigh heavily in our consideration of how freely the courts ought to award damages in substitution of an injunction. Nonetheless, as a matter of principle it is not correct to say that such damages involve an appropriation of the claimant's primary rights. Thus in *Anchor Brewhouse* Scott J said, 'Whether or not an injunction was granted, the defendant's use of the right of way

[164] *Jaggard v Sawyer* [1995] 1 WLR 269, 291; *Morris-Garner* (n 1).
[165] *Morris-Garner* (n 1) [53], [69], [95](4).
[166] See *Morris-Garner* (n 1) [69] ('The claimant does not literally lose the right in question').

would, after the judgment as well as before, represent trespass unless and until he were granted a right of way.'[167] Millett LJ echoed this analysis in *Jaggard*:[168]

> [T]he court could not by an award of damages put the defendant in the position of a person entitled to an easement; whether or not an injunction were granted, the defendant's conduct would still constitute a trespass … This reasoning strikes at the very heart of the statutory jurisdiction; it is in marked contrast to the attitude of the many judges who from the very first have recognised that, while the Act does not enable the court to license future wrongs, this may be the practical result of withholding injunctive relief … Thereafter the defendant may have no right to act in the manner complained of, but he cannot be prevented from doing so.

In this light, the more accurate explanation of what the claimant is being forced to give up – what the claimant has lost – is the *liberty* to enforce his or her primary rights against the defendant. As a result of the court's refusal to grant the injunction and its decision to grant damages instead, the defendant shall, into the future, be *immunised* from suit – any claim would be struck out[169] – and the claimant shall be *disabled* from bringing a claim against the defendant in respect of the subject matter of the damages award. Such damages are often drawn together with and analysed alongside other types of damages relating to proprietary interests and which have proven challenging to explain, such as user damages for trespass. However, damages in lieu are different in nature, in that they do not compensate for a one-off intrusion upon a protected interest (and are awarded in a unique statutory jurisdiction, which is equitable in nature).[170] Rather they compensate for the loss of the liberty to enforce a primary right into the future.

The different nature of such damages in turn explains why they are calculated differently from user damages. In trespass, user damages are assessed according to parameters that measure the seriousness or extent of the defendant's interference with the claimant's interests, such as duration of use and amount of land used. However, there are no such parameters when assessing damages for the loss of the liberty to enforce a primary right. Furthermore, while there is a rental market for land, by reference to which interests in possession and use can be valued, there is no such market for trading in liberties to enforce primary rights. As such, the courts resort to a different measure: a hypothetical bargain between the claimant and the defendant for the 'purchase' of the claimant's liberty to enforce.[171]

[167] *Anchor Brewhouse Developments Ltd v Berkley House (Docklands Developments) Ltd* (1987) 38 BLR 97, 101.

[168] *Jaggard* (n 164) 285–86.

[169] ibid 280–81.

[170] See *Morris-Garner* (n 1) [46]–[47], [55]–[56], [62], [71]; cf K Barker, '"Damages Without Loss": Can Hohfeld Help?' (2014) 34 *OJLS* 631.

[171] Albeit, as noted in *Morris-Garner* (n 1) [63], [95](5), while negotiating damages are the common measure applied in property tort cases, they may not be the invariable measure for damages under the Lord Cairns' Act jurisdiction; it is ultimately for the court to judge the most appropriate method of quantification in the circumstances.

Put another way, damages are akin to the 'price of [the claimant] waiving their rights' *to sue*.[172] Thus such damages have commonly been referred to as 'negotiating damages'.[173] Having said this, within any hypothetical negotiation, what the claimant may reasonably have demanded for waiver of the right to sue will naturally be informed by the value of what the claimant is giving up through not being able to protect his or her primary rights.[174] This explains why Brightman J in *Wrotham Park* took into account, in setting damages in lieu, the profits the defendant would make from use of the land in breach of the restrictive covenant.[175] Contrary to the claims of restitution theorists, it is obvious that Brightman J's consideration of the profits the defendant could make through use did not suggest damages were a form of disgorgement damages. As Bingham LJ said in *Jaggard*, Brightman J

> paid attention to the profits earned by the defendants, as it seems to me, not to strip the defendants of their unjust gains, but because of the obvious relationship between the profits earned by the defendants and the sum which the defendants would reasonably have been willing to pay to secure release from the covenant.[176]

Millett LJ echoed this view:

> It is plain from his judgment … that Brightman J's approach was compensatory, not restitutionary … He did not award the plaintiff the profit which the defendant had made by the breach, but the amount which he judged the plaintiff might have obtained as the price of giving its consent.[177]

Kennedy LJ agreed with Bingham LJ. In the more recent case of *Force India*, Arnold J, distilling from the authorities the principles applicable to assessment of 'negotiating damages', could not have been clearer when he said '[t]he overriding principle is that the damages are compensatory'.[178] That these damages are compensatory has now been authoritatively confirmed by the Supreme Court, consonant with the statements of principle in *Jaggard*: such damages compensate for 'what is lost by the withholding of' an injunction.[179]

Thus damages in lieu of an injunction compensate for the loss of the liberty to sue, not the loss of primary rights as such. Nonetheless, as noted above, it is significant that the *practical effect* of a grant of damages in lieu is that the claimant is unable to enjoy his or her primary rights and must endure an ongoing wrong. The courts have taken these effects seriously, and generally injunctions have been granted as of course for ongoing nuisances and trespasses. The courts

[172] *Jaggard* (n 164) 289. And see ibid [69].
[173] *Lunn Poly Ltd v Liverpool & Lancashire Properties Ltd* [2006] 2 EGLR 29, [22]. And see now *Morris-Garner* (n 1) [3] *et passim*, the Supreme Court endorsing this terminology.
[174] See *Morris-Garner* (n 1) [95](4).
[175] *Wrotham Park Estate Co Ltd v Parkside Homes Ltd* [1974] 1 WLR 798, 815–16.
[176] *Jaggard* (n 164) 281–82.
[177] ibid 291.
[178] *Force India Formula One Team Ltd v 1 Malaysia Racing Team SDN BHD* [2012] EWHC 616, [386](i) (appeal dismissed [2013] EWCA Civ 780).
[179] *Morris-Garner* (n 1) eg [44], [58]–[61], [95](3)–(4), [114].

have been reluctant to allow a defendant to effectively buy his or her way out of complying with legal duties: 'the Court has always protested against the notion that it ought to allow a wrong to continue simply because the wrongdoer is able and willing to pay for the injury he may inflict'.[180] Lord Kingsdown in *Imperial Gas Light* said that for an ongoing wrong an injunction should issue 'as of course', unless there 'is something special in the case'.[181] In *Shelfer* it was observed that 'very exceptional circumstances'[182] would be required before damages were given in lieu, and the working rule enunciated by AL Smith LJ in that case indicates that this will only be where it is oppressive to the defendant to grant the injunction.[183] There is another reason why courts should be reluctant to grant damages in lieu. The court's refusal to grant an injunction de facto – albeit not de jure – effects a redistribution of proprietary rights. Damages in lieu may not grant a defendant a right of way over the claimant's land as a matter of law, but as a matter of fact the practical effects are not dissimilar. Courts are not well placed institutionally, and they lack constitutional legitimacy to effect such redistributions. Allocation of rights ought first and foremost to be for the political branches of government. Furthermore, there *is* a de jure redistribution of sorts in that the claimant loses a legal liberty to sue.

If the courts have been reluctant to allow ongoing nuisances or trespasses to continue, which involve interferences with proprietary interests (recall nuisance is a tort *against land*), they should be even more reluctant to allow an ongoing interference with dignitary interests such as liberty, physical integrity *or privacy* to continue for a fee. The idea of being disabled from enforcing one's basic personal or privacy rights is unpalatable in a liberal democracy. This was recognised by Lord Mance in *Fen Tigers*. Albeit the Supreme Court in that case suggested (in my view wrongly, with respect), at least in cases of private nuisance, that the criteria for granting damages in lieu need not be as strict as AL Smith LJ's working rule suggested,[184] Lord Mance observed that 'the right to enjoy one's home without disturbance is one which I believe many, indeed most, people value for reasons largely if not entirely independent of money'.[185] This suggests where the subject matter of the claimed injunction is something other than land or goods, which can be valued in market terms, the courts should be even slower to grant damages in lieu than they typically would be, as damages are an even less satisfactory remedy for an ongoing interference with dignitary interests. This point was echoed specifically in the context of privacy in *PJS*, again by Lord Mance.[186] One may analogise

[180] *Shelfer v City of London Electric Lighting Co* [1895] 1 Ch 287, 315–16.
[181] *Imperial Gas Light and Coke Company v Broadbent* (1859) 7 HL Cas 600, 612.
[182] *Shelfer* (n 180) 316.
[183] ibid 322–23; and see *Jaggard* (n 164) 287–88.
[184] The Court did, however, maintain that 'the prima facie position is that an injunction should be granted' (*Fen Tigers* (n 122) [101], [121]).
[185] ibid at [168], and see also [127], [247].
[186] *PJS* (n 35) [41].

here with the great writ of habeas corpus, itself a type of specific relief constituted to address ongoing interferences with a basic interest. The writ issues *as of right* where it is proven that a person is being deprived of liberty without lawful justification.

V. Conclusion

Given the protective and vindicatory policies that underpin creation of privacy rights, damages for both normative and factual losses ought to be available, and clearly are available following *Gulati*. Compensatory damages should not follow the ECtHR's approach to money awards under Article 41 of the Convention.

Exemplary damages ought to be available. But care must be taken to ensure that quantum is not so high as to constitute a disproportionate interference with freedom of expression. An account of profits is an unnecessary remedy in the light of the availability of normative damages, coupled with exemplary damages in the second category of *Rookes*; exemplary damages in the second category also have many advantages over the remedy of an account of profits. However, if an account of profits were to be made available, the remedy ought to be exceptional, and the criteria for its award should follow the normative concerns that underpin creation of the primary rights in privacy. Reasonable fee or user damages are one way of measuring normative damage in property torts. They are not restitutionary. They ought not to be available for breach of privacy, as it would be inapt to treat dignitary interests as if they were interests in tradeable commodities. The novel head of vindicatory damages ought not to be available. Such damages add nothing to established remedies.

Damages in lieu of an injunction compensate for the loss of the legal liberty to enforce a primary right. They are not restitutionary. Where a privacy claimant proves an ongoing wrong, an injunction should be granted as of course to restrain that wrong. A court should be extremely reluctant to refuse a final injunction and grant damages in substitution.

4

Damages for Wrongdoing in the Absence of Loss

ROBERT STEVENS

I. Introduction

The purpose of this chapter is to examine the basis for the award of damages in cases of violation of a right to privacy. It proceeds in six stages.

First, it is necessary to carefully differentiate between wrongdoing and the causation of loss. Second, an explanation for the award of general damages in the absence of consequential loss for *some* torts is given. Third, an explanation for the scope and legitimacy of judge-made rights in general, and of rights to privacy in particular, is offered. Fourth, the possibility that human rights legislation mandates or requires the creation of privacy rights at common law is rejected. Fifth, the historical provenance of the modern law of privacy within our law in common will be briefly sketched, and it will be argued that given the radical developments it is no longer helpful to look back towards its equitable source. Sixth, the question of how damages that are not quantified by reference to consequential harm are to be assessed is sketched out.

The conclusion is in Australia a conservative one, in England reactionary. The difficulties with justifying the newly created judge-made privacy right(s) both historically and normatively should lead to the courts being cautious in the remedies awarded. It would be better if such wrongs were not actionable per se (ie they should require proof of consequential loss).

II. Wrongs

In order to understand the law of wrongs in general and the law of privacy in particular, it is essential to understand the distinction between the violation of a right and the causation of loss.[1] An earlier generation of lawyers would have recognised this distinction as being that between *iniuria* and *damnum*.

[1] The conceptual distinction drawn in this chapter is subject to an exemplary dissection in D Nolan, 'Rights Damage and Loss' (2016) 36 *OJLS* 1.

Some wrongs are actionable per se. A successful claim based upon the wrong is not conditional upon proof of consequential loss. Sometimes substantial damages are available for a wrong, regardless of consequential loss. *Damnum sine iniuria* is not actionable; *iniuria sine damno* sometimes, but not always, is.

Where does the law of privacy fit within this division? Is consequential loss required, or not? The answer to this question is complicated by the fact that 'privacy' as a distinct category within our law in common is of relatively recent origin, with different possible reasons justifying it.

The law of privacy poses many further puzzles. Does it refer to one reason for the imposition of a duty, and hence one class of rights, or many such reasons and so many classes of rights? Why did it take the common law such a long time to recognise such a class of rights, and is its recognition by the courts today legitimate? Has a new tort or wrong now been recognised separate from the old categories, and is such recognition dependent upon the existence of human rights legislation? Are all, some or none of the claims for violation of privacy actionable per se? Should they be? How are claims for damages and other monetary awards to be quantified? As a comparative matter, have English and Australian law diverged? Can any such divergence be justified?

III. Wrongs and Loss

I have long been professionally employed in the deliberate infliction of misery on the young. From the other side, a succession of women have made me miserable down the years in my now accustomed role as dumpee. None of this behaviour, by myself or others, was prima facie wrongful either as a matter of law or otherwise, despite the causation of harm.

To suffer loss is to be factually worse off, in relation to some kind of baseline. Usually, in law, the baseline comparison is between the plaintiff as he or she is at the time of judgment, and as he or she would have been if some event (typically a wrong) had not occurred.[2] The comparison is between the world as it is and the hypothetical world as it would have been. The relevant comparator is not as between the world as it was pre-wrong and the world today. The plaintiff seeks to be placed in the position he or she expected to be in, not that in which he or she was in the past. The use of the word 'loss' in law is therefore confusing: in the English language it imports no longer having something I once had, whereas in law it includes not obtaining benefits that would otherwise have accrued.[3] The law's concept of loss is ambulatory: it changes over time. As perceived from

[2] Loss can be used in other contexts, such as statutory compensation schemes.

[3] So a disappointed history graduate is currently suing the University of Oxford for the poor tuition he received which, he claims, led to his being denied the first he deserved and, as a result, the career in commercial law he would have obtained. He is claiming for the life he would have had, not the one that he once possessed.

any particular moment, it may have increased, decreased or even disappeared altogether. Such loss may be economic or non-economic, the latter typically taking the form of distress.

In private law, a wrong is a breach of a duty owed to another. A breach of a duty owed to another is, synonymously, a violation of a right that other has. If I owe you a duty not to punch you on the nose, you have a right against me that I do not. Such wrong is suffered in a moment of time (though it may be repeated, or may, as with a nuisance, be continuous). It is conceptually impossible to speak of a right not to suffer loss. The relevant baselines for the two enquiries are completely different. For wrong we ask whether the defendant's actions have, looking back, infringed a right that the plaintiff had. We compare the actual world as it was with that as it now is. For loss we ask, at the time of judgment, whether the defendant is, and will be, worse off than he or she would have been in the counterfactual world absent the wrong. We compare the world as it is and will be with the world as it otherwise would have been.

Whether such a wrong causes the plaintiff consequential loss is always a contingent matter. If I punch you on the nose that will wrong you but, as things turn out, may, albeit unusually, leave you no worse off. Indeed, sometimes you may be left better off. You may initially suffer pain, but then may obtain valuable and rewarding work as a movie star because of your interestingly rearranged face. Who knows?

A tort is a species of the private law wrongs recognised in common law systems (the others are breaches of contract and equitable wrongs). The gist of all private law wrongs is the violation of a right, not the causation of loss. Where loss is caused without violating a right, it is not actionable as a tort. It is *damnum sine iniuria*. If we both see a $100 bill in the street and reach to grab it, the person who obtains it first will have left the other worse off than he or she otherwise would have been, but does not wrong the other. If you win a race, your competition may cause distress to those you defeat, but that is not even prima facie a form of wrongdoing. That some act may cause another to be worse off is not sufficient for it to constitute wrongdoing, either within or without the law.

IV. A Great Case

One of the great cases that all lawyers ought to take in with their mother's milk, whether in Australia or anywhere else which has the law in common with it, is *Victoria Park Racing & Recreation Grounds v Taylor*.[4] The plaintiffs operated a racetrack and charged spectators to see the spectacle. The first defendant, Taylor, owned land neighbouring the racetrack on which he allowed the second defendant, a radio station, to erect an observation tower, using which the station

[4] *Victoria Park Racing & Recreation Grounds v Taylor* [1937] HCA 45, (1937) 58 CLR 479.

broadcast details of races. As a result, the number of punters going through the plaintiffs' turnstiles declined, causing them consequential loss, and they sought an injunction restraining the broadcasts.

In order for this claim to succeed it needed to be based upon a right recognised by the law. The majority (Latham CJ, Dixon and McTiernan JJ) rightly held that they could not identify one. The plaintiffs had no intellectual property right by way of copyright to the information as to the order in which the horses crossed the line. Reporting a factual occurrence does not give you a copyright over that information. A claim based upon nuisance failed because there had been no interference with the plaintiffs' use and enjoyment of their land, which is the essence of the right's scope of protection. Today, as we shall see, there is scope for developing a right to privacy to prevent the media broadcasting to the world details of our activities in our homes, but it is very doubtful indeed whether any such right is or ought to be recognised for the protection of commercial enterprises, who are not thereby inhibited from doing anything they choose.

The plaintiffs had suffered what an earlier generation would have described as *damnum sine iniuria:* loss without the infringement of a right. Even where such loss is deliberately inflicted, for no good commercial reason, it is not actionable. Without the right, there is no wrong. Although what was sought was an injunction, there is no doubt that a claim for damages would also have failed.

V. Damages: General Principles

How, regardless of the law, do we think someone ought to behave after he or she has wronged another? Once I have punched you on the nose, is the blow so much spilled milk so far as I am concerned? Do my duties disappear upon my breaching them?

The answer is, of course, no. The reason I had for my duty not to punch you does not evaporate. Although I can no longer perfectly comply with my duty, I can do the next best thing: usually this would involve an apology and the making good of any harm I have caused. If you need to go to hospital, I should take you there, and any costs you incur should be met by me.

The positive law takes the same approach.[5] The underlying reason for the duty persists, creating a new duty of next-best compliance. As this is to be enforced through a court order, it places limitations on the form in law it can take (ordered apologies are not true apologies, they merely have the form not the substance of sincerity). Usually the courts order the payment of damages because that is the next best thing that they can compel, not because that is the next best thing I could do.

[5] The classic statement of principle is that of Lord Blackburn in *Livingstone v Rawayards Coal Co* (1880) 5 App Cas 25, 39. Precisely the same 'next best' principle applies to claims for breach of contract. This may sometimes give rise to different results in contract and torts not because the remedial principle differs, but because the duty that ought to have been fulfilled is not the same.

How are such damages to be quantified? Say you are distressed by the blow I have delivered, should damages be awarded to reflect this?

One answer, quite different from that above, is that we should award damages for distress when doing so will cheer the plaintiff up. If we thought damages are awarded to eradicate harm, this would be a necessary condition of their being awarded. But what if you are inconsolable, or if you have died before trial so that it is now too late to improve your happiness? Are damages now pointless?

One response might be to claim that money and happiness are commensurable. One day's severe misery is equivalent to $1,000. So, although the award of a sum of money could not eradicate the misery, it would appear on the other side of the balance sheet and be equivalent to it. If we took such a view then the quantum of damages awarded to reflect consequential distress should vary according to the wealth of the plaintiff. For those, such as myself, who earn a notional academic salary, a few dollars may be equivalent to a day of anguish. For another, such as Mark Zuckerberg, a vast sum may be required to be equivalent, to him.

I would suggest that this 'eradication of harm' view of damages is implausible. Money and misery are not commensurable in this way, and it will often be impossible for an award of damages to make good or extinguish a harm suffered. Rather, the sum awarded is simply the next best thing now available to the wrong not having been suffered. Such a duty to pay damages may indeed look radically different from the original duty (here not to punch), but it is the form it now takes because it is the best now possible.

Accepting that damages are justifiable even where they do not eradicate or counterbalance consequential harm, opens the door to the award of damages *for the wrong itself* regardless of consequential harm. Torts lawyers are most familiar with this idea within the law of defamation. The traditional rule within the law of libel is that *general damages* are available for the wrong regardless of its consequences. This was best expressed by Windeyer J in *Uren v John Fairfax Pty Ltd*:[6]

> Apart from special damages strictly so called and damages for a loss of clients or customers, money and reputation are not commensurables. It seems to me that, properly speaking, a man defamed does not get compensation for his damaged reputation. He gets damages because he was injured in his reputation, that is simply because he was publicly defamed. For this reason, compensation by damages operates in two ways – as a vindication of the plaintiff to the public and as consolation to him for a wrong done. Compensation is here a solatium rather than a monetary recompense for harm measurable in money.

This does not mean that (*general*) damages are only ever awardable on this basis, and that consequential loss is ignored. Rather, where consequential loss is suffered,

[6] *Uren v John Fairfax Pty Ltd* [1996] 117 CLR 118, 150, approved *Broome v Cassell* [1972] AC 1027, 1071 *per* Lord Hailsham.

as it would be where, for example, a plaintiff is libelled and loses his or her job as a result, such consequential loss may be claimed as *special* damages.

Further, substantial damages are not always capable of being claimed for all wrongs regardless of the absence of adverse consequences. Sometimes the wrong itself is so notional that only nominal damages should be awarded. Trespass is actionable per se, but if I fleetingly take one step into your garden without permission, that should not result in a substantive award against me. In the context of libel an illustration is the award of £1 made in favour of the former Liverpool football club goalkeeper Bruce Grobbelar.[7] Whilst strictly speaking he was defamed, with regard to accepting bribes for throwing football matches, he had no further reputation to lose.

In a way, both damages for the wrong and its consequences are compensatory. They are both caught by the 'next best' justification for the award. Failing to distinguish the two can, however, quickly lead to confusion. When assessing consequential losses, we have a variety of limitations upon the amount recoverable (it must not be too remote, the plaintiff is under a 'duty to mitigate' his or her loss, collateral benefits will usually reduce what is recoverable). In relation to damages for the wrong itself, such limitations are irrelevant. The timing of assessment also differs. Consequential losses are assessed at the time of trial, and take into account events that may have increased or decreased the loss expected to have been suffered in the interim.[8] Damages for the wrong itself are calculated at the time of the wrong. If I convert your gold coins, I must pay you their value at the date of conversion, even if their value falls between that time and the date of judgment and you would not have disposed of them in the interim. Other incidental rules (such as interest) can also only be understood once this distinction is recognised.

In order to avoid confusion and reflect these differences between damages for the wrong and for consequential loss, we should use different words for each. The traditional language of damages for the wrong itself is the one used by Windeyer: a *solatium*. This may confuse, however, as it may indicate that it is awarded to console or give solace to the plaintiff, which may not be true. Sometimes the language of 'general damages' as distinguished from 'special damages' has been adopted, but unfortunately not consistently. More modern terminology is 'vindicatory damages'. Sometimes damages justified on this basis are lumped into an award for 'exemplary damages', which is unfortunate as their rationale is not the instrumentalist one of seeking to make an example of anyone in order to deter further wrongdoing. I have in the past suggested the label 'substitutive damages', but I cannot pretend that this has found universal favour. The label is, however, much less important than the idea.

[7] *Grobbelar v Mirror Group Newspapers* [2002] UKHL 40, [2002] 1 WLR 3024.
[8] See, eg, *Golden Strait Corp v Nippon Yusen Kubishka Kaisha, The Golden Victory* [2007] 2 AC 353.

VI. Per Se or Not Per Se

Do all private law wrongs follow the pattern of allowing damages for the wrong itself, without more? The answer is no: some are actionable per se, while some are actionable only upon proof of consequential loss.[9] Traditionally, this was the major significance of the divide between libel and slander.[10] Libel, defamation in print, is traditionally actionable per se, so that general damages for the wrong itself are available. Slander, oral defamation, generally required proof of special damage, or consequential loss.[11] Some slanders, but not all, such as the imputation of a crime or of unchaste behaviour (of a woman), were considered more serious and so were also actionable without more.

Deceit is similar to slander. Lies that are believed are not themselves actionable, consequential loss is required. It would be perfectly possible to imagine legal systems where consequential losses were necessary for the actionability of all wrongs, and they were all that were ever recoverable. But the distinction between a wrong and its consequences is a conceptual one, that is true in all times and places: it is not based in the history of any particular legal system and is just as true outside of the positive law.

Notice that the proof of loss does not go to the question of whether a wrong has been suffered, but rather to *actionability* for the wrong (ie the power to sue for it). All wrongs are wrongful per se; not all wrongs are actionable per se. Just as the expiry of a limitation period does not render earlier tortious conduct non-wrongful, the fact that no consequential loss is suffered does not mean that slandering someone is not, in law, wrongful. The slander may also have other legal consequences, such as constituting unlawful means where it is used to cause loss to a third party.

Why does the common law draw this distinction, and not adopt a uniform approach of always either requiring or not requiring loss? It is suggested that the distinction turns upon the gravity of the wrong. So, a defamatory statement in writing has a permanence and a possibility of wide dissemination that the same statement made orally does not have (at least in the era when the division arose, before mass communications and audio recording). Lies which have no adverse consequences are insufficiently serious to merit the law's concern.

[9] Confusion is caused in England, and to a lesser extent Australia, by the tort of negligence. The modern law of negligence covers many claims that were traditionally within the law of trespass (eg negligent shooting of someone with a bow and arrow). Other claims had to be brought within the action on the case (eg injuring someone indirectly, by, eg, leaving roller skates lying around for them to trip over). Trespass claims were and are actionable per se, whilst the action on the case required proof of consequential loss. In Australia where 'negligent trespass' survives, that distinction survives even within negligence.

[10] Abolished in Australia, see Defamation Act 2005, s 7.

[11] The traditional rule is that these must be readily measurable in money. In England, libel now requires proof of serious harm to reputation, see Defamation Act 2013 (UK), s 1; *Lachaux v Independent Print Ltd* [2015] EWHC 2242.

In the context of privacy two questions then arise: is it actionable per se, and ought it to be? Should privacy be like libel or slander? Is it sufficiently serious that substantive damages should be recoverable for the wrong itself, regardless of its consequences? This in turn requires us to answer the question of why violations of privacy should be actionable at all. That the common law was making a mistake by for centuries not allowing such a wrong to be actionable is not obvious.

VII. Why Do We Have the Rights We Do?

It is characteristic of our rights that we have against persons generally that they protect our ability to choose how to live our lives. Here we need to draw the Hohfeldian conceptual distinction between (claim-) rights and liberties.

At first sight, the claim that (claim-) rights protect our freedom to choose is a paradoxical one. If I have a liberty with respect to you to eat my lunch, you have no right with respect to me that I do not eat a cheese sandwich after midday. It follows from your having a right with respect to me that I do *X*, not only that I have a duty to you to do *X*, but also that I have no liberty with respect to you not to do *X*. Our rights one against another restrict the liberty of each other to choose to behave in certain ways.

However, in a world of absolute liberties each of us would be free to stab one another in the neck, to steal a farmer's crops and to shout 'Fire!' in crowded theatres. Freedom for the pike is death for the minnow,[12] but we are all of us both pikes and minnows. In order for each of us to be able to choose how to live our own lives, it is necessary that we have rights against others that they refrain from interfering with this freedom. We have a right to be secure from interference in order that we may be independent of others. The correlative general duties are ones to refrain from behaving in certain ways. This results in a system of equal freedom for all.

If we see rights as justified by seeking to ensure that each of us has equal freedom to live our lives, the absence of general rights that others take positive steps to confer benefits upon us follows as a matter of course. The point here is not that positive duties limit the freedom of the person subject to the duty, when a duty to refrain from acting in a certain way does not. All rights limit the freedom of others. Rather, your damaging my lorry interferes with my independence, my freedom to choose how to live my life, whereas your not repairing my bicycle does not.[13] Further we are not concerned with whether I would or would not have made use of the undamaged lorry. Whether, as a matter of fact, the consequence of your wrong removes from me options that I would in fact have exercised is irrelevant. It is for me to choose how to use my body and my things, not you. We are unconcerned

[12] I Berlin, *Two Concepts of Liberty* (Oxford, Clarendon, 1958).

[13] Thinking in terms of 'loss' and not 'rights' obscures this distinction because, as we have seen, not obtaining a benefit that would have counterfactually accrued can constitute 'loss'.

here with whether the plaintiff is, as a matter of fact, worse off as things turn out than he or she otherwise would be.

The position of the positive law is, I suggest, reflected in the position as a matter of morality. The maxim of Jesus that we should 'Do unto others as you would have them do unto you'[14] is, on this view, a maxim of *virtue* not interpersonal *right*. The man who fails to pick up the baby drowning in an inch of water when he could, if he chose, easily rescue it, is what is technically known as an 'arsehole'. He behaves in a way that is, as a matter of personal morality, deeply wrong and reprehensible. However, he does not, by his failure to rescue, wrong the child. Although he has caused loss in the law's sense (the child is in a worse position than he or she would have been if rescued), there is no right violation.

These rights required by equal freedom justify the category of basic rights with which we are all familiar at common law. You must not tell me lies I believe. You may not burn down my crops, or enter my home. You may not detain me against my will. You must not damage my reputation with others. You must keep the agreements you make.

This does not entail that courts should recognise and enforce this class of rights regardless of any countervailing considerations. So we may refuse to enforce an otherwise good claim because the defendant is having to rely upon his or her own criminal conduct in order to establish it. Or we may have a public interest in parliamentarians being able to speak freely, and so may give them a blanket privilege to defame citizens.

Further, although we may accept this minimal list of rights, or something very similar to it, we need positive law to give *determinatio* in cases of uncertainty. Where does my land end and yours begin? When is it permissible to damage another's reputation when the truth is important? Over time, the judge-made law has answered most of these kind of questions for us. The judge-made positive law still has many gaps, and so is still being created, but it has no gaps in the sense that the judge is required to give an answer to every case with which he or she is presented according to what justice requires.

There are also other rights in law that are not required by but are compatible with a system of equal freedom. The creation of such rights is not the proper province of the courts. It is impossible to imagine a civilised society with no law giving individuals the right to exclude others from physical things they own. A world where we are free to burn a farmer's crops, or break into a stranger's home at night, or steal lollipops from babies, or rip the clothes from one another's backs is not a just one. In relation to some property, usually land, many societies have communal rights where no individual has the right to exclude others: a village green is an English example. However, it is impossible to imagine any society we could consider just that recognised *no* right to personal property whatsoever.

By contrast, it is perfectly possible to imagine a civilised society that did not possess any patent, trade marks or copyright law at all. Copying a Picasso means

[14] Matthew 7:12; Luke 6:31.

that we now have two. The Australian Pirate Party state 'We in the Pirate Party have simply decided that if sharing a love for culture, knowledge and information with our friends and family makes us pirates, then that's what we are and we're proud of it.' This is a legitimate viewpoint (albeit not one I share, even if my own royalties as an author are somewhat modest). The justification for patents is that they encourage innovation, for copyright that it enables creative work to be funded, for trade marks that they allow us to have confidence in the things we consume. They are dependent for their justification upon the instrumental goals they seek to pursue. It is no accident that the origins of the general law of patents was in the Statute of Monopolies 1624, of copyright in the Copyright Act 1709 and of trade marks in the Trade Marks Registration Act 1875. Because these rights cannot be justified absent instrumental reasoning, their recognition was the proper province of the legislature. One thing moral rights are not is moral rights (absent the law).

VIII. Why Don't We Have the Rights We Don't?

Another way of illustrating the importance of the distinction between rights and loss is insulting behaviour. Insults are, or almost always are, wrongful as a matter of virtue. Being offensive and insulting is a very bad way to behave. Similarly, deliberately making others miserable is, generally, reprehensible. The journalists of the *Sunday Sport* behaved in the most disgusting manner when they sneaked into the hospital bedroom of the actor Gordon Kaye,[15] but lack of virtue is not enough to establish that another had a right that they did not so act.

The law of insults is interesting both comparatively and, more importantly, theoretically. In common law jurisdictions insults alone are not actionable. True, the publication of a defamatory statement to a third party potentially is, but the gist of the wrong here is the infringement of the right to one's correct reputation. Communications to the plaintiff alone do not suffice, and truth provides a defence. If we are to be able to pursue our ends, this will require the trust of others. If other people believe I am a mass murderer, I will not be able to obtain a mortgage, get a job, marry, have children and so on. Conversely, we all of us have an interest in knowing the truth so that we can decide who to interact with. It is possible to imagine a universe where we could all pursue our ends as hermits without needing to interact with others, but that is not our world. The principle of equal freedom *necessitates* a law of defamation.

However, common law systems do not recognise any generalised right to one's emotional wellbeing. Upset alone is not actionable. Why not?

The Scots and South Africans, unlike the English, received Roman-Dutch law into their legal system. One part of this reception was the Roman *actio iniuriarum*. The gist of this wrong was never, or at least never solely, the reputation that the

[15] *Kaye v Robertson* [1991] FSR 62.

victim had, but rather his or her honour or dignity. At the time of the Roman-Dutch reception into Scotland prior to The Enlightenment, honour and dignity were more prized than they are today. Duels were fought, and men and women died fighting for this interest in a way that seems alien to us today.

In still having the *actio iniuriarum* within their legal system, the Scots and South Africans are relatively unusual. The Germans, who like the Scots were never a geographical part of the Roman world but inherited its law, entirely abolished the Roman *actio* by legislation by the end of the nineteenth century. Post-war, the German courts have again recognised rights to reputation and privacy at large, but this has not been done through the resurrection of the long-dead Roman rule protecting honour and dignity.

Now, looked at from a common law perspective, most of the situations where the *actio iniuriarum* could be and can be invoked under Roman, Scots and South African law are covered by other torts. So, physical assault was and is one form of the wrong. The original Roman sanction for the *actio iniuriarum* was a penalty of 25 *asses*. Because of inflation this sum became derisory, and so we are told the well-known story of Lucius Veratius, who amused himself by slapping the faces of those he met, followed by a slave who would pay the 25 *asses* to the startled victims.[16] For those lawyer-economists who see the law as simply about price signalling there was presumably nothing wrong with this behaviour, it was just that the price had been set too low.

In the common law, conduct such as this would clearly be trespass to the person. Although the gist of the wrong would be different, one's right to the integrity of one's body rather than to dignity, the consequential emotional distress should be recoverable for this wrong. Similarly, other forms of the *actio iniuriarum*, such as wrongful imprisonment, defamation and – at least historically – some forms of interference with family relations, such as enticing away a wife or husband, were actionable in England, and in principle at least consequential distress recoverable.

So, from a comparative perspective, the most interesting category of case is the category of abusive language, as insults have never been actionable in the common law. Similarly in the common law, truth will always be a defence in cases of defamation, whereas in Scotland and South Africa, in principle at least, it remains possible that the *actio iniuriarum* may be available where, say, a conviction in a juvenile court from many years ago is publicised in order to humiliate someone.[17] Unless we think all legal rules are simply arbitrary line drawing (as sometimes they are, as with the decision on which side of the road to drive), we need to decide which legal system is making the right choice.

My independence is not diminished by an insult, however offensive, or by misery alone, however deeply it is suffered. It should be emphasised here that it is not enough that we would not choose to be subject to the conduct complained

[16] Aulus Gellius, *Noctes Atticae*, Lib XX, [13].

[17] *Mackay v M'Cankie* (1883) 10 R 537; Lord Kilbrandon 'The Law of Privacy in Scotland' (1971) 2 *Cambrian Law Review* 35, 38.

of, but rather that the conduct complained of does not constrain my independent action. Damaging my reputation with others impairs my future self's ability to choose how to live my life. My options are diminished if I am widely believed to be a paedophile. Insults and misery do not constrain me.[18] Equal freedom, or independence, cannot justify a wrong of this kind.

In the United States, the negligent infliction of emotional distress is sometimes actionable. In England and Australia, by contrast, in a claim for so-called nervous shock, recovery is limited to cases of a recognised psychiatric illness.[19] Why does our law draw this distinction between illness and misery?

Yet again, impairing someone else's mental health will seriously set back that person's independence. In the marvellous 1940 British film *Gaslight*, starring Anton Walbrook and Diana Wynyard, rather flatly remade by Hollywood in 1944 with Charles Boyer and Ingrid Bergman, a husband does everything short of physical violence to psychologically torture his wife in order to drive her mad. Although I know of no case like this, if he had succeeded I have no doubt that he would today have been liable for a tort.

It is sometimes claimed that in England, the deliberate infliction of misery is actionable following the decision in *Wilkinson v Downton*.[20] The defendant, as a practical joke, told the plaintiff that her husband had been seriously injured in an accident. This was untrue and the plaintiff suffered a serious reaction: vomiting, other physical side-effects, weeks of suffering and a threat to her reason. The recovery for the mental distress can be seen either as consequent upon the adverse physical consequences the deceit induced, or as loss consequent upon deceit, which need not of course be economic loss. Lies which are believed do inhibit our ability to choose, and are rightly actionable. There is little authority here for the idea that the infliction of misery is itself a wrong.

Similar is *Janvier v Sweeney*.[21] Here the defendant had told the plaintiff that she was wanted for communicating with a German spy, and she suffered what was then called nervous shock but what we would now call a recognised psychiatric illness. Impairing *my ability to reason* does inhibit our equal freedom, indeed in perhaps the most fundamental way possible. Distress, however deeply felt, does not violate my independence.

When the issue came before the House of Lords in *Wainwright v Home Office*, Lord Hoffmann, whilst leaving open the possibility of recovery for intentional inflicted emotional distress, stated:

> In institutions and workplaces all over the country, people constantly do and say things with the intention of causing distress and humiliation to others. This shows lack of

[18] Cf J Raz, *The Morality of Freedom* (New York, Oxford UP, 1986) 421.

[19] *Alcock v Chief Constable of South Yorkshire Police* [1992] 1 AC 310, HL (the law of torts); *R v Burstow, R v Ireland* [2001] 3 WLR 534, HL (criminal law); *Tame v New South Wales* (2002) 211 CLR 317. Some Australian State legislation expresses this obscurely by requiring the damage to be 'serious'.

[20] *Wilkinson v Downton* [1897] 2 QB 57.

[21] *Janvier v Sweeney* [1919] 2 KB 316.

consideration and appalling manners but I am not sure that the right way to deal with it is always by litigation.[22]

In *Giller v Procopets*,[23] a majority[24] of the Victoria Court of Appeal ruled out recovery for intentionally inflicted emotional distress without more, and four members of the UK Supreme Court in *Rhodes v OPO* took the position that recognised psychiatric injury was still required,[25] whilst two did not.[26]

The law's long-standing distinction between recognised psychiatric illness and simple misery is not merely cultural, with the latter not being seen as sufficiently important nowadays. Nor is it based upon a 'policy', such as trying to limit the number of claims. Rather it is more basic to what law in general, and private law in particular, is all about.

IX. Abuse of Rights?

What happens where the law has said that the plaintiff has no right that the defendant does not do a particular action, and the defendant performs an action that does not constitute the violation of a right with respect to the plaintiff with the sole purpose of inflicting harm? Some legal systems permit the loss caused in such a situation to be recoverable, under a doctrine of 'abuse of rights' that would be more accurately called 'abuse of liberty'. The point of an 'abuse of rights' doctrine is that the defendant has done something that he or she has the liberty to do (ie that the defendant's actions are non-wrongful with respect to the plaintiff). *Should* such a general doctrine be recognised by common law systems?[27]

The classic example of the kind of scenario caught by this doctrine would be that of *Tuttle v Buck*.[28] Ned Tuttle was the only barber in the village of Howard Lake, Missouri. He made profits of $800 per annum. Cassius Buck[29] opened premises which he owned at a nominal rent to barbers whom he paid a wage in return for their work. Tuttle claimed that this was done maliciously with the sole purpose of driving him out of business. The court accepted as a matter of principle that if this malice could be established, there was an actionable tort.

[22] *Wainwright v Home Office* [2003] UKHL 53, [46].
[23] *Giller v Procopets* [2008] VSCA 236.
[24] Neave and Ashley JJA, Maxwell P dissenting on this point.
[25] *Rhodes v OPO* [2015] UKSC 32, [88] *per* Baroness Hale and Lord Toulson, Lords Clarke and Lord Wilson agreed.
[26] Lord Neuberger at [116]–[119], with whom Lord Wilson also agreed.
[27] Again, failing to distinguish rights and loss results in a failure to understand the justification for an 'abuse of rights' doctrine and why it requires intention to harm.
[28] *Tuttle v Buck* 119 NW 946 (Minn 1909). But see *Eldridge v Johndrow* 345 P 3d 553 (Utah 2015), where the Utah Supreme Court refused to follow *Tuttle v Buck*.
[29] 'Mega Buck'. The joke is Tony Weir's.

The position in England, and other systems that follow it,[30] is quite different. This was firmly established in the 1890s in a trio of decisions of the House of Lords: *Mogul Steamship Co v McGregor Gow & Co*,[31] *Bradford v Pickles*,[32] and *Allen v Flood*.[33]

Taking the last alone as illustrative, the plaintiffs were shipwrights, engaged each day to work on their employer's ship. The defendant was the secretary of a union, who informed his employer that if the plaintiffs continued to be re-engaged, the union members would not work. The employer consequently refused to re-engage the plaintiffs, who claimed their consequent economic loss from the defendant. The claim failed. The intentional infliction of economic harm is not actionable.

No doubt someone who acts with the purpose of inflicting harm on another without good motive is lacking in virtue. This is, as a matter of personal morality, a very bad way to behave. However, we cannot justify using the force of the state to enforce virtuous behaviour where no right violation occurs. Those who deliberately do not pick up babies drowning in an inch of water may be appalling and disgusting individuals, but it should not be the job of the law to make us be good.

Nonetheless, if rights afford us the space within which we may pursue our own ends, using the freedom the law accords us *solely* for the purpose of harming others may be thought to be contrary to the law.

However, that there may be good reasons for our law in common not to have developed such a doctrine is well illustrated by *Tuttle v Buck* itself. The defendant's behaviour enhanced the competition in the area for the provision of haircuts. The price fell, benefiting everyone other than Tuttle. What kind of competitive practice should and should not be allowed is a matter of public policy, largely driven by economic concerns. Judges are peculiarly ill-suited to judge these matters, lacking both the political legitimacy and technical competence to engage in the line-drawing exercise that is required. Similarly, a *general* doctrine of abuse of rights would seem to endanger all forms of industrial action by trade unions. What should and should not be permitted, and the procedural hurdles that such unions should have to clear (through balloting) are questions for a democratic legislature, not a judge.

Applied to the intentional infliction of *emotional* harm, the judges would, as Lord Hoffmann warned, be forced to adjudicate on when it is acceptable for us to upset one another. Were the women who dumped me and thereby made me miserable acting reasonably?[34] There seem therefore to be good *prudential* reasons why the common law refused to recognise any general doctrine of abuse of rights, as this would have forced judges into answering questions they are not equipped to answer.

[30] See, eg, *Victoria Park Racing and Recreation Grounds Co Ltd v Taylor* (1937) 58 CLR 479 (High Ct of Australia).

[31] *Mogul Steamship Co v McGregor Gow & Co* [1892] AC 25.

[32] *Bradford v Pickles* [1895] AC 587.

[33] *Allen v Flood* [1898] AC 1.

[34] Yes.

X. Intimidation

However, there will be situations where the conduct goes further than merely causing upset, and instead *intimidates* or *inhibits* another so as to constrain his or her ability to act. A stalker constantly outside someone's home may prevent him or her leaving the house, a campaign of telephone calls by a silent caller may menace someone into being unable to pick up the receiver. Cases such as these are now covered by legislation in the United Kingdom (UK), through a statutory tort.[35] The legislation's requirement that the tort is constituted by a 'course of conduct' (ie not a one-off act) is sensible, as the gist of the wrong is the constraint caused by repeated conduct.

In Australia no equivalent statutory tort of harassment has been created, but there are criminal offences of stalking at State level, so the *Crimes Act 1958* (Vic), section 21A provides that (so long as the offender knew or ought to know of the likely consequences) the offence of stalking is committed

> if the offender engages in a course of conduct which includes [any of a wide range of types of conduct] ... [with] the intention of causing physical or mental harm to the victim, including self-harm, or of arousing apprehension or fear in the victim for his or her own safety or that of any other person.

Whether a victim could rely upon this provision for the purpose of bringing a claim based upon the principle of liability for loss caused by unlawful means depends upon whether Australia follows England in confining 'unlawful means' to civil wrongdoing and excluding crimes.[36] There seems to be no good reason why such a principle should be confined to *economic* loss caused by unlawful means.

In 2003, a Queensland District Court[37] recognised a right to privacy in the context of stalking (loitering outside the plaintiff's home, following her to shopping malls, repeated offensive phone calls, offensive language to the plaintiff and her friends). Skoijen SJDC referred to the American authorities regarding the tort of privacy, and found that a cause of action was available involving (i) a willed act by the defendant; (ii) which intrudes on the privacy or seclusion of the plaintiff; (iii) in a manner considered highly offensive to a reasonable person of ordinary sensibilities; and (iv) which causes the plaintiff detriment in the form of mental, physiological or emotional harm or distress, or which hinders or prevents the plaintiff from doing an act she or he is otherwise lawfully entitled to do. The disjunctive last test is too broad. The essence of the wrong is not, and should not be, the distress but rather the inhibition from action.

[35] Protection from Harassment Act 1997 (UK).
[36] *OBG v Allen* [2007] UKHL 21.
[37] *Grosse v Purvis* [2003] QDC 151.

XI. Consequential Harm

Why are damages for misery or distress ever recoverable, if they cannot form the gist of a wrong? As we have seen, it is a common, if mistaken, view that damages are awarded in law to make good the wrong that has been suffered, when in fact this is frequently impossible. Severed limbs cannot grow back, the time spent wrongfully detained cannot be restored, months of misery cannot be recovered. Rather, damages are awarded as the next best thing to the wrong's not having been suffered in the first place. If we had judges with magical powers, they would enjoin the pile-up on the road caused by the drunken driver, the television programme from claiming that a former politician is a paedophile, the negligent smashing of priceless porcelain. Once the injuries have happened, the reputation been besmirched or the vase smashed, the duty of the wrongdoer not to behave in these ways does not simply disappear. Instead, he or she is now under a duty to do the next best thing now possible to perfect compliance with his or her duty. To the extent that the plaintiff is factually worse off as a result of the wrong, this harm must be compensated. This includes consequential misery that is not too remote. For consequential harm of this kind, it is essential that this plaintiff is in fact worse off. *Pure* misery, like pure economic loss, is not in principle recoverable. It is *damnum sine iniuria*. *Consequential* misery is recoverable because that is what compliance with the duty that has been breached now requires. Just as *pure* economic loss is not in principle actionable, so *pure* misery does not suffice.

Importantly, where a wrong has been suffered, consequential misery should be recoverable regardless of whether such harm was intended by the defendant. The relevant question is whether such loss is too remote, not whether it was intended to be caused. In cases of deliberate wrongdoing (as in the case of a spurned lover who posts compromising photos of his or her ex on the Internet), all direct (ie non-coincidental) consequential loss should be recoverable, regardless of whether it was reasonably foreseen or not.

Pure misery is not and should not be actionable. Misery *consequential* upon a wrong is actionable, and should be.

XII. Offence, Distress, Preference, Dignity, Reputation

The preceding discussion helps us to exclude several plausible reasons that can be given for grounding a right to privacy. In trying to demarcate a separate and freestanding role for privacy, it is nowadays common to focus on two related kinds of case: unwanted intrusion and the disclosure of private information. An example of the former would be photos taken without consent (typically of celebrities whilst on holiday); of the latter, publication of information that is true but embarrassing (an addiction to heroin).

Distress and offence cannot, alone, suffice. If they did, we would have much wider rights to protect us from suffering such forms of harm in general, and this is not required by any principle of equal freedom.

The preference that each of us may have not to have our privacy invaded similarly cannot be enough. I frequently commute by coach from my home in Oxford to London. The coach is rarely full and, like many others, I would prefer it if other passengers did not sit next to me so that I have the space to spread out. This preference cannot be enough to ground a right, even if everyone has the same preference.

Dignity has also been frequently given as a reason grounding the right,[38] and no doubt it did ground the old Roman rule, but it may be doubted whether this suffices. Many acts damage the dignity of others, but these acts do not inhibit or set back the ability of those persons to interact with others, or generally inhibit how they lead their lives. The politicians and celebrities who have been lampooned by cartoonists such as Gillray, or by modern-day television satirists who strip their victims of their dignity in the eyes of others, no doubt often find this hurtful, but it seems wrong to conceive of this as being even prima facie wrongful. Dignity is our sense of ourselves as deserving of attitudinal respect from others. *Alone*, why should this suffice?

Loss of reputation is clearly related to dignity, but we have long-standing torts reflecting this (libel, slander), and, as I have sought to show, it is justifiable based upon the requirement of equal freedom. It seems difficult to justify the right to privacy on the basis that it interferes with reputation. First, the privacy wrong as it exists in the positive law does not seem to require that anyone does or would think worse of the person who is intruded upon or has private information about him or her revealed. Second, if reputation is the gist of the wrong, we seem to be circumventing the defence of justification or truth by allowing a new free-standing tort to come into being that is not subject to these limits. Changing the label on the bottle cannot justify such a change.

XIII. Autonomy

Returning to our equal freedom principle, the most plausible candidate as a reason for grounding the privacy right is autonomy, in the sense of our ability to lead independent lives, in most cases. Dignity and autonomy are not the same. If I attended the conference at which this chapter was delivered in the nude, that would be a forceful expression of my autonomy but it would offend my dignity. Autonomy may be thought to justify a right to privacy because each of us has an interest in forging for ourselves an independent self outside of the bounds of

[38] eg, *Campbell v MGN* [2004] 2 AC 457, [50], [51], [53] and [56] *per* Lord Hoffmann.

public scrutiny. If, say, someone wishes to pursue an activity that wrongs nobody else, but will be inhibited from doing so by public disclosure, should the law afford that person protection? This justification relies upon embarrassment and shame. Some might say that individuals should just toughen up, and that the resultant inhibition on your ability to act is insufficiently serious to warrant the law's intervention. This may seem unrealistic.

If, however, this is to be the basis of our right, certain carve-outs will have to be made. So, with the law of defamation, if publication is made of a matter of public interest, such as that revealing the gross hypocrisy of a politician campaigning to reinstate traditional moral values, then there will be no liability. Such policy carve-outs are better left to the legislature; but where it is silent, it may be argued that the courts have no option but to act.

Further, in some cases, autonomy alone will not do. Paul Weller's infant children were photographed while out and about in Santa Monica, the photographs being published online by an English newspaper. The children were allowed to recover damages in their own right,[39] but it seems implausible that the children themselves were inhibited from acting in any way. They never knew what had happened. Autonomy could have justified a claim by the celebrity or his partner, as they themselves might wish to spare their children the public gaze and so be reluctant otherwise to go out in public, but this was not the reasoning of the court. For those more persuaded than me that dignity suffices, the children, unconscious of what happened, did not have this sense of themselves set back. Has the law gone too far here, and transformed what should have been a matter of press regulation into a matter of private right?

We can imagine hypothetical claims for the publication of pictures of the dying or dead celebrity, where it is implausible to ground the claim in the autonomy of the individual, where we are forced back on to the (in my view weaker) ground of dignity. We could choose to deal with such problem cases through public regulation, in order to maintain the kind of society where corpses, the mentally ill and children are afforded respect. It seems harder to justify this in terms of the *rights* of those whose choices are not inhibited, and whose independence is not set back.

It is to be hoped that enough has now been said to establish that the normative justification for a right to privacy is not easy, and although there may be such good reasons, the judges' hesitation in creating such rights has not been simply cruel or cultural. If this is so, the right to privacy is not as basic as but is more contentious than, say, the right not to be detained against our will. If it is to be actionable then should it not, like deceit, require proof of consequential loss?

[39] *Weller v Associated Newspapers Ltd* [2014] EWHC 1163, affirmed [2015] EWCA Civ 1176, [2016] 1 WLR 1541.

XIV. Do Human Rights Make the Difference?

Section 13 of the Victorian Charter on Human Rights and Responsibilities Act 2016 provides:

> A person has the right—
>
> (a) not to have his or her privacy, family, home or correspondence unlawfully or arbitrarily interfered with; and
> (b) not to have his or her reputation unlawfully attacked.

Article 8 of the European Convention on Human Rights, given effect in UK domestic law by the Human Rights Act 1998, states:

> **Article 8 – Right to respect for private and family life**
>
> 1. Everyone has the right to respect for his private and family life, his home and his correspondence.
> 2. There shall be no interference by a public authority with the exercise of this right except such as is in accordance with the law and is necessary in a democratic society in the interests of national security, public safety or the economic well-being of the country, for the prevention of disorder or crime, for the protection of health or morals, or for the protection of the rights and freedoms of others.

In England, the latter proved important in encouraging the courts to develop a right to privacy not just against the state but against persons generally.[40] Until recently, it was the UK Government's policy to repeal the Human Rights Act and replace it with a British Bill of Rights. This change has, for now, been delayed by the imperative need to give substance to the statement that 'Brexit means Brexit'. If, as seems probable, any such future repeal removed the incorporation of Convention rights from UK domestic law, this raises the question of whether privacy rights at common law fall with the Act that encouraged their development. It also raises the possibility that any divergence between Australian and English law is justified by our different human rights regimes.

The label 'human rights' lays claim to the idea that these are rights that all humans have in all times and places, regardless of what the positive law in any particular place might say. Although this is often stated as if it were axiomatically true of the rights contained in human rights conventions, it is obviously false. These are rights against a state that secure for us a number of human goods. As they are dependent upon the existence of a state against which they are exigible, they are not held universally. The rights in relation to a criminal trial in section 25 of the Victorian Act makes this clear: these are rights against the state, not persons generally. Even the right in Article 2 of the European Convention on Human Rights (the equivalent is section 9 of the Victorian Act), which protects the right to life, does not merely give us a right not to be killed, as might naively

[40] *Campbell v MGN* (n 38) [49]–[50] *per* Lord Hoffmann.

be expected. The state is not only obliged not to kill me (as all people are), it is also obliged to take positive steps to protect me from death (by, for example, setting up a police force). These rights are quite different in their content from those found at common law. 'Human rights', as that label is now used to refer to the various rights in international instruments, are not necessitated by the equal freedom principle, and are the proper province of constitutions and legislation, not judge-made law.

The difference between the basis of our judge-made rights and those under the Convention is well illustrated by the UK Supreme Court's decision in *Michael v The Chief Constable of South Wales Police*.[41] The police failed to respond promptly to an emergency 999 call and, as a result, Joanna Michael was murdered by her partner. At common law, do we have rights generally against persons, that they take care to protect us from other people? Clearly not: the equal freedom principle does not require that we take positive steps to pick up a stranger's baby drowning in an inch of water. If we do not have such rights against persons generally, do we have such rights against the police specifically? The only legitimate source of such a right would be found in legislation. We cannot jump from the premise that the police are under a *public* duty to protect the community, to the conclusion that any individual within society has a *private* right to protection enforceable against them. Nor can we simply assume, as one member of the court did, that because the police had been negligent, and this had left the plaintiff worse off than he or she otherwise would have been, the claim should be allowed unless there was a good countervailing reason why not. The claim at common law was rightly dismissed.

The claim under the Human Rights Act was allowed to proceed to trial. What is the best justification for the extra rights the legislation confers? One answer is found in considerations that apply in the UK but not in some other common law jurisdictions such as Australia. The case for having constitutional constraints on state power within the wholly domestic context of a liberal democracy is difficult and controversial. Within an international context it is much easier. If we in the UK think that there are certain human goods all societies should seek to secure for their citizens, how can we apply pressure on, say, Belarus to meet those standards? As Syria currently demonstrates, even from a wholly selfish perspective it is in our interests if our near neighbours meet certain standards in relation to the treatment of their citizens. Absent military force, the only tool available is international agreement. This is the primary justification for the European Convention on Human Rights and the United Nations Declaration. If these rights are to be meaningful for citizens, this further requires both that there be an international forum for determining what they require (because if the UK is free to determine their meaning for itself, so would other states be) and that they be enforceable within each member state's own domestic legal order. That is what the UK Human Rights Act seeks to achieve. This provides a powerful internationalist justification

[41] *Michael v The Chief Constable of South Wales Police* [2015] UKSC 2.

for a Bill of Rights that is absent in relation to, say, the (wholly domestic) Canadian Charter of Rights and Freedoms or the legislation in the State of Victoria. The result in *Michael* justifiably differs between the minimalist approach of the common law and the more generous approach of the legislation. The judges could not have done this.

It is sometimes claimed, as a justification either for or against having them, that rights against the state that are found in Bills of Rights either have their origins in or are found within the common law. An examination of the different rights contained within the European Convention and United Nations Declaration and their scope, shows this not to be so. There is nothing in the common law that restricts Parliament's power to, say, abolish freedom of assembly. Rights of this form are again the proper province of the legislature, not the courts. This is another proof of the falsity of the proposition that there is anything particularly fundamental or essentialist about such rights. It is perfectly possible to imagine civilised societies that do not possess a general Bill of Rights of this kind, and we have a name for one: Australia.

Domestic private law rights that track Convention rights are neither a necessary nor a sufficient condition for a state to be Convention-compliant. For example, in relation to the prohibition on torture, it would obviously not be sufficient that individuals have a private law right against the state that they are not tortured, with a secondary right to damages when they are. If someone is in fact tortured on behalf of the state, this will constitute a violation of the prohibition of torture in Article 3, notwithstanding the existence of a parallel domestic right not to be tortured. Conversely, a domestic law provision permitting torture will not offend anyone's Convention right if no one is in fact tortured.

However, prior to the Human Rights Act, the UK courts were under pressure to expand the common law in order to ensure that the UK was in compliance with its international obligations. Under Article 13 of the Convention, signatory states are obliged to provide an effective remedy for the violation of the rights in other articles before their own domestic courts. Before the Human Rights Act, the only way of doing this was through the expansion of the common law. If the case had arisen in a pre-Act world, therefore, the only way of avoiding the conclusion that the UK was in breach of Article 13 in *Michael* would have been to expand (distort?) the common law of negligence in order to allow a claim to succeed by that route. Today no such expansion of the common law is required, as the Human Rights Act ensures that the UK is in compliance with Article 13.

The effect of the Human Rights Act properly understood is therefore to diminish, not increase, the importance of the Convention in developing the common law. It is somewhat ironic, then, that the House of Lords in *Campbell v MGN* took the Act as being one of the developments that justified a new right to privacy.

In *Campbell v MGN*, Lord Hoffmann asked why we should have a different right to privacy against the state than we do against persons generally? Once the Act had recognised such a right against the state, why not extrapolate from it? The same answer can be given as it is in relation to the right to education.

With regard to the state, we do not have the concern of using someone as a means to another's ends. So, as in *Michael*, whereas it may be objectionable to require a private person to come to another's rescue, no such problem arises with regard to the state. Indeed, we might say that the entire purpose of the state is that it is used as means to further the ends of citizens. We require the state to set up a police force, provide schools, guarantee healthcare and so on. Similarly, the European Convention imposes *positive* duties on states to secure the private and family life of citizens that would be wholly unacceptable as a model between private persons. We can and should expect more from the state than we do from each other. That we have a right to privacy against the state does not, alone, justify a right to privacy against persons generally.

Worse, we cannot use the jurisprudence of the European Court of Human Rights to determine the boundaries of interpersonal wrong between persons, as different considerations are in play. The European Court of Human Rights is not concerned to tell signatory states what its law on privacy should be. The ways in which states may secure family or private life may be diverse, and how each state may choose to do so is subject to a margin of appreciation (ie there is a wide range of possible options). In 'balancing' the right to freedom of expression against the right to private life, the European Court of Human Rights is not engaged in the bright-line drawing required in private law, but rather in setting the boundaries beyond which no state may go. As a result, the deference UK courts have shown to decisions of the European Court of Human Rights in this area is misguided: the courts are engaged in answering fundamentally different questions.

The conclusion is that our right to privacy, if justified, should not stand or fall with the existence of human rights legislation. If it can be justified at all, it can only be justified independently.

XV. Confidence

In England, the historical source of what has become our right to private information is the old law of confidence. At one time the law of confidence was confined to cases of confidential relationships. The law recognises many rights that are voluntarily assumed by one party to another, and which are not imposed upon persons generally without more. The most obvious are contractual duties, but there are many more outside of contract. Bailees owe positive duties of care to bailors, hospitals to patients they admit, schools to children they accept, agents owe positive duties of action to their principals, as do trustees to their beneficiaries. In none of these cases is there any necessity to point to any contract between the parties. The duty of confidence could at one time have been seen as part of the same family of voluntarily assumed duties arising from entering into a relationship. Third parties could, in certain circumstances, be held liable on the basis of their accessorial involvement in the breach by the principal, as is a dishonest assistant in the breach of a fiduciary duty.

Historically, as with fiduciary duties, the duty of confidence arose in the Chancery Division, rather than in the common law, but without further justification this appears to have little normative significance.

Confidence of this relational kind is enough to explain why there is a wrong in cases such as the Victoria Court of Appeal decision in *Giller v Procopets.* During a relationship, the defendant had videotaped sex with the plaintiff, which tapes he had either shown to others or threatened to do so. This is a clear breach of the undertaking of confidence between sexual partners, and although a relatively modern phenomenon on its facts, very old in relation to the underlying principle.

A much more revolutionary step had been taken by Lord Goff in *Attorney-General v Observer Newspapers Ltd (No 2) ('Spycatcher')*,[42] where he reformulated the right to confidential information without reference to any prior relationship at all, it being sufficient that the person receiving the information had notice that it was intended to be confidential. It was this reformulation that enabled the claim of Ms Naomi Campbell in relation to private (but true) information about her private life: her visiting a drug rehabilitation clinic. The gist of the wrong is nicely illustrated by the facts of the case: Ms Campbell would be inhibited from visiting drug a rehabilitation centre if paparazzi could photograph and then publish her every move; this would constrain her ability to act. This rule can be reconciled with the law that we have no general proprietary right to information[43] on the basis that it concerns a species of information (that we expect to be private).

This may be contrasted with the recent and difficult decision of the Supreme Court in *PJS v News Group Newspapers.*[44] The plaintiff was the partner of a well-known celebrity in the entertainment business with whom he had children. He had been engaged in sexual activity with others outside of this relationship, the details of which a newspaper threatened to publish. An interim injunction was obtained, and upheld before the Supreme Court. The identity of the plaintiff and the outline of the facts were well known, having been widely distributed on social media. (So widely in fact that I inadvertently discovered who the litigant was, despite not having the remotest interest in the story itself. If unworldly Oxford law professors know, who does not?) A claim based upon breach of confidence was, it was accepted, bound to fail as the information was no longer confidential. The claim based upon the now independent right to privacy succeeded, despite the fact that the information had by now been widely circulated.

For our purposes it is enough to note that as a matter of history, this right to information about one's own life, although it had its origins in the equitable duty of confidence, now has little or nothing to do with either that equitable duty or the original justification that underlay that equitable rule. It is no longer anything to do with the old law of confidence. The radical nature of this new tort has been hidden by its introduction through the baby steps of incrementalism, rather than through

[42] *Attorney-General v Observer Newspapers Ltd (No 2) ('Spycatcher')* [1990] 1 AC 109, 281.
[43] See, eg, *Farah v Say-Dee* [2007] CLR 89, [2007] HCA 22.
[44] *PJS v News Group Newspapers* [2016] UKSC 26.

one large change. That a change is made in small stages does not mean, however, that we are absolved from providing the same kind of justification as would be required for one large one. Further, the rule as now recognised in England is so far removed from the old law of confidence that it is unsafe to analogise across from one area to the other.

XVI. Damages in Equity

At one time it was thought that for equitable wrongdoing, the only remedies available were an injunction and, where appropriate, an account.[45] This seemed to provide a barrier to recovery where damages were sought for breach of confidence.

Lord Goff in *Spycatcher* suggested that such damages were now available through 'a beneficent interpretation of the Chancery Amendment Act 1858 (Lord Cairns' Act)'.[46] This cannot be correct.

Lord Cairns' Act did two important things. First, it enabled common law damages to be awarded before the courts of equity. A litigant who sought an injunction in the courts of Chancery, but lost, was not thereby forced to re-litigate the point in a separate claim for damages before the common law courts. Since the Judicature Acts, and the procedural unification of the courts of common law and equity, this justification for damages in lieu of an injunction has fallen away. The same court, acting in its common law jurisdiction, is able to award damages anyway.

Second, and still importantly today, it enabled damages to be awarded *before* a wrong had in fact been suffered. If a neighbour is about to open a pig slaughterhouse next door, you may seek an injunction to restrain the nuisance before it has occurred. If an injunction is refused, does the unsuccessful plaintiff have to wait until the wrong occurs before bringing a claim in separate proceedings (as would be necessary at common law)? The answer is no: damages can be given in lieu of the injunction now. It is in such cases that Lord Cairns' Act is still of significance today.

The effect of the Act is not, therefore, to allow damages to be recovered for causes of action that do not, independently, sound in damages. Indeed, the principles for the assessment of damages under the Act are identical to those applicable at common law.[47] Rather, it allows damages for wrongs that have not yet happened, but which are inevitable.

[45] Eg, *Proctor v Bayley* (1889) 42 Ch D 390, 401.
[46] *Spycatcher* (n 42) 286.
[47] *Johnson v Agnew* [1980] AC 367 (HL).

XVII. Equitable Compensation

Once we have accepted that there *is* a private law wrong of violation of privacy, damages, whether we call them equitable compensation or not, seem inevitably to follow. Allowing compensation in equity for wrongdoing is nowadays accepted by all.[48] There are, today, many cases that assume such compensation is available for both breach of confidence and its privacy offspring.

However, that does not determine the question with which we started. Should such damages be available for the wrong itself, or only for consequential losses? Indeed, if history is a guide, making an award of 'equitable compensation' where no consequential loss has been suffered is a very radical step. Given the difficulty we have seen in articulating the reason for the right to privacy itself, its doubtful provenance within human rights legislation and the law of confidence, its late recognition within the common law world, the more cautious approach would have been to confine recovery to consequential loss. This was not the approach of the English Court of Appeal (affirming the decision of Mann J) in *Gulati v MGN*.[49] Should celebrities who were the victims of phone hacking, which on several occasions led to the publication of private information, be able to recover damages in the absence of proof of consequential loss? General damages for such conduct, described as vindicatory damages, were awarded. Leave to appeal to the Supreme Court was refused. Violations of privacy have, in England at least, overcome doubts as to their wrongfulness, and historical doubts as to the availability of damages, to become actionable per se.

XVIII. Quantification

Once the law has taken this bold step, the question arises as to how such damages are to be quantified?

In relation to some wrongs, placing a figure on the value of the right violated is easy. There is a ready market for the right infringed and we can use that market to set the figure. This is straightforwardly the case in regard to many property rights. If you destroy my seven-year-old Hyundai i30, you must pay me its market price. In some privacy cases this will also work, as where a celebrity's photographs could have been sold to a gossip magazine, and in the United States this measure seems to predominate.

In some cases there is no market, or the right is of less value to others than it is to the plaintiff (as, for example, in relation to the publication of naked pictures of non-celebrities). One option for the purposes of calculation is then to ask what a reasonable release fee would be (sometimes called *Wrotham Park* damages).

[48] *Smith Kline v Department of Community Services* (1990) 22 FCR 73, 121 *per* Gummow J.
[49] *Gulati v MGN* [2015] EWCA Civ 1291.

The enquiry here is not to ask what the plaintiff would himself or herself have accepted as a price for consent (he or she may be either idiosyncratically bloody-minded, or oddly free and easy). Rather, it is to ask what reasonable people situated in the parties' position would have paid.

Again, this form of quantification is also sometimes unavailable, perhaps because no reasonable person would ever have consented to the invasion or disclosure, as is often the case in the most embarrassing scenarios. It is in such circumstances tempting to look to the factual gain made by the defendant in committing the wrong. Tempting, but incorrect.

The leading English decision is that of the House of Lords in *Attorney-General v Blake*.[50] Mr Blake, a notorious spy, was paid a large sum by the publisher Jonathan Cape for his memoirs. There is no market for the UK Government's consenting to release spies from their agreements not to publish their memoirs. No reasonable government would ever have agreed a fee with Mr Blake to release him from his commitments. No provable consequential loss could be shown by the publication of information that was long since in the public domain. The court awarded an account of profits in order to ensure that an adequate remedy was available for the breach of contract committed.

In the context of breach of privacy, it is tempting to think that an account of profits is similarly an appropriate remedy, especially as its origins lie in the equitable duty of confidentiality. It seems unjustifiable, however, that the result should turn on *any* actual profits made by Blake.

What if the same facts were to recur, but with one difference. In Blake II, the contract-breaking spy turns down the offer from the publisher on the basis that he knows that if he accepts it, he will have to hand the fee over to the UK Government. What remedy should be available to the Government in such circumstances?

The better view is that Blake should be liable for the amount he was offered. It should not matter whether Mr Blake personally made a gain. He should have to pay what he was offered, regardless of whether he accepted it. What matters is what someone was prepared to pay him to commit the wrong, not whether he did in fact gain from doing so. This is so because, in the absence of a market, or a reasonable release fee, this provides the best valuation of general damages that is available. What someone was prepared to pay Blake to breach his agreement is the best available evidence of what the Government's right was worth.

In yet other cases (often those of private individuals whose secret personal lives are of no interest to strangers), this form of quantification is also impossible. Here the law may be forced to adopt a tariff system. Just as we know that the loss of two arms is worse than the loss of one, and this can be reflected in the award of general damages, so we know that some invasions of privacy are worse than others, and so deserving of a greater award. How this tariff is fixed is more or less arbitrary, however. We need to ensure that the tariff is consistent with that applied

[50] *Attorney-General v Blake* [2001] 1 AC 268.

in other cases. Some certainty can be achieved over time, as it has been in the context of personal injuries, but that is all.

Lastly, the issue of double recovery arises. Can a plaintiff recover vindicatory damages and damages for consequential loss, or does this entail over-compensation? One answer might be to consider the wrong and the loss consequent upon it to be wholly distinct, so that recovering both is acceptable.

The better view is that recovery under one head reduces the damages under the other. Every penny recovered by the plaintiff by way of vindicatory damages reduces the loss he or she has suffered by virtue of the wrong by one penny. Recovery under one head reduces the damages payable under the other. These should be seen as alternative, not cumulative, ways of calculating damages, with the plaintiff confined to whichever of the two is the greatest.

XIX. Were We Wrong?

It is a sad fact of life that litigation is carried on by the wealthy, who are often the drivers of change in our law. The law of privacy has changed. Few of us will have much sympathy for the likes of the *Sunday Sport* or the *Daily Mirror*, publishing the prurient details of the lives of others, where no public good is furthered by their so doing. Their lack of virtue, and the misery they cause, however, cannot alone be enough to justify the law as it now stands in England.

There is a case to be made that we have gone too far. Maybe we should seek to create a more civilised public arena by regulating what the press can publish, but the correct vehicle for this is not private rights (with consequential claims for damages). Nobody has been a stauncher advocate of damages in the absence of consequential loss than I have, but it should not be thought that it is appropriate in every case. In deciding that breach of privacy should be actionable per se, the courts have gone further than the creation of a new form of wrongdoing, but have also treated it more seriously than other longer-established categories. It cannot be assumed that in doing so we have grown wiser than our legal forebears.

5

Compensating for Loss of Dignity and Autonomy

NA MOREHAM*

I. Introduction

According to recent English authority, if someone breaches your privacy and you can establish the requirements of the misuse of private information tort then that person has to pay you compensation for the loss of privacy you suffer, regardless of whether you have suffered any distress or other consequential harm. In other words, damages are payable for the loss of privacy per se.

This chapter will argue that this position is conceptually sound. Further, it argues that it is sound for the very reasons that the courts give in privacy damages decisions themselves; namely, that even in the absence of distress, all actionable breaches of privacy interfere with the dignity and autonomy of the individual. This position is in turn is consistent with widely-held philosophical, sociological and psychological understandings of nature of privacy harms and, as a result, with the reasons why English courts developed the misuse of private information action in the first place. This includes reasoning derived from the jurisprudence on the right to respect for private life in Article 8 of the European Convention on Human Rights 1950, the incorporation of which into English domestic law formed part of the impetus for introducing the privacy right into English privacy law.

The chapter will develop these arguments in three sections. The first section briefly discusses the leading decisions on damages for misuse of private information and examines the bases on which courts have held privacy damages to be available as of right. Section III then shows how those reasons for protecting privacy breaches align with dominant theoretical conceptions on the relationship between privacy and the protection of dignity and autonomy. Finally, the chapter

* I would like to thank Dr Normann Witzleb of Monash University and the participants in the *International Workshop on Remedies for Breach of Privacy* at Melbourne University in December 2016 for helpful feedback on this chapter. Thanks also to Etienne Wain of Victoria University of Wellington for copy-editing assistance. I take full responsibility for all content.

will briefly reflect on how damages for loss of dignity and autonomy fit with other types of damages, including those awarded for distress.

II. Damages for Loss of Privacy Per Se

Damages have been a part of the misuse of private information action since its inception. The claimants in the seminal case of *Douglas v Hello! Ltd* were awarded £7,250 each for the distress and inconvenience resulting from publication of unauthorised photographs of their wedding ceremony,[1] and in *Campbell v MGN Ltd*, the claimant received £2,500 (plus £1,000 aggravated damages) for distress and injury to feelings following the publication of details of her drug addiction treatment and images of her leaving a Narcotics Anonymous meeting.[2] It took some time, however, before either substantial monetary awards or detailed reasoning on the basis on which they were granted became established features of the misuse of private information action. No early privacy award exceeded £7,500, and the courts' reasoning was invariably limited to short statements explaining that claimants were being compensated for distress, injury to feelings or inconvenience.[3]

All this changed in the 2008 case of *Mosley v News Group Newspapers Ltd*. In that case, Eady J not only awarded the claimant £60,000 for publication of images and recordings of his participation in a sado-masochistic orgy, he gave detailed reasons for doing so.[4] This began the dual trend of increased awards and more nuanced consideration of damages issues, culminating in Mann J's decision in *Gulati and others v MGN Ltd*, upheld by the Court of Appeal in 2015, to award of tens, and in some cases hundreds, of thousands of pounds in damages to victims of a systematic campaign of telephone hacking conducted by Mirror Group Newspapers Ltd.[5]

Most significantly for the purposes of this chapter, these new more nuanced damages decisions make it clear that damages for misuse of private information

[1] *Douglas v Hello! Ltd* [2003] EWHC 2629 (Ch), [2003] All ER (D) 110 (Nov) (Lindsay J), [56]–[57] (described as 'unassailable in principle' by the Court of Appeal in [2005] EWCA Civ 595, [2006] QB 125, [259]).

[2] *Campbell v MGN Ltd* [2002] EWHC 499 (QB), [2002] EMLR 30, [136].

[3] See, eg, *McKennitt v Ash* [2005] EWHC 3003 (QB), [2006] EMLR 10, [162] (£5,000 for 'hurt feelings and distress') and *Applause Store Productions Ltd v Raphael* [2008] EWHC 1781 (QB), [2008] Info TLR 318, [80]–[81] (£2,000 for 'hurt feelings and distress' including 'shock and upset') and, in the context of contractual breach of confidence, *Archer v Williams* [2003] EWHC 1670 (QB), [2003] EMLR 38, [74]–[78] (£2,500 for 'injury to feelings') and *Cornelius v De Taranto* [2000] EWHC 561 (QB), [2001] EMLR 12, [77]–[84] (£3,000 for 'injury to her feelings' (upheld by the Court of Appeal in [2001] EWCA Civ 1511, [2001] All ER (D) 227 (Oct))).

[4] *Mosley v News Group Newspapers Ltd* [2008] EWHC 1777 (QB), [2008] EMLR 20, [212]–[231] and [236].

[5] *Gulati and others v MGN Ltd* [2015] EWHC 1482 (Ch), [2015] All ER (D) 199 (May) (*Gulati* (HC)), upheld by the Court of Appeal in *Gulati v MGN Ltd and other cases* [2015] EWCA Civ 1291, [2015] All ER (D) 193 (Dec) (*Gulati* (CA)).

are no longer just compensating for distress, hurt feelings or inconvenience. They are also compensating for the loss of privacy itself. So in the leading statement on the issue, Arden LJ said, speaking for the Court of Appeal in *Gulati*:

> In the present context, the damages are an award to compensate for the loss or diminution of a right to control formerly private information and for the distress that the respondents could justifiably have felt because their private information had been exploited, and are assessed by reference to that loss.[6]

In other words, damages for misuse of private information are compensating for two types of loss: the loss of privacy itself and any distress (and presumably other harm)[7] which results from it.

Mann J also recognised these two components of privacy damages in his High Court judgment in *Gulati*. (Indeed, much of the Court of Appeal's analysis is based on Mann J's thoughtful judgment in that case.) Explaining why breach of a right to privacy is worthy of compensation independent of any distress which might have been caused, he said:

> The tort is not a right to be prevented from [being] upset in a particular way. It is a right to have one's privacy respected. Misappropriating (misusing) private information without causing 'upset' is still a wrong. I fail to see why it should not, of itself, attract damages. Otherwise the right becomes empty, contrary to what the European jurisprudence requires. Upset adds another basis for damages; it does not provide the only basis.[8]

This approach, as Mann J says, 'leaves distress where it should be – one of the consequences (perhaps in many cases the prime consequence) of the wrong'.[9] It also avoids what he calls the 'the undesirable consequences of using distress as some sort of measure of the seriousness of the wrong, for which purpose it is highly imperfect'.[10] The shortcomings of using distress in this way is demonstrated in cases that involve young children. Mann J regards as 'quite right' the decision to award £15,000 to the young child in *AAA v Associated Newspapers Ltd*

[6] *Gulati* (CA) (n 5) [48]. See also *Burrell v Clifford* [2015] EWHC 2001 (Ch), [2015] All ER (D) 63 (Nov), [28] (unsuccessful strike out application); *Burrell v Clifford* [2016] EWHC 294 (Ch), [2016] All ER (D) 206 (Feb) (*Burrell*), [133] and [138]; and *Brown v Commissioner of the Police of the Metropolis* (County Court at Central London, 7 October 2016) [43]–[45] and [62].

[7] See further NA Moreham and M Warby (eds), *The Law of Privacy and the Media*, 3rd edn (Oxford, Oxford UP, 2016) [12.95] et seq.

[8] *Gulati* (HC) (n 5) [143]. In *Spelman v Express Newspapers Ltd* [2012] EWHC 355, [2012] All ER (D) 51 (Mar), [114], Tugendhat J said in terms that it should no longer be assumed that damages for misuse of private information would continue to be awarded at the 'very low' levels set in cases like *Campbell*. See also *Cooper v Turrell* [2011] EWHC 3296 (QB), [2011] All ER (D) 82 (Dec) (award of £30,000); *WXY v Gewanter* [2013] EWHC 589 (QB), [2013] All ER (D) 222 (Mar) (award of £19,450 plus £5,000 of aggravated damages); and the decisions discussed in the next section.

[9] *Gulati* (HC) (n 5) [135]. Although compare Eric Descheemaeker's argument (in 'Claimant-focused Damages in the Law of Privacy', ch 6 of this book) that courts need to compensate either for the wrong itself *or* for resulting distress.

[10] *Gulati* (HC) (n 5) [135].

whose photograph was published alongside articles speculating about her father's identity, even though she was too young to be distressed by the publication.[11] Not even counsel for the defendant, he said, suggested that there was any less of an invasion of privacy because the child did not suffer distress.[12] Rather, as Nicola Davies J says in *AAA*, the damages reflect the fact that 'the rights of the claimant have been breached … and serve as notice … as to how seriously the court regards infringement of a child's rights'.[13]

Gulati also makes it clear that damages for loss of privacy per se can be substantial. Explaining that damages for the loss of privacy itself in that case were going to be 'significant', Mann J said:

> Each of the claimants (in differing degrees) had their private information rendered freely available, on a daily basis … to journalists who used it as they thought fit … This was not a situation in which there was a one-off, or two-off, penetration of private information … the claimants' right to control their information was taken from them. It would be quite wrong to confine any damages to compensation for distress, or injured feeling, which they experienced from articles published at this time, and then for additional distress when the enormity (which in my view is the right word) of what happened to them was slowly revealed … For reasons already given, there ought to be some compensation for this invasion per se, and it will inevitably be significant.[14]

Spearman QC has subsequently said, in *Burrell v Clifford*, that the nature of the information disclosed and the extent of any misuse should bear on a court's assessment of compensation for the 'wrong itself'.[15] This reflects, he said, the fact that 'a disclosure to the world at large involves a greater loss of control than a disclosure to, for example, a small number of journalists'.[16] Where the interference is a significant one then, independent of any distress caused, damages will also be substantial.

A. What is the Nature of the Inherent Loss?

So, in an appropriate case, significant damages will be awarded for the loss of privacy itself, independent of any distress or other harm caused. In other words, the breach of privacy itself will give rise to a right to potentially substantial compensation. Questions remain, however, about the conceptual basis for this approach. What reasons have courts given for the award of damages for loss of privacy per se, and are those reasons defensible?

[11] ibid [115].
[12] ibid.
[13] *AAA v Associated Newspapers Ltd* [2012] EWHC 2103 (QB), [2012] All ER (D) 303 (Jul), [127], cited in *Gulati* (HC) (n 5) [114]. As discussed further in section III.A, the same argument would apply to other vulnerable claimants.
[14] *Gulati* (HC) (n 5) [169].
[15] *Burrell* (n 6) [138].
[16] ibid.

i. 'Vindicating' the Breach of the Privacy Right

The first way courts have rationalised damages awards for loss of privacy per se is by referring to the need to 'vindicate' breach of the privacy right. This idea was most clearly articulated by Eady J in *Mosley*. He said that

> it is reasonable to suppose that damages for such an infringement may include distress, hurt feelings and loss of dignity … Apart from distress, there is another factor which probably has to be taken into account of a less tangible nature. It is accepted in recent jurisprudence that a legitimate consideration is that of vindication to mark the infringement of a right … It is simply to mark the fact that either the state or a relevant individual has taken away or undermined the right of another – in this case taken away a person's dignity and struck at the core of his personality.[17]

Similar reasoning can also be seen in Nicola Davies J's reasoning in *AAA* that privacy awards recognise that 'the rights of the claimant have been breached … and serve as notice … as to how seriously the court regards infringement of a child's rights'.[18] This kind of language also appears in some passages of Mann J's judgment in *Gulati*. He says, for example, that whilst 'the law is used to awarding damages for injured feelings, there is no reason in principle … why it should not also make an award to reflect infringements of the right itself, if the situation warrants it'.[19]

Some – most notably Lord Dyson in *R (on the application of Lumba) v Secretary of State for the Home Department* – have seen this reference to 'vindicating' the privacy right as an attempt to introduce into private law a special species of damages, designed not to compensate the claimant but to 'reflect the sense of public outrage, emphasise the importance of the constitutional right and the gravity of the breach, and deter further breaches'.[20] In his view, such damages have no place in private law:

> It is one thing to say that the award of compensatory damages, whether substantial or nominal, serves a vindicatory purpose: in addition to compensating a claimant's loss, it vindicates the right that has been infringed. It is another to award a claimant an additional award, not in order to punish the wrongdoer, but to reflect the special nature of the wrong.[21]

Lord Dyson was prepared to contemplate the first type of award in private law but not the second.[22] And in his view, Eady J's award in *Mosley* was an example of

[17] *Mosley* (n 4) [216].

[18] *AAA* (n 13) [127], cited in *Gulati* (HC) (n 5) [114].

[19] *Gulati* (HC) (n 5) [111].

[20] *Attorney-General of Trinidad and Tobago v Ramanoop* [2005] UKPC 15, [2006] 1 AC 328, [19], cited in *R (on the application of Lumba) v Secretary of State for the Home Department* [2011] UKSC 12, [2012] 1 AC 245, [98].

[21] *Lumba* (n 20) [100].

[22] Instead, he said that the need to vindicate a claimant's common law rights would be sufficiently met by an award of compensatory damages, 'including (in the case of strict liability torts) nominal damages where no substantial loss is proved', a declaration in suitable terms 'where appropriate' and an award of exemplary damages, again 'where appropriate' (*Lumba* (n 20) [101]).

the second type of award – one designed to reflect the special nature of the wrong rather than compensate the claimant. Detailed discussion of *Lumba* and the role of vindicatory damages in other areas of law is beyond the scope of this chapter.[23] Suffice it to say that, contrary to Lord Dyson's suggestion, Eady J was not using the term 'vindicatory damages' to refer to Lord Dyson's second category of award but his first. In other words, Eady J was discussing an award of *compensatory* damages that serves a vindicatory purpose; they were compensatory damages 'to mark the fact that either the state or a relevant individual has taken away or undermined the right of another – in this case taken away a person's dignity and struck at the core of his personality'.[24] As Mann J says in *Gulati*:

> This conclusion is not to reintroduce vindicatory damages by the back door … What is still open is to allow for compensation to be given for the act of misuse itself, where appropriate. I do not see in principle why that should not be allowed, and good reasons why it should be. If one assumes for the moment that what each claimant alleges to have happened has happened, the defendant will have helped itself, over an extended period of time, to large amounts of personal and private information and treated it as its own to deal with as it thought fit. There is an infringement of a right which is sustained and serious. While it is not measurable in money terms, that is not necessarily a bar to compensation (distress is not measurable in that way either). Damages awarded to reflect the infringement are not vindicatory in the sense of *Lumba*. They are truly compensatory.[25]

This is, with respect, correct. *Lumba* does not rule out an award of compensatory damages for breach of the privacy right itself. Nonetheless, it is suggested that the language of vindication does not fully capture the reasons why losses of privacy should be compensable per se. Whilst recognition of the need to vindicate the loss of privacy itself is welcome, describing the harm caused by breaches of privacy as a 'breach of the right itself' can render the harm somehow abstract and impersonal; it risks disconnecting the right from the individual it is designed to protect. This in turn encourages the viewpoint, expressed by Lord Dyson in *Lumba*, that there can be situations where an individual's rights – specifically in that case, the right to be free from false imprisonment – are interfered with but 'no substantial harm follows from the breach'.[26] As the rest of this chapter will show, this will never be the case where misuse of private information is concerned. It is perhaps unsurprising then that Dingemans J held in the first-instance decision in *Weller* that the term 'vindicatory damages' is 'unhelpful and liable to mislead' in misuse of private information, and that it creates a risk of both over-compensation

[23] See further JNE Varuhas, *Damages and Human Rights* (Oxford, Hart Publishing, 2016) especially 125–29.

[24] *Mosley* (n 4) [216].

[25] *Gulati* (HC) (n 5) [132]. See further *Gulati* (CA) (n 5) [48].

[26] He says there was no harm in that case because the claimants could have been detained lawfully under another policy. But could the harm in *Lumba* not be seen as the indignity of being detained under an unlawful secret policy?

(because of double counting) and of under-compensation 'because relevant features about the conduct are not considered'.[27]

The rest of this chapter delves beneath the idea that privacy damages awarded as of right are vindicating the breach of the privacy right itself and it asks *why* we regard a loss of privacy as worthy of vindication. Is it because there are further interests underpinning the privacy right which are harmed if someone interferes with it? And if so, do we in fact protect against losses of privacy themselves because of the harm a loss of privacy will always cause to these fundamental interests?

ii. The Harm to Dignity and Autonomy Inherent in All Breaches of Privacy

When one looks at recent privacy decisions themselves, one sees that rather than talking in terms of vindication, judges in fact discuss damages for loss of privacy per se in terms of the harm caused to the claimant. Damages, they say, are being awarded in these situations to compensate for the loss of dignity and autonomy that is present in all actionable breaches of privacy.

In the first instance judgment in *Gulati*, for example, Mann J set out clearly three types of loss that flowed from the telephone hacking at issue in that case. He said:

> There is compensation for loss of privacy or 'autonomy' resulting from the hacking or blagging that went on; there is compensation for injury to feelings (including distress); and there is compensation for 'damage or affront to dignity or standing'.[28]

Indeed, even when he frames the discussion in terms of 'mak[ing] an award to reflect infringements of the right itself', Mann J takes care to point out that it is harm to dignity and autonomy which is ultimately being compensated. For example, he says:

> While the law is used to awarding damages for injured feelings, there is no reason in principle, in my view, why it should not also make an award to reflect infringements of the right itself, if the situation warrants it. The fact that the loss is not scientifically calculable is no more a bar to recovering *damages for 'loss of personal autonomy' or damage to standing* than it is to damages for distress … If one has lost 'the right to control the dissemination of information about one's private life' then I fail to see why that, of itself, should not attract a degree of compensation, in an appropriate case. A right has been infringed, and loss of a kind recognised by the court as wrongful has

[27] *Weller v Associated Newspapers Ltd* [2014] EWHC 1163 (QB), [2014] All ER (D) 142 (Apr), [191]. This decision was upheld on appeal in *Weller v Associated Newspapers Ltd* [2015] EWCA Civ 1176, [2016] 1 WLR 1541.

[28] *Gulati* (HC) (n 5) [108]. *Gulati* is the first case in which English courts have provided a remedy for a breach of privacy that did not involve the dissemination of private information, ie for the unauthorised listening itself. See further NA Moreham, 'Liability for Listening: Why Phone Hacking is an Actionable Breach of Privacy' (2015) 8 *Journal of Media Law* 155.

> been caused. It would seem to me to be contrary to principle not to recognise that as a potential route to damages ...[29]

This characterisation of privacy harms as the 'loss of personal autonomy', 'loss of the right to control dissemination of information' and 'damage to standing' is consistent with courts' stated reasons for protecting privacy in the first place. As Mann J points out, the values of dignity and autonomy underpin both Article 8 of the European Convention and the misuse of private information tort which it helped create. He cites, for example, Lord Hoffman's statement in *Campbell* that

> [w]hat human rights law has done is to identify private information as something worth protecting as an aspect of human autonomy and dignity ... it focuses upon the protection of human autonomy and dignity – the right to control the dissemination of information about one's private life and the right to the esteem and respect of other people.[30]

According to Mann J's reasoning, then, the reason that a claimant should be compensated for loss of 'the right to control the dissemination of information about one's private life' is because 'loss of personal autonomy' or 'damage to standing' will inevitably flow from it.

The Court of Appeal in *Gulati* agreed with Mann J's analysis. As already outlined, Adern LJ said in terms that damages in misuse of private information are not just for distress but also to compensate 'for the loss or diminution of a right to control formerly private information'.[31] She explains how in that case that loss of control led, inter alia, to the release of information about an actor's plans to leave a television show, the publication of the fact that a public figure had sought legal advice on a possible divorce, and the exposure of an otherwise secret wedding venue. Although Arden LJ does not articulate exactly *why* loss of control over information about one's career plans, marital difficulties or wedding is harmful, she does go on to say that privacy is a fundamental right and that the reasons for protecting it are manifold. She also cites Lord Nicholls's statement in *Campbell* that privacy lies at the heart of liberty in a modern state, and that the proper degree of liberty is 'essential for the well-being and development of an individual'.[32] All this seems to imply that the Court of Appeal was willing to adopt not just Mann J's conclusion about damages for the loss of privacy per se, but also his reasons for awarding them, at least in so far as they relate to liberty and autonomy.

Concern about the dignity of the individual also clearly underpinned Eady J's reference to the need to vindicate the breach of the privacy right in *Mosley*.

[29] *Gulati* (HC) (n 5) [111] (emphasis added).

[30] *Campbell v MGN Ltd* [2004] UKHL 22, [2004] 2 AC 457, [50]–[51], cited in *Gulati* (HC) (n 5) [110]. Peter Birks agreed that privacy and dignity are inherently connected. He argued that privacy infringements should be seen as part of a more general tort of *iniuria* or contemptuous harassment, which had at its heart the 'right to equality of respect': see P Birks, 'Harassment and Hubris: The Right to an Equality of Respect' (1997) 32 *Irish Jurist* (NS) 1.

[31] *Gulati* (CA) (n 5) [48].

[32] ibid [46], citing *Campbell* (HL) (n 30) [12].

Although Lord Dyson in *Lumba* focused on Eady J's reliance on the concept of vindicatory damages, Eady J himself was emphasising the dignity interests at stake in privacy claims. To repeat the 'vindication' passage, this time with emphasis added:

> It is reasonable to suppose that damages for such an infringement may include distress, hurt feelings and *loss of dignity* ... Apart from distress, there is another factor which probably has to be taken into account of a less tangible nature. It is accepted in recent jurisprudence that a legitimate consideration is that of vindication to mark the infringement of a right ... It is simply to mark the fact that either the state or a relevant individual has taken away or undermined the right of another – *in this case taken away a person's dignity and struck at the core of his personality.*[33]

This focus on the intangible harms that inevitably *flow* from a loss of privacy, rather than on the breach or the loss of privacy itself, is welcome for a number of reasons. First, it avoids the risk that the privacy right becomes something that can be violated in circumstances where 'no substantial harm follows from the breach' (as Lord Dyson argued in respect of false imprisonment in *Lumba*). Rather, it recognises that (in the privacy context at least) if there is a breach there is harm, even if it is harm to intangible interests. Second, seeing privacy damages as compensation for harm suffered fits comfortably with the conventional rationale for private law damages. Harms to dignity and autonomy might be intangible but, like other types of harm (distress, harm to reputation and financial damage), they are *suffered by* the claimant. They therefore fit into traditional harm-focused analysis in a way that descriptions of harm by reference to the breach of a right itself do not. Perhaps most significantly though, conceiving of the harms inherent in breaches of privacy as interference with dignity and autonomy accords with both theoretical and doctrinal accounts of why privacy is important in the first place. It is to that consideration that we now turn.

III. The Relationship Between Privacy and Dignity and Autonomy

Jurists, philosophers and social scientists have consistently held that the right to privacy – to be free from unwanted access to oneself[34] – is an essential part of what it is to be human: to be treated as an end, not a means, and to have the freedom to choose how to live one's own life. It follows that judges are acting consistently with accepted conceptual thinking when they suggest that interferences with these interests automatically flow from any actionable privacy breach.

[33] *Mosley* (n 4) [216] (emphasis added).
[34] NA Moreham, 'Privacy in the Common Law' (2005) 121 *LQR* 628, 636 et seq.

A. Dignity

The close relationship between privacy and dignity is widely recognised. Indeed, the need to protect the dignity of the individual was identified as one of the key reasons for recognising a right to privacy in English private law in the leading privacy cases. As mentioned, when referring to the incorporation into domestic law of the right to respect for private life in Article 8 of the European Convention, Lord Hoffmann said in *Campbell v MGN Ltd* that human rights law has identified private information 'as something worth protecting as an aspect of human autonomy and dignity'.[35] Lord Walker similarly said in *Douglas v Hello! Ltd* that the law's protection of the confidentiality of individuals' private lives is 'based on the high principle of respect for human autonomy and dignity'.[36] All of this is consistent with the European Court of Human Rights' (ECtHR's) interpretation of the rights underpinning Convention interests. As the Court held in *Pretty v United Kingdom*, '[t]he very essence of the Convention is respect for human dignity and human freedom'.[37]

Commentators agree that privacy and dignity are closely related. In their celebrated article on American law, Warren and Brandeis describe the interests protected by privacy as 'spiritual'[38] and as closely connected with an individual's 'inviolate personality'.[39] Peter Cane has identified privacy as a 'dignitary tort',[40] and in his response to William Prosser's fragmentary analysis of the US privacy torts,[41] Edward Bloustein argues that the coherence of privacy lies in the fact that all privacy interferences are 'an affront to dignity':

> [J]ust as we may regard [assault, battery, or false imprisonment] as offences 'to the reasonable sense of personal dignity', as offensive to our concept of individualism and the liberty it entails, so too should we regard privacy as a dignitary tort ... The injury is to our individuality, to our dignity as individuals, and the legal remedy represents a social vindication of the human spirit thus threatened rather than a recompense for the loss suffered.[42]

[35] *Campbell* (HL) (n 30) [50]. See also ibid [51].

[36] *Douglas v Hello! Ltd* [2007] UKHL 21, [2008] 1 AC 1, [275]. See also *HRH Prince of Wales v Associated Newspapers Ltd* [2006] EWHC 522 (Ch), [2008] EMLR 3, [133], cited in *HRH Prince of Wales v Associated Newspapers Ltd* [2006] EWCA Civ 1776, [2007] 2 All ER 139, [70]; *Mosley v News Group Newspapers Ltd* [2008] EWHC 1777 (QB), [2008] All ER (D) 322 (Jul), [7] and [214]; and, in the New Zealand context, *Hosking v Runting* [2004] NZCA 34, [2005] 1 NZLR 1, [239] and *Brooker v Police* [2007] NZSC 30, [2007] 3 NZLR 91, [182] and [252].

[37] *Pretty v United Kingdom* (2002) 35 EHRR 1, [65]. See also ibid [61].

[38] S Warren and L Brandeis, 'The Right to Privacy' (1890) 4 *Harvard Law Review* 193, 197.

[39] ibid 205.

[40] P Cane, *The Anatomy of Tort Law* (Oxford, Hart Publishing, 1997) 71–74.

[41] W Prosser, 'Privacy' (1960) 48 *California Law Review* 383.

[42] E Bloustein, 'Privacy as an Aspect of Human Dignity: An Answer to Dean Prosser' (1964) 39 *New York University Law Review* 962, 1002–03 (see also 1000–07).

Other jurists agree that, to quote Harry Kalven, privacy is 'deeply linked' to individual dignity and the needs of human existence.[43] Philosophers like Jeffrey Reiman and Stanley Benn also identify the protection of dignity as the principal reason why privacy is important,[44] and sociologist Edward Shils says that the social space around individuals, the recollection of their past, their conversations, and their body and image, belong to them by virtue of their 'humanity and civility'.[45]

This relationship between privacy and dignity is usually linked to Immanuel Kant's ideas about entitlement to respect – the right to be treated as an 'end' and not simply as a 'means'. As Kant famously argued,

> the human being and in general every rational being *exists* as an end in itself, *not merely as a means* to be used by this or that will at its discretion; instead he must in all his actions, whether directed to himself or to other rational beings, always be regarded *at the same time as an end* … [Rational beings], therefore, are not merely subjective ends, the existence of which as an effect of our action has a worth for us, but rather *objective ends*, that is, beings the existence of which is in itself an end, and indeed one such that no other end, to which they would serve *merely* as a means, can be put in its place, since without it nothing of *absolute worth* would be found anywhere.[46]

The philosopher Stanley Benn applies this idea – that one should '[a]ct that you use humanity, whether in your own person or in the person of any other, always at the same time as an end, never merely as a means'[47] – to privacy interferences. Reflecting on the possible basis for the objection of a bystander to a researcher's recording a woman's working-class accent on the street (more specifically, to Professor Higgins' recording of Eliza Doolittle's accent in *Pygmalion*), he says:

> What this man resents is surely that Higgins fails to show a proper respect for persons; he is treating people as objects or specimens – like 'dirt' – and not as subjects with sensibilities, ends, and aspirations of their own, morally responsible for their own decisions, and capable, as mere specimens are not, of reciprocal relations with the observer … These resentments suggest a possible ground for a prima facie claim not to be watched,

[43] H Kalven Jr, 'Privacy in Tort Law: Were Warren and Brandeis Wrong?' (1966) 31 *Law and Contemporary Problems* 326, 326. See also D Feldman, 'Secrecy, Dignity or Autonomy? Views of Privacy as a Civil Liberty' (1994) 47 *Current Legal Problems* 4, 54–58 (especially 55). See also NA Moreham, 'Why is privacy important? Privacy, Dignity and the Development of the New Zealand Breach of Privacy Tort' in J Finn and S Todd (eds), *Law, Liberty, Legislation* (Lexis Nexis, 2008) 231.

[44] See S Benn, 'Privacy, Freedom and Respect for Persons' in JR Pennock and JW Chapman (eds), *Privacy: NOMOS XIII* (New York, Atherton Press, 1971) 1, 3–13; and J Reiman, 'Privacy, Intimacy and Personhood' (1976) 6 *Philosophy and Public Affairs* 26, 39. Jurist Hyman Gross says that privacy interferences always 'humiliate' their subjects because they shift control over personal matters away from them and on to someone else. Breaches of privacy therefore always result in the individual being shamed, not because of what others learn about him or her, but because someone other than the victim is determining what will be done with what is learnt (H Gross, 'Privacy and Autonomy' in JR Pennock and JW Chapman (eds), *Privacy: NOMOS XIII* (New York, Atherton Press, 1971) 169, 177).

[45] E Schils, 'Privacy: Its Constitution and Vicissitudes' (1966) 31 *Law and Contemporary Problems* 281, 306.

[46] I Kant, *Groundwork of the Metaphysics of Morals* (M Gregor (tr), Cambridge University Press 1996) 4:399 and 4:428 (original emphasis).

[47] Kant, *Groundwork* 4:399 and 4:429.

> at any rate in the same manner as one watches a thing or an animal. For this is to 'take liberties', to act impudently, to show less than a proper regard for human dignity.[48]

The idea that privacy damages should compensate loss of dignity – and that that is why it is necessary to compensate for the loss of privacy per se – is therefore consistent with the way privacy is understood by jurists, philosophers and social scientists. To use another person's private experience to further one's research, to make money, to titillate, to entertain or to make a point is to treat that person as a means to your ends rather than to respect that individual's inherent value as a person. And that lack of respect is inherent in breaches of privacy independent of any distress or other consequential harm suffered. Such harm will therefore be suffered – and should be compensated – whenever there is an actionable breach.[49]

This dignity-based account of privacy harm helps explain why individuals should be compensated for loss of privacy even if they lack legal capacity. People are no more entitled to use a child or an unconscious grown up as a means to their ends than they are a competent adult. Such a person's inherent right to respect is no less affected by a privacy breach than a competent adult's. Courts are therefore acting entirely consistently with theoretical privacy thinking when they award privacy damages to those who were too young or who otherwise lack the capacity to know that the breach was taking place.[50] As these decisions recognise, such individuals have a compensable right to be treated with respect – as an end and not a means – whether they get distressed by privacy interference or not.

B. Autonomy

Courts and commentators have also consistently echoed Mann and Eady JJ's view that privacy breaches undermine individual autonomy. In addition to the observations of Lords Walker and Hoffmann outlined in section III.A, in *Douglas v Hello! Ltd* Sedley LJ referred to privacy as 'a legal principle drawn from the fundamental value of personal autonomy',[51] and in *Campbell* Lord Nicholls held that privacy 'lies at the heart of liberty in a modern state'.[52] This is again consistent with the jurisprudence of the ECtHR, which has said that 'the notion of personal autonomy is an important principle underlying the interpretation of

[48] Benn (n 44) 6–7.

[49] Noting that there will not be an actionable breach if the infringement is trivial or *de minimis*.

[50] See, eg, *Murray v Express Newspapers Plc* [2008] EWCA Civ 446, [2009] Ch 481; *Reklos and Davourlis v Greece* App no 1234/05 (ECHR, 15 January 2009); *AAA* (n 13); and *Kaye v Robertson* [1991] FSR 62 (CA) (in which the badly impaired claimant succeeded in malicious falsehood in the absence of a privacy action).

[51] *Douglas v Hello! Ltd* [2000] EWCA Civ 353, [2001] QB 967, [126].

[52] *Campbell* (HL) (n 30) [12].

[Convention] guarantees'[53] and confers on individuals 'the ability to conduct one's life in a manner of one's own choosing'.[54] As the ECtHR said in *Pretty*:

> The very essence of the Convention is respect for human dignity and human freedom. Without in any way negating the principle of sanctity of life under the Convention, the Court considers that it is under Article 8 that notions of the quality of life take on significance.[55]

A similar approach has been adopted in domestic Human Rights Act 1998 cases, where 'autonomy' has often been equated with self-determination.[56] In *R (on the application of Pretty) v DPP*, for example, four of their Lordships accepted that 'the guarantee under article 8 prohibits interference with the way in which an individual leads his life'.[57]

Privacy enhances autonomy in this sense because it protects a claimant's ability to determine whether, when and to whom he or she is accessible. More particularly, it protects the claimant's right to determine whether and in what circumstances others have access to his or her physical self and private affairs. Cobb J eloquently explains why this is an important feature of personal liberty (which for current purposes can be used interchangeably with 'autonomy') in the American misappropriation case of *Pavesich v New England Life Insurance Co*:

> Liberty includes the right to live as one will, so long as that will does not interfere with the rights of another or of the public. One may desire to live a life of seclusion; another may desire to live a life of publicity; still another may wish to live a life of privacy as to certain matters, and of publicity as to others. One may wish to live a life of toil, where his work is of a nature that keeps him constantly before the public gaze, while another may wish to live a life of research and contemplation, only moving before the public at such times and under such circumstances as may be necessary to his actual existence. Each is entitled to a liberty of choice as to his manner of life, and neither an individual nor the public has a right to arbitrarily take away from him this liberty.[58]

Every interference with the privacy of a competent adult will therefore undermine an aspect of his or her autonomy, that is, the ability to be as accessible or

[53] *Goodwin v United Kingdom* (2002) 35 EHRR 18, [90]; and *I v United Kingdom* (2003) 36 EHRR 53, [70]. See also *Pretty v UK* (n 37) [61]; and *Van Kück v Germany* (2003) 37 EHRR 51, [69].

[54] *Pretty v UK* (n 37) [62].

[55] ibid [65].

[56] Lord Hope expressly referred to 'self-determination' in *R (on the application of Purdy) v DPP* [2009] UKHL 45, [2010] 1 AC 345 [36] and *Pretty v DPP* [2001] UKHL 61, [2002] 1 AC 800 [100]. See also *Montgomery v Lanarkshire Health Board (Scotland)* [2015] UKSC 11 [80].

[57] *Pretty v DPP* (n 56) [61] (Lord Steyn). See also ibid [23] (Lord Bingham); [100] (Lord Hope); and [124] (Lord Scott). See also *R (on the application of Purdy) v DPP* [2009] UKHL 45, [34]–[39] (Lord Hope) and [66]–[67] (Baroness Hale) and *R (on the application of Wood) v Metropolitan Police Commissioner* [2009] EWCA Civ 414, [2009] 4 All ER 951, [20]–[21] (Laws LJ).

[58] *Pavesich v New England Life Insurance Co* 69 LRA 101, 50 SE 68 (SC Ga 1905), 70. See also *Hosking* (n 36) [239], where Tipping J says that '[i]t is of the essence of the dignity and personal autonomy and well-being of all human beings that some aspects of their lives should be able to remain private if they so wish'.

inaccessible as he or she chooses. And in the areas of our lives where we have reasonable expectations of privacy – matters relating to the body, personal relationships, sexual expression, domestic affairs[59] – we regard choices about accessibility as particularly important. Even in the absence of distress, then, actionable breaches of privacy will interfere with important aspects of individual autonomy; with important choices that people make about their lives.

Privacy also enhances autonomy in a second way – namely, by creating a space or a realm of life in which individuals are free from the inhibiting scrutiny of others and can therefore 'be themselves'. As Benn says, one of the ideals served by privacy is the idea of an independently-minded individual whose actions are governed by principles that are his or her own, in the sense that he or she has subjected them 'to critical review, rather than taking them over unexamined from his social environment'.[60] Privacy is seen to serve this ideal because it enables people to retreat to a zone where they can act according to their *own* principles and desires without concern for the views of others. As Benn says,

> the man who is truly independent – the autonomous man – is the one who has the strength of mind to resist the pressure to believe with the rest, and has the courage to act on his convictions … For the rest of us, the freedom we need is the freedom to be something else – to be ourselves, to do what we think best, in a small, protected sea, where the winds of opinion cannot blow us off course. We cannot learn to be autonomous save by practising autonomous judgment.[61]

This idea that people need a protected space in which they can relax and act without concern for the views or opinions of others is widely shared. As legal philosopher, Thomas Nagel has said, it is important for human freedom that we are not merely social or political beings.[62] Although awareness of how one appears from the outside is a constant of human life, there are aspects of life, such as sexual relations, that require that people can live and react entirely from the inside.[63] People also need an opportunity to relax. As privacy scholar Alan Westin says, people needs moments 'off stage' when they can be 'themselves': '[t]o be always "on" would destroy the human organism'.[64]

The long-term negative impacts of constant scrutiny for both the individual and society as a whole are said entrench this need for privacy further. Consistently

[59] See further NA Moreham, 'Unpacking the Reasonable Expectation of Privacy Test' (2018) 134 *LQR* (forthcoming).

[60] Benn (n 44) 24. See also R Gavison, 'Privacy and the Limits of the Law' (1980) 89 *Yale LJ* 421, 449.

[61] Benn (n 44) 25–26. As Gavison says, 'societies should enable all, not only the exceptional, to seek moral autonomy' (Gavison (n 60) 450). See also A Westin, *Privacy and Freedom* (New York, Atheneum, 1970) 33–34.

[62] T Nagel, 'Concealment and Exposure' (1998) 27 *Philosophy & Public Affairs* 3, 17.

[63] ibid 18.

[64] Westin (n 61) 35. Warren and Brandeis agree that '[t]he intensity and complexity of life, attendant upon advancing civilisation, have rendered necessary some retreat from the world' (Warren and Brandeis (n 38) 196). See also M Konvitz, 'Privacy and the Law: A Philosophical Prelude' (1966) 31 *Law & Contemporary Problems* 272.

conforming to the expectations and values of others is seen to undermine an individual's capacity for autonomous thought and action. Thus psychologist Sidney Jourard observed that '[i]f a person practises role-conformity faithfully and long enough, he will lose the capacity to recognize as his own those experiences – of impulses and feelings – that are incongruent with his desired role', and his wish to appear as a certain kind of person, not only to others but also to himself, will lead him to repress feelings and urges that are inconsistent with that role.[65] Bloustein eloquently agreed:

> The man who is compelled to live every minute of his life among others and whose every need, thought, desire, fancy or gratification is subject to public scrutiny, has been deprived of his individuality and human dignity. Such an individual merges with the mass. His opinions, being public, tend never to be different; his aspirations, being known, tend always to be conventionally accepted ones …[66]

In contrast, privacy allows people the space for 'sheltered experimentation and the testing of ideas, for preparation and practice in thought and conduct, without fear of ridicule or penalty, and for the opportunity to alter opinions before making them public'.[67] This in turn is seen to encourage diversity and meaningful participation in Western liberal democratic society.[68]

All this suggests that, as with dignity, an individual's interest in personal autonomy is going to be affected by an interference with privacy even if no distress or other harm is caused. Every actionable breach of privacy is going to undermine an important decision the subject has made about his or her inaccessibility, and hence to narrow the scope of the realm into which individuals can retreat to 'be themselves'. It is unsurprising, then, that courts have recognised this as one of the bases for awarding damages for loss of privacy itself.

There is one area, however, where the connection between privacy and autonomy causes some difficulties; namely, when the subject of the breach was a child or an adult who lacks capacity. It is difficult to argue that a defendant who publishes an unauthorised intimate photograph of a very young child or severely mentally impaired adult has interfered with the subject's autonomy of thought or action. Such individuals lack the capacity to make decisions about the scope of their private sphere, and may even be unable to appreciate that the publication has occurred. In the case of a young child or an adult whose competency is likely to be restored one could meet this argument by pointing out that disseminating

[65] S Jourard, 'Some Psychological Aspects of Privacy' (1966) 31 *Law & Contemporary Problems* 307, 308–09. See also Westin (n 61) 34.

[66] Bloustein (n 42) 1003. See also Gavison (n 60); and P Freund, 'Privacy: One concept or many?' in Pennock and Chapman (eds) (n 44) 182, 195.

[67] Westin (n 61) 34. Thus, as Gavison says, by 'insulating the individual against ridicule and censure at early stages of groping and experimentation', privacy encourages people to 'dare' more and to extend themselves beyond what they know they can do well (Gavison (n 60) 448).

[68] See, eg, Westin (n 61) 34; and H Fenwick and G Phillipson, 'Breach of Confidence as a Privacy Remedy in the Human Rights Act Era' (2000) 63 *MLR* 660, 682–83.

private material about an individual forecloses choices that would have otherwise been available to him or her on maturity or the return to capacity. For example, a child who has been subjected to widespread media attention before he or she is old enough to object will, to a large degree, have lost the ability to choose a life of anonymity when he or she comes of age. His or her autonomy in this broader sense will therefore be affected by the privacy breach. Where the subject's incapacity is permanent (when a person is in a permanent coma, for example) courts could address his or her lack of capacity in one of two ways. First, they could ascribe to the incompetent individual the wishes of his or her legal guardians, and say that an interference with those wishes is an interference with the individual's autonomy. Alternatively – and perhaps preferably – damages could be awarded for the interference with individual dignity which, as discussed, is clearly established in these cases.

IV. Conclusion and a Postscript on Distress

There is nothing like the need to award damages to focus the mind on what legal action is all about. Compensation awards under the English misuse of private information tort are no exception. This chapter has argued that courts are right to award damages for the loss of privacy itself, independent of any distress or tangible harm that flows from it. This is because all actionable breaches of privacy cause loss of dignity and autonomy. This is not to say that all breaches should be actionable – trivial or *de minimis* breaches should be excluded from liability and therefore be ineligible for damages awards. But when there has been an actionable breach, awarding damages for the loss of privacy itself is consistent both with theoretical accounts of the privacy interest and with the doctrinal rationales (including those derived from Article 8 of the Convention) for recognising a privacy tort in the first place.

It is suggested, then, that in future cases, the need to protect autonomy and dignity should be expressly adopted by appellate courts as a reason for awarding damages even in the absence of distress or other harm. Detailed discussion of how these interests fit with existing conceptions of tortious damages (or indeed damages for breach of confidence) is beyond the scope of this chapter. Suffice it to say that the privacy action's origins in European human rights law mean that the fit might not be immediately apparent, although the dignitary basis of traditional common law torts such as assault, battery and false imprisonment provides an obvious point of convergence. The starting point for any consideration of these issues – and other questions about how the misuse of private information action will embed itself into the existing English tort law – must be a clear articulation of what the privacy interest is about.

Two final points remain. The first is that although the preservation of dignity and autonomy are the most widely recognised of the reasons for protecting privacy – and always at stake, regardless of the nature of the interference – other important values are also at issue in privacy claims. In particular, the impact that privacy interferences can have upon the formation and maintenance of intimate relationships and on feelings of safety and security needs to be recognised in appropriate cases. It follows that as well as compensating for the loss of dignity and autonomy inherent in a breach of privacy, courts should also compensate (as Mann J did in *Gulati*) for any harm caused to relationships and emotional equilibrium.

Second, in many cases the relationship between the loss of dignity and autonomy and the distress or loss of emotional equilibrium that results from it is very close. People do not like to be commodified. It is humiliating to be used by someone else to make money, obtain sexual gratification, garner sympathy for a cause, to ridicule or to entertain without consent. As a result, this kind of treatment can cause anger, outrage, depression and fear, as well as harm to one's relationships, mental health and ability to work effectively.[69] Mann J noted in *Gulati*, for example, that many of the claimants felt 'violated' and 'sickened' by the systematic telephone hacking at issue in that case.[70] One, for example, felt 'that the newspaper considered that he and [his former wife] were just pieces of news to be played with',[71] whilst others explained how the sense that they were under surveillance exacerbated existing mental health problems[72] or interfered with relationships with family and friends.[73] It is unsurprising, then, that when Mann J made his awards in *Gulati*, he took account of the impact of the hacking not only on the claimants' dignity and autonomy but also on their emotional equilibrium.[74]

Inevitably in some cases it will be difficult – and perhaps unnecessary – to separate the distress that flows from a loss of dignity and autonomy from the loss of dignity and autonomy itself. Mann J acknowledges that in *Gulati*:

> As already observed, it will not be in all cases that it will be necessary or appropriate to consider separating the misuse from the distress, because the infringement and its consequences will be so wrapped up. Mr Sherborne runs his case consistently with that. While he seeks compensation for the misuse of private information as such, in general terms, when it comes to his claims on an article by article basis he does not seek one figure for the distress and a separate award for acquiring the information wrongly and another for actually using it to produce an article. He claims one overall figure per article which reflects all elements, including the seriousness of the misuse.[75]

[69] See, eg, *Wilson v Ferguson* [2015] WASC 15.

[70] See, eg, the summary of the evidence of Alan Yentob (*Gulati* (HC) (n 5) [247]) and Lucy Taggart (ibid [407]), and Mann J's general summary (ibid [32(i)]). The words 'sick' or 'sickening' were also used by four other claimants to describe their response to the hackers' activities (see the summary of the evidence of Lauren Alcorn (ibid [273]), Shane Roche (ibid [513]), Paul Gascoigne (ibid [571]) and Sadie Frost (ibid [661]).

[71] ibid [336] (Robert Ashworth).

[72] ibid [569] (Paul Gascoigne).

[73] See, eg, ibid [335] (Ashworth), [406] (Taggart), and [645] (Frost).

[74] See ibid [108]–[145].

[75] ibid [134].

No doubt there will be cases where this is the right approach; judges often observe that awarding damages for breaches of privacy is an imprecise science.[76] In all privacy cases, however, the fundamental interests that underpin the action should be at the forefront of judges' minds, and the nature of the harm the claimant has suffered should be identified as precisely as possible. Otherwise, the less tangible – but nonetheless significant – costs of privacy interferences can be forgotten, including, of course, the loss of dignity and autonomy, which has been the subject of this chapter.

[76] See, eg, HHJ Luba QC's observation in *Brown* (n 6) [62], that even before one adds on compensation for the loss of control of personal information itself, compensating for 'the shock, distress and upset' caused by a breach of privacy 'cannot be an exact science'.

6

Claimant-Focused Damages in the Law of Privacy

ERIC DESCHEEMAEKER

I. Introduction

Chief among remedies for breach of privacy, as indeed for any other tort,[1] are damages. Damages can be simply defined as a money award granted in response to a wrong.[2] But if, as Montesquieu opined (and the common law appears to have always believed), 'money is the measure of all things',[3] then the transfer of money from the losing defendant to the successful claimant is not, in itself, going to tell us why the transfer is taking place. To make sense of damages, we need to draw further distinctions.

The most common distinction is between compensatory damages – which are uncontroversially regarded as the core, and in many ways the default, type of damages (to the point where the two, 'damages' and 'compensatory damages', are sometimes assumed to be synonymous)[4] – and all other types, that is, all species of damages that can be described as non-compensatory. The line drawn in this

[1] That breach of privacy, at least under the guise of misuse of private information, has been recognised as a civil wrong is undeniable in English law (on which lies the jurisdictional focus of this chapter). Whether it is a tort *stricto sensu* has been disputed but now appears to have been settled – rightly – in the affirmative: see *Google Inc v Vidal-Hall* [2015] EWCA Civ 311, [2016] QB 1003, [43]: 'if one puts aside the circumstances of its "birth", there is nothing in the nature of the claim itself to suggest that the more natural classification of it as a tort is wrong'. The only alternative would be to hold that it is an equitable wrong, an argument that should be firmly rejected despite the genealogical link between breach of privacy and the equitable action for breach of confidence. Dr Turner, 'Privacy Remedies Viewed Through an Equitable Lens', in ch 11 of this book, makes a powerful argument to the effect that nothing would be gained from developing a form of equitable compensation for breach of privacy.

[2] J Edelman, 'The Meaning of "Damages": Common Law and Equity' in A Robertson (ed), *The Law of Obligations: Connections and Boundaries* (London, UCL Press, 2004) 31; J Edelman et al, *McGregor on Damages*, 20th edn (London, Sweet & Maxwell, 2018) para 1-001.

[3] C-L de Secondat, Baron de Montesquieu, *De l'esprit des loix*, vol 2 (Barrillot 1748) bk XXII, ch 3, 88 (my translation).

[4] eg Edelman, 'The Meaning of "Damages"', (n 2) 31.

chapter is different: it is between claimant- and defendant-focused damages. The distinction is between monetary awards granted in response to a wrong, which are assessed with reference to factors concerned with the claimant, and those that depend on considerations pertaining to the defendant.[5] The focal point of this chapter is the former.

In both cases, what is lying immediately underneath this first-level division is one based on the different functions served by the monetary awards: what is it that they are designed to achieve? How many such functions exist in the abstract is an intriguing question; for all intents and purposes, four have been recognised in the common law tradition: damages can serve a compensatory, vindicatory, punitive or restitutionary function. Straightforwardly, the last two are defendant-focused, in the sense that they are to be measured in accordance with some characteristic of the defendant – their conduct, their gain; accordingly they are excluded from the scope of this chapter. Our focus will be on the first two, which are defined by reference to some feature of the claimant: their loss, their right. This common focus links up the two not only formally but substantively: as will be explored in this chapter, one can in fact hardly be understood in isolation from the other.

Types of awards, as traditionally labelled, form a separate (and longer) series. While so-called 'compensatory' and 'vindicatory' damages are evidently serving, respectively, a compensatory and a vindicatory function, they need not occupy the whole territory by themselves: the function is, at least potentially, broader than the namesake categories of awards. As a matter of fact, looking at the – ill-ordered – list of types of damages, as recognised by courts and scholars, there are two others that we need to include in our study: damages known as 'aggravated', which also serve a – now well-established – compensatory function; and awards referred to as 'nominal damages', which are typically understood (even though the point is not beyond dispute) as vindicatory in nature. Accordingly, the twofold function fulfilled by claimant-focused damages maps on to four types of damages as traditionally defined: compensatory, aggravated, nominal and vindicatory.

This chapter examines these four sorts of awards in the specific context of the action for breach of privacy: when and why are they available, how do they operate, and what is the relationship between them? The analytical and normative aspects of this enquiry can hardly be studied in isolation from the rest of the law of torts. Indeed a theme underpinning this chapter is that there is not, or at least should not be, anything specific with that cause of action: despite the constant temptation to treat wrongs such as breach of privacy and defamation as laws unto themselves,

[5] Some types of damages, like those known as '*Wrotham Park*' or 'user fee' damages, cannot easily be located in respect of this distinction: they might be placed on one side of the line or the other, or be thought to straddle the division. But they have no application in the context of privacy; accordingly, the difficulty can be ignored in the present enquiry.

there is no reason why they should behave differently from other tortious causes of action, or derogate from principles generally recognised within the law of torts – at the very least, not until a positive and cogent reason to the contrary has been established. What makes the present study especially relevant is that courts seem, precisely, to be in the process of imposing on breach of privacy a micro-rationality that is at odds with the rest of tort law. This ought to be resisted: for it to happen, the necessary first step is to identify and explain this discrepancy. As we do so, insights of general interest for the law of damages can be gathered.

The chapter proceeds in three sections: it starts in section II with vindicatory damages – which didactically should come first, because it is in their context that we can identify the theoretical issues against which compensatory damages, dealt with in section III, can be analysed. Section IV turns briefly to aggravated damages, which raise no particular difficulties, and then section V to nominal damages, which provide additional insights into the vindicatory and compensatory functions of money awards in the privacy context.

II. Vindicatory Damages

A. Definition

Money awards now referred to by scholars and courts as 'vindicatory damages' are, at least under that name, a recent development. Although the expression is older,[6] it was not until the first decade of the twenty-first century that it was pressed into service in the sense (with which we are concerned here) of 'damages that aim to vindicate a right that has been infringed, independently of any consequences'.[7] While not much can be said with confidence about this – at least apparently – novel type of damages, for neither their definition nor, especially, the circumstances in which they are available are agreed upon, it would seem that the core idea underpinning what Lord Dyson has described as an 'unruly horse'[8] is in fact reasonably straightforward: we are talking about damages awarded to mark the infringement of a right apart from any loss. Importantly, it does not seem to have ever been doubted that vindicatory damages must be *substantial*: indeed this is what distinguishes them from the older-established category of nominal damages, which are also typically understood as having the aim of marking the infringement of a right of the claimant in circumstances where no loss is averred.[9]

[6] This was helpfully traced by Lord Collins of Mapesbury in *R (Lumba) v Secretary of State for the Home Department* [2011] UKSC 12, [2012] 1 AC 245, [223] et seq.

[7] J Edelman, 'Vindicatory Damages' in K Barker, K Fairweather and R Grantham (eds), *Private Law in the 21st Century* (Oxford, Hart Publishing, 2017) 343.

[8] The horse analogy is from Lord Dyson: *Lumba* (n 6) [101].

[9] See section V, 'Nominal Damages'.

B. Relationship with Compensatory Damages

This immediately raises the question of their relationship with compensatory damages, to which, as mentioned, it is difficult to deny a central position in the lawyer's toolbox. Logically, like any type of damages, each will have a prima facie scope of application, which we can define as situations where, apart from any consideration pertaining to the availability of other remedies, the claimant will be entitled to them. For compensatory damages, this is relatively straightforward, namely, the existence of relevant loss that was wrongfully caused according to the rules governing the cause(s) of action relied upon: if the claimant can prove the existence of such loss, they are entitled to compensation according to the general principles of the law. For vindicatory damages it is, as explained, much less straightforward; but this difficulty need not detain us here. Suffice it to accept that the law considers that, by establishing the existence of a relevant set of facts (like *x*, *y* or *z* – whatever these might actually cover), the claimant has established their entitlement to a remedy known as 'vindicatory damages'.

The question for us is whether the availability of one type of damages impacts on that of the other. Given the centrality of compensatory damages, the question really needs to be asked in one direction only: does the availability of compensatory damages affect that of vindicatory ones? Vindicatory damages being shrouded in much uncertainty, it is not surprising that the question of their relationship with other types of awards has not been authoritatively settled. Yet despite the lack of clear judicial pronouncement on the matter, one cannot but observe a striking dimension of *subsidiarity* underpinning much of the discussion surrounding vindicatory damages. The reasoning, to the extent that we can reconstruct it, would seem to run as follows:

- The claimant who has successfully established the existence of a – relevant – wrong committed against them is entitled to an 'effective remedy', to use a concept originating in the European Convention on Human Rights.[10] This means a substantial award of damages, neither nominal damages nor declaratory relief being sufficient to redress the wrong effectively.[11]
- However, the need to redress the wrong through the award of substantial damages does not necessarily mean awarding vindicatory damages in the

[10] Convention for the Protection of Human Rights and Fundamental Freedoms (European Convention on Human Rights, as amended), Art 13. It would be tempting to say that what justifies the special treatment given to the right to privacy is precisely the fact that it is covered by the European Convention on Human Rights. But, besides all the principled issues that such a 'two stream' approach would raise, there never was any equivalence drawn (either analytically or in terms of the history of the concept) between vindicatory damages on the one hand and this subclass of rights on the other. This approach would also probably mean that *Lumba* (n 6) was wrongly decided.

[11] *Mosley v News Group Newspapers Ltd* [2008] EWHC 1777 (QB), [2008] EMLR 20, [217]: 'If the objective is to provide an adequate remedy for the infringement of a right, it would not be served effectively if the court were merely to award nominal damages'.

technical sense of the term. Other awards, in particular compensatory ones, can also fulfil – indirectly – a vindicatory role.[12]

- Therefore vindicatory damages (as a type of award) are a subsidiary remedy, in the etymological sense of the term: a *support* or *reserve*. If the claimant can establish substantial loss (or any other basis for obtaining an effective remedy apart from this novel doctrine), they should do so and then neither need, nor indeed will be allowed, to claim vindicatory damages in addition.[13]

Even though this is not stated in so many words, the logical implication of this reasoning is that loss becomes irrelevant, at least up to a certain point, within the scope of application of vindicatory damages. The claimant does not need to aver any in order to recover substantial damages (since they are entitled to vindicatory damages, which, by construction, will be more than nominal); and if they do in fact suffer loss they will not recover more – at least not until the threshold of the 'effective remedy' is reached – since, as mentioned, the availability of (sufficient) compensation is implicitly taken, despite the claimant's having established *x*, *y* or *z*, to dislodge their entitlement to vindicatory damages. On this logic, vindicatory damages effectively provide a 'baseline' money award, which can be claimed whenever other established remedies do not allow the claimant to recover a similar amount. However, how this neutralisation of loss can be reconciled with some of the most basic tenets of tort law remains, to say the least, unclear.

C. Vindicatory Damages in the Law of Privacy

Within privacy, the concept of vindication-apart-from-compensation was touched upon, if with a level of ambiguity, by the High Court in *Mosley*, where Eady J opined that, when it came to assessing quantum of damages, there was, '[a]part from distress … another factor which probably has to be taken into account … that of vindication to mark the infringement of a right … to mark the fact that … [an] individual has taken away or undermined the right of another – in this case taken away a person's dignity'.[14] This reasoning was later applied in *AAA* to award a substantial sum to an infant who had suffered neither pecuniary nor non-pecuniary loss as a result of her invasion of privacy.[15] However, in the wake of

[12] ibid [216]: 'If other factors mean that significant damages are to be awarded, in any event, the element of vindication does not need to be reflected in an even higher award. As Lord Scott observed in *Ashley*, "… there is no reason why an award of compensatory damages should not also fulfil a vindicatory purpose".' (The reference is to *Ashley v Chief Constable of Sussex Police* [2008] UKHL 25, [2008] 1 AC 962, [22].).

[13] *Mosley* (n 11) [216].

[14] ibid [216]. 'Dignity', in this context, can be understood as an overarching interest encompassing the right to privacy.

[15] *AAA v Associated Newspapers Ltd* [2012] EWHC 2103 (QB), [2013] EMLR 2, [126]–[127].

Weller[16] and *Gulati*[17] (which themselves followed on the important judgment of the Supreme Court in *Lumba*),[18] it would appear that vindicatory damages are, as a matter of principle, no longer available in breach of privacy actions. The significance of this will be explored when we turn to compensatory damages in the next section; for now let it simply be noted.

Whether they *ought* to be allowed is probably a moot point given how little is common ground in terms of their general availability. What can profitably be done, however, is to point out two simple but important issues:

- First, the need for coherence across the law of torts. This need not entail that all causes of action be treated identically, but it does mean that whatever normative concern underpins our answer – positive or negative – in respect of breach of privacy ought to be transferrable over the rest of the law. Nothing would be worse than allowing privacy (or more generally a subset of wrongs) to develop a separate and incompatible logic, a danger all the more present given that 'mainstream' tort scholars rarely have a sustained interest in privacy, while privacy scholars are not typically interested, it seems fair to say, in private law theory.
- Second, the fact that, in the common law, the acknowledgement of the existence of a wrong in the absence of loss is exactly the function that was traditionally devolved to *nominal* damages. Again, we need to sort out their relationship: does breach of privacy entitle the claimant, in the absence of (or apart from) loss, to nominal damages, or to vindicatory damages, or does it depend and, if so, on what? Here too, we need to make sure that whatever answer we give in the context of breach of privacy maps on to other causes of action.

III. Compensatory Damages

A. Definition

The second, and principal, type of claimant-focused award is compensatory damages. Again the underlying idea is simple: it is that of making up for a detriment through a monetary award. The claimant, as a result of the wrong inflicted on them, is worse off than they would otherwise have been and seeks a money award to restore the balance – the assumption being that all detriments recognised by the law can be given a monetary value. The underlying metaphor is that

[16] *Weller v Associated Newspapers Ltd* [2014] EWHC 1163 (QB), [2014] EMLR 24, [190].
[17] *Gulati v MGN Ltd* [2015] EWHC 1482 (Ch), [2016] FSR 12, [128].
[18] *Lumba* (n 6).

of scales: the loss or harm is laid on one side, while money is added on to the other. As the scales balance out, compensation has been achieved.[19]

We can take it as apodictic that compensation is for loss and for loss only: any loss can, in principle, be compensated; only something characterised by the law as a loss can be. Immediately this raises the question of what loss is, or what counts as loss. This is a question that is, of course, not specific to breach of privacy, but here too, a focus on that wrong is especially helpful. It is remarkable, and not to the credit of our law, how much uncertainty has been allowed to linger regarding this question within tort law as a whole. Perhaps because it is forced to confront directly, without much opportunity to fudge the issues, the types of harm it is least comfortable with – losses that do not flow from tangible damage and are non-pecuniary, often in the absence of any allegation of financial detriment on which it could 'piggyback' – breach of privacy forces the law to confront, and make decisions concerning, foundational issues. The question is how and whether these answers are, or should be, specific to the law of privacy, or simply the application of principles common to the whole law of torts.

B. A Taxonomy of Losses

I have developed and defended in another context the idea that what courts and scholars have called 'loss' consists of three, and only three, types of detriment:[20] pecuniary losses;[21] concrete losses that are not pecuniary and are, in the final analysis, reducible to emotional harm broadly construed;[22] and, lastly, abstractly defined losses, sometimes referred to as 'normative' or 'legal' losses, which are defined as the very invasion (or, to use language inspired by Grotius that has now been picked up by the Court of Appeal), the 'diminution' of the claimant's right, that is, the setback to the claimant's interest.[23] This model applies to all causes of actions.

In the context of privacy, the types of detriment that courts have described as 'losses' and compensated as such can be mapped straightforwardly on this model. Besides pecuniary loss (on which, remarkably, there does not appear to be a single successful case)[24] and emotional harm (referred to under a variety of labels,

[19] Etymologically, *compensāre* is to weigh one thing against another (OED, qv 'compensate').

[20] E Descheemaeker, 'Unravelling Harms in Tort Law' (2016) 132 *LQR* 595, 597ff.

[21] That is to say, loss that is directly valuable in money or, to put the same point in layman's language, which leaves the claimant 'out of pocket'. Where the line is drawn raises difficulties, but these are irrelevant for the present purpose.

[22] Descheemaeker (n 20) 597.

[23] Hugo Grotius, *De Iure Belli ac Pacis* (Blaeu 1646) 2.17.2; *Gulati v MGN Ltd* [2015] EWCA Civ 1291, [2017] QB 149, [48].

[24] E Descheemaeker, 'The Harms of Privacy' (2016) 8 *Journal of Media Law* 278, 281. In particular, *Douglas v Hello! Ltd (No 3)* [2007] UKHL 21, [2008] 1 AC 1, which might be the most obvious case to spring to mind, was not in fact an instance of economic loss consequential upon breach of privacy (Descheemaeker, 'The Harms of Privacy' at 281).

such as 'distress',[25] 'hurt' or 'injured' 'feeling[s]',[26] 'pain',[27] 'embarrassment'[28] or 'humiliation'),[29] courts have also recognised and compensated losses defined not in terms of the concrete consequences of the wrong on the claimant – what makes the claimant, in Professor Stevens' words, 'factually worse off'[30] – but as the loss of the right itself: the 'loss of privacy',[31] 'loss of dignity'[32] or, as the Court of Appeal put it in *Gulati*, 'loss of control of information'[33] – legal losses that all characterise, at various levels of generality, the setback to the privacy interest. Accordingly, losses in privacy cases are reducible to three sorts: pecuniary loss and emotional harm (as under any cause of action), and loss of privacy per se (ie the violation of the specific right on which the action is based).

C. Three Key Questions

Three principal issues arise, which are key to making sense of compensatory damages in the law of privacy: the relationship between concretely and abstractly defined losses; the extent to which compensatory awards are a standardised award for what an ordinary claimant would have suffered, as opposed to what the specific claimant did suffer; and the relationship between vindication of the right violated and compensation of the abstract right-diminution. Again, while these questions apply across the law of torts, they arise with particular sharpness in the context of breach of privacy, making it especially important to consider them in this context.

i. Relationship Between Abstract and Concrete Losses

a. Unipolar and Bipolar Models of Tort Law

Probably the most important issue concerns the relationship between loss of privacy as an abstract or legal loss, and the concrete losses which flow from the

[25] eg *Gulati* (n 17) [168]; *Mosley* (n 11) [216], [224]; *Campbell v MGN Ltd* [2004] UKHL 22, [2004] 2 AC 457, [33], [34].

[26] eg *Gulati* (n 17) [169]; *Mosley* (n 11) [216].

[27] eg *Campbell* (n 25) [33].

[28] eg *Mosley* (n 11) [235]; *Weller* (n 16) [196]; *Campbell* (n 25) [75].

[29] eg *Campbell* (n 25) [75].

[30] R Stevens, *Torts and Rights* (Oxford, Oxford UP, 2007) 59: 'although loss is not limited to financial loss, in principle it requires proof that the claimant was factually worse off as a result of the infringement of the right'.

[31] eg *Gulati* (n 17) [168]: 'damages should compensate not merely for distress … but … also … for the loss of privacy … as such'.

[32] eg *Mosley* (n 11) [216], [224]; *Gulati* (n 17) [108], [141]. This is best understood as the same abstract loss construed on a higher level of generality, privacy being regarded as a subset of the 'right to dignity'. (To the extent that it is understood as a concrete detriment, it would be a form of emotional harm: Descheemaeker (n 24) 284–85.).

[33] *Gulati* (n 23) [45]; cf *Weller* (n 16) [192]: 'damages for misuse of private information should compensate the [c]laimants for the misuse of their private information'. At first instance, it was referred to as 'the right to control the dissemination of information about one's private life' being 'lost': *Gulati* (n 17) [111].

invasion to the privacy interest, whether these be to the pocket (pecuniary losses) or to the mind (non-pecuniary ones). I have argued elsewhere that these two forms of harm are incompatible because they are two ways of approaching the same detriments, one from the perspective of the breach itself and the other from that of its consequences.[34] The argument cannot be reopened in the present context, and its conclusion will simply be restated in the specific context of breach of privacy.

The traditional approach of English law is to follow a model I described as 'bipolar', whereby the wrong itself is transparent – it is a mere peg, which renders the detriments flowing from it wrongful and therefore (prima facie) compensable – and what the law looks to, in order to compensate them, is the concrete *consequences* of the wrong, whether these be economic or emotional. Once the consequences of the wrong, on the wallet and the mind, have been translated into monetary terms and paid for, for all intents and purposes the wrong has been blotted out.

Another model, however, was said to exist, described as 'unipolar' because it conflates the loss with the wrong, construing the claimant's loss as the very violation of (encroachment upon, diminution of, setback to) their right – in this case to privacy: having had their phone hacked, the claimant now has less privacy, just as the person whose leg was broken has less physical integrity; and *that* is the detriment which the law characterises as a loss and puts a monetary value on in order to compensate it. This second model has been making significant inroads in a variety of contexts in the recent past, hand-in-hand with the rise of rights-based conceptions of tort; but it is of ancient pedigree, being traceable at least, through Grotius, to Thomas Aquinas and his understanding of loss (*damnum*) as the deprivation of what is 'one's own' – in modern language, the claimant's protected rights or interests.

A principal cause of the muddle that the law has walked itself into, in particular in the field of privacy, is that such abstractly defined losses have tended – unsurprisingly perhaps in a context where damages remain significantly under-conceptualised – to be added on by courts and scholars to pre-existing conceptions of loss: a third concentric circle, as it were, beyond financial loss (*damnum*: historically the core of the concept) and emotional harms. The underlying assumption seems to be that, by so doing, the law is extending the scope of liability for consequences in the same way as it is familiar with pushing back the boundaries of actionability through the recognition of new rights or causes of action. In reality, allowing in these abstract forms of harm amounts to switching from one analytical framework to a completely different, indeed incompatible, model. 'Loss of privacy' is not another consequence of the wrong of breach of privacy that can be added to the others and compensated alongside them. It *is* the breach of privacy itself, seen from a different perspective: saying that the claimant has suffered the wrong of breach of privacy and that they have been deprived of

[34] Descheemaeker (n 20) 603ff.

(some of) their privacy is exactly the same proposition. The loss is now construed as the wrong itself; the *damnum* has become the *iniuria*. This is not an extension but a change of logic.

b. Incompatibility

The key point is that one ought to choose, lest double-counting should arise. One does not – should not – get one award for breach of privacy and one for the consequences of the breach, any more than one gets an award for the cost of repairing one's damaged car *and* a second award for the very fact that it was damaged; or an award for pain and suffering and loss of amenities *and* (leaving aside financial considerations) another one for the fact that one suffered a physical injury. There is therefore a simple argument from consistency at work here: unless one can explain why breach of privacy should behave differently from other rights, it ought not to follow a discrepant logic.

But there is also a deeper substantial argument. Unless the law grants a fixed award for the wrong itself, valuing all infringements of privacy equally, the amount of the award is bound to be predicated on an evaluation of the seriousness of the breach; this, in turn, will necessarily look ahead to the consequences – at least potential – of the wrong: consequences both economic and emotional, which, as was said, are what all the (concrete, as opposed to abstract) detriments flowing from the wrong boil down to on the dominant bipolar model. All other things being equal, disclosing a private fact to an audience of millions is worse than in a private conversation because, financial considerations apart, the emotional consequences on the claimant can be presumed to be more significant. *This* is the reason why we consider that the claimant has suffered a 'greater' invasion of privacy or (which is to say exactly the same thing) has been deprived of 'more' of it. It is the same logic that tells us that smashing a car is worse than scratching it: it will cost more to repair it; a proposition that can be translated in unipolar language as saying that the claimant has suffered a greater setback to their property right. In other words, the valuation of normative losses does not in fact follow a deontic logic, in the sense in which moral philosophers use the term; it is consequentialist too. But the reason why the two approaches do not necessarily yield the same result is because they do not approach consequences in the same way. What the unipolar does is essentially to neutralise the specificities of the instant case and look to typical consequences of the infringement, which in turn become the flipside of how serious the infringement is deemed to be. For instance, an invasion of privacy could be regarded as serious, hence worthy of substantial damages for the claimant's loss of privacy, because it would *ordinarily* lead to significant distress on the claimant's part, even though no such distress would have been experienced on the facts of the case (for instance because, as happened with the Weller twins, the claimant was a young child, unaware of being wronged). In the same way, smashing the claimant's car can still be regarded as more serious, and worth more damages, than scratching it, even if the instant owner happened to be on their way to the skip when the damage occurred and will not, therefore, be any more 'out of pocket' as a result of the invasion of their right.

c. Conflation of the Two Models

Accordingly, we are in the presence of two frameworks to analyse tort, each with its distinct logic and history. Both have merits; and while to-ing and fro-ing between them is permissible (albeit unhelpful if one seeks to achieve consistency across the law), mixing and matching them in respect of the same cause of action is not. Yet conflating the two models is precisely the path that English courts have set off on. As the Court of Appeal put it in *Gulati*, ratifying the long judgment of Mann J at first instance (itself prompted, as will be explained, by the very unusual circumstances of the case) and turning it into the fledging orthodoxy in the field, claimants 'are entitled to be compensated for [the] loss of control of information as well as for any distress':[35] in other words, for their abstract loss of privacy *and also* for the concrete consequences of the breach. After permission to appeal to the Supreme Court was denied, this has become the established judicial stance in respect of actions for breach of privacy.

It was not always thus. In the early days the action could be seen to follow, as if as a matter of course, the dominant bipolar model whereby, having established the wrong (the invasion of their privacy), the claimant would then seek to recover for the factual losses or harms suffered as a result of the invasion. Thus, in the seminal *Campbell* case, the claimant sought, and was allowed, to recover for the 'distress, embarrassment and anxiety' caused by the wrongful publication of photographs of her: an alleged breach of confidence which morphed, in the course of the procedure, into the misuse of her private information.[36] She did not recover for her 'loss of privacy' or 'loss of the right to control the dissemination of information about her private life', even though, by construction, she suffered them every bit as much as the phone-hacked claimants in *Gulati*. This accords with the dominant understanding of English law whereby, having compensated her for the consequences of the invasion, there was nothing left for the law to redress.

d. Lingering Doubts

Interestingly, however, doubts can be observed within the courts' own pronouncements as to whether their cumulative approach really is quite right. We saw earlier that the idea of right-vindication was regarded, if implicitly, as subsidiary to the compensation of – concrete – losses: it should step in only when there is no, or not enough, loss for the compensatory award to be regarded as an 'effective remedy'.

[35] *Gulati* (n 23) [45] (Arden LJ). Naturally, pecuniary loss would also be recoverable, within the usual parameters, if it flowed from the wrong.

[36] *Campbell v MGN Ltd* [2002] EWHC 499 (QB), [2002] EMLR 30, [2].

A similar idea can be seen to operate in the context of compensation for abstract losses.[37] Thus Mann J's judgment in *Gulati* is replete with markers of uncertainties as to the availability of such awards, making it clear, at the very least, that to his mind they ought not always to be recoverable (even though the loss will, by construction, be there in every instance):

> While the law is used to awarding damages for injured feelings, there is no reason in principle, in my view, why it should not also make an award to reflect infringements of the right itself, *if the situation warrants it* … If one has lost 'the right to control the dissemination of information about one's private life' then I fail to see why that, of itself, should not attract a degree of compensation, *in an appropriate case*.
>
> …
>
> [T]he damages should compensate not merely for distress … but should also compensate (*if appropriate*) for the loss of privacy or autonomy as such arising out the infringement by hacking (or other mechanism) as such. (This may include, *if appropriate*, a sum to compensate for damage to dignity or standing, so far as that is meaningful in this context and *is not already within the distress element*.)[38]

The same idea surfaces in *TLT*:

> I accept [the claimant's] submission that in principle damages can be awarded in respect of the loss of control of personal and confidential information … On the facts of these cases, as [the claimant] accepts, *it is neither necessary nor desirable to make a separate award* in respect of this head of damage.[39]

As a matter of logic this is extremely puzzling. Courts seem to be saying that there exist losses which, by construction, will be present in a case but may or may not be recoverable depending on the existence of *other losses*. Abstract, legal losses are seen, in some unarticulated but clear sense, as subsidiary to – default, ordinary, older-established – concrete, factual losses. It is not hard to read this as giving away the fact that they are not, contrary to the stated logic, independent heads of loss meriting compensation within the ordinary parameters of the law, but distinct ways of construing the same detriment. Normative loss, on this reading, would act as a *gap-filler*, allowing courts to grant substantial damages (an 'effective remedy') for serious invasions where there is no, or at least not enough, concrete loss to reach the desired result through the ordinary template of English law.

e. Origins

These developments become easier to understand if we observe that the change of paradigm occurred in the context of cases we could describe as 'ill-fitting'. In *Weller* and *Gulati*, the courts were faced with claimants who had suffered what

[37] Perhaps unsurprisingly, if the two really are practical substitutes one for the other: see section III.C.iii, 'Compensation for Abstract Losses and Vindication'.
[38] *Gulati* (n 17) [111], [168] (emphasis added).
[39] *TLT v Secretary of State for the Home Department* [2016] EWHC 2217 (QB), [17] (Mitting J).

intuitively appeared to be serious breaches of privacy but had little, or no, harm – in the ordinary sense of 'factual worse-offness' – to show for it because, due to unusual circumstances, they were not aware (at least not until a late stage) that they had been wronged.

Faced with such circumstances, there are three main routes the courts could have taken:[40]

- They could have accepted the result: that, according to well-established principles of English law, the claimants would only get nominal damages (or a very small quantum of damages compared to the perceived seriousness of the wrong). This was clearly regarded as unsatisfactory, not granting them the 'effective remedy' to which they were entitled and, perhaps, failing in the prophylactic role of the law.
- They could have granted vindicatory damages: had the door not been closed,[41] it seems likely that this is the route that would have been followed.
- Lastly, they could have switched over to the loss-as-wrong approach, characterising the setback to the interest itself as the loss: a serious loss, by construction, given that the wrong was itself regarded as serious. As mentioned, this is what they did – but only in part, mixing it with the traditional model (ie compensation for factual consequences) and expressing, as observed, uncertainty about the relationship between the two.

f. Problems

The problems with the solution adopted (the 'cumulative approach') have already been mentioned, but it is worth returning to them. One is that it is bound to take consequences into account twice, once to determine the intrinsic seriousness of the infringement and the other when looking at the effects of the wrong on the claimant. The courts seem, as highlighted, to be aware (if in an inchoate way) of the potential for double-counting; but their resorting to control devices such as the 'appropriateness' of combining the two approaches in any given instance is no more than an attempt to alleviate the practical consequences of the conflation of logics on an ad hoc basis. Things would be different if one found a way to determine the seriousness of the injury independently of its potential consequences – but it is not clear how this could be achieved, indeed what 'seriousness' even *means* apart from (potential) consequences; or if the law genuinely gave an award for the injury per se independently of any consequences, actual or potential. This, presumably,

[40] There are least two further routes that would, in principle, have allowed the courts to grant a substantive award of damages. One is that of punitive damages, a route that – like vindicatory damages – appears to have been closed (*Mosley* (n 11) [197]; but see *PJS v News Group Newspapers Ltd* [2016] UKSC 26, [2016] AC 1081, [42], [92]). The other would have been to deem the claimant's distress: see section III.C.ii, 'Standardised or Personalised Awards'.

[41] Section II.C, 'Vindicatory Damages in the Law of Privacy'.

would entail granting the same award for all invasions of privacy: not something anyone appears to have ever suggested.

Even if one disagreed with the above argument and favoured the approach in principle, there would still remain a very significant problem, namely, the development of a micro-rationality in the context of the law of privacy. Unless one can explain on what normatively convincing basis we ought to distinguish between them, logically, if the violation of the right to privacy entitles the claimant to damages, in itself and on top of any concrete consequences, the same reasoning should apply to any right-violation. But clearly this is not the case. Admittedly, there is no cut-and-dried judicial dissonance between privacy on the one hand and all other rights on the other. There do exist other causes of action in respect of which similar strands of reasoning had already made an appearance – defamation and false imprisonment in particular – but never in a way that was so clear as to threaten the internal coherence of the law of torts. The cases in question could either, despite appearances, be reconciled with principle,[42] or else they concerned the very specific issue of 'vindication of reputation' in the tort of defamation – where 'vindication' is used in an idiosyncratic sense. If *Gulati* is rightly decided then it is very difficult to understand why the owner of the damaged car and the physically injured claimant do not also get two separate awards, one for their loss (economic and/or emotional), the other because they have lost (some of) their physical integrity or property right: a result that everyone would regard as wrong or even absurd.[43]

ii. Standardised or Personalised Awards

Even though it is inextricably intertwined with the first point, it is easier to keep this second difficulty separate. The question is whether the claimant in a privacy, or indeed any tort, action gets compensated for their actual loss or for something else, akin to what an 'ordinary' claimant, placed in the same objective circumstances,

[42] For instance, cases where damages said to be for distress are in reality aggravated damages, to the effect that the recovery of 'ordinary' emotional harm – ie that part which is independent of the defendant's conduct – has to be shifted to another category. The only possibility being the abstract right-violation, we end up with an appearance of damages for abstract loss combined with damages for mental distress, when in fact what we have is two types of damages for emotional harm – the 'ordinary' (disguised as damages for interference with a right, for example loss of liberty) and the 'extraordinary' one (compensated *qua* distress).

[43] What makes these two examples easier is that, in the first case, the loss is pecuniary hence – despite complications – objective: we know how much the claimant should get, and therefore we can easily spot over- (or indeed under-) compensation. The same is true in the second case because, even though the loss is non-pecuniary, and therefore the amount of compensation arbitrary, the arbitrariness has been stabilised through a tariff system, which makes it possible to prove, or at the very least to give strong indicators of, a discrepancy between what the claimant receives and what the law says they should receive. The difficulty with breach of privacy is that, because the amount of the awards is arbitrary and there is no mechanism for stabilisation, it is all but impossible to prove or disprove any such disparity. But the tort should not be allowed to hide behind the arbitrariness of awards to reach results it never would if these could be compared with some external yardstick.

would have suffered. In other words, is the award personalised or standardised? The reason why this – remarkably underexplored[44] – question matters a great deal to the present enquiry is because, as can easily be seen, the more the law standardises the award, that is, affixes a monetary value to a set of facts regardless of the claimant's idiosyncrasies (such as their sensitivity), the more the bipolar model will converge with the unipolar one. It has been explained that the Weller twins could get substantial damages *for their loss* on the unipolar model because the wrong was regarded as serious in itself (in turn, because an ordinary claimant – presumed not to be a toddler – would have suffered significant distress, as indeed the twins' half-sister did). But the very same idea could work itself out on the bipolar model: the law could presume, even irrebuttably, the twins' distress to have been serious on the basis that that of an ordinary claimant would have been. Intuitively this is less appealing than detouring through the compensation for an abstract loss-wrong (the very reason why the latter route would be preferred); but the reasoning is an outworking of the same logic and the result would be the same: granting substantial compensatory damages in the absence of any concrete 'worse-offness'. Again, we see that the two analytical frameworks are not cumulative but alternative.

Where, then, does the law stand? Unsurprisingly perhaps, it does not appear to speak with one voice on this topic, but even this is difficult to establish with much precision given the arbitrary quantum of awards for non-patrimonial losses: because we cannot convert emotions into money in a systematic way, we cannot compare what the claimant receives with what they ought to have received on any given model.

What can safely be said, however, is that the default self-understanding of the law is that the claimant gets compensated for their actual loss (subject, of course, to control mechanisms such as remoteness, etc). Any other starting point would probably be regarded as unorthodox. Yet a striking feature of the common law is the extent to which damages can in fact be shown to be standardised, even on the dominant bipolar model. This is true, first, on the side of pecuniary losses, where we would least expect it. Thus it is well-established that, if it costs £2,000 on the market to repair a damaged car, but a friend did it for £500, the claimant is entitled to the full £2,000 by way of compensatory damages for their economic loss, despite being out of pocket for only a quarter of this. (This would remain true if the claimant was an unemployed mechanic who could do it for free and enjoyed the work: they would still recover £2,000, despite having suffered *no* actual detriment, financial or emotional.)

On the side of non-pecuniary losses things are, for the reasons explained, more difficult to establish, but the existence of *tariffs* putting a price tag on the non-patrimonial consequences of the wrong are a very clear sign of the process of standardisation at work. In the much more developed field of damages for personal

[44] See, however, J Edelman, 'The Meaning of Loss and Enrichment' in R Chambers, C Mitchell and J Penner (eds), *Philosophical Foundations of the Law of Unjust Enrichment* (Oxford, Oxford UP, 2009) 216ff.

injury, we have examples of the law's putting a specific figure on damages for 'pain and suffering and loss of amenities' in respect of given injuries: an incontrovertible example of standardisation based on the perceived intrinsic seriousness of the injury.[45] The wrong has a value that is independent of the individual claimant. Even though these do not exist at this stage for invasions of privacy, some writers have argued in their favour, and it seems inevitable that, as the body of case law grows, a system of award stabilisation will emerge.[46] Although the matter is not beyond contention, the dominant view is also that, generally speaking – hence logically in the tort of privacy as well – given two claimants who have been exposed to the same injury, the one who presents a long face to the court will not get more than a stoic one.[47]

Again, the more distress is standardised on the basis of what we would expect an ordinary person placed in the same objective circumstances as the claimant to have suffered,[48] the more it becomes the flipside of the intrinsic seriousness of the wrong, which itself provides the yardstick for valuing the wrong under the 'unipolar' model – thereby reducing the practical difference between the two approaches, potentially down to nothing.

iii. Compensation for Abstract Losses and Vindication

At this stage, we can return to the issue of vindication of right and its relationship with compensatory awards. The parallel between the two that can be drawn from court dicta is striking and deserves examination. Compare, for instance, Eady J in *Mosley*:

> Apart from distress, there is another factor which probably has to be taken into account … that of vindication to mark the infringement of a right … to mark the fact

[45] Judicial College, *Guidelines for the Assessment of General Damages in Personal Injury Cases*, 13th edn (Oxford, Oxford UP, 2015); Descheemaeker (n 20) 600–01. More often it works with brackets, which allow the ambiguity to persist: do some claimants get more than others because their injury was objectively worse, or because they subjectively suffered more from it?

[46] PR Handford, *Tort Liability for Mental Harm*, 3rd edn (Pyrmont, NSW, Law Book Co, 2017) 592 (with cross-reference to fuller developments in the previous edition of the book).

[47] A Burrows, *Remedies for Torts and Breach of Contract*, 3rd edn (Oxford, Oxford OUP, 2004) 31; Law Commission, *Damages for Personal Injury: Non-Pecuniary Loss* (Law Com CP No 140, 1995) 14; Handford (n 46) 607–08. It is interesting that a suggestion to the contrary was made by Mann J in *Gulati* at the same time as he endorsed the existence of the abstract loss of privacy (*Gulati* (n 17) [229]: 'A thinner-skinned individual may be caused more upset, and therefore receive more compensation, than a thicker-skinned individual who is the subject of the same intrusion'). This is not surprising if we accept that the two mechanisms – standardising awards for emotional harm based on what an ordinary claimant would have been expected to suffer, and granting damages for the wrong itself – fulfil the same function and are therefore alternatives. If the unbothered (because, for instance, unaware) claimant is already receiving substantial damages as 'compensation for the wrong itself', this relieves the pressure to make a substantial award as – standardised – distress (and vice versa); indeed combining the two would be much more likely to appear as double-counting.

[48] Of course, the key question is what counts as an objective circumstance as opposed to an idiosyncrasy. Being oversensitive would certainly be discounted, but a pianist would get more damages for PSLA than a non-pianist if they lost a finger; the injury is regarded as objectively worse for the pianist. Where the line is drawn is a difficult question that admits of no self-evident answer and which will need to be grappled with.

> that … [an] individual has taken away or undermined the right of another – in this case taken away a person's dignity.[49]

with Mann J in *Gulati*:

> [T]he damages should compensate not merely for distress … but should also compensate (if appropriate) for the loss of privacy or autonomy as such arising out the infringement.[50]

We can see how vindication of right in *Mosley* maps exactly on to loss of privacy in *Gulati* as the remedial dimension over and above compensation for distress (ie for the consequences of the wrong, it being implicit in both cases that no financial loss was averred) to which the claimant should be entitled. In the same way, it was highlighted above how the two doctrines are both regarded, clearly if implicitly, as subsidiary remedies, which should only step in when the default remedy of compensatory damages for factual losses flowing from the wrong is not – whatever exactly this might mean – an 'effective' one.

Analytically, there is no doubt that the two are independent of one another. However, if we accept that vindicatory damages were thought of as a means to award substantial damages in situations where there was no – concrete – loss (or only disproportionately little compared to the perceived gravity of the infringement), it is clear that the recognition of abstract losses renders vindicatory awards superfluous. By construction, a serious wrong will lead to serious – legal – loss, hence a substantial award of damages. There will be no situation where courts would need to resort to vindicatory damages (narrowly so called) so as to award substantial damages to the claimant in the absence of loss. Although there is no incompatibility of principle between the two, it suggests that these are alternative strategies, rooted in two different logics, which ought not to be combined. To put the same point differently, it is an unlikely commentator who would not find it inappropriate, in a more or less articulated way, for the likes of Max Mosley or Shobna Gulati to receive an award of damages 'to mark the infringement of [their] right' (to privacy) – as he did – *and* another one for the 'loss of privacy … arising out [of] the infringement' – as she did. It is therefore not altogether surprising that, in judicial practice, the latter followed chronologically on the demise of the former.

IV. Aggravated Damages

After vindicatory and compensatory damages, we turn in this section and the next to types of awards that do not immediately map, through semantic similarity, on to either of the two functions – compensation and vindication – that were assigned at the outset to claimant-focused damages: the so-called 'aggravated' and

[49] *Mosley* (n 11) [216].
[50] *Gulati* (n 17) [168].

'nominal' damages. The first type does not pose any particular difficulty for the present purpose and only deserves brief examination here.

As is well known, Lord Devlin in *Rookes v Barnard* clearly separated out aggravated from punitive (or exemplary) damages, with which they had been inextricably entwined since the eighteenth century, recognising that the former were of a compensatory nature for a further loss suffered by the claimant due to the manner in which the wrong was committed: the mental distress caused by the high-handed conduct – in a broad sense – of the defendant.[51] This 'extra-ordinary' distress comes, and is compensated, on top of the 'ordinary' distress, that is, the emotional harm suffered by the claimant independently of any such aggravating factors. The only reason, on this reading, why they are treated as a separate category today is due to their distinctive history. Once we accept that emotional harm which flows from the violation of a right entitles the claimant to compensation, and that distress caused by the defendant's insulting or oppressive conduct counts as a form of emotional harm, aggravated damages become a simple application of general principles.

Consonant with such principles, aggravated damages are straightforwardly available in actions for breach of privacy. They were awarded, among others, in *Campbell*,[52] *Mosley*[53] and *Gulati*;[54] and it does not appear to have ever been doubted that this was the right approach.

V. Nominal Damages

Lastly, nominal damages. Despite their ancient pedigree, they are surprisingly under-conceptualised and raise interesting issues that allow us to reconsider certain topics pertaining to the compensatory and vindicatory functions of damages already touched upon.

A. Definition

What are nominal damages? The dominant (and to my mind correct) view that emerged from history is that they are symbolic, non-compensatory damages designed to mark a wrong in the absence of loss, in the usual sense of factual worse-offness:[55] a form of declaration of wrong, hence right, in a legal system

[51] *Rookes v Barnard* [1964] AC 1129 (HL), 1221: 'the manner of committing the wrong may be such as to injure the plaintiff's proper feelings of dignity or pride' (Lord Devlin).

[52] *Campbell* (n 36).

[53] *Mosley* (n 11) [222]–[223].

[54] *Gulati* (n 17) [203]–[215].

[55] Obviously this requires that the cause of action should be complete without the allegation of such loss, hence the fact that they are only available for torts actionable per se.

where this form of declaratory redress was unknown. Like compensation, or indeed any remedy for a wrong, this quasi-declaratory function can be seen, in turn, as a form of vindication of the right.[56]

There exists, however, another view, which sees them as compensatory damages, the nugatory amount of the award reflecting the nugatory extent of the loss: a trifling award for a trifling loss. This is how they were described, for instance, by Lord Dyson in *Lumba*.[57] If this were true, the category would have no separate existence and should be abolished: it would simply, like aggravated damages, be an exemplification of ordinary principles. The overwhelming weight of authority is, however, against this view, which seems to betray a lingering confusion between nominal damages and a low quantum of – ordinary, that is, compensatory – damages. But it is well-established that, as Lord Halsbury put it in *The Mediana*, '"nominal damages" does not mean small damages'.[58] They do not serve a compensatory function at all; if they did, they would work themselves out of existence.

B. Availability

De lege lata, nominal damages do not appear to have been awarded in privacy cases. Even though no official pronouncement has been made by courts, there does not seem to be any suggestion that this would be because breach of privacy requires proof of – concrete – loss flowing from the right invasion in order to be actionable: all the authorities point to the fact that it is actionable per se.[59] Indeed this is implicit in Eady J's view in *Mosley* that nominal damages would not be an 'effective remedy' for the infringement of the claimant's right: this assumes that they are, in principle, available in a privacy action.[60] Accordingly, the debate over the availability of nominal damages is not whether, in the absence of concrete loss, the claimant should get them (as opposed to nothing), but whether there could ever be situations where a successful claimant would get *no more* than nominal damages.

On the logic of what was said above, following *Gulati* it is hard to see how nominal – that is, non-substantial – damages could ever be granted in a privacy action: if the wrong entitles the claimant, apart from any concrete consequences,

[56] N Witzleb and R Carroll, 'The Role of Vindication in Tort Damages' (2009) 17 *Tort Law Review* 16, 41.

[57] *Lumba* (n 6) [100].

[58] *Mediana (Owners of Steamship) v Comet (Owners of Lightship)* [1900] AC 113 (HL), 116; McGregor (n 2) paras 12-006–12-007.

[59] eg Australian Law Reform Commission, *Serious Invasions of Privacy in the Digital Era* (ALRC DP No 80, 2014) para 7.36; N Moreham, 'Why Is Privacy Important? Privacy, Dignity and Development of the New Zealand Breach of Privacy Tort' in J Finn and S Todd (eds), *Law, Liberty, Legislation: Essays in Honour of John Burrows QC* (Wellington, LexisNexis, 2008) 244.

[60] See n 11.

to a substantial award for the loss of privacy itself, then awarding nominal damages would be a contradiction in terms: it would signal that there was no loss, hence, on this reading of loss, no wrong. Privacy could not be violated without the claimant's losing, by construction, at least some of it, hence suffering loss sounding in substantial damages. (Assuming that no *de minimis* principle applies, there could of course be small, even insignificant, damages in response to trivial invasions, but this is an altogether separate issue.)

C. Nominal Damages, Compensation for Abstract Losses and Vindication

Again, we are back to a question of coherence. Nominal damages are one of the best-established doctrines of the common law. We know that they are available in causes of action actionable per se – whether torts, equitable wrongs (like breach of confidence),[61] statutory wrongs or breach of contract – and we know that, on the prevailing view, they are not compensatory for loss: indeed they are awarded precisely because there is no compensable loss. For this to be meaningful, it must be the case that such wrongs can exist in the absence of loss (in the sense of a compensable detriment).[62] Yet, post-*Gulati*, it seems to have become a logical impossibility when it comes to breach of privacy.

The obvious question becomes, why would the infringement of the right to privacy amount to a loss in itself but not that of other rights? (As mentioned earlier, this form of thinking has made inroads, albeit much less clearly, in other causes of action; but this does nothing to solve the issue: it simply broadens it.) It seems that, on the logic underpinning this case, the violation of *any* right recognised by the law should amount to a – legal, abstract, normative – loss and therefore merit substantial damages. In order to reconcile the post-*Gulati* understanding of damages for breach of privacy with the orthodoxy of tort, we would need to find a reason why privacy (or a wider subset of rights) should behave differently from the others. But it is difficult to think of any. The most plausible line would be one relating to the relative importance of rights. It is not clear, however, that it would even get off the ground: the decision whether an infringement of right

[61] *Woodward v Hutchins* [1977] 1 WLR 760 (CA), 765; *Hannon v News Group Newspapers Ltd* [2014] EWHC 1580 (Ch), [2015] EMLR 1, [34]. This is especially relevant, of course, given the genealogical link between the two actions.

[62] This is phrased in such a way as to avoid saying that the recognition of right-violation as a form of loss makes the distinction between torts that are actionable per se and torts that are not meaningless, on the basis that any wrong would definitionally be accompanied by loss. It would still be intelligible (if admittedly a little odd) to say that loss – legal loss – is inherent in the commission of any wrong yet does not constitute, in itself, the sort of loss (often termed, mysteriously enough, 'special loss') required in certain causes of action to render the infringement actionable. There could still be wrongs not actionable in the absence of a special type of loss, even if we accepted that the violation of a right is by construction a harm or loss.

constitutes a loss, in and by itself, seems to be of an ontological nature: it depends on what we understand a right to be, not what its object is. Even if that hurdle was overcome, the argument would immediately backfire: how could a right so comparatively unimportant that, until very recently, English law refused to grant it any direct protection be treated more favourably than even the 'sacred' right to property (which follows the mainstream orthodoxy and merits no more than nominal damages when an interference with it causes no concrete detriment to the right-holder)? In the absence of a way to reconcile the two approaches, we would be forced to conclude that those recent cases have introduced an incompatible micro-rationality into a section of the law of torts. This would be indefensible.

VI. Conclusion

The law of privacy has been developing spectacularly quickly. It did not exist in any meaningful sense at the turn of the century, and was still largely embryonic at the turn of the present decade: this chapter could hardly have been written then. Yet, today, breach of privacy has become a principal battleground for foundational issues of tort theory, regarding in particular the law of damages. What does loss mean? How do concretely and abstractly defined losses relate to one another? What is the relationship between abstract losses and vindication, or between vindication and nominal damages? Following some recent hard cases, which as we all know make bad law, English courts have allowed a discrepant logic to enter their midst and, it seems, dominate – for the time being – their decision-making on claimant-focused damages in the law of privacy. Clarification is needed, not simply for the sake of that specific wrong, but because no part of the law exists in isolation from the others, and whatever happens in that (admittedly peripheral) part of the law of tort is bound, if it is not addressed, to have a ripple effect which, sooner or later, will attack some of the very foundations of the discipline.

7

Invasion of Privacy and Recovery for Distress

MEGAN RICHARDSON, MARCIA NEAVE
AND MICHAEL RIVETTE

We have come a long way since 1861, when, as Lord Wensleydale said in *Lynch v Knight*,[1] 'mental pain … the law cannot value'. As discussed in this chapter, awards for 'mental pain' are now being made in English and Australian cases where the essential complaint is invasion of privacy, whether framed in terms of a privacy tort (specifically a tort of misuse of private information) in the United Kingdom (UK) or equitable breach of confidence in Australia. Nevertheless, as we consider, there are some unresolved questions regarding the award that still need to be addressed. First, how should the value of distress or other mental harm ('pain') be assessed, and what guidance should awards in contiguous fields, such as defamation, copyright, contract and trespass (including false imprisonment), provide here?[2] Second, should such mental harm be seen as a primary harm associated with invasion of privacy, or as consequential on some more basic harm or impairment that results from the breach, such as a loss of privacy or incursion on a *right* to privacy? A question we come back to at the end of the chapter.[3] And, perhaps

[1] *Lynch v Knight* (1861) 10 HLC 576, 598, *per* Lord Wensleydale (although adding that 'where a material damage occurs, and is connected with it, it is impossible a jury, in estimating it, should altogether overlook the feelings of the party interested').

[2] See, eg, *Monroe v Hopkins* [2017] EWHC 433, where £24,000 damages were awarded for libel in respect of two tweets published on Twitter (combining serious harm to reputation and 'injury to feelings [that] was real and substantial, and has continued'). As to additional damages for distress involving an 'intrusion into [a man's] life, deeper and graver than an intrusion into a man's property' in a copyright case, see *Williams v Settle* (1960) 1 WLR 1072, 1082, *per* Sellers LJ; and cf *Milpurrurru v Indofurn Pty Ltd* (1994) 30 IPR 207, 245–47, *per* von Doussa J. For contract cases, where damages were awarded for distress on the basis that the contract was for an enjoyable experience and this was fundamentally not provided, see *Jarvis v Swans Tours* [1973] QB 233; *Baltic Shipping Co v Dillon* (1993) 176 CLR 344. For trespass to the person, specifically false imprisonment, see *McDonald v Coles Myer Ltd (t/as K-Mart Chatswood)* (1995) Aust Torts Reports 81-361 (additional damages for loss of 'liberty' and 'injury to the plaintiff's feelings' assessed at unspecified shares of general damages of $25,000 for false imprisonment by store detective). See generally PR Hanford, 'Damages for Injured Feelings in Australia' (1982) 5 *University of New South Wales Law Journal* 291, 303–04.

[3] See discussion at p 179.

most significantly for present purposes, should a remedy that seeks to compensate for mental harm only be awarded through the development of a privacy tort, or should it be available for equitable breach of confidence, as held by an Australian court?[4] To put it another way, should a plaintiff in an Australian breach of confidence action be deprived of a remedy because equity does not generally provide damages or compensation for distress, as argued by one well-known Australian textbook?[5] If so, does the unavailability of an appropriate remedy provide another reason for reform of the law of privacy in Australia?[6]

In this chapter, we argue that enabling recovery for distress or other mental harm as a result of a breach suffered is an appropriate function of any privacy doctrine whose significant purpose is the avoidance or alleviation of such harm. Moreover, the point has been recognised implicitly or explicitly in historical and recent cases.

I. Recent Cases

In the UK, it is clear that the tort of misuse of private information may result in damages for distress or other mental harm (such as embarrassment and anger). The availability of the remedy has been treated as a logical consequence of the privacy tort developed by English courts in the period after the Human Rights Act 1998 made the European Convention on Human Rights, including its Article 8 right to respect for private life, part of English law.[7] The existence of the tort has been recognised at the highest level, including in the recent decision of the Supreme Court in *PJS v News Group Newspapers Ltd*.[8] In this case the remedy sought was not one of damages but rather an interlocutory injunction to prevent the *Sun* from publishing a scandalous story about the plaintiff's alleged sexual encounters with a male couple and identifying him by name as the partner of a famous celebrity. The injunction was awarded, despite the newspaper's argument

[4] *Giller v Procopets* (2008) 24 VR 1.

[5] JD Heydon, MJ Leeming and PG Turner, *Meagher, Gummow and Lehane's Equity: Doctrines and Remedies*, (Chatswood, NSW, LexisNexis Butterworths, 2015) 882–83, [24-085].

[6] See Australian Law Reform Commission, *Serious Invasions of Privacy in the Digital Era* (ALRC Report 123), 2014, ch 12, and especially recommendation 12.1 and discussion at [12.31].

[7] See *Google, Inc v Vidal-Hall* [2016] QB 1003, 1021–26, [21]–[37] *per* Lord Dyson MR and Sharp LJ, detailing the history of the development of the misuse of private information tort in a case where service out of jurisdiction was sought against the defendant, Google, in order to enable proceedings to continue in a class action brought after the plaintiffs discovered that Google had bypassed the security measures on their Apple devices to monitor their accounts and target advertising to them. The Court acknowledged that there may be implications of this development for issues such as remedies, limitation and vicarious liability, which would need to be considered 'as and when they arise': ibid. But there is no suggestion that any question remained as to the availability of an award of damages for distress or other mental harm, as claimed in that case. Leave to appeal to the Supreme Court was denied on this aspect of the Court of Appeal's decision: see www.supremecourt.uk/news/permission-to-appeal-decisions-28-july-2015.html.

[8] *PJS v News Group Newspapers Ltd* [2016] AC 1081.

that the information enabling identification of PJS had been published extensively overseas and discussed on social media (an argument the Court of Appeal had accepted). As the Supreme Court pointed out, publication in the newspaper would still be an 'intrusion' on the plaintiff's privacy in breach of his Article 8 right to respect for his private life, regardless of whether secrecy could or could not be maintained, 'intrusion' being an important focus of a modern privacy tort.[9] There was no suggestion that damages for mental harm would not be available if the injunction had been denied. Rather, the only debate about damages in the *PJS* case was whether these could include an award of exemplary damages to mark a defendant's egregious conduct. Here there was clear support for an expansive approach. Both Lord Mance, in the majority, and Lord Toulson, in the minority, indicated that the Court would be open to the award of exemplary damages, 'in order to deter flagrant breaches of privacy and provide adequate protection for the person concerned', as Lord Toulson said.[10] Thus it appeared to be accepted that a logical implication of Article 8's becoming part of English law is that where invasion of privacy is found, appropriate remedies should be developed to give the Article its effect.

On the other hand, the development of a privacy tort in the UK has not removed the possibility of also arguing breach of confidence – a doctrine that has been broadly construed in modern times to include the publication of confidential information obtained with notice or knowledge of confidence. This is how Lord Goff framed it in *Attorney-General v Guardian Newspapers Ltd* (commonly known as the *Spycatcher* case), giving the example of a document wafted out of a window or a diary dropped in the street.[11] Indeed the action for breach of confidence has continued to function as an equitable doctrine alongside the tort in recent cases, with both able to be called in aid of a right to privacy (to the extent their doctrinal parameters allow). While in *PJS* breach of confidence seemed to have been ruled out because of the extent of the disclosures that had already occurred, in other cases claims for breach of the privacy tort and breach of confidence may run in tandem, with similar remedies awarded for both claims. For instance, in the well-known case of *Mosley v News Group Newspapers Ltd*,[12] misuse of private information as well as breach of confidence were found, and damages of £60,000 were awarded to acknowledge the invasion of privacy and to compensate for the

[9] ibid. See the extensive discussion in the leading judgments of Lord Mance and Lord Neuberger, Lady Hale and Lord Reed concurring, Lord Toulson dissenting, and especially Lord Mance at 1099–1100, [29]–[30], citing with approval Eady J in *CTB v News Group Newspapers Ltd* [2011] EWHC 1326, [23]–[26] and Tugendhat J in *CTB v News Group Newspapers Ltd* [2011] EWHC 1334, [3].

[10] ibid 1104, [42] *per* Lord Mance and 1116, [92] *per* Lord Toulson (both indicating that such damages might still be held awardable in a future appropriate case for breach of privacy, notwithstanding Eady J's decision to the contrary in *Mosley v News Group Newspapers Ltd* [2008] EWHC 1777).

[11] *Attorney-General v Guardian Newspapers Ltd (No 2)* [1990] 1 AC 109, 281–83 *per* Lord Goff. The formulation, said Laws J in *Hellewell v Chief Constable* [1995] 1 WLR 804, revealed breach of confidence as a doctrine that protected what might reasonably be called 'a right to privacy' in all but name.

[12] *Mosley* (n 10).

embarrassment and distress caused to the plaintiff Max Mosley, after his private sexual encounters were the subject of a scandalous exposé in the notorious (and now defunct) *News of the World*.[13] Moreover, even before the development of the misuse of private information tort, breach of confidence was relied on in cases that were essentially about 'intrusions' on privacy, relying on the authority of Lord Goff in the *Spycatcher* case.[14] Thus the courts treated their approach in these cases as not just as a matter of giving effect to Article 8, but as part of a development that began before the Human Rights Act came into operation, as signalled by Lord Goff in *Spycatcher*.[15] And damages for distress were awarded in some of these cases, a development that Lord Goff also anticipated, stating that damages under 'a beneficent interpretation' of Lord Cairns' Act were 'now available' despite the 'equitable nature of the wrong'.[16] For instance, in *Campbell v Mirror Group Newspapers Ltd*, relying, inter alia, on Lord Goff in *Spycatcher*, a modest sum of £2,500 in damages was awarded to Naomi Campbell for the distress occasioned by the *Mirror*'s breach of confidence in publishing an exposé of her treatment for drug addiction, complete with surreptitiously obtained photographs showing her leaving a Narcotics Anonymous meeting in London.[17] And although Lord Nicholls in this case foreshadowed a tort framed as 'misuse of private information', suggesting this would be a more 'natural description' of the law's focus here,[18] the development that occurred largely after the case did not end up annihilating the breach of confidence doctrine, which continued on intact.

In Australia, the main judicial mechanism for the protection of privacy continues to be the equitable action for breach of confidence. And courts – at least for the time being – have preferred to adopt a flexible approach to this traditional cause of action to deal with new situations and circumstances involving invasions of privacy, rather than declare a new privacy tort. This is in line with a general

[13] ibid [214]–[221], [234]–[236] *per* Eady J, adding 'there is nothing "landmark" about this decision'.

[14] See, eg, *Douglas v Hello! Ltd* [2001] QB 967, 1000–01, [122]–[126] *per* Sedley LJ (citing Lord Goff in *Attorney-General v Guardian Newspapers* as speaking to the protection of privacy under breach of confidence and identifying the breach in such cases as involving not just a breach of trust but 'an unwanted intrusion into [people's] personal lives'); *Campbell v MGN* [2004] 2 AC 457, 480, [85] *per* Lord Hope ('if there is an intrusion in a situation where a person can reasonably expect his privacy to be respected, that intrusion will be capable of giving rise to liability unless the intrusion can be justified: see also the exposition in *Attorney General v Guardian Newspapers Ltd (No 2)* [1990] 1 AC 109, 282').

[15] See *Campbell* (n 14) 472, [46] *per* Lord Hoffmann, pointing to 'two developments': the first, 'an acknowledgment of the artificiality of distinguishing between confidential information obtained through the violation of a confidential relationship and similar information obtained in some other way', citing Lord Goff in *Spycatcher*; and the second, 'the acceptance, under the influence of human rights instruments such as Article 8 of the European Convention, of the privacy of personal information as something worthy of protection in its own right'. And note generally the reliance on Lord Goff's statement in *Spycatcher* as a starting point for analysis in the House of Lords in the post-Human Rights Act *Campbell* case.

[16] *Attorney-General v Guardian Newspapers Ltd* (n 11) 286 *per* Lord Goff. See also *Douglas v Hello! Ltd* (n 14) 1000, [122] *per* Sedley LJ (citing the above statement as to available remedies).

[17] *Campbell* (n 14), Lord Hope, Lady Hale and Lord Carswell, Lord Nicholls and Lord Hoffmann dissenting.

[18] ibid 465, [14] *per* Lord Nicholls.

preference of Australian courts to adapt existing causes of action to deal with new situations and circumstances rather than declaring new law.[19] The doctrine's importance was acknowledged by the High Court in the leading case of *Australian Broadcasting Corporation v Lenah Game Meats Pty Ltd*.[20] As Gleeson CJ put it, '[i]f the activities filmed [in that case] were private, then the law of breach of confidence is adequate to cover the case',[21] treating confidentiality and privacy as largely aligned here.[22] The Chief Justice noted that the doctrine covers not just cases of imparting and receiving in confidence, but also surreptitious or improper obtaining, pointing out that this was a position that some earlier cases also supported.[23] And he referred also, with apparent approval, to Lord Goff's broad framing of the doctrine in the *Spycatcher* case.[24] Likewise, Gummow and Hayne JJ observed that privacy is dealt with in Australia under 'recognised causes of action', including 'confidential information and trade secrets (in particular, as extending to information respecting the personal affairs and private life of the plaintiff, and the activities of eavesdroppers and the like)'.[25] They added that, while not ruling out the future development of a privacy tort in an appropriate case, '[i]t may be that development is best achieved by looking across the range of already established legal and equitable wrongs' to protect the interests of the individual in 'leading, to some reasonable extent, a secluded and private life, … "free from the prying eyes, ears and publications of others"'.[26] Courts must also take into account, they said, the fact that 'the sensibilities, offence and injury [that an individual may suffer] provide [the] staple value for any developing law of privacy'.[27] While Gummow and Hayne JJ may have had the prospect of the award of an injunction for breach of confidence especially in mind when they talked of equity protecting 'the sensibilities, offence

[19] See *Moorgate Tobacco Ltd v Philip Morris Ltd (No 2)* (1984) 156 CLR 414, 448 *per* Deane J.

[20] *Australian Broadcasting Corporation v Lenah Game Meats Pty Ltd* (2001) 208 CLR 199.

[21] ibid 225, [39] *per* Gleeson CJ.

[22] ibid 225–26, [36], [40]–[42] *per* Gleeson CJ.

[23] ibid 224, [34] *per* Gleeson CJ, citing *Lord Ashburton v Pape* [2013] 2 Ch 469, 475 *per* Swinfen-Eady LJ, and *Commonwealth v John Fairfax & Sons Ltd* (1980) 147 CLR 39, 50 *per* Mason J.

[24] *Lenah* (n 20) 224–25, [34]–[36] *per* Gleeson CJ, noting the development of breach of confidence in Lord Goff's statement in *Attorney-General v Guardian Newspapers* and endorsing the statement of Laws J in *Hellewell v Chief Constable* about its scope and effect.

[25] *Lenah* (n 20) 255, [123] *per* Gummow and Hayne JJ, citing F Gurry, *Breach of Confidence* (Oxford, Clarendon Press, 1984) 162–68 and M Richardson, 'Breach of Confidence, Surreptitiously or Accidentally Obtained Information and Privacy: Theory Versus Law' (1994) 19 *Melbourne University Law Review* 673, 684–97; and ibid 250, [110], noting that this is in line with the general preference of Australian courts to adapt traditional causes of action, *per* Deane J in *Moorgate Tobacco Ltd v Philip Morris Ltd* (n 19). Elaborating further in *Roads and Traffic Authority of New South Wales v Dederer* (2007) 324 CLR 330, 350, [57], Gummow J said 'the common law … looks to precedent and operates analogically … Equity, by contrast, involves the application of doctrines themselves sufficiently comprehensive to meet novel cases'. In other words, a distinction may be drawn between the adaptability of common law as based on incremental adaptation and the inbuilt adaptability of equity as part and parcel of its inherent flexibility: and see Heydon, Leeming and Turner (n 5) 415, [12-045] (although we might query whether the distinction in practice is quite as absolute).

[26] *Lenah* (n 20), 258, [132].

[27] ibid, 256 [126].

and injury' that a plaintiff might suffer,[28] they cannot have overlooked the significant possibility that in a number of cases a plaintiff may be left to a claim for a remedy after the fact – for instance, because publication has occurred at the time the proceedings are initiated, or because an injunction is denied on the basis that the plaintiff will suffer only limited harm from publication and this is outweighed by a hardship to the defendant if publication is stopped.[29]

Later, in *Giller v Procopets*,[30] the Victorian Court of Appeal in Australia took the reasoning of the High Court in *Lenah* to its logical conclusion, holding that a remedy should be available for the mental harm occasioned by a breach of confidence involving the defendant's distribution of a video to the plaintiff's friends, family and employer, showing the plaintiff and defendant engaged in sexual activity following the break-up of the relationship.[31] In that case, an injunction was not sought as the matter by this stage was in the hands of the police.[32] Nevertheless, as Gillard J said at first instance, the plaintiff was left feeling 'extremely angry, annoyed, upset, concerned, anxious, distressed, humiliated and embarrassed by what the defendant did'.[33] In the Court of Appeal, damages under the Victorian version of the Lord Cairns' Act, assessed at $40,000 (including $10,000 for aggravation), were awarded for the 'mental distress' suffered by Alla Giller (using the term here in a global sense to cover the range of mental harm).[34] Special leave to appeal to the High Court was subsequently denied in this case.[35] Nevertheless, some commentators, including the current authors of *Meagher, Gummow and Lehane's Equity: Doctrines and Remedies*, argue that Lord Cairns' Act did not support the award of damages for distress for a wholly equitable claim in this case, as the statute was concerned rather with the grant of a remedy by a court of equity for a legal 'wrong'.[36] The authors of *Meagher, Gummow and Lehane* went further, to argue:

> The reason equity has not explicitly denied power to make such awards is that they concern claims which at all relevant times have been foreign to equity's concerns.

[28] The remedy of an interlocutory or final injunction was specifically mentioned: see ibid, 255, [123].

[29] As, for instance, in the earlier case of *Douglas v Hello! Ltd* (n 14), where an interlocutory injunction was denied to the plaintiffs, who at short notice sought to prevent *Hello!* magazine from publishing surreptitiously obtained photographs of their carefully guarded wedding party, claiming breach of confidence.

[30] *Giller v Procopets* (n 4).

[31] At least two people viewed the video before the matter was placed in the hands of the police: see Gillard J at first instance in *Giller v Procopets* [2004] VSC 113, [273]–[274].

[32] Gillard J said that, 'Early on 10 December 1996 the police took the defendant into custody and from then on the risk of the defendant continuing with the threats to distribute or show the video or the risk of him actually distributing it was remote': ibid, [147].

[33] ibid, [147].

[34] See especially discussion of Neave JA in *Giller v Procopets* (n 4) 133–52, [394]–[446].

[35] *Procopet v Giller* [2009] HCASL 187 *per* Heydon J (concluding that '[t]he papers [the applicant] has filed in support of his application for special leave raise no question of law on which, if special leave were granted, an appeal could enjoy any real prospects of success').

[36] See Heydon, Leeming and Turner (n 5) 882, [24-085]. In earlier editions, a similar line was taken on the availability of Lord Cairns' Act damages for a wholly equitable claim: see RP Meaghar, WMC Gummow and JRF Lehane, *Equity: Doctrines and Remedies* (Sydney, Butterworths, 1975) 524, [2317].

> Equity does not stand still. However, the value of legal coherence … suggests that such legal developments, if they are to occur in the judge-made law, ought to occur at common law not in equity … It does not follow from the fact that the equitable duty of confidence may concern sensitive personal information in a particular case that equitable compensation or damages under Lord Cairns' Act are, or ought to be, available – let alone for distress or in an aggravated measure.[37]

However in *Giller*, the Victorian Court was able to refer to the line of English authorities, including *Campbell* in the House of Lords,[38] where awards of damages for mental harm flowing from breach of confidence had been made relying generally on Lord Cairns' Act in the period of transition after the Human Rights Act 1998 and before the full development of a separate tort of misuse of private information (the development flagged by Lord Nicholls in *Campbell*).[39] Notably, there was no concern expressed in these English decisions of high authority that 'legal coherence' might require the developments to be in common law rather than equity – and even when later on the English courts took the step of declaring a misuse of private information tort, they did not do so on the basis of the need for 'coherence' regarding remedies, but rather for the reason given by Lord Nicholls in *Campbell*, that a tort would be a more natural way to give effect to the Article 8 right to respect for private life in the European Convention.[40] Further, this approach has found support in leading English textbooks.[41]

In the alternative, the Court in *Giller* also relied on the inherent jurisdiction of an equity court to award equitable compensation for claims falling within the exclusive jurisdiction of equity.[42] The use of this jurisdiction to award compensation

And it does seem clear that historically, Lord Cairns' Act was not considered as having this function: see K Barnett and M Bryan, 'Lord Cairns's Act: A Case Study in the Unintended Consequences of Legislation' (2015) 9 *Journal of Equity* 150, considering the history of Lord Cairns' Act and concluding that its purpose was to enable legal wrongs to be made the subject of an injunction or damages in lieu of an injunction in a court of equity. In fact, the current Victorian Supreme Court Act provision (s 38) under discussion in *Giller* does not include the word 'wrong' but, as Barnett and Bryan point out, the redrafting was not intended to effect a substantive change.

[37] Heydon, Leeming and Turner (n 5) 882–83, [24-085].

[38] *Campbell* (n 14). See also *Cornelius v de Taranto* [2001] EMLR 12 (damages of £3,000 awarded by Morland J to Cornelius for distress after her medical records were circulated without consent to her general practitioner and a consultant psychiatrist: the decision was upheld on this aspect in the Court of Appeal ([2001] EMLR 12)) and *Douglas v Hello! Ltd* [2003] QB 633, following the failure of the plaintiffs' attempt to obtain an interlocutory injunction in *Douglas v Hello! Ltd* (n 14) (damages of £3,750 awarded by Lindsay J to each of the plaintiffs Michael Douglas and Catherine Zeta Jones for distress occasioned by *Hello!*'s breach of confidence in publishing surreptitiously obtained photographs of their carefully guarded wedding party: the judgment was upheld on this aspect by the Court of Appeal ([2006] QB 125)).

[39] As Neave JA points out in *Giller v Procopets* (n 4) 142, [418].

[40] See (n 15).

[41] For instance, RG Toulson and CM Phipps, *Confidentiality* (London, Sweet & Maxwell, 2012) 229–32; T Aplin et al, *Gurry on Breach of Confidence* (Cambridge, Cambridge UP, 2012) 764–66 ('whatever the intended effect in 1858, it is clear that courts have applied Lord Cairns' Act in relation to purely equitable rights, including breach of confidence') and 772–73 ('damages are awarded to cover hurt feelings and mental distress as well as loss of dignity and the vindication of a right').

[42] For an earlier decision in the Victorian County Court, awarding equitable compensation of $25,000 for breach of confidence causing 'hurt, distress, embarrassment, humiliation, shame and

in breach of confidence cases follows a traditional approach of English cases of the nineteenth century, an approach reaffirmed by the House of Lords in *Nocton v Lord Ashburton* in 1914.[43] Those cases were concerned with compensation for loss of commercially valuable information, but Viscount Haldane LC's observation in *Nocton*, that the remedy extended to 'mak[ing] compensation' for 'losses' that may be incurred as a result of a breach, may be taken to suggest a potentially broader application in cases of breach of personal confidence.[44] Further, there is nothing in those cases to suggest that the courts would be averse to making compensation awards for distress or other mental harm: their concern was rather to frame a remedy that could speak to the case before them, where commercially valuable information was involved. Nevertheless, the above quotation suggests that the authors of *Meagher, Gummow and Lehane* do not consider that equitable compensation (as opposed to Lord Cairns' Act damages) should be available. They attribute the awards that had been made in recent English cases to the influence of Article 8 of the Convention on Human Rights, noting that courts were 'sometimes professing that influence, sometimes not'.[45] As such, the authority of these cases is said to be inapplicable in Australia. That is a debatable proposition. As we have noted above, while human rights jurisprudence was influential in the English cases, especially in the development of the misuse of private information tort, in *Campbell* the award of damages for Ms Campbell's distress caused by the disclosure of her attendance at Narcotics Anonymous was based solely on her breach of confidence claim.[46]

Giller is a decision of an intermediate appellate court in Australia, and such decisions are generally binding on other intermediate appellate courts.[47] Its holding that equitable compensation should be available for emotional distress has already been followed in the more recent case of *Wilson v Ferguson* in Western Australia,[48] a case involving the unauthorised publication of private sexual images

guilt' to a rape victim whose identity was published in breach of the *Judicial Proceedings Reports Act 1958* (Vic), see *Doe v Australian Broadcasting Corporation* [2007] VCC 281, [186], judgment of Judge Hampel.

[43] See *Nocton v Lord Ashburton* [1914] AC 932, 956–57 *per* Viscount Haldane LC ('Courts of Equity had jurisdiction to direct accounts to be taken, and in proper cases to order the solicitor to replace property improperly acquired from the client, or to make compensation if he had lost it by acting in breach of a duty which arose out of his confidential relationship to the man who had trusted him').

[44] Although Haldane LC uses the more particular language of a loss of 'property'. Even then, the term 'property' may be broadly construed, encompassing, for instance, creation of intellectual property, such as a photograph or film, 'in circumstances involving the invasion of the legal or equitable rights of the plaintiff or a breach of the obligations of the maker to the plaintiff': see *Lenah* (n 20) 247, [102] *per* Gummow and Hayne JJ, adding that '[t]he maker may be regarded as a constructive trustee of an item of personal (albeit intangible) property, namely the copyright'. On like reasoning, might loss of control over the copyright (held under a constructive trust for the benefit of a plaintiff) arguably be a basis for awarding equitable compensation in such cases? Of course, a plaintiff might alternatively elect for a gain-based remedy such as account of profits in such cases (assuming profits can be assessed).

[45] Heydon, Leeming and Turner (n 5) 881, [24-085].

[46] See *Giller v Procopets* (n 4) 99, [418] *per* Neave JA.

[47] See *Farah Constructions Pty Ltd v Say-Dee Pty Ltd* (2007) 230 CLR 89, 151–52, [135].

[48] *Wilson v Ferguson* [2015] WASC 15.

on the defendant's Facebook page after his relationship with the plaintiff ended. The judge held that the defendant had breached confidence both in respect of images that had been imparted to him in confidence by the plaintiff and in respect of two videos that he had surreptitiously obtained by borrowing the plaintiff's phone and sending the videos to himself while she was out of the room.[49] Compensation of $35,000 (including an unspecified amount for aggravation) was awarded to the plaintiff for the 'significant embarrassment, anxiety and distress [suffered by her] as a result of the [defendant's] dissemination of intimate images of her in her workplace and among her social group'.[50] As Mitchell J said, the Court of Appeal in *Giller* was not 'plainly wrong' in extending the award of equitable compensation to include non-economic loss occasioned by a breach of confidence, and the decision should be treated as good authority on the question.[51] The view that compensation for distress can be awarded has also been adopted by a number of leading Australian textbooks (although with the notable exception of *Meagher, Gummow and Lehane*), with several also endorsing the view that damages would be available under Lord Cairns' Act.[52]

II. Older Cases

In any event, is the argument put forward by the authors of *Meagher, Gummow and Lehane*, that distress was historically 'foreign' to equity's concerns, historically accurate? Or is a more obvious explanation a practical one, namely, that courts did not turn their minds to the question of compensation for distress in privacy cases until recently, because an injunction could be and was granted to avoid or alleviate the prospect of such harms arising? In our view, there is much to commend the latter interpretation.

Consider, for instance, the three leading 'privacy' cases of the nineteenth century – *Gee v Pritchard*,[53] *Prince Albert v Strange*[54] and *Pollard v Photographic*

[49] ibid, especially discussion of Mitchell J, [67]–[85].

[50] ibid [85] *per* Mitchell J.

[51] ibid [76] *per* Mitchell J.

[52] See, eg, ICF Spry, *The Principles of Equitable Remedies*, 9th edn (Sydney, Lawbook Co, 2014) 647 ('[c]ourts of equity have always had it within their jurisdiction or power to award damages') and 658 ('the question in any particular circumstances is simply whether "the best justice of which the case is capable will be done by giving damages"', here talking about the Lord Cairns' Act); GR Dal Pont, *Equity and Trusts in Australia*, 6th edn (Sydney, Thomson Reuters, 2015) 220 ('[a]lthough the award of equitable damages for mental distress and embarrassment represents a distinctly non-traditional application of Lord Cairns' Act, the reasoning is compelling … To the extent that breaches of confidence align with unconscionable conduct … the award of damages here is not far removed from equity's recognised ability to award of compensation for emotional distress in cases of equitable estoppel … With it the law of confidentiality takes a step further from fiduciary law which retains an economic focus') and 222 (the same might be done by way of equitable compensation as indeed was held in *Giller v Procopets*). See also Barnett and Bryan (n 36) 165 (compensation preferable).

[53] *Gee v Pritchard* (1818) 2 Swans 403.

[54] *Prince Albert v Strange* (1849) 1 H & Tw 1.

Company[55] – all discussed in Samuel Warren and Louis Brandeis's seminal article on 'The Right to Privacy' in the (1890) *Harvard Law Review.*[56] Indeed, they are still commonly cited today.[57] The central question the courts had to resolve in these cases was the extent to which existing doctrines of a common law property right in unpublished works and equitable breach of confidence could be drawn on and refashioned to accommodate contemporary problems of invasions of privacy involving, respectively, unwanted publications of personal correspondence, 'surreptitiously and improperly obtained' family etchings and a photographic portrait.[58] A significant concern in granting a remedy was avoidance or alleviation of 'wound[ed] feelings', as Lord Eldon put it in *Gee v Pritchard.*[59] Because notice was given of the defendants' publications in these cases (in the first with an announcement published in the *Morning Post*, in the second with advance copies of the defendant's catalogue sent to the plaintiff, and in the third with the plaintiff's noticing that the defendant had begun exhibiting her photograph in his shop window), the plaintiffs were able to obtain injunctions to stop the publications.[60]

[55] *Pollard v Photographic Company* (1888) 40 ChD 345.

[56] SD Warren and LD Brandeis, 'The Right to Privacy' (1890) 4 *Harvard Law Review* 193.

[57] Especially the leading case of *Prince Albert v Strange*: see, eg, *Douglas v Hello! Ltd* (n 14) 998, [116] *per* Sedley LJ (noting, inter alia, *Prince Albert v Strange*); *Campbell* (n14) 471, [43] *per* Lord Hoffmann (*Prince Albert v Strange* a 'seminal' case).

[58] See M Richardson, *The Right to Privacy: Origins and Influence of a Nineteenth-Century Idea* (Cambridge, Cambridge UP, 2017), for discussion of the broader social context of these cases.

[59] *Gee v Pritchard* (n 54) 422, 426 *per* Lord Eldon. In *Prince Albert v Strange* 2 de G & Sm 652, the Solicitor-General John Romilly argued before Knight Bruce VC that 'the result of destroying privacy may be to inflict pain upon the feelings of the individual, or, as in the present case, to increase the honour and affection in which he is held', adding, however, that this was 'altogether immaterial to the question at issue' of the propriety of privacy's protection: ibid, 677–78. Nevertheless, there would arguably be some mental anguish suffered by the plaintiff and his wife if the defendant's exhibition of their family etchings was allowed to proceed without their authority, and likewise if the catalogue that was still at issue in the case was allowed to be published without their authority. As to *Pollard v Photographic Company*, as North J put it, 'a lady's feelings are shocked by finding that the photographer she has employed to take her likeness for her own use is publicly exhibiting and selling copies thereof': *Pollard* (n 55) 352.

[60] In the lead-up to *Gee v Pritchard*, an advertisement published in the *Morning Post* of Friday, 10 July 1818 heralded the forthcoming publication of Pritchard's Memoir, with its 'interesting correspondence', as 'in the press and speedily [to] be published'. Proceedings were launched on 17 July 1818, a preliminary injunction was awarded and, on the motion of the defendant to dissolve the injunction, judgment for the plaintiff was given on 28 July. Advance notice was also given leading to the proceedings in *Prince Albert v Strange*. According to Strange's answer to the plaintiff's Bill, recorded in the report of the trial (2 de G & Sm 652), 'on the 9th day of October 1848, the [second] Defendant, Jasper Tomsett Judge, with a view of bringing the subject of the exhibition to the notice of the Plaintiffs Consort and the Plaintiff, and of ascertaining whether the exhibition would be objected to by the Plaintiff's Consort and the Plaintiff, sent copies of the catalogue to the Plaintiff's Consort and the Plaintiff, and to various other persons mentioned, who were connected by family and service with the Plaintiff and his Consort, and that all such copies were sent under cover in the usual way': ibid, 662. The package arrived on 11 October, according to the plaintiff: ibid, 655. A preliminary injunction was applied for on 20 October 1848 and was granted; then on application by the defendant Strange to dissolve it was confirmed by Knight Bruce VC on 12 January 1849, and upheld by Lord Cottenham LC on appeal on 8 February 1849. In the case of *Pollard v Photographic Company*, proceedings were launched in November, after the plaintiffs became aware of the defendant's display of a Christmas Card featuring her photograph in his shop window. Judgment was handed down awarding the injunction sought on 21 December.

And the courts went out of their way to award the injunction requested at relatively short notice, with Lord Cottenham LC noting in *Prince Albert v Strange* that where privacy is 'the right invaded', postponing of the injunction 'would be equivalent to denying it'.[61] Nevertheless, there is no suggestion in these cases that had the injunction been denied, or had publication already occurred, another remedy might not have been found to alleviate or assuage the plaintiffs' mental harm resulting from publication.

The traditional cases just noted provide the backdrop for the more recent privacy–breach of confidence cases, such as *Campbell*[62] in the UK and *Giller*[63] in Australia. In the more recent cases, the nineteenth-century cases continue to be cited along with decisions of the twentieth century, such as the marriage secrets case of *Argyll v Argyll*,[64] the personal identity case of *G v Day*[65] and the telephone surveillance case of *Francome v Mirror Group Newspapers Ltd*,[66] to demonstrate the flexibility of the breach of confidence doctrine and that it is an apposite way to deal with invasions of privacy. The twentieth-century cases were also cases where injunctions were sought and granted. For at this stage still, plaintiffs were in a position to become aware of the impending publication before the fact, and so an injunction could be obtained to avoid an anticipated breach, sometimes at very short notice.[67] It is only when we come to the post-Human Right Act cases in the UK that we see more than passing attention paid to the question of damages for distress, following a change to the prior practices of giving notice of an impending publication, so that significant damage may already have been suffered by the time the case came to court.[68] By this time, the English courts, to the extent

[61] *Prince Albert v Strange* (n 55) 26 *per* Lord Cottenham.

[62] *Campbell* (n 14).

[63] *Giller v Procopets* (n 4).

[64] *Duchess of Argyll v Duke of Argyll* [1967] Ch 302.

[65] *G v Day* (1982) 1 NSWLR 24, concerning protection of the plaintiff's identity as an informant. Note also *Foster v Mountford and Rigby Ltd* (1976) 14 ALR 71 – a rare example of a claim for cultural privacy brought on behalf of a community (namely the Pitantjara community in the Northern Territory).

[66] *Francome v Mirror Group Newspapers Ltd* [1984] 1 WLR 892, distinguishing *Malone v Metropolitan Police Commissioner* [1979] Ch 344 where an injunction had been denied against surreptitious telephone tapping as a case where the police were acting under a lawful warrant (in contrast to the press in Francome's case).

[67] Indeed, in *G v Day* (n 65), despite the fact that the plaintiff's identity had been revealed on television, considered a fleeting transient revelation, the injunction was awarded against the defendant newspaper: and see, for the same approach taken to suspicions voiced about a plaintiff's identity (as a sports figure who had tested positive for drugs) on social media in a case where the claimed injunction was also awarded against the defendant newspaper, *Australian Football League v The Age* (2006) 15 VR 419.

[68] In fact, very late notice was given in both *Douglas* and *Campbell*: in *Douglas* it was given after the photographs were taken at the plaintiffs' wedding party on 18–19 November and then sold to the defendant *Hello!*, leading to an urgent application for an interlocutory injunction on 20 November, which was granted on 21 November but discharged on appeal on 21 December; in *Campbell*, notice of the impending story in the *Mirror* was given the day before publication, but it was not passed on to Naomi Campbell by her employees in time for her to apply for an injunction. But by the time of *Mosley* (n 10), the press practice was clearly one of not giving notice – a practice to which Mosley later objected, but without success, before the European Court of Human Rights: *Mosley v United Kingdom*

they considered the question of their jurisdiction to do so (and mostly they did not),[69] had the ready answer that '[u]nder Article 8 of the European Convention on Human Rights "everyone has the right to respect for his private and family life"' and 'it would be hollow protection of that right if in a particular case in breach of confidence without consent details of [the plaintiff's] private and family life were disclosed by the confidant to others and the only remedy that the law of England allowed was nominal damages', as Morland J put it in *Cornelius v de Taranto*.[70]

That answer was not available in *Giller* (where the damage had also been suffered by the time the case came to court),[71] as Australia was not a party to the European Convention nor bound by the Human Rights Act, with all that that entailed for domestic law. The right to privacy was identified as a human right in Article 17 of the International Covenant on Civil and Political Rights (ICCPR), a Covenant implemented in Victoria through the Victorian *Human Rights and Responsibilities Act 2006* (the Charter).[72] The Charter does not create legally enforceable rights and remedies between individuals, although it may be taken into account in developing the common law.[73] Because it could not rely directly on legislation equivalent to the Human Rights Act, in *Giller* the Court reverted to the question that was still in Australia 'at large',[74] *viz* the logical and policy arguments for awarding damages under Lord Cairns' Act, or alternatively equitable compensation, in a case where a claim for breach of confidence involved breach of an equitable right and the damage suffered was one of mental harm.

III. Arguments from Logic and Policy

So what are the arguments from logic and policy for allowing an award for mental harm caused by the unwanted publication of private information? In *Giller*, a number of reasons were identified for holding that damages under Lord Cairns' Act or equitable compensation should be available for breach of confidence where the plaintiff suffers distress or some other kind of mental harm. And these provide a useful starting point for the further discussion below.

[2011] 53 EHRR 30. In *Cornelius v de Taranto*, the plaintiff only discovered that her medical file had been shared when she was in hospital subsequently with pneumonia. In *Giller*, the plaintiff had no notice that the video would be circulated in the way it was, but once that occurred, it was placed in the hands of the police and the videotapes handed over (the reason an injunction was not sought).

[69] And recall here Lord Goff's passing comment in *Attorney-General v Guardian Newspapers*, that damages under 'a beneficent interpretation' of Lord Cairns' Act were 'now available': see n 16.

[70] *Cornelius v De Taranto* (n 39) [66] *per* Morland J.

[71] *Giller v Procopets* (n 4).

[72] See the *Charter of Human Rights and Responsibilities Act 2006* (Vic), s 13 (privacy and reputation).

[73] See M Rivette, 'Privacy as a Human Right' (2017) *Privacy Law Bulletin* 22, noting that Australian courts may nevertheless choose to reference the rights in the ICCPR (and the Charter in Victoria), and have occasionally done so: and see, eg, *Lenah* (n 20) 279, [190] *per* Kirby J at (citing the ICCPR as reflecting 'universal principles of fundamental rights' that may influence the common law on privacy).

[74] *Giller v Procopets* (n 4) 99, [419] *per* Neave JA.

First, the remedy for breach of a protected interest should be commensurate with the interest that the claim is designed to address – or, as Ashley JA put it in *Giller*, 'I think it should not be held that equity is incapable of moulding relief appropriate to the circumstances',[75] adding that it would also be 'anomalous' or 'odd' if it failed to do so.[76] Conversely, we might add here, lack of power to order compensation for breach of confidence would deprive the claim of any worth in cases where it was too late to award an injunction. To adapt the words of Morland J in *Cornelius v de Taranto*,[77] denial of a compensatory remedy would render hollow the equitable principles protecting confidential information. Or as Gummow and Hayne JJ explained in *Lenah*, 'the sensibilities, offence and injury [that an individual may suffer] provide [the] staple value for any developing law of privacy'.[78] Of course, this does not mean that there should be free rein in awarding damages, or equitable compensation for distress and the like.[79] Rather, in the particular circumstances in which a defendant's conduct violates a plaintiff's interest in, or right to, privacy, and if an action framed as breach of confidence also satisfies the parameters of that action, a remedy should be available. Thus, even if another Australian court in another State or Territory were not prepared to find that the local version of Lord Cairns' Act supported an award of damages for distress,[80] equitable compensation should be considered an appropriate remedy to develop for distress-type cases[81] – as indeed was held in *Wilson v Ferguson*.[82]

Second, equitable remedies should respond to current problems.[83] One current set of problems obviously is the increase in the number of privacy cases compared to in the fairly recent past – indeed, Ashley JA noted in *Giller* that 'there has been a veritable explosion in causes of action of that kind' in recent years.[84] As a result of this 'explosion', the prospects of a privacy case involving something that has already been published are significantly greater than in a time where the pool of privacy cases was relatively small. Further, changes in technologies and social

[75] ibid 32, [146] *per* Ashley JA.

[76] ibid [150]–[151]. Cf Mitchell J in *Wilson v Ferguson* (n 48) [82] (referencing the 'cardinal principle of equity that the remedy must be fashioned to fit the nature of the case and the particular facts', citing *Warman International Ltd v Dyer* (1995) 182 CLR 544, 559).

[77] *Cornelius v De Taranto* (n 39) [60]–[67], [69] *per* Morland J.

[78] See n 28.

[79] That is, accepting the argument of *Meagher, Gummow and Lehane's Equity: Doctrines and Remedies* that 'damages for distress are available very narrowly in [common law fields of tort and contract]' and '[i]t is an accepted principle in Australian law that the validity of proposed judicial extensions of the law of compensatory remedies depends on the coherence of the proposal with existing rules and principles of the legal system': Heydon, Leeming and Turner (n 5) 882, [24-085].

[80] The Australian Law Reform Commission has noted this possibility (especially in States or Territories whose provisions vary from that in Victoria, more explicitly referencing a 'wrong'): see ALRC Report 123 (n 6) 268, fn 20.

[81] See Barnett and Bryan (n 36) 165 (taking the view that, regardless of the wording of the Lord Cairns' Act provision, this would be preferable), and further texts noted in n 53.

[82] See *Wilson v Ferguson* (n 48).

[83] See *Giller v Procopets* (n 4) 32, [146] *per* Ashley J.

[84] ibid (this is the particular example that Ashley JA gives in *Giller v Procopets*).

practices have meant that privacy invasions can be both deeply invasive and widely disseminated, as in the Australian revenge-porn cases of *Giller* and *Wilson* (the latter especially showing how the Internet and social media can exacerbate the situation).[85] And, as explained earlier in this chapter, changes in practices around notice have put new pressures on remedies. While in the older cases plaintiffs were notified of potential breaches of privacy in time to seek injunctions, prior notification is becoming increasingly rare. And the rise of individual defendants who control publication, for instance through their use of social media, makes notice even less likely. These changes make it desirable to provide compensation for plaintiffs whose privacy has already been breached by the misuse of the private information in question.

Third, although it may be argued that compensation should not be payable because of the difficulties in assessing quantum, we note that damages for distress and mental upset are available, inter alia, in actions for defamation, copyright infringement, certain cases of breach of contract (where the contract is specifically for a pleasurable experience) and false imprisonment as a species of trespass to the person.[86] Further, English and Australian courts have already shown themselves able to make awards for mental harm in privacy cases, including breach of confidence cases. Principles to govern such awards can be developed in future cases.[87] Ideally, such principles should look across the whole experience of assessing damages for mental harm, whether the cause of action takes the form of a common law claim or an equitable claim – in other words, the approach adopted to the assessment of damages or compensation in these cases should be focused on the nature and extent of the harm rather than the formalities of the claim.

Fourth, awarding compensation for mental harm would help to remove the stigma associated with this harm, sometimes characterised as 'mere distress', without acknowledgement of the depth and range of emotions that may be involved or their significance for the individual concerned. We may recall here, for instance, the finding of Gillard J in *Giller* at first instance that the plaintiff was left feeling 'extremely angry, annoyed, upset, concerned, anxious, distressed, humiliated and embarrassed by what the defendant did'.[88] Similarly, as found by Mitchell J in *Wilson v Ferguson*, the plaintiff suffered 'significant embarrassment, anxiety and distress' as a result of the defendant's posting of her intimate photographs and films on his Facebook page.[89] The fact that injury to feelings may be

[85] A point especially noted by Mitchell J in *Wilson v Ferguson* (n 48) [79] and [80] (pointing to technological advances with the advent of the Internet, social media platforms and portable devices, as well as evolving social practices of sharing intimate communications and images).

[86] See, eg, cases noted in n 2.

[87] In fact fairly consistent awards have been made in the Australian cases, with $40,000 awarded in *Giller v Procopets*, $35,000 in *Wilson v Ferguson*, and $25,000 in *Doe v ABC*, all cases of serious privacy breaches.

[88] See n 33. Cf Hampel J in *Doe v ABC* (n 42), characterising the plaintiff's harm as 'hurt, distress, embarrassment, humiliation, shame and guilt' after her public identification as a rape victim.

[89] See n 50.

harmful and debilitating and may affect the whole of a person's later life is one that the Victorians were prepared to recognise in fashioning breach of confidence as a doctrine to avoid or minimise the prospects of this occurring, and finding ways to grant an injunction at very short notice – and, as Maxwell P pointed out in *Giller*, surely, with our greater knowledge of the harmful effect of a prolonged negative emotional state on human health and welfare, the social value of a remedy in the absence of strong countervailing arguments on the other side should now be recognised?[90]

Fifth, adaptability has been a hallmark of breach of confidence, and thus applying the same approach to its treatment of remedies should not be seen as anomalous but rather as a logical continuation. As discussed in this chapter, the doctrine of breach of confidence has been refashioned to accommodate privacy concerns from the nineteenth century onwards – including in cases where the information published was not imparted in a confidential relationship, as in *Wilson*, where some of the information was surreptitiously obtained (and in *Campbell*, where the surreptitious obtaining occurred on a public street). Similarly, we have pointed to important statements in Australian cases of high authority supporting the extension of the duty of confidence to accommodate privacy interests, as, for instance, with Gleeson CJ's comment in *Australian Broadcasting Corporation v Lenah Game Meats Pty Ltd*[91] that '[i]f the activities filmed were private, then the law of breach of confidence is adequate to cover the case'.[92] In light of these flexibilities found at the doctrinal level, the flexibilities identified with respect to remedies in *Giller* and *Wilson* (as well as numerous English cases) seem quite consistent. That is not to say that breach of confidence will always be sufficient to protect privacy interests in Australian cases, or that remedies could not be improved with a different legal approach. There may still be good reasons found for an Australian court to recognise a privacy tort (or torts) in a future case, as flagged, for instance, by Gummow and Hayne JJ in *Lenah*,[93] or for an Australian legislature to take the step of enacting a statutory tort (or torts), as recommended by various law reform commissions.[94] For instance, as intimated in the English *PJS* case, a tort might be thought a better way to deal with a situation, where a plaintiff's private information has been so widely published that it is hard to argue the information is still confidential but the defendant's publication would nevertheless amount to an 'intrusion' on privacy – or where a court wishes to award exemplary damages to take into account the egregious character of the defendant's conduct.[95] Or it may finally be that an Australian

[90] *Giller v Procopets* (n 4) [31] (making the point in the context of an argument that the tort of intentional infliction of emotional distress should be given a wider application, but it is equally applicable in characterising the mental harm associated with breach of confidence).

[91] *Lenah* (n 20).

[92] See n 21.

[93] See n 26.

[94] See, eg, ALRC Report 123 (n 6).

[95] See n 10 and further n 12.

court or legislature takes the view that Lord Nicholls took in *Campbell*,[96] namely, that it seems 'unnatural' to force a complaint about invasion of privacy, with all its dignitarian and liberal trappings,[97] into a doctrine that is framed in the language of breach of confidence. Even so, it seems a feeble argument to accept that the doctrine of breach of confidence is sufficiently flexible to deal with modern cases of invasion of privacy in doctrinal terms but its remedies are locked in some imagined restrictive past.

IV. Conclusion

We have argued in this chapter that English and Australian courts have appropriately awarded damages or compensation for mental harm in invasion of privacy cases, whether the law is couched in terms of a privacy tort (as in the UK) or continues to be framed in terms of equitable breach of confidence (as is currently the case in Australia). Along the way, we have suggested that mental harm is a natural and obvious consequence of an invasion of privacy, and that this provided a basis both for some significant doctrinal development over the last two centuries and for a range of remedies recognised to date – including not only damages or compensation for distress or other mental harm, but also the award of an injunction, which may sometimes be granted at very short notice with the express desire of alleviating or minimising the prospect of an invasion of privacy. In short, we have argued that, given the close nexus between a person's loss of privacy and the mental harm that a person may suffer as a result, to say the harm cannot be remedied under a cause of action concerned with privacy is not only illogical, it strikes at the heart of the idea that law (including here equity) should render justice in a case, one of the most fundamental aspirations of the law.

As a final word, we note that we are not necessarily arguing that mental harm is the *most* natural and obvious harm that will flow from an invasion of privacy. Rather, we are inclined to think that harm to privacy (and more generally to liberty/dignity) is the harm that most naturally follows from an invasion of privacy, whether the action is framed in terms of a privacy tort or breach of confidence, with other injuries such as distress consequential on that. Thus the situation may be comparable to defamation or copyright infringement, where the

[96] See n 18.

[97] See, eg, *Douglas v Hello! Ltd* (n 16) 1001, [125] *per* Sedley LJ ('privacy' a 'legal principle … drawn from the fundamental value of personal autonomy'); *Campbell* (n 15) 473, [51] *per* Lord Hoffmann (the cause of action now focuses on 'the protection of human autonomy and dignity – the right to control the dissemination of information about one's private life and the right to the esteem and respect of other people'); *Lenah* (n 20) 226, [43] *per* Gleeson CJ ('the foundation of much of what is protected, where rights of privacy, as distinct from rights of property, are acknowledged, is human dignity'), 256, [125] *per* Gummow and Hayne JJ ('a concern for privacy "as a legal principle drawn from the fundamental value of personal autonomy"', citing Sedley LJ in *Douglas v Hello!*); and see further generally for these values recognised historically, Richardson (n 59).

primary harm is loss of reputation or appropriation of property, with mental harm treated as a form of consequential loss (and where liberty/dignity may also be in play).[98] This possibility may be easy to overlook for the simple reason that harm to privacy is difficult to value, and so typically there may be no damages award for invasion of privacy per se, unlike in defamation and copyright cases where damages awards may be based on the cost of retrieving a reputation (in the case of defamation) or hypothesising a market transaction under which the property is sold or licensed (in the case of copyright infringement – and similarly, it may be added, in the case of misuse of commercial secrets, another head of breach of confidence).[99] Recognising that an award may be made for loss of privacy or, as sometimes said, in vindication of the right to privacy,[100] may be a better way to explain why damages or compensation may be appropriate where plaintiffs seem to suffer relatively little mental harm – for instance because they are unaware of a breach until significantly later, or have difficulty comprehending how their lives will be affected.[101] Perhaps such awards should be more generally applied.[102] Then damages or compensation for mental harm can be more clearly distinguished from a remedy that is sometimes treated as a catchall remedy,[103] forming a particular response to a particular kind of harm that is increasingly coming to be recognised as important in its own right.

[98] See, eg, the defamation and copyright cases noted at n 2.

[99] See *Seager v Copydex Ltd (No 2)* [1969] 2 All ER 718; and cf *Talbot v Television Corporation Ltd (No 2)* [1980] VR 242, where in the absence of a clear market, Marks J considered a number of factors in assessing the 'depreciation' in the value of the plaintiff's right suffered as a result of the breach of confidence (including the plaintiff's lost opportunity to exploit his idea for a television programme on a commercial basis).

[100] See JNE Varuhas, *Damages and Human Rights* (Oxford, Oxford UP, 2016); and further Jason NE Varuhas, 'Varieties of Damages for Breach of Privacy', in ch 3 of this book.

[101] As, for instance, the damages awarded by Mann J for 'loss of privacy' to various plaintiffs who had been unaware of the defendants' phone hacking until later but nevertheless had been impeded in their ability to reveal the information (or not) on their own terms, in *Gulati v MGN Ltd* [2015] EWHC 1482, affirmed [2017] QB 149. Note that in *Gulati*, the Court of Appeal was careful to say that it was not awarding a purely vindicatory remedy, such remedies being ruled out for private claims by the Supreme Court in *R (WL (Congo)) v Secretary of State for the Home Department* [2012] 1 AC 245.

[102] For instance, consider cases of false imprisonment where, as Powell JA put it in *McDonald v Coles Myers Ltd* (n 2) 62,690, damages may be awarded taking into account 'the injury to liberty, the injury to the plaintiff's feelings, ie the indignity, mental suffering, disgrace and humiliation, with any attendant loss of social status, and where it can be demonstrated that the imprisonment has had a deleterious effect on the plaintiff's health, any resultant physical injury, illness or discomfort', but in practice these elements may not be clearly distinguished in the actual award made, as indeed in that case.

[103] As, for instance, Mann J suggests in *Gulati v MGN* with respect to the award in *Cornelius v De Taranto* (n 38) – noting that 'I accept that in most cases of that kind, and indeed in most cases of invasion of privacy involving a publication which becomes known to the claimant, the focus will be on feelings, and other factors are likely to be swept up into the damages in an unbroken-down sort of way': n 101 [121].

8

Gain-Based Relief for Breach of Privacy

KATY BARNETT*

I. Introduction

The call for an account of profits or other gain-based relief for breach of privacy is not new.[1] Nonetheless, gain-based relief has only rarely been awarded for breach of confidence,[2] and has never been awarded for breach of privacy, although it has recently been acknowledged as a possibility by the English Supreme Court in *PJS v News Group Newspapers Ltd*.[3] It is vastly more common for a claimant to seek an injunction restraining further breaches. As Lord Mance observed in *PJS*, while a defamatory statement can be undone when the defendant acknowledges it to be false, a breach of privacy cannot be undone, and hence injunctive relief preventing the breach in the first place is preferred.[4] However, in cases where the breach of privacy has already occurred, gain-based relief may have more traction.

As the Australian Law Reform Commission has noted, there are two forms of breach of privacy that are potentially deserving of relief: misuse of private information and intrusion into seclusion. If courts choose to award gain-based relief, it will mostly likely occur in media cases: when a formerly intimate friend or partner disseminates private information to the media,[5] or when a member of the press intrudes upon an individual's privacy and disseminates the information (photographs, recordings etc) so obtained.[6] A claimant may sue both the friend

* Thank you to Jason Varuhas and Megan Richardson for very helpful comments on earlier versions of this paper.

[1] See, eg, N Witzleb, 'Justifying Gain-Based Remedies for Invasions of Privacy' (2009) 29 *OJLS* 325; S Harder, 'Gain-Based Relief for Invasion of Privacy' (2011) 1 *DICTUM–Victoria Law School Journal* 63.

[2] *Attorney-General v Observer Ltd* [1990] 1 AC 109, 262 (Lord Keith), 292 (Lord Goff).

[3] *PJS v News Group Newspapers Ltd* [2016] AC 1061, [2016] UKSC 26, [42] (Lord Mance, with whom Lord Neuberger, Baroness Hale and Lord Reed agreed).

[4] ibid [41]. Interestingly in that case, while an injunction was granted, the celebrities in question were repeatedly identified in jurisdictions not covered by the injunction, including Scotland and Australia.

[5] eg, *Duchess of Argyll v Duke of Argyll* [1967] 1 Ch 302; *McKennitt v Ash* [2006] EWCA Civ 778, [2008] QB 73; *Mosley v News Group Newspapers Ltd* [2008] EWHC 1777, [2008] EMLR 679.

[6] *Francome v Mirror Group Newspapers Ltd* [1984] 2 All ER 408; *Campbell v MGN Ltd* [2004] UKHL 22, [2004] 2 AC 457; *Hosking v Runting* [2004] NZCA 34, [2005] 1 NZLR 1; *Douglas v Hello! Ltd*

or partner and the media outlet for gain-based relief where there has been misuse of private information. By contrast, a claimant may simply sue the media outlet for gain-based relief in a case of intrusion upon seclusion. Gain-based relief may also be sought in a classic breach of confidence case where there is exploitation of private information more generally.

In this chapter, I focus on English and Australian law, and explore why gain-based relief is uncommon for breach of privacy. The difficulties facing courts are numerous. First, there are arguably two possible measures of gain-based relief: the reasonable fee and the account of profits. In relation to the latter, the account of profits is a personal remedy, but the proprietary constructive trust can also sometimes be used to achieve a similar result. Second, there is uncertainty about the nature of the cause of action, particularly in Australia. The availability of specific kinds of gain-based relief has generally been predicated on the historical origin of the particular cause of action.[7] Unfortunately, the categorisation of breach of privacy is uncertain, and it has been seen both as a tort and as a species of equitable breach of confidence. This has ramifications for the availability of remedies, particularly in Australia. The equitable remedy of account of profits is more likely to be awarded for equitable causes of action, and only exceptionally for common law causes of action, if at all. By contrast, reasonable fee awards are more likely to be available for certain torts. Thirdly, accounts of profits are generally unwieldy and difficult to calculate, and courts find it difficult to apportion profits to the breach.

I suggest that the remedies available for breach of privacy should be uncoupled from the debates about historical origin. In Tugendhat J's vivid words in the *Vidal-Hall v Google Inc* first-instance decision, 'history does not determine identity. The fact that dogs evolved from wolves does not mean that dogs are wolves.'[8] Instead the focus should be upon the normative basis of the cause of action (whether it is conceived of as equitable or tortious, or as a mixture of both), as this will determine what remedies should be available. It will be suggested that accounts of profit *should* be available for breach of privacy, but only exceptionally, where compensatory damages are inadequate, an injunction is unavailable, the defendant's breach was advertent and the defendant made a profit. Given this, it may be queried why gain-based relief has not been awarded more often. One reason is that in cases where the court would have been likely to award gain-based relief if asked to do so, the defendant had not profited.[9] But another reason relates to the difficulties of calculation mentioned above, which should be dealt with by reversing the burden of proof, and requiring the defendant to show that any net profit was *not* attributable to the breach.

(No 3) [2005] EWCA Civ 595, [2006] QB 125; *Murray v Big Pictures (UK) Ltd* [2008] EWCA Civ 446, [2009] Ch 481.

[7] See B McDonald and D Rolph, 'Remedial Consequences of Classification of a Privacy Action: Dog or Wolf? Tort or Equity?', in ch 10 of this book.

[8] *Vidal-Hall v Google Inc* [2014] 1 WLR 4155, [2014] EWHC 13, [57] (QB).

[9] See, eg, *Giller v Procopets* [2008] VSCA 236, (2008) 24 VR 1; *Wilson v Ferguson* [2015] WASC 15.

By contrast, it will be argued that reasonable fee awards should not be made, and nor should Lord Cairns' Act be used (even in a beneficent interpretation) to enable gain-based awards.

II. Shackles of History: Tort or Equitable Cause of Action?

Breach of privacy in Anglo-Australian law is in some ways a *sui generis* action, although its origins are found in equitable breach of confidence. Recently, in England and Wales at least, it has been held to be tortious, despite its beginnings. Consequently, there is radical uncertainty as to whether breach of privacy should be treated as a species of breach of confidence or as a tort. There is also an overlap with contract, as some obligations of privacy are based in contract,[10] although this area is generally less problematic and will be set aside for present purposes.

The historical origins of breach of privacy matter, because if breach of privacy develops as a tort, it may be more difficult to obtain an account of profits. Historically, accounts of profits have not been available for common law torts, apart from passing off[11] and rare cases of trespass.[12] However, if privacy protection develops through breach of confidence law, it may be easier to claim an account of profits, because historically, accounts of profits have generally been available for equitable causes of action. Despite this, accounts of profits are not always available as of right for breach of confidence in England and Wales,[13] and the availability of reasonable fee awards for breach of confidence is also unclear.[14]

It is necessary to outline how breach of confidence and breach of privacy became entangled in Anglo-Australian law. It was not inevitable that the two would develop together: in the United States, breach of privacy developed as a tort through the influence of Brandeis and Warren's seminal article, although breach of confidence was an important inspiration for those authors.[15]

Breach of confidence law was used to prevent dissemination of private information from the nineteenth century onwards.[16] In *Prince Albert v Strange*,[17]

[10] See, eg, *HRH Prince of Wales v Associated Newspapers Ltd* [2006] EWCA Civ 1776, [2008] Ch 57.

[11] *My Kinda Town Ltd v Soll* [1983] RPC 15.

[12] *Philips v Homfray* (1871) LR 6 Ch App 770, (1883) 24 Ch D 439, [1892] 1 Ch 465. See JD Heydon, MJ Leeming and PG Turner, *Meagher, Gummow and Lehane's Equity: Doctrines and Remedies*, 5th edn (Sydney, LexisNexis, 2015) [26-050].

[13] *Vercoe v Rutland Fund Management Pty Ltd* [2010] EWHC 424 (Ch), [2010] Bus LR 141.

[14] *Seager v Copydex* [1967] 1 WLR 923, *Seager v Copydex (No 2)* [1969] 1 WLR 809 and *Vercoe* (n 13) all suggest reasonable fee awards are available for breach of confidence. The *Seager* cases are criticised in Heydon, Leeming and Turner (n 12) [2–235], [42–190].

[15] S Warren and LD Brandeis, 'The Right to Privacy' (1890) 4 *Harvard Law Review* 193. See also W Prosser, 'Privacy' (1960) 48 *California Law Review* 383.

[16] M Richardson, M Bryan, M Vranken and K Barnett, *Breach of Confidence: Social Origins and Modern Developments* (Cheltenham, Edward Elgar, 2012) 123–30.

[17] *Prince Albert v Strange* (1849) 1 H & Tw 1; 47 ER 1302.

a mid-nineteenth-century case involving etchings of Queen Victoria and her consort, an injunction was issued to restrain a breach of confidence out of a concern to protect, amongst other things, Prince Albert's privacy.[18] Subsequently, in *Argyll v Argyll*,[19] the Duchess of Argyll was able to restrain her former husband from publishing scandalous details about the breakdown of their marriage in a newspaper. Ungoed-Thomas J said that the confidential nature of the marital relationship 'is of its very essence and so obviously and necessarily implicit in it that there is no need for it to be expressed'.[20] Nonetheless, the case law on breach of confidence was contradictory, and did not clearly indicate a right to privacy.[21]

In England and Wales, a 'partial law of privacy'[22] has developed via a peculiar melding of breach of confidence and the European Convention on Human Rights.[23] Article 8 of the Convention, which enshrines the right to respect for private and family life, the home and correspondence, was used as a vehicle to introduce privacy concerns into breach of confidence. The seminal case, *Campbell v MGN Ltd*, arose when a newspaper published photos of a model attending a drug rehabilitation clinic.[24] She had previously denied having a drug problem. The court held that breach of confidentiality covered infringement of an individual's right to privacy and considered that the future development of the law should be informed by Article 8, such that it would be a breach of confidentiality when the person publishing the information knew or ought to know that the other person could reasonably expect the information to be kept confidential because of its private nature.[25] However, the Article 8 rights had to be balanced against the right to freedom of expression in Article 10. In the event, a majority decided that the defendants had breached Ms Campbell's right to privacy.[26]

In Australia, the position is less clear. While the High Court has said in *Australian Broadcasting Corporation v Lenah Game Meats Pty Ltd*[27] that its prior decision in *Victoria Park Racing and Recreation Grounds Co Ltd v Taylor*[28] does not stand in the way of the development of a tort of privacy, no tort has arisen. There are signs in *Giller v Procopets*[29] and other cases[30] that Australian courts are

[18] (1849) 1 H & Tw 1, 23–24; 47 ER 1302, 1311.

[19] *Argyll v Argyll* (n 5).

[20] ibid 322.

[21] *Malone v Metropolitan Police Commissioner* [1979] Ch 344 and *Kaye v Robertson* [1991] FSR 62 suggested that there was not, while *Francome v Mirror Group Newspapers Ltd* (n 6) suggested there was.

[22] RG Toulson and CM Phipps, *Confidentiality*, 3rd edn (London, Sweet & Maxwell, 2012) 161.

[23] The Human Rights Act 1988 (UK) gives effect in domestic law to the Convention for the Protection of Human Rights and Fundamental Freedoms 1950 (the European Convention on Human Rights).

[24] *Campbell* (n 6).

[25] ibid [20]–[21] (Lord Nicholls); [85] (Lord Hope); [134] (Baroness Hale).

[26] Lord Hope, Baroness Hale and Lord Carswell in the majority, Lord Nicholls and Lord Hoffmann in dissent.

[27] *Australian Broadcasting Corporation v Lenah Game Meats Pty Ltd* [2001] HCA 63, (2001) 208 CLR 199, [105]–[111] (Gummow and Hayne JJ, with whom Gaudron J agreed), [313]–[320] (Callinan J).

[28] *Victoria Park Racing and Recreation Grounds Co Ltd v Taylor* (1937) 58 CLR 479.

[29] *Giller v Procopets* (n 9).

[30] *Grosse v Purvis* [2003] QDC 151; *Doe v Australian Broadcasting Corporation* [2007] VCC 281.

(like English courts) prepared to use breach of confidence as a vehicle to allow remedies for breach of privacy.[31] However, there remains significant doubt and confusion about the status of the cause of action, with some courts finding that an action for breach of privacy is an open possibility,[32] but others finding that it is either nascent or non-existent.[33] Most Australian courts appear unwilling to develop a law of breach of privacy without legislative intervention.[34] This may be because Australian law does not have a Federal equivalent of the Human Rights Act,[35] and thus Australian courts cannot readily draw on English authorities such as *Campbell* and *Douglas v Hello! Ltd (No 3)*. It has nonetheless been argued that breach of confidence alone allows for the development of breach of privacy, even absent the Human Rights Act, because of its consistent protection of privacy.[36] The 2014 Australian Law Reform Commission Report on Privacy also suggested that a statutory tort of breach of privacy should be enacted in Australia to deal with both misuse of private information and intrusion upon privacy.[37] However, no legislation has yet been passed.

The English courts have been prepared to use breach of confidence to give redress against news outlets for publishing details about celebrities which constitute a breach of privacy.[38] In *Douglas v Hello! Ltd*, Lord Nicholls summarised the development of English law as follows:

> As the law has developed, breach of confidence, or misuse of confidential information, now covers two distinct causes of action, protecting two different interests: privacy and secret ('confidential') information. It is important to keep the two distinct. In some instances information may qualify for protection both on grounds of privacy and confidentiality. In other instances, information may be in the public domain, and not qualify for protection as confidential, and yet qualify for protection on the grounds of privacy. Privacy can be invaded by further publication of information or

[31] See M Richardson, 'Towards Legal Pragmatism: Breach of Confidence and the Right to Privacy' in E Bant and M Harding (eds), *Exploring Private Law* (Cambridge, Cambridge UP, 2010) 109. Cf M Tilbury, 'Privacy and Private law: Developing the Common Law of Australia' in E Bant and M Harding (eds), *Exploring Private Law* (Cambridge, Cambridge UP, 2010) 86.

[32] *Maynes v Casey* [2011] NSWCA 156, [35] (Basten J); *Saad v Chubb Security Australia Pty Ltd* [2012] NSWSC 1183, [183] (Hall J); *Gee v Burger* [2009] NSWSC 149, [53] (McLaughlin AsJ); *Dye v Commonwealth* [2010] FCA 720, [290] (Katzmann J); *Doe v Yahoo!7 Pty Ltd* [2013] QDC 181, [310]–[311] (Smith DCJ).

[33] *Kalaba v Commonwealth of Australia* [2004] FCA 763, [6] (Heerey J); *Chan v Sellwood; Chan v Calvert* [2009] NSWSC 1335, [34] (Davis J); *Sands v State of South Australia* [2013] SASC 44, [35] (Kelly J).

[34] P Bartlett, 'Privacy Down Under' (2010) 3(1) *Journal of International Media and Entertainment Law* 145, 162–63; Harder (n 1) 64.

[35] Although Victoria and the Australian Capital Territory have Charters of Human Rights: see *Charter of Human Rights and Responsibilities Act 2006* (Vic) and *Human Rights Act 2004* (ACT).

[36] *Giller v Procopets* (n 9); Richardson (n 31).

[37] Australian Law Reform Commission (ALRC), *Serious Invasions of Privacy in the Digital Era*, Report No 123 (2014), ch 1. See also New South Wales Law Reform Commission (NSWLRC), *Invasion of Privacy*, Report No 108 (2009) [4.14], [4.16].

[38] *Campbell* (n 6); *Douglas v Hello! Ltd (No 3)* (n 6); *McKennitt v Ash* (n 5); *Mosley v News Group Newspapers Ltd* (n 5); *Murray v Big Pictures (UK) Ltd* (n 6).

> photographs already disclosed to the public. Conversely, and obviously, a trade secret may be protected as confidential information even though no question of personal privacy is involved.[39]

In England, it is still unclear whether the cause of action is a tort[40] or remains grounded in its equitable origins,[41] although the English Court of Appeal in *Vidal-Hall* has recently held that the balance has tipped in favour of misuse of private information as tort.[42] Nonetheless, as Jason Varuhas has noted in his chapter in this collection, the label 'tort' covers a great many forms of wrongdoing, and important questions remain as to the nature of breach of privacy even if it is conclusively labelled as a tort.[43] It appears that breach of confidence and the tort of breach of privacy are coterminous and sometimes overlapping,[44] although as Lord Mance noted in *PJS*, breach of privacy covers situations which breach of confidence does not, particularly where there is the dissemination of information that is no longer confidential.[45]

III. Two Different Gain-Based Measures

There are (arguably) two or three gain-based remedies for private law breaches. The primary contenders are the account of profits and the reasonable fee award. The availability of these two awards varies according to the historical origin of the cause of action. The account of profits is grounded in equity, whereas the reasonable fee award is grounded in common law. Thus, the categorisation of the cause of action is prima facie pivotal to the availability of gain-based relief, and the choice between which relief is possible. I shall also briefly canvass the possibility of a constructive trust when discussing the account of profits, as it also effects profit stripping.

Ultimately, however, I suggest that these remedies should be cut from their historical moorings and, instead, their award should depend upon a deeper inspection of the normative concerns at the heart of privacy law.

[39] *Douglas v Hello! Ltd* [2007] UKHL 21, [2008] 1 AC 1, [255]. See also *Vidal-Hall* [2015] EWCA Civ 311, [2016] QB 1003, [21].

[40] *Murray v Big Pictures (UK) Ltd* (n 6); *Lord Browne of Madingley v Associated Newspapers Ltd* [2007] EWCA Civ 295, [2008] QB 103, [22]; *McKennitt v Ash* (n 5) [8]; *Venables v Newsgroup Newspapers* [2001] Fam 430, 447 (Butler-Sloss P); *Campbell v MGN Ltd* [2002] EWCA Civ 1373, [2003] QB 633, [60], [69] (Lord Phillips MR); *Campbell* (n 6) [14] (Lord Nicholls); *Imerman v Tchenguiz* [2011] Fam 116, [65] (Lord Neuberger); *PJS* (n 3) [32].

[41] *Douglas v Hello! Ltd* [2003] EWHC 786 (Ch), [2003] 3 All ER 996, [193] (Lindsay J).

[42] *Vidal-Hall* (n 39) [51]. See also JNE Varuhas, 'Varieties of Damages for Breach of Privacy', in ch 3 in this book.

[43] Varuhas (n 42).

[44] See, eg, *Mosley v News Group Newspapers* [2008] EMLR 20 and *McKennitt v Ash* (n 5), both of which involved concurrent claims for breach of confidence and breach of privacy.

[45] *PJS* (n 3) [57]–[61] (Lord Mance).

A. Account of Profits – Availability in Practice

The account of profits is incontrovertibly gain-based.[46] It effects a disgorgement of net profits, and is primarily available in equity, although there is some availability through equity's auxiliary jurisdiction. Present authority suggests that an account of profits may be awarded for breach of privacy,[47] although no awards have been made in practice. It is also possible that a constructive trust may be awarded over confidential material obtained by a breach of privacy, and even the property created by use of the private material,[48] although a court may also choose to award an additional account of profits in respect of profits made by use of the material.[49]

The nature of the relationship between breach of confidence and privacy is important here. It is necessary to divert into the way in which accounts of profit are awarded for breach of confidence in England and Australia respectively, as this may be relevant if breach of privacy is conceived of as a species of breach of confidence. Because breach of confidence is an equitable cause of action, it has been suggested that claimants may elect between an account of profit and compensation.[50] However, English law appears to be changing on this point. In *Vercoe*,[51] which involved a concurrent breach of contract and breach of confidence, it was suggested that, following *Blake*,[52] accounts of profit should only be awarded exceptionally for breach of confidence. Sales J said that the cases that merited accounts of profits were those involving proprietary rights,[53] particularly non-commercial cases where the right would never have been sold, or where the right was exceptional and quasi-fiduciary, as in *Blake* itself. By contrast, Sales J suggested that if the right was one that would be sold in the market, it may be more appropriate to award a reasonable fee.[54] In England and Wales, breach of privacy appears to have diverged from breach of confidence in any case.

No awards have yet been made in practice for breach of privacy in England and Wales, although *Douglas v Hello! Ltd (No 3)* might have seemed at first blush to be a prime vehicle for an account of profits.[55] In that case, Hollywood celebrities Michael Douglas and Catherine Zeta-Jones were married in New York, and granted *OK!* magazine an exclusive licence to take photographs of the wedding.

[46] Although cf *WWF-World Wide Fund for Nature v World Wrestling Federation Entertainment Inc* [2007] EWCA Civ 286, [2008] 1 WLR 445, [73]–[75] (Chadwick LJ).

[47] *Douglas v Hello! Ltd (No 3)* (n 6) [249]; *PJS* (n 3) [42].

[48] [2001] HCA 63; (2001) 208 CLR 199, [103] (Gummow and Hayne JJ, with whom Gaudron J agreed), [311] (Callinan J).

[49] ibid [311] (Callinan J).

[50] *Peter Pan Manufacturing Corporation v Corsets Silhouette Ltd* [1964] 1 WLR 96, 106 (Pennycuick J); *Siddell v Vickers* [1892] RPC 152, 162 (Lindley LJ); *Attorney General v Observer Ltd* [1990] 1 AC 109, 262 (Lord Keith), 292 (Lord Goff).

[51] *Vercoe* (n 13) [341].

[52] *Attorney-General v Blake* [2001] 1 AC 268.

[53] He cites *Siddell v Vickers* [1892] RPC 152; *Blake* (n 52); and *Devenish Nutrition Ltd v Sanofi-Aventis SA* [2008] EWCA Civ 1086, [2009] Ch 390, [75], [155], cf [144].

[54] *Vercoe* (n 13) [340].

[55] *Douglas v Hello! Ltd (No 3)* (n 6).

A freelance photographer infiltrated the wedding and took unauthorised photos, which he sold to *Hello!* magazine. *Hello!* magazine published the unauthorised photos. *OK!* magazine then brought forward its own publication and incurred expenses as a result. The Douglases had not vetoed all media from taking photographs of their wedding, but they had not authorised *Hello!* magazine to do so. They were attempting to forestall media interest by controlling who was present at the wedding. It was said, 'If, however, *Hello!* had made a profit on the publication we would have had no hesitation in accepting that the Douglases would have been entitled to seek an account of that profit.'[56] In fact, *Hello!* magazine made a loss, because it failed to recoup the £125,000 it paid for the photos, and so an account of profits was not sought.[57] The claimants sought a notional licence fee, but this claim was rejected. This will be discussed further in section III.B.

The Australian position with regard to the availability of accounts of profit differs from the English position. Not only is the very existence of any cause of action uncertain, but the way in which the cause of action develops will have greater consequences because of the emphasis on the historical bases for remedies and causes of action in Australia. In particular, there is a strong tradition in New South Wales of paying attention to the historical origin of cause of action and remedy, such that any attempt to apply a remedy that has traditionally been awarded in equity to a common law claim is said to involve 'fusion fallacy'.[58] If breach of privacy develops as a tortious cause of action in Australia, it may be difficult to obtain accounts of profit for breach of privacy, because Australian courts tend not to award accounts of profit for tort.[59] Conversely, if breach of privacy develops as a species of breach of confidence in Australia, it is easier to argue that an account of profits should be available, because in Australian law, they are available for breach of confidence as of right.[60] As noted above, there is also the possibility (particularly in Australia) that a constructive trust may attach to information or property obtained in breach of privacy.[61] However, it is suggested that a constructive trust is unlikely to be awarded over any profits made using that property or information, unless there is a concurrent breach of fiduciary duty.[62] Instead, it is likely that if any profit-stripping award were made, it would be the personal remedy of an account of profits.[63]

Heydon, Leeming and Turner suggest that if there is a concurrent breach of a common law claim and breach of confidence in Australian law, an account of

[56] ibid [249].

[57] ibid [245].

[58] Heydon, Leeming and Turner (n 12) [2-140].

[59] *Hospitality Group Pty Ltd v Australian Rugby Union Ltd* [2001] FCA 1040, (2001) 110 FCR 157, [162] (Hill and Finkelstein JJ), cf [166]–[173] (Emmett J, dissenting).

[60] *Peter Pan Manufacturing v Corsets Silhouette* [1964] 1 WLR 96.

[61] *Lenah Game Meats Pty Ltd* (n 27) [103] (Gummow and Hayne JJ, with whom Gaudron J agreed), [311] (Callinan J).

[62] Heydon, Leeming and Turner (n 12) [42-200]; M Conaglen, 'Thinking about Proprietary Remedies for Breach of Confidence' [2008] *Intellectual Property Quarterly* 82. See, eg, *Snepp v United States* 444 US 507 (1980).

[63] *Lenah Game Meats Pty Ltd* (n 27) [311] (Callinan J).

profits should only be awarded if damages are inadequate because of the presence of the common law claim.[64] This in fact squares in part with the approach suggested by Sales J in *Vercoe*. *Vercoe* also suggests that if an account of profits is unavailable then a reasonable fee should be considered. It is unlikely that Australian courts would follow the latter line of authority because, first, the *Seager v Copydex* cases have not traditionally been accepted in Australian and, second, *Vercoe*'s reasoning depended heavily on *Attorney-General v Blake*,[65] and *Blake* has been rejected in Australia.[66]

There have been two Australian cases that arguably involved a breach of privacy shoehorned into breach of confidence, in which it is likely that the court would have awarded an account of profits if asked to do so.[67] However, the defendants in each case had made no profit, and breached privacy purely to gain revenge against a former lover, and so accounts of profit were not available. This highlights one of the drawbacks of an account of profits; an actual profit must be made for an account to be awarded. In such a case, exemplary damages might be more appropriate given the contumelious and distressing nature of the breaches involved, and the lack of profit-making intention.[68]

The other reason why courts have not awarded accounts of profits readily is because they have had difficulty with causation and remoteness and attributing profits to the breach. Aplin, Bently, Johnson and Malynicz have noted in the context of breach of confidence:

> The remedy of account has proven to be a most unsatisfactory and cumbersome one in practice. The cases are replete with references to the practical difficulties associated with the calculation of the defendant's wrongful profits, and the courts have often impressed on litigants the expedience of a compromise instead of following the procedure of the account through its maze of intricacies. This means that it is rare for a claimant to pursue an account of profits save where the defendant's profits are substantial and clearly evident.[69]

[64] Heydon, Leeming and Turner (n 12) [42-190]. Cf *Peter Pan Manufacturing v Corsets Silhouette* (n 60), in which an account of profits was awarded as of right despite a contractual and equitable aspect.

[65] *Blake* (n 52).

[66] *Hospitality Group Pty Ltd v Australian Rugby Union Ltd* [2001] FCA 1040, (2001) 110 FCR 157, [155]–[162] (Hill and Finkelstein JJ); *Town & Country Property Management Services Pty Ltd v Kaltoum* [2002] NSWSC 166, [85]; *Biscayne Partners Pty Ltd v Valance Corp Pty Ltd* [2003] NSWSC 874, [232]–[235]; *Dalecoast Pty Ltd v Guardian International Pty Ltd* [2003] WASCA 142, [103]–[107]; *Short v Crawley* [2005] NSWSC 928, [24]; *Testel Australia Pty Ltd v Krg Electrics Pty Ltd* [2013] SASC 91, [99]–[109]; *Hydrofibre Pty Ltd v Australian Prime Fibre Pty Ltd* [2013] QSC 163, [91]–[94].

[67] *Giller v Procopets* (n 9); *Wilson v Ferguson* (n 9).

[68] *PJS* (n 3) [92] (Lord Toulson dissenting). But cf *Mosley* (n 44). In Australia, exemplary damages are not available for breach of fiduciary duty, and possibly not for any equitable causes of action (including breach of confidence) if the broader approach of Heydon JA is taken: *Harris v Digital Pulse Pty Ltd* [2003] NSWCA 10, (2003) 56 NSWLR 298, [28]–[44] (Spigelman CJ), [343]–[353] (Heydon JA) (Mason P dissented).

[69] T Aplin, L Bently, P Johnson and S Malynicz, *Gurry on Breach of Confidence*, 2nd edn (Oxford, Oxford UP, 2012) [20.06].

Similar difficulties have been observed in relation to the tort of passing off,[70] and in intellectual property cases more generally.[71] Breach of privacy actions may also face the same problems. As Aplin et al later observe, in cases of misuse of personal information by a media outlet, it is hard to ascertain what proportion of the media outlet's sales stemmed from the breach of confidence.[72] Profit in media outlets is usually obtained from either sales or an increase in advertising revenue. Even if sales increase for an issue of a newspaper, for example, this may be because of some other unrelated story or event, which reflects the difficulty of attributing a gain to a part of a whole publication. Advertising revenues are usually based on average readership (or listeners), and occasional peaks in sales because of a story are unlikely to directly affect that profit. Thus it is also difficult to attribute advertising profits to the breach. The High Court of Australia has recognised the difficulties in calculating profit and noted that 'mathematical exactitude is generally impossible'.[73]

B. Reasonable Fee – Availability in Practice

English courts have sometimes been prepared to award reasonable fee awards for breach of confidence,[74] but not generally for cases which edge into breach of privacy.[75] Before going further, issues of nomenclature and categorisation must be cleared up. Reasonable fee awards have also been called 'restitutionary damages', '*Wrotham Park* damages', 'licence fee damages', 'user awards' and 'bargaining damages'. Their normative basis is uncertain, but they are generally available for proprietary torts, particularly for the torts actionable per se, which have a strong vindicatory aspect.[76] They are usually calculated objectively, to reflect the amount the claimant would have asked for the use of his or her property, or relaxation of a negative covenant or the like. There is an overlap with Lord Cairns' Act cases discussed in section III.C, as sometimes reasonable fee awards are made in lieu of specific performance or injunctions.[77]

In *Blake*, Lord Nicholls saw the reasonable fee cases, the user awards and the Lord Cairns' Act cases as an essential step towards recognition of gain-based relief in common law. It appears (although it is not entirely clear from the speech itself)

[70] *My Kinda Town Ltd v Soll* [1983] RPC 15, 58.

[71] M Gronow, 'Restitution for Breach of Confidence' (1996) 10 *Intellectual Property Journal* 219.

[72] Aplin et al (n 69) [20.13].

[73] *Dart Industries Inc v Décor Corporation Pty Ltd* (1993) 179 CLR 101, 111 (Mason CJ, Deane, Dawson and Toohey JJ); *Warman International Ltd v Dwyer* (1995) 182 CLR 544, 558.

[74] *Seager v Copydex* (n 14); *Seager v Copydex (No 2)* (n 14); *Vercoe* (n 13).

[75] *Douglas v Hello! Ltd (No 3)* (n 6) [246]–[249].

[76] JNE Varuhas, 'The Concept of "Vindication" in the Law of Torts: Rights, Interests and Damages' (2014) 34 *OJLS* 253.

[77] See, eg, *Wrotham Park Estate Co Ltd v Parkside Homes Ltd* [1974] 1 WLR 798; *Bracewell v Appleby* [1975] Ch 408; *Jaggard v Sawyer* [1995] 1 WLR 269.

that Lord Nicholls envisaged reasonable fees as a form of gain-based relief measured according to the benefit received by the defendant by use of property or breach of a duty.[78] Thus, when choosing a gain-based remedy, there appears to be a choice between full accounts of profit and gain-based relief measured by a reasonable fee. However, while Lord Nicholls clearly conceived of the reasonable fee as gain-based (perhaps including expenses saved), this is controversial. Reasonable fees do not have a clear normative basis in case law or academic literature. They have been argued to be compensatory,[79] vindicatory,[80] restitutionary,[81] a combination of restitution and compensation,[82] based upon proprietary or quasi-proprietary entitlements,[83] or as effecting partial disgorgement.[84] Nonetheless, despite this, reasonable fee damages will be considered in this chapter because there is sufficient

[78] See *Kuwait Airways Corp v Iraqi Airways Corp (Nos 4 & 5)* [2002] UKHL 19, [2002] 2 AC 883, [87].

[79] Lost opportunity to bargain theory: RJ Sharpe and SM Waddams, 'Damages for Lost Opportunity to Bargain' (1982) 2 *OJLS* 290; A Phang and PW Lee, 'Rationalising Restitutionary Damages in Contract Law – An Elusive or Illusory Quest?' (2001) 17 *Journal of Contract Law* 240, 252–53. Loss of a right: M McInnes, 'Account of Profits for Common Law Wrongs' in S Degeling and J Edelman (eds), *Equity in Commercial Law* (Sydney, LBC, 2004) 416–18; M McInnes, 'Gain, Loss and the User Principle' (2006) 14 *Restitution Law Review* 76, 84–86; F Giglio, *The Foundations of Restitution for Wrongs* (Oxford, Hart Publishing, 2007); P Benson, 'Disgorgement for Breach of Contract and Corrective Justice: An Analysis in Outline' in J Neyers, M McInnes and S Pitel (eds), *Understanding Unjust Enrichment* (Oxford, Hart Publishing, 2004) 311; A Botterell, 'Contractual Performance, Corrective Justice, and Disgorgement for Breach of Contract' (2010) 16 *Legal Theory* 135. Loss of a claim-right: K Barker, "Damages Without Loss': Can Hohfeld Help?' (2014) 34 *OJLS* 631. Cases: *Strand Electric & Engineering Co Ltd v Brisford Entertainments Ltd* [1952] 2 QB 246, 256 (Romer LJ); *Jaggard v Sawyer* (n 77) 291 (Millett LJ); *Gafford v Graham* (1999) 77 P & CR 73, 86 (Nourse LJ); *Experience Hendrix LLC v PPX Enterprises Inc* [2003] EWCA Civ 323, [2003] 1 All ER (Comm) 830, [45], [57] (Mance LJ); *WWF-World Wide Fund for Nature v World Wrestling Federation Entertainment Inc* [2007] EWCA Civ 286, [2008] 1 WLR 445, [58] (Chadwick LJ); *Smith v Landstar Properties Inc* [2011] BCCA 44; *Bunnings Group Ltd v Chep Australia Ltd* [2011] NSWCA 342, (2011) 82 NSWLR 420, [173] (Allsop P, with whom McFarlan JA agreed); *Morris-Garner v One Step (Support) Ltd* [2016] EWCA Civ 180, [81] (Christopher Clarke LJ), [145] (Longmore LJ).

[80] R Stevens, *Torts and Rights* (Oxford, Oxford UP, 2007) 60; Varuhas (n 76). Case: *Hampton v BHP Billiton Minerals Pty Ltd (No 2)* [2012] WASC 285, [342]–[354] (Edelman J).

[81] J Edelman, *Gain-Based Damages – Contract, Tort, Equity and Intellectual Property* (Oxford, Hart Publishing, 2002) 65–78; J Beatson, 'The Nature of Waver of Tort' in J Beatson (ed), *The Use and Abuse of Unjust Enrichment* (Oxford, Clarendon Press, 1991) 232; S Worthington, 'Reconsidering Disgorgement for Wrongs' (1999) 62 *MLR* 218. Cases: *Strand Electric* [1952] 2 QB 246, 254–55 (Denning LJ); *LJP Investments v Howard Chia Investments* (1989) 24 NSWLR 499; *Gaba Formwork Contractors Pty Ltd v Turner Corp Ltd* (1991) 32 NSWLR 175 (Giles J); *Ministry of Defence v Ashman* [1993] 2 EGLR 102, 104, 105; *Esso v Niad* [2001] EWHC 458 (Ch), [2001] 1 All ER (D) 324; *Bunnings Group Ltd v Chep Australia Ltd* [2011] NSWCA 342, (2011) 82 NSWLR 420, [194]–[199], [205] (Giles JA); *Esperance Cattle Co Pty Ltd v Granite Hill Pty Ltd* (2014) 47 WAR 318, [454]–[456].

[82] KFK Low, 'The User Principle: *Rashomon* Effect or Much Ado about Nothing' (2016) 28 *Singapore Academy of Law Journal* 984. Cases: *Hampton v BHP Billiton Minerals Pty Ltd (No 2)* [2012] WASC 285, [355]–[359], [342]–[354] (Edelman J); *ACES System Development Pte Ltd v Yenty Lily* [2013] 4 SLR 1317, [38] (Phang JA).

[83] P Jaffey, 'Licence Fee Damages' [2011] *Restitution Law Review* 95; S Harder, *Measuring Damages in the Law of Obligations: The Search for Harmonised Principles* (Oxford, Hart Publishing, 2010) 216–18. Cases: *Hospitality Group Pty Ltd v Australian Rugby Union Ltd* (2001) 110 FCR 157, (2001) 110 FCR 157, [167]–[168] (Emmett J, dissenting).

[84] K Barnett, *Accounting for Profit for Breach of Contract: Theory and Practice* (Oxford, Hart Publishing, 2012) ch 6. Cases: *Kansas v Nebraska*, 135 Sup Ct 1042 (2015); *Marathon Asset Management LLP v Seddon* [2017] EWHC 300 (Comm), [192]–[202].

judicial acceptance of these awards as restitutionary for them to be classed as gain-based in at least some sense.[85]

Thus far, courts have not awarded a reasonable fee award for breach of privacy. It may help to envisage the kind of situation where a reasonable fee may be sought. *Douglas v Hello! Ltd (No 3)* provides a useful example. As noted earlier, the claimants had sold the right to photograph their wedding to *OK!* magazine, but *Hello!* magazine took unauthorised photographs and published them. In the event, *Hello!* magazine had made no actual (positive) profit that could be disgorged. The claimants attempted to argue that they should be entitled to a reasonable fee award reflecting the notional fee they would have sought from the defendant for permission to publish the photos. The court characterised the reasonable fee award as compensatory in nature, and found that there was no loss because the claimants would never have granted a licence to the defendant.[86] This represents one of the problems with simplistic compensatory analyses of reasonable fee awards: often the cases when reasonable fee awards are most needed are those where there has been no factual loss because the claimant would never have agreed to bargain with the defendant for any money.[87] It could be argued that *Hello!* magazine saved an expense by failing to pay for the right to take photos at the wedding, and thus made a (negative) profit. However, one could equally well argue (and it has been argued) that the same problem applies to gain-based analyses as applies to compensatory analyses.[88] No expense was saved because the claimants would never have granted a licence. In such circumstances, any gain can only really be understood as a normative, objective gain rather than as a factual gain. In other words, *Hello!* magazine did not make any actual profit as a result of its conduct at all, because the prospect of actually being able to pay for the right to access the wedding was hypothetical.

In any case, whether they are gain-based, loss-based or vindicatory, reasonable fee awards are generally awarded in cases involving rights that are marketable commodities, and which can be objectively valued. In *Marathon Asset Management LLP v Seddon*,[89] Leggatt J proposed the following scheme for the award of gain-based relief:

1. If there was an alternative means by which the defendant could have obtained the benefit, the benefit will be valued on the market value.[90]
2. If the defendant could not have obtained the benefit from another source, it should be asked whether it was reasonable to expect the claimant to sell the

[85] See the cases mentioned at nn 81 and 84.
[86] *Douglas v Hello! Ltd (No 3)* (n 6) [246]–[249].
[87] C Rotherham, '"*Wrotham Park* Damages" and Accounts of Profits' [2008] *LMCLQ* 25, 31; R Cunnington, 'The Assessment of Gain-based Damages for Breach of Contract' (2008) 71 *MLR* 559, 562–63; R Cunnington, 'The Measure and Availability of Gain-based Damages for Breach of Contract' in D Saidov and R Cunnington (eds), *Contract Damages: Domestic and International Perspectives* (Oxford, Hart Publishing, 2008) 221.
[88] Varuhas (n 76) 286–87; Barker (n 79) 643–44.
[89] *Marathon Asset Management* (n 84).
[90] ibid [232].

benefit to the defendant for a reasonable fee. In this case, the benefit will be valued by the reasonable fee that the claimant could have charged.[91]

3. If the defendant could not reasonably have been expected to purchase the benefit from elsewhere, or where it was not reasonable for the claimant to sell, the benefit should be assessed according to the amount of profit made by the wrongdoer which is fairly attributable to the breach (either through an account of profits and apportionment, or through a percentage of profits through a licence fee).[92]

Although this scheme has not yet been accepted by any courts in England or Australia, the important point to take from Leggatt J's scheme is that reasonable fee awards depend upon the presence of a market for the right in question. While there may well be a market for confidential information, it is usually inappropriate to put an objective market value on a breach of privacy unless the information is also commercial confidential information. Perhaps the exception may be a case like *Douglas v Hello! Ltd (No 3)*, where the claimants *were* clearly interested in entering the market to allow certain people to intrude upon their privacy, but this still leaves one with an uneasy feeling: the claimants' complaint is not specifically that their privacy was invaded, but that they could not sell that right exclusively to the magazine they chose.

In any case, it is highly unlikely that Australian courts will be prepared to award a reasonable fee for breach of privacy so long as that action remains grounded in breach of confidence, because of the perception that such an award rests on an impermissible 'fusion fallacy'.[93] It will also be argued in section IV.B that a reasonable fee should not be awarded even if breach of privacy is conceptualised as a tort.

C. Lord Cairns' Act – Gain-Based Relief in Lieu of an Injunction?

A third possibility, which overlaps with the previous discussion, is that courts may use Lord Cairns' Act provisions to award gain-based relief. These provisions allow courts to award damages in lieu of an injunction.[94] As noted previously, Lord Nicholls in *Blake* saw the damages awarded in lieu of an injunction pursuant to Lord Cairns' Act in *Wrotham Park* as gain-based in nature. Thus, it is possible that courts may attempt to award reasonable fee awards calculated on the basis of gains to defendant pursuant to Lord Cairns' Act. It is also possible that it could be

[91] ibid [233].
[92] ibid [236].
[93] Heydon, Leeming and Turner (n 12) [2–235], [42–190].
[94] Australia: *Supreme Court Act 1933* (ACT), s 34; *Supreme Court Act 1970* (NSW), s 68; *Supreme Court Act* (NT), s 14(1)(b); *Civil Proceedings Act 2011* (Qld), s 8; *Supreme Court Act 1935* (SA), s 30; *Supreme Court Civil Procedure Act 1932* (Tas), s 11 (13); *Supreme Court Act 1986* (Vic), s 38; *Supreme Court Act 1935* (WA), s 25(10). UK: Judicature (Northern Ireland) Act 1978, s 92; Senior Courts Act 1981 (UK), s 50.

used to award an account of profits for a broad range of breaches of confidence, particularly because of the statement of Lord Goff in *Attorney-General v Guardian Newspapers (No 2)*:

> Th[e] remedy of account is alternative to the remedy of damages, which in cases of breach of confidence is now available, despite the equitable nature of the wrong, through a beneficent interpretation of the Chancery Amendment Act 1858 (Lord Cairns' Act), and which by reason of the difficulties attending the taking of an account is often regarded as a more satisfactory remedy, at least in cases where the confidential information is of a commercial nature, and quantifiable damages may therefore have been suffered.[95]

This has been followed in some English cases,[96] although not in Australia. However, if a court took a leaf from Lord Goff, and adopted an expansive or 'beneficent' view of the word 'damages' as representing *any* monetary award for a wrong, all kinds of gain-based relief could be covered.[97] The attraction of Lord Cairns' Act, particularly in an Australian case, is that it allows a limited form of apparently statutorily-sanctioned fusion.[98]

Thus far, Lord Cairns' Act has not been used to award gain-based relief for breach of privacy. However, it has been used to award damages for distress (or aggravated damages) in *Giller v Procopets*, a case which was effectively a breach of privacy, although it was pleaded as breach of confidence. The Victorian Court of Appeal used the Victorian Lord Cairns' Act provision to facilitate the award of damages for distress for breach of confidence.[99] After their relationship broke down the defendant disclosed videos of sexual activity between himself and the claimant to the claimant's friends and family. Damages for distress are not traditionally available as a head of equitable compensation, and Lord Cairns' Act allowed the court to argue that there had been an inherent jurisdiction to award an injunction restraining the breach of confidence and, in lieu of that injunction, damages for distress could be awarded.

Despite this, Lord Cairns' Act should not be used to award gain-based relief for a number of reasons. First, I argue that some aspects of the use of Lord Cairns' Act in *Giller v Procopets* were based upon a common misconception. In particular, the court held that the absence of the reference to 'wrongful act' in the updated Victorian Act[100] evinced an intention to expand the application of the Act to

[95] *Attorney-General v Guardian Newspapers (No 2)* [1990] 1 AC 109, 286.

[96] See, eg, *Douglas v Hello!* [2001] QB 967, [122]–[123] (Sedley LJ); *Campbell v MGN* (QBD, 21 December 2001, Morland J), cited in Aplin et al (n 69) [19.14]. Cf *Cadbury Schweppes v FBI Foods* [2000] FSR 491.

[97] P Birks, 'Equity in the Modern Law: An Exercise in Taxonomy' (1996) 26 *University of Western Australia Law Review* 1, 29.

[98] JA Jolowicz, 'Damages in Equity – A Study of Lord Cairns' Act' (1975) 34 CLJ 224, 227.

[99] *Giller v Procopets* (n 9). See the discussion in M Richardson, M Neave and M Rivette, 'Invasion of Privacy and Recovery for Distress', ch 7 in this book.

[100] *Supreme Court Act 1986* (Vic), s 38. See also *Supreme Court Act 1933* (ACT), s 34; *Civil Proceedings Act 2011* (Qld), s 8; cf *Supreme Court Act 1970* (NSW), s 68; *Supreme Court Act* (NT), s 14(1)(b);

equitable wrongdoing.[101] However, the second reading speeches of the redrafted provision do not indicate that the change in wording was intended to expand the availability of Lord Cairns' Act.[102] The intention seems simply to have been to introduce a 'plain English version'.

Second, as the Victorian Court of Appeal acknowledged, there is no need to use Lord Cairns' Act to award remedies to vindicate breaches of privacy. In *Wilson v Ferguson*, a case otherwise very similar to *Giller v Procopets*, the court was prepared to award damages for distress for breach of confidence based on the court's inherent jurisdiction.[103] As in *Wilson v Ferguson*, courts could make distress damages and other forms of equitable awards under provisions originally enacted in the Judicature legislation.[104] Specifically, in most states and territories, there are legislative powers for courts to make orders to achieve 'full and complete justice' between the parties, such as section 29(2) of the *Supreme Court Act 1986* (Vic), which obliges the Supreme Court to exercise its jurisdiction in every civil proceeding before it so 'as to secure that, as far as possible, all matters in dispute between the parties are completely and finally determined, and all multiplicity of proceedings concerning those matters is avoided'.[105] In fact, Lord Cairns' Act provisions are, as I have argued elsewhere with Michael Bryan, largely redundant.[106] When courts use Lord Cairns' Act, it obscures what is really going on, and means that courts fail to engage with the normative basis of causes of action. Just as distress damages should be awarded without recourse to Lord Cairns' Act, so also should gain-based relief.

Third, as will become evident in what follows, I argue that reasonable fee awards are inappropriate for breaches of privacy because they presume a market basis for rights, and do not reflect the dignitary basis of breach of privacy.

However, my scheme for how gain-based relief would work for breach of privacy broadly mirrors the Lord Cairns' Act jurisprudence. Regardless of whether the normative basis of the claim is in common law or equity, gain-based relief for breach of privacy should be exceptional, although it should be available in lieu

Supreme Court Act 1935 (SA), s 30; *Supreme Court Civil Procedure Act 1932* (Tas), s 11(13); *Supreme Court Act 1935* (WA), s 25(10).

[101] *Giller v Procopets* (n 9), [403] (Neave JA).

[102] K Barnett and M Bryan, 'Lord Cairns's Act: a Study in the Unintended Consequences of Legislation' (2015) 9 *Journal of Equity* 150, 159–62.

[103] *Wilson v Ferguson* (n 9) [74]. For another example of a case (albeit in common law) where it was not necessary to have recourse to Lord Cairns' Act and compensatory damages were sufficiently flexible, see *Tabcorp Holdings Pty Ltd v Bowen Investments Pty Ltd* [2009] HCA 8, (2009) 236 CLR 272, [22]–[23].

[104] Supreme Court of Judicature Act 1873 (UK), s 24(7). See also *Sayers v Collyer* (1884) 28 Ch D 103, 108 (Baggallay LJ).

[105] See also Senior Courts Act 1981 (UK), s 49(2); *Federal Court of Australia Act 1976* (Cth), s 22; *Supreme Court Act 1933* (ACT), s 32; *Supreme Court Act 1970* (NSW), s 63; *Supreme Court Act 1979* (NT), ss 61–68; *Civil Proceedings Act 2011* (Qld), s 7; *Supreme Court Act 1935* (SA), s 27; *Supreme Court Civil Procedure Act 1932* (Tas), s 10(7); *Supreme Court Act 1935* (WA), s 24(7).

[106] Barnett and Bryan (n 102) 154–55; M Bryan, 'Injunctions and Damages: Taking *Shelfer* off the Shelf' (2016) 28 *Singapore Academy of Law Journal* 921, 927–28.

of or in addition to an injunction. In the majority of circumstances, as I noted at the outset, the most appropriate remedy will be an injunction. I argue in the next section that this is the appropriate way to approach the award of gain-based relief for breach of privacy given the normative basis of the cause of action. This will be discussed next.

IV. Normative Bases for Gain-Based Relief for Breach of Privacy

In shaping the relief to be awarded for breach of privacy, it is important to look to the normative basis of the action of breach of privacy. Privacy has been recognised as a fundamental human right,[107] and as necessary to promote dignitary interests, human flourishing and autonomy.[108] It is also particularly important in intimate relationships or relationships of trust and confidence, as indicated by the early breach of confidence cases, including *Prince Albert v Strange*[109] and *Duchess of Argyll v Duke of Argyll*,[110] and thus there remains an overlap with the concerns which inform breach of confidence, including conscience and the ability to confide to one's fellows. Privacy is generally not conceived of as a proprietary right but as a personal right.[111] Technological and media advances, and the rise of social media have made protection of privacy all the more necessary. Thus, for the reasons pointed out by the Australian Law Reform Commission, breach of privacy should be an available cause of action in Australian law,[112] and it should protect intrusions upon privacy and misuse of private information. It is already entrenched in English law, probably as a tortious cause of action. The normative basis of the cause of action shapes the availability of relief in important ways. I argue in this section that an account of profits should be available for breach of privacy for two reasons: deterrence and coherence. However, I shall argue that reasonable fees should *not* be awarded in most cases for breach of privacy. Thus, I agree with the position of the ALRC, which suggested that accounts of profit should be an available remedy for a statutory tort of breach of privacy as an alternative to damages,[113] particularly where the breach of privacy was commercially motivated, and where the gain to the defendant is greater than the loss caused to the claimant (or the claimant's losses are difficult to calculate). It was also suggested that the account

[107] International Covenant on Civil and Political Rights (16 December 1966) 999 UNTS 171 (entered into force 23 March 1976), Art 17.

[108] Witzleb (n 1) 337.

[109] *Prince Albert v Strange* (1849) 1 H & Tw 1; 47 ER 1302.

[110] *Duchess of Argyll v Duke of Argyll* [1967] Ch 302.

[111] Witzleb (n 1).

[112] ALRC (n 37) ch 1. See also NSWLRC (n 37) and Australian Law Reform Commission (ALRC), *For Your Information*, Report No 108 (2008).

[113] ALRC (n 37) ch 1, [12.102]–[12.111]. See also NSWLRC (n 37) [4.14], [4.16] and ALRC, *For your Information* (n 112), Rec 74-5.

of profit might have a deterrent effect, both specifically on recidivist media outlets and more generally.[114] However, the 2014 ALRC Report on Privacy recommended that notional licence fees should not be awarded for any statutory breach of privacy tort.[115]

A. Deterrence and Coherence

There are two ways of looking at whether gain-based relief should be awarded for breach of privacy as a matter of principle.[116] First, one could argue that gain-based relief is necessary for breach of privacy because of dignitary concerns specifically associated with the nature of breach of privacy itself, and the need to deter such breaches.[117] Deterring breaches of privacy would be both general (in that it would deter the general public) and specific (in that it would deter individuals and media outlets from breaching privacy in specific instances). Thus, it is argued that profitable invasions of privacy (through either misuse of private information or intrusion upon privacy) should be deterred by profit-stripping, particularly where the gain made is greater than any loss to the claimant.[118] However, it should be noted that deterrent justifications for gain-based relief have been questioned on the basis that profit-stripping is not sufficiently deterrent,[119] and it has been argued that exemplary damages would be a more appropriate deterrent.[120] In response, I argue that exemplary damages represent a 'blunt axe', whereas profit-stripping represents 'the sharp axe'.[121] It is well for a court to have several remedial options in its armoury. In circumstances where a breach of privacy is particularly egregious, I agree that courts *should* be able to award exemplary damages to a claimant. However, in other situations, the very wrong that has occurred is that the defendant has made a profit by committing a breach of the claimant's privacy. It should be open to a court to remove only the actual profit made, thus putting the defendant in the position as if he had not committed the wrong. In those cases, I argue that profit-stripping has a vindicatory function, where the importance of the claimant's interest is signalled by the court's response to a privacy breach.[122]

Second, gain-based relief could also be said to be necessary for broader reasons of coherence and consistency.[123] English courts have noted in this area

[114] ALRC (n 37) [12.104]–[12.107].

[115] ibid [12.112]–[12.117].

[116] Harder (n 1) 70–71.

[117] ibid 70; Witzleb (n 1) 352–54; ALRC (n 37) [12.102], [12.104], [12.107].

[118] Witzleb (n 1) 352, ALRC (n 37) [12.103].

[119] L Smith, 'Deterrence, Prophylaxis and Punishment in Fiduciary Obligations' (2013) 7 *Journal of Equity* 87, 91–93.

[120] JNE Varuhas, 'Varieties of Damages for Breach of Privacy', ch 3 in this book.

[121] Edelman (n 81) 17.

[122] I use vindication in the sense suggested by Varuhas (n 76) 258, although he does not agree with me that gain-based relief should be a vindicatory response in this area.

[123] Harder (n 1) 71.

that it is important to ensure coherence across the law, and to ensure that like cases are treated alike. In *Vercoe*, Sales J observed that Lord Nicholls' speech in *Blake*[124] had opened the way to a more principled examination of the circumstances where accounts of profits would be awarded by courts. In his view, the reasoning 'flow[ed] in both directions'.[125] It raised the possibility that accounts of profit could be awarded for common law causes of action, but also led him to question whether accounts of profit should be awarded as of right simply because a cause of action had originated in equity. Sales J argued that the award of an account of profits should depend upon the facts and nature of the rights affected, not on the historical origin of the cause of action. This relates back to the normative basis of the cause of action: the award of gain-based relief should depend not on the historical accident of the origin of a cause of action, but on the nature of the interests protected and what is necessary to vindicate those interests.

Thus, I would argue that gain-based damages should be available where the defendant has breached privacy with a subjective intention to make a profit, or where the gain to the defendant was greater than the loss caused to the claimant. It may also be appropriate to impose accounts of profits on media outlets that repeatedly breach privacy for profit.

B. The Availability of Account of Profits

In my view, the historical origin of the cause of action should not be the sole basis for determining whether an account of profits is available. The normative basis of the cause of action should also be pivotal. It is probable that it will develop as a tort in England, and unclear whether breach of privacy will develop at all in Australia. I argue that it is preferable for it to develop as a stand-alone tort, separate from breach of confidence, although overlapping with it to some degree. But if so, it is perhaps best conceived of as an 'equi-tort', a tort shaped by equity in important ways.

This is not without precedent. The tort of passing off has also been greatly shaped by equitable principle. Equity contributed to the tort of passing off in three ways: it alleviated the need to prove 'fraud'; it found a basis for judicial intervention in the goodwill of business; and it allowed for the grant of *quia timet* injunctions.[126] Accounts of profits have always been available for passing off in equity's auxiliary jurisdiction,[127] although Heydon, Leeming and Turner stipulate that this is only available where 'the defendant continues its activities after notice of the plaintiff's rights',[128] and there is a necessity to elect. Although the

[124] *Blake* (n 52).
[125] *Vercoe* (n 13) [339].
[126] Heydon, Leeming and Turner (n 12) [43-015].
[127] *My Kinda Town Ltd v Soll* [1983] RPC 15.
[128] Heydon, Leeming and Turner (n 12) [43-095]. The authors do not cite any authority for this proposition.

explanation for equity's intervention into the law of passing off has sometimes been said to be the property in a claimant's business, there are problems with this explanation given the breadth of circumstances in which courts will offer relief for passing off.[129]

Even if breach of privacy develops as a tort, an account of profit should be available in appropriate circumstances. The question of whether breach of privacy is a tort or an equitable wrong is likely to matter more in Australia than England, because of the Australian concern with 'fusion fallacy'. Breach of privacy has its origins in breach of confidence, but also has considerable similarities with tort.[130] As McDonald and Rolph have noted, the notion of intrusion into privacy, in particular, seems to have kinship to the tort of trespass, and thus breach of privacy is best treated as a tort.[131] However, privacy remains entwined with equity, and has been shaped by it from the beginning. Accordingly, I would argue that it should be treated as a tort for which gain-based relief is available exceptionally through equity's auxiliary jurisdiction.

Under my scheme, accounts of profit would be available where compensatory damages were inadequate and an injunction was unavailable. An injunction would still be the preferred remedy for breach of privacy because, as Pomeroy puts it, 'a remedy which *prevents* a threatened wrong is in its essential nature better than a remedy which permits the wrong to be done, and then attempts to pay for it'.[132] In this way, breach of privacy shares some characteristics with the torts actionable per se, as Varuhas has noted in his chapter in this collection. In other ways it is dissimilar, because many of the torts actionable per se involve proprietary interests (although not all do). If one focuses on proprietary interests as the determinant of awards of accounts of profit then it is more difficult to argue that breach of privacy should give rise to disgorgement, because there is not usually a proprietary interest in privacy.[133] However, I suggest that the focus should be on the exceptional dignitary character of the interest, and argue that it should be vindicated by an award of profits, particularly where an injunction was unavailable and damages were inadequate or difficult to calculate. It would also be necessary for any breach to constitute a conscious and advertent disregard of the claimant in order for the intervention of equity to be justifiable. I have argued elsewhere that there is a slightly punitive aspect to accounts of profit awarded for breach of contract, and thus advertence is required – otherwise the disgorgement of profit would not be deserved.[134] The same holds in the present context.

[129] ibid [43-015], [43-060].

[130] In fact, breach of confidence also has tortious aspects, including, eg, the borrowing of the 'reasonable man': see, eg, *Coco v AN Clark (Engineers) Ltd* [1968] FSR 415, 420–21 (Megarry J).

[131] McDonald and Rolph (n 7).

[132] J Norton Pomeroy, *Equity Jurisprudence*, vol 3 (1887) §1357 (emphasis in original).

[133] Witzleb (n 1) 337.

[134] Barnett (n 84) 40–46.

There would be room for courts to award both an injunction and account of profits where there were past profitable breaches of privacy which could not be rectified, and a threat of future breaches of privacy which needed to be restrained.

As noted earlier, a further argument against the recognition of an account of profits for breach of privacy is the difficulty in calculating the profits that flow from a breach. In the 2014 ALRC Report on privacy, these difficulties in calculation were noted but not regarded as insurmountable,[135] and it was suggested that a court should determine the reasonableness of the connection between the invasion of privacy and the profit.[136] In other words, there has to be a sufficiently direct causal link between the invasion of privacy and the profit made. These difficulties already exist for other causes of action for which accounts of profit are available (including breach of confidence).

This issue could be dealt with by saying that looser causation rules applied, as per profits made from a breach of fiduciary duty (and indeed, for losses made because of deceit[137]). For breaches of fiduciary duty, the causation test is liberal, and there is no need to make out the 'but for' test.[138] The breach need only be 'a cause' of the gain, not the predominant cause,[139] although there must be 'some reasonable connection' between the breach and the profits.[140] This would be appropriate given the requirement that any breach be advertent and conscious. There is a similar requirement of advertence for common law torts such as deceit, although they have a higher burden of proof given the necessity to also establish fraud. The burden of proof should then shift to the defendant to prove that the breach of privacy did not cause the gains in question, as the defendant will always possess better information about the gain than the claimant. However, it may be feared that a looser causation test will cause accounts of profits to operate too harshly, so it should follow that allowances and the usual equitable defences (including hardship, delay and acquiescence and lack of clean hands) should apply, but that the defendant has the burden of proving those.

C. The Availability of Reasonable Fees

By contrast with the argument regarding accounts of profits, I argue that reasonable fee awards should generally *not* be available for breach of privacy.[141] The reason for this links back to the nature of a claimant's interest in privacy, and the way in which reasonable fee awards are calculated.

[135] ALRC (n 37) [12.109].
[136] ibid [12.108], citing *CMS Dolphin Ltd v Simonet* [2001] 2 BCLC 704, [97].
[137] *Doyle v Olby (Ironmongers) Ltd* [1969] 2 QB 158, affirmed in *Gould v Vaggelas* (1985) 157 CLR 215.
[138] See, eg, *Industrial Development Consultants Ltd v Cooley* [1972] 1 WLR 443.
[139] C Mitchell, 'Causation, Remoteness, and Fiduciary Gains' (2006) 17 *Kings College Law Journal* 325, 332; *Fexuto Pty Ltd v Bosnjak Holdings Pty Ltd (No 2)* (1998) 29 ACSR 290, 297.
[140] *CMS Dolphin Ltd v Simonet* [2001] EWHC 415, [97] (Ch) (Lawrence Collins J).
[141] See also ALRC (n 37) [12.112]–[12.117].

The interest in privacy protects dignity and autonomy. The reasonable fee award, on the other hand, is concerned with the market value of an infringement of a right. Thus, in order to award a reasonable fee, the court is required to consider how much a claimant would have charged to allow a breach of privacy in the market. However, (most) claimants would never agree to sell the right not to have their privacy invaded or their private information misused,[142] precisely because human dignity and autonomy are involved.

Breach of privacy could be analogised to trespass to the person. I have an interest in personal autonomy which prevents people from trespassing to my person, but I suggest that a court would be highly unlikely to award a reasonable fee for trespass to the person. How would a court calculate the fee someone would accept to be punched in the face? It is argued that for similar reasons, courts would not wish to put a licence fee on a breach of privacy. In both instances, it is inconsistent with the dignitary concern at the heart of the doctrine, and an injunction should be awarded if the action can still be restrained. And, as already argued, Lord Cairns' Act provisions should not be used to facilitate the award of a reasonable fee.

V. Conclusion

Accounts of profits should be available for actions for breach of privacy (regardless of the normative basis of the cause of action), but only where an injunction is not possible, damages are inadequate, and the defendant has acted in conscious and advertent disregard of the claimant's rights with a view to making a profit. This is because we wish to deter interferences with the important dignitary interest claimants have in privacy. However, accounts of profits are the 'sharp axe' in the court's armoury; courts should also be able to award the 'blunt axe' of exemplary damages in situations where the breach was contumelious and no profit was made (as in *Giller v Procopets* and *Wilson v Ferguson*, the revenge porn cases considered earlier in this chapter).[143] This reflects the normative concerns at the heart of breach of privacy. The historical evolution of the action should not constrain courts, but the normative concerns at the heart of the action should.

[142] The exception is *Douglas v Hello! Ltd (No 3)* (n 6), where the claimants sold the right to take photos of their wedding, thus arguably commercialising it.

[143] My argument here is normative. Of course, the difficulty with this assertion is that the law does not reflect that position. In Australia, exemplary damages are not available for breach of fiduciary duty, and possibly not for any equitable causes of action: *Harris v Digital Pulse Pty Ltd* (n 68). In the UK, the availability of exemplary damages is constrained by the three categories in *Rookes v Barnard* [1964] AC 1129, 1226–27 (Lord Devlin). The categories are (1) oppressive, arbitrary or unconstitutional acts by servants of the government, (2) cynical breaches by a defendant who calculated that his profit would exceed any compensation payable to the claimant, and (3) where statute authorises awards of exemplary damages.

It is for this reason that reasonable fee awards and awards made in lieu of an injunction pursuant to Lord Cairns' Act should not be made for breach of privacy. Reasonable fee awards are inconsistent with the fundamental nature of breach of privacy. They presume that there is a market for interference with certain interests; but breach of privacy is more akin to interference with the person, for which reasonable fees are not available. Similarly, Lord Cairns' Act should not be used in this area to award reasonable fees, or indeed to award any other kind of measure, such as distress damages, aggravated damages or an account of profits. To award remedies by that mechanism obscures what is really happening, and means that a court does not consider the normative basis of the cause of action.

9

Apologies and Corrections as Remedies for Serious Invasions of Privacy

ROBYN CARROLL*

> In any context, an apology is a way of recognising wrongdoing (large or small, moral, personal, social, public or legal) and acknowledging hurt and grievance caused or felt in others because of that wrongdoing.[1]

I. Introduction

In a statement in open court in the High Court of Justice in London on 26 May 2016, counsel for Sir Cliff Richard OBE stated the facts surrounding his claim against the BBC and the Chief Constable of South Yorkshire Police ('SYP') for misuse of private information and breach of Article 8 of the European Convention of Human Rights and the Data Protection Act 1998. The claims arose out of unlawful disclosures by the SYP to the BBC that led to headline news coverage of a search of the claimant's apartment and naming him as under police investigation for an alleged historic sexual offence against a boy aged under 16. The statement, which was made jointly with SYP, referred to the 'profound and long-lasting damage and distress' caused to the claimant, and to his reputation as being 'forever tainted'. It also announced that SYP agreed to pay the claimant a substantial sum by way of general and aggravated damages as compensation, as well as appropriate sums for financial damage and legal costs incurred by the claimant. Following this statement, counsel for SYP acknowledged that its conduct as described was unlawful, and offered 'its sincere apologies to the Claimant for the distress and humiliation he has suffered'.[2]

* I would like to thank Jason Varuhas and Nicole Moreham for hosting the *International Workshop on Remedies for Breach of Privacy* at the Melbourne University Law School in December 2016, at which I presented a paper on this subject. I also thank Nicole Moreham and Normann Witzleb for their valuable comments on an earlier version of this chapter, while acknowledging that any errors or omissions are my own.

[1] *Wotton v State of Queensland (No 5)* [2016] FCA 1457 (5 December 2016) [1589] *per* Mortimer J.

[2] *Richard v BBC* [2017] EWHC 1648 (Ch) (26 May 2017) Appendix *per* Mann J.

Apologies have a long-standing and well-recognised role in torts that protect dignitary interests, such as false imprisonment and trespass, and especially in defamation, where a prompt correction and apology for defamatory publication is considered an effective way to restore an injured party's reputation and provide consolation for injury to that party's feelings. When the law protects the dignitary interest in privacy, apologies and corrections can also play a role in this tort, through judicial remedies and in negotiated settlements, as demonstrated by the case of *Richard v BBC*. An apology, as Mortimer J says, is 'a way of recognising wrongdoing (large or small, moral, personal, social, public or legal) and acknowledging hurt and grievance caused or felt in others because of that wrongdoing'.[3] An apology for invasion of privacy is an acknowledgement of wrongdoing and 'may assist in rectifying a plaintiff's feelings of embarrassment and distress'.[4] A correction can 'set the record straight' and reduce the harm caused by a breach of privacy where false information has been published or otherwise disclosed.[5]

Although privacy rights are recognised in a number of common law jurisdictions, there is no privacy tort action available in Australia. The common law in Australia provides no incentive, therefore, for apologies and corrections to be made in response to a complaint of breach of privacy.[6] This will change if a common law tort is developed by the courts or a statutory tort is introduced. There have been numerous calls in Australia for a statutory tort action for invasion of privacy that confers broad remedial powers on courts.[7] In the *Serious Invasions of Privacy in the Digital Era Final Report* ('Privacy Report'), the Australian Law Reform Commission ('ALRC') proposes the enactment of the tort of serious invasion of privacy.[8] The proposed remedies for a tort of serious invasion of privacy recognise that apologies and corrections can contribute to redress for emotional distress. In the event of reform we can expect, therefore, to see further development of legal principles concerning these remedies.

[3] *Wotton v State of Queensland (No 5)* (n 1) [1589].

[4] Australian Law Reform Commission, *Serious Invasions of Privacy in the Digital Era* (Australian Law Reform Commission Report No 123, 2014) 254, [12.160] ('Privacy Report').

[5] ibid 252–53, [12.154].

[6] Apologies and other non-compensatory remedies are available under privacy legislation – see section V. See also N Witzleb, 'Determinations under the Privacy Act 1988 (Cth) as a Privacy Remedy', in ch 15 of this book.

[7] eg, ALRC, Privacy Report (n 4) 13. See also ALRC, *For Your Information: Australian Privacy Law and Practice* (Australian Law Reform Commission Report No 108, 2008); New South Wales Law Reform Commission, *Invasion of Privacy* (NSW Law Reform Commission Report No 120, 2009) ('Invasion of Privacy'); Victorian Law Reform Commission, *Surveillance in Public Places* (Victorian Law Reform Commission Report 18, 2010); South Australian Law Reform Institute, *A Statutory Tort for Invasion of Privacy* (South Australian Law Reform Institute Final Report 4, 2016); Parliament of New South Wales Standing Committee on Law and Justice, *Remedies for the Serious Invasion of Privacy in New South Wales* (New South Wales Legislative Council 2016).

[8] ALRC, Privacy Report (n 4). In this chapter I use 'invasion of privacy' to refer to the action for serious invasion of privacy proposed in the ALRC's Privacy Report and, more generally, tort actions for misuse of private information and intrusion into seclusion that exist in other common law jurisdictions.

The ALRC proposes that apologies and corrections be factors considered in the assessment of damages for serious invasion of privacy.[9] This is consistent with principles applied to the assessment of damages for other torts that protect dignitary interests and assessment of damages principles for breach of privacy in other jurisdictions. The Commission also proposes that the legislation confer on courts the power to order a correction where false private information has been published and to order a defendant to apologise.[10] The latter proposal would create a more extensive role for these non-monetary remedies than in other common law jurisdictions.

This chapter identifies and discusses the principles and factors that need to be considered to give effect to these proposals. It proceeds on the basis, as does the ALRC, that there are sound reasons for conferring broad powers on the courts to grant non-monetary remedies that vindicate the right to privacy and provide redress for emotional harm. The central inquiry is into the ways that an apology can serve these purposes. The analysis of the proposals in this chapter shows that there are similarities as well as important differences in the legal principles and considerations that apply to apologies and corrections in the assessment of damages, on the one hand, and court-ordered apologies and corrections, on the other. In both instances, the insights provided by research into the meaning and function of an apology in addressing emotional distress can be employed in the formulation of principles and judicial decision-making.

Section II of this chapter sets out the ALRC's proposal for a tort of serious invasion of privacy, the proposed roles for apologies and corrections, and the way in which the law encourages apologies and corrections in the settlement of privacy disputes. This discussion provides context for the discussion in later sections of the chapter. Section III discusses the meaning and functions of apologies in a legal context, drawing on research on apologies that provides insights into the functions of apologies after a harmful event and into the complexity of apologies. Section IV identifies principles and considerations that apply to apologies and corrections as factors in the assessment of damages for invasion of privacy. Section V examines the purposes for which a court might make an apology or a correction order and the principles it is likely to apply. I conclude that while apologies and corrections are appropriate factors to consider in the assessment of damages for breach of privacy, close attention must be paid to the circumstances of the invasion of privacy, the parties and their relationship, and the plaintiff's experience of the apology. I also conclude that there are benefits of conferring power on courts to order corrections and apologies for invasion of privacy, but that the circumstances in which it will be appropriate to make orders of this nature are limited by a number of important considerations.

[9] ALRC, Privacy Report (n 4) 226–28. See specifically Recommendation 12-2(a), (b).
[10] ibid 254–56.

II. The ALRC Proposals

The ALRC proposals provide a convenient framework for discussing the role of apologies and corrections in privacy law for several reasons. First, the proposals identify ways in which the law can encourage these responses to invasions of privacy and assess their 'remedial fit' once liability has been determined in a plaintiff's favour.[11] Second, the significance of apologies and corrections as factors in the assessment of damages for breach of privacy can be expected to develop in a similar way at common law or under legislation, and therefore the discussion of this ALRC proposal is relevant to other common law jurisdictions. Third, the ALRC proposal that courts be given power to order corrections and apologies in appropriate circumstances draws largely on legislative developments in Australian law, although it may not reflect current law in the common law jurisdictions that protect privacy. Discussion of this proposal will allow comparisons to be drawn should other jurisdictions adopt these remedies in the future.

A. Tort of Serious Invasion of Privacy

Despite multiple inquiries into privacy law in Australia and recommendations for the introduction of a statutory cause of action for invasions of privacy, it remains the case that there is no cause of action for serious invasion of privacy. While there are avenues open to a person to seek redress for breach of information privacy under legislation or through complaint mechanisms available voluntarily or in industry codes of conduct, these do not provide tortious remedies. This is highly significant to the remedies that will be available to a person whose privacy has been invaded in a serious manner.

The essential elements and features of the tort of serious invasion of privacy as recommended by the ALRC are:[12]

- the invasion of privacy must be either by intrusion into seclusion, or by misuse of private information;
- a person in the position of the plaintiff must have had a reasonable expectation of privacy in all of the circumstances;
- the invasion must have been committed intentionally or recklessly – mere negligence is not sufficient;
- the invasion must be serious;

[11] It is not the aim of this chapter to evaluate the liability rules (elements and defences) proposed by the ALRC, nor the development of liability rules in other countries. Even if the recommendation for the tort is never enacted, the recommendations in the Privacy Report will be relevant to courts fashioning a cause of action at common law and awarding remedies in the future.

[12] Australian Law Reform Commission, *Serious Invasions of Privacy in the Digital Era: Summary Report* (Australian Law Reform Commission Summary Report No 123, 2014) 7 [1.11] ('Summary Report').

- the court must be satisfied that the public interest in privacy outweighs any countervailing public interests; and
- the invasion need not cause actual damage and damages for emotional distress may be awarded.

Intrusion upon seclusion occurs by, for example, physically intruding into the plaintiff's private space, or by watching, listening to or recording the plaintiff's private activities or private affairs.[13] Misuse of information can occur, for example, by collecting or disclosing private information about the plaintiff.[14]

A number of defences are proposed, including lawful authority, where the conduct was incidental to defence of persons or property, consent, necessity, absolute privilege, the publication of public documents and fair reporting of public proceedings.[15] A wide range of remedies would be available when liability is made out, to take account of the different objectives, experiences and circumstances of plaintiffs who may pursue privacy actions.[16] These include damages, including damages for emotional distress, an account of profits, injunctions, delivery up, destruction and removal of material, declarations, as well as apology orders and correction orders.[17] Exemplary damages would be available in exceptional circumstances.[18]

The ALRC also considers the advantages and disadvantages of allowing a tort of misuse of private information to be developed by the courts under common law. It concludes that the tort should be created by legislation.[19] One obvious advantage of this approach, from a remedies perspective, is that legislation is able to confer on the courts power to grant remedies that are not available at common law.

B. Encouragement and Protection of Apologies and Early Settlement of Disputes

There are various ways other than monetary payments in which the law encourages resolution of disputes and settlement of proceedings. The procedure for making a statement in open court, referred to in the opening paragraph of this chapter, for example, supports settlement by providing an opportunity for parties to defamation and privacy actions to set out the terms of their negotiated settlement and make any agreed apology or correction in court.[20] This procedure supports

[13] See Recommendation 5-1(a): ibid 17.
[14] See Recommendation 5-1(b): ibid.
[15] ibid 7–8, [1.14].
[16] ALRC, Privacy Report (n 4) 219, [12.2].
[17] ALRC, Summary Report (n 12) 8, [1.15].
[18] ALRC, Privacy Report (n 4) 220, [12.5].
[19] ibid 59, [4.1]–[4.4].
[20] See M Collins, *Collins on Defamation* (Oxford, Oxford UP, 2014) 413. Collins explains that statements to the effect that defamation proceedings have been settled are particularly common where settlement is achieved shortly before or during the trial: ibid 413.

settlement of proceedings as a 'public good'.[21] The parties are free to express in their own words what they wish to say about the settlement in court. The statement then becomes available to the public and the media.[22] It is regarded as a valuable means of vindication for the parties in libel cases.[23] In *Richard*, the claimant and the second respondent, the BBC, availed themselves of this vindicatory procedure in settlement of an action for breach of privacy.[24] In the event that a tort of serious invasion of privacy is introduced in Australia, consideration could be given to extending this procedure to privacy cases.

The ALRC recommends other measures aimed at encouraging settlement of privacy disputes, including a proposal to allow a court to take into account in the assessment of damages whether either party took reasonable steps to settle their dispute before litigation.[25] A proposal that has direct significance to apologies is Recommendation 7-2, which states 'The Act should provide that an apology made by the defendant does not constitute an admission of fault or liability and is not relevant to the determination of fault or liability.' Such a provision would prevent a plaintiff from relying on an apology made by a defendant that is an express or implied admission of serious invasion of privacy as evidence of the defendant's liability. This Recommendation is intended to encourage the early resolution of disputes without recourse to litigation.[26] Provisions to this effect have previously been introduced for this purpose in defamation law and other areas of civil liability in Australia.[27]

The benefits of apologies offered in the settlement of tort claims are well documented in the dispute resolution literature.[28] It is also well documented by proponents of law reform that the fear that an apology will be treated as an admission of liability can discourage apologetic behaviour when there is potential for civil disputes to arise.[29] A key aim of the legislation (often referred to as 'apology legislation') is to remove, or at least lessen, the 'chill' that prevents an early apology

[21] *Barnet v Crozier* [1987] 1 WLR 272 (CA) 280 *per* Ralph Gibson LJ.

[22] *Murray v Associated Newspapers Limited* [2015] EWCA Civ 488, [2015] CN 836, [25] *per* Sharp LJ, Ryder LJ and Longmore LJ agreeing.

[23] ibid. See also Collins (n 20) 413: 'The reading of an apology by the defendant's counsel in open court, can be a powerful form of vindication for a claimant.'

[24] *Richard v BBC* [2017] EWHC 1648 (Ch) (26 May 2017).

[25] ALRC, Privacy Report (n 4) 226–27. Refer to Recommendation ch 12, 12-2.

[26] ibid 128, [7.88].

[27] eg, *Civil Liability Act 2002* (NSW), s 69 (regarding civil liability) and *Defamation Act 2005* (NSW), s 20 (regarding defamation).

[28] See, eg, JR Cohen, 'Advising Clients to Apologize' (1999) 72 *Southern California Law Review* 1009; P Vines, 'The Power of Apology: Mercy, Forgiveness or Corrective Justice in the Civil Liability Arena?' (2007) 1 *Public Space* 1; R Carroll, C To and M Unger, 'Apology Legislation and its Implications for International Dispute Resolution Practitioners' (2015) 9 *Dispute Resolution International* 115.

[29] See, eg, British Columbia Ministry of Attorney-General, *Discussion Paper on Apology Legislation* (Ministry of Attorney-General, September 2006); British Columbia Office of the Ombudsman, *The Power of an Apology: Removing the Legal Barriers* (Special Report No 27 to the Legislative Assembly of British Columbia, British Columbia Office of the Ombudsman, February 2006).

by a willing defendant.[30] Similar protections apply to privacy proceedings in most Canadian provinces and in Hong Kong.[31]

There was some concern expressed to the ALRC about the protection of apologies in privacy cases, because some defendants might use an apology as a vehicle to exacerbate the harm caused by the initial invasion. For example, publishing an apology might reconvey the improperly disclosed private information to a wider audience. That is particularly likely to be the case where a more prominent location within a website or media publication is used for the apology.[32] To address this valid concern, the ALRC recommends that a factor in the assessment of damages should be whether there was unreasonable conduct following the invasion of privacy that subjects the plaintiff to additional embarrassment, harm, distress or humiliation.[33] This and other assessment of damages factors are discussed in section IV.

C. Court-ordered Apologies and Correction Orders as Remedies for Serious Invasions of Privacy

The New South Wales Law Reform Commission ('NSWLRC') and the ALRC have recommended that courts be conferred with broad power to award remedies for invasion of privacy.[34] When assessing damages, a court would be able to consider whether the defendant had made an appropriate apology to the plaintiff, whether the defendant had made a correction, and whether the defendant's unreasonable conduct following the invasion of privacy subjected the plaintiff to particular or additional embarrassment, harm, distress or humiliation.[35]

The remedial functions of damages for emotional distress in combination with the non-monetary remedies of apology and correction include:

- mitigation of injury to dignity and feelings, thereby reducing the amount of compensatory damages needed by a plaintiff;[36]
- vindication of the right to privacy and the hurt or distress caused to the plaintiff by the invasion;[37] and

[30] See, eg, JR Cohen, 'Legislating Apology: The Pros and Cons' (2002) 70 *University of Cincinnati Law Review* 819; P Vines, 'Apologizing to Avoid Liability: Cynical Civility or Practical Morality?' (2005) 27 *Sydney Law Review* 483; JC Kleefeld, 'Thinking Like a Human: British Columbia's Apology Act' (2007) 40 *University of British Columbia Law Review* 769; C Brown, 'Apology Legislation: Oiling the Wheels of Tort' (2009) 17 *Tort Law Review* 127.

[31] eg, British Columbia, Apology Act, SBC 2006, c 19. In Hong Kong, see Apology Ordinance (Cap 631).

[32] eg, ALRC, Privacy Report (n 4) 129 [7.95].

[33] ibid 227, [12.42].

[34] ibid ch 12; NSWLRC, Invasion of Privacy (n 7) ch 7.

[35] See Recommendation 12-2: ALRC, Privacy Report (n 4), [12.40]–[12.45].

[36] ibid 228, [12.42].

[37] ibid 254, [12.160].

- furtherance of the public interest by upholding the right to privacy, educating the public about the right and potentially deterring others from serious invasions of the right to privacy.[38]

An apology order as described in the Privacy Report might only be 'a public acknowledgement of wrongdoing'.[39] It is implicit, however, that the meaning of 'apology' in the Report is not limited to acknowledgement and would include expressions of regret, remorse, contrition and sympathy. Corrections, as noted in the Privacy Report, have the ability to 'set the record straight' where 'false private information is published or otherwise disclosed'.[40] The ALRC recommends that the legislation provide that 'private information', for the purposes of the tort of serious invasion of privacy, includes untrue information, but only if the information would be private if it were true.[41] Therefore, where such untrue information is disclosed in circumstances where the other elements of the tort of invasion of privacy are satisfied, the plaintiff would have an action under this tort and a correction order could be made.

In practical terms, we can expect that a correction will be suitable less often than an apology as a remedy for invasion of privacy. This is because in many cases, an invasion of privacy does not involve the wrongful disclosure of untrue information, and to the extent that it does, an apology can acknowledge the untruth. In any event, where the defendant has published untrue facts and the plaintiff is seeking a correction in order to vindicate his or her reputation, the action may well lie in defamation rather than invasion of privacy.[42] Sections IV and V of this chapter examine the reasoning behind the recommendations outlined in this section, and how the remedial purposes of apologies and corrections might be achieved. Before turning to consider this, the next section explores the meaning and function of apologies in a legal setting.

III. Meaning and Function of Apologies in Resolution of Privacy Torts and Other Civil Actions

To understand the meaning of 'apology' one needs to draw on many disciplines, including sociology, medicine, philosophy, psychology, criminal justice and law. It is important for lawyers to understand the meaning and function of apologies

[38] ibid 255, [12.163].
[39] ibid 254, [12.161].
[40] ibid 252–53, [12.154].
[41] ibid 83. See especially Recommendation [5-2].
[42] For discussion of the relationship between privacy and defamation in this context, see R Parkes QC, 'Privacy, Defamation, and False Facts' in N Moreham and M Warby (eds), *Tugendhat and Christie, The Law of Privacy and The Media*, 3rd edn (Oxford, Oxford UP, 2016) 349; D Rolph, 'The Interaction Between Defamation and Privacy' in K Barker, K Fairweather and R Grantham (eds), *Private Law in the 21st Century* (Oxford, Hart Publishing, 2017) 474.

in a civil society, and to appreciate that each of these disciplines has an important perspective to offer. There is theoretical and empirical support for a meaning of 'apology' that recognises that there are multiple components to an apology.[43] Psychological research also tells us that what constitutes an apology for the recipient in any particular situation and context is a highly unique and subjective experience.[44] Whether it will be acceptable to that person depends on many variables.[45]

Alfred Allan and others have identified three key features of an apology that are significant to how it will be perceived by a victim: the content of the apology, the sincerity of the apology and the focus of the apology.[46] The content of an apology is comprised of three components, which can be described in general terms as an acknowledgement of wrongdoing (admission), an expression of regret or remorse (affect), and a willingness to act in some way that is consistent with being sorry (action). Indicators of sincerity include the cost to the wrongdoer of making the apology, how the apology is communicated, the timing of the apology and whether it is given spontaneously. Apologies can range along a continuum from self to self–other focused. Victims prefer a self–other focused apology, because this indicates that the wrongdoer recognises the physical and/or psychological impact of his or her wrongdoing on the victim and feels regret for the other, rather than focusing primarily on his or her own needs. Important variables that influence how a victim feels about the wrongdoer's apology include the victim's perception of the wrongfulness of the behaviour, the level of responsibility he or she attributes to the wrongdoer, the perceived wrongfulness of the behaviour, and the nature and severity of the harmful consequences.[47]

This research into the meaning of 'apology' helps us understand why one person might be willing to settle on the basis of an apology that another person, the first person's lawyer for example, considers inadequate. It also explains why an apology that is considered sufficient for legal purposes to reduce the damages awarded against the defendant might not be sufficient to satisfy the plaintiff's emotional needs. A distinction is sometimes made in the legal context between 'full' and 'partial' apologies. Whether an apology is full or partial depends on the content of the apology. There is consensus that a 'full' apology incorporates an expression of heartfelt regret and remorse for what has happened, sympathy for the victim and acknowledgement of the wrongdoer's transgression.[48] For some people, it must

[43] See, eg, N Smith, *I Was Wrong: The Meanings of Apology* (Cambridge, Cambridge UP, 2008); see generally, D Slocum, A Allan and MM Allan, 'An Emerging Theory of Apology' (2011) 63 *Australian Journal of Psychology* 83.

[44] A Allan and R Carroll, 'Apologies in a Legal Setting: Insights from Research into Injured Parties' Experiences of Apologies after an Adverse Event' (2016) 24 *Psychiatry, Psychology and the Law* 1, 9.

[45] A Allan, 'Functional Apologies in Law' (2008) 15 *Psychiatry, Psychology and Law* 369.

[46] Allan and Carroll (n 44) 5–7.

[47] Slocum et al (n 43) 90.

[48] A Allan, 'Apology in Civil Law: A Psycho-Legal Perspective' (2007) 14 *Psychiatry, Psychology and Law* 5, 7.

also offer some form of recompense and a commitment to change in the future.[49] A 'partial' apology will consist of some, but not all, of these components. A partial apology might include an expression of sympathy or empathy alone ('I am sorry you were upset when I disclosed private information about you'), an expression of regret for the act or its outcome alone ('I regret that I disclosed private information about you'), an expression of sorrow alone ('I am very sorry I disclosed your private information') or an acceptance of responsibility for wrongdoing ('I was wrong to disclose your private information') without any expression of apology. A full apology would encompass all of these: 'I am sorry that you were humiliated, embarrassed and hurt as a result of my wrongful disclosure of your private information. I regret that you have suffered as a result of my actions. I am responsible for your distress and suffering and I want to make it up to you.'

When parties are endeavouring to resolve their dispute, they can decide together what would be a mutually acceptable apology. A plaintiff might be willing to accept an expression of regret and sympathy (the affect component), even if the defendant is not willing to admit to legal wrongdoing (the admission component). Alternatively, it might be more important to the plaintiff to receive an undertaking by the defendant to take steps to prevent similar harm to others in the future (the action component) than an admission. For this reason, settlements of legal disputes are sometimes accompanied by a 'partial' apology. It will be evident that this terminology does not sit well with the statement by Mortimer J at the start of this chapter that '[i]n any context, an apology is a way of recognising wrongdoing (large or small, moral, personal, social, public or legal) and acknowledging hurt and grievance caused or felt in others because of that wrongdoing'.[50] This reflects the fact that for many people, an acknowledgement of the hurt and emotions experienced by another person without acknowledgement of wrongdoing is not an apology at all. Nonetheless, parties are free to accept an acknowledgement of hurt or a mere expression of regret as an 'apology'.

If a dispute is not settled and liability is determined in favour of a plaintiff, a court will decide the legal significance of an apology for the purpose of determining judicial remedies. Where damages are available for emotional distress, a court may be required to decide whether an apology should be taken into account in the assessment of damages.[51] A court might be empowered to make an apology order. As we shall see, the meaning of 'apology' in this context may differ in important respects, particularly in relation to voluntariness and sincerity. In both situations, however, the court will expect defendants to make an apology that acknowledges wrongdoing and the harm they have caused to the plaintiffs.

When assessing an apology as a factor in mitigation of non-pecuniary damage to a person's reputation or right to liberty or privacy, a court will look at whether

[49] ibid.

[50] *Wotton v State of Queensland (No 5)* (n 1) [1589] *per* Mortimer J.

[51] An offer to publish a correction or an apology may also be relevant in a defamation case to a claim for the award of indemnity damages under s 40 of the *Defamation Act 2005* (NSW) and corresponding legislation in other Australian States and Territories.

the defendant has clearly acknowledged the wrongdoing (the defamation, the false imprisonment, the invasion of privacy) and has expressed regret and remorse or contrition for the distress and injury caused by the wrong. Something less than a 'full' apology in these terms might not be considered effective to mitigate the damage caused by the defendant. In defamation, for example, the courts say that the apology should contain 'a full and frank withdrawal of the charges or suggestions conveyed',[52] and it should contain an expression of regret that the matter complained of had been published.[53] The extent to which a correction or an apology is effective to vindicate and restore a plaintiff's reputation and provide consolation for distress and hurt experienced by a plaintiff will depend on multiple factors, including the timeliness of publication, the prominence given to the response and the content of the correction or apology.[54]

When deciding whether to make an apology order, the meaning of 'apology' takes on a very different complexion. This is because, as is universally acknowledged, a court cannot compel the defendant to convey sincere emotions. Even though an apology is usually intended to do so when it is offered in response to a serious breach of the plaintiff's rights, it has been recognised that this may not be essential for ordered apologies. This was the approach taken by the New South Wales Administrative Decisions Tribunal in *Burns v Radio 2UE Sydney Pty Ltd (No 2)*.[55] In this case, the second and third respondents, two radio presenters, made comments during a morning broadcast that were held to be unlawful vilification pursuant to section 49ZT(1) of the *Anti-Discrimination Act 1977* (NSW), because they were capable of inciting severe ridicule of gay men. The Tribunal granted the applicant's request for these respondents to be ordered to broadcast an apology. The Tribunal defined an 'apology' for the purposes of the *Anti-Discrimination Act* as an 'acknowledgement of the wrongdoing' that is a 'fulfilment of a legal requirement rather than as a statement of genuinely held feelings'.[56] In this way the Tribunal distinguished between a personal apology, which is an expression of sincere feelings of remorse and regret incapable of being coerced by a court order, and an apology ordered for statutory purposes. This approach has been applied in subsequent tribunal decisions in Australia.[57] In other anti-discrimination cases a court or tribunal may decline to order an apology at all when it is not satisfied that it would be made with sincerity[58] or voluntarily.[59]

[52] *Risk Allah Beh v Johnstone* (1868) 18 LT 620, 621.

[53] *Associated Newspapers Ltd v Dingle* [1964] AC 371 (HL), 400 *per* Lord Radcliffe, 419 *per* Lord Morris.

[54] These factors are reflected in the considerations to which a court is to have regard when determining whether an offer to make amends is reasonable, pursuant to s 18(2) of the *Defamation Act 2005* (NSW) and corresponding legislation in other Australian States and Territories.

[55] *Burns v Radio 2UE Sydney Pty Ltd (No 2)* [2005] NSWADT 24 (16 February 2005).

[56] ibid [29].

[57] *Sunol v Collier (EOD)* [2006] NSWADTAP 51 (27 September 2006), [54]; *Menzies v Owen* [2008] QADT 20 (19 September 2008).

[58] eg, *Jackson v Ilievski* [1996] HREOCA 18 (17 July 1996).

[59] eg, *Jones v Scully* (2002) 71 ALD 567, [245].

Turning from the meaning to the function of apologies, research shows that people from most, if not all, cultures learn to use apologies as a mechanism to acknowledge their mistakes, repair their own reputation and the reputations of injured parties, and re-establish relationships where required.[60] They might apologise because they feel morally obliged to do so or feel contrite, but they often apologise automatically to be polite and/or sympathetic without necessarily admitting responsibility. Wrongdoers sometimes apologise when injured parties do not expect them to do so, but victims generally want apologies after wrongdoing. Victims often experience a wrongdoer's failure to apologise as a violation of the social norm that wrongdoers should apologise for their wrongs, which makes them even angrier. Victims may, however, sometimes find apologies less satisfying than they expected, accept them conditionally or reject them explicitly. When a victim's psychological and social needs remain frustrated he or she may experience a 'state of unforgiveness'.[61] He or she may also experience a 'fight response', leading to the use of formal complaint processes or litigation against the wrongdoer.[62] Regardless of whether a fight or, instead, a flight response is invoked, researchers have found that victims believe that apologies will assist them to forgive. There is evidence of an association between apologies and forgiveness, but an apology does not appear to be a prerequisite for forgiveness nor lead automatically to forgiveness.[63]

There is potential, therefore, for apologies to restore social standing, repair relationships, and promote healing and forgiveness. Research shows that there are many variables that will influence the way a victim responds to an apology. The law cannot compel personal and social healing, but it can promote these processes while advancing the law's goals of protecting and vindicating legal rights, offering consolation for emotional distress, and educating the community about rights and societal values as expressed by the law. We shall return to consider the remedial functions attributed to apologies and correction orders in section V.

IV. Apologies and Corrections as a Factor in the Assessment of General Damages for Invasion of Privacy

Damages are available to compensate a plaintiff for the infringement of his or her right to privacy and for emotional distress inflicted by the invasion of that right in similar common law jurisdictions.[64] The ALRC's recommendation for damages

[60] The findings reported in this paragraph are reproduced from Allan and Carroll (n 44) 3–5 (footnotes omitted).

[61] ibid 5.

[62] ibid.

[63] ibid.

[64] *MGN v Gulati* [2015] EWCA Civ 1291, [2017] QB 149 (17 December 2015) [48] *per* Arden LJ, Rafferty LJ and Kitchen LJ agreeing (UK); *Jones v Tsige* 2012 ONCA 32, [74]–[77] (Ontario).

to be available for emotional distress as a remedy for serious invasion of privacy is consistent with these developments in privacy law. Although damages will be available at trial, a prompt apology is likely to be a more effective remedy. This is for similar reasons identified in defamation, where corrections and apologies are thought to vindicate reputation and provide consolation for hurt feelings and distress for defamation more promptly and more directly than an eventual award of damages.[65] Neither damages nor an apology or a correction can completely reverse the effect of the invasion and the emotional distress experienced by the plaintiff. Nor will the courts require a plaintiff to accept an apology offered by the defendant instead of monetary compensation for the invasion of privacy. Nonetheless, the courts will assess whether and the extent to which an apology has reduced the harm to the plaintiff. In so doing, the law provides an incentive for wrongdoers to mitigate the damage caused by their tortious conduct. This section identifies the principles applied to apologies and corrections in the assessment of damages for emotional distress for torts actionable without proof of actual damage, and discusses the application of those principles to invasion of privacy cases.

A. Apologies and Corrections as Mitigating and Aggravating Factors in the Assessment of Tort Damages for Emotional Distress

Courts take apologies into account when assessing damages for torts such as false imprisonment, assault and defamation, which aim to compensate for indignity, mental suffering, disgrace and humiliation suffered by the plaintiff.[66] Courts, tribunals and administrative decision makers are also empowered to take account of apologies in assessing damages for emotional distress for claims arising from breach of privacy legislation, unlawful discrimination and breach of the moral rights of an author under copyright legislation.[67]

A court can take into account 'the whole of the conduct of the defendant to the time of verdict which may have the effect of increasing the injury to the person's feelings'.[68] In defamation, an apology is addressed both to the person defamed, in

[65] *Robins v Kordowski* [2011] EWHC 1912 (QB) (22 July 2011), [82] *per* Tugendhat J; *Cerutti v Crestside Pty Ltd* [2014] QCA 33 (28 Feburary 2014) [44] *per* Applegarth J; JG Fleming, 'Retraction and Reply: Alternative Remedies for Defamation' (1978) 12 *University of British Columbia Law Review* 15, 24; D Milo, *Defamation and Freedom of Speech* (Oxford, Oxford UP, 2008) 270.

[66] *Spautz v Butterworths* (1996) 41 NSWLR 1, 17–18 *per* Clarke JA. Section 38(1) of the *Defamation Act 2005* (NSW) confirms that evidence is admissible on behalf of the defendant, in mitigation of damages for the publication of defamatory matter, that (a) the defendant has made an apology to the plaintiff about the publication of the defamatory matter; and (b) the defendant has published a correction of the defamatory matter.

[67] See, eg, *Privacy Act 1988* (Cth), s 52(1)(b)(ii) (privacy legislation); *Equal Opportunity Act 1984* (WA), s 127(b)(iii) (discrimination); *Copyright Act 1968* (Cth), s 195AZA(1)(d) (author), s 195AZGC(1)(d) (performer); see also *Perez v Fernandez* (2012) 260 FLR 1, [107] *per* Driver FM (copyright).

[68] *Spautz v Butterworths* (1996) 41 NSWLR 1, 8.

order to appease his or her injured feelings, and to those to whom the defamatory words were published, to undo the harm.[69] Non-pecuniary damages for a defamatory publication aim to compensate for personal distress and hurt, as well as to vindicate the plaintiff's reputation. An apology that is not an attempt to right a wrong but instead an attempt to escape from the consequences of wrongdoing therefore is unlikely to mitigate damages.[70] The law is concerned with the effectiveness of an apology to mitigate damages, which are awarded to compensate for distress and hurt caused to the plaintiff by the publication, provide reparation for the harm done to the plaintiff's reputation and to vindicate the plaintiff's reputation.[71] The extent to which a correction or an apology is effective in achieving these remedial objectives will be determined by the court's taking account of multiple factors, including the timeliness of publication, the prominence given to the response and the content of the correction or apology.[72]

B. Apologies and Corrections as Mitigating and Aggravating Factors in the Assessment of Damages for Emotional Distress for Invasion of Privacy

The ALRC's recommendation that courts consider any correction or apologies when assessing damages is consistent with the principles for assessment of damages for other torts where damages are available for emotional distress. In section III we saw that the effectiveness of an apology to reduce a plaintiff's emotional distress depends on the content of an apology, sincerity, its focus and many variables, including the plaintiff's perception of the wrongfulness and the nature and severity of the harmful consequences. This section identifies case law and legislative factors that are relevant to the assessment of damages for invasion of privacy. These provide the context in which courts will take apologies and corrections into account as mitigating or aggravating factors. The section then discusses some issues affecting the significance of apologies and corrections for the assessment of damages.

In *Gulati v MGN*, Mann J identified a number of principles that apply to the assessment of damages for wrongful disclosure of private information.[73] In this case, eight claimants were awarded substantial damages against the defendant, the owner of the *Daily Mirror*, *The Sunday People* and *The Sunday Mirror*, for misuse of private information obtained through phone hacking – that is, intercepting

[69] *Cerutti v Crestside Pty Ltd* [2014] QCA 33 (28 February 2014) [44] *per* Applegarth J.

[70] *Uren v John Fairfax and Sons Pty Ltd* (1966) 117 CLR 118, 141 *per* Menzies J.

[71] *Carson v John Fairfax and Sons Ltd* (1993) 178 CLR 44, 60, 66 *per* Mason CJ, Deane, Dawson, Gaudron JJ.

[72] See text accompanying n 54.

[73] *Gulati v MGN* [2015] EWHC 1482 (Ch) (17 December 2015) [229]. These principles were referred to and not disputed by the Court of Appeal in *MGN v Gulati* [2015] EWCA Civ 1291, [2017] QB 149, 164, [32] *per* Arden LJ, Rafferty LJ and Kitchen LJ agreeing.

voicemail messages left on the claimants' mobile telephones. Damages were awarded to compensate for distress and for the invasion of the claimant's privacy.[74] In assessing damages, Mann J took into account the wrongfulness of the general hacking activity, as well as the effect of the published articles.[75] When assessing individual claims, consideration was given to the subject matter of the information and to whether the information was about matters internal to a relationship.[76] Further considerations included the effect of the disclosure on the victim and whether the intrusions by publication were repeated.[77] Consistent with damages-assessment principles more generally, His Honour accepted that the extent of the damage may be plaintiff-specific, and that a 'thinner-skinned individual may be caused more upset, and therefore receive more compensation, than a thicker-skinned individual who is the subject of the same intrusion'.[78]

To similar effect, the Manitoba *Privacy Act* provides specific guidance with regard to the factors relevant to a determination of damages.[79] Section 4(2) states:

> In awarding damages in an action for a violation of privacy of a person, the court shall have regard to all the circumstances of the case including
>
> (a) the nature, incidence and occasion of the act, conduct or publication constituting the violation of privacy of that person;
>
> (b) the effect of the violation of privacy on the health, welfare, social, business or financial position of that person or his family;
>
> (c) any relationship, whether domestic or otherwise, between the parties to the action;
>
> (d) any distress, annoyance or embarrassment suffered by that person or his family arising from the violation of privacy; and
>
> (e) the conduct of that person and the defendant, both before and after the commission of the violation of privacy, including any apology or offer of amends made by the defendant.

In assessing the effectiveness of any particular apology or offer to make amends to reduce the harm caused to the plaintiff as invited to by paragraph (e) of the subsection, a court will need to take into account all the circumstances of the invasion of privacy, including those referred to in paragraphs (1)(a)–(d).

The ALRC Privacy Report does not set out factors similar to those identified in *Gulati* or the Manitoba *Privacy Act*. There are other indicators, however, of the factors relevant to the effectiveness of an apology. In particular, a court will need to consider whether, and to what extent, there was a 'reasonable expectation of privacy' and whether the invasion of privacy was 'serious' when determining if the

[74] *Gulati v MGN* (Ch) (n 73) [144].
[75] ibid [155].
[76] ibid [229].
[77] ibid.
[78] ibid.
[79] Manitoba, *Privacy Act*, RSM 1987, c P125. The other provincial statutes leave this determination to judicial discretion. Case law indicates that courts will consider the same factors enumerated in the Manitoba *Privacy Act* when applying common law principles: see, eg, *Jones v Tsige* (2012) 108 OR (3d) 241, [82] *per* Sharpe JA.

cause of action is made out. The ALRC identified a number of factors relevant to determining whether there was a reasonable expectation of privacy, including:[80]

- the nature of the private information, including whether it relates to intimate or family matters, health or medical matters, or financial matters;
- the means used to obtain the private information or to intrude upon seclusion, including the use of any device or technology;
- the place where the intrusion occurred, such as in the plaintiff's home;
- the purpose of the misuse, disclosure or intrusion;
- how the private information was held or communicated, such as in private correspondence or a personal diary;
- whether and to what extent the private information was already in the public domain;
- the relevant attributes of the plaintiff, including the plaintiff's age, occupation and cultural background; and
- the conduct of the plaintiff, including whether the plaintiff invited publicity or manifested a desire for privacy.

In determining whether the invasion was 'serious' a court would need to consider:

- the degree of any offence, distress or harm to dignity that the invasion of privacy was likely to cause to a person of ordinary sensibilities in the position of the plaintiff; and
- whether the defendant was motivated by malice or knew the invasion of privacy was likely to offend, distress or harm the dignity of the plaintiff.

It is suggested that a court's findings on the evidence relating to a plaintiff's reasonable expectation of privacy and the seriousness of the invasion will be relevant to an assessment of the effectiveness of an apology or correction to reduce the plaintiff's damages. In other words, the effectiveness of an apology or correction in reducing the emotional harm inflicted on the plaintiff needs to be evaluated in light of all of the circumstances surrounding the invasion of privacy.

A number of observations can be made from a comparison with the principles applied to mitigation of damages in defamation and discrimination and other statutory actions. First, where awards of non-pecuniary damages are small (by reason of convention or caps or otherwise), an apology as vindication and as consolation for distress may assume greater importance to a plaintiff than damages only. Second, in the absence of a suitable voluntary apology or correction, a plaintiff may need a higher damages award for consolation and vindication. With these observations in mind, it will be in the interests of both parties to take account of these non-monetary remedies in settlement negotiations for a claim for serious invasion of privacy.

[80] See Recommendation 6-2: ALRC, Privacy Report (n 4) 96.

C. Apologies and Corrections in the Assessment of Damages – Points for Consideration

It is reasonable to predict that where an invasion of privacy is serious, the defendant's apology or correction will need to be full and timely for a court to find it had a mitigating effect. Each case will turn on its own facts, and one would not expect any fixed discount to apply for an apology. A court will take into account all the evidence, including the plaintiff's evidence, as to the impact of an apology or correction on the level of the emotional distress he or she experienced. In this section I identify three interrelated points for consideration when assessing the significance of an apology or correction for an award of damages for invasion of privacy.

First, the research referred to in section III confirms that the seriousness of the invasion of privacy and the circumstances in which it occurred are likely to affect how an apology by the defendant will be perceived by the plaintiff. Victims of wrongdoing take account of the degree of culpability and seriousness of the offence in their response to apologies. Where the conduct is deliberate, even if the harm is not inflicted deliberately and more so where it is, it may take a lot more for an apology to convey to a plaintiff that the defendant is sorry and remorseful than if the conduct were accidental. For an apology to reduce the emotional harm to a plaintiff for deliberate conduct, one would expect that the defendant would need to offer an apology in a timely way that is full in every sense. An understanding of what this means in terms of the content, focus and sincerity of an apology, discussed in section III, will assist in evaluating the mitigating effect of an apology for the purposes of assessing damages.

This point is illustrated by the facts and decision in *Gulati v MGN*.[81] In this case, the defendant submitted that apologies tendered ought to be taken into account when assessing the distress and hurt caused to the plaintiffs. Mann J agreed that in some circumstances apologies would be capable of having this effect, but not in this case.[82] The defendant's apologies, when they finally came, were held to be ineffective to reduce the hurt and the amount of damages necessary to compensate the victims of sustained and serious invasions of privacy. The Mirror Group 'firmly and publicly' denied knowledge of any phone hacking by its newspapers until court proceedings were well advanced.[83] As the proceedings approached, the defendant added apologies to admissions made in the proceedings, and published admissions and a public apology in its newspapers, which expressed 'sincere apologies' for the 'wholly unacceptable intrusions to which the claimants were subjected' that were 'improper and should never have happened'.[84] Most of the claimants were

[81] *Gulati v MGN* (Ch) (n 73).
[82] ibid [216].
[83] ibid [19].
[84] ibid [26]. A further apology was made by counsel in his opening at trial for the defendant's wrongful conduct: ibid [18].

'distinctly unimpressed' by the apologies and their timing, believing the apologies were 'triggered by the approach of the court proceedings'.[85]

Mann J found that the public apologies were made at least partly as a tactical matter with an eye to the forthcoming trial. While this did not mean the apologies were not genuine, in the result, his Honour concluded that it was 'quite understandable that the apologies have done nothing to mollify the claimants or reduce their level of hurt, which I find is the case'.[86] The facts and decision in *Gulati* illustrate that an apology that offers too little or comes too late to satisfy the victim may also be regarded by a court as ineffective to reduce the hurt caused by the defendant, and thereby to justify a reduction in the amount of damages awarded for emotional distress.

A second point is that the question of whether an apology or a correction was effective to reduce the emotional harm inflicted on the plaintiff is for the court to decide. A court will take into account the circumstances of the invasion of privacy and the evidence of the plaintiff, but ultimately the court will decide whether a correction or apology has reduced the harm caused to the plaintiff.[87] The Court's approach is illustrated by *Jones v Tsige*.[88] The plaintiff Jones and the defendant Tsige worked for different branches of the same bank. They did not know each other. Tsige had formed a de facto relationship with the plaintiff's ex-husband. For about four years, the defendant used her workplace computer to access the plaintiff's personal bank accounts at least 174 times. She did not publish, distribute or record the information in any way. When she discovered the conduct, the plaintiff brought an action for damages for invasion of privacy.

The Ontario Court of Appeal upheld the plaintiff's claim at common law for invasion of privacy by intrusion upon seclusion. The Court took into account a number of factors in the assessment of damages, including that Tsige's actions were deliberate, repeated and arose from a complex web of domestic arrangements likely to provoke strong feelings and animosity. Speaking for the Ontario Court of Appeal, Sharpe JA concluded that Jones was understandably very upset by the intrusion into her private financial affairs. On the other hand, the Court took into account that Jones suffered no public embarrassment or harm to her health, welfare, social, business or financial position, and that Tsige had apologised for her conduct and made genuine attempts to make amends.[89] The Court awarded damages to Jones of $10,000, described by Sharpe JA as being at the mid-point of the usual range of up to $20,000 for breach of the right to privacy. The Court apparently took into account that Tsige was 'apologetic and contrite', but also that her actions were 'deliberate, prolonged and shocking'.[90] His Honour

[85] ibid [28]–[29].
[86] ibid [216]. The defendant did not rely on the content of those apologies in oral arguments on appeal: see *MGN v Gulati* (CA) (n 73).
[87] *Jones v Tsige* (n 79) [90].
[88] ibid.
[89] ibid.
[90] ibid [69].

concluded that '[a]ny person in Jones' position would be profoundly disturbed by the significant intrusion into her highly personal information'.[91] It appears that the Court regarded the defendant's apology and contrition as a mitigating factor in the assessment of damages.

A plaintiff's evidence of his or her personal experience of the invasion of privacy, of particular sensitivities that affect the degree of emotional distress suffered and of his or her response to any apology by the defendant will be relevant. As Mann J notes in *Gulati*, some individuals will be more upset than others by the same intrusion on their privacy. It follows that the distress experienced by some individuals will be ameliorated less by an apology than others. In cases of serious invasion of privacy, like *Gulati*, courts are likely to place significant weight on the plaintiff's evidence as to whether his or her feelings of emotional distress were lessened by an apology.

The third point is that an apology is not always welcome to a victim, and it cannot be assumed that it will reduce the emotional distress caused by a serious invasion of privacy. In some scenarios, in particular revenge-porn cases, it is not difficult to imagine the emotional distress, hurt and humiliation experienced by a plaintiff being increased as a result of an insensitive, insincere, untimely and incomplete apology. Publication of an apology concerning highly sensitive private information that was unlawfully disclosed and the circumstances of the invasion of privacy, for example, particularly where there is an existing or previous relationship between the parties, could re-victimise the plaintiff and add to his or her distress.

For this reason it is significant that the ALRC recommends that the defendant's unreasonable conduct following the invasion of privacy that subjected the plaintiff to particular or additional embarrassment, harm, distress or humiliation is a factor to be taken into account in the assessment of damages.[92] Conduct relating to the offer or publication of an apology may well be unreasonable in all the circumstances and be a factor that increases the amount of damages awarded. The ALRC's recommendation acknowledges the potential for an apology, whether it is made publicly or in private, to increase the emotional distress caused to the plaintiff.

Further, it cannot be assumed that a plaintiff is seeking to achieve forgiveness as an outcome of the legal process, particularly in proceedings between previous intimate partners or where there is a history of family violence by the defendant against the plaintiff. There are lessons to be gained from research on restorative justice, which points to the need to avoid expecting this of victims and the importance of not pressuring victims to accept apologies. There is a risk that doing so will result in failure to respect their reasons for rejecting a defendant's offer of apology and cause greater harm to victims.[93] This is an important consideration in the assessment of damages, where assumptions might be made about the ability of an apology to reduce the emotional harm experienced by a person in the plaintiff's

[91] ibid.

[92] ALRC, Privacy Report (n 4) 227, [12.42].

[93] J Stubbs, 'Beyond Apology? Domestic Violence and Critical Questions for Restorative Justice' (2007) 7 *Criminology and Criminal Justice* 169.

position. It is also a significant reason why an order to apologise should not be made in lieu of damages unless that is a remedy sought by the plaintiff.

In summary, the circumstances in which a serious invasion of privacy occurred and the effectiveness of an apology by the defendant in terms of sincerity, fullness, timing and respect for the plaintiff's privacy in the manner in which the apology is communicated, will be highly relevant to a court's assessment of damages. The developing case law indicates that the courts, quite properly, take into account evidence of the plaintiff's subjective experience of embarrassment, indignity, hurt and humiliation resulting from an invasion of privacy. A court needs to consider all the features of a defendant's apology, as well as the plaintiff's experience of the apology. This approach is supported by empirical research, which shows that the content, sincerity and focus of an apology affect the likelihood that an apology for wrongdoing in any particular situation will reduce the emotional harm inflicted by a wrongdoer on an injured party.

V. Apology Orders and Correction Orders

Recognition of the tort of privacy and consideration of apologies and corrections in the assessment of damages provide incentives for parties to negotiate with each other for remedies other than damages. At present, in the absence of a tort action, a victim of serious invasion of privacy is reliant on a defendant's civility or other motivation to offer an apology. Pressure may be applied on a person who has invaded another's privacy to apologise or publish a correction through complaint mechanisms and codes of conduct, including codes that apply to the press, but these mechanisms provide insufficient protection for serious invasions of privacy, particularly when the wrongdoer is not amenable to any form of regulatory remedy or sanction.

This section discusses the ALRC's recommendations that courts be given the power to order a defendant to publish a correction and to order an apology. In the first two subsections, I discuss areas of the common law and legislation where these or similar orders are available, in order to identify the principles for determining whether and when to order a defendant to apologise. The cases reveal a number of purposes that might be achieved by orders of this type. In the last subsection, these insights are applied to orders for an apology or correction in cases of serious invasion of privacy.

A. Apology and Correction Orders – Common Law Torts and Remedies

Correction and apology orders are rarely ordered by courts in common law jurisdictions. Even in defamation cases where corrections and apologies feature most prominently in settlements and assessment of damages, courts in the

United Kingdom (UK), Australia and other common law countries generally do not regard these remedies as available to a plaintiff. One reason is that coercive remedies will not be awarded where compensatory damages would be adequate to compensate the plaintiff.[94] Another reason is the view that courts do not have the power to order a defendant to publish an apology due to constitutional protections of freedom of expression.[95] Over the years, legislative reform proposals have called for greater emphasis to be placed on remedies that provide prompt and vindicatory responses to defamatory publications, including by correction orders, vindication orders, declarations of falsity, and retraction and apology orders.[96] These recommendations have not been taken up. Instead, the importance of early and effective correction, vindication of reputation and consolation for injury to feelings is acknowledged by provisions in defamation legislation that encourage rather than coerce corrections and apologies. These include 'offer to make amends' provisions and the ability of courts to award costs on an indemnity basis against a party who refuses an offer to settle on reasonable terms.[97]

A defamation plaintiff can achieve vindication of his or her reputation by means other than an award of damages. One is by a court order for a defendant to publish a summary of the court's judgment. Section 12 of the *Defamation Act 2013* (UK) was introduced as one of a number of reforms to defamation law in the UK to give a court the power to make this order. There is also scope for a reasoned judgment to provide some vindication of a claimant's reputation.[98]

It remains the case, however, that in Australia and other common law countries, damages are the primary judicial remedy for defamation.[99] With this said, some

[94] See generally, N Witzleb et al, *Remedies: Commentary and Materials*, 6th edn (Thomson Reuters, 2015) 25, [1.110].

[95] In Australia, see, eg, *Summertime Holdings Pty Ltd v Environmental Defender's Office Ltd* (1998) 45 NSWLR 291, 297; *Cerutti v Crestside Pty Ltd* (2016) 1 Qd R 89, 110, [36] *per* Applegarth J; *VTS IT Pty Ltd v Russell* [2015] ACTSC 230 (14 August 2015) [41] *per* Refshauge J; D Rolph, *Defamation* (Thomson Reuters, 2015) 350, [17.10]. In the UK see, eg, *Loutchansky v Times Newspapers Ltd (Nos 2, 3, 4 and 5)* [2001] EWCA Civ 1805, [2002] QB 283, [99] *per* Phillips MR. The legitimacy of arguments based on freedom of expression in this context has been questioned: see, eg, Milo (n 65) 271–72; Dario Milo, 'It's Hard for Me To Say I'm Sorry: Apology as a Remedy in the South African Law of Defamation' (2012) 4 *Journal of Media Law* 11, 16.

[96] eg, Australian Law Reform Commission, *Unfair Publication: Defamation and Privacy* (Australian Law Reform Commission Report No 11, 1979) 141–42, [257]–[258]; Australian Government, Attorney-General's Department, *Revised Outline of a Possible National Defamation Law*, July 2004, 34 (Attorney-General's *Revised Outline*) (correction orders); Attorney-General (ACT), *Defamation Report in the ACT* (September 1998) 6–8 (vindication orders). See also Recommendation 13 of New South Wales Law Reform Commission, *Defamation* (NSW Law Reform Commission Report No 75, 1995); Milo (n 65) 273.

[97] See, eg, *Defamation Act 2005* (NSW), Part 3 Division 1 (offer to make amends), s 40 (costs).

[98] See, eg, *Purnell v Business Magazines* [2007] EWCA Civ 744, [2008] 1 WLR 1. See further R Carroll and N Witzleb, 'It's Not Just About the Money – Enhancing the Vindicatory Effect of Private Law Remedies' (2011) 37 *Monash University Law Review* 216, 237–38.

[99] In Canada, for instance, the general rule is that a court will not order a defendant to publish a retraction or publish an apology. See, eg, *Hunger Project v Council on Mind Abuse (COMA) Inc* (1995) 22 OR (3d) 29 (Gen Div). See also dicta in *John v Lee* (2009) BCCA 313, [11]. In Australia, see *Pingel v Toowoomba Newspapers Pty Ltd* [2010] QCA 175 (16 July 2010), [137]–[138] *per* Applegarth J.

courts have endorsed the use of apology orders. In *Ottawa-Carlton District School Board v Scharf*,[100] the defendants, as parents of a child who made defamatory remarks on a website about a school principal and a superintendent of instruction, were ordered to publish a retraction and apology in two local newspapers in addition to paying damages.[101] In South Africa, where, like most Commonwealth countries, damages are the primary remedy for defamation, the Constitutional Court in *Le Roux v Dey* ordered the defendants, three schoolboys who were held to have defamed the deputy headmaster at their high school, to pay damages and 'to tender an unconditional apology to the plaintiff for the injury they caused him'.[102] In deciding that an apology could be ordered for defamation despite authority to the contrary, Froneman J and Cameron J (with whom the other members of the Court agreed) stressed the importance of remedies that create the best possible conditions for reconciliation between members of society, stating:

> Part of reconciliation, at all different levels, consists of recantation of past wrongs and apology for them. That experience has become part of the fabric of our society. The law cannot enforce reconciliation but it should create the best conditions for making it possible. We can see no reason why the creation of those conditions should not extend to personal relationships where the actionable dignity of one has been impaired by another.[103]

In another defamation case the same year, *The Citizen 1978 (Pty) Ltd v McBride*,[104] the Constitutional Court reiterated the view that there may be cases where a plaintiff should be entitled to remedies that include a suitable apology, stating 'the importance of apology in securing redress and in salving feelings cannot be under-estimated'.[105] The Court noted in this case the complexities of ordering a media defendant to apologise, and concluded that 'the question of an apology where a media defendant has defamed another must await another day'.[106]

Cases in which courts have been willing to entertain making an apology order against a defamation defendant, despite being rare and few in number, are significant for a number of reasons. First, they indicate the potential for the apology order to be developed by the courts as a remedy for defamation, and therefore for other torts such as invasion of privacy. Second, they highlight the need for careful examination of the circumstances in which a court might make such an order, and the implications of an order for freedom of expression and – in the case of media

[100] *Ottawa-Carlton District School Board v Scharf* [2007] OJ No 3030, affirmed 2008 ONCA 154, leave to appeal refused [2008] SCCA No 285.

[101] See also *Moore v Canadian Newspapers Co* (1989) 69 OR (2d) 262 (HC) expressing the opinion in dicta that the Court did have the power to order an apology and that such an act would not violate the Canadian *Charter.*

[102] *Le Roux v Dey* 2011 (3) SA 274 (CC), [206]. For discussion, see Milo, 'It's Hard for Me To Say I'm Sorry' (n 95) 13–14.

[103] *Le Roux v Dey* (n 102) [202].

[104] *The Citizen 1978 (Pty) Ltd v McBride* 2011 (4) SA 191 (CC).

[105] ibid 231.

[106] ibid 232.

defendants – a free press. Lastly, the decisions in *Ottawa-Carlton District School Board* and *Le Roux* raise questions about the extent to which an order compelling a natural person to apologise is an unjustifiable restriction on that person's constitutional right to freedom of conscience.[107]

B. Apology and Correction Orders– Statutory Actions and Remedies

There are a number of statutes in Australia that confer power on a court to make an apology order as a remedy for interference with dignitary interests. For example, when granting relief under the *Copyright Act 1968* (Cth) for infringement of an author's moral rights in respect of a work or for infringement of a performer's moral rights, a court has the power to order that the defendant make a public apology for the infringement.[108] There is also provision for apology orders to be made in some Australian jurisdictions under privacy legislation that regulates disclosure of private information by government and specified entities.[109] In *NZ v Director General, Department of Housing*, for example, pursuant to section 55(2)(e) of the *Privacy and Personal Information Protection Act 1998* (NSW), the New South Wales Administrative Appeals Tribunal ordered a government department to tender a written apology to the applicant for disclosing personal information about the applicant to a third person without lawful authority.[110] There does not appear to be a similar power to order an apology under data protection legislation in the UK, New Zealand or Canada.

Orders to apologise are also available under anti-discrimination legislation in Australia and some other countries.[111] In some jurisdictions the legislation makes express reference to orders to apologise, in others apology orders and related orders are made pursuant to a power to order a respondent 'to perform any reasonable act or course of conduct to redress any loss or damage suffered by the

[107] Milo, 'It's Hard for Me To Say I'm Sorry' (n 95) 16. See also BT White, 'Say You're Sorry: Court Ordered Apologies as a Civil Rights Remedy' (2006) 91 *Cornell Law Review* 1261; D-K Choi, 'Freedom of Conscience and the Court-Ordered Apology for Defamatory Remarks' (2000) 8 *Cardozo Journal of International and Comparative Law* 205.

[108] *Copyright Act 1968* (Cth), s 195AZA(1)(d) (author) and s 195AZGC(1)(d) (performer).

[109] eg, pursuant to s 55(2) of the *Privacy and Personal Information Protection Act 1998* (NSW); *Privacy Act 1988* (Cth), s 52(1)(b)(ii). For discussion of the remedies available in federal privacy legislation in Australia and the availability of apologies, see N Witzleb, 'Determinations under the Privacy Act 1988 (Cth) as a Privacy Remedy' in ch 15 of this book.

[110] *NZ v Director General, Department of Housing* [2006] NSWADT 173 (7 June 2006).

[111] A comprehensive list of federal and State anti-discrimination legislation in force is set out in *CCH: Australian and NZ Equal Opportunity Commentary* ¶2–720. The power to order apologies is conferred on courts and tribunals exercising anti-discrimination jurisdiction in a number of overseas jurisdiction. In Hong Kong, see *Disability Discrimination Ordinance* (Hong Kong) cap 487, s 72(4)(b). In the Republic of South Africa, s 21(2) of the *Promotion of Equality and Prevention of Unfair Discrimination Act 2000* (South Africa) confers power on the Equality Court to make a wide range of remedies orders, including 'an order that an unconditional apology be made': s 21(2)(j).

complainant'.[112] The ALRC's recommendation that courts be given the power to make an apology and similar orders against defendants for serious invasion of privacy draws on cases decided under anti-discrimination law in Australia and Hong Kong. In what follows I refer to three cases that provide guidance on the circumstances in which a court might make such an order, before turning to consider these orders in the context of serious invasion of privacy in the next subsection.

In *Ma Bik Yung v Ko Chuen*, the Hong Kong Court of Final Appeal held that the Hong Kong *Disability Discrimination Ordinance* conferred power on a court to make an order against an unwilling defendant.[113] An unwilling defendant was described by the Court as 'one who does not feel sorry'.[114] The Court stated that when addressing the question of remedies for unlawful conduct, a court must bear in mind the legislative purpose of eliminating discrimination and the prejudicial attitudes that may exist in society.[115] In doing so, the Court stated that it should be prepared to be innovative, and at the same time flexible and pragmatic in its approach.[116] As for when a court should order an unwilling defendant to apologise, the Court of Final Appeal said 'it will be a rare case where enforcement of an apology order will not be futile or disproportionate and contrary to the interests of administration of justice'.[117] In making an order, the circumstances to be considered include 'the nature and aim of the legislation, the interest of the community, the gravity of the unlawful conduct and the plaintiff's circumstances, including the extent of the loss and damage suffered'.[118] Only then can the question be answered whether in the particular instance the guaranteed freedoms of the applicant justify the making of an order, notwithstanding the interference it constitutes with the guaranteed freedoms, including freedom of expression, of the respondent. The Court concluded that to make an order against an unwilling defendant, the circumstances would have to be 'exceptional'.[119]

One can foresee a court ordering a defendant to publish a correction or make an apology where the defendant has not already done so voluntarily but is willing to do so once he or she has been found to have acted unlawfully. Beyond this situation, the question narrows to what constitutes 'rare' and 'exceptional' circumstances for the purposes of ordering a defendant who remains unwilling to apologise for unlawful discrimination? Two Australian cases shed some light on this question.[120]

[112] *Equal Opportunity Act 1984* (WA), s 127(b)(iii). In contrast, s 108(2)(d) of the *Anti-Discrimination Act 1997* (NSW) and s 209(1)(d)–(e) of the *Anti-Discrimination Act 1991* (Qld) expressly confer the power to make an apology order.

[113] *Ma Bik Yung v Ko Chuen* [2002] 2 HKLRD 1.

[114] ibid 11, [25].

[115] ibid 14.

[116] ibid.

[117] ibid 20–21.

[118] ibid 19.

[119] ibid 19.

[120] See R Carroll 'You Can't Order Sorriness, So Is There Any Value in an Ordered Apology? An Analysis of Apology Orders in Anti-discrimination Cases' (2010) 33 *University of New South Wales Law*

In the Federal Court of Australia decision in *Eatock v Bolt*, Bromberg J held that the respondent newspaper proprietor, *Herald and Weekly Times* ('HWT'), had contravened section 18C of the *Racial Discrimination Act 1975* (Cth) by publishing in print and online in the *Herald Sun* articles written by the first respondent, Andrew Bolt, which unlawfully vilified '[s]ome aboriginal persons of mixed descent who have a fairer, rather than darker skin, and who by a combination of descent, self-identification and communal recognition are, and are recognised as aboriginal persons'.[121] The plaintiffs sought an apology order against the newspaper as second respondent, which was strongly resisted by HWT. His Honour found force in the contention that an apology should not be compelled by an order of the Court, 'because that compels a person to articulate a sentiment that is not genuinely held'.[122]

In *Eatock v Bolt (No 2)*, rather than order an apology, Bromberg J ordered HWT to publish a corrective notice in the *Herald Sun* newspaper and online.[123] The notice was required to refer to the proceedings, the order requiring its publication and set out the declaration made by the Court. The prominence and frequency of the published notice were also stipulated in the order. His Honour considered that a corrective notice could serve a number of purposes, namely:

> redressing the hurt felt by those injured; restoring the esteem and social standing which has been lost as a consequence of the contravention; informing those influenced by the contravening conduct of the wrongdoing involved; and helping to negate the dissemination of racial prejudice.[124]

His Honour ordered the publication of the corrective notice because he was not satisfied that media coverage of the Court's decision could be relied upon to achieve all of the purposes of a corrective notice. His Honour reached this view based on evidence of media coverage of the case received by the Court and the concern that a reader would be exposed to 'competing and often conflicting media commentary made upon the Court's judgment'.[125] The corrective notice is neither an ordered correction of false statements nor a published apology. Essentially, it performs the same function as ordering a defendant to publish a summary of a court's judgment.

More recently, in *Wotton v State of Queensland (No 5)*, Mortimer J in the Federal Court of Australia considered once again what purposes an apology order might serve in an anti-discrimination case, and when it might be appropriate to make such an order.[126] The applicants sought a public apology from the State of Queensland and the Commissioner of the Queensland Police Service under

Journal 360 for circumstances in which courts and tribunals in Australia have determined whether it is, or is not, appropriate to order a defendant to anti-discrimination cases to apologise to the plaintiff.

[121] *Eatock v Bolt* (2011) 283 ALR 505, 598.

[122] ibid 601.

[123] *Eatock v Bolt (No 2)* (2011) 284 ALR 114, 118.

[124] ibid 118, [15].

[125] ibid 119, [23].

[126] *Wotton v State of Queensland (No 5)* (n 1).

section 46PO(4) of the *Australian Human Rights Commission Act 1986* (Cth), for having engaged in unlawful discrimination through officers of the Queensland Police Service ('QPS'). Complaints of racial discrimination under section 9(1) of the *Racial Discrimination Act 1975* (Cth) were made by members of the Palm Island community for actions taken by the police following the death in custody of a member of the community. The Court held that the action for racial discrimination against the QPS was made out. Mortimer J awarded Mr Wotton (and other defendants) damages for the way he was treated when arrested, and 'for the interference with his home, family and privacy'.[127]

Her Honour saw much force in the views expressed by Froneman J and Coleman J in *Le Roux v Dey* that a public statement about past wrongs is capable of creating the best conditions to make reconciliation possible, even though the law cannot enforce reconciliation. She also recognised that the principles identified by Li CJ in *Ma Bik Yung*, when considering whether to order an unwilling defendant to apologise, were consistent with the approach taken by Bromberg J in *Eatock*, in concluding:[128]

> The principal reason tending against ordering an apology in relation to an unwilling respondent is that the court has other remedies at its disposal that could better achieve the objectives of such an order. Nevertheless, in some cases it may well be appropriate to order an apology.

The critical questions, therefore, as identified by Mortimer J, are 'whether a court-ordered apology is an act which the Court is satisfied would redress damage suffered by the applicants' and whether 'more appropriate methods of achieving that redress are available'.[129]

Mortimer J concluded that a more appropriate method of redress than an apology order or a corrective notice in this case would be a public statement by QPS about the Court's findings in the case, published in the same way as the apology would have been published. The statement would be in a similar form to that ordered in *Eatock v Bolt (No 2)*, adapted to the circumstances of this case.[130] The distinction was made in this case between a 'correction' of conduct held by the court to be unlawful in the same media in which the conduct occurred and a 'statement' unconnected to a previous publication. Ultimately, Mortimer J declined to make an apology order in *Wotton (No 6)* because the proceedings before her, as a class action, were yet to be completed.[131]

These cases demonstrate the range of declaratory and vindicatory orders that a court can make in anti-discrimination cases, instead of an apology order, when a defendant is unwilling to apologise. A media defendant can be ordered to publish a corrective notice, or a public authority ordered to publish a public statement to

[127] ibid [12].
[128] ibid [1577].
[129] ibid [1584].
[130] ibid [1596].
[131] *Wotton v State of Queensland (No 6)* [2017] FCA 245 (15 March 2017) [36]–[38].

ensure that the public is informed about the unlawful conduct in terms stipulated by the court. The purposes of the orders referred to in *Eatock* and *Wotton* include redressing the hurt felt by those injured, restoring the esteem and social standing that has been lost as a consequence of the contravention conduct, and helping to negate the dissemination of racial prejudice. These orders aim to vindicate the plaintiff's right not to be discriminated against and to inform the public about the protection of this right by the law and the court's orders. These purposes are similar to those attributed to an order to apologise for unlawful discrimination by the New South Wales Administrative Decisions Tribunal in *Burns v Radio 2UE*. They are examples of remedial orders, other than damages, that vindicate the protected right and in doing so protect dignitary and other interests.

C. Apology and Correction Orders – Tort of Serious Invasion of Privacy and Remedies

As the law stands, courts do not order apologies and corrections as remedies in jurisdictions that have recognised common law or legislative torts that protect privacy. Given that a tort of serious invasion of privacy has not been recognised under common law in Australia, questions as to the courts' powers to make such orders and the circumstances in which they would be appropriate remain moot. In the absence of legislative power to order these remedies, there is little prospect that they will be developed as a remedy by the courts. Both the NSWLRC and the ALRC have recommended that courts be conferred with broad power to award remedies for invasion of privacy. In keeping with the decision in *Eatock*, the ALRC recognises that there will be cases where a coercive order can vindicate the plaintiff's rights and serve the public interest in ways that do not force a defendant who is unwilling and not remorseful to make an apology.[132]

The NSWLRC has proposed that courts be given a broad discretion to award remedies, including 'such other relief as the court considers necessary in the circumstances', which includes court-ordered apologies and correction orders.[133] The advantage of expressing the power in this or in similarly broad terms is that it allows a court to fashion orders that may achieve some of the purposes of an apology order while not compelling an unwilling defendant to apologise. This is evident from *Eatock* and *Wotton*, discussed in the previous section. It affords a court the remedial flexibility to distinguish between a correction order, an order to apologise, a corrective notice and a public statement of liability, or to fashion an order to fit the circumstances. There would be further advantages of conferring remedial power using the same language as existing privacy legislation and

[132] ALRC, Privacy Report (n 4) 256, [12.169].

[133] NSWLRC, Invasion of Privacy (n 7) 48–49, [7.7]. The ALRC also envisages that an apology order will be only one of many available remedies for serious invasion of privacy: see ALRC, Privacy Report (n 4) 256, [12.168].

anti-discrimination legislation in Australia, namely, that the court can order that 'the respondent must perform any reasonable act or course of conduct to redress any loss or damage suffered by the complainant'. This will allow for consistency in the developing case law in these areas of the law that both seek to protect dignitary interests and redress non-pecuniary loss.

In the event that the power to make these types of orders is conferred by legislation, courts will need to consider what purposes might be served by an apology or correction order, and the principles and considerations to apply when exercising their powers. The following subsections discuss these, and identify a number of concerns likely to be raised and the implications for coherence among tort remedies.

i. Purposes of Making an Apology or Correction Order for Invasion of Privacy

Case law, law reform reports and academic commentary point to a number of remedial purposes that might be achieved by court-ordered apologies and correction orders. These include vindication of the plaintiff's right to privacy and acknowledgement of the defendant's wrongdoing, and consolation for humiliation and emotional distress.[134] In some circumstances, as found by Bromberg J in *Eatock*, these orders can also serve to restore the plaintiff's esteem and social standing and achieve wider informational and educative purposes. These informational and educative purposes can be seen to benefit the public interest, as well as the personal interests of the plaintiff.

The argument might also be made that the sentiment expressed by the Constitutional Court in *Le Roux v Dey* and endorsed by Mortimer J in *Wotton*, that an apology order ought to be considered where 'the actionable dignity of one has been impaired by another' and this order will create 'the best conditions' for making reconciliation of personal relationships possible,[135] could apply to a serious invasion of privacy case. A number of points would need to be addressed before advancing this argument. First, these judicial statements about the public interests that can be served by private law remedies that protect dignitary interests go beyond those identified in *Eatock* and by the ALRC and other reform bodies advocating for privacy law reform. Second, the significance of what constitutes 'actionable dignity' under South African law, as the basis of defamation in that jurisdiction, as compared to the protection of reputation by the law of defamation in common law countries including Australia, would need to be considered. Lastly, careful analysis of the similarities and differences between the legislative objectives of anti-discrimination law, on the one hand, and the aims of

[134] ALRC, Privacy Report (n 4) 254, [12.160]; R Carroll, 'Beyond Compensation: Apology as a Private Law Remedy' in J Berryman and R Bigwood (eds), *The Law of Remedies: New Directions in the Common Law* (Irwin Law, 2010) 323, 352–69; see generally Carroll and Witzleb (n 98).

[135] *Le Roux v Dey* (n 102) [202].

privacy law, on the other, is needed before 'reconciliation of personal relationships' can be confirmed as a general remedial purpose of the tort of serious invasion of privacy. This is not to say that in an individual case a court might not decide there was some factual basis for deciding that an apology order would serve the purpose of reconciling the relationship between the plaintiff and defendant, and make an order with this in mind.

ii. Principles for Determining When to Make an Apology Order or a Correction Order

It is assumed that the question of whether it is appropriate to make a correction order will be answered, first, by whether the defendant has published untrue information about the plaintiff on a personal and private matter, and, subsequently, by an exercise of discretion as to what order would be just in all the circumstances. It is also assumed in this discussion that it is appropriate for a court to make these orders with the consent of the parties, in which case the parties will comply voluntarily, albeit grudgingly. The more contentious issue, on which guidance is provided by the cases discussed in this subsection, is when the court should exercise its discretion to order an unwilling defendant to apologise or publish a correction.

First, a court must have regard to the aims and purposes of the legislation under which the power is conferred.[136] In this case the legislative purpose would be to protect the right to privacy and the underlying interests of dignity and autonomy affected by intrusion upon seclusion or misuse of information. In considering this, as in the case of anti-discrimination legislation, courts should be prepared to be innovative, and at the same time flexible and pragmatic.[137]

Second, a court must ask the questions stated in *Wotton*, namely: 'whether a court-ordered apology is an act which the Court is satisfied would redress damage suffered by the applicants' and '[w]hether more appropriate methods of achieving that redress are available'.[138] In considering the benefit of the order to the plaintiff, a court can have regard to the research referred to in section III that explains why an involuntary apology might achieve redress for one plaintiff even if it would not do so for another in the same circumstances. A court would need to consider the nature of the invasion of privacy and whether a private or public apology is appropriate, the nature of the relationship (if any) between the plaintiff and the defendant, and whether the defendant is a natural person, a media organisation or other corporate entity. Where there are multiple defendants, the court must decide against which of them, if any, the order should be made. Whenever a court exercises a discretionary power to grant a coercive remedy, it will need to take these and many other factors into account in deciding what orders meet the justice of the case.

[136] *Ma Bik Yung v Ko Chuen* (n 113) 14.
[137] ibid.
[138] *Wotton v State of Queensland (No 5)* (n 1) [1584].

iii. General Concerns Likely to be Raised About These Orders

There are many important issues that arise when a court is contemplating making orders that compel a defendant to publish a correction or apologise for his or her wrongful conduct and other similar orders.[139] Each of these deserves considerably more attention than is possible here. Based on historical concerns about such orders expressed in the defamation and anti-discrimination contexts, it is likely that three particular concerns will arise in the privacy context to which courts will need to respond.

a. Sincerity

It is often said that an apology has no meaning if it is not offered with sincerity. This returns us to the question of what 'apology' means in a legal setting, discussed in section III. There is no doubt that a court cannot order a defendant to apologise with sincerity. There are a number of ways that this reality can be addressed while still achieving some or all of the purposes of an apology order already discussed. First, a court should only consider making an apology order when one is sought by the plaintiff. A plaintiff can judge for himself or herself whether an ordered apology would provide redress, even if the defendant is not willing to make it voluntarily. Even though a plaintiff might be willing to accept a partial apology in settlement of his or her claim against the defendant, he or she might prefer to receive damages after a trial, instead of an apology made by the defendant only to comply with a court order.

Second, a court might order the defendant to publish an apology as defined by the NSW Administrative Decisions Tribunal in *Burns v Radio 2UE Sydney Pty Ltd (No 2)*, namely, as an 'acknowledgement of the wrongdoing' that is not 'a statement of genuinely held feelings'.[140] This would address to some extent at least the concern expressed by Mortimer J in *Wotton* that

> [i]f an apology is seen as some kind of admission of personal responsibility or wrongdoing, or a statement of personal regret, then in a dispute between private individuals (or entities) it may well be inappropriate to force an individual to say something she or he does not really mean.[141]

Third, instead of an apology, a court can order the defendant to publish a corrective notice or public statement that sets out the facts and findings in a case and the orders made by the court. In each situation it is important that the court clearly sets out what the defendant is being ordered to do and avoid any impression that the court is compelling the defendant to express insincere personal emotions.

[139] eg, see Carroll (n 134) 369–76.
[140] *Burns v Radio 2UE Sydney Pty Ltd (No 2)* (n 55) [29].
[141] *Wotton v State of Queensland (No 5)* (n 1) [1590].

b. Freedom of Expression and of the Press

The cause of action proposed by the ALRC would require a court to find that in all the circumstances the plaintiff's right to privacy outweighs the defendant's right to freedom of expression as an element of tort.[142] When liability is determined in the plaintiff's favour and the court is deciding the most appropriate method of achieving redress, a court will again weigh freedom of expression and freedom of the press against the right to privacy. This is a significant factor that a court must consider when ordering the defendant to speak or publish words that he or she is unwilling to speak or publish voluntarily. The decision in *Eatock v Bolt (No 2)* is indicative of a strong judicial reluctance to order the press to publish an apology. A court will be concerned not to place a 'chill' on the press. The NSWLRC acknowledges that freedom of speech considerations mean that orders to apologise in invasion of privacy cases would be exceptional.[143] Free speech considerations do not necessarily mean that an order to apologise should never be made.[144] In all the circumstances of the case, the defendant's interest in freedom of expression may be outweighed when regard is had to the 'nature and aim of the legislation, the interests of the community, the gravity of the unlawful conduct and the plaintiff's circumstances, including the extent of the loss and damage suffered'.[145] In response to concerns that these orders would unduly interfere with a free press, the ALRC rightly notes, however, that the remedy would only be one of many available remedies, and in any event it would only be considered where the plaintiff has made out a serious, unjustifiable, intentional or reckless invasion of privacy.[146]

c. Enforcement

The ability of a court to enforce and supervise an order to provide a written apology to a plaintiff, or to publish a public correction or apology, is unlikely to present an obstacle where the wording and manner of publication has been agreed to by the parties[147] or the wording is determined by the court. As the ALRC notes, some legislation anticipates potential breaches of apology (and other) orders by providing that orders must be satisfied within a specified time period or the defendant

[142] Freedom of expression and other competing freedoms and interests would be considered when determining whether the plaintiff has a cause of action – it is an element of the tort, rather than a defence. A plaintiff will not be able to claim that a wrong has been committed – that his or her privacy has been seriously invaded – where there are strong public interest grounds justifying the invasion of privacy. See ALRC, Privacy Report (n 4) 19, [1.12].

[143] NSWLRC, Invasion of Privacy (n 7) 56, [7.26].

[144] A Zwart-Hink et al, 'Compelled Apologies as a Legal Remedy: Some Thoughts from a Civil Law Jurisdiction' (2014) 38 *University of Western Australia Law Review* 100; G van Dijck 'The Ordered Apology' (2017) 37 *OJLS* 562.

[145] *Ma Bik Yung v Ko Chuen* (n 113) 19 *per* Li CJ.

[146] ALRC, Privacy Report (n 4) 256, [12.168].

[147] eg, as was the case in *Summertime Holdings Pty Ltd v Environmental Defender's Office Ltd* (1998) 45 NSWLR 291, 298 *per* Young J.

will be subject to a fine.[148] In *Corbett v Burns*, the New South Wales Civil and Administrative Tribunal identified this and other ways in which an order to publish an apology under New South Wales anti-discrimination legislation can be enforced without invoking contempt proceedings.[149] Ultimately, a defendant who does not comply with a court order will be vulnerable to contempt proceedings, and this possibility will remain a weighty factor against the exercise of coercive power.[150] Arguably, however, contempt proceedings will be of less concern with corporate and media defendants than with natural persons, because the former will face a fine rather than imprisonment.

iv. Coherence Among Remedies for Torts That Protect Interests in Dignity, Autonomy and Reputation

An obvious implication of conferring power on the courts to make apology and correction orders for the tort of serious invasion of privacy is that these orders will be available even though they are not awarded for torts of false imprisonment, trespass and defamation. Apologies and corrections are not generally available as judicial remedies for these (or any other torts) where general damages are awarded in Australia, the UK, Canada and New Zealand. Without legislative intervention, it is unlikely that these remedies will be awarded for defamation or other dignitary torts, due to concerns about constitutional implications for a free press and freedom of expression. The availability of these orders by legislation for serious invasion of privacy will therefore have implications for the coherence of remedies for torts that protect dignity, autonomy and reputation. By the same token, conferring broad statutory remedial powers on courts to redress serious invasions of privacy provides an opportunity for rights and freedoms and the underlying interests that the law seeks to protect to be judicially articulated, weighed against one another and upheld by non-monetary orders.

VI. Conclusion

With the development of tortious actions for invasion of privacy comes the opportunity for legislatures and courts to consider what remedies will best support the right that is being protected. In jurisdictions where the privacy tort is recognised, the question of 'remedial fit' of available remedies is already under consideration. In Australia, the express intention of the recommendations in the ALRC's *Serious Invasions of Privacy in the Digital Era Final Report* is to reform the law to prevent and remedy serious invasions of privacy. There are sound reasons for conferring

[148] ALRC, Privacy Report (n 4) 256, [12.170]. See, eg, *Anti-Discrimination Act 1977* (NSW), s 108(7).
[149] *Corbett v Burns* [2015] NSWCATAP 188, [79]–[90].
[150] R Carroll, 'Apologies as a Legal Remedy' (2013) 35 *Sydney Law Review* 317, 342.

broad remedial powers on the courts in such cases. It is important that courts have available to them the power to order remedies other than damages, to vindicate the right that has been breached and redress the emotional distress caused by the defendant.

This chapter has focused on two of the ALRC's proposals. The first proposal is for courts to take account of apologies and corrections as a factor in the assessment of damages. This is an uncontroversial proposal that is consistent with the principles that apply to other torts where general damages for emotional distress are available. In defamation, for example, publication and dissemination of appropriate apologies and corrections play a central role in mitigating damage to reputation and reducing the hurt, embarrassment and humiliation inflicted on the plaintiff. They have a similar role to play in privacy cases by reducing, to some extent at least, emotional distress resulting from the invasion of privacy. It cannot be assumed that an apology by a defendant who has committed a serious and intentional invasion of a plaintiff's privacy will have this effect, however, particularly where the parties have a prior personal relationship. The timing of the apology, the fullness of the apology and accompanying offers of additional ways to make amends, including monetary compensation, will be relevant to any assessment of whether an apology is regarded by the plaintiff, and the court, as a sincere attempt to remedy the wrong. A grudging, poorly constructed or poorly conveyed apology might increase the emotional distress experienced by the plaintiff and justify an increased award of damages. Given that the tort arises where a defendant has intentionally or recklessly invaded the plaintiff's privacy in a serious way, it is appropriate that the court place considerable weight on the value attributed to the apology by the plaintiff.

The second proposal, more controversial in nature, is to confer on the court power to order the defendant to apologise and to order the publication of a correction where false private information has been published. In Australia, the UK, New Zealand or Canada, where apologies and corrections have a well-recognised role in the settlement of defamation claims and assessment of damages, there is little likelihood that courts will make orders in these terms. Similarly, there is little prospect in the absence of a statutory power that courts will make these coercive orders for invasion of privacy without legislative reform. For Sir Cliff Richard and other privacy plaintiffs, it remains the case for the time being that the only way to obtain an apology or a correction is to negotiate one. If legislation is enacted in Australia creating a tort action for serious invasions of privacy and conferring power on the courts to make these and other similar orders, courts can look to the case law decided under other legislation referred to in this chapter for guidance as to when they might be appropriate. The power to order corrections and apologies for breach of privacy, or to publish a corrective notice or make a public statement for similar purposes, is likely to be exercised rarely and in exceptional circumstances. Conferral of the power would signal, however, a legislative expectation that there are cases where redress of this type will benefit a plaintiff and the wider public interest in protecting the right to privacy.

10

Remedial Consequences of Classification of a Privacy Action: Dog or Wolf, Tort or Equity?

BARBARA McDONALD AND DAVID ROLPH

I. Introduction

> There can be no real dispute that a claim for breach of confidence is not a claim in tort … [H]istory does not determine identity. The fact that dogs evolved from wolves does not mean that dogs are wolves. … I conclude that the tort of misuse of private information is a tort within the meaning of ground 3.1 (9) [of the Civil Procedure Rules].[1]

In *Google Inc v Vidal-Hall*,[2] the Court of Appeal affirmed Tugendhat J's determination that misuse of private information was a tort for the purposes of the Civil Procedure Rules and was distinct from the equitable cause of action for breach of confidence. This was a significant development in the evolution of misuse of private information, which had originated a little over a decade earlier out of breach of confidence. The transformation of misuse of private information from equitable wrong to tort could be expected to have an impact on the remedies available and the principles upon which they are granted.

This chapter considers some of the remedial consequences of classifying 'wrongful misuse of private information' as a cause of action in tort, rather than as the basis of a claim for relief in equity. Many of these consequences are more than merely procedural: they affect the substance of the parties' rights and obligations. In particular, we consider issues relating to choice of law, vicarious liability, damages and injunctions. This chapter argues that a number of significant doctrinal issues about the remedies for misuse of private information have not been identified, let alone adequately addressed, in this cause of action's transformation from equitable to tortious.

[1] *Vidal-Hall v Google Inc* [2014] EWHC 13 (QB), [2014] 1 WLR 4155, [52], [57] [70] *per* Tugendhat J (*Vidal-Hall* (QB)).

[2] *Google Inc v Vidal-Hall* [2015] EWCA Civ 311, [2016] QB 1003 (*Vidal-Hall* (CA)).

A. Background

The decision in *Google Inc v Vidal-Hall* that misuse of private information is a tort was the culmination of a process of tentative reclassification that had begun over a decade earlier. Yet *Google Inc v Vidal-Hall* was the first case in which the classification of misuse of private information was of practical importance to the outcome of a dispute, rather than forming mere obiter dicta.

The issue in the case was whether the claimants could rely on the Civil Procedure Rules (CPR), which allowed a court to give leave to serve a tort claim outside the jurisdiction. The question therefore was whether the claimants' claim against Google – that it had misused their private information – was a claim in 'tort'. Tugendhat J draws a distinction between an historical approach taken by courts to the meaning of legal terminology ('to look back to the history or evolution of the disputed term')[3] and an approach that looks forward to the legislative purpose underlying the relevant rule in which the term appears. The former has been the more common approach in cases dealing with the CPR. Yet, as quoted at the start of this chapter, while he eschewed the history of the common law and equity as explaining why service outside the jurisdiction should be denied for an equitable claim, his judgment does not otherwise delve into legislative purpose in relation to the rule. Having decided that he was not bound by the approach of the Court of Appeal in *Douglas v Hello! Ltd (No 3)*,[4] limited as it was to the traditional action for breach of confidence, Tugendhat J rested his classification of the action for misuse of private information on the use of the word 'tort' to describe the action in a number of recent cases. In none of these, it should be noted, did anything turn on the classification. It is also arguable, as we discuss later, that even a tort classification in *Douglas v Hello! (No 3)* may have made no difference to the choice of law issue discussed there if it could have been successfully argued that the key 'event' in the 'tort', using the language of the relevant statute on choice of law,[5] was the disclosure of the private information in the United Kingdom (UK),[6] regardless of whether a prior wrong was committed in New York.[7]

It was at the very outset of the 'extended'[8] action for breach of confidence – the well-established action having been given new life in *Campbell v MGN Ltd*[9] in 2004 – that Lord Nicholls had embraced the 'tort' nomenclature. His Lordship

[3] *Vidal-Hall* (QB) (n 1) [54].

[4] *Douglas v Hello! Ltd (No 3)* [2005] EWCA Civ 595, [2006] QB 125 (*Douglas* (CA)).

[5] Private International Law (Miscellaneous Provisions) Act 1995, s 11.

[6] *Vidal-Hall* (QB) (n 1) [65], citing *Douglas* (CA) (n 4) [100]–[101].

[7] The double-actionability rule was abolished for most torts by the Private International Law (Miscellaneous Provisions) Act 1995 (UK), s 10. See further NA Moreham and Sir Mark Warby, *Tugendhat and Christie: The Law of Privacy and the Media*, 3rd edn (Oxford, Oxford UP, 2016) [13.85].

[8] Here we adopt the terminology used by T Aplin, L Bentley, P Johnson and S Malynicz, *Gurry on Breach of Confidence: The Protection of Confidential Information*, 2nd edn (Oxford, Oxford UP, 2012), eg [7.147].

[9] *Campbell v MGN Ltd* [2004] UKHL 22, [2004] 2 AC 457.

described the nomenclature of 'breach of confidence' as misleading, because the modern cause of action 'has now firmly shaken off the limiting constraint of the need for an initial confidential relationship'.[10] He went on:

> The continuing use of the phrase 'duty of confidence' and the description of the information as 'confidential' is not altogether comfortable. Information about an individual's private life would not, in ordinary usage, be called 'confidential'. The more natural description today is that such information is private. The essence of the tort is better encapsulated now as misuse of private information.

Lord Nicholls' 'tort' nomenclature was not picked up by the other judges in *Campbell*, who, rather, discussed the nature and changing rationale of the modern action for breach of confidence. While the new nomenclature was increasingly raised as a classification query or possibility by courts and academic commentators alike,[11] the Court of Appeal in *Douglas v Hello! Ltd (No 3)*[12] preferred to see the Douglases' claim as resting on the equitable action for breach of confidence rather than as a tort, for the purposes of determining the applicable law to determine the dispute, an issue discussed later in this chapter.

In the Douglases' appeal to the House of Lords, heard together with *OBG v Allan* and other actions,[13] Lord Nicholls went further than merely reclassifying the existing cause of action. He stated (obiter):

> As the law has developed breach of confidence, or misuse of confidential information, now covers two distinct causes of action, protecting two different interests: privacy, and secret ('confidential') information. It is important to keep these two distinct.[14]

Treating the extended action as an entirely new cause of action rather than as a new formulation of an existing one was contrary to the express views of other members of the House of Lords in *Campbell*, for example Baroness Hale:

> The 1998 Act does not create any new cause of action between private persons. But if there is a relevant cause of action applicable, the court as a public authority must act compatibly with both parties' Convention rights. In a case such as this, the relevant vehicle will usually be the action for breach of confidence.[15]

Further, in dismissing an appeal from Tugendhat J's judgment, the Court of Appeal of England and Wales in *Google Inc v Vidal Hall* adopted the new nomenclature, while at the same time insisting that, in doing so, they were not creating a new

[10] ibid [14].

[11] As early as 1972: PM North, 'Breach of Confidence: Is there a New Tort?' (1972) 12 *Journal of the Society of Public Teachers of Law* 149, after Lord Denning in *Seager v Copydex Ltd* [1967] 1 WLR 923 (CA) had awarded 'damages' or equitable compensation. See further M Richardson, M Bryan, M Vranken and K Barnett, *Breach of Confidence: Social Origins and Modern Developments* (Cheltenham, Edward Elgar, 2012) 138.

[12] *Douglas* (CA) (n 4).

[13] *OBG v Allan* [2007] UKHL 21, [2008] AC 1 ('*Douglas* (HL)').

[14] ibid 72, [255].

[15] *Campbell* (n 9) [132].

cause of action. They felt the references to the action as a tort by various judges could not be dismissed as 'mere loose use of language; they connote an acknowledgment, even if only implicitly, of the true nature of the cause of action':[16]

> Against the background we have described, and in the absence of any sound reasons of policy or principle to suggest otherwise, we have concluded in agreement with the judge that misuse of private information should now be recognised as a tort for the purposes of service out the jurisdiction. *This does not create a new cause of action.* In our view, it simply gives the correct legal label to one that already exists. We are conscious of the fact that there may be broader implications from our conclusions, for example as to remedies, limitation and vicarious liability, but these were not the subject of submissions, and such points will need to be considered as and when they arise.[17]

It may be that, despite the absence of any significant discussion of the legislative purpose behind the CPR, the decision in *Google* is confined to its statutory context. This may explain both the apparent ease of coming to the result and also the otherwise puzzling rejection of the leave application by the Supreme Court of the UK on the classification point, on the basis that there was not 'an arguable point of law'.[18] It would seem odd indeed that the substantive and procedural differences of claims in tort and claims in equity do not raise any arguable points of law.

Tugendhat J noted that '[a] term may have different meanings in different contexts'.[19] It is possible that, for other purposes, a court may come to a different conclusion on the classification of the cause of action for misuse of private information. While this now seems unlikely, the implications identified by the Court of Appeal in the passage above as arising out of classification, and other issues of substance, remedy and procedure, are bound to arise in the future.

While the Court of Appeal insisted, in the passage quoted above, that it was not thereby creating a new cause of action, the judgment also adopts what it described as the 'highly influential'[20] view of Lord Nicholls in *OBG v Allan* that 'there are now two separate and distinct causes of action: an action for breach of confidence; and one for misuse of private information'.[21] Given the explicit statements to the contrary or the silence on this point by other members of the House of Lords in the foundational cases, it is not just the point of transformation from a wolf into a dog, but also the birth of the new species of action that remains a mystery. While no modern common lawyer would doubt that judges can make new law,[22] judges

[16] *Vidal-Hall* (CA) (n 2) [26].

[17] ibid [51] (emphasis added).

[18] Supreme Court, 'Google Inc (Appellant) v Vidal-Hall and others (Respondents)' (*Permission to appeal decisions by UK Supreme Court*, 28 July 2015), www.supremecourt.uk/news/permission-to-appeal-decisions-28-july-2015.html.

[19] *Vidal-Hall* (QB) (n 1) [54].

[20] *Vidal-Hall* (CA) (n 2) [22] *per* Dyson MR and Sharp LJ.

[21] ibid [21].

[22] *Prince Alfred College v ADC* [2017] HCA 37, (2016) 258 CLR 134, [127] *per* Gageler and Gordon JJ, citing O Dixon, 'Concerning Judicial Method' in *Jesting Pilate and Other Papers and Addresses*, 2nd edn (Melbourne, Law Book Co, 1997) 152, 155, 157–58.

do need to be explicit when they are doing so, rather than hiding new law under the subterfuge that it already existed.

For Australia, the issue of classifying privacy claims remains partly hypothetical. Although the High Court in 2001 opened the door to possibly radical development in *Australian Broadcasting Corporation v Lenah Game Meats Pty Ltd*,[23] the common law has so far seen only a modest (but nonetheless significant) extension of the traditional equitable action of breach of confidence,[24] and no development at a superior court level of any separate tort or torts of invasion of privacy.[25] No doubt, at some point in the future, the right case will put the issue as to how a court should respond to the High Court's open door squarely in contention: by fashioning a new tort, or by extending existing actions? If an Australian State or the Federal Government does one day decide to follow the proposal of the Australian Law Reform Commission (ALRC) and design a new statutory action for invasion of privacy, many of the questions raised in this chapter and the prospect of unnecessary litigation should be seen as further support for the ALRC's recommendation that the action be called a 'tort' in any legislation.[26]

The ALRC also recommended that the statutory tort make actionable two types of invasion of privacy, broadly defined: misuse of private information and intrusion into seclusion. This was intended to increase certainty as to the proposed legislation's scope of application (in an environment where there would be general reluctance to support a broad-based right of action with components left undefined), and also to give priority (in an environment of caution as to *any* legislative intervention) to the types of serious privacy invasion that had most commonly occurred in other countries. For the purposes of common law development, we wonder whether the wrong should be more broadly defined as wrongful 'dealing' to capture not just wrongful disclosure and/or misuse of private information, but also a broader range of privacy invasions, including wrongful snooping and collection of private information. There is a difficult issue of whether different forms of invasion of privacy should found separate causes of action. Certainly, an 'intrusion' into privacy, being analogous to trespass, seems most obviously classified as tort.[27] While there may be an intrusion into privacy without actual collection, use or disclosure of information, and conversely there may be a wrongful

[23] *Australian Broadcasting Corporation v Lenah Game Meats Pty Ltd* [2001] HCA 63, (2001) 208 CLR 199.

[24] That is, in allowing compensation for mental distress in the equitable claim: *Giller v Procopets* [2008] VSCA 236, (2008) 24 VR 1 ('*Giller* (CA)'); *Wilson v Ferguson* [2015] WASC 15.

[25] Cf *Grosse v Purvis* [2003] QDC 151, (2003) Aust Torts Reports 81-706; *Doe v Australian Broadcasting Corporation* [2007] VCC 281. Australian Law Reform Commission, *Serious Invasions of Privacy in the Digital Era* (ALRC Report 123, 2014).

[26] ALRC (n 25) recommendation 4-2. The Court of Appeal in *Vidal-Hall* (n 2) referred to this recommendation in support of its conclusion at [44].

[27] There is some debate as to whether, even if the extended action encompasses the deliberate collection of private information, as held in *Imerman v Tchenguiz* [2010] EWCA Civ 908, [2011] 2 WLR 592, [68], the traditional action for breach of confidence does too.

disclosure without a preceding wrongful intrusion or collection, it may seem quite artificial, or unnecessarily duplicative, for the purposes of damages, to keep the various forms of invasion of privacy as separate causes of action. On the other hand, particularly in cross-border disputes or for the purposes of limitation periods, there may be a significant advantage for a claimant in treating each stage of an invasion as giving rise to a separate action. A statutory action can build in some limitations on multiple actions arising out of related matters, such as a first publication rule,[28] but the common law is less able to do so, and courts and defendants can rely only on rules against abuse of process to discourage an overly litigious or persistent claimant.

Like any aspect of law, the remedial and substantive consequences of classification of privacy claims may not be uniform across jurisdictions. They may vary according to the law of the forum or the applicable law. There are now clear differences of approach on a number of issues in the law of obligations and remedies between the courts of the UK, Canada, New Zealand and Australia, to name a few jurisdictions. The approach of the jurisdiction in which the dispute is brought may govern several questions: for a start, the first question in a cross-border dispute, of which law the court should apply. For this reason, we begin with the difficult issue of choice of the proper law of the dispute, and then move on to two issues identified by the Court of Appeal in *Google Inc v Vidal Hall*: vicarious liability and remedies.[29] The last can obviously be divided into many sub-issues relating to injunctions, damages, and the availability of gain-based remedies such as an account of profits and so on. The availability of defences may also depend on classification, but we do not consider that issue here.[30]

Broader questions underlie the specific remedial issues. When is the cause of action complete: on 'breach', or on loss? Is it actionable per se? Where claims fit within both the traditional and the extended action, as in *Campbell v MGN* itself, will the claimant have concurrent or multiple claims?[31] We cannot answer all these questions, but we do pose them to illustrate that classification of the wrong in broad terms as a tort is only a starting point.

[28] eg Defamation Act 2013 (UK), s 8(4).

[29] As to the third issue identified by the Court of Appeal in *Vidal-Hall*, limitation periods, see Moreham and Warby (n 7) [11.217] et seq.

[30] See further B McDonald, 'Privacy Claims: Transformation, Fault and the Public Interest Defence' in A Dyson, J Goudkamp and F Wilmot-Smith (eds), *Defences in Tort* (Oxford, Hart Publishing, 2015) 297, noting that the issue of defences requires the identification of key elements of any new tort: Is it one of strict liability? If not, on what fault does it rest: lack of conscience or lack of care or intent/recklessness?

[31] Lord Hoffmann observed in *Campbell* (n 9) [53], 'the cause of action fits squarely within both the old and the new law. The judge found that the information about Ms Campbell's attendance at NA had been communicated to the *Mirror* in breach of confidence and that the *Mirror* must have known that the information was confidential. As for human autonomy and dignity, I should have thought that the extent to which information about one's state of health, including drug dependency, should be communicated to other people was plainly something which an individual was entitled to decide for herself'.

II. Choice of Law

Classification of a cause of action is of course fundamental to the choice of the appropriate law to be applied to the dispute. If, for example, an obligation of privacy or confidence had its source in a contract between the parties, as is often the case, the applicable substantive law would be the 'proper law of the contract', however that is determined.[32]

But where there is no contract involved, will it make a difference if a privacy cause of action is classified as a tort or an equitable action? The authors of *Gurry* merely identify the problem:

> Once more, the important matter is characterization. If breach of confidence is a matter related to tort then the choice of law rules are those set out in [the 1995 Act] or if not, the 'proper law' of the equitable obligation applies. There is some confusion in the area … It is therefore clearly worth considering both potential characterizations (tort and equitable obligations) before considering which is the most appropriate.[33]

A. Choice of Law in Tort

If the wrongful disclosure of private information is, or is to be treated as, a tort then the relevant choice-of-law rule in Australia is now clear: the forum must apply the substantive law[34] of the place of the tort, the *lex loci delicti*.[35] Such a simple rule will not, however, resolve all practical problems because of the operation of the doctrine of *renvoi*,[36] or because it may be difficult in multi-jurisdictional events or transactions to determine precisely where the tort occurred.[37] The situation will become more complicated if the invasion of the claimant's privacy involved multiple successive forms – perhaps first an intrusion into seclusion

[32] See further M Davies, AS Bell and PLG Brereton, *Nygh's Conflict of Laws in Australia*, 9th edn (Chatswood, NSW, LexisNexis, 2013) ch 19. See Moreham and Warby (n 7) [13.83] as to the impact of the Rome I Regulation (Council Regulation (EC) 593/2008 of 17 June 2008 on the law applicable to contractual obligations [2008] OJ L177/6) for claims in Europe.

[33] Aplin et al (n 8) [23.75].

[34] Some uncertainty remains in distinguishing substantive and procedural aspects of law: see, eg, *Dyno Wesfarmers v Knuckey* [2003] NSWCA 375, [45] *per* Handley JA.

[35] *John Pfeiffer Pty Ltd v Rogerson* [2000] HCA 36, (2000) 203 CLR 503 in respect of torts within Australia; *Regie Nationale des Usines Renault SA v Zhang* [2002] HCA 10, (2002) 210 CLR 491 in respect of international torts. See further Davies, Bell and Brereton (n 32) [20.1]–[20.4].

[36] *Renvoi* (meaning 'return' or 'reference back') is a conflict of laws doctrine that is concerned with whether a reference to a foreign legal system includes reference to that foreign legal system's conflict-of-laws principles. If the reference to that foreign legal system includes its conflict-of-laws principles, that foreign legal system may refer the case back to the original legal system or on to a third legal system. See *Neilson v Overseas Projects Corporation of Victoria Ltd* [2005] HCA 54, (2005) 223 CLR 331, [86] *per* Gummow and Hayne JJ. See also R Mortensen, R Garnett and M Keyes, *Private International Law in Australia*, 3rd edn (Chatswood, NSW, LexisNexis, 2015) 427.

[37] Mortensen, Garnett and Keyes (n 36) 433.

to collect information, then some misuse or private viewing of the information (for example, viewing of private images), then communication of those images in various formats and across boundaries, including on the Internet.

Even identifying the place of an intrusion may be problematic: while physical intrusions are easy enough to locate by reference to the claimant's and defendant's location, things become more complicated with electronic remote intrusions. Where is the tort committed by a person in one jurisdiction hacking into a person's personal computer located in another? Or where the perpetrator – assuming the film *Snowden* was not mere science fiction when describing the excesses of the US National Security Agency – uses software in one jurisdiction to control a webcam from a person's computer in another jurisdiction to capture footage or recordings of the latter's activities and conversations? Conclusions on these questions would require analysis of analogous situations in other multi-jurisdictional tort claims.

However, at least as far as *publication* of private information is concerned, the law can take some guidance from decided cases in defamation, misrepresentation and breach of confidence. In defamation law, the approach of the High Court of Australia in *Dow Jones v Gutnick* to determining the place of an Internet publication is well-accepted at common law: applying *Duke of Brunswick v Harmer*,[38] the tort is complete when and wherever the defamatory statement is downloaded, in that case, the State of Victoria.[39] The same principles still apply in English defamation law,[40] despite the introduction of a limitation period based on the first publication of substantially the same matter.[41]

Presumably, the same approach would apply to publication or use of private information if it is the publication or use that is tortious,[42] although Moreham and Warby note that it could be argued that, if the essence of the wrong is seen to be hurt to feelings, the place where the harm is suffered may be the more appropriate location of the action.[43]

But what of collection in one jurisdiction and misuse or disclosure in another? Will they each found a cause of action, with potentially different law applying to each? By contrast to Australian law, which looks to the place of the tort, the approach under the European Rome II convention is to look primarily, but not exclusively, to the law of the place where the damage occurred.[44] However, this rule applies to

[38] *Duke of Brunswick v Harmer* (1849) 14 QB 185.

[39] *Dow Jones & Co Inc v Gutnick* [2002] HCA 56, (2002) 210 CLR 575. See also *Berezovsky v Michaels* [2000] UKHL 25, [2000] 1 WLR 1004; *Lewis v King* [2004] EWCA Civ 1329; *Douglas* (CA) (n 4). Cf actions based on publications in more than one Australian State, now governed by the uniform Defamation Acts, eg Defamation Act 2005 (NSW), s 11, which requires the court to apply the law of the State with which the harm has the closest connection. See further D Rolph, *Defamation Law* (Pyrmont, NSW, Thomson Reuters, 2016) [8.160].

[40] *Shevill v Presse Alliance SA* [1996] AC 959.

[41] Defamation Act 2013, s 8.

[42] *WXY v Gewanter* [2012] EWHC 1601 (QB).

[43] Moreham and Warby (n 7) [13.59].

[44] Regulation (EC) 864/2007 of 11 July 2007 on the law applicable to non-contractual obligations (Rome II) [2007] OJ L199/40, Art 4(1).

torts and other non-contractual obligations, except those 'arising out of violations of privacy and rights relating to personality, including defamation'.[45] We gather that privacy and defamation claims were excepted because consensus could not be reached.[46] Because of this exception, a claim in the UK for breach of confidential information that is *not private* information will (currently, at least) be determined by Rome II, while a claim for misuse of *private* information will have the applicable law determined, if a tort or delict, by Part III of the Private International Law (Miscellaneous Provisions) Act 1995. The latter generally applies the *lex loci delicti*, unless displaced by a substantially more appropriate law.[47] But it is worth noting the full provision as it applies to multi-jurisdictional 'events', particularly given that most privacy breaches result in mental distress, which, as arguably a form of impairment of one's mental condition, is treated as personal injury.[48] In such a case, the law of the place where the individual sustained the injury might prevail:

> **11 Choice of applicable law: the general rule**
>
> (1) The general rule is that the applicable law is the law of the country in which the events constituting the tort or delict in question occur.
>
> (2) Where elements of those events occur in different countries, the applicable law under the general rule is to be taken as being—
>
> (a) for a cause of action in respect of personal injury caused to an individual or death resulting from personal injury, the law of the country where the individual was when he sustained the injury;
>
> (b) for a cause of action in respect of damage to property, the law of the country where the property was when it was damaged; and
>
> (c) in any other case, the law of the country in which the most significant element or elements of those events occurred.
>
> (3) In this section 'personal injury' includes disease or any impairment of physical or mental condition.

B. Choice of Law in Equity

How would the situation differ if the claim for misuse of private information were characterised as still lying in equity? While the rules with respect to tort are clear in principle (even if difficult in practice), the same cannot be said about choice

[45] ibid, Art 1(2)(g).

[46] A Dickinson, *The Rome II Regulation* (Oxford, Oxford UP, 2008) 57, fn 389.

[47] Aplin et al (n 8) [23.80].

[48] In this way, cases in New South Wales dealing with mental distress resulting from breach of contract have come within restrictions under the *Civil Liability Act* 2002 (NSW), which relate to negligence: eg *Insight Vacations Pty Ltd v Young* [2010] NSWCA 137, (2010) 78 NSWLR 641 (appeal to High Court of Australia on other grounds dismissed); *Flight Centre Ltd v Louw* [2011] NSWSC 132, (2010) 78 NSWLR 656.

of law in equity. The rules are commonly described as 'ill defined'.[49] Questions about choice of law in equity elicit responses such as, 'Ah, you're getting into unexplored territory there.' Or, 'That's a difficult and uncertain issue.' There seems to be a much higher level of theory and commentary than settled legal principle.[50] *Gurry*, in the passage quoted at the start of section II, refers to the 'proper law' of the equitable obligation. In obligations having some foundation in contract, this makes sense: it is said that separate characterisation of an equitable claim makes no sense when other key issues in the same action fall to be decided under other fields.[51] However, the difficulty lies in circumstances that do not have a foundation in contract, agreement or some other nominate classification. Is the best classification of such freewheeling obligations or wrongs that they fall in tort? Yeo posits that fine and difficult distinctions will fade

> once we accept that 'torts' here is not used as a legal term of art in the domestic law sense of wrongs recognised by the common law courts, but a category containing functionally equivalent rules for solving particular kinds of social problem. If necessary, the torts category could be re-labelled 'wrongs' to remove any possible misconception of doctrinal connections with torts in the narrow meaning in the domestic common law.[52]

In *Google Inc v Vidal Hall*, the Court of Appeal quoted the authors of the 15th edition of *Dicey, Morris & Collins on the Conflict of Laws*, who argued that all non-contractual claims to protect privacy should be treated as involving issues of tort under the Private International Law (Miscellaneous Provisions) Act 1995 (UK).[53]

C. *Douglas v Hello! (No 3)*

The Court of Appeal in *Google Inc v Vidal Hall* obviously had to deal with the effect of the decision in *Douglas v Hello! Ltd (No 3)*.

In relation to the action for breach of confidence, the Court of Appeal in *Douglas v Hello! (No 3)* had applied English law to the 'privacy' action brought by Michael Douglas, Catherine Zeta-Jones and *OK!* magazine, notwithstanding that the intrusion occurred in New York. It was there, in a room of the Plaza Hotel they

[49] A Dickinson, 'Reading the Tea Leaves: Private International Law in England after EU Exit' (*Oxford Business Law Blog*, 26 October 2016) www.law.ox.ac.uk/research-subject-groups/commercial-law-centre/blog/2016/10/reading-tea-leaves-private-international.

[50] Yeo describes three approaches to characterising and dealing with such issues. See TM Yeo, 'Choice of Law for Equity' in S Degeling and J Edelman (eds), *Equity in Commercial Law* (Pyrmont, NSW, Law Book Co, 2005) 147; R Stevens, 'Choice of Law for Equity: Is it Possible?' in S Degeling and J Edelman (eds), *Equity in Commercial Law* (Pyrmont, Law Book Co, 2005) 173.

[51] See further Davies, Bell and Brereton (n 32) [21.12]–[21.13].

[52] Yeo (n 50) 167–70.

[53] Lord Collins of Mapesbury and Jonathan Harris, *Dicey, Morris & Collins on the Conflict of Laws*, 15th edn (London, Sweet & Maxwell, 2012) vol 2, [34-091]–[34-092], [35-141]. It was pointed out that this was a revision of a tentative view expressed in an earlier edition, and relied upon by the Court of Appeal in *Douglas* (CA) (n 4), that a claim for breach of confidence could be categorised as a claim for unjust enrichment.

had hired for the celebration, that confidential and private information – photographs of their wedding celebrations – was collected by a trespasser, a paparazzo disguised as a waiter. However, that information was published in the UK by *Hello!* magazine. This event was considered sufficient to treat the action for breach of confidential information as having occurred in England, so as to attract the application of the law of England and Wales. Critically, the fact that no tort against the Douglases might have been committed in New York, either by the intrusion or by subsequent publication in New York, was not enough to defeat the Douglases' claim of unlawful publication in the UK.[54]

Lord Phillips had commented:

> The Douglases' claim in relation to invasion of their privacy might seem most appropriately to fall within the ambit of the law of delict. We have concluded, however, albeit not without hesitation, that the effect of shoe-horning this type of claim into the cause of action of breach of confidence means that it does not fall to be treated as a tort under English law …[55]

Commenting on that earlier case, the Court of Appeal in *Google Inc v Vidal-Hall* noted that no party in *Douglas v Hello! Ltd (No 3)* had argued that the claim was one in tort, or that the Private International Law (Miscellaneous Provisions) Act 1995, dealing with tort claims, was relevant. Therefore, Lord Phillips' comments were obiter. Effectively, the Court of Appeal distinguished the decision in *Douglas* as one dealing with the traditional, equitable action for breach of confidence, thus leaving the way open to a different classification for the new 'extended' action.

The Court of Appeal also distinguished *Kitechnology BV v Unicor GmbH Plastmaschinen*[56] on this basis. That case concerned the issue of whether English courts had jurisdiction to hear the particular dispute under Article 5(3) of the Brussels Convention 1968, which then applied to matters of tort.[57] The Court of Appeal in *Kitechnology* had held that claims for breach of confidence do not arise in tort for historical reasons:

> The decision in *Kitechnology*, therefore, turned on the historical distinction that existed before the Judicature Act 1873 between the courts of common law and the Court

[54] A similar approach was taken more recently in *Weller v Associated Newspapers Ltd* [2015] EWCA Civ 1176, [2016] 1 WLR 1541.

[55] *Douglas* (CA) (n 4) [96].

[56] *Kitechnology BV v Unicor GmbH Plastmaschinen* [1995] FSR 765.

[57] See now Civil Jurisdiction and Judgments Act 1982. As to when a court will have jurisdiction to hear a multi-state or international dispute, see further Moreham and Warby (n 7) [13.56]: 'In privacy, as in defamation claims, the court will assume jurisdiction provided the tort committed within its territory is "real and substantial"'. Contrast [13.65]: defamation claims are now subject to a 'clearly the most appropriate place' test under s 9 of the Defamation Act 2013 (UK), to prevent so-called 'libel tourism'. In Australia, jurisdiction in actions *in personam*, including tort, contract or equitable claims for relief, depends on service of the process. See further Davies, Bell and Brereton (n 32) ch 3. A defendant disputing the appropriateness of the forum must satisfy a test that it is a 'clearly inappropriate forum': *Voth v Manildra Flour Mills Pty Ltd* [1990] HCA 55, (1990) 171 CLR 538, discussed in Davies, Bell and Brereton (n 32) [8.13]–[8.23]. The authors note, at [8.22], that this case presumably overrides the previous practice, whereby equitable relief in respect of events occurring abroad could be refused on the ground that the foreign court was the more appropriate forum.

> of Chancery. It would seem an odd and adventitious result for the defendant, if the historical accident of the division between equity and the common law resulted in the claimants in the present case being unable to serve their claims out of the jurisdiction on the defendant. …
>
> We accept that the decision in *Kitechnology* would be binding on us if the cause of action for misuse of private information were an action for breach of confidence. But for the reasons already given, it is not.[58]

The Court concluded, much as Tugendhat J had done, that 'in the absence of any sound reasons or policy or principle to suggest otherwise … misuse of private information should now be recognised as a tort for the purposes of service out the jurisdiction'.[59]

The Court did not include choice of law (or other conflict-of-laws issues) in its list of still-to-be-worked-out ramifications of categorising the wrongful disclosure of private information as a tort. Presumably, this is because its classification, for the purposes of allowing service outside the jurisdiction under the CPR, would also bring the tort within the Private International Law (Miscellaneous Provisions) Act 1995. However, any assumption as to the application of the 1995 Act would be, strictly speaking, obiter, and it is just as possible that another court could come to a stricter view as a matter of statutory interpretation. Even if the legislative term 'tort' is ambulatory and new torts coming into being after 1995 are encompassed in its application, it is difficult, as we point out at the beginning of this chapter, to see how this action has become a tort when the courts keep denying, as the Court of Appeal did here, and as members of the House of Lords had done previously, that they have created a new cause of action, while at the same time distinguishing it from a well-established equitable one.

Perhaps the issue would be side-stepped, for private international law purposes at least, if a court could conclude that the legislator of the 1995 Act intended to use 'tort' in the wider sense of all non-contractual wrongs, as Yeo suggests. *Gurry* supports Yeo's position on breach of confidence claims where liability results from fault.[60] But in many cases of breach of confidence, liability for active disclosure or misuse is strict,[61] once there is knowledge or notice, 'objectively assessed', of the information's confidential character.[62] Again, this illustrates that it may be premature to classify the cause of action for misuse of

[58] *Vidal-Hall* (CA) (n 2) [48]–[50].

[59] ibid [51].

[60] Aplin et al (n 8) [23.81].

[61] *Seager v Copydex Ltd* [1967] 1 WLR 923; *Interfirm Comparison (Aust) Pty Ltd v Law Society of New South Wales* [1975] 2 NSWLR 104; *Talbot v General Television Corp Pty Ltd* [1980] VR 224. See further Aplin et al (n 8) [15.31]–[15.41].

[62] Aplin et al (n 8) [15.05], citing *Re Smith Kline and French Laboratories (Australia) Ltd* [1990] FCA 206 *per* Gummow J. On the issue of knowledge of confidentiality as binding the conscience of the defendant, see *Vestergaard Frandsen A/S v Bestnet Europe Ltd* [2013] UKSC 31, [2013] 1 WLR 1556, [25] *per* Lord Neuberger.

private information, new or not, before its elements – including the element of fault or strict liability – have been clearly defined by the courts. Yeo's suggestion would seem to be supported by other academic commentators, who argue that the term 'tort' is 'underdetermined'.[63] It would have ramifications beyond privacy actions, and have the advantage of giving some certainty as to the applicable law in other cross-border equitable claims. However, it seems inconsistent with the approach taken in *Kitechnology*, which the Court of Appeal in *Google Inc v Vidal Hall* was at pains to distinguish.

As the Court of Appeal implicitly acknowledged by expressly putting to one side 'the circumstances of its "birth"',[64] the mystery of the birth of the new tort, in both time – occurring sometime between 2004 and 2015 – and judicial method, is an obstacle, some might think more than just an inconvenient detail, in the broader classification of this modern-day action. As Lord Millett said in another context, 'The correct classification of the claimants' cause of action may appear to be academic, but it has important consequences … causes of action have different requirements and may attract different defences.'[65]

It is noteworthy that, despite *Google Inc v Vidal Hall*, Moreham and Warby still refer to the 'remaining uncertainties as to the correct categorisation of the causes of action for misuse of private information and breach of confidence' before discussing applicable law in international disputes.[66]

III. Vicarious Liability

One of the implications the Court of Appeal identified as potentially arising out of classifying the privacy action as a tort was vicarious liability.

Many disclosures or misuses of private information may occur in contexts where various parties have responsibility for or access to the information, and questions may arise as to whether a defendant is vicariously liable for the tort of another person due to the defendant's relationship with that person. Vicarious liability for the tort of another person arises in three situations: where the actor was an employee (not an independent contractor) of the employer and was acting in the course of employment; where the actor was acting as agent of the defendant as principal; and where the tort was committed by a partner of the defendant.

The doctrine has been a significant and perennially contentious issue in the law of torts, but is one that is not generally mentioned in treatises on contract law or equitable principles. We briefly consider here why this might be so, and again what difference, if any, classification of the action might make.

[63] J Edelman, 'Equitable Torts' (2002) 10 *Torts Law Journal* 1.
[64] *Vidal-Hall* (CA) (n 14) [43].
[65] *Foskett v McKeown* [2000] UKHL 29, [2000] 2 WLR 1299, 1324, cited in Edelman (n 63) 3.
[66] Moreham and Warby (n 7) [13.82].

A. Vicarious Liability in Equity?

Perhaps the key reason why vicarious liability is not discussed in the context of contractual or equitable claims is that it is usually unnecessary for a claimant to rely upon the doctrine. First, it will be the employer (as defendant) who owes the relevant contractual or equitable obligation to the claimant. Secondly, it may be obvious that the relevant breach – the publication, communication or misuse of confidential information – was committed by the defendant in its own name. Thirdly, even where another person commits the relevant act, the issue will be whether the act of that other person, such as an employee or agent, can be *attributed* to the employer/principal so that it is *treated* as a breach by the employer/principal of its own personal obligation.[67] Such legal rules of attribution vary in different contexts.[68] A law firm has contractual and equitable obligations to its clients: a breach of those obligations by an employed solicitor is treated as a breach by the firm. Where a journalist employed by a media organisation is given or acquires confidential information, it may be the media organisation itself that is regarded as the confidant. In that sense, the contractual or equitable obligation to keep the information confidential is, to use terminology more accustomed in tort, a 'non-delegable' obligation.[69] If on the other hand, the act of the employee is not treated as a disclosure of confidential information *by* the employer, there will be no attribution to the employer and liability will rest on the employee alone.

A further reason why vicarious liability does not arise for discussion in equity claims is that equity has, at least since the second half of the seventeenth century, formulated its own basis for accessorial liability. It was recently noted in the context of an equitable claim:

> [T]he problem is that to apply the doctrine of vicarious liability in order to impose upon an employer, liability for a breach of trust (or fiduciary duty) by an employee, without more, would go beyond the ambit of accessorial liability as identified in *Barnes v Addy* (1874) LR 9 Ch App 244 and subsequent cases.[70]

Equitable liability thus rests squarely on the state of knowledge and level of participation of the particular party in the wrong. In that sense, liability in equity is based on personal conscience.

[67] This is a separate issue to the basis of liability, strict or 'fault' based, discussed in section II.C.

[68] *Director General, Department of Education and Training v MT* [2006] NSWCA 270, (2006) 67 NSWLR 237, applying *Meridian Global Funds Management Asia Ltd v Securities Commission* [1995] UKPC 5, [1995] 2 AC 500. See also Richardson et al (n 11) 78–79.

[69] A non-delegable duty may in fact be delegated, but the employer cannot escape liability for breach by delegating. See *Woodland v Essex County Council* [2013] UKSC 66, [2013] 3 WLR 1227.

[70] *Oliver Hume South East Queensland P/L v Investa Residential Group P/L* [2017] FCAFC 141 *per* Dowsett J, citing *Lifeplan Australia Friendly Society Ltd v Ancient Order of Foresters in Victoria Friendly Society Ltd* [2017] FCAFC 74, (2017) 250 FCR 1, [123], in which the Full Court described the issue of vicarious liability as important. Leave to appeal to the High Court of Australia has been granted from the latter decision on issues of accessorial liability: [2017] HCATrans 210.

B. Vicarious Liability for a Tort of Misuse of Private Information?

Arguably, issues of attribution of conduct will also arise where misuse of private information as a tort is concerned. But because liability will generally arise from the nature of the information rather than from any pre-existing personal obligation of the employer or principal, different considerations may become relevant. Further, if misuse is treated as a tort then tort principles of vicarious liability would seem to apply as a matter of course.

It has been said that the doctrine of vicarious liability 'lies at the heart of all common law systems of tort law'.[71] Gilliker notes that while vicarious liability may appear fundamentally at odds with tort's traditional focus on individual responsibility, under both the common law and civil law systems, it may be best seen as a rule of responsibility rather than of attributed fault.[72] The long-established rationale of vicarious liability was stated by Isaacs J in the High Court of Australia thus:

> The principle on which the responsibility rests is that it is more just to make the person who has entrusted his servant with the power of acting in his business responsible for injury occasioned to another in the course of so acting, than that the entirely innocent party should be left to bear the loss.[73]

In other words, it can be seen as a form of enterprise liability, whereby the employer must carry the risks of its delegates being at fault in the course of the conducting of the enterprise. It is sometimes described as a strict liability in the sense that there is no personal fault on the part of the employer, yet there must be a tort committed by the employee, and most torts involve fault in the form of intent or negligence.

The most litigated issue in recent times in tort claims concerning vicarious liability has been the issue of whether deliberate, possibly criminal, conduct may fall within the 'course of employment'. The traditional approach, traced back to the first edition of Salmond's *Law of Torts* in 1907,[74] has been to identify whether the employee's conduct was an authorised act (clearly within), an improper, even a prohibited, mode of committing an authorised act (still within) or, on the other hand, an entirely remote and disconnected act, a 'frolic of his own'[75] as if a stranger to the employer (outside). While this approach may yield an answer as to on which side of the line many acts of an employee may fall, particularly in cases of

[71] P Gilliker, *Vicarious Liability in Tort: A Comparative Perspective* (Cambridge, Cambridge UP, 2010) [1.1].

[72] ibid ch 1.

[73] *Bugge v Brown* [1919] HCA 5, (1919) 26 CLR 110, 117. See also *Hollis v Vabu* [2001] HCA 44, (2001) 207 CLR 21, [35] *per* Gleeson CJ, Gaudron, Gummow, Kirby and Hayne JJ: 'A fully satisfactory rationale for the imposition of vicarious liability in the employment relationship has been slow to appear in the case law.'

[74] JW Salmond, *The Law of Torts* (London, Stevens and Haynes 1917) 83, cited in *New South Wales v Lepore* [2003] HCA 4, 212 CLR 511, [42] *per* Gleeson CJ.

[75] *Joel v Morison* (1834) 6 Car & P 501, 503; 172 ER 1338, 1339 *per* Parke B.

negligence, the approach has proved unhelpful when considering certain examples of intentional, criminal behaviour, such as sexual assault by teachers or other carers in institutional settings. The trouble with such cases is that the employee is doing the opposite of what he or she was entrusted to do: protect the child or the patient. Yet the courts have not been prepared to dismiss the claim of vicarious liability, given that the child or patient came to harm while entrusted into the care of the employer. In such cases, Canadian and English courts have now formulated a test that asks whether there was such a close connection between the duties of the employee and the position in which he or she was placed vis-à-vis the victim, with English courts also asking whether it is therefore fair, just and reasonable in the particular circumstances to hold the employer vicariously liable.[76] The High Court of Australia, taking a slightly different approach, requires the court to look at whether the employee was placed in a position of power and intimacy, and whether the employer provided not merely the opportunity for the tort to be committed, but also the 'occasion' for the tort.[77]

How will these principles operate in respect of a tort of misuse of private information? If misuse encompasses intrusion or *collection* of private information, where there is no pre-existing obligation, the action is clearly analogous to existing torts, and the traditional test should yield a logical and just answer. Arguably, phone hacking or trespassing by an employed journalist is merely an unauthorised, possibly prohibited, mode of committing an authorised act: collecting information for a story. There are numerous examples of actions against media employers for trespass committed by employees.[78] Even though it involves criminal conduct, such conduct is nevertheless pursued for the employer's business and benefit, and would logically seem to fall within the course of employment and thus the employer's vicarious liability.

What of misuse by publication or communication? In any claim, it will become critical to determine whether a defendant is to be treated as having committed the new tort itself (including by the acts of people whose conduct is attributed to it). If so, vicarious liability may be redundant.

C. The Role of Fault in Liability

A related issue is whether some sort of fault is required for liability under the new tort.[79] Torts are generally divided into intentional torts, torts founded on negligence or strict liability torts, the last category increasingly rare at common law. In contrast, as previously mentioned, equitable liability is either strict or

[76] *Lister v Hesley Hall Ltd* [2001] UKHL 22, [2002] 1 AC 215.
[77] *Prince Alfred College Inc v ADC* [2016] HCA 37, (2016) 258 CLR 134. See also *Bazley v Curry* [1999] 2 SCR 534; *Jacobi v Griffiths* [1999] 2 SCR 570.
[78] See, eg, *TCN Channel Nine Pty Ltd v Anning* [2002] NSWCA 82, (2002) 54 NSWLR 333.
[79] See further McDonald (n 30).

conscience-based, with conscience, and thus liability, dependent on the state of a party's knowledge.[80] The basis of liability in tort affects defences and issues of remoteness of damage, and may also impact on an employer's liability.

For example, let us assume a wrongful disclosure of private information is committed by an employee of a bank or a doctor's surgery. To sue the employer on a 'personal' basis, the claimant would have to show both that the acts of the employee could be attributed to the employer and, unless the new tort is one of strict liability, some fault on the part of the employer. If either factor was missing, the claimant would need to fall back on vicarious liability and prove that the employee at fault was acting in the course of employment when he or she wrongfully disclosed the information. Either the traditional test for 'course of employment' or the local variant of the newer 'close connection' test would apply. The fact that the employee was acting deliberately, or even criminally, would not foreclose the issue.

D. Conclusion on Vicarious Liability

How vicarious liability will operate in the context of the new tort will depend on whether the wrong is fault-based or strict liability, and on whose duty or obligation is breached by a perpetrator in committing the wrong: only his or her own duties, or those of another party too? There is still much to be worked out, if misuse of information is indeed a tort for all purposes.

IV. Injunctions

The principal remedy for misuse of private information has been the injunction, sought on an interim or an interlocutory basis. It is fair to observe that the cause of action for misuse of private information has developed around the injunction as the main form of relief, shaping its current form. This is understandable in that, privacy, once invaded, can never be entirely restored.[81] For the orderly and principled development of the law relating to misuse of private information, however, the cause of action must be formulated to support a range of remedies that operate coherently against the background of other legal wrongs. Injunctions are sought

[80] *Vestergaard Frandsen A/S v Bestnet Europe Ltd* [2013] UKSC 31, [2013] 1 WLR 1556. See also Aplin et al, (n 8) [15.31]–[15.44].

[81] See, eg, *Mosley v News Group Newspapers Ltd* [2008] EWHC 1777 (QB), [230] *per* Eady J; *Cooper v Turrell* [2011] EWHC 3269 (QB), [102] *per* Tugendhat J. In *Attorney-General v Newspaper Publishing Ltd* [1988] Ch 333, 358, Sir John Donaldson MR remarked that '[c]onfidential information is like an ice cube … Give it to the party who has no refrigerator … and by the time of trial you just have a pool of water'. See also New South Wales Law Reform Commission, *Invasion of Privacy* (NSWLRC Report 120, 2009) [7.16]–[7.18]; D Rolph, 'Irreconcilable Differences? Interlocutory injunctions for defamation and privacy' (2012) 17 *Media and Arts Law Review* 170, 191.

urgently, often with little time for detailed consideration of, and reflection upon, the legal issues and their implications.[82] There have been a number of appeals, to the Court of Appeal and to the UK Supreme Court, which have allowed for some deeper analysis.[83] Still, because the evolution of the cause of action for misuse of private information has been significantly through applications for injunctions, some fundamental doctrinal questions have remained unanswered.

Consistently with other wrongs, the classification of misuse of private information as either a common law or an equitable wrong will generally have an effect on the availability and grant of injunctive relief. Yet the evolution of misuse of private information from its origins in breach of confidence to a tort has not squarely identified this as an issue. It is settled that breach of confidence arises in equity's exclusive jurisdiction, being based on conscience, rather than being grounded in contract or property.[84] If misuse of private information is to be treated as an equitable wrong, like breach of confidence, it would also arise in equity's exclusive jurisdiction. A consequence for a claimant seeking injunctive relief in equity's exclusive jurisdiction is that he or she does not have to address whether or not damages would be an adequate remedy.[85] By contrast, if misuse of private information is properly classified as a tort, the grant of injunctive relief arises in equity's auxiliary jurisdiction, with the consequence that the adequacy of damages as a remedy should be a consideration on any application for an injunction.[86] The case law on injunctions for misuse of private information, though, suggests that the adequacy of damages has rarely been considered in this context.[87]

A. Injunctions and Breach of Confidence

The readiness with which injunctions are granted for misuse of private information is in part derived from the origins of the cause of action in breach of confidence.[88]

[82] See JD Heydon, MJ Leeming and PG Turner, *Meagher, Gummow & Lehane's Equity: Doctrines & Remedies*, 5th edn (Chatswood, NSW, LexisNexis Butterworths, 2015) [42-055].

[83] For England and Wales Court of Appeal decisions, see, eg, *AAA v Associated Newspapers Ltd* [2012] EWHC 2224 (QB); *JIH v News Group Newspapers Ltd* [2011] EWCA Civ 42, [2011] 2 WLR 1645; *Ntuli v Donald* [2010] EWCA Civ 1726, [2011] 1 WLR 294; *Ash v McKennitt* [2006] EWCA Civ 1714, [2008] QB 73. For UK Supreme Court decisions, see *PJS v News Group Newspapers Ltd* [2016] UKSC 26, [2016] AC 1081.

[84] Heydon, Leeming and Turner (n 82) [42-040] (citing *McKaskell v Benseman* [1989] 3 NZLR 75, 88), [42-060] (citing *Moorgate Tobacco Co Ltd v Philip Morris Ltd (No 2)* (1984) 164 CLR 414, 438).

[85] Heydon, Leeming and Turner (n 82) [21-015], [42-075].

[86] ibid [21-040], citing *Wood v Sutcliffe* (1851) 2 Sim (NS) 263; *Imperial Gas Light & Coke Co v Broadbent* (1859) 7 HLC 600, 612; *London & Blackwall Railway Co v Cross* (1885) 31 Ch D 354; *Fielden v Cox* (1906) 22 TLR 411; *Stollmeyer v Trinidad Lake Petroleum Co* [1918] UKPC 8, [1918] AC 485, 489; *Lawrence v Fen Tigers Ltd* [2014] UKSC 13, [2014] AC 822, [159]–[160], [171]. See also *Australian Broadcasting Corporation v O'Neill* [2006] HCA 46, (2006) 227 CLR 57; *Lenah Game Meats* (n 23).

[87] See, eg, *Terry v Persons Unknown* [2010] EWHC 119 (QB).

[88] Rolph (n 81), citing *Douglas v Hello! Ltd* [2001] QB 967 (CA); *Theakston v MGN Ltd* [2002] EMLR 22, [2002] EWHC 137 (QB); *A v B plc* [2002] EWCA Civ 337 [2003] QB 195 (CA).

Courts have always been ready to grant injunctions, or to make suppression or non-publication orders in claims involving confidential information. These routine derogations from the principle of open justice have been considered necessary to preserve the subject matter of the proceedings: once confidential information had entered the public domain, it loses its quality of confidence and there is nothing left for the court to protect. For a court to permit the subject matter of a claim to be destroyed, in advance of a trial on the merits of the claim, would be inimical to the proper administration of justice.[89] It is a small step from protecting confidential information in this way to protecting private information.

Further, even in those jurisdictions, unlike Australia, where a broad public interest defence is recognised to a claim for breach of confidence, the courts have recognised that there also is a public interest in protecting confidences.[90] The same applies in privacy claims, in which courts and commentators have stressed the public value of protecting privacy.[91] Thus, public interest considerations are a double-edged element in a claim for an injunction, whether the claim is one of confidence or of privacy.

B. Injunctions and Human Rights

The other impetus for the ready use of injunctions on an interim or interlocutory basis to protect private information is Article 13 of the European Convention on Human Rights (ECHR). This article requires signatory countries to ensure that individuals have an effective remedy for a breach of rights and freedoms protected under the ECHR. United Kingdom human rights jurisprudence readily accepts that an injunction is the most effective, or sometimes the only effective, remedy for misuse of private information.[92] Interestingly, the European Court of Human Rights is more open on this point.[93] For example, in *Mosley v NGN Ltd*, Eady J considered that 'it has to be accepted that an infringement of privacy cannot ever be effectively compensated by a monetary award', and that 'the only realistic course

[89] See, eg, *Scott v Scott* [1913] UKHL 2, [1913] AC 417; *Nagle-Gillman v Christopher* (1876) 4 Ch D 173; *Mellor v Thompson* (1885) 31 Ch D 55; *Hogan v Hinch* [2011] HCA 4, (2011) 423 CLR 506, 531.

[90] *Attorney-General v Guardian Newspapers Ltd (No 2)* [1988] UKHL 6, 29; [1990] 1 AC 109, 282.

[91] E Barendt, 'Privacy and Freedom of Speech' in AT Kenyon and M Richardson (eds), *New Dimensions in Privacy Law* (Cambridge, Cambridge UP, 2006) 11, 30–31. As to claims for misuse of private information where a public interest defence was established at trial, see *Ferdinand v MGN Ltd* [2011] EWHC 2454 (QB); *Spelman v Express Newspapers* [2012] EWHC 255 (QB).

[92] See, eg, R Clayton and H Tomlinson (eds), *Privacy and Freedom of Expression* (Oxford, Oxford UP, 2010); H Fenwick and G Phillipson (eds), *Media Freedom under the Human Rights Act* (Oxford, Oxford, 2006). See also D Eady, 'Injunctions and the protection of privacy' (2010) 29 *Civil Justice Quarterly* 411. This is reflected in statistics on injunctions granted in the UK in respect of misuse of private information: see, eg, Ministry of Justice, 'Statistics on privacy injunctions January to June 2013' (*Statistics Bulletin*, 19 September 2013), www.gov.uk/government/uploads/system/uploads/attachment_data/file/243813/privacy-injunctions-bulletin-jan-jun-2013.pdf.

[93] *Mosley* (n 81) [231].

is to select a figure which marks the fact that an unlawful intrusion has taken place while affording some degree of *solatium* to the injured party. That is all that can be done in circumstances where the traditional object of *restitutio* is not available.'[94] Eady J also considered that pre-publication notification was likely necessary for the granting of an injunction.[95] However, in *Mosley v United Kingdom*, the European Court of Human Rights rejected the submission that Article 8 of the ECHR requires pre-publication notification.[96]

Tending against the ready grant of injunctive relief for misuse of private information is section 12 of the Human Rights Act 1998 (UK). This section is engaged where the grant of relief 'might affect the exercise of the Convention right to freedom of expression'.[97] A court is not to grant an injunction before the trial unless it is satisfied that, at the trial, the claimant is likely to succeed.[98] In assessing this, the court is specifically directed to have particular regard to the Convention right of freedom of expression and whether what is sought to be published is in the public interest.[99] The working out of the principles relating to the grant of injunctions for misuse of private information not only involves ordinary equitable principles, but also entails a complex interplay with human rights instruments and legislation.

In countries such as Australia, without the underlying imperatives and authority of an instrument such as the Human Rights Act 1998 (UK), the development of the remedy of injunctions to protect privacy will take place against the historical division between equity's exclusive and auxiliary jurisdictions. It was decided in *Lenah Game Meats* that even broadly expressed statutory powers endowed on courts to grant injunctions do not expand the jurisdiction of the courts, and must be construed against the background of recognised legal or equitable rights and causes of action.[100] Whether the claim is based on a tort or contract[101] or on some grounds for equitable relief will therefore, theoretically at least, govern the factors the court must consider when adjudicating on the application for an injunction. However, the authors of Meagher, Gummow and Lehane note that

> [s]o strong has been the tendency of the courts to view almost any damage as irreparable, and so undemanding the requirement that irreparable damage must be demonstrated, that in recent years one might have categorised the test as being merely nominal.[102]

[94] ibid.

[95] ibid [209].

[96] *Mosley v United Kingdom* App 48009/08 [2012] EMLR 1, [132]. See also *Representatives Claimants v MGN Ltd* [2015] EWCA Civ 1291, [2016] 3 All ER 799, [89], where it was held that the adequacy of damages is a matter for national courts.

[97] Human Rights Act 1998, s 12(1).

[98] ibid, s 12(3). As to the meaning of 'likely' in this context, see *Cream Holdings Ltd v Banerjee* [2004] UKHL 44, [2005] 1 AC 253.

[99] Human Rights Act 1998, s 12(4).

[100] *Lenah Game Meats* (n 23), considering *Supreme Court Civil Procedure Act 1932* (Tas), s 11(12).

[101] Where injunctions may be given to restrain the breach of an express or implied negative covenant without requiring proof of inadequacy of damages: *Doherty v Allman* (1878) 3 App Cas 709, 719–20.

[102] Heydon, Leeming and Turner (n 82) [21-040].

C. Injunctions and Tort

More contentious, particularly if the action is considered to be a tort, and in circumstances where the court is not concerned with enforcing a pre-existing obligation to keep information private, will be the issue of whether applications for injunctions for misuse of private information or other invasions of privacy should be treated with the same caution by the courts as applications for injunctions in defamation cases. Indeed, the interaction between the approaches to injunctive relief in defamation and privacy has only recently begun to be explored. It is well-established that an interim or interlocutory injunction is difficult to obtain for defamation, given the public interest in freedom of speech and the common law's aversion to prior restraint.[103] The issue of claimants' impermissibly circumventing defamation law's balancing of the defendant's freedom of speech[104] by framing the claim for an injunction as one to protect privacy rather than reputation is a real one, and has begun to be debated in the English courts.[105] The working test, such as it is, is that a court should not permit a claimant to circumvent the restrictive approach to injunctive relief in defamation by framing a claim in some other cause of action. However, where the facts would support a cause of action in defamation and equally in some other cause of action, the claimant could obtain an injunction on that other cause of action, even if the effect of the injunction is to restrain an arguably defamatory publication that could not be restrained by relying upon defamation alone.[106] The test then resolves itself to whether the essence of the claimant's claim is the protection of reputation or some other interest.[107] The courts have offered no real guidance as to when a matter is concerned essentially with reputation and when it is not. It is very much a matter of the judge's characterisation of the claims before the court, on the partial basis disclosed on an interim or interlocutory application. It is not difficult to imagine scenarios in which a person's reputation and privacy are both equally implicated by a threatened publication. After all, reputation and privacy are simply the public and private aspects of an individual's persona. Allowing for the ready grant of injunctions for misuse of private information provides claimants with an incentive to frame their claim in that cause of action, even if the claim is arguably one in defamation and would previously have been dealt with on that basis. Unsurprisingly, claims for defamation have been declining markedly in London, formerly the libel capital of the world, eclipsed by claims in privacy. The remedial advantages offered by a cause of action in privacy are a significant reason for this development.

[103] See *Bonnard v Perryman* [1891] 2 Ch 269; *O'Neill* (n 86) [17]–[19] *per* Gleeson CJ and Crennan JJ, [80]–[82] *per* Gummow and Hayne JJ.

[104] As to which in Australia, see *O'Neill* (n 86).

[105] *Terry v Persons Unknown* [2010] EWHC 119 (QB).

[106] See Rolph (n 81), quoting *Service Corp International Plc v Channel Four Television Corp* [1999] EMLR 83.

[107] *Woodward v Hutchins* [1977] 1 WLR 760, 764 *per* Lord Denning MR.

V. Damages

The focus on injunctive relief as the principal remedy for misuse of private information has had the effect that the principles relating to the award of damages for this cause of action are comparatively underdeveloped. There are now a number of claims in which damages have been awarded for misuse of private information,[108] but these are few in comparison to the vast case law on injunctions. Unsurprisingly, then, fundamental doctrinal questions have not been resolved about the principles governing damages for misuse of private information. Many of those questions arise from the uncertainty as to whether misuse of private information should be classified as an equitable wrong or a tort.

This uncertainty raises a threshold question as to whether damages, properly speaking, are a remedy for this cause of action at all. If misuse of private information is an equitable wrong, derived from breach of confidence, then equitable compensation, rather than common law damages, would seem to be the proper remedy. This has not emerged as a doctrinal problem in the English case law on misuse of private information[109] but will likely be an issue under Australian law. Indeed, it may be an impediment to Australian law's developing a more direct and effective protection of privacy through the preferred judicial method of extending and adapting breach of confidence.[110]

If misuse of private information is equitable, equitable compensation may be awarded in a straightforward manner if equity recognises the underlying interest as worthy of its protection. This has not yet happened under Australian law outside traditional breach of confidence cases. The leading Australian case on protecting private information through breach of confidence, the Victorian Court of Appeal decision in *Giller v Procopets*,[111] suggested that a claimant's entitlement to equitable compensation was to be determined under a form of *Lord Cairns' Act*. In *Giller v Procopets*, the trial judge, Gillard J, was prepared to accept that the claimant had a prima facie claim for breach of confidence: the sex tapes that were the subject of that claim constituted information with the necessary quality of confidence; they were imparted in a de facto relationship, being a relationship importing an obligation of confidence; and their unauthorised disclosure caused the claimant relevant detriment in the sense of her humiliation in the eyes of her family, friends and work colleagues.[112] However, as the claimant had not sought an injunction and as there was no scope for specific performance, His Honour found that damages could not be awarded 'in addition to, or in substitution for, an injunction or specific

[108] See, eg, *Campbell* (n 9); *Mosley* (n 81); *Weller* (n 54).

[109] For examples of damages for distress being awarded for misuse of private information in English case law, see NA Moreham, 'Compensating for Loss of Dignity and Autonomy', in ch 5 of this book.

[110] *Lenah Game Meats* (n 23) [40] *per* Gleeson CJ), [110] *per* Gummow and Hayne JJ); *Giller* (CA) (n 24) [430]–[431].

[111] *Giller* (CA) (n 24).

[112] *Giller v Procopets* [2004] VSC 113, [149], [153], [156].

performance' for the purposes of section 38 of the *Supreme Court Act 1986* (Vic), the *Lord Cairns' Act* provision in that jurisdiction.[113] On appeal, the Victorian Court of Appeal found that compensation could be granted under section 38 of the *Supreme Court Act 1986* (Vic) because it was not necessary that the claimant had in fact applied for an injunction; all that was required was that the court had the jurisdiction to entertain such an application. Notwithstanding the majority's reliance on the *Supreme Court Act 1986*, and the rather odd analogy with existing tort law (which would *not* have given the claimant a remedy), the best argument in favour of the award of equitable compensation for mental distress in a breach of confidence claim would seem to be equity's remedial flexibility to protect the underlying interest. As Neave JA said in that case, 'An inability to order equitable compensation to a claimant who has suffered distress would mean that a claimant whose confidence was breached before an injunction could be obtained would have no effective remedy.'[114] As equity has protected personal private information since the very earliest cases of breach of confidence, such as *Prince Albert v Strange*,[115] that protection must support a right to compensation for harm caused. This of course gives rise to the question of why distress should be treated as harm in this but not other legal contexts.

If misuse of private information is properly characterised as a tort, the availability of damages as a remedy is not necessarily less problematic. Again, a threshold issue will be whether mere mental distress as a result of misuse of privacy can be treated as actual damage. To do so would be contradictory to a long line of established cases based on any form of the 'action on the case': for example, the action based on the principle in *Wilkinson v Downton*[116] and the action of negligence.[117] If the same approach is followed in a privacy tort, then the only way that tort law could, coherently and consistently, allow compensation for distress would be to treat the privacy tort as analogous to trespass and other torts actionable per se.[118]

Although compensation or damages may be available as a remedy on some juridical basis, the heads of damages and the purposes for which they may be awarded remain problematic. Compensation for actual damage, whether in the form of equitable compensation or common law damages, will be available. Aggravated damages are likely to be available at common law, given that aggravated damages are compensatory in purpose. Indeed, aggravated damages are likely to be

[113] ibid [162]–[165].

[114] *Giller* (CA) (n 24) [424]. See also *Wilson v Ferguson* (n 24) [82].

[115] *Prince Albert v Strange* (1848) 2 DeG & Sm 652; 64 ER 293, affirmed (1849) 1 H & Tw 1; 47 ER 1302.

[116] *Wilkinson v Downton* [1897] 2 QB 57.

[117] Cases arising out of negligence may also be limited by the civil liability legislation in most Australian States and Territories, which requires claimants to have suffered a recognised psychiatric illness and also limits damages recoverable in more minor claims. See, eg, *Civil Liability Act 2002* (NSW), pts 2, 3.

[118] It was for reasons of consistency and practical justice that the ALRC recommended that any statutory tort in Australia should be actionable per se, once other elements of the tort had been made out: ALRC (n 25) [8.39] et seq.

readily awarded in light of the nature of the impact of privacy breaches.[119] Again using the tort analogy, the Victorian Court of Appeal accepted in *Giller v Procopets* that aggravated damages are available for breach of confidence.[120]

The more difficult issue is whether exemplary damages are available for misuse of private information. Both Eady J in *Mosley v NGN Ltd* and the Victorian Court of Appeal in *Giller v Procopets* conclude that exemplary damages are not available to privacy claimants.[121] In these cases, the fact that the cause of action is equitable in origin is viewed as a bar to an award of exemplary damages. In *Giller v Procopets*, the Court, somewhat reluctantly, recognised that there was authority of a co-ordinate court – the New South Wales Court of Appeal in *Harris v Digital Pulse Pty Ltd*[122] – to the effect that exemplary damages could not be awarded for breach of fiduciary duty.[123] As equity is not a punitive jurisdiction, the Victorian Court of Appeal held, by parity of reasoning, that exemplary damages were not available for breach of confidence.[124] In *Mosley v NGN*, Eady J noted that misuse of private information had been incidentally referred to as a tort but that it had not been definitively established as such.[125] The original characterisation of the cause of action as equitable was influential upon Eady J's conclusion that exemplary damages could not be awarded for it. If misuse of private information is now properly characterised as tortious, this may necessitate the revisiting of this issue of principle.[126]

The distinction between equitable and tortious causes of action also affects the availability of restitutionary remedies, such as an account of profits. For claimants, the remedy is a valuable part of the armoury of equitable remedies in its exclusive jurisdiction for equitable wrongs. Traditionally only available in equity suits, it was also awarded for a (common law) breach of contract in the exceptional circumstances of *Attorney-General v Blake*,[127] but that is not a precedent followed in contract cases in Australia. However, if misuse of private information is a tort, there should be no barrier to an award of exemplary damages, which may have the similar intent and effect of stripping the defendant of his or her ill-gotten gain in contumelious disregard of the claimant's rights.[128]

[119] Indeed, they are sometimes referred to as 'aggravated compensatory damages'. See, eg, *Amalgamated Television Services Pty Ltd v Marsden (No 2)* [2003] NSWCA 186, [18]. See also *Gulati v MGN Ltd* [2015] EWCA Civ 1291, [2017] QB 149, [45]–[48] *per* Arden LJ). See further JNE Varuhas, 'Varieties of Damages for Breach of Privacy', in ch 3 of this book.

[120] See also *Mosley* (n 81) [176], [193] *per* Eady J.

[121] *Mosley* (n 81) [197] *per* Eady J; *Giller* (CA) (n 24) [156]–[158].

[122] *Harris v Digital Pulse Pty Ltd* [2003] NSWCA 10, (2003) 56 NSWLR 298.

[123] ibid [292]–[342] *per* Heydon JA.

[124] *Giller* (CA) (n 24) [158].

[125] *Mosley* (n 81) [182].

[126] See *PJS v News Group Newspapers Ltd* [2016] UKSC 26, [2016] AC 1081, [92], where Lord Toulson JSC (dissenting) observed that Eady J's decision on exemplary damages in *Mosley* may not be 'the final word on the subject'.

[127] *Attorney-General v Blake* [2000] UKHL 45, [2001] 1 AC 268.

[128] *Whitfeld v De Lauret & Co Ltd* (1920) 29 CLR 71, 77 *per* Knox CJ. Cf *Rookes v Barnard* [1964] AC 1129, 1227 *per* Lord Devlin; *AB v South West Water Services Ltd* [1993] QB 507.

VI. Conclusion

Other chapters in this book deal in depth with the many interesting issues – both real and so-far hypothetical – that are engendered by the recognition of a cause of action for misuse of private information and other forms of invasions of privacy. Many of these will arise whatever the classification of the action. However, there are many issues as to which the outcome may depend on classification, not just as a matter of legal history and precedent, but also in the context of international disputes, where complex rules of private international law have developed. While no one should doubt the law-making capacity of judges in a common law system, their creativity is not at large, so that the development of the action must be coherent and, at least, not inconsistent with the law's treatment of other analogous wrongs.[129] It should be recognised that the task of developing a new cause of action, which is coherent in and of itself as well as being consistent with existing private law principles and doctrines and consonant with human rights obligations, is a difficult one. Sometimes pragmatic choices have been, or will be, made; sometimes decisions relating to classification and their attendant doctrinal consequences might need to be revisited and revised. The Court of Appeal in *Google Inc v Vidal Hall* was clearly alive to possible implications of its decision operating in a broader context. Whether that classification will be revisited in another context remains to be seen. There is still much to be worked out in the substantive and remedial content of any new tort of misuse of private information.

[129] PG Turner, 'Rudiments of the Equitable Remedy of Compensation for Breach of Confidence' in S Degeling and JNE Varuhas, *Equitable Compensation and Disgorgement of Profit* (Oxford, Hart Publishing, 2017) 239, argues that equitable compensation for breach of confidence should develop without reference to common law analogues, eg torts protecting purely personal interests (see esp 269ff).

11

Privacy Remedies Viewed Through an Equitable Lens

PG TURNER

I. Introduction

With the aid of an equitable lens, this chapter examines how privacy interests might in future be protected through the grant of relief by courts of law. It eyes the potential law of the future, rather than concentrate alone on the present, for two reasons. The first is change. On matters more basic than relief, some common law jurisdictions have moved from the traditional position of the common law, in which privacy interests were only protected incidentally, to a position in which courts strive to protect privacy interests in law – or, rather, within equitable principles. Courts have extended equitable doctrines of confidentiality, by which equitable obligations constrain one who receives information in confidence from another, to constrain those who receive inherently 'private' information regardless of how that private information was received.[1] An 'extended action'[2] for breach of confidence has been developed, which, in a further change, English courts now incline to call a (common law) tort.[3] The result is to lengthen the list of arguable propositions as to the available relief for infringement of privacy, and to place many conflicting propositions on that register of potential arguments. A second reason to eye the potential future law rather than look alone at the present law is that there has not been the number and variety of cases to reach into all the crevices of relief. The time is yet to come when the courts closely consider what rules and principles might apply to relieve infringements of privacy, and what such

[1] *Sim Kon Fah v JBPB & Co (a firm)* [2011] HKCFI 396, [2011] 4 HKLRD 45, [38]–[41].

[2] See *Campbell v MGN Ltd* [2004] UKHL 22, [2004] 2 AC 457, [44], [51] *per* Lord Hoffmann. The term 'extended action' is attributed to this case, though it features in none of the judgments.

[3] *PJS v News Group Newspapers Ltd* [2016] UKSC 26, [2016] AC 1081, [32], [33], [38], [44]; *Vidal-Hall v Google Inc* [2015] EWCA Civ 311, [2016] QB 1003, [21], [25], [43], [50]–[51]; but see *Tchenguiz v Imerman* [2010] EWCA Civ 908, [2011] Fam 116, [65], [69]. The conviction expressed in [69] of *Tchenguiz*, that actions for infringements of privacy should continue to be kept within the equitable doctrine of confidentiality, was misunderstood or overlooked in *Vidall-Hall* [2016] QB 1003, [31]–[42].

relief reveals of the true nature of liability for infringing another's privacy and the entitlement beneath.

As Maine noticed, equity is an agent of change in legal systems.[4] An equitable lens may show whether a fully grown body of privacy remedies – be it limited or great – is likely to develop from existing laws and ideas through the agency of equity jurisprudence. Equity is a series of glosses and appendices to the common law,[5] including statute. When looking through equity to the potential legal developments of the future, it is inevitable that some such developments will be found unsuited to equity jurisprudence. Equity jurisprudence is a series of glosses and appendices to the law because it is not a complete parallel system of law. Equity jurisprudence is an incomplete system in that sense, because the many grounds on which equity jurisdiction can be objected to in many situations ensure that the system of equity contains gaps. Much of what follows therefore addresses the common law because of, rather than despite, the use of an equitable lens. For consideration of how privacy remedies might develop in the judge-made law brings into sight both equity's limits and the special capacity of equity to effect legal change.

The limits of equity are such that in several respects the topic of remedies for infringements of privacy might be expected to become a topic principally of the judge-made common law. That suggestion is offered on the basis of the case law of Australia, Canada, England, Hong Kong and New Zealand. (The case law of the United States has developed on such distinct lines as to make immediately useful comparisons difficult, and cases in point do not exist in such pertinent common law jurisdictions as Singapore.) The chapter advances the following particular points. If the 'extended action' for breach of confidence remains the chief means of directly protecting interests in privacy, the forms of available relief will include the standard equitable remedies for breach of confidence: injunctions, accounts of profits, equitable compensation, and delivery up and destruction of documents or goods. However, because the nature of the interest or interests protected by a judge-made law of privacy is akin to the interests protected by the common law of torts yet quite unlike the interests protected by obligations which arise only in equity, it might be expected that infringement of an entitlement to privacy will become actionable as a common law tort. Unlike equitable principles, which centre on conduct in good conscience, the concern of a law of privacy is a certain kind (or certain kinds) of harm. That harm is akin to the concerns of torts rather than other bodies of judge-made law. The available remedies for infringement of privacy, it is suggested, should therefore be developed by reference to the remedies

[4] HS Maine, *Ancient Law* (London, Murray, 1861) ch 3. See A Diamond, 'Fictions, Equity and Legislation: Maine's Three Agencies of Change' in A Diamond (ed), *The Victorian Achievement of Sir Henry Maine* (Cambridge, Cambridge UP, 1991) ch 15.

[5] FW Maitland, *Equity[:] Also the Forms of Action at Common Law*, AH Chaytor and WJ Whittaker (eds) (Cambridge, Cambridge UP, 1909) 18–19.

for torts. The most important equitable weapon in the protection of privacy would in that case be the remedy of injunction.

But it is as well to begin with a position quite different from the remedially narrow position ultimately advanced here, by considering an argument that has been found attractive in at least one other area of recent legal development: the argument that a full range of relief ought to be available to remedy infringements of entitlements to privacy in a court's discretion.

II. Full Range of Relief

The attraction of equipping the courts to do justice as the circumstances require, in an area of quickly changing social customs and technology, is unlikely to become weak as populations increase. Arguments for a discretionary power in judges to grant a full range of relief, as the circumstances may require, have a precedent in the case law on the doctrine through which private interests have been indirectly protected: the equitable doctrine of confidentiality.

Once the modern equitable doctrine of confidentiality was recognised in *Saltman Engineering Co Ltd v Campbell Engineering Co Ltd*,[6] injunctions were found to be available to protect confidences enforceable only in equity.[7] In other respects, the uncertainty over the available remedies, and the rules relating thereto, was high until the end of the twentieth century. Accounts of profits were found to be available, as might be expected where the obligation is an equitable obligation of conscience, though a poor report of *Seager v Copydex Ltd (No 1)*[8] left doubt over whether the ordering of the account is a subject of wide judicial discretion or is a prima facie entitlement in the election of a claimant.[9] The availability of proprietary relief was accepted in Canada but rejected elsewhere.[10] Compensation – be it equitable compensation, 'damages' under Lord Cairns' Act, common law damages or damages of no fixed address – has been the most troublesome form of relief. From the 1980s, litigation concerning these various remedies was influenced at key points by the idea that a full range of relief was, or should be, available for breach of an equitable obligation of confidence.[11] The idea was accompanied by

[6] *Saltman Engineering Co Ltd v Campbell Engineering Co Ltd* (1948) 65 RPC 203, 213.

[7] *Argyll v Argyll* [1967] Ch 302.

[8] *Seager v Copydex Ltd (No 1)* [1967] 1 WLR 923.

[9] See below, text to n 50.

[10] See M Conaglen, 'Thinking about Proprietary Remedies for Breach of Confidence' [2008] *Intellectual Property Quarterly* 82.

[11] *Lac Minerals Ltd v International Corona Resources Ltd* [1989] 2 SCR 574, 615; *Aquaculture Corp v New Zealand Green Mussel Co Ltd* [1990] 3 NZLR 299, 301; *Cadbury Schweppes Inc v FBI Foods Ltd* [1999] 1 SCR 142, [26]; *Vercoe v Rutland Fund Management Ltd* [2010] EWHC 424 (Ch), [333]–[346]. See F Gurry, *Breach of Confidence* (Oxford, Oxford UP, 1984) 58 and discussion in PG Turner, 'Rudiments of the Equitable Remedy of Compensation for Breach of Confidence' in S Degeling and JNE Varuhas (eds), *Equitable Compensation and Disgorgement of Profit* (Oxford, Hart Publishing, 2017) 244 and *passim*.

a suggestion that judges ought to have wide discretion to decide, independent of any asserted entitlements in the litigants, whether to grant relief and, if relief were to be granted, in what form. Professor Birks called adherence to this view 'discretionary remedialism'.[12] It would be understandable if counsel were to adapt these ideas to argument in a case concerning the remedies available for infringement of entitlements to privacy.

The persuasiveness of the suggestion that judges should hold such a wide discretion over the full range of remedies, however, is not high in relation to infringements of entitlements to privacy or, indeed, generally. The suggestion is incongruent with the powers of superior courts in most common law Commonwealth jurisdictions, either (as in England and Wales) through the Judicature Acts 1873 and 1875 and their modern successors or through enactments that copy and adapt the English provisions. More modest attempts to derive widened discretionary powers to grant injunctions from the Judicature Acts (for want of a more promising source) have been denied by the courts. It has been held that modern equity in 'Judicature Act courts', in England and Wales and comparable jurisdictions, is to be understood as the continuation of the jurisprudence and tradition of equity adjudication of the old Court of Chancery in England at the time of its abolition by the Judicature Act 1873 in November 1875. In that jurisprudence and tradition, a court of equity is not permitted to grant equitable relief where a judge exercising equitable jurisdiction thinks it just and equitable to do so, without more.[13]

Among the jurisdictions that have equitable traditions of long standing, New Zealand is the jurisdiction where a wide discretion to grant relief in the form of a wide range of equitable remedies is most likely to find favour. Some New Zealand judges have been drawn to discretionary remedialism. But even in New Zealand that discretion has limits. For while a claim that a person's entitlement to privacy was infringed will typically lie outside contract, the ruling in *Paper Reclaim Ltd v Aotearoa International Ltd*,[14] that exemplary damages are never available for breach of contract, shows that discretionary remedialism in New Zealand is not absolute. In Canada, wide remedial discretion is recognised and applied with

[12] Birks' views are set out and considered by S Evans, 'Defending Discretionary Remedialism' (2001) 23 *Sydney Law Review* 463.

[13] The Judicature Act 1873, s 25(8) only continued power to grant interlocutory injunctions and receivers by interlocutory order where 'it appears to the Court to be just and convenient to do so', and those powers, in any case, continued the principles that pre-dated the Judicature Acts as to the availability of those remedies: eg *North London Railway Co v Great Northern Railway Co* (1883) 11 QBD 30, 37–38, 39; *Holmes v Millage* [1893] 1 QB 551, 557; *Bremer Vulkan Schiffbau und Maschinenfabrik v South India Shipping Corp Ltd* [1981] AC 909 (HL); *Fourie v Le Roux* [2007] 1 WLR 320, [26]. Cf *Bremer Vulkan* at 933ff (CA); *Japan Line Ltd v Aggehki Charis Compania Maritima SA* [1980] 1 Lloyd's Rep 288 (CA). Although the terms of the Senior Courts Act 1981, s 37(1) (UK) extend these provisions explicitly to include final and interlocutory grants of injunctions or appointments of receivers, the provision effects no change of the substantive law.

[14] *Paper Reclaim Ltd v Aotearoa International Ltd* [2006] 3 NZLR 188, [181]–[183].

respect to equitable remedies.[15] The discretion may be narrower than that in New Zealand: the Supreme Court of Canada's most important declarations of wide discretion over equitable remedies have been in cases where concurrent legal and equitable causes of action – and concurrent legal and equitable remedies – were in question.[16] Elsewhere in the Commonwealth, wide equitable discretion for the court to choose an appropriate remedy unconstrained by the lines of doctrine[17] is contrary to the settled position. Were it otherwise, quips as to the length of the Chancellor's foot would become mirthless. Rather than operate within the constraints of the principles, doctrines and practices of a developed system of equity, equity would be the mere dispensation of palm-tree justice and its concomitant, palm-tree injustice.

Arguments for a full range of remedies are unpersuasive for the separate reason that a full range of remedies, or even of equitable remedies, is nonsense in respect of infringements of privacy. A 'full' range of remedies available in private law disputes would include specific performance, rectification and rescission. Those remedies must be put aside as unsuited to protecting entitlements of privacy as such. Of course, a range of remedies arguably suited to protecting entitlements of privacy can be found. Orders for specific delivery or the appointment of receivers may not commonly be useful to protect entitlements to privacy, but could conceivably be of use on occasion: an infringement may involve property the claimant owns or to which he or she claims to be ultimately entitled. And a group of remedies – in particular, equitable remedies – with the potential of powerful weapons – equitable compensation, 'equitable' damages under Lord Cairns' Act, accounts of profits, liens and constructive trusts – could in theory form part of that range. However, because the full range of remedies available in private law disputes is notably larger than the range of remedies arguably suited to protecting privacy entitlements, it must be acknowledged that the appeal of claims to a full range of relief for infringement of privacy is partly rhetorical.

Rhetoric can be a legitimate tool of legal advocacy. But it will be more useful if this chapter pursues detached legal reasoning. In expounding the law on remedies for infringement of privacy, the courts are likely to evaluate the suitability of each remedy separately. Attention will now turn individually to remedies whose invocation in privacy cases is likely to require the elaboration of principle: equitable relief by injunction, equitable compensation, equitable damages, account of profits, liens and constructive trusts, as well as common law damages and restitution.

[15] In Canada, a common law tort of intruding upon seclusion has been recognised in Ontario (*Jones v Tsige* (2012) 108 OR (3d) 241) but not, to date, in any other common law province.

[16] *Lac Minerals Ltd v International Corona Resources Ltd* (n 7); *Cadbury Schweppes Inc v FBI Foods Ltd* (n 7), [24]–[25]; *Strother v 3464920 Canada Inc* [2007] 2 SCR 177, [156]–[158].

[17] This is not to say that the award of relief under a wide discretion of this kind would be unconstrained by judicial method: see M Harding, 'Equity and the Rule of Law' (2016) 132 *LQR* 278, 293–95. Rather, it is to say that the judicial grant of relief would be entirely a matter for the judge, acting judicially, rather than constrained or more or less predetermined by equitable principles.

III. Injunction

Like other interests that have come to receive protection through the establishment of legal entitlements, the legal protection of privacy in its early stages has begun with appeals to the equitable jurisdiction to grant the ancient remedy of injunction. In the first such cases in England, the protection was not grounded in an entitlement to privacy. In *Prince Albert v Strange*,[18] the Prince's interest in keeping private certain etchings by Queen Victoria was protected on the ground that a third party's publication of a catalogue describing the etchings and advertising their exhibition would be an abuse of the confidence or trust placed by Prince Albert in Mr Brown, from whom the third party, Mr Strange, had obtained them. Each pleaded ground fell outside established doctrine: the relief, which stimulated the genesis of a unitary equitable doctrine of confidentiality in the twentieth century,[19] was granted under an innominate head of jurisdiction. By the time Ungoed-Thomas J granted an injunction to the Duke of Argyll to restrain his estranged wife from revealing the pair's marital secrets to the press in the classic case of *Argyll v Argyll*,[20] the protection of privacy came on the ground of a unitary equitable doctrine of confidentiality. A further stage of development has witnessed the seeking and granting of injunctions to protect privacy interests as such, not merely under other innominate heads or a nominate head focused on another topic, viz confidentiality, but through the 'extended action' for breach of equitable obligations of confidence mentioned earlier.

Whether privacy interests can now be protected by injunctions to protect privacy interests directly, apart from the equitable doctrine of confidentiality, is uncertain. English case law could move from the Court of Appeal's decision in *Vidal-Hall v Google Inc*[21] – that an action for invasion of privacy under the 'extended action' for breach of confidence is a 'tort' for the purposes of service out of the jurisdiction – to the more absolute proposition that such an action is for all purposes a tort at common law. However, that implies a teleology according to which a legal entitlement to privacy is sure to emerge, fully formed and independent of other doctrines. The teleology may be false. Claims can be torts for the purpose of jurisdiction and choice of law, in private international law, without being torts in the ordinary municipal common law. Provisionally true doctrines of the municipal common law of torts can prove false after the testing of litigation over a decade or longer.

Nevertheless, equitable relief in the form of injunction would be present at the creation of such an independent entitlement. It was present before the modern

[18] *Prince Albert v Strange* (1849) 1 Mac & G 25; 41 ER 1171; 1 H & Tw 1; 47 ER 1302.

[19] See L Bently, '*Prince Albert v Strange* (1849)' in C Mitchell and P Mitchell (eds), *Landmark Cases in Equity* (Oxford, Hart Publishing, 2012) ch 8.

[20] *Argyll v Argyll* (n 7).

[21] *Vidal-Hall v Google Inc* (n 7), [21], [25], [43], [51]. See also *Gulati v MGN Ltd* [2015] EWCA Civ 1291, [2017] QB 149, [88]. Cf *Kitechnology BV v Unicor Gmbh Plastmaschinen* [1995] FSR 765, 777–78.

equitable doctrine of confidentiality was born. In Australia, when the High Court refused an injunction to restrain the filming and televised broadcast of the operation of a brushtail possum 'processing facility', the High Court effectively invited lower courts to develop a novel tort of invasion of privacy.[22] In the UK, the Supreme Court's continuation of the injunction granted by the primary judge in *PJS News Group Newspapers Ltd* may in future come to be seen as an act of creation of an independent entitlement to privacy. But while injunctions may be present at the birth of an independent entitlement to privacy, the substantive elements of the entitlement may remain obscure if applications for injunctions are the main source of curial proceedings on such entitlements. That has been true of innocent passing off, whose origins and continuing ambivalence are due in part to the fact that interlocutory injunctions are the principal relief in innocent passing-off cases.[23]

Uncertainty attends the requirements of injunctive relief in protection of independent entitlements to privacy, whereas equivalent uncertainty does not affect injunctive relief in protection of equitable obligations of confidentiality. The adequacy of relief at law is not in issue when injunctions are sought to protect equitable obligations of confidentiality, since the entitlement arises only in equity. On the other hand, if independent entitlements to privacy should subsist at common law then the inadequacy of damages and other relief at law must be material. But the requirement is uncertain because of uncertainty as to whether independent entitlements to privacy subsist at law or in equity. Again, how specifically must the subject matter of the injunction be defined? If entitlements to privacy are only protectable under the extended equitable obligation of confidentiality, it is arguable that the subject matter must be defined just as specifically – no more and no less – as confidential information which a claimant seeks to protect by injunction. But if entitlements to privacy subsist under a distinct equitable obligation or at common law then the specificity with which the entitlement must be defined on a motion for injunctive relief may be different and, it seems likely, lesser.[24] Also uncertain is what degree of publication of the subject matter will deny a claimant's entitlement to injunctive relief. As confidentiality is readily enough lost, a title to injunctive relief to protect privacy might also be readily lost if the entitlement to privacy rests in the equitable doctrine of confidentiality. But if an entitlement to privacy is separate, including if it is a tort at common law, a different test may apply.

Notwithstanding those uncertainties, injunctions are one (equitable) remedy that, in principle, is certain to be available to protect entitlements to privacy.

[22] *Australian Broadcasting Corp v Lenah Game Meats Pty Ltd* [2001] HCA 63, (2001) 208 CLR 199, [40]–[43], [107]–[111], [129]–[132], [328]–[336].

[23] JD Heydon, MJ Leeming and PG Turner, *Meagher, Gummow and Lehane's Equity: Doctrines and Remedies*, 5th edn (Sydney, LexisNexis, 2015) [43-015].

[24] See *PJS* (n 3) [25]–[35].

IV. Compensation for Loss

Apart from injunctions, compensation must be the most important possible remedy for infringements of entitlements to privacy. Compensation has already been awarded to protect interests in privacy in numerous cases. The numerousness of the cases suggests that compensation is a natural remedy, irrespective of whether the legal protection of entitlements to privacy is housed in the equity jurisdiction as the 'extended action' for breach of confidence, or at common law in the house of torts as a new tort of infringement of privacy. However, the principles and rules according to which such compensation ought to be awarded are in their early development. A sign of this early stage of development is the relative shapelessness at present of the compensatory remedy, both as to when it will be available and as to its quantification. Whereas the absence of constraints on the remedy has been emphasised, it is suggested that a remedy of compensation must be given shape.

A. Equitable Compensation for Torts

The need to give shape to a remedy of compensation can be illustrated, first, by an argument the logic of which would require equitable compensation to be available for, it seems, all torts except the torts of negligence and defamation.

The argument is that equitable compensation ought to be available to remedy infringements of privacy, since a party who could have obtained an injunction to restrain an apprehended infringement of his or her entitlements to privacy should not be denied a remedy merely because he or she did not seek an injunction in time. Lord Scott of Foscote is one who made this argument. Speaking of the extended (equitable) action for breach of confidence – an extension specifically to protect an entitlement to privacy – Lord Scott said that monetary relief for loss (which he called 'damages') ought to be available in equity where a claimant could have obtained an injunction protecting his or her entitlement supposing he or she had moved for an injunction in time.[25] The same argument was also adopted by the Victorian Court of Appeal in the leading Australian case of *Giller v Procopets*.[26]

The argument ought to be credited with pragmatically seeking to state why an undoubted impulse to remedy past infringements of privacy ought to be remedied through compensation. While this pragmatism may satisfy the demands of justice in the instant case, particularly at an early stage in the development of judge-made entitlements to privacy, a stronger reason for the remedy will in time be required. The argument is an argument of symmetry and form: if an injunction could have

[25] R Scott, 'Confidentiality' in J Beatson and Y Cripps (eds), *Freedom of Expression and Freedom of Information: Essays in Honour of Sir David Williams* (Oxford, Oxford UP, 2000) 267, 267–72.

[26] *Giller v Procopets* (2008) 24 VR 1, [145], [150], [151].

prevented the given harm then compensation should be available to repair such harm as has happened in the absence of timely injunctive relief. As such, the argument at least applies with equal weight to established torts against the commission of which an injunction may issue. Injunctions generally do not issue to restrain breaches of duties of care in the common law of negligence or for defamation. Accordingly, the argument would generally not apply so as to make equitable compensation available for damage suffered by reason of breach of a common law duty of care or defamation. However, the argument would apply so as to make equitable compensation available for damage suffered by reason of such other torts as trespass to land, trespass to goods, trespass to the person, inducement to breach a contract, conspiracy and deceit.

It is difficult to see a sound argument of principle or practicality for compensating torts through equitable doctrines and remedies.[27] Awards of equitable compensation for common law torts, including any possible common law tort of infringing entitlements to privacy, would require a new branch of equitable remedies to be established in equity's concurrent jurisdiction: that is, remedies in aid of common law rights where the common law itself provides a remedy. If the awards of equitable compensation would be the same in all respects as the awards of common law damages for the same tort – including in their measure – the equitable award would not be aiding the protection of common law rights, for the relief in equity would be of no practical advantage to a claimant. Awards of equitable compensation for torts could aid a claimant's common law rights if they were made to differ in incidence (including measure) from awards of damages in the law of torts. Thus, equitable awards might be available subject to looser[28] rules of causation, remoteness, foreseeability and contributory fault than awards of common law damages for the same tort. If not in form then in substance, that would involve the establishment of an equitable law of torts.

Against that enterprise a good deal could be said. The most telling reason against establishing an equitable law of torts – be it general in scope or confined to infringements of privacy – is superfluity. Almost all equity jurisprudence has this property: it exists because there is a shortcoming in the common law (or, occasionally, statute law), which shortcoming is then overcome by the establishment of an equitable doctrine and attendant equitable relief. Unless a critical injustice occurs in the common law, and unless it is otherwise a fit occasion on which for equity to intervene, a judge exercising equitable jurisdiction will tend to stay his or her hand. A judge who is asked to develop the law to permit equitable compensation to be awarded for torts would tend to decline the invitation because such developments would be superfluous. That is particularly so given that the common law

[27] 'Equitable damages' in addition to or in lieu of an injunction stand outside this argument since such damages derive from statutory powers. See also P Birks, 'Equity in the Modern Law: An Exercise in Taxonomy' (1996) 26 *University of Western Australia Law Review* 1, 49–52.

[28] Or, indeed, tighter – though equitable awards more restrictive than common law damages awards could not be said to aid the enforcement of the claimant's rights in a practical sense.

recognises so many torts, all of which the common law remedies through awards of damages. The point is not the narrow point that equitable compensation would only avoid superfluity if in some way, in some cases, it could be awarded differently from damages at common law, or where common law damages might not be available at all. The point is broader: the law of torts effectively pre-empts equitable intervention by occupying the field of justice-concerns so fully as to make equitable intervention, by granting compensation for torts, unnecessary. The law of torts has developed so as to protect basic interests of dignity and autonomy from others' unauthorised interference outside the law of contract by awarding compensation. Equity is only required in such cases where the common law remedies, especially damages, are inadequate to do justice.

The argument of symmetry, that *equitable* compensation ought to be available after the event if an (equitable) injunction could have forestalled the event, reveals an impulse to do justice. However, the argument reveals no adequate reason or principle by which courts may say when or why equitable compensation ought to be available for torts, or for infringements of privacy (irrespective of whether the liability properly sits in the common law of torts or in equity). It is suggested that the immediate pragmatism of the argument of symmetry will prove deficient in the long term. The impulse to do justice by compensation must be given shape by some other reason or principle.

B. Equitable Damages for Infringement of Privacy

An alternative to equitable compensation for infringements of privacy would be to permit the recovery of 'equitable damages' under the modern equivalents of Lord Cairns' Act.[29] Section 2 of the original enactment empowered the Court of Chancery, 'if it shall think fit, to award damages to the party injured either in addition to or in substitution for' an 'injunction … against the commission or continuance of any wrongful act' in 'all cases' in which that court 'has jurisdiction to entertain' such an application. In the State of Victoria, this and its modern Victorian counterpart[30] have been viewed as freeing relevant courts of constraints in deciding whether compensation is available for infringements of privacy and in deciding the quantum of compensation to be awarded.

Lord Cairns' Act was intended as liberal legislation of a sort. How far it liberates the courts, and how far it empowers courts subject to constraints, are difficult questions. But it is suggested that it would probably empower courts to award damages in addition to or in substitution for an injunction against the commission or continuance of an infringement of privacy, supposing infringement of privacy to become a tort at common law. This suggestion assumes that Lord Cairns' Act

[29] Chancery Amendment Act 1858 (21 & 22 Vict c 27).
[30] Supreme Court Act 1986 (Vic), s 38.

should be read in ambulatory fashion (as a dictum in *Aid/Watch Inc v Commissioner of Taxation*[31] arguably requires of Australian courts) and, particularly, that while infringement of privacy was no wrong in law as contemplated when the 1858 Act was made, the statute can have become applicable to new torts as new wrongs within the legal meaning of the Act. Such damages in aid of a common law entitlement to privacy would be in a court's discretion, but otherwise shaped by analogies from the decided cases – especially as to quantum.

Can Lord Cairns' Act enable compensation for infringements to be awarded more broadly, irrespective (for example) of whether entitlements to privacy are equitable or subsist at common law? The difficulty is to know how the Act and its modern equivalents should properly be construed. In particular, what is the respective significance of (i) the original mischief of Lord Cairns' Act, (ii) its original subject matter, and (iii) latter-day views of how empowering statutes are to be construed?

The first and second items just mentioned would hold no significance if the third – latter-day views of how empowering statutes are to be construed – inhibited reference thereto. Understood literally, reference to the original mischief and subject matter of Lord Cairns' Act would be inhibited in Australia under a principle the High Court of Australia has latterly often employed to construe statutory powers: that '[i]t is quite inappropriate to read provisions conferring jurisdiction or granting powers to a court by making implications or imposing limitations which are not found in the express words'.[32] Although the court in *Giller v Procopets* did not invoke that principle, its evident assumption that the words of Lord Cairns' Act and its modern Victorian equivalent should take their widest possible meaning is consonant with the High Court's principle of construction. However, that principle can only be a presumption: it would be odd to construe a statutory power more broadly than is known to have been intended. Hence, in conformity to English authority, the High Court of Australia has declined to construe at its widest the 'Judicature Act power' to grant interlocutory injunctions[33] where 'just and convenient', because it is known that that statutory power was not intended to

[31] *Aid/Watch Inc v Commissioner of Taxation* [2010] HCA 42, (2010) 241 CLR 539, [23]. However, the width of the exception applicable in the presence 'of a contrary indication in the statute' likewise appears open to argument.

[32] *Owners of the Ship 'Shin Kobe Maru' v Empire Shipping Co Inc* (1984) 181 CLR 404, 421. See also *PMT Partners Pty Ltd (In Liq) v Australian National Parks and Wildlife Service* (1995) 184 CLR 301, 313; *Oshlack v Richmond River Council* [1998] HCA 11, (1998) 193 CLR 72, [21]; *Australasian Memory Pty Ltd v Brien* [2000] HCA 30, (2000) 200 CLR 270, [17]; *The Commonwealth v SCI Operations Pty Ltd* [1998] HCA 20, (1998) 192 CLR 285, [26]; *Macedonian Orthodox Community Church St Petka Incorporated v His Eminence Petar The Diocesan Bishop of The Macedonian Orthodox Diocese of Australia and New Zealand* [2008] HCA 42, (2008) 237 CLR 66, [55]; *Campbell v Backoffice Investments Pty Ltd* [2009] HCA 25, (2009) 238 CLR 304, [178]; *Weinstock v Beck* [2013] HCA 14, (2013) 251 CLR 396, [55]–[56].

[33] Or, under the Senior Courts Act 1981, s 37(1), final injunctions: see n 13; *Australian Broadcasting Corp v Lenah Game Meats Pty Ltd* (n 22) [10], [59]–[60], [87]–[92], [97]; *Cardile v LED Builders Pty Ltd* [1999] HCA 18, (1999) 198 CLR 380, [31]–[35].

erase from the legal system the principles according to which interlocutory injunctions had previously been granted and denied.[34] Accordingly, courts in Australia and elsewhere are not in principle barred from considering the original mischief and subject matter of Lord Cairns' Act. Indeed, the High Court of Australia itself did so in *Wentworth v Woollahra Municipal Council*[35] to hold that Lord Cairns' Act does not empower courts to award damages in addition to or in substitution for an injunction against the commission or continuance of any act that infringes a public rather than a private right.[36]

At the same time, it seems unlikely that courts today would construe the power given by Lord Cairns' Act as applying only to such 'wrongs' as existed in 1858, which would place motions for injunctive relief in respect of later-developed common law entitlements outside the power granted by Lord Cairns' Act. It also seems unlikely – despite its attractions – that a modern Judicature Act court, seized of common law and equitable jurisdiction, should hold that the modern equivalents of Lord Cairns' Act only empower modern courts to grant relief that overcomes the original mischief of Lord Cairns' Act. That original mischief was mainly or only to overcome the injustice by which the Court of Chancery, when refusing an injunction in its discretion, necessarily sent an otherwise deserving plaintiff away with no remedy since that court maintained a lack of power to award damages. To recover, the plaintiff in Chancery then had to sue out an action at law.[37] This mischief ceased to exist on the day the Courts of Chancery, King's Bench and Common Pleas themselves ceased to exist, 1 November 1875.[38] By a fiction that Lord Cairns' Act was merely preserved after that date, for the greater part of the Act's existence the power it confers has been exercised under conditions in which justice is administered in single courts, such that the Act's original mischief does not exist.

The upshot is that the power conferred by Lord Cairns' Act and its equivalents has, and must have, some limits; those limits derive at least in part from the Act's original subject matter; but those limits are not fixed simply according to the original subject matter and mischief of the Act. Hence the relevance of Lord Cairns' Act to this discussion of compensation for infringement of privacy. As far as subject matter is concerned, reliable limits on the power conferred by Lord Cairns' Act can perhaps be found by asking (i) to what wrongs it was envisaged Lord Cairns' Act should apply,[39] (ii) what damages it was intended the Act should make recoverable, and (iii) what later additions to (i) and (ii) are required

[34] See n 13.

[35] *Wentworth v Woollahra Municipal Council* (1982) 149 CLR 672.

[36] See ibid 683 (consideration of 'the history and terms of' corresponding legislation in aid of its construction).

[37] ibid 676.

[38] PD Finn, 'A Road Not Taken: The Boyce Plaintiff and Lord Cairns' Act' (Pt I) (1983) 57 *Australian Law Journal* 493, 505–06.

[39] Consider, eg, W Blackstone, *Commentaries on the Laws of England* (Oxford, Clarendon Press, 1768), book III ('Of Private Wrongs').

or made plausible by reading the words of the Act (and its modern counterparts) in an ambulatory manner.

From the original mischief of the Act, it is relatively clear that the original subject matter of Lord Cairns' Act comprised actions for breach of covenant, breach of contract and the various torts. Updated as an ambulatory construction requires, that subject matter must now include post-1858 common law innovations, such as several economic torts and, supposing it to be a tort at common law, infringement of privacy. It is also relatively clear that moral wrongs were only within the power given by Lord Cairns' Act in 1858 if they were also wrongs actionable at common law. Further, because injunctions can properly issue to restrain conduct that is not actionable at law, the class of claims to which the Act was originally intended to apply was narrower than the class of claims that in principle attracts injunctive relief. Conduct in the actual or purported exercise of public power, and conduct regulated by principles of equity but not the common law, could attract injunctive relief without being actionable at law – and so fell outside the intended scope of Lord Cairns' Act.[40]

It is respectfully suggested that these principles should lead a modern court to conclude that, as already mentioned, compensation for infringement of privacy could properly be awarded under Lord Cairns' Act if the infringement were to be a common law tort; but that if the infringement should be a default only in equity, the Act and its modern counterparts are improper support for a compensatory award. It is acknowledged that some authorities are against this last point. In particular, the various authorities to the effect that damages may be awarded under Lord Cairns' Act for the infringement of a restrictive covenant[41] – a covenant enforceable only in equity, the infringement of which is not actionable at common law – are contrary to the position advanced here. Those decisions cannot be ignored without undermining the doctrine of *stare decisis*. However, decisions such as *Wentworth v Woollahra Municipal Council*[42] do support the position advanced here so far as they admit that the original mischief and subject matter of Lord Cairns' Act can be significant when construing the Act. Though decisions exceeding the Act's original mischief and subject and matter should not be ignored, it is respectfully suggested that those constructions which implausibly stretch the meaning of the Act's words should be extended no further.[43]

[40] Cf *Wentworth* (n 35) 676 (a dictum).

[41] Particularly *Wrotham Park Estate Co Ltd v Parkside Homes Ltd* [1974] 1 WLR 798, 811 (seemingly the point was undisputed). See also *Talbot v General Television Corp Ltd* [1980] VR 242 (confidential information in equity); *Gas & Fuel Corp (Vic) v Barba* [1976] VR 766 (equitable easement) (varied on appeal on other grounds: (1976) 136 CLR 120).

[42] But not every dictum therein: *Wentworth* (n 35) 676 (relief in respect of purely equitable claims thought to be an 'incidental object' of Lord Cairns' Act).

[43] For instance, the influential reasoning of Marks J shows, with great respect, an implausible interpretation of the words of the Act. His substantive reasoning for rejecting a submission that the provision applies only to common law wrongs was that, although courts of equity lacked power to grant damages, a grant of damages under Lord Cairns' Act in aid of an equitable entitlement would be in accordance with equity's award of compensation in its exclusive jurisdiction in which it 'restored

C. Compensation through Damages in the Common Law of Torts

The common law of torts would be better able to recognise and enforce entitlements to privacy than can the doctrines and remedies of equity, or the provisions of Lord Cairns' Act. This may be seen, first, from the types of harm involved.

The types of harm that would tend to follow the infringement of another's entitlement to privacy are closely akin to the types of harm recognised and remedied by the existing, elaborate common law of torts and little like the concerns of doctrines of equity. An infringement of privacy might well cause financial harm. However, the commonest type of harm would be non-financial: it would consist of the seeing or telling or accessing or relaying that transgresses the other's entitlement to privacy. As that harm requires proof of nothing more, it is like what one scholar has called 'normative harm':[44] harm taken to exist by the law regardless of the fact that no financial harm may have been caused. Examples are associated with the 'vindicatory' function of certain torts: chiefly the torts of trespass to land, trespass to goods, assault, battery and false imprisonment.

Harm to emotions and reputation is also apt to follow certain kinds of conduct in infringement of privacy. The relaying of reports, images, sound and other information concerning what one person saw, accessed or obtained contrary to another's entitlement to privacy will tend to harm the emotions and reputation of the person to whom the relayed information relates, especially where the information is relayed to numerous persons. Inevitably a desire follows to seek compensation for infringement of privacy for harm done to interests in dignity, autonomy and reputation. Whether compensation for harm should be available in respect of each and all those interests through novel remedies has been doubted.[45] But it is notable that the existing, elaborate law of torts already speaks in detail of those interests.

Secondly, the interests awards of damages are made to protect in the common law of torts also point to the capacity of the common law of torts to recognise and enforce entitlements to privacy better. The interests are various. Some torts protect proprietary interests. Others protect personal interests: those relating to bodily integrity (battery) and reputation (defamation, slander). In some

to an owner property or rights of which that owner according to equity have been deprived': *Talbot* (n 41) 243. This assumes that Lord Cairns' Act extended the equitable principles of compensation for breach of trust and fiduciary to settings calling for an award of damages, whereas the Act was designed to empower courts of equity to grant the damages previously available only in common law courts. See also K Barnett and M Bryan, 'Lord Cairns's Act: A Case Study in the Unintended Consequences of Legislation' (2015) 9 *Journal of Equity* 150, 158–63.

[44] JNE Varuhas, 'The Concept of "Vindication" in the Law of Torts: Rights, Interests and Damages' (2014) 34 *OJLS* 253, 255 and *passim*.

[45] M Tilbury, 'Coherence, Non-Pecuniary Loss, and the Construction of Privacy' in J Berryman and R Bigwood (eds), *The Law of Remedies: New Directions in the Common Law* (Toronto, Irwin Law, 2010) ch 5.

circumstances, damages may be recovered for mental harm and, where a tort has been committed in aggravating circumstances, in an aggravated compensatory measure. So may exemplary damages. The economic torts are viewed as exceptional within the law of torts, since the economic torts protect economic interests alone: the interest in upholding contracts (inducement of breach of contract), the interest in conducting a business (passing off, unlawful means conspiracy), and so on.

Those various interests include interests akin to the interests that entitlements to privacy could protect. Viewed on that general level, placing liability to compensate for losses caused by infringing a person's privacy alongside these torts would not be strange. It would admittedly prompt questions as to the relation of the new tort to its tortious neighbours. Would harm to reputation as a result of infringement of privacy be remediable through relief for infringement of privacy as such, or only through the law of defamation? Would recovery be possible for mental distress – and if yes, would the recovery be substantial or minor? However, those questions are akin to the questions that arise whenever an extension is proposed of an existing tort: such questions are native, not alien, to the law of torts.

It is no coincidence that equity contains no law of torts, nor that equity declares itself unable to award damages. The diversity of the interests protected by the law of torts – and the consequently wide reach of the law of torts – overwhelmingly suggests that, in the structure of the civil law, there is here no call on equity to gloss the common law or fulfil it. Liability to compensate for loss caused by infringing another's privacy contains no quality alien to the common law, unable to be accommodated by it. Since the liability is akin to liabilities at common law, compensation would best be awarded according to rules of the judge-made common law. And if the common law itself refuses to protect a given interest in some way, it does not follow that it should be protected in equity. Where the law of torts refuses to further one of those interests in some way, that lack of protection is spoken for. If the law of torts, which addresses a certain set of harms through rules of damages, is set against remedying some harm by awarding damages, for equity – which lacks rules of damages and contains no power to grant damages – to be called on to grant compensation would be curious. Further, gaps in the relief afforded by the law of torts or by equity should not be thought to exist through the inattention of lawyers and judges. Unless shown otherwise, those gaps should be assumed to result from series of small, deliberate judicial decisions, which together amount to a legal balance of liability and immunity that draws a line limiting persons' entitlements to recover for certain kinds of harm.

Equity is ill-equipped to protect against the kinds of harm that will tend to result from infringements of privacy. As already noted, equity does not award damages. Like the common law, equity protects economic and proprietary interests by means of compensation: in particular, compensation for breach of trust and fiduciary duty. But the reasons for equity's doing so are revealing. Trusts and fiduciary obligations are not recognised at common law. Each is a relation depending on principles the common law did not develop, yet which courts of equity found it necessary to develop. There was a special call on equity, and equitable remedies and procedures aided these peculiarly equitable developments. Observing that proprietary and economic interests are protected exclusively by equity through compensatory awards does not undermine the distinctness of equitable principles, since those equitable forms of protection are beyond the common law.[46] No other types of interest – particularly, personal interests – are protected as such[47] by awards of compensation in equity's inherent jurisdiction. Harms to the person, reputation and otherwise personal interests are likewise outside equity's purview since they are within that of the common law. In the parlance of torts, equitable compensation is not at large. And, to recall another point made earlier, the fact that equity has and will protect the interests that any law of privacy protects, at least by injunctions, is beside the point of whether equity will or ought to grant compensation for infringements of privacy. It is respectfully suggested that the reasoning in the leading Australian case of *Giller v Procopets*, which proceeds on a view of harms and interests different from that offered here, will in time require to be revisited.

V. Account of Profits

An account of profits is common equitable relief for breach of fiduciary duty and breach of equitable obligations of confidence. So far as an 'extended action' for breach of confidence is the means of protecting entitlements to privacy, it seems likely that an account of profits would be available in those situations too, given its equitable nature. As seen earlier, it was long thought that a special, unusually wide, discretion to refuse an account of profits applied to cases of breach of confidence in equity.[48] Conceivably, such a discretion could be exercised to withhold accounts of profits in cases where the complaint is, in substance, of infringement of privacy – rather than a breach of a commercial confidence. However, Arnold J has shown[49] that this wide discretion rested on a misunderstanding of *Seager v Copydex Ltd (No 1)*.[50] That being so, an account of profits should be no easier to defeat where it is sought under the 'extended action' for breach of confidence than in a commercial case.

[46] As to the availability of monetary relief for loss caused by fraud, concurrently at law and in equity, see Heydon, Leeming and Turner (n 23) [24-010]–[24-015].

[47] An award of equitable compensation to satisfy an estoppel could in effect protect a claimant's personal interest and repair emotional harm. However, that would be fortuitous. On equitable compensation to satisfy estoppels, see J Hudson, 'Equitable Compensation for Equitable Estoppels' in Degeling and Varuhas (eds) (n 11) ch 11.

[48] eg PD Finn, *Fiduciary Obligations* (Sydney, Law Book Co, 1977) [383]. See Turner (n 11) 264–65.

[49] *Force India Formula One Team Ltd v 1 Malaysia Racing Team Sdn Bhd* [2012] EWHC 616 (Ch), [2012] RPC 29, [396].

[50] *Seager v Copydex Ltd (No 1)* (n 8).

What if entitlements to privacy should be established either as an equitable doctrine separate from breach of confidence, or, alternatively, as a (common law) tort? The situations in which an account will be ordered are not closed. However, the recognised situations do not favour an account of profits in either of the situations just mentioned. Should the entitlement to privacy be placed in equity separately from breach of confidence, the difficulty would be that accounts of profits derived from equitable misconduct have been confined to situations in which the accounting protects a proprietary entitlement – which an entitlement to privacy is not, and is unlikely substantially to become – or (as Jackman puts it) protects a small number of other 'facilitative relationships' in the law: those between the privies to a trust, between principal and fiduciary, and between a confidant and the confider.[51] Entitlements to privacy are a few degrees removed from that circle. Although trust-like and fiduciary-like liabilities can be imposed on those who are not strictly trustees or fiduciaries, the root of those liabilities is the notion that these extended liabilities facilitate the legal relations between a real trustee and beneficiary, principal and fiduciary, and confidant and confider. All refer back to a voluntary undertaking of sorts.[52] Obligations to afford privacy would be imposed by law. They would not depend, as such, on a facilitative relationship voluntarily created by relevant parties.

In the English law of torts, the availability of accounts of profits is the subject of conflicting Court of Appeal decisions. In *Forsyth-Grant v Allen*,[53] the Court of Appeal thought that there is no jurisdiction to order an account of profits in respect of a tort (in that case, private nuisance) absent the infringement of a relevant proprietary interest.[54] However, in *Devenish Nutrition Ltd v Sanofi-Aventis SA*,[55] the Court of Appeal held accounts of profits to be available on the same principles as accounts of profits for breach of contract as stated by the House of Lords in *Attorney-General v Blake*.[56] Thus, the Court of Appeal thought that an account of profits could be ordered, in the court's discretion, in an exceptional case where the tort infringed no proprietary interest.[57]

The conflict of decisions is unfortunate and confusing, including with regard to entitlements to privacy. The former decision dictates that no account of profits could be available for infringements of privacy, unless privacy becomes proprietary in the requisite sense. The latter decision dictates that an account of profits may be ordered for an infringement of a tortious entitlement to privacy in any exceptional case. In the terms of precedent, *Forsyth-Allen* seems the stronger authority: *Devenish* widely extends *Attorney-General v Blake* beyond what the House of

[51] IM Jackman, *The Varieties of Restitution*, 2nd edn (Sydney, Federation Press, 2017) ch 8.

[52] See M Conaglen, 'Fiduciary Duties and Voluntary Undertakings' (2013) 7 *Journal of Equity* 105; J Edelman, 'The Importance of the Fiduciary Undertaking' (2013) 7 *Journal of Equity* 128.

[53] *Forsyth-Grant v Allen* [2008] EWCA Civ 505, [2008] Env LR 41.

[54] ibid [31], [33], [43].

[55] *Devenish Nutrition Ltd v Sanofi-Aventis SA* [2008] EWCA Civ 1086, [2009] Ch 390.

[56] *Attorney-General v Blake* [2001] 1 AC 268.

[57] *Devenish Nutrition Ltd v Sanofi-Aventis SA* (n 55) [88], [104], [111], [145], [152], [156]–[157].

Lords ruled, and incorrectly treats the decisions that underpin *Forsyth-Allen* as having been impliedly overruled. Accounts of profits for common law misconduct in the form of infringement of privacy might be ordered in New Zealand under the wider judicial discretions as to relief favoured there. In other Commonwealth jurisdictions that is less likely. In Australia, it would require the addition of a new ground to the stable list of situations in which accounting on equitable principles is ordered in aid of common law rights.[58]

Viewed generally, the possibility that accounts of profits should be available for any tort of infringement of privacy would face an obstacle in principle. In a case of deceit, the only account of profits normally considered to be available is an account of profits ancillary to rescission. Absent rescission, an account of profits is unavailable for fraud.[59] That being so, a court would find it difficult to accept that an account of profits should be available for conduct, in the form of infringement of privacy, which is less pernicious than fraud. Certainly, the common law has seen infringements of privacy as less pernicious than fraud to date: while fraud has long been remediable at common law (and in equity), infringements of privacy have not.

VI. Restitution

Restitution under this heading is used in the narrow sense adopted by the American Law Institute's *Restatements of the Law* and academic writers working in the field of that name or its nominal successor, the field of 'unjust enrichment'. Whereas restitution had previously (and naturally) been understood to mean restoration, in the narrower sense to be used here the word means a reversal of a gain made by one person at the expense of another under a more widely defined 'transfer principle'.[60] Restitution in this sense presents two arguable avenues of recovery. Neither is equitable in relating to the subject matter jurisdiction derived from the old Court of Chancery, but each will be discussed, as each touches on equity in a more general sense sometimes elided with Chancery equity.

The first is equitable in the loose sense associated with relief in the form of recovery on an action for money had and received: a 'kind of equitable action', Lord Mansfield called it.[61] Suppose that infringements of privacy become actionable as common law torts. Might the action for money had and received lie where one

[58] See the list of instances in Heydon, Leeming and Turner (n 23) [26-025]–[26-075].

[59] *Halifax Building Society v Thomas* [1996] Ch 217, 227–28 (CA). The status of this case since *Devenish* is unclear.

[60] See A Burrows, *The Law of Restitution*, 3rd edn (Oxford, Oxford UP, 2011) 66.

[61] *Moses v Macferlan* (1760) 2 Burr 1005, 1012; 97 ER 676, 680–81. On this 'equitable' quality, see B Kremer, 'Equity and the Common Counts: The Development of the Action for Money Had and Received' in JC Goldberg, HE Smith and PG Turner (eds), *Equity and Law: Fusion and Fission* (Cambridge, Cambridge UP, forthcoming) ch 8.

person has infringed another's entitlement to privacy? The portents are discouraging. The action would be for money had and received following waiver of tort: correctly, that is, to recover the profits made by the tortfeasor by reason of the commission of the tort in the alternative to recovery of damages for loss sustained by that tort. Waiver of tort classically lies as an alternative to a claim to damages for conversion of chattels (including cheques). Its character is proprietary, as is seen particularly from its role in common law tracing. As well as for conversion,[62] the action can lie for trespass to goods,[63] trespass to land[64] and the tort of seduction,[65] in the last instance presumably on the ground that the employer has a quasi-proprietary interest in continued service by the employee.[66] On the other hand, the action does not lie for the torts of battery, false imprisonment or deceit. Waiver of tort is confined to cases in which the tort protects a proprietary or (in the case of seduction) a quasi-proprietary interest.[67]

The possibility of recovering money had and received following waiver of the tort of infringement of an entitlement to privacy grows and shrinks according to whether the interest – or interests – at the heart of the entitlement is – or are – seen to have a proprietary character. In this, the situation corresponds to that pertaining to accounts of profits. Should the interest (or interests) develop to acquire the characteristics of the interests protected by trespass to land and trespass to goods, the infringement of the entitlement protecting that interest (or those interests) would lend itself to correction through suing out an action for money had and received. However, should the privacy-interest remain largely personal to the exclusion of proprietary concerns, it would be odd to permit recovery on this restitutionary action: like the tort of deceit, a tort of infringement of entitlements to privacy would in that case lack the proprietary qualities that to date have been found essential to ground waiver of tort. Further, the theory of money had and received upon waiver of tort is that the claimed money represents the claimant's proprietary interest, which the defendant infringed.[68] In order for money had and received to lie in respect of infringements of privacy, the defendant must have derived from the infringement money that represents a proprietary interest of the claimant. The nature of privacy and infringements of privacy makes it improbable that that requirement of the theory of waiver of tort could be fulfilled.

[62] *Lamine v Dorrell* (1706) 2 Ld Raym 216; 92 ER 303; *United Australia Ltd v Barclays Bank Ltd* [1941] AC 1.

[63] *Oughton v Sepping* (1830) 1 B & Ad 241; 109 ER 776; *Neate v Harding* (1851) 6 Exch 349, 351; 155 ER 577.

[64] *Powell v Rees* (1837) 7 Ad & E 426; 112 ER 530.

[65] *Lightly v Clouston* (1808) 1 Taunt 112; 127 ER 774; *Foster v Stewart* (1814) 3 M & S 192; 105 ER 582.

[66] See now *Zhu v Treasurer of New South Wales* [2004] HCA 56, (2004) 218 CLR 530.

[67] It is not suggested that waiver of tort therefore applies to the tort of inducing a breach of contract, although it is arguable that waiver of tort should be available either for both seduction and inducing a breach of contract, or for neither. See Jackman (n 51) 155–56.

[68] Under a rival theory, that the claim is in substance to damages (eg *Hart v EP Dutton & Co Inc*, 93 NYS (2d) 871, 878 (DCNY 1949), affirmed 98 NYS (2d) 773 (SDNY App 1950)), even after 'waiver' of the tort, it might not strictly be required that the claimed money represent the claimant's proprietary interest. But see the text to n 72.

The second possible remedy to mention here has been termed 'restitutionary damages'. Restitutionary damages are equitable in so far as they may be awarded in equity and they are legal in so far as they may be awarded at common law.[69] In his important monograph, Justice Edelman defined restitutionary damages in contradistinction to 'disgorgement damages': he pointed out that the latter should be calculated by reference to all a defendant's profits, whereas the former are limited by whether a gain of the defendant was obtained 'at the expense of' the claimant, as writers in the fields of restitution or unjust enrichment define that 'expense of' requirement.[70] (The more familiar name of disgorgement damages where the relief is equitable is an account of profits.)

Within the case law, the status of restitutionary damages is obscure. At any rate, it is obscure under that name. As academic writings well show, awards of damages whose function is restitutionary are notable (but, until relatively recently, little noted) in the case law. Several English decisions now speak of restitutionary damages; the term occurs more sparsely in other jurisdictions. What continues to be obscure, in apparently all Commonwealth common law jurisdictions, is whether 'restitutionary damages' is a functional description only, of awards made under sundry doctrines, or whether restitutionary damages are awarded under a unitary doctrine. Opinions diverge. It is respectfully suggested, however, that restitution in this instance follows from several distinct doctrines and instances of relief, rather than a unitary doctrine.[71] For example, some awards of damages made in lieu of an injunction have been named as awards of restitutionary damages. However, the law that supports those awards is the statutory power under Lord Cairns' Act and its successors to award such damages; and under that power, awards of damages in lieu of an injunction can have a compensatory function. The fact that some awards placed under the heading 'restitutionary damages' are made under judge-made common law, while others are made under Lord Cairns' Act,[72] also indicates that restitutionary damages have several distinct roots. Further, while a unitary category of restitutionary damages would seem to require all the forms of relief to which it relates to be damages, and while it has been argued that money had and received after waiver of tort is properly an award of damages, English authorities treat a restitutionary liability for money and received as a liquidated liability.[73]

The uncertainty over the status of restitutionary damages is such that a plain view of whether restitutionary damages might properly be granted to remedy the infringement of entitlements to privacy cannot yet be seen. If restitutionary damages form a heterogeneous category, as it is suggested they currently do, then

[69] J Edelman, *Gain-Based Damages* (Oxford, Hart Publishing, 2002) 68–69; Jackman (n 51) 147–52.

[70] Edelman (n 69) 72.

[71] For a similar analysis of 'user damages' and 'negotiating damages', see *One Step (Support) Ltd v Morris-Garner* [2018] UKSC 20, [2018] 2 WLR 1353.

[72] eg *Wrotham Park Estate Co Ltd v Parkside Homes Ltd* (n 41) 811; *Carr-Saunders v Dick McNeil Associates Ltd* [1986] 1 WLR 922, 932.

[73] eg *Watson v Holliday* (1882) 20 Ch D 780, 784; *BP Exploration Co (Libya) Ltd v Hunt (No 2)* [1979] 1 WLR 783, 835.

their availability for infringement of privacy will depend on whether analogies lie from any of the individual doctrines – waiver of tort, the wayleave cases, Lord Cairns' Act, etc – sometimes grouped together under the one functional heading. In general terms, that is unlikely unless privacy entitlements take on a proprietary character.[74] Restitutionary damages for infringement of privacy might become readily available under some alterations and rearrangements of the law, but those possibilities are too speculative for further discussion of them here to be of help.

VII. Aggravation

In the common law of obligations, aggravation is a term of legal art that denotes aggravated mental harm, particularly where a tort has been committed with spite. Once a common law system has accepted a legal entitlement to privacy and that compensation is available to remedy loss suffered through an infringement thereof, it might be odd to preclude awards for aggravation (assuming that aggravated awards are compensatory). Infringing another's entitlement of privacy with spite seems merely a worse way of infringing an entitlement and harming an interest that is harmed by any infringement of privacy. But aggravated damages will only become available for any tort of infringement of privacy if damages for that tort are at large. That general limit dictates two particular limits which become important below: that if damages are not at large because the law denies recovery on a particular head of loss, then aggravated damages cannot be available for that type of loss; and that if damages are not at large because the manner of a defendant's conduct is legally irrelevant under that tort, then aggravated damages cannot be available at all. These elementary principles would, of course, apply to claims to damages for any tort of privacy.

Although the concepts of the common law of torts are mostly absent from equity jurisprudence, a short-term loan of them shows why, it is suggested, awards for aggravation are unsupportable in equity. Regarding the tortious idea of harm, it is certainly so that equitable relief can relieve emotional harm.[75] An injunction can forestall conduct that would inflict emotional distress on the claimant, for example. But effects should not be mistaken for causes. Where an injunction forestalls conduct that would inflict emotional distress on the claimant, the injunction is nevertheless granted to protect some other entitlement, not to protect the claimant from emotional distress as such. Regarding tortious ideas of loss, it is certainly so that compensation can be awarded in equity for certain types of loss.[76] However, not all losses relating to quasi-'heads' of proprietary and economic loss

[74] See *Devenish Nutrition Ltd v Sanofi-Aventis SA* (n 55) [81], [93], [98], [106]–[109].

[75] See *Giller v Procopets* (n 26), [131], [396], [423]–[424].

[76] The meaning of 'loss' in the setting of breach of trust, however, is controversial: see PG Turner, 'Want of Causation as a Defence to Liability for Misapplication of Trust Assets' in P Davies, S Douglas and J Goudkamp (eds), *Defences in Equity* (Oxford, Hart Publishing, 2018) ch 9.

are compensable in equity, even where such losses arise, say, from a breach of trust. And compensation for emotional distress is not available in equity.[77] Establishing aggravated awards of equitable compensation would be an unsound development. In contrast, awards of aggravated damages in cases of infringement of privacy could become established on the basis of sound principle in the common law. The torts in which aggravated damages have been awarded include deceit,[78] trespass to goods,[79] defamation[80] and malicious prosecution.[81] To award compensation for the loss suffered as a result of the aggravated nature of the misconduct is within the purview of the common law, and could be coherently done within the common law. The introduction of such awards in equity would inevitably lead to the assimilation of equitable relief and equitable liability to the common law of torts. Given that the civil law's variety is a product of the differentiation of principle and legal doctrines to address different legal concerns, reversing that differentiation would seem unwise in societies which are not becoming simpler.

If infringement of privacy were to become established as a (common law) tort, could a component for aggravation be included in an award of damages in addition to or in substitution for an injunction under Lord Cairns' Act and its modern equivalents? In *Giller v Procopets*, where the defendant's relevant acts were wholly past, it was held that damages under the local equivalent of Lord Cairns' Act (in Victoria) may 'include a component for aggravation'.[82] It was stressed that aggravation went to the extent of the claimant's loss and, thus, to what compensation the claimant ought to be awarded.[83] The inclusion of such a component, with respect, would appear justifiable should the past conduct of a defendant be actionable under a tort of infringement of privacy. Where compensation is claimed in lieu of an injunction to restrain an apprehended commission of such a tort, however – which the court was not required to consider in *Giller v Procopets* – it may be that no component for aggravation can be included in an award of damages under Lord Cairns' Act or its equivalents. Elsewhere in the law of torts, equity is generally unwilling to countenance the possibility that a defendant will make a defamatory statement so as to be willing to enjoin the defendant not to utter defamatory words. Similarly, it might be thought odd that a court should countenance the possibility that any apprehended breach of obligation by a defendant will be done in a manner that will aggravate the wrongdoing: that would assume ill of the defendant's temper, if not his or her character. By declining to make such assumptions, it is unlikely that a court could be said to err.

[77] *Paramasivam v Flynn* (1998) 90 FCR 389, 505; *Brown v New South Wales* [2008] NSWCA 287, [40]. Cf *Wilson v Ferguson* [2015] WASC 15, [74]–[85].

[78] eg *Archer v Brown* [1985] QB 401.

[79] eg *Owen and Smith v Reo Motors (Britain) Ltd* (1934) 151 LT 274.

[80] eg *McCarey v Associated Newspapers Ltd (No 2)* [1965] 2 QB 86.

[81] eg *Thompson v Metropolitan Police Commissioner* [1998] QB 498.

[82] *Giller v Procopets* (n 26) [439].

[83] ibid [438].

In either case, awards of damages under Lord Cairns' Act ought to include no component for aggravation if the hypothetical injunction would be to restrain a tort for which aggravated damages are unavailable. To include a component for aggravation in such a situation would, it is suggested, exceed what the words of Lord Cairns' Act and its modern counterparts can plausibly be taken to mean in law.[84]

VIII. Exemplary Awards

Exemplary components have been said to be impermissible in England under the 'extended action', in equity, for breach of confidence.[85] The reasons for equity's antipathy towards exemplary awards have deep roots, which suggests that, if exemplary awards come to be made in respect of infringements of privacy, those awards will be made through developments in the common law of torts. For the aphorism of Somers J – 'Equity and penalty are strangers'[86] – is accurate for modern equity as established beginning in the Restoration, and especially from Lord Nottingham's tenure in the Court of Chancery.[87] It is consistent with equity's methods. As already seen, equitable principles take form and operate within a certain structure within the legal system. Only where the common law and statute are inadequate to address some critical legal need are equitable principles activated. Since those *principles* are only activated where critical shortcomings in justice are found to have been left by statute and the common law, equitable *doctrines* embodying those principles – and affording relief from injustice – are only created where such shortcomings are found. Wherever equity addresses the impropriety of defendants' conduct – to make things as they ought to be – equity's exclusive concern is with the state of defendants' consciences, according to the objective standards of equity courts. Exertions beyond the instruction and correction of that conscience are beyond the jurisdiction of equity.

Indeed, such matters are contrary to tenets of the equitable system itself. Defendants may be coerced into restoring property to another, or surrendering documents for destruction, or refraining from exercising their strict legal rights, and so on. Coercing a defendant under threat of contempt into discharging his or her obligations of conscience is at the heart of equity's methods. Coercing a defendant into accepting punishment, however, has never been part of modern

[84] Cf ibid [428], [442] (aggravated damages for distress in lieu of an injunction to restrain a breach of confidence under the 'extended' equitable action).

[85] *Campbell v MGN Ltd* [2002] EWHC 499 (QB), [2002] EMLR 30, [143] *per* Morland J.

[86] *Aquaculture Corp v New Zealand Green Mussel Co Ltd* (n 11) 302. As to punishment in the 17th-century Chancery, see *Harris v Digital Pulse Ltd* [2003] NSWCA 10, (2003) 56 NSWLR 298, [423]–[433] *per* Heydon JA.

[87] Lord Keeper 1673–75; Lord Chancellor 1675–82.

equity.[88] Exemplary equitable 'compensation' would be beyond the area in which awards of exemplary damages are acceptable. The arguments of principle against exemplary awards thus apply to check the idea that equitable 'compensation' could be awarded to punish a defendant who infringes another's privacy. Appeals to the ingenuity of equity in support of such awards evidently suppose that in the exercise of equitable powers, anything should be possible.

Unlike in equity, at common law there are at least avenues for pursuing awards of exemplary damages. In the nature of things, infringements of privacy lend themselves to forms of misconduct that are hurtful, highly embarrassing, offensive to public morals or terribly misuse public power.[89] Nevertheless, the avenues towards the recovery of exemplary damages in such a case may be blocked, should infringement of privacy be recognised as a tort. The anomalous nature of exemplary damages in the modern law places a heavy burden on arguments for increasing their availability. The burden of argument suggests that counsel who moves a court to award exemplary damages for an infringement of privacy under any new tort of infringement of privacy, would require energy and great persuasiveness. Quite remarkable persuasiveness would be required to prompt a court to admit a *non-tortious* cause of action for infringement of privacy into the group of situations in which exemplary damages are available in principle.

This is true of English law, too, notwithstanding the House of Lords' decision in *Kuddus v Chief Constable of Leicestershire Constabulary*.[90] The ratio of that decision is that exemplary damages may be awarded in the law of torts, even though evidence showing that exemplary damages were awarded for that tort before 1964 cannot be found.[91] The case was intended to rationalise, and perhaps to liberalise, the availability of exemplary damages. But the judgments give no strength to the suggestion (sometimes heard) that *Kuddus* decides that exemplary damages might be awarded on any cause of action. Two reasons especially show why that is not so. First, the argument and reasoning in the case were observably[92] and consciously[93] narrow: narrower than can could support a ratio that exemplary damages might be awarded on any cause of action. Secondly, in abandoning that 'cause of action requirement', the House was addressing only the law of torts.[94] Odd results would come of treating the case as having decided that the nature of a claimant's cause of action is wholly irrelevant to whether exemplary damages are available. A claimant can have a cause of action for rescission or rectification, for example, or to

[88] The instances of punishment in Chancery in the 17th century are *inter alia* to be understood in the setting of the exceptional civil unrest of that period: *Harris v Digital Pulse Ltd* (n 85). Then and thereafter, it was recognised that such punishment was foreign to the equitable tradition and to equitable tenets.

[89] See Turner (n 11) 270.

[90] *Kuddus v Chief Constable of Leicestershire Constabulary* [2001] UKHL 29, [2002] 2 AC 122.

[91] ibid [8], [21], [27], [38], [44], [80], [111], [122]. The year 1964 is the date of the decision in *Rookes v Barnard* [1964] AC 1129.

[92] eg *Kuddus v Chief Constable of Leicestershire Constabulary* (n 89), [26]–[27], [45], [49], [68], [80].

[93] eg ibid, [26]–[27], [35], [60], [68], [80].

[94] See especially ibid [60], [89], [122].

marshal securities. A cause of action 'is simply a factual situation the existence of which entitles one person to obtain from the court a remedy against another person'.[95] Facts the existence of which entitle a person to obtain orders for rescission, rectification and to marshal are causes of action, on that definition. Yet a court is virtually certain to refuse a claim of exemplary damages on such causes of action, even where the defendant's conduct is akin to the conduct of defendants in prior cases in which exemplary damages have been given. The cause of action must therefore be significant in deciding whether exemplary damages are in principle available and should be given on the facts.

More still than awards of compensation in an aggravated measure, awards of damages under Lord Cairns' Act and its equivalents to punish and make an example of the defendant are doubtful. However tentative and provisional arguments must be as to the proper construction of those Acts today, it is uncontroversial that those Acts were not intended to confer a novel power to punish on the courts. Indeed, clear words would be needed to evidence an intention that courts should have power to punish by awarding damages under this provision. Such a clear intention is missing. In the Australian case of *Giller v Procopets*, two members of the court held no such award should be made on the facts of the case, but left open the possibility that it might be proper to do so (or to grant equitable compensation in such a form) in some other case.[96] The third member of the court was worried by the proposition, but considered that exemplary awards of either equitable compensation or equitable damages under Lord Cairns' Act should be treated as unavailable.[97] It is respectfully suggested that Lord Cairns' Act and its modern equivalents do not confer the power that such awards would require.

IX. Proprietary Relief

Returning from monetary relief to specific relief, to which some attention was given early in this chapter, equitable relief relating to property may be expected to be straightforwardly given where it amounts to orders for the delivery up and cancellation or destruction of documents or chattels (as the case may be), where the documents or chattels are a means of infringing a claimant's entitlement to privacy. Indeed, once a legal entitlement to privacy is recognised in the judge-made law of a common law jurisdiction, the availability of such equitable relief in principle would seem to lack all controversy. The equitable or legal source of the entitlement would be immaterial on that count.

Otherwise, equitable proprietary relief for infringement of privacy should be doubtful or, at the minimum, contestable – and it would be so irrespective of

[95] *Letang v Cooper* [1965] 1 QB 232, 242–43.

[96] *Giller v Procopets* (n 26) [434]–[437] (Neave JA); see also ibid [1] (Maxwell P agreeing generally with Neave JA).

[97] ibid [157].

whether entitlements to privacy sit in the law of torts or in equity. Aside from obviously irrelevant grounds on which equitable proprietary relief can be obtained – as where a person is entitled to the due administration of a fund of property, or to rescission or to the satisfaction of an estoppel by encouragement – equitable relief in respect of property generally requires: (i) that the claimant had or has an equitable interest or estate in the claimed asset, or in an asset now represented by the property in a defendant's hands; or (ii) that the defendant obtained the property by reason of breach of a fiduciary duty owed to the claimant. However, the means of obtaining proprietary relief would not avail one who complains that his or her privacy has been infringed. Unless privacy interests and entitlements come to be seen as proprietary, assets acquired by a defendant will not be seen as the proceeds or fruit of a proprietary interest in even a loose sense – let alone as an interest or estate in a technical sense – so as to avail the claimant of equitable proprietary relief.

Nor will an infringement of privacy, as such, be a breach of fiduciary duty so as to make the proprietary relief so accessible through fiduciary doctrine easily accessible to the claimant in a privacy action. Further, the strong equitable remedies given to correct breaches of such facilitative legal relationships as fiduciary relationships and equitable obligations of confidence[98] cannot be expected to apply to infringements of privacy. The former typically arise between particular parties and from some undertaking. Any duty not to infringe another's privacy would instead be imposed by law. Further, such a privacy-duty would evidently be *in rem* or, in Hohfeldian terms, multital; whereas fiduciary and confidential relations arising from undertakings are *in personam* or, in Hohfeldian terms, paucital: they bind the parties thereto only.[99] Moreover, since an entitlement to protect privacy would protect personal rather than proprietary interests, the likelihood is low that infringements of privacy would lead those who infringe others' privacy to acquire property by reason of their commission of the tort. The frequency of cases in which the defendant acquires property by reason of a privacy infringement is likely to be so low that a need to widen the availability of equitable proprietary relief by altering these principles will not arise. Beyond relief in the form of delivery up and cancellation, the doubts over the availability of equitable proprietary relief for infringement of privacy outweigh the confidence one might have that such relief could be available.

X. Conclusion

Following the establishment in the judge-made law of liability for infringing another's entitlement to privacy, the resolution of basic questions of relief

[98] See n 51.

[99] Third parties' liability is in rem and imposed by law, but that does not alter the distinction drawn in the text here.

will – or would – be required. Among those are several questions of relief in equity but also, it has been argued, questions of the judge-made common law. An equitable perspective on the relief that might in future come to be developed to remedy infringements of privacy should indicate whether any such legal developments are a fit subject of equitable principles. Where the thresholds of equitable innovation and relief are not met, that perspective should also indicate what parts of the common law might instead speak to the situation.

A future body of law on remedies for infringement of privacy would differ according to whether a legal entitlement to privacy should be established in equity, as a source of liability distinct from equitable obligations of confidentiality and other sources of equitable liability, or at common law, as a further accession to the library of torts. As equity is ill placed to develop an equitable law of torts, it is suggested that any liability for infringement of privacy ought to be established at common law, should the liability be established by judge-made law at all. The common law of torts protects economic, proprietary and personal interests through numerous torts: the law of torts, and thus the common law, has successfully accommodated the concerns that justice be done with respect to these kinds of interests in many situations. To establish liability for infringement of privacy and to afford monetary relief for such infringements would be a notable legal step, and would be controversial. Should that step be taken, however, the placing of the liability and relief therefor at common law, in the law of torts, would attract no notable controversy – because doing so seems obvious. That is but one sign that the reform would be highly coherent with the existing law. Unlike the only other obligations for which equity furnishes compensation for loss – breaches of trust, of fiduciary obligations and of equitable obligations of confidentiality – the interests at the heart of an entitlement to privacy are fully serviceable at common law. Except where an entitlement to privacy is substantially an entitlement to a voluntarily assumed equitable obligation of confidentiality – and except where equitable relief might issue in aid of common law rights – the interests protected by an entitlement to privacy make no call on equity to correct the conscience of one who infringes another's entitlement to privacy.

Should entitlements to privacy be protected through a (common law) tort, equity could intervene in appropriate cases to grant relief in aid of a party's common law rights. Equitable compensation would be unavailable. But 'equitable damages' under Lord Cairns' Act and its modern equivalents – which are truly statutory relief – could be available within bounds. Accounts of profits would doubtfully be available. Proprietary relief would also be doubtful. However, equity's oldest remedy, the injunction, would commonly be available both as interim and permanent relief. Orders for delivery up and cancellation of documents – or, more probably, the destruction of chattels – would be available. At common law, compensatory damages would be available as of right, including aggravated damages; and there is a possibility that exemplary damages could be available at common law.

12

Remedies for Breach of Privacy: A Study of a Different Hedgehog

DAVID PARTLETT

Privacy is a moving frontier. The growth of electronic media, of social media, and the capacity of government and corporations to pry into the lives of individuals have threatened the accepted boundaries of privacy. Those boundaries have deep and ancient roots in the common law. Recall the old nineteenth-century Michigan case of the doctor who takes his untrained assistant on a house call to attend to the birth of the patient's child. The case, although not couched in terms of privacy, turns on the zone of privacy that can be expected during the birth of a child.[1] That event, in that time and place, required an express and punctilious consent if the usual social norms surrounding childbirth were not to be transgressed.[2] In the age-old process by which the law of torts has expanded to meet current-day demands of changing social norms, protections extended to traditional interests were recognised in respect of new interests. The example beyond the present was the extension of the intentional torts to recognise directly protection of emotional tranquility.

Likewise, interstitial protections of privacy eventually saw the interest as directly protected.[3] In one of the noteworthy wins by academics, the tort was to

[1] *De May v Roberts*, 9 NW 146 (Mich 1881).

[2] It is noteworthy that these norms governed conduct by the hoi polloi. For royalty, it was different: Queen Victoria gave birth with many male courtiers in attendance. This conformed with the tradition that no trickery was engaged in to confuse the royal succession. See J Baird, *Victoria: The Queen* (London, Little Brown, 2016) 166, describing the birth of Queen Victoria's first born and the entourage assembled. The doctor told Victoria, 'Oh, Madam, it is a Princess'. She responded, 'Never mind, the next time will be a Prince' (at 167).

[3] This is a process still in development elsewhere in the common law world. Recognition of the tort of invasion of privacy has had it fits and starts in England and Australia, for example. In England one sees the gradual stirrings of the tort in *Wainwright v Home Office* [2004] 2 AC 406; in Australia, *Australian Broadcasting Corporation v Lenah Game Meats* (2001) 208 CLR 199. The New Zealand courts have been more welcoming: see *Hosking v Runting* [2005] 1 NZLR 1. Outside judicial development, Law Reform bodies have taken up the work. See Australian Law Reform Commission, *Serious Invasions of Privacy in the Digital Era: Final Report*, ALRC Report No 123 (2014) (recommending a cause of action for invasion of privacy with a broad range of remedies).

be launched as a separate field in the famous article by Brandeis and Warren.[4] It was to be formalised by William Prosser,[5] and was vigorous and robust until the discombobulating, epoch-making 1964 case of *New York Times v Sullivan*.[6] Private facts were facts, and the First Amendment notion was that, if of public interest, they should see the light of day despite their capacity to damage persons. The law, then, has been molded in conformity with the changing terrain of the free-speech clause of First Amendment jurisprudence. The law of privacy, as with the law of defamation, has been recast by the US Supreme Court to be a creature of federal law ripped from its State law roots. This has deeply influenced the substance of the law of privacy and its remedies.[7]

In this chapter, my aim is to give a sense of what makes the available remedies for breach of privacy rather peculiar: they unearth a different kind of hedgehog not found in the other jurisdictions examined in this book.

To explicate this, I will take the reader through a number of steps. In section I, I show how the tort emerged and was changed by the strong hand of the First Amendment. In section II, concentrating on the law of remedies, I explain the pragmatic realist foundations of remedies in private law. I submit that remedies (secondary rights) attach to the substantive rights (primary rights) in an orderly cogent manner, reflecting the underlying systematic pattern of the common law. As private law, current social concepts are instantiated in the fabric of privacy law.[8] In section III, turning to remedies in privacy, I describe how the substantive interests touch the available remedies that courts are prepared to grant individuals. Here I take the categories put forward by Prosser as encompassing the tort law of privacy. These categories are well-known and adopted as a starting point throughout the common law world. The emergence of privacy protection as a right to be encompassed by tort liability rules, with the panoply of remedies usually attending thereto, still remains uncertain in numbers of important common law jurisdictions.[9] But even with that unevenness, the march towards a wider protection is clear, even though in the UK, the European Convention on Human Rights, with the concomitant Human Rights Act 1998, may, with Brexit, wane in influence. In conclusion, in section IV I note that the common law of torts is rooted in the community locally and nationally.[10] The purposes of a variety of remedial tools,

[4] SD Warren and LD Brandeis, 'The Right to Privacy' (1890) 4 *Harvard Law Review* 193.

[5] WL Prosser, 'Privacy' (1960) 48 *California Law Review* 383.

[6] *New York Times v Sullivan* 376 US 254 (1964).

[7] See JCP Goldberg and BC Zipursky, 'The Supreme Court's Stealth Return to the Common Law of Torts' (2016) 65 *DePaul Law Review* 433, 437–43.

[8] CC Tilley, 'Tort Law Inside Out' (2017) 127 *Yale LJ* 1320, 1343–45.

[9] See, eg, *Google Inc v Vidal-Hall* [2015] EWCA Civ 311 (England); *Australian Broadcasting Corporation v Lenah Meats Pty Ltd* (2001) 208 CLR 199. Gleeson CJ specifically referred to Prosser's (n 5) classification and the *Restatement (Second) of Torts*. See generally R Stevens, 'Damages for Wrongdoing in the Absence of Loss', in ch 4 of this book.

[10] Tilley (n 8) (discussing tort law's internal structure as drawing on local morality norms for some torts and national efficiency norms for others).

and the imperative of the First Amendment of the US Constitution, shape remedies that, while familiar, are applied differently. In the end, as the law is debated and developed elsewhere, we should be mindful that substantive privacy rights should be considered along with the structure of the remedies.[11]

I. The Tort Emerges

Some exploration of this must be canvassed before we engage in our inquiry into remedies. The great divide is between remedies in property protective cases and that area where the central interest is personal dignity.

Prosser's division in his famous article, adopted by the *Restatement (Second) of Torts*, was fourfold:

1. Appropriation of name or likeness.
2. Intrusion upon seclusion.
3. Public disclosure of private facts.
4. False light publicity.

The first is strongly, but not solely, based in protection of property rights. It has to do with the creation of intellectual property at a time that pre-dated the statutory protections via copyright, patents and trademarks. The rights go beyond the corporeal to the intellectual when the importance of such rights in promoting free markets grows apace. To create property rights undergirds markets, giving consumers assurances of quality. It encourages innovation by giving returns to holders of the rights. It promotes trades for mutual gains. But an individual's image and personality have a dignitary aspect too.

The other branches identified by Prosser are less property-based and more protective of human dignity. For example, the law governing the public disclosure of private facts in one dimension extends to protect confidential information. This, non-American readers will immediately grasp, incorporates the law of confidence, as where information is given over in a relationship that demands such confidentiality.[12] Note here, as in the first category, that this protection is justified on the basis that the law encourages the transmission of information for mutual gain.

[11] RJ Krotoszynski, *Privacy Revisited: A Global Perspective on the Right to be Left Alone* (Oxford, Oxford UP, 2016).

[12] The English courts developed the duty of confidentiality from relationships that demand confidence. The jurisdiction was in equity. Thus, a breach of the obligation would bring into force equitable remedies. The privacy action, while first developed as a form of breach of confidence, is now tentatively situated in tort despite its equitable roots: *Vidal*-Hall (n 9). Such is the hold of tort reasoning and amnesia about equity in the United States that confidentiality without debate became an avenue to a form of tort liability for breach of privacy. And, ironically, this route was taken in England, even though those courts are more attentive to the sources of causes of action. See *Murray v Big Pictures (UK) Ltd* [2008] EWCA Civ 446.

The rule undergirds trust, resting on the foundation that in human interactions, valuable, expensively generated information must be imparted to others. A strong rule protecting against the disclosure of that information will promote mutually beneficial relationships. Furthermore, the tort provides an individual with protection of his or her dignity, so as not to have exposed to public view aspects of his or her life that are private, and necessarily so for human flourishing.

Similarly, in the tort of false light, we find that the investment in a public identity is protected from intentional, or sometimes negligent, miscasting.

In the aspect of intrusion upon seclusion we find a tort akin to the Fourth Amendment of the US Constitution. Under the Amendment, 'the right of the people to be secure in their persons, houses, papers, and effects … shall not be violated'.[13] The Amendment is directed to protect persons in their freedom from a felt abuse by government, at the time bolstered by Lockean and Whig notions of liberty.[14] Protection of property interests was fundamental in ordered liberal society.[15]

The other peculiarly American aspect of any considered remedy is the close association of the protection of privacy and the law of defamation. This will be immediately apparent in the tort of false light. This tort touches on the protection of an individual's reputation in society. It protects that individual's interest 'in not being made to appear before the public … otherwise than he is'.[16] It is clear that liability is established upon a showing by 'clear and convincing evidence' that the defendant acted with actual malice under the standard set forth in *New York Times v Sullivan*.[17]

The sweep of the First Amendment extends to other aspects of the privacy tort, as in disclosure of true private facts.[18] It also confines the scope of the tort of intentional infliction of emotional distress, as seen in the two expansive opinions in

[13] US Constitution, 4th amendment.

[14] M Cloud, 'Property is Privacy: Locke and Brandeis in the Twenty-First Century' (2018) 55 *American Criminal Law Review* 37.

[15] J Ely, *The Guardian of Every Other Right: A Constitutional History of Property Rights*, 3rd edn (Oxford, Oxford UP, 1992) (arguing that protection of property rights was not revolutionary but was present in time-honoured concepts of English liberties); D Partlett, 'Remedies in a Wide-angle Lens: Observations on Remedial Consilience' (2014) 63 *Emory Law Journal Online* 2053 ('There is in this world no difference between the right and the remedy') (citing *Chase Manhattan Bank v Israel British Bank* [1981] 1 Ch 105, 124), available online at http://law.emory.edu/elj/elj-online/remedies-in-wide-angle-lens.html.

[16] *Restatement (Second) of Torts*, § 652E.

[17] *Sullivan* (n 6) 280 (requiring 'knowledge that the [actionable] statement was false or [made] with reckless disregard of whether it was false or not'). See also *Time Inc v Hill*, 385 US 374 (1967) (applying *Sullivan* in holding that constitutional protections of speech and press precluded the application of a statute to redress false reports of matters of public interest in the absence of proof that the appellant acted with malice or knowledge). See *Cantrell v Forest City Publishing Co*, 419 US 245 (1974), applying the actual malice standard to a story in which the plaintiff and her family were featured in a follow-up about the family's plight after a notorious bridge collapse. The story contained misrepresentations about the plaintiff's coping with the consequences.

[18] See *Hall v Post*, 372 SE 2d 259 (1988) (stressing that even 'false statements which cause actual harm must be given limited breathing space').

Hustler Magazine v Falwell[19] and, more recently, *Snyder v Phelps*.[20] The domain of protection provided by the States in consumer protection and privacy are severely confined by the First Amendment.[21] To the extent that the substantive law bends to the demands of the First Amendment, so must the remedies if the action can be made out.

It follows that, as we shall see, any damages are constrained and that injunctive relief is frowned upon as prior restraint and inconsistent with the heart of free speech under the First Amendment. However, injunctive relief is available, albeit narrowly, where property rights and harm to dignity combine with little risk to free speech.

Various States have adopted statutes to codify rights to privacy.[22] They do not depart materially from the usual Prosserian classification. The statutory language may, however, fashion the remedies that may be available.[23] In the United States, efforts in State tort reform to blunt claim frequency and severity, mainly in product liability and in medical malpractice, have broad-brush restricted remedial rights in tort actions generally, touching privacy actions.

The intimate association of privacy protection in tort law has had a profound influence on differences between United States and European law. In Europe and to a lesser extent in the rest of the Commonwealth, privacy protection flows from a concept of human rights and contends on a level playing field with free speech. The rights are balanced. In the United States following *New York Times v Sullivan*, tort law is a nuanced form of state action that carries no equal weight. There is no balance.[24]

II. A Journey into the American Law of Remedies

The realists have left a long shadow in American law. The field of remedies is a great exemplar of that legacy. Remedies have never been carefully theorised by the courts or by the academy. Signs of change are in the wind. The Canadians, led by Jeff Berryman, have been pathfinders. In the United States, Sam Bray has made significant contributions in throwing light on equity jurisprudence.[25]

[19] *Hustler Magazine v Falwell*, 485 US 46 (1988).

[20] *Snyder v Phelps*, 562 US 443 (2011).

[21] *Sorrell v IMS Health Inc*, 564 US 552 (2011).

[22] eg California Constitution, art I, § 1 (proclaiming privacy to be an inalienable right); California Penal Code, § 630 (stating an intention to protect the right of privacy of the people of California); New York Civil Rights Law, § 50 (Consol 2017).

[23] See New York action for injunction and for damages: New York Civil Rights Law, § 51 (Consol 2017).

[24] K Hughes and N Richards, 'The Atlantic Divide on Privacy and Free Speech' in AT Kenyon (ed), *Comparative Defamation and Privacy Law* (Cambridge, Cambridge UP, 2016) 164 (recommending that conflicts between concepts be understood in a world of modern communications).

[25] S Bray, 'The System of Equitable Remedies' (2016) 63 *UCLA Law Review* 530; S Bray, 'The Supreme Court and the New Equity' (2015) 68 *Vanderbilt Law Review* 99; S Bray, 'Remedies, Meet Economics; Economics, Meet Remedies' (2018) 38 *OJLS* 71.

On the whole, however, like the neglect of restitution, lack of careful thought about remedies and their relationship to substantive rights has left a hole in American Private Law.[26] History and theory are absent in most court decisions and academic discussions. The realists and the following pragmatic schools of thought such as law and economics simply treat the remedy to be attached to a breach of a right as a grab-bag of wide and unexamined judicial discretion.[27] American private law has never had a systematiser, a taxonomist, like Peter Birks.[28]

Scholars in remedies have provided a number of matrices and schemas for categorising remedies. The law of remedies can be conceptualised as secondary rights to support primary substantive rights. The debate, as Degeling and Varuhas state, has been about the relationship between rights and remedies.[29]

The school that prevails is that of the dualist or modified dualists. The dualist would see a river between the right and the remedy, and the remedy is drawn from a grab-bag, but subject to defined principles, to suit the exigencies of the day. Rights, in contrast, are ideal and abstract. Most theorists, however, who have given thought to the relationship, subscribe to a category that Berryman dubs the 'integration model'.[30] These scholars are structurally dualist but draw a closer nexus between the right and the remedy. As I stated in commenting on the divide, the contending schools of thought can be described as Isiah Berlin's hedgehogs and foxes.[31]

The strong force, I contend, is a reverence for the common law method. Peter Birks wished to introduce rigour and certainty. Like cases ought to be treated alike. Birks's map provides a certainty not given, he and his disciples argue, by the common law.[32] The careful mapping avoids a world in which remedial volcanoes erupt without appropriate systematic justification.[33] But the deficiencies of the

[26] As is often the case in American legal thought, the realm of public law has a more highly developed schema and has closely distinguished between rights and remedies. See DJ Levinson, 'Rights Essentialism and Remedial Equilibration' (1999) 99 *Columbia Law Review* 857.

[27] The most influential example of American scholarship is G Calabresi and A Douglas Melamed, 'Property Rules, Liability Rules, and Inalienability: One View of the Cathedral' (1972) 85 *Harvard Law Review* 1089, wherein property rights are associated with injunctive relief while tort rights, as liability rules, are associated with damages. The discussion of this has filled the pages of law reviews ever since. For a follow-up, see E Sherwin, 'Property Rules as Remedies' (1997) 106 *Yale LJ* 2083. The theory is in the American realist vein of law and economics, where rules serve the exterior goal of efficiency.

[28] P Birks, 'Equity in the Modern Law: An Exercise in Taxonomy' (1996) 26 *University of Western Australia Law Review* 1.

[29] S Degeling and JNE Varuhas, 'Equity's Personal and Monetary Remedies' in S Degeling and JNE Varuhas (eds), *Equitable Compensation and Disgorgement of Profit* (Oxford, Hart Publishing, 2017) 7.

[30] J Berryman, 'The Law of Remedies: A Prospectus for Teaching and Scholarship' (2010) 10 *Oxford University Commonwealth Law Journal* 125.

[31] Partlett (n 15).

[32] Berryman (n 30) 128 (citing P Birks, 'Three Kinds of Objection to Discretionary Remedialism' (2000) 29 *University of Western Australia Law Review* 1).

[33] Oliver Cromwell (and possibly all those of a military stamp) made order and close classification his mantra: RF Horton, *Oliver Cromwell: A Study in Personal Religion* (London, James Clarke and Co, 1897) 144; TE Holland, *Essays Upon the Form of the Law* (1870) 171 (describing the common law as 'chaos with a full index').

common law are a straw man, and are more a product of a want of understanding of its internal rigour.[34] Those that would dismiss the common law method do not adequately grasp its systemetacity.[35] The common law adheres cohesively through its disciplined practice of deliberate, practical reasoning; this is the artificial reason of the common law.[36]

The system is denoted by public-mindedness in solving problems with a regard to justice, a reasoned discourse in shaping its rules and doctrines, a common endeavour by exercise of common practice, a forging of rules and principles in court, and a discourse disciplined by its focus on concrete cases tethered to past decisions and 'structured by (a) analogical reasoning, (b) mindfulness of the temporal aspect of law, and (c) a keen sense of its practical task of ordering and coordinating social interaction in the community'.[37] Subjects, providing, as Waldron says, 'a unified realm of legal meaning and purpose'.[38] The best scholarship in the common law realm shares these indicia of artificial reason. It strengthens our understanding of the law and reinforces its systemetacity. It will show within the discourse how doctrine can be changed to accommodate change over time. It will identify the path of normative guidance: inconsistencies and coalescence. And of vital importance is the role of private law in particular in 'ordering and coordinating social interaction in the community'.[39]

The Birkian model building enterprise attempts, as Postema dubs it, an '*elegantia juris*' that smothers the expression of practical values concerning justice, integrity or the rule of law.[40] The Birkian model freezes the common law's ability to change over time, constrained, as it is, by the terms of the system or taxonomy within which it operates. Criticism of the common law method, we shall see, is apparent as the Supreme Court derides the capacity of that law to keep constitutional values safe. The common law of torts is too pliable, the Court asserts, to properly guard free speech. Yet its evolution and accretion of wisdom by reasoned elaboration may be a tonic against a one-dimensional and wooden idea of free speech under the Constitution.[41] For example, privacy rights may be entirely consistent with the First Amendment if privacy is viewed as protecting a space for intellectual development of ideas vital to the public marketplace of ideas.[42]

[34] See BC Zipursky, 'Philosophy of Private Law' in J Coleman and S Shapiro (eds), *Oxford Handbook of Jurisprudence and Philosophy of Law* (Oxford, Oxford UP, 2002) 624.

[35] J Waldron, '"Transcendental Nonsense" and System in the Law' (2000) 100 *Columbia Law Review* 16.

[36] G Postema, 'Law's System: The Necessity of System in Common Law' [2014] *New Zealand Law Review* 69.

[37] ibid 16.

[38] J Waldron, 'Torture and Positive Law: Jurisprudence for the White House' (2005) 105 *Columbia Law Review* 1681, 1722; see also J Waldron, 'The Concept of the Rule of Law' (2008) 43 *Georgia Law Review* 135.

[39] Postema (n 36) 16.

[40] ibid 24–29.

[41] D Partlett, 'New York Times v Sullivan at Fifty Years' in Kenyon (ed) (n 24) 58.

[42] N Richards, 'Intellectual Privacy' (2008) 87 *Texas Law Review* 387; see also N Richards, 'The Dangers of Surveillance' (2013) 126 *Harvard Law Review* 1934.

Broadly, I would contend that privacy is essential to human flourishing and is an entirely supportive concomitant of the underlying value of free speech. A reading of the remedies attaching to the tort law of privacy exposes this battle line.

III. Remedies for Breach of Privacy: Wherein the Elegance

Professor Jimenez, in the American context, has usefully begun to explore the proper fundamentals between substantive rights and interests, suggesting that courts engage in a matching of remedies to the interests underlying the cause of action.[43] He suggests that remedies should be conceptualised as falling into four boxes: protection, restoration, coercion, and retribution. These have a temporal and victim/wrongdoer aspect, and may overlap. Protection may also draw on retribution and coercion on restoration. He suggests that judges ought to go through a process of categorisation in bestowing remedies. In these terms, we may usefully explore the remedial aspects of privacy protection in tort law. Throughout the protection of privacy, we witness that the courts draw lines according to evolving community standards. The function of tort liability is multiple, but in the end is to devise liability rules that smooth coordination of individuals in society, reflecting deep values of individual dignity. Does the hedgehog of privacy law hide an elegance that reconciles rights to remedies in this fashion?[44] Property, social cohesion and justice operate as cohesive principles.[45] Whether the right is based in property or dignity to encourage human thriving, the right is actionable upon its invasion; that is actionable per se. In privacy, as with the intentional torts, it is the invasion of the right and not the damage that is the gist of the action.[46] Where the right attaches to protection of human dignity, it is defined in each of its guises as depending on a flouting of an individual's reasonable expectations of privacy. The community standard employed borrows from the intentional torts and, like them, is actionable upon such invasion. The damages in touching dignity will be measured according to the defendant's departure from the social norm. An outrageous departure will bring in its train compensatory and super compensatory damages and coercive remedies to prevent continuing violations. In each of its manifestations, the hedgehog of privacy law demonstrates an elegance that reconciles rights to remedies.

[43] M Jimenez, 'Remedial Concilience' (2013) 62 *Emory Law Journal* 1309.

[44] M Barbery, *L'Elegance du herisson* (Paris, Gallimard, 2006) (trans, *The Elegance of the Hedgehog*).

[45] Tilley (n 8) (suggesting a recasting of tort law and remedies to view it from the inside, taking account of its community-reflecting guise where the material is local and its wider utilitarian role when the view is wider).

[46] D Rolph, 'Vindicating Reputation and Privacy' in Kenyon (ed) (n 24) 291. See also JNE Varuhas, 'The Concept of "Vindication" in the Law of Torts: Rights, Interests, and Damages' (2014) 34 *OJLS* 253.

A. Appropriation of Name or Likeness

In this subsection, I examine the tort of appropriation of identity or personality. In the first place, a property interest is apparent. A person who invests in an identity has a right to be protected in his or her investment. That person's image should not be expropriated by another. To protect that property in full, a coercive remedy of injunction is presumed. And in a temporal sense, a threat should be warded off by the granting of a temporary injunction in order to avoid aggravating harm to the interest. The courts are particularly willing to grant an injunction where the appropriation is committed knowing that the owner would be unwilling to let his or her image be used by defendant.[47]

If the tort has already taken place, the strong remedy of injunction will be futile and restoration and/or retribution may be appropriate. Thus, the damages remedy will be backward-looking, in the sense that it is designed to put the wronged person in the position he or she occupied prior to the commission of the wrong. But the measure may be difficult to calculate, and a remedy that strips the wrongdoer of a gain made in the wrong may be more satisfactory in protecting the right,[48] restoring the person and exacting some measure of retribution where the breach is accompanied by some atrocious behaviour. In *Rohrbaugh v Wal-Mart*,[49] the court found that nominal damages were available despite considerable authority requiring proof of harm following the invasion. The court determined that the invasion of privacy, forcing the plaintiff, an employee, to be drug tested and for disclosure of the results, was reprehensible in itself. No compensable damage could be shown, but punitive damages were nevertheless awardable. Presumed damages play a similar role and, as we shall see, the US case law favours such damages.[50] In *Ainsworth v Cent Supply*,[51] the plaintiff was filmed installing ceramic tiles, believing that the footage would be used for instructional purposes. The footage later appeared on an advertisement for his employer. It was conceded that he suffered no tangible harm from the filming. Nevertheless, the Illinois court, on appeal from a lower court, found that this was actionable, as 'vindicating plaintiff's right to use his image against this deliberate violation, even if plaintiff cannot prove actual damage'.[52] The appeal court sent the matter back for determination on the basis that nominal damages could be awarded and that that could form the basis of punitive damages.

[47] *Onassis v Christian Dior-New York Inc*, 472 NYS 2d 254 (NY 1984).

[48] For discussion of the potential role of gain-based remedies see, eg, K Barnett, 'Gain-Based Relief for Breach of Privacy', in ch 8 of this book; PG Turner, 'Privacy Remedies Viewed Through an Equitable Lens', in ch 11 of this book; JNE Varuhas, 'Varieties of Damages for Breach of Privacy', in ch 3 of this book.

[49] *Rohrbaugh v Wal-Mart*, 572 SE 2d 881, 887 (W Va 2002).

[50] See Varuhas (n 48).

[51] *Ainsworth v Cent Supply*, 295 Ill App 3d 644 (1998).

[52] In this sense, the tort operates in the same way as the traditional trespass torts in allowing an action despite the lack of proof of actual damages. In a similar vein, see *Manville v Borg-Warner Corp*, 418 F2d 434, 434–437 (10th Cir 1969).

Also note that in respect of the property right reflected, that right may have to give way to other interests. Take, for example, the case of the human cannon ball. In *Zacchini v Scripps-Howard Broadcasting*,[53] the plaintiff was an entertainer who made his living by being shot from a cannon into a net some 200 feet away. The defendant broadcasting station, though requested not to film the act, showed it on the evening news. Justice White emphasised that the right of publicity protected the property interests of the individual. It is akin to patent and copyright law. The tort contrasts with false light, where the information is to be repressed. Here the 'owner' of the information has no objection to the publication of the information, provided he or she obtains the economic reward. Indeed, here the plaintiff simply sought damages that would cover his loss of commercial interest. Justice Powell, in dissent, would presume a 'newsworthy' defence, a protection by the First Amendment, unless the plaintiff could show that the news broadcast was a 'subterfuge or cover for a private or commercial exploitation'.[54]

The line to be drawn is not always clear. Justice White opined:

> Wherever the line in particular situations is to be drawn between media reports that are protected and those that are not, we are quite sure that the First and Fourteenth Amendments do not immunize the media when they broadcast a performer's entire act without his consent. The Constitution no more prevents a State from requiring respondent to compensate petitioner for broadcasting his act on television than it would privilege respondent to film and broadcast a copyrighted dramatic work without liability to the copyright owner, or to film and broadcast a prize fight, or a baseball game, where the promoters or the participants had other plans for publicizing the event. There are ample reasons for reaching this conclusion.[55]

Speaking for the dissenters, Justice Powell said:

> Rather than begin with a quantitative analysis of the performer's behavior – is this or is this not his entire act? – we should direct initial attention to the actions of the news media: what use did the station make of the film footage? When a film is used, as here, for a routine portion of a regular news program, I would hold that the First Amendment protects the station from a 'right of publicity' or 'appropriation' suit, absent a strong showing by the plaintiff that the news broadcast was a subterfuge or cover for private or commercial exploitation.[56]

Pursued by many but attained by few, fame is often accompanied by the price of others' exploitation of such status. In the course of public speech, celebrities commonly sell products, influence attitudes and affect public discourse. The balance between free speech under the First Amendment on the privacy right is often at issue. In *White*, the court held that Vanna White, a well-known media figure in 'Wheel of Fortune', a long-running and successful quiz show, had made a

[53] *Zacchini v Scripps-Howard Broadcasting*, 433 US 562 (1977).
[54] ibid 581 *per* Powell J.
[55] ibid 575 *per* Powell J.
[56] ibid 581 *per* Powell J.

supportable claim when a robot identifiable as a representation of her was featured in an ad for the defendant's product. The Ninth Circuit rejected the application for rehearing en banc.[57] Judge Kozinski, joined by others, dissented, finding that the right to publicity had become too expansive and inconsistent with free-speech notions, where actionability rests simply on the invocation of the 'celebrity's image in the public's mind'.[58] The use of a bewigged robot might be a powerful way of expressing the durability of the defendant's product: as the 'Wheel of Fortune' had survived, so would the defendant's product.

The line drawn between protection of the right of publicity and legitimate free expression has produced a plethora of authorities mainly in the Ninth Circuit, the Hollywood Circuit as many dub it, where the entertainment law docket is large.[59] The courts have found images protected if they contain 'significant expressive content'.[60] An entire world of sports heroes and film and stage stars beat a path to the court room door.[61]

It seems plain that the strong protective remedy of injunction would not be available given the thirst in the public for such information. Any prior restraint faces severe First Amendment objections if there is an element of public interest or concern in the information.[62] Where the matter is clearly commercial and the information is not blocked in coming into the public forum, an injunction may be given. In Martin Luther King, Jr Center for Social Change,[63] the defendants argued that public figures have a right to publicity. The defendants here marketed plastic busts of Dr King and pamphlets containing his speeches. Dr King's estate and the plaintiff organisation had refused to allow the defendants to engage in this trade. Although Dr King had not exploited those opportunities during his lifetime, the court found that the right could pass as property in his estate. The plaintiff was able to sustain an injunction against the defendants' marketing the busts and pamphlets.

As the cases concede, the tort is not confined to protection of property interests. In *Dickerson v Dittmar*,[64] the plaintiff brought, inter alia, a claim for appropriation where the defendant had published in his widely disseminated report a purportedly factual account of the plaintiff's involvement in a fraudulent scheme. The name and photograph of the plaintiff were included. The issue raised before the Colorado court was whether the claim was actionable. The lower court had found

[57] *White v Samsung Elecs Am Inc*, 989 F2d 1512 (9th Cir 1993).

[58] ibid 1514.

[59] *Downing v Abercrombie & Fitch*, 265 F3d 994 (9th Cir 2001) (holding the use of a well-known surfer's image actionable under the Lanham Act).

[60] *Winter v DC Comics*, 69 P3d 473 (2003). But cf *Doe v TCT Cablevision*, 110 SW3d 363 (MO 2003) (holding differently on facts similar to *Winter* by adopting a 'predominant use test').

[61] See also *Tiger Woods in ETW Corp v Jireh Pub Inc*, 332 F3d 915 (6th Cir 2003); *Comedy III Productions v Gary Saderup*, 106 21 P3d 797 (2001).

[62] *Zacchini* (n 53).

[63] *Martin Luther King Jr Cntr For Soc Change Inc v American Heritage Products Inc*, 250 Ga 135 (1982).

[64] *Dickerson v Dittmar*, 34 P3d 995 (2001).

that the plaintiff had no valuable interest in her name. The appeal court found this mistaken. A person need not prove that she has acquired a commercially valuable image or name. The tort, it may be said, recognises the dignitary aspect of the tort of privacy.[65]

Aligning the remedies with the substantive tort damages may trace the loss of commercial value (restorative), or allow recovery of profits gained by the plaintiff (protective). In addition, non-economic losses can be recovered, that is for humiliation and mental distress, as in *Abdul-Jabbar v General Motors*,[66] where the words used in an advertisement were capable of indicating that the plaintiff had lost his religion. The advertisement had used the famous basketballer's name as it was in college, before he had converted to Islam and had changed his name. In order to fill the gaps in proof of actual loss, a court, for the purpose of effectively delivering restoration and deterrence, will give presumed damages on intangible losses flowing from humiliation and emotional harm.[67]

In the result, in *Dickerson* the court found that the publication was not actionable because the speech was constitutionally protected. It was a publication concerning a newsworthy matter or one of legitimate public concern. The question here turns on its primary import. Thus, an advertisement using the photograph of a child for promoting a business has no news moment.[68] The norms of public discourse with the modern turn to celebrity have arguably confined the tort. Much of what is newsworthy begins with celebrity.[69]

One last word on the tort and its remedies in relation to defamation. An observer outside the United States could make the observation that the tort of appropriation sails very closely to the old tort of defamation. Take the old English case of *Tolley v Fry*.[70] In this case the defendant had used the plaintiff's image in an advertisement. Tolley was a well-known amateur golfer. His appearance in an advertisement carried the imputation that he was a professional, according to the reasonable standards of the day. His reputation was besmirched in the eyes of the relevant reading public. Actions in defamation are rare in the United States because of the strict proof fetters flowing from *New York Times v Sullivan*.[71] Remedies are restricted to take account of First Amendment requirements.

[65] Prosser (n 5) (emphasising the property aspect of the appropriation tort confusing the waters).

[66] *Abdul-Jabbar v General Motors*, 85 F3d 407 (9th Cir 1996).

[67] *Petty v Chrysler Corp*, 799 NE2d 432 (2003); see also *Waits v Frito-Lay Inc*, 978 F2d 1093, 1103 (9th Cir 1992) (finding damages for the 'humiliation, embarrassment, and mental distress' where the advertisement cut asunder the plaintiff's reputation for non-commercial songs and career posture).

[68] Of course, as in the famous case of *Slocum v Sears Roebuck*, 542 So 2d 777 (La 1989), the photo may not be of sufficient circulation or disputable quality to be actionable.

[69] *White* (n 57) (Kozinski J dissenting). Outside the US, see P Loughlan, B McDonald and R van Krieken, *Celebrity and the Law* (Annandale NSW, Federation Press, 2010); D Rolph, *Reputation, Celebrity, and Defamation Law* (Ashgate, Routledge, 2008). Celebrity is also an aspect of the other categories of privacy protection: see *Tolley v JS Fry & Sons Ltd* [1931] AC 333.

[70] *Tolley* ibid.

[71] A recent exemplar is the failure of Sarah Palin to survive summary judgment in her action against the *New York Times*, where the court concluded that the offending assertion in the editorial resulted from mistake and not malice: *Palin v New York Times Co*, US Dist LEXIS 139847 (2017).

Where the appropriation tort is available, the aggrieved person will likely take the route of privacy rather than defamation.[72] This may leave the door ajar for the protective remedy of injunction in the event that damages may be inadequate. The essential interest at stake is the same: it is the dignity of the individual.

Note here that the usual concern of remedies to protect, compensate and deter contend with the public interest in free speech, a public purpose for which a private individual may be required to concede in whole or in part a remedy for the private hurt. That hurt is usually cured by compensation, the bailiwick of the common law. More forcefully, injunctive relief, the mark of a strong property right, bends before the imperative of free speech.

B. Intrusion Upon Seclusion or Solitude

In the collective American mind, the ideal of Walden Pond looms large. Henry James Thoreau's book in the transcendental school still holds the imagination of Americans.[73] The right to let alone finds its most honoured place in the right to protect one's home from invasion. It carries the interest in human dignity, as well as an aspect of property when tied to the right to enjoy property ownership. Clearly the tort of nuisance touches this latter property interest. It has a firm place in the law and public consciousness because of its incorporation in the Fourth Amendment.[74]

The tort is defined in one leading case[75] as 'unconsented to intrusion into the home, hospital room or other place the privacy of which is legally recognized, as well as unwarranted sensory intrusions such as eavesdropping, wiretapping, and visual or photographic spying'. A good deal of the debate about this tort surrounds the requirement of reasonable expectation of privacy.[76] The other aspect of the tort is the requirement that the intrusion be highly offensive to a reasonable person. The issue with the tort in the modern world is that we have come far from *Walden*: American society is suffused with the noise of the news and mass voyeurism. Its coarseness was seen but dimly by Warren and Brandeis in their attack on the yellow press of the day.[77] The job of the press is to satisfy the appetite of the public. How far should the modern-day Thoreau expect that his solitary behaviour will

[72] The alternative tort label has failed to deter the Supreme Court from its faithful adherence to *Sullivan* (n 6). See *Hustler Magazine v Falwell*, 485 US 46 (1988); *Snyder v Phelps*, 580 F3d 206 (4th Cir 2009).

[73] F Montaigne, 'American Surveyor: On Thoreau's 200th Birthday A New Biography Pictures Him as a Man of Principle' *NY Times: Sunday Book Review* (23 July 2017) BR17, available online at www.nytimes.com/2017/07/12/books/review/henry-david-thoreau-a-life-laura-dassow-walls.html?mcubz=0.

[74] Ely (n 15).

[75] *Shulman v Group W Productions Inc*, 955 P2d 469, 489 (Cal 1998) (citing *Restatement (Second) of Torts*, § 652B, com b).

[76] *Sanders v Am Broad Companies Inc*, 978 P2d 67, 79 (Cal 1999).

[77] Warren and Brandeis (n 4); see N Richards, 'The Puzzle of Brandeis, Privacy, and Speech' (2010) 63 *Vanderbilt Law Review* 1295.

become a legitimate item of interest of the public, and that he will be pulled into the public light by the press? Thus, the boundaries of the tort have been strictly tailored to accommodate the social milieu, with the reasonableness standard and the First Amendment brought in aid to accommodate reasonable newsgathering. A person does not have to expect complete privacy to be protected. In the work place for example, although conversations may be overheard, one could still expect not to be secretly taped and recorded by way of a 'hat cam'.[78] The material need not be published. The intrusion into the plaintiff's home to film her in the throes and aftermath of a heart attack is enough. The dignity interest and the property right involved is vindicated through damages not requiring proof of special harm.[79] That is, they are presumed. To place a camera, although not capable of operation, in a bathroom is actionable if a reasonable person would believe that his or her privacy had been invaded.[80]

Where newsgathering is involved, the First Amendment looms large. Still, the media has no immunity from the general law. The media cannot trespass or commit other torts to gather information.[81] In *Food Lion v Capital Cities/ABC Inc*,[82] the supermarket chain was the subject of a primetime exposé on meat handling. On false pretences, employees of ABC obtained employment. They filmed activities with a hidden camera. The plaintiff sued in trespass, claiming that the employees had gained entry to the meat-packing and deli areas by fraud. The defendant was held liable.[83] In turning to damages, the court, for First Amendment reasons, disallowed damages flowing from the publication. If reputational damages were to be recovered, the standard of proof would have to reach that of actual malice under the *New York Times v Sullivan* standard.[84] This in effect de-tooths the tort. The damages from directly caused loss, wasted wages etc, would be *de minimus*.[85] However, in *Dietemann v Time Inc*,[86] the court found that the subsequent publication could enhance the damages, and indeed was the very essence of the fraudulent invasion into the quack doctor's office when examining clients. The dignity interests of the clients and the nature of the public interest play a crucial role.[87] The measure of damages expands and contracts accordingly.[88]

[78] *Sanders* (n 76).

[79] *Miller v Nat'l Broad Co*, 232 Cal Rptr 668, 680 (Cal App 2d Dist 1986); 157 F Supp 240 (Del 1957).

[80] *Koeppel v Speirs*, 808 NW2d 177 (Iowa 2011).

[81] The principle is established in *Cohen v Cowles Media Company*, 501 US 663 (1991).

[82] *Food Lion v Capital Cities/ABC Inc*, 194 F3d 505 (4th Cir 1999).

[83] *Accord, Copeland v Hubbard Broadcasting Inc*, 526 NW2d 402 (Minn 1995).

[84] *Smithfield Foods v United Food and Comm Workers*, 584 F Supp 2d 838 (ED VA 2008).

[85] No restitution claim was made, although it may be viable; if so, *Food Lion* could be distinguished on the grounds that reputational damages are not sought but rather recovery of ABC's gain from a wrongful act.

[86] *Dietemann v Time Inc*, 449 F2d 245, 250 (9th Cir 1971).

[87] Food safety and purity has a high place in the protective pecking order. Recall that negligence law, even in the days of laissez faire in the 19th century, moved to protect the consuming public and their health: see *Donoghue v Stevenson* [1932] AC 562; *MacPherson v Buick Motor Co*, 111 NE 1050 (1916).

[88] For a nuanced treatment, see LB Lidsky, 'Prying, Spying, and Lying: Newsgathering and What the Law Should Do About It' (1999) 73 *Tulane Law Review* 173.

The boundaries of defamation have been carefully guarded by the courts intent on preventing plaintiffs from circumventing the strong constitutional protections of *New York Times v Sullivan*. At the same time, the courts have been willing to protect privacy interests through damages, provided newsworthiness is weighed in the balance. As in much of American tort law, the courts are flexible in choosing the tort under which privacy will be protected. Often here, trespass to land may be the cause of action, and accordingly, as Varuhas would say, the invasion is actionable per se: it does not depend on proof of harm. However, the measure of the damages will reflect the characterisation of the nature of the harm and the interests at play in the balance of the interests, both private and public.

Take cases at the opposite end of the spectrum where the press is not involved. Here the protective role of remedies can be muscular. In *Nader v General Motors*,[89] the defendant engaged in a campaign of harassment, including lengthy surveillance, probing inquiries about the plaintiff's political, social, racial and religious views and beliefs, and his sexual proclivities, and attempts to entrap him in illicit relationships. The court, applying DC law, found this constituted a breach of the plaintiff's privacy. The opinion did not consider the remedies. To be completely protective of Nader's rights, a court would grant both damages and an injunction against the defendant's continuing infringing actions. Where the intrusion knowingly invades property rights and does not hinder unduly proper newsgathering, injunctive relief is available.[90] No intrusion such as picketing can be enjoined by reference to its content.[91] Prior restraint is invoked where the media are restrained from publishing newsworthy material.[92] In another case involving harassment Jacqueline Onassis and her children were tracked and photographed constantly by Galella, a paparazzo. A temporary restraining order had been issued against Galella, the terms of which he flouted. The court found that the injunction had been appropriately drawn to protect the plaintiff. The functioning of the press was not unduly crimped.[93] The malicious or knowingly tortious nature of the breach will swell the damages that may be awarded in addition to the injunction. Where a plaintiff was sexually harassed, the conduct could be regarded as a breach of privacy and would be productive of punitive damages.[94] Again, we may observe the balance between private rights and public interests in the remedies to be given. The harassing behaviour of General Motors in the *Nader* case in fact was designed to repress the release of information to the public about the inferior and dangerous defects of its motor vehicles. Although this is not within the First

[89] *Nader v General Motors*, 255 NE2d 765 (1970).

[90] *Webb v Glenbrook Owners Ass'n Inc*, 298 SW3d 374, 392 (Tex App Dallas 2009); *Wolfson v Lewis*, 924 F Supp 1413, 1435 (ED Pa 1996).

[91] *City of Seven Hills v Ayran Nations*, 667 NE2d 942 949 (Ohio 1996).

[92] *Cox Broadcasting v Cohn*, 420 US 469 (1975).

[93] The case is usually looked at as an example of the court's discretion in framing injunctions. For general principles see *Madsen v Women's Health Center Inc*, 512 US 753 (1994).

[94] *CP&B Enterprises v Mellert*, 762 So2d 356 (2000) (awarding $25,000 in compensatory damages and $250,000 in punitive damages).

Amendment's free speech purview, since General Motors is a private actor, it is clearly a public factor to be weighed in granting an injunction. It also supports the goal of aligning a remedy to deter and punish conscious wrongdoing. The courts in the usual vein do not make a distinction between punitive or exemplary damages and aggravated damages. The two are rolled in together, leading to some confusion.[95] In a warrantless police search, punitive damages would only be awarded if malice or improper motive were conclusively proved by the plaintiff. Separately, and correctly, the court could award damages for hurt feelings, anxiety or embarrassment. No special damages would have to be proved.[96]

C. Public Disclosure of Private Facts

In this category, the potential of the tort is at its maximum in colliding with First Amendment principles. Some courts have held that the delicate flower of the First Amendment can only be protected by not recognising the tort.[97] The Supreme Court in *Cox Broadcasting Corp v Cohn*[98] left unanswered the 'question whether truthful publication of very private matters unrelated to public affairs could be constitutionally proscribed'. The answer to the question is nowadays put in terms of whether the material is 'newsworthy or in the public interest'.

The line is drawn according to a community standard. The *Restatement (Second) of Torts*[99] states that 'publicity ceases to be the giving of information to which the public is entitled, and becomes morbid and sensational prying into private lives for its own sake, with which a reasonable member of the public, with decent standards, would say he had no concern'. Much time and effort has gone into drawing the line.

The tort in this guise has the function of protecting an individual's dignity, and also the function of promoting an individual's ability to live fully and fruitfully in society without being dogged by the past. In other words, he or she may begin afresh. This social function is confirmed by the wide and relevant publicity requirement.[100] The classic case stressing the force of the fresh starts is *Melvin v Reid*,[101] wherein the California Supreme Court found that the plaintiff, who had been a prostitute and was tried for murder and acquitted in a notorious case, had a good cause of action where her identity was revealed in a movie, *The Red Kimono*, which disclosed her name, claiming the film was a true account. After the trial,

[95] C Sharkey, 'Punitive Damages as Societal Damages' (2003) 113 *Yale LJ* 347 (discussing punitive damages as properly incorporating wider harm that should be recognised in the calculation).

[96] *Monroe v Darr*, 559 P2d 322 (Kansas 1977) (warrantless police search of plaintiff renter's apartment).

[97] *Hall v Post*, 372 SE2d 711 (NC 1988).

[98] *Cox Broadcasting Corp v Cohn*, 420 US 469 (1975).

[99] Section 652D, comment h.

[100] *Pachowitz v Ledoux*, 666 NW2d 88, 97 (Wis App 2003); *Restatement (Second) of Torts*, § 652D comment a.

[101] *Melvin v Reid*, 112 Cal App 285 (1931).

she had lived an 'exemplary, virtuous, honorable and religious life'. Likewise, the courts have been sensitive to the privacy of victims of sexual abuse, even though the newsworthiness quotient is high.[102] Persons who voluntarily put themselves in the public eye, or indeed are swept up in an event of public interest, are regarded as ceding a large measure of privacy.[103] In America, as elsewhere, the private sexual peccadillos of persons of some fame are a target of the press goaded by public thirst.[104] The nexus between private lives and public activities varies according to time and place. Changing modes of creating and translating information – cameras, video, possibly drones, voice-overs and aggressive journalism – have an impact on the zone of life that can be expected to be private and sealed off from the prying eyes of the press.

Of paramount importance in the United States was the change of judicial mood wrought by *New York Times v Sullivan* in 1964.[105] The time-honoured idea in defamation law that publishers ought to bear the costs of harmful publications was changed on a dime. The ability of an aggrieved defamed person to hold the press liable was severely curtailed on the reasoning that persons, particularly public officials and figures, ought to bear the costs to the end of not putting a chill on free speech. The marketplace of ideas rather than the court room was given the task of encouraging accurate information. It was inevitable that privacy interests, to the extent they protected the individual, would give way to the full force of such a constitutional gale. The privacy interest in *Melvin v Reid*, of promoting the end of social rehabilitation, could not stand against the presumption that society is better off with true information.[106]

Accordingly, the tort, in this guise, has become less certain and is subject to direct attack as not being consistent with First Amendment jurisprudence. The Supreme Court has stopped short of constitutional condemnation.[107] The reluctance to let go of privacy completely is seen also in *Bartnicki v Vopper*.[108]

[102] *People v Bryant*, 94 P3d 624 (Colo 2004).

[103] The reasoning is redolent of defamation jurisprudence flowing from *Sullivan* (n 6) in finding that public figures deserve little protection because they voluntarily put themselves before the public: *Heath v Playboy Enterprises Inc*, 732 F Supp 1145 (1990).

[104] In the UK, the President of the Fédération Internationale de l'Automobile, Max Mosley, brought a successful action: *Mosley v News Group Newspapers Ltd* [2008] EMLR 20; see further JE Stanley, 'Max Mosley and the English Right of Privacy' (2011) 10 *Washington University Global Studies Law Review* 641. As noted in the text to nn 112–17, in the discussion of Gawker and harassment online, the US courts have taken an admonishing attitude even to public figures. But the availability of a super injunction flies in the face of established American doctrine. Contrast the approach in the UK: M Tugendhat, 'Privacy Injunctions and the Rule of Law', in ch 2 of this book.

[105] D Partlett, 'New York Times v Sullivan at Fifty: Defamation in Separate Orbits' in Kenyon (ed) (n 24) 58.

[106] Take Chief Justice Roberts in *McCutcheon v Federal Election Commission*, 134 S Ct 1434 (2014), the second campaign financing case, arguing that individual dignity is supported by a maximal reading of the First Amendment (at 1448).

[107] *Florida Star v BJF*, 491 US 524 (1989). But Justice White was sceptical. Joined by the Chief Justice and Justice O'Connor, Justice White stated: '[T]he trend in "modern" jurisprudence has been to eclipse an individual's right to maintain private any truthful information that the press wished to publish … Today we hit the bottom of the slippery slope.'

[108] *Bartnicki v Vopper*, 532 US 514 (2001).

The defendants broadcast taped cellphone conversations that had been illegally intercepted. The tape had been left with Vopper, a radio talk-show host who, knowing of its illegal origin, broadcast it, revealing the plaintiff's telephone numbers, together with private information about the teacher's union tactics in a labour dispute. The majority of the Justices found that the legality of garnering the tape was critical. Vopper used it but did not illegally purloin it. In addition, in the mind of Justices Breyer and O'Connor, the privacy interest was eroded by the threat of violence in the conversation, giving weight to free speech. The dissenting Justices noted that the finding undermined the deterrence of illegal scanning, the purpose of the criminal statute. The insecurity of conversations would reduce the flow of information. Defendants could prosper, moreover, from the fruit of the illegality.[109] The trend is unmistakable. The requirements of 'offensiveness and newsworthiness' leave little room to protect private and true facts.[110] The state interest in protecting the information must be compelling or paramount to repress the publication of true facts, as where the information is protected by the state's witness protection program.[111] It follows that for claims established, free speech would still cast a shadow, restricting the measure of damages to non-reputational foreseeable consequences.

This at least is the accepted wisdom. Yet some recent cases show that the disclosure tort has life in two circumstances, both in the realm of sexual behaviour; for some it is the emerging field of sexual privacy that is stimulated by the power of the Internet and social media. The first is the publication of revenge porn and other online sexual assault, where the traditional role of tort law is clear. The harm is real and often intended.[112] The second carries the same concerns without the same animus. It concerns use of videos of sexual behaviour where the public has an abiding but prurient interest. A famous and notorious case is *Gawker*, which resulted in a win for Hulk Hogan, the well-known wrestler.[113] His real name is Terry Bollea. The media website Gawker published images of the plaintiff in a sex act with his 'best friend's wife'. His erstwhile best friend was known as Bubba the Love Sponge. The litigation was financed by Peter Theil, a Silicon Valley billionaire, who had a virulent distaste for the publications of Gawker's proprietor. Theil had

[109] RA Smolla, 'Information as Contraband: The First Amendment and Liability for Trafficking in Speech' (2002) 96 *Northwestern University Law Review* 1099, arguing that the Justices had endorsed the tort with its newsworthiness defence.

[110] *Haynes v Alfred A Knopf*, 8 F3d 1222 (7th Cir 1993). Posner J trenchantly discusses the law. The publication uncovering the plaintiff's distant past was protected speech, even though it was deeply offensive, where the public had a legitimate interest. See also *Gates v Discovery Communications Inc*, 101 P3d 552 (Calif 2004) (publication of crime committed 12 years before).

[111] *Capra v Thoroughbred Racing Ass'n of North America Inc*, 787 F2d 463 (9th Cir 1986) (vindication of a paramount public interest: here to protect identity in the federal witness protection program).

[112] M Talbot, 'Taking Trolls to Court' *The New Yorker* (5 December 2016).

[113] *Bollea v Gawker Media*, 105 US PQ 2d 1496, 40 Media L Rep 2601, 2012 WL 5509624 (MD Fla 2012). Unpublished documents: No 12-02348 (MD Fla). See R Holiday, *Conspiracy: Peter Theil, Hulk Hogan, Gawker, and the Anatomy of Intrigue* (London, Portfolio, 2018), describing the extraordinary events and personalities involved in this litigation.

also been the subject of publications. The litigation shows the power of the jury in the American court room and the criticality of high-level legal representation. In essence, Bollea was able to avoid summary judgment and get to the jury by showing that the tape had no connection to his public persona. Hogan was a wrestler, with everything that portrayed; that character was loud, overbearing and exhibited sexual braggadocio. The private sphere was Bollea's, a somewhat retiring, self-conscious and sensitive person, with a compelling personal story of the Horatio Alger type so admired by Americans. He should be entitled as a private person to keep his sex life private. To a private person the depiction was entirely despicable and added nothing to the news in which the public would have a legitimate interest.[114] Of importance would be the fact that a person had injected himself into public life and put his own persona into the public marketplace. As Hogan, Bollea had certainly become a general public figure. But intimate images of his sex life were not voluntarily injected into the public sphere.[115] He had not put his sex life in issue either in boasting about his conquests, or in insisting on his faithfulness, a perception that could have been legitimately corrected. The Florida court dismissed on constitutional grounds Bollea's application for a temporary injunction to prevent distribution of the sex tape by Gawker.[116] However, damages were very high, sufficient to cause the financial demise of Gawker and Denton the owner. The jury awarded $55 million in compensatory damages, and an additional $60 million for emotional distress. (The division here does not accord with the usual nomenclature, which would include both heads as compensatory.) In a further hearing, a sum of $25.1 million was awarded in punitive damages. Negotiations followed that reduced the quantum; the damages were nevertheless financially ruinous.[117]

One last category arises from breach of confidence, as Commonwealth scholars would describe the action. For non-American readers, the jurisprudence dwelling in equity is well known and has been fully explicated by Justice Paul Finn.[118] Information given over in a confidential relationship may be impressed with a duty incumbent on the person receiving the information. He or she may not reveal that information to a third party.[119] The duty was in equity, inviting equitable remedies. The expansion by the English court of the duty to a wide class of recipients of the

[114] *Vigil v Time Inc*, 527 F2d 1122, 1129 (1979) (the line is crossed when 'publicity ceases to be the giving of information to which the public is entitled, and becomes a morbid and sensational prying into private lives for its own sake, with which a reasonable member of the public, with decent standards, would say that he had no concern').

[115] *Bret Michaels v IEG Inc*, 5 F Supp 2d 823 (SD Cal 1998) (sex tapes of Pamela Anderson, a famous model, were private and not newsworthy).

[116] *Gawker Media v Bollea*, 129 So 3d 1196 (Dist Ct App 2d, 2014) (rejecting the application for a temporary restraining order on the basis of prior restraint under the First Amendment).

[117] For a detailed and fascinating account, see J Toobin, 'When Truth is Not Enough: Sex Tapes, the Demise of Gawker, and What the Trump Era Means for the First Amendment' *The New Yorker* (19 and 26 December 2016) 96.

[118] P Finn, *Fiduciary Obligations: 40th Anniversary Republication with Additional Essays* (Annandale, NSW, Federation Press, 2016) 141–81.

[119] See the discussion by R Stevens, 'Damages for Wrongdoing in the Absence of Loss', in ch 4 of this book.

information forms the basis of the English cause of action for breach of privacy.[120] American courts and commentators only recently recognised the equitable roots of the action in breach of confidence.[121] In the following cases the courts have loosely defined the causes of action as a tort of breach of confidentiality, or as invasion of privacy.

In *Humphreys v First Interstate Bank of Oregon*,[122] the plaintiff birth mother agreed to place her child, born out of wedlock, for adoption. An anonymous adoption was effected. Later, the child approached the doctor who had delivered her, seeking her birth mother's identity. The doctor gave her a letter to the hospital, which enabled her to obtain release of the sealed information by falsely stating that the plaintiff had taken Diethylstilbestrol (DES) during pregnancy and that her daughter needed the records for medical reasons. The plaintiff was distressed when located, and sued the doctor's estate (he had died) for invasion of privacy and for unauthorised disclosure of the confidential information. The court held that there could be no recovery for invasion of privacy, but held for the plaintiff, awarding her damages, on her confidentiality claim. Similarly, in *Doe v Portland Health Centers*,[123] a hospital employee disclosed information about a patient's suicide attempt to a person who subsequently publicised it widely. The patient's mother sued in breach of confidentiality and invasion of privacy, among other causes of action. The court agreed that plaintiff had no action under invasion of privacy, because the defendant's disclosure was not made to the public or a large number of persons. She also failed in her confidentiality action, since it was not her confidence that had been breached, although her claim in breach of contract, and the duty arising therefrom, was allowed to proceed.

Not all courts have maintained the distinction between the two actions: often the action, in substance for breach of confidence, is labelled an action for invasion of privacy.[124] The confluence of the two actions may be observed in the following cases on disclosure of HIV status: in *Behringer*, disclosure of a private fact that may give rise to a breach of confidentiality claim;[125] in *Urbaniak*, disclosure may also give rise to an invasion of privacy claim.[126] The latter case was characterised as one of 'public disclosure of true, embarrassing private fact'. But a better characterisation would be as a breach of confidence claim, where the information was disclosed

[120] *Campbell v Mirror Group Newspapers* [2004] 2 AC 457; *Douglas v Hello!* [2006] QB 125.

[121] DJ Solove and NM Richards, 'Privacy's Other Path: Recovering the Law of Confidentiality' (2007) 96 *Georgetown Law Review* 123.

[122] *Humphreys v First Interstate Bank of Oregon*, 298 Or 706, 696 P2d 527 (1985).

[123] *Doe v Portland Health Centers*, 99 Or App 423, 782 P2d 446 (1989).

[124] See *Doe v Roe*, 93 Misc 2d 201, 400 NYS2d 668 (1977) (psychiatrist published a book recording the plaintiff patient's thoughts, feelings and fantasies; actionable although patient not named).

[125] *Estate of Behringer v Medical Center at Princeton*, 249 NJ Super 597, 592 A2d 1251 (1991) (hospital failed to preserve confidentiality of HIV antibody test results of the patient).

[126] *Urbaniak v Newton*, 226 Cal App 3d 1128, 277 Cal Rptr 354 (1991) (disclosure of HIV status by the defendant physician violated privacy rights of the plaintiff when information was revealed by the plaintiff to protect others who might come into contact with the examining instrument).

within a relationship of confidence constituted by the physician–patient relationship. Information on a patient's HIV status generated within the relationship falls squarely within the duty of confidence.

The action in breach of confidence may arise from a fiduciary relationship between the parties or from a confidential relationship.[127] In the United States, the accumulating law, forgetting or ignoring equitable roots, has been conceptualised as providing a new action in tort: the relationship establishes a tort duty of confidentiality[128] based on the relationship established between the person entrusting the information and the person receiving it. The courts often have a shot-gun approach, allowing the pleading of breaches of privacy from statute to common law and generally overlooking that that division may clarify available remedies. Thus, in *Doe v Roe*,[129] the Supreme Court of New York dealt with the disclosure of revelations in the psychiatrist–patient relationship, made by a husband and wife, of their sexual life. The defendants had published a book that thinly covered the plaintiffs' identities. The Court found that the New York privacy statute prevented punitive damages but, having determined that damages would be inadequate, held that profits on the publication should be disgorged and an injunction given to prevent further publication of the book.

The courts have addressed the First Amendment's fit within breach of confidence. In *Cohen v Cowles Media Company*,[130] the plaintiff gave information about a political candidate to reporters of the defendant newspapers, conditioned upon the promise that his identity would remain confidential. The defendant newspapers published stories identifying the plaintiff as the source of the information. The plaintiff was fired by his employer. The majority found the plaintiff to have a good cause of action in damages for the loss occasioned by the breach. The Court's opinion distinguished *The Florida Star*[131] line of cases, which held that reporting the identity of a sexual assault victim while prohibited by statute was protected when the records had been given over mistakenly by the police. The disclosure clearly breached the plaintiff's privacy, secured by the statutory protection. Yet the publication, having lawfully reached the defendant's hands, and hence the public domain, was constitutionally protected. The distinguishing mark in *Cohen* was that Minnesota law 'simply requires those making promises to keep them'. It was a neutrally applicable law that had no reference to content. In the same vein, in *Ruzicka v Conde Nast Publications Inc*,[132] *Glamour* magazine published a story about therapist–patient sexual abuse. The plaintiff gave information to the story's author on condition that she not be identified or identifiable. The story was published, changing the plaintiff's name but supplying details allowing

[127] *Horne v Patton*, 291 Ala 701 (1973) (physician revealing information).
[128] Note, 'Breach of Confidence: An Emerging Tort' (1982) 82 *Columbia Law Review* 1426.
[129] *Doe v Roe* (n 124).
[130] *Cohen v Cowles Media Company*, 501 US 663 (1991).
[131] *Florida Star v BJF*, 491 US 524 (1989).
[132] *Ruzicka v Conde Nast Publications Inc*, 999 F2d 1319 (8th Cir 1993).

a reasonable recipient of the communication to identify her. (She was the only female law student or lawyer serving on the Minnesota Task Force Against Sexual Abuse.) Liability was based on a promissory estoppel theory. Contract damages would place the plaintiff in the position she would have been in if the promise had been observed. Thus, if she lost employment opportunities, those would have been recoverable. But to so characterise the cause of action crimps the damages usually available in privacy invasions. American courts have usually been reluctant to give damages for emotional distress in breach of contract. If the promise is one to assume a duty to protect the emotional and physical wellbeing of the promisee, liability may reside in tort. The failure to perform could be construed as a misrepresentation of fact.[133] The case could be seen as the obligee's profiting from a misrepresentation of fact, and in consequence, profits garnered could be sought in a breach of confidence claim.[134]

In a special group of cases, the government typically contracts with its employees to keep information secret. An employee subject to such a contract occasionally, as we know, discloses the information. Is the employee (or former employee) liable for breach of confidence? Can a publisher of the information, knowing of its confidential nature, be held liable? May that publisher be enjoined from publication? These issues were aired in *United States v Marchetti*[135] and *United States v Snepp*.[136] The English and Commonwealth courts in the *Spycatcher* litigation wrestled with the same issues, when a former MI5 agent in retirement in Tasmania wrote a book disclosing intelligence secrets. The British Government waged a global campaign to suppress the publication: *Attorney-General v Guardian Newspapers (No 2)*.[137] An injunction will not be awarded where such would be futile, as where the information has been widely disseminated.[138]

In terms of remedies, if it is conceded that the action is entirely in conformity with constitutional constraints, the traditional coercive remedy of injunction ought to be available as upholding an obligation that will maximise the flow of information. The injunction may prevent the disclosure of the information, which is often the details of plaintiffs' sex lives. In a development deeply surprising to American lawyers, the English courts, as several chapters in this book point out, have invented a particularly muscular remedy – the super-injunction – in such

[133] *City of New York v Lead Indus Ass*, 241 AD2d 387 (NY App Div 1997). The statement relied upon, albeit indirect, may then be regarded as a misfeasance upon which to base a duty in tort. The measure of damages will be limited by the usual concepts surrounding causation.

[134] W Farnsworth, *Restitution* (Chicago, IL, University of Chicago Press, 2014) 64.

[135] *United States v Marchetti*, 466 F2d 1309 (4th Cir 1972), cert denied: 409 US 1063 (1972) (former CIA agent revealed secrets in book in violation of agreement).

[136] *United States v Snepp*, 897 F2d 138 (4th Cir 1990) (similar facts).

[137] *Attorney-General v Guardian Newspapers (No 2)* [1990] 1 AC 109.

[138] But contrast the insistence of the UK court in *A-G v Guardian Newspapers* (ibid), maintaining the injunction despite the widespread dissemination (and see now also *PJS v News Group Newspapers Ltd* [2016] UKSC 26). The High Court of Australia took an opposite view: *Attorney-General (United Kingdom) v Heinemann Publishers Australia Pty Ltd* (1987) 61 ALJR 612.

cases. A court may order that the identity of the plaintiff be kept secret.[139] Where damages are the appropriate remedy, the scope of recovery in terms of compensation may be confined if they rest on a claim that the plaintiff's reputation has been besmirched by the publication. If the publication is of and concerning a public figure, the actual malice standard will apply. In the Hulk Hogan/Gawker case, the plaintiff was able to persuade the court that he was a private individual in his sex life, as he had not injected that subject into the public arena. Embarrassment and humiliation not a product of reputational loss are recoverable for breach of privacy.

On the other hand, the contractual relationship is one of good faith. A promisor may opportunistically take advantage of later changed circumstances. (No one can anticipate and contract for all contingencies in long-term contracts.) In order to shore up the relationship, to inculcate trust, a remedy in damages beyond the conventional is called for: an accounting of profits is appropriate. In the United States, as in the Commonwealth, a person who has signed a contract to keep information confidential, as does a CIA agent, may be stripped of any profits on sales of books he or she publishes that use the information. The remedy is protective of the interest where the plaintiff's harm is impossible to show in court. American courts in a broader way are beginning to award such wrongful gain more often as a remedy. They have been spurred by the adoption by the American Law Institute of section 39 of the *Restatement (Third) of Restitution and Unjust Enrichment*.[140] The rationale is to devise a remedy that will help to ensure the maintenance of mutually advantageous relationships where the ex-post forces to exploit the relationship loom large.[141] The tort of inducement to breach of contract has the same rationale, allowing essentially for tortious damages against a defendant who interferes with such relational contracts. The remedy obliges an intending inducer to bargain with the promisee.[142] These super-compensatory recoveries are justifiable in protecting contractual/property rights. The profits unjustly garnered are subject to a constructive trust to effectuate recovery.[143] On the other hand, courts will set their face against even compensatory damages where free-speech rights are impinged upon.

Punitive damages have been a particular focus of the US Supreme Court in testing their compatibility with due process under the Fourteenth Amendment of

[139] See, eg, M Tugendhat, 'Privacy Injunctions and the Rule of Law' in ch 2 of this book; R Stevens, 'Damages for Wrongdoing in the Absence of Loss' in ch 4 of this book. American readers would immediately see this as anathema. And of course, as Stevens points out, even cloistered Oxford dons knew the identity of the plaintiff. The subject has been much discussed in the Commonwealth.

[140] See *Kansas v Nebraska and Colorado*, 135 S Ct 1042 (2015). The finding that benefits from breach should be disgorged because of opportunism, by Nebraska under § 39 of the *Restatement*, was criticised by Chief Justice Roberts in his opinion as an example of the American Law Institute straying far outside its mission of restating the law: ibid at 1069.

[141] The formal argument to ground such reparation is founded on agency-cost theory that underpins broad restitutionary recoveries in breaches of fiduciary relations.

[142] D Partlett, 'The Republican Model and Punitive Damages' (2004) 41 *San Diego Law Review* 1409.

[143] See *Patton v Mid-Continent Systems Inc*, 841 F2d 742 (7th Cir 1988).

the Constitution. The Court has insisted that they are to punish a proven arrogant disregard of the rights of the plaintiff. They are reviewable so as to avoid arbitrariness under substantive due process requirements of the Fourteenth Amendment of the US Constitution. The Court requires a review of the award to measure it as comporting with the guideposts of reprehensibility, the ratio between the compensatory damages and punitive damages, and the disparity between civil penalties in comparable cases and the punitive damages.[144] Some States have reformed their law to further control the treatment and availability of such damages.[145] This is not the place to retrace the morass this intrusion by the Supreme Court has created. Breach of privacy actions have not featured prominently in the theatre of punitive damages. It will be immediately observable that the availability of punitive damages in the absence of compensatory damages in some breach of privacy cases ill fits the second proportionality guidepost, which requires a low ratio between the actual or potential harm suffered and the punitive damages award.[146] If the damages for invasion of the right are nominal, as we have already noted, the ratio makes no sense. Yet an arrogant and contumelious disregard of a person's privacy may warrant censure through the imposition of super-compensatory damages, even in the absence of proven actual harm.[147]

D. False Light

Prosser conceptualised a group of cases as being the fourth category of privacy. They may be described as placing a person in a false light in the public eye. Drawing on the old English case of *Lord Byron v Johnston*,[148] the *Restatement (Second) of Torts* explains that the interest to be protected is 'not being made to appear before the public … otherwise than he is'. Lord Byron was able to enjoin the circulation of a bad poem that had been attributed to his pen. It is an action that is close to defamation, in the sense that such falsity diminishes a person in the eyes of others

[144] *State Farm Mutual Automobile Ins Co v Campbell*, 538 US 408 (2003).

[145] *Cheatham v Pohl*, 789 NE2d 467 (Ind 2003) (reviewing the constitutionality of the Indiana provision that splits the award of punitive damages between the plaintiff and a State fund to compensate the victims of violent crimes). In Arizona, the State constitution was amended to prohibit illegal aliens from recovering punitive damages: Ariz Rev Stat Constitution, Art 11, s 35. See also D Partlett, 'Punitive Damages: Legal Hot Zones' (1996) 56 *Louisiana Law Review* 781; see *Zaffuto v City of Hammond*, 308 F3d 485 (5th Cir 2002) ('punitive damages for breach of privacy are not allowed under Louisiana law in absence of a particular state statute') (quoting *Fowler v Western Union Telegraph Co*, 357 So 2d 1305, 1309 (La App 3d Cir 1978)).

[146] *Campbell* (n 144). The requirement of reasonable relation to the compensatory award is commonly found in directions to the jury, although the guideline is sometimes firmer, eg Florida Stat, s 768.73 (greater of three times compensatory or $500,000, except in certain circumstances when it is greater than four times or $2 million). Some impose a cap, eg Va Code Ann, s 8.01-38.1 ($350,000).

[147] eg *Mathias v Accor Econ Lodging Inc*, 347 F3d 672 (7th Cir 2003) (applying Illinois law). Posner J emphasises the need for punitive damages where the scope of compensable damages would be inadequate to promote private enforcement of clear wrongs. In these cases, public enforcement is too costly and generally not 'worth the candle' (ibid 677).

[148] *Lord Byron v Johnston* (1816) 35 ER 851.

in the community. The privacy aspect turns on the right of an individual to control the spread of false statements about him or her; to correct the way that person is presented to the world.[149] A false light claim in this sense is a 'natural extension' of the right to privacy.[150] Thus it promotes social cooperation upon the assumption of true and accurate information. Most of the American commentary has been directed to the question of whether the standards of defamation actions have been imported into false light cases. The arcane issues are imported to the tort, such as: the status of the plaintiff – public figure/official or private person – and matters of public concern import the requirement, or not, of proof of malice on convincing evidence.[151]

For our purposes the question is whether proof of damage is required, or may it be assumed? The answer varies. The Ohio Court, in *Welling v Weinfeld*, describing the elements of the cause of action, did not require pleading and proof of actual damages suffered from the invasion of privacy. Other courts require the plaintiff to prove that actual damage was caused, but in one case this was satisfied by demonstrating a 'diminished standing in the community, humiliation, or emotional distress'.[152] At common law, once the plaintiff had established that he or she was defamed, damage was assumed. Damages are said to be at large. Under the *Gertz*[153] standard, in US law, a private plaintiff must establish, inter alia, actual damage and fault (negligence) if the publication was of 'public concern'. If the plaintiff is a public official or figure, he or she must show, in addition, actual malice.[154] The plaintiff, private or public, must also prove falsity, which at common law was assumed.[155] If the action is sounded in false light, the plaintiff must still hew to the constitutional requirements in defamation law.[156] The harm, however, will be tied to showing false light, but will by necessity show the plaintiff's diminished social standing resulting from the offending statement.

Once the constitutional hurdles have been surmounted, the plaintiff may obtain full compensatory damages and super-compensatory (punitive) damages if the publication was made with arrogant disregard of the plaintiff's rights, which includes actual malice. The courts here reflect a rare retributive purpose. As in defamation, an irony stalks American law: the chances of success in navigating the eye of the needle for substantive grounding of a false light case are statistically small[157] but the rewards in terms of damages are substantial. The remedies are

[149] I thank Jason Varuhas for this suggestion.

[150] *Welling v Weinfeld*, 866 NE 2d 1051, 1053, 1057 (Ohio 2007).

[151] *Time Inc v Hill*, 385 US 374, 397 (1967).

[152] *West v Media General Convergence Inc*, 53 SW3d 640, 648 (Tenn 2001).

[153] *Gertz v Robert Welch Inc*, 418 US 323 (1974).

[154] The availability of nominal damages has not been decided: it should be favoured if the law aims to vindicate reputations or accurate information. The court could render what is in essence a declaratory judgment, thus vindicating the interest at stake while not trenching upon free speech through a damages-rich liability rule. This was discussed in *Hearst v Hughes*, 466 A2d 486 (Md 1983).

[155] *Philadelphia Newspapers v Hepps*, 475 US 767 (1986).

[156] *Hill* (n 151).

[157] D Logan, 'Libel Law in the Trenches: Reflections on Current Data on Libel Litigation' (2001) 86 *Virginia Law Review* 503 (citing statistics on libel litigation demonstrating a very low success rate).

not nuanced to reflect the public/constitutional imperative of free speech protection. Indeed, on the contrary, reform of the remedial law has been thwarted by the First Amendment in refusing to countenance apology, right of response, retraction and other redress as restricting freedom of the press.[158] Defamation and its close cousin false light employ a strangely inconsistent balance of remedy and substantive cause of action to protect the interests at play.

IV. A Conclusion on Remedies

If the four categories are taken, what commonalities and differences are to be observed? Can we discern an elegance in this hedgehog? In the first place, the courts hew to the American realist tradition of loosely tying remedies to the interests protected by the substantive rights. The dualist tradition is observed. No broad systematic rationales are given; rather, remedies as secondary rights are founded on a tradition that declares rights heavily constrained by public values.[159] The interest at stake in privacy invasions is akin to that in the intentional torts, and is complete upon the invasion, except on those occasions where the right overlaps with the boundaries of defamation. Here proof of actual damage is demanded where the speech is of public concern. The invasion is otherwise actionable per se, the remedy and its measure in terms of damages being dependent on the departure of the breach from the observance of the social norm.

Second, the remedies fit Jimenez's four boxes: protection, restoration, coercion and retribution, and in their interaction with one another. To preserve individual dignity requires a remedy that protects, and which may draw upon restitution when damages cannot be estimated and will always fall short, coercion when an injunction will more fully protect, and retribution that will reflect a disapprobation of malicious invasions. To protect the property interest, we see the same interaction but with a greater willingness, amounting to a presumption, to employ injunctions, unless public policy obliges a retreat to an estimation of damages.[160] This would provide for compensation in lieu of injunction.[161]

[158] See DA Anderson, 'Is Libel Law Worth Reforming?' (1991) 140 *University of Pennsylvania Law Review* 487, 550–54 (viewing the present law as a failure in that it denies defamation victims any remedy, but at the same time it chills free speech by encouraging high litigation costs and occasional large judgments).

[159] The most pertinent example, beyond the confines of the topic at hand, is the willingness to fashion property rights and liability rules to fulfil public values or policy. See *Boomer v Atlantic Cement Co Inc*, 257 NE2d 870 (1970); L Kaplow and S Shavell, 'Property Rules versus Liability Rules: An Economic Analysis' (1996) 109 *Harvard Law Review* 713.

[160] ibid.

[161] The remedy is usually associated with nuisance law: see J Lewin, 'Compensated Injunctions and the Evolution of Nuisance Law' (1986) 71 *Iowa Law Review* 775. But because breach of privacy often involves speech with its special protection, such trade-offs are uncomfortable within prevailing American constitutional doctrine, which would not contemplate compensation for exposure to privacy invading First Amendment speech.

Third, throughout the tort's remedial apparatus, we have witnessed a tension between the private rights of the individual and the public imperative of free speech. In the United States, this has particular force through a muscular First Amendment jurisprudence. At times, injunctive relief, robust compensatory damages or disgorgement of profits would most adequately protect privacy interests in the dignitary and property guises. But the private rights are trumped by the public imperative of the First Amendment. This, we have observed, has led to an enfeebling of the tort of public disclosure of private facts, and to a reluctance to compensate fully for intrusion upon seclusion when newsworthiness is a factor.[162] Where the tort stands it is hemmed in by restrictive remedies, particularly the sacrosanct prohibition against prior restraint.[163] False light, which has been reduced to a fiefdom of defamation, shares, with it, the paradox of expansive damages constrained by the Cerberus of the need, in the case of public officials and figures, to prove by clear and convincing evidence that the publication was actuated by malice. It is with regard to those aspects of privacy that protect property rights and serve a public function of encouraging the production of information, most particularly appropriation of name or likeness in the commercial space, that the remedies are most robust, even to the issuing of preliminary and permanent injunctions.

Fourth, in reinforcement of my last conclusion, the major observation on American privacy law is that, despite its early acceptance and its influential endorsement by William Prosser, its vitality is remarkably fragile and its power is qualified by tentative remedies that weaken privacy at the 'sticking place' of free speech.[164] The institution of the jury has had an ironical influence on the formulation of remedies. The jury is the touchstone of the community values that the law of torts deeply reflects. The jury, articulating the ethos of the community, is a cornerstone of republican values as non-domination.[165] Yet unruly juries can, as *New York Times v Sullivan*[166] recognised, upset broader, more universal rights in the Constitution. Here the rhetoric of chilling free speech becomes critical. In the fashioning of the law of remedies, it is therefore noticeable that prescriptive rules are used to curb the wide discretions of the jury. Although privacy rights elsewhere in the common law world are more tentative and formative, remedies are unlikely to be impinged upon as thoroughly. The jury, in the rest of the common law world, has little role in most tort cases. Judges there view cases in an iterated game, and become sensitive to the stakes in setting damages. Juries do not have this advantage.[167] Moreover, other common law nations' jurisprudence exhibits more

[162] See nn 84–88.

[163] See n 116. In *Bollea*, the refusal to grant a temporary restraining order preventing the distribution of the sex tape acted to swell the quantum of damages recovered by Bollea, alias Hulk Hogan.

[164] Shakespeare's Lady Macbeth, when admonishing her wavering husband to murder Duncan, used the term to mean a steadfast and firm rock that does not yield.

[165] P Pettit, *Republicanism: A Theory of Freedom and Government* (Oxford, Oxford UP, 1997) 51–78.

[166] *Sullivan* (n 6).

[167] JF Blumstein, RR Bovbjerg and FA Sloan, 'Beyond Tort Reform: Developing Better Tools for Assessing Damages for Personal Injury' (1991) 8 *Yale Journal on Regulation* 171.

trust in governmental interventions in speech. The strongest coercive remedy, the injunction, is not the bête noir in Commonwealth law when free speech is at stake.

Fifth, in terms of privacy as a segment of tort law, throughout the development of the tort and the reflective remedies, the courts have striven to reason how rules and remedies will operate in society to accommodate citizens' expectations about operative norms.[168] Privacy is deeply imbedded, but it is not immutable. Ideas change with changes in information technology and the capacity of governments to capture and control data. The short history of tortious protection of privacy nicely shows the common law's strengths in the terms articulated at the outset of the chapter, that is, the artificial reason of the law. The law constructs community both locally, its moral base, and nationally, its rationalisation with governing public norms and legal efficiency.[169]

The American tort law of privacy instantiates that society's widely disparate balance of interests. Public values differ from those prevailing in other common law nations. Faith in government action is present in other nations, a faith eschewed by American political theory, practice and prejudice. To a remarkable degree American courts have collapsed the strongly individualistic and protean tort system into state action when liability concerning information is involved. There is a deep suspicion of local social norms, upon which rest the tort of privacy. Thus, defamation liability is seen as state action, akin to government fiat, and subject to suspicion concerning repression of information.[170] In private law, the jury is still ubiquitous; indeed, it is constitutionally mandated under the Sixth and Seventh Amendments (for the latter in 'suits at common law'), and is required under many State constitutions.[171] But local norms of community mix uneasily with constitutional commitments to a broad view of First Amendment values.[172] Tort rights are forfeited or reduced on the altar of the First Amendment for no compensation other than a lottery ticket in the marketplace of ideas.[173] I wrote at the end of section II of the battle line between free speech and human flourishing. These are consistent goals if First Amendment dogma is ameliorated to dovetail

[168] Tilley (n 8).

[169] ibid.

[170] F Schauer, 'On the Distinction Between Free Speech and Action' (2016) 65 *Emory Law Journal* 427 (discussing the difficulty of distinguishing legal regulation of speech from action).

[171] For discussion see RL Weaver, D Partlett, MB Kelly and WJ Cardi, *Remedies: A Contemporary Approach* (St Paul, MN, West, 2016) 87–108. Under the Seventh Amendment, the US courts have been obliged to differentiate between suits at common law and in equity.

[172] *Snyder v Phelps*, 562 US 443 (2011), dismissing the tort of intentional infliction of emotional distress as too loose and open-ended to provide a remedy comporting with the rigours of the First Amendment, wherein free speech of public concern should not be crimped. The harm long recognised by the common law visited upon grieving persons at a funeral was set aside as creating a risk to speech on such public matters. The remedy suggested by the Chief Justice, citing *Erznoznik v Jacksonville*, 422 US 205, 210–211 (1975), is for the 'viewer to avoid further bombardment of [his] sensibilities simply by averting [his] eyes'.

[173] The egalitarian foundations of the marketplace, that all may participate, are flouted in everyday experience, and the concept of debate leading to enlightenment is a chimera. See D Partlett, 'New York Times v Sullivan at Fifty Years: Defamation in Separate Orbits' in Kenyon (ed) (n 24) 74–75.

with the reality of individual flourishing in communities. It does seem fatuous to suggest a change of course in First Amendment jurisprudence. The force of the First Amendment juggernaut shows no signs of fatigue. Protective remedies have been and will continue to be crimped as a result.

This is American exceptionalism. The law of privacy and remedies shows how fundamental social norms have been shaped and changed. To take the law of battery: that intentional tort, in its practice and consequences, will vary from New York to London or Sydney for the reason of prevailing social norms.[174] Crocodile Dundee arriving in New York City will have to conform with the social norms of that city. Consent is socially constructed, presumed, in the intentional torts.[175] And so it is with the law of privacy and its accepted panoply of remedies. The American path will always be of great interest to outside observers, but its idiosyncratic public weighing of values should be recognised as creating an unreliable model to be applied elsewhere. Every hedgehog is elegant in its own way.

[174] *O'Brien v Cunard SS Co*, 28 NE 266 (Mass 1891).

[175] ibid. Consent may be implied to meet utilitarian ends in social coordination. The more intrusive the invasion, the more explicit consent must be: *Mohr v Williams*, 104 NW 12 (Minn 1905). For discussion, see S Hershovitz, 'The Search for a Grand Unified Theory of Tort Law' (2017) 130 *Harvard Law Review* 942 (disputing Ripstein's thesis on the inviolability of bodily integrity: A Ripstein, *Private Wrongs* (Cambridge, MA, Harvard UP, 2016)).

13

Remedies for Breach of Privacy in Canada

JEFF BERRYMAN*

I. Introduction

In 2012, the Ontario Court of Appeal quietly ushered into Ontario's common law a free-standing tort, intrusion upon seclusion. The tort can trace its parentage to the four torts delineated by Prosser in 1960. Prosser argued that within the law of privacy, there were to be recognised four distinct torts:

1. Intrusion upon the plaintiff's seclusion or solitude into his private affairs.
2. Public disclosure of embarrassing private facts about the plaintiff.
3. Publicity which places the plaintiff in a false light in the public eye.
4. Appropriation, for the defendant's advantage, of the plaintiff's name or likeness.[1]

Prosser also discussed both commonalities and divergence within the four torts. With respect to remedies for infringement, he noted that the first tort, intrusion, is clearly linked to the wrong of intentional infliction of mental distress and damages for non-pecuniary losses. The second and third torts engage reputation and are closely aligned to defamation, absent the defence of justification, because the defendant is liable for the publication of entirely truthful statements, and where the damages are at large. The fourth tort is similar to infringement of trademark, and engages remedies of account of profits and damages.[2]

In section II of this chapter, I first catalogue Canadian developments of Prosser's first two torts, intrusion upon seclusion based upon the decision in

* I wish to thank my research students, Mitchell Fournie and Adam Lawson, for their most helpful assistance in preparing this chapter. This paper was first delivered at the *International Workshop on Remedies for Breach of Privacy*, Faculty of Law, University of Melbourne, December 2016. I also appreciate the work of Jason Varuhas for his most helpful editing and comments.

[1] W Prosser, 'Privacy' (1960) 48 *California Law Review* 383, 389.

[2] ibid 409, 422.

Jones v Tsige[3] and then the tort of public disclosure of private facts.[4] In section III, I raise the issue of class actions in both privacy torts, and in section IV, I discuss some elements of injunctive relief and privacy.

II. Canadian Developments of Prosser's First Two Torts

A. What was Decided in *Jones v Tsige*?

The Ontario Court of Appeal decision in *Jones v Tsige* dealt only with intrusion upon seclusion. The defendant, Tsige, became involved in a relationship with the claimant's former husband, Uton Moodie. Both Tsige and Jones were employees of the Bank of Montreal but worked in different branches. Tsige used her workplace computer to access Jones's bank account on 174 occasions, ostensibly to see whether Uton Moodie was still making maintenance payments to Jones. Tsige maintained that she had a financial dispute with Moodie. After extensive discussion of developments in the protection of privacy and the particular tort of intrusion upon seclusion, Sharpe J, giving a unanimous decision, and paraphrasing the *Restatement (Second) of Torts*, described the key features of the new tort as:

1. That the defendant's conduct must be intentional, including recklessness.
2. That the defendant must have invaded without lawful justification the plaintiff's private affairs or concerns.
3. That a reasonable person would have regarded the invasion as highly offensive causing distress, humiliation or anguish, although proof of loss to a recognised economic interest is not an element of the cause of action.[5]

Sharpe J implied that such an action was actionable per se, as he indicated that 'proof of harm to a recognized economic interest is not an element of the cause of action'.[6] He also qualified the reach of this new tort to prevent a 'floodgate' of claims, by stating that 'only intrusions into matters such as one's financial or health records, sexual practices and orientation, employment, diary or private correspondence that, viewed objectively on a reasonable person standard, can be described as highly offensive'[7] were covered.

Sharpe J was clear to confine the court's actual ruling to the tort of intrusion upon seclusion, but throughout the discussion there is extensive reference to the

[3] *Jones v Tsige* (2012) 108 OR (3d) 241 (CA).

[4] Most privacy theorists agree that these two forms of the privacy interest dominate what is termed a right to privacy. See C Hunt, 'The Common Law's Hodgepodge of Privacy' (2015) 66 *University of New Brunswick Law Journal* 161.

[5] *Jones* (n 3) [71].

[6] ibid [71].

[7] ibid [72].

development of privacy, and to specific developments in other jurisdictions of the second tort, the public disclosure of private facts.[8] I believe this to be a clear signal from the court that such an action should also be brought to Ontario's shores.

Sharpe J supported the common law development with reference to four other Provinces that have enacted a statutory tort of privacy, but which have largely then left development of it to the respective courts, the statutes providing little in the way of prescriptive guidance.[9] In addition, he drew support from the plethora of privacy legislation of federal and provincial acts that have been geared towards the protection of personal data held by corporations or other public bodies. For example, in Ontario, in addition to the federal *Personal Information Protection and Electronic Documents Act* SC 2000, c 5,[10] there are the *Personal Health Information Protection Act 2004* SO 2004, c 3 (essentially covering health providers), the *Freedom of Information and Protection of Privacy Act* RSO 1990, c F.31 (essentially covering information held by government ministries, boards and agencies), the *Municipal Freedom of Information and Protection of Privacy Act* RSO 1990, c M.56 (essentially covering municipal governments, boards and agencies) and the *Consumer Reporting Act* RSO 1990, c C.33 (covering private consumer credit reporting agencies). Similar provisions prevail in the other Provinces.

Turning to the issue of remedy for breach of intrusion upon seclusion, Sharpe J took a novel, although predictable, approach to assessment of damages. He made a number of categorical statements. First, that proof of actual loss is not an element of the cause of action for intrusion upon seclusion. Second, where the damages fall under the head of non-pecuniary loss, the award of damages is symbolic or constitutes 'moral damages', awarded to vindicate rights or symbolise recognition

[8] In particular, Sharpe J discusses (ibid [64]) the New Zealand Court of Appeal's decision in *Hosking v Runting* [2004] NZCA 34, [109] (CA), which embraced two elements of the tort: (i) the existence of facts in respect of which there is a reasonable expectation of privacy; and (ii) that the publicity given to those facts must be considered highly offensive to an objective reasonable person. In addition, further references were made to the UK decision in *Campbell v Mirror Group Newspaper Ltd* [2004] 2 AC 457 (HL) and the Australian decision in *Lenah Games Meats Pty Ltd v Australian Broadcasting Corp* (2001) 185 ALR 1 (HCA), which deal with the public disclosure of private facts.

[9] British Columbia *Privacy Act* RSBC 1996 c 373, s 1; Saskatchewan *Privacy Act* RSS 1978, c P-24, s 2; Newfoundland *Privacy Act* RSNL 1990, c P-22, s 3; and Manitoba *Privacy Act* CCSM 1987, c P125, s 2(1). Manitoba is the only legislation that does not require the actions of the defendant to be 'wilful', but does require the infringement to be 'substantial or unreasonable'. Quebec adopts a civilian approach to privacy, where the right is enshrined in the notion of personhood: *Civil Code of Quebec* CQLR, c CCQ-1991, Art 3, 'Every person is the holder of personality rights, such as the right to life, the right to the inviolability and integrity of his person, and the right to the respect of his name, reputation and privacy.' See K Eltis, 'The Anglo-American/Continental Privacy Divide? How Civilian Personality Rights Can Help Reconceptualize the "Right to be Forgotten" Towards Greater Transnational Interoperability' (2016) 94 *Canadian Bar Review* 1.

[10] Section 3, a purposive section, states: 'The purpose of the Part is to establish, in an era in which technology increasingly facilitates the circulation and exchange of information, rules to govern the collection, use and disclosure of personal information in a manner that recognizes the right to privacy of individuals with respect to their personal information and the need of organizations to collect, use or disclose personal information for purposes that a reasonable person would consider appropriate in the circumstances.'

of infringement.[11] Third, awards of aggravated and exemplary damages were to be neither encouraged or excluded but are justified only in exceptional cases.[12]

With these three points in mind, Sharpe J endorsed an approach that quantified damages according to a 'conventional range', designed to ensure 'consistency, predictability, and fairness between one plaintiff and another'.[13] This approach was drawn from Waddams.[14] Sharpe J spent considerable time reviewing case law of analogous torts where a nascent form of intrusion upon seclusion had been part of the action, namely, cases drawn from trespass and nuisance. Sharpe J then analysed decisions under the respective Privacy Acts of the four Provinces that have such legislation, and in particular the Manitoba legislation, because that is the only Act to actually articulate damages quantification principles. The Act states:

> 4(2) In awarding damages in an action for a violation of privacy of a person, the court shall have regard to all the circumstances of the case including:
>
> (a) the nature, incidence and occasion of the act, conduct or publication constituting the violation of privacy of that person;
> (b) the effect of the violation of privacy on the health, welfare, social, business or financial position of that person or his family;
> (c) any relationship, whether domestic or otherwise, between the parties to the action;
> (d) any distress, annoyance or embarrassment suffered by that person or his family arising from the violation of privacy; and
> (e) the conduct of that person and the defendant, both before and after the commission of the violation of privacy, including any apology or offer of amends made by the defendant.

Sharpe J assembled the cases he discussed in two appendices attached to the judgment: Ontario damage awards; and damages awarded under provincial legislation. From this study, he determined a conventional range was up to $20,000, and that the provisions from the Manitoba *Privacy Act* should be used by later courts to guide assessment. In the case before the court, an award of $10,000 was justified. The actions of the defendant were deliberate and repeated, and arose from a complex and acrimonious domestic dispute. The plaintiff was very upset, but had suffered no public embarrassment or actual harm to her health or business interests. The defendant had apologised for her conduct and made genuine attempts to amend.[15]

[11] *Jones* (n 3) [74]–[75]. The term 'moral damages' was used by the Supreme Court of Canada to describe damages for mental distress arising as a result of wrongful dismissal causing distress from the manner of dismissal: *Honda Canada Inc v Keays* [2008] 2 SCR 362, [59].

[12] *Jones* (n 3) [88].

[13] ibid [75].

[14] S Waddams, *The Law of Damages*, looseleaf edn (Toronto, Canada Law Book, 2011) [10.05].

[15] *Jones* (n 3) [90].

Resort to a 'conventional range' has been adopted by a number of courts, particularly concerning the assessment of non-pecuniary damages.[16] Arguably, the approach adopted by the Supreme Court of Canada with respect to assessing non-pecuniary damages for personal injury has evolved into such an approach, although the range is considerably higher, somewhere in the vicinity of $350,000.[17] Other commentators have endorsed such an approach as a pragmatic solution for courts, particularly where assaults to dignity are the primary injury in the action.[18] The difficulty with a conventional range is that it allows the first litigant to the court to have an undue impact on setting the range. Similarly, without appropriate adjustment mechanisms, the range can be left behind general inflationary pressures and changes in social mores.[19] With the top of the range set at $20,000 in Ontario, litigants will likely have their actions heard in the Small Claims Court.[20]

B. Post-*Jones v Tsige* Decisions: Intrusion Upon Seclusion

Perhaps as expected, the adoption of a new tort has generated significant attention in practice circles, and pleadings of the action, as an accompanying cause with other actions, are frequently found. In most cases, the reported decisions are of these claims being struck out as having no prospect of success because the facts do not actually identify an intrusion upon seclusion, or because the intrusion does not meet the requisite level of 'highly offensive'. What is left are two decisions of the Ontario Superior Court of Justice and several arbitral decisions.

McIntosh v Legal Aid Ontario[21] shares remarkably similar facts to *Jones v Tsige*. In this case, the defendant, who worked for Legal Aid Ontario, accessed the plaintiff's case records. With this information, the defendant threatened to report the

[16] For example, see the work of the Ontario Human Rights Commission discussed in J Berryman, 'Remedies before Administrative Tribunals: What Can be Learned from the Common Law?' (2010) 24 *Canadian Journal of Administrative Law and Practice* 129, 148.

[17] See *Zurich Life Insurance Co v Branco* (2015) 460 Sask R 176 (CA). I have discussed this approach in J Berryman, 'Non-pecuniary Damages for Personal Injury: A Reflection on the Canadian Experience' in E Quill and R Friel (eds), *Damages and Compensation Culture* (Oxford, Hart Publishing, 2016) 95, and J Berryman, 'Rethinking Damages for Personal Injury: Is it Too Late to Take the Facts Seriously?' in R Sharpe and K Roach (eds), *Taking Rights Seriously* (Ottawa, Canadian Institute for the Administration of Justice, 2009) 167.

[18] See G Hammond, 'Beyond Dignity' in J Berryman and R Bigwood (eds), *The Law of Remedies: New Directions in the Common Law* (Toronto, Irwin Law, 2010) 171.

[19] Arguably, this is what happened in the UK with respect to non-pecuniary damages and personal injury, prompting the significant increase in these damages taken by the Court of Appeal in *Heil v Rankin* [2001] QB 272 (CA). Similarly in New Zealand, with respect to damages under the *Employment Relations Act* 2000, s 123(1)(c)(i), damages for humiliation, loss of dignity and injury to feelings, were significantly revised in *Telecom New Zealand Ltd v Nutter* [2004] 1 ERNZ 315 (CA).

[20] Under rule 57.05(1) of the *Rules of Civil Procedure*, plaintiffs risk a no cost ruling if they win but are awarded less than the monetary jurisdiction of the Small Claims Court, which is currently set at $25,000.

[21] *McIntosh v Legal Aid Ontario* 2014 ONSC 6136.

plaintiff to the Children's Aid Society, in an attempt to have the plaintiff's children removed from her. The defendant, who was the new girlfriend of the plaintiff's former boyfriend, had learnt, from accessing the plaintiff's legal aid file, that the plaintiff had previously been the subject of a Children's Aid file. The breach of privacy was investigated by the Office of Information and Privacy Commissioner of Ontario and by Ontario Legal Aid, who apologised to the plaintiff for the privacy breach. In addition to claiming general damages for breach of privacy, the plaintiff argued for a number of pecuniary special damages flowing from her loss of employment, which she attributed to the depression, anxiety and injury experienced as a result of the intrusion upon seclusion. The pecuniary claims were all dismissed on the bases that no causative chain linked the inability to continue employment with the intrusion upon seclusion. However, on the general damages, the court awarded $7,500 for the distress, annoyance and anxiety caused by the defendant, who had not offered an apology. The court characterised the invasion as affecting the plaintiff's emotional state in a minor fashion, and her physician's note indicated anxiety, and that this was a pre-existing condition.

The second decision is an appeal from a Small Claims Court, awarding $1,500 general damages for intrusion upon seclusion. In *Stevens v Walsh*[22] the plaintiff, an Air Canada pilot, brought an action against the defendant, also an Air Canada Pilot, alleging that she intruded upon his privacy when she disclosed records to the plaintiff's estranged wife about his flight schedules and movements. Air Canada operated a password-protected website that logged the flight schedules of pilots. Pilots could give access to the system to friends and family, which the plaintiff had done with respect to the defendant. The alleged intrusion was not that the defendant accessed the plaintiff's flight schedules, but that she gave them to the plaintiff's estranged wife, who used the material in subsequent divorce proceedings. The Small Claims Court judge awarded $1,500 for the intrusion, stressing the moral and symbolic nature of the damages. An appeal was brought on whether the grounds of the tort had been made out, the parties accepting that the amount of damages would be appropriate if the appeal were to be dismissed, which it was.

Three labour arbitration awards, two from outside Ontario (Alberta and British Columbia) and one from within, raise some interesting issues on how the damages can escalate because of the number of employees involved. In *Alberta v Alberta Union of Provincial Employees (Privacy Rights Grievance)*,[23] the intrusion upon seclusion came about when a provincial employee was brought in to investigate operations surrounding the issue of fraudulent maintenance enforcement program cheques. The Province ran a program under which it sought to recover from those who were delinquent in paying support and maintenance payments. In return for assuming the burden of collection, the Province would pay out

[22] *Stevens v Walsh* 2016 ONSC 2418.

[23] *Alberta v Alberta Union of Provincial Employees (Privacy Rights Grievance)* (2012) 221 LAC (4th) 104.

maintenance and support cheques directly to beneficiaries. Upon discovering that fraudulent cheques were being issued, the Province brought in a zealous investigator, who promptly accessed personal employment data on ministry employees and ran unauthorised credit checks on them. This was ostensibly to discover whether any employee might have harboured a motive for fraudulent behaviour. None was found. However, upon finding that their privacy had been invaded, the 26 employees in the maintenance program promptly filed a grievance. The arbitrator found that the tort of intrusion upon seclusion, as voiced in *Jones v Tsige*, was made out. On the assessment of damages, the arbitrator awarded each employee $1,250. Although there was a lack of tangible harm to each employee, the invasion had created a climate of mistrust. The Province had admitted error and apologised, and this went a long way to rectifying the climate in the department. By mentioning these factors, the arbitrator specifically embraced the factors specified in the Manitoba *Privacy Act* and endorsed in *Jones v Tsige*.

In *Re Rio Tinto Alcan v Unifor, Local 2301*,[24] a grievance was filed by employees who worked in a remote mining camp. The employer, without reasonable cause, had engaged a private company to conduct a sweep of the employee's camp living quarters in a search for illicit drugs. None were found. In fact, after the sweep, the employees were brought together so that the sniffer dog could demonstrate how it could identify drugs. The employer left the impression that it had the right to do what it had just undertaken at any time. The employer had apologised for the privacy infringement only at the commencement of the grievance proceedings. Following the decision in *Alberta v Alberta Union of Provincial Employees*,[25] the arbitrator awarded each employee $1,250 for the infringement. This award was justified on the basis that: while the actual infringement had been of an extremely momentary period of time, and had not engaged any lasting harm, it had affected the employer/employee relationship; it was performed against the background of a previous grievance, which had determined that the employer had no right to arbitrarily conduct searches without reasonable cause; and the employer had taken no steps for over two years to apologise or otherwise quell the distress and annoyance caused by the recent search.

The final arbitration case is *St Patrick's Home of Ottawa Inc v Canadian Union of Public Employees, Local 2437*.[26] In this case, the grievor argued that her privacy had been intruded upon when her employer released confidential information about her to another employer, for whom she also worked. The information released concerned the extent to which the employer had made any accommodation for the employee based upon any disclosed medical condition. The employer released to the other employer a medical certificate provided by the grievor's physician, to the effect that the grievor was able to perform her duties without accommodations.

[24] *Re Rio Tinto Alcan v Unifor, Local 2301* 2014 CanLII 95110 (BC LA).
[25] *Alberta v Alberta Union of Provincial Employees* 2012 CanLII 47215 (AB GAA).
[26] *St Patrick's Home of Ottawa Inc v Canadian Union of Public Employees, Local 2437* 2016 CanLII 10432 (ON LA).

When the other employer received this information, it dismissed the grievor. The grievor had requested, and received, accommodations from the work schedule of the other employer for work that was identical in nature. The grievor argued that the employer had breached a specific confidentiality provision in her collective agreement, the *Ontario Health and Safety Act*, and committed the tort of intrusion upon seclusion. The arbitrator decided to award damages under the tort principles and awarded the grievor $1,000. Again, resort was made to the factors specified in the Manitoba legislation.[27] In addition, counsel provided the decisions just discussed from the labour arbitral jurisprudence involving disclosure of information, and which had resulted in only modest damages awards.

Apart from British Columbia, which has specifically rejected *Jones v Tsige*, there is only one Province's courts – those of Nova Scotia – that have specifically referenced the decision with approval.[28] Despite the fact that four Provinces have privacy legislation, the legislation appears to anticipate the development of the privacy right to accord with common law methodology. Courts in Newfoundland and Labrador suggest that the common law and statutory provision create concurrent rights.[29]

C. Post-*Jones v Tsige* decisions: Intrusion Upon Seclusion in British Columbia

British Columbia merits specific treatment because it has advanced the right to privacy exclusively through its legislative provision. This has resulted in a different approach to damages for infringement, the level of compensation awarded and the specific rejection of the common law development outlined in *Jones v Tsige*.[30] One immediate difference is that, under section 4 of the *Privacy Act*, claims under the Act are required to be brought in the British Columbia Supreme Court. Combined

[27] The factors were applied as follows: (i) *The nature of the wrong* – it was a violation of the collective agreement confidentiality provision as well as the tort of intrusion upon seclusion. In the context of a healthcare facility, the employer should have been more sensitive to privacy issues. (ii) *The effect on the health of the grievor* – this did cause the grievor to feel embarrassed, humiliated and disrespected by the employer. However, any economic loss occasioned from losing employment with the plaintiff's other employer could not be taken into account, because any loss had been compensated for in the grievance that had resulted from her termination of employment with the other employer. (iii) *The relationship between grievor and employer* – the relationship required mutual trust and respect. (iv) *The distress and annoyance to the grievor* – distress had been occasioned to the grievor, but this was not solely attributable to the actions of this particular employer. (v) *The conduct of the parties* – the employer had apologised to the grievor, but this apology had only been offered once the issues of the grievance had been narrowed by the union.

[28] *Trout Point Lodge Ltd v Handshoe* 2014 NSSC 62; *Murray v East Coast Forensic Hospital* 2015 NSSC 61 (renamed on appeal *Captial District Health Authority v Murray* 2017 NSCA 28), upholding class action certification on whether the tort claim of intrusion upon seclusion exists in Nova Scotia.

[29] *Hynes v Western Regional Integrated Health Authority* (2014) 64 CPC (7th) 150 (Nfld&Lab SC); *Dawe v Nova Collection Services (Nfld) Ltd* (1998) 160 Nfld & PEIR 266.

[30] See most recently affirmed in *Ladas v Apple Inc* 2014 BCSC 1821, [76].

with the interplay of the Small Claims Court monetary jurisdiction set at $25,000, the claimant must be successful in receiving a damages claim in excess of that amount to win its costs.

A common feature of the British Columbia cases is that they concern invasions of privacy where the defendant is engaged in 'peeping-tom' activities, often involving the videotaping of the claimants in their bedrooms or bathrooms. An egregious infringement occurred in *Malcolm v Fleming*.[31] The plaintiff was a nursing student at the time, and rented a room in the defendant's home where he lived with his family. The plaintiff discovered hidden cameras throughout the home, including in the bathroom, and further discovered that the defendant had recorded her and her friends at various times while she had lived in his home. In awarding the plaintiff $15,000 compensatory damages and a further $35,000 punitive damages, Downs J drew support from an earlier 'peeping-tom' case in British Columbia, *Lee v Jacobson*.[32] The factors identified in both cases justified both general and punitive damages. First, the privacy was violated in the room in the home where the most intimate acts can be expected. Second, the plaintiff had paid for accommodation and reasonably expected privacy. Third, the defendant had made elaborate arrangements that required premeditation to execute. Fourth, the defendant had lied about his participation, which demonstrated lack of remorse. The plaintiff had been put through the embarrassment of discoveries involving others witnessing the tapes. Fifth, there was the potential that the tapes had been viewed by others, thus crossing the line into the public disclosure of private facts. In conclusion, Downs J saw some parallel between cases on sexual assault and the level of trauma experienced by the plaintiff.

Similar levels of damages have been awarded in two other 'peeping-tom' cases, *M (LA) v I (JE)*[33] and *TKL v TMP*.[34] In the former case, the plaintiff adduced evidence that she had taken anti-depressants following discovery of the events, although she had stopped taking them by the time of the trial and the trial judge found that she was more motivated to see the defendant punished. However, the court still awarded $20,000 general damages, a further $5,000 for loss of income-earning opportunity and punitive damages of $35,000. In the latter case, the determinative causes of action were both an infringement of privacy as well as breach of fiduciary duty, following the position taken by the Supreme Court of Canada in *KM v HM*.[35] More evidence supported the plaintiff's claim of suffering from depression, anxiety and inability to trust others in a relationship, although the judge also noted that she was well on the way to recovery following treatment and psychotherapy. The court awarded general damages of $85,000.

[31] *Malcolm v Fleming* [2000] BCJ No 2400 (BC SC).
[32] *Lee v Jacobson* (1992) 87 DLR (4th) 401 (BC SC).
[33] *M (LA) v I (JE)* 2008 BCSC 1147 (involving the secret videotaping of the plaintiff and her infant daughter).
[34] *TKL v TMP* 2016 BCSC 789 (stepfather surreptitiously videotaping his stepdaughter).
[35] *KM v HM* [1992] 3 SCR 6; see also *SY v FGC* (1986) 26 BCLR (3d) 155 (CA).

At the other end of the scale, British Columbia's courts have also awarded nominal or symbolic damages in a case involving a school house-master, who searched an off-campus student's house to determine if on-campus boarding students were present without permission;[36] where a landlord placed a video camera in a corridor outside the plaintiff's property to see who was gaining entry to the premises;[37] and where the defendant, an adjoining neighbour, placed surveillance cameras aimed at the plaintiff's windows.[38]

The British Columbia courts appear to show more willingness to entertain pecuniary claims for general damages associated with the trauma that may accompany an infringement of privacy, and are more likely to consider a plea for punitive damages. It may be sheer happenstance, but the cases that have come before British Columbian courts raising intrusion upon seclusion have in general provided a stronger evidential foundation that links the infringement of privacy to a particular trama or psychological injury. More often, the damages awarded are intended to compensate for a harm that has generated physical symptoms of distress, and thus there is a closer analogy to the classic award for non-pecuniary losses arising in personal injury claims.[39] In contrast, the award in *Jones v Tsige* has usually been characterised as comprising symbolic or moral damages and is akin to a solatium. The injury suffered, while experienced as annoyance or embarassment, does not evoke the same physical reactions of emotional distress.

D. The Public Disclosure of Private Facts

Given the court in *Jones v Tsige* referenced Prosser's classification, it is not surprising that a claim for public disclosure of private facts has recently been advanced.

In *Jane Doe 464533 v ND*,[40] the plaintiff brought an action claiming intentional infliction of mental suffering, breach of confidence and breach of privacy, namely publication of private facts. The plaintiff and defendant had been in a relationship since high school. At age 18, the defendant left to take up studies at university in Nova Scotia, but kept in close contact with the plaintiff. Over the course of several phone calls, the defendant persuaded the plaintiff to make a sexually explicit video of herself and send it to the defendant. Upon receipt, the defendant promptly

[36] *Getejanc v Brentwood College Association* 2001 BCSC 822 ($2,500 damages awarded).

[37] *Heckert v 5470 Investments Ltd* 2008 BCSC 1298 ($3,500 damages awarded).

[38] *Wasserman v Hall* 2009 BCSC 1318 ($3,500 damages awarded).

[39] Interestingly, while the Supreme Court of Canada has capped the level of non-pecuniary damages in personal injury cases across Canada (the current maximum stands at approximately $350,000 (see *Zurich Life Insurance* (n 17)), there has been a vociferous call by the Bench and Bar in British Columbia to eliminate the cap and raise this level of damages. See British Columbia Law Reform Commission, *Report on Compensation for Non-Pecuniary Loss*, LRC No 76 (1984).

[40] *Jane Doe 464533 v ND* (2016) 128 OR (3d) 352 (Sup Ct J).

posted the video to a pornographic site and shared it with friends. Upon becoming aware of this activity, the plaintiff took efforts to have the video removed, which was done after three weeks, but she also experienced severe humiliation and embarrassment, causing serious depression and emotional upset. The plaintiff commenced the action, which was ultimately undefended. At the time of the action, the plaintiff had finished her own undergraduate university studies and had started a graduate degree.

Stinton J described the facts of this case as raising a legal first in Canada – to seek civil liability for the publication of private facts. He found liability under all three heads: intentional infliction of mental suffering,[41] breach of confidence[42] and breach of privacy. Drawing support from *Jones v Tsige*, the court saw in the facts of this case elements of the tort of intrusion upon seclusion, that is, parallels to the 'peeping-tom', video surveillance type of cases. But the Court considered the case to be a better fit with Prosser's second tort, public disclosure of private facts. Stinton J accepted, with one qualification, the criteria from the *Restatement (Second) of Torts*,[43] that the tort is proved where the plaintiff can establish that 'the matter publicised or the act of the publication (a) would be highly offensive to a reasonable person, and (b) is not of legitimate concern to the public'.[44] The underlined additional qualification would allow liability even where publication does not actually occur but where the defendant attempts to post the highly offensive material, or where the material is made available to a secured smaller group. The provision in the *Restatement* requires 'publicity' in the sense that the matter is certain to become one of public knowledge.[45] This is different from 'publication', which simply requires communication to a third person.[46]

Turning to appropriate remedies, the court drew parallels between this case and tort liability for sexual assault for the reason that, while there is no actual physical battery to the plaintiff, the harm claimed is most often for the psychological impact and consequences of the offensive conduct. The violation was of the plaintiff's personal and sexual integrity, which caused an emotional and psychological effect justifying an award of non-pecuniary damages. In *Blackwater v Plint*,[47]

[41] ibid [26]–[33]. The Canadian test requires conduct that is flagrant and outrageous, calculated to produce harm, and resulting in a visible and provable injury. See *Prinzo v Baycrest Centre for Geriatric Care* (2002) 60 OR (3d) 474 (CA).

[42] *Jane Doe 464533* (n 40) [20]–[25]. The Canadian test requires that the information has the necessary quality of confidence, imparted in circumstances importing an obligation of confidence, and that there must be unauthorised use of that information to the detriment of the plaintiff. See *Cadbury Schweppes Inc v FBI Foods Ltd* [1999] 1 SCR 142.

[43] *Restatement (Second) of Torts* (2010) § 652D.

[44] *Jane Doe 464533* (n 40) [46] (original underline).

[45] *Restatement* (n 43) § 652D (comment).

[46] ibid § 577 (comment).

[47] *Blackwater v Plint* [2005] 3 SCR 3, [39]. This case dealt with damages for sexual assault and abuse that happened in Canada's residential schools' system set up as government policy to educate indigenous students between the 1940s and 1960s.

the Supreme Court of Canada approved three factors to be considered in quantifying damages in sexual assault cases:

- First, the circumstances of the assault, the frequency and extent of the violence, degradation and invasion. In this case, the plaintiff was at a vulnerable age, control of the video had been lost, and no one could be assured of how many copies of it existed or who had viewed it. The video was highly personal and involved an invasive portrayal. Some of the defendant's friends were also friends of the plaintiff. The court likened each viewing as akin to a new assault on the plaintiff.
- Second, the circumstances of the defendant and whether there was a position of trust. In this case, although the defendant was the same age as the plaintiff, the relationship had been a long one and was imbued with trust.
- Third, the consequences for the victim. In this case the plaintiff had experienced psychological harm and emotional distress.

Applying these criteria, the court saw an award of $50,000 compensatory damages and $25,000 aggravated damages as being appropriate. The latter were justified on the grounds that the posting of the video had been a particularly arrogant breach of trust, bearing in mind that the defendant had repeatedly assured the plaintiff, despite her misgivings, that he alone would watch the video and keep it private. In addition, the court saw this as a case warranting $25,000 punitive damages for the malice and blameworthiness of the defendant's conduct, which passed the proportionality analysis now used by Canadian courts when considering punitive damages awards.[48] Stinton J also saw the need for deterrence. The total amount awarded, $100,000 plus interest and costs, was the maximum claim the plaintiff could bring under the simplified procedures she had used to prosecute her claim.

In this case, the court also granted an injunction directing the defendant to destroy any copies of the video, and prohibiting any further publishing or posting of intimate images of the plaintiff. The plaintiff also sought anonymisation of the order using the Jane Doe appellation, as well as initials for the defendant, and a sealing of the file; all of which were granted. Following the initial default judgment, the defendant successfully moved to have the judgment set aside, and the matter has now been set down for a full hearing.[49] The matter has yet to be reported.

Jane Doe 464533 v ND[50] has been followed in one other case, *Halley v McCann*.[51] The plaintiff voluntarily entered a crisis mental health facility for treatment. The

[48] The Supreme Court, in *Whiten v Pilot Insurance* [2002] 1 SCR 595, [74], asserted that awards of punitive damages must be proportionate: 'The overall award, that is to say compensatory damages plus punitive damages plus any other punishment related to the same misconduct, should be rationally related to the objectives for which the punitive damages are awarded (retribution, deterrence and denunciation).'

[49] *Doe v ND* 2016 ONSC 4920. A subsequent motion brought by the plaintiff to appeal the motion to set aside the default judgment was also lost: *Jane Doe 464533 v ND* 2017 ONSC 127.

[50] *Jane Doe 464533* (n 40).

[51] *Halley v McCann* [2016] OJ No 4672 (Small Claims Ct).

defendant, the plaintiff's half-sister, worked in the same treatment facility. The relationship between the sisters was one of acrimony and bitterness. The defendant avoided contact with the plaintiff for the six days she was in the facility, and the plaintiff never knew of the fact that her half-sister was aware of her admission to the facility. Regrettably, and in breach of the facility's confidentiality policy, the defendant told her husband, her brother and her daughter of her half-sister's presence in the facility. After checking-out of the treatment facility and returning to her boyfriend's home, the plaintiff was confronted by the former spouse of the defendant's brother, who indicated that she knew the plaintiff had been in the treatment facility. This revelation exacerbated the plaintiff's fragile condition, causing depression, stress and anxiety. McGill J first asked whether the disclosure of the fact that the plaintiff was in a crisis facility constituted disclosure of private information. The *Personal Health Information Protection Act* provides that visits to a health facility constitute private information. The fact that the plaintiff had only granted limited access to this information to her boyfriend and housing worker, and the existence of the facility's confidentiality policy, were conclusive evidence that the matter was private. Was the disclosure highly offensive to a reasonable person? A reasonable person in the shoes of the plaintiff, and who had taken steps to ensure that her treatment remained a secret from her family, would find this disclosure highly offensive. There was no lawful reason for the disclosure that provided a defence, and the court found the defendant had acted with malice. General damages were assessed at $7,500 for embarrassment, humiliation and the physiological (the judge is likely to have meant, psychological) harm. An additional $1,500 punitive damages were awarded.

As with the tort of intrusion upon seclusion, where development in British Columbia departs from the common law as articulated in *Jones v Tsige*, section 1 of the British Columbia *Privacy Act* has also been interpreted as covering public disclosure of private facts, and thus creates a statutory tort claim. *Griffin v Sullivan*[52] supports the view that a statutory breach of privacy can be argued together with a defamation suit and, if the elements of the privacy tort are present, can support a distinct award of damages in addition to any award that may arise from the defamation. In this case, the plaintiff alleged defamation against the defendant for a number of postings on the Internet in which the defendant had described the plaintiff as a 'stalker, abuser, harasser, criminal, liar, killer, sexual predator, pervert, pedophile, coward, manipulator, and hate monger'. Separate from these allegations were further allegations that the defendant had acquired from the plaintiff's former girlfriend personal information, including photographs, which the defendant posted to an anonymous online suicide support group that the plaintiff frequented under a pseudonym, thus revealing his identity. The chat group posted very revealing, intimate, explicit and vulgar messages, and thus valued anonymity very highly. In addition to awarding the plaintiff $150,000 damages for libel,

[52] *Griffin v Sullivan* 2008 BCSC 827.

the court awarded $25,000 for breach of privacy without any evidence of particular psychological or other emotional harm suffered by the plaintiff.[53] The latter award was made without discount to account for any potential of double recovery with the damages awarded for libel. The two harms are seen as distinct injuries, libel compensating for the fact that untruths have been said about the plaintiff, and damages for the disclosure of otherwise truthful private facts where there is a reasonable right to privacy.

E. Discussion

The cases discussed all present a fairly obvious claim for breach of privacy, and I do not imagine readers find the fact that liability was demonstrated as being extraordinary or inappropriate. Canadian courts have, up to now, not experienced difficulty in, first, accepting Prosser's and the *Restatement (Second) Law of Torts* formulation of intrusion upon seclusion, and then applying that criterion, either as part of the common law or in exposition of a statutory tort of privacy. What is interesting is the regional variety in the types of cases. Why the higher number of 'peeping-tom' cases in British Columbia? Can this be explained on the basis of the increased levels of damages awarded in the Province, and why the higher levels in the first place? The cases also exhibit a tendency to eschew protracted debates about what constitutes privacy. As part of Canada's *Charter* jurisprudence, courts have readily accepted the guidance provided by the Supreme Court that a right to privacy can be divided into territorial privacy, protecting physical spaces from prying eyes where there is a reasonable expectation of privacy; personal privacy, protecting bodily integrity against being touched, searched or exposed; and informational privacy, protecting the documentary and image record of how we project ourselves to others.[54] All forms of privacy engage both intrusion and disclosure, and questions of justification.[55]

British Columbia parts company from the other common law Provinces in the level of awards. There is a far greater willingness to entertain suits that argue for higher levels of compensatory damages for a variety of non-pecuniary losses that have been occasioned to victims, although the harms incurred seem to justify those awards because they are more closely analogous to sexual assaults. This mirrors a similar trend in non-pecuniary awards in personal injury claims generally, where British Columbia's courts appear to push the envelope on the cap on such awards.

[53] In contrast, note the earlier decision in Ontario in *Warman v Grosvenor* (2008) 92 OR (3d) 663 (Sup Ct J) which also included both defamation and privacy actions similar to *Griffin v Sullivan* (ibid), but opined that even if such a privacy action was part of Ontario law, the damages flowing from the breach of privacy would be subsumed in the action for defamation.

[54] *R v Tessling* [2004] 2 SCR 432, [20]–[24]; *R v Spencer* [2014] 2 SCR 212, [34] et seq.

[55] See C Hunt, 'Conceptualizing Privacy and Elucidating its Importance: Foundational Considerations for the Development of Canada's Fledgling Privacy Tort' (2011) 37 *Queen's Law Journal* 167.

The propensity to award aggravated and punitive damages also distinguishes British Columbia. While punitive damages may be appropriate where they meet the criteria and proportionality tests outlined in *Whiten v Pilot Insurance*,[56] the awarding of aggravated damages is problematic. Problematic, because Canadian courts have yet to articulate the underlying rationale for these damages. The current test for these damages mirrors the test for punitive damages rather than focusing upon the true compensatory aspect of compensating for additional harm as a result of the defendant's conduct adding insult to injury.

The creation of a 'conventional award', as previously indicated, results in the problem of allowing the first case to the court to set the range, and omits a mechanism for subsequent adjustments. Adopting a conventional approach is a pragmatic solution to the issue of how to compensate for a non-pecuniary loss. As yet, Canada has no systematic way of informing judges how the conventional approach is to be used to standardise awards across the Provinces, other than in depending on the research of counsel to inform the court. The actual upper level of the award, $20,000, in effect means that this cause of action will not be argued before a superior court as a single cause of action. The resultant payout, if successful, will not justify the costs incurred in litigation.

The action for public disclosure of private facts is very much a work in progress in Canada. Unlike the UK and New Zealand, Canada has not yet experienced claims brought by celebrities who seek to control their image,[57] or their family members' image.[58] One can only speculate why this has not occurred in Canada, although it is suspected that for Canadian celebrities, who tend to be overshadowed by their American counterparts, there may be much truth in Oscar Wilde's admonition, that 'only one thing in life is worse than being talked about and that is not being talked about'. Canada does not have aggressive tabloid news media, and news gathering, both in print and on television, is highly concentrated in risk-averse business entities. Telecommunication, including cable and digital broadcasting, is regulated by the Canadian Radio-television and Telecommunications Commission, which monitors privacy practices, particularly those associated with spam e-mail. Canadians do not seem to have any preoccupation with the sexual orientation or proclivities of Canada's celebrities or politicians. Recall that it was Pierre Trudeau, when Justice Minister, who said in 1967 that 'there's no place for the state in the bedrooms of the nation',[59] and Ontario has its first openly gay premier, Kathleen Wynne, elected in 2013. Canadians also appear to lack an appetite for political satire on television or radio to the same extent as found in other Commonwealth countries. Perhaps the fact that Canadians pay some of the highest cellular data rates in the world also curbs participation in newsfeeds or

[56] *Whiten v Pilot Insurance* (n 48).
[57] As in *Campbell* (n 8).
[58] *Hosking v Runting* [2005] 1 NZLR 1 (CA).
[59] CBC 21 December 1967. Archive available online at http://www.cbc.ca/archives/entry/omnibus-bill-theres-no-place-for-the-state-in-the-bedrooms-of-the-nation.

other programs that require high bandwidths of data transfer, which impacts on the propensity to publicise or become a market for celebrity gossip.

The first reported case of public disclosure of private facts, *Jane Doe 464533 v ND*,[60] demonstrates some of the difficulties with this action in a digital world. The element of public disclosure was expanded to include the act of 'publication', used as in the defamation sense, as well as to 'publicise', used in the sense of dissemination to a broader section of the public. This was the distinguishing feature of the Federal Court of Appeal's decision in *Canada v John Doe*.[61] The expanded notion of publication in *Jane Doe 464533* makes a better fit with the digital world, where the offending video can be removed but those who have downloaded it before removal always retain the ability to resurrect it and give it new currency. This change in the focus of what can constitute publicity also shifts the analogy of the action away from defamation, as contemplated by Prosser, to the intentional infliction of mental distress, similar to the tort of intrusion upon seclusion. However, as noted in *Jane Doe 464533*, the damage assessment process far exceeded the conventional range because the plaintiff could adduce stronger evidence of psychological impact, akin to the sexual assault awards. This seems quite appropriate on the facts of the case, but the other recent Ontario decision to embrace public disclosure of private facts, *Halley v McCann*,[62] underpins the need to have a conventional award approach, particularly if these actions, as will shortly be discussed, become grist for the class action regime. In addition, it should be noted that the Federal Government has shown a willingness to criminalise egregious behaviour overlapping with privacy claims, as in the criminalisation of cyber-bullying and revenge porn.[63]

III. Class Actions in Both Privacy Torts

A. Privacy and Class Actions

Ontario's class action regime is similar to those of most other Provinces in Canada.[64] It allows for the certification of class action proceedings where the notice discloses a cause of action, there is an identifiable class of two or more persons that would be represented by a representative plaintiff, the claims of the class members raise common issues, and the class proceedings would be a preferable procedure for the

[60] *Jane Doe 464533 v ND* (n 40).
[61] *Canada v John Doe* 2016 FCA 191.
[62] *Halley v McCann* (n 51).
[63] *Protecting Canadians from Online Crime Act* 2014, c 31.
[64] To help understand the extent to which privacy and class actions are rapidly becoming part of the legal scene in Canada, see the following site run by Sutts Strosberg, one of the pioneering and well respected plaintiff class action firms in Canada, at https://www.strosbergco.com/practices/class-actions/.

resolution of the common issues.[65] The class action must be a preferable way to handle the litigation when viewed through the lenses of access to justice, judicial economy and behavioural modification.[66]

In *Evans v Bank of Nova Scotia*,[67] the plaintiff representative sought certification of a class action to represent a group of the bank's customers who had been the victims, or could possibly be the victims, of identity theft as a result of the bank's wrongdoing. A bank employee had provided private and confidential information on 643 of the bank's customers to his girlfriend, who had then given the information to third parties for fraudulent purposes. Of the 643 customers, 138 reported they had been victims of identity theft, for which the bank had compensated them for any pecuniary losses. The representative plaintiff sought certification of a class action, alleging the tort of intrusion upon seclusion, negligence, breach of fiduciary duty and the duty of good faith, and waiver of tort. The bank resisted certification on the grounds that the bank could not be held vicariously liable[68] for the actions of its employee for the tort of intrusion upon seclusion, and that if damages were to be awarded for emotional suffering and inconvenience then the harm did not reach the level of a recognised psychiatric illness or serious prolonged psychological injury as a result of the defendant's conduct. In addition, the bank argued that because damages under *Jones v Tsige* were characterised as 'moral or symbolic' damages, this was synonymous with punitive damages, and thus could not be awarded pursuant to a claim that depended upon vicarious liability.

[65] *Class Proceedings Act 1992* SO 1992, c 6, s 5(1). In addition, there must be a representative plaintiff who will fairly represent the interests of the class and has a plan for the proceedings that sets out a workable method to proceed. Section 6 further liberalises the ability to certify the class by stating that the certificate will not be denied simply because the claim for damages would require individual assessment; the relief claimed relates to separate contracts; different remedies are sought for different members of the class; the number of class members or the identity of each class member is not known; or that the class includes subclasses.

[66] *Hollick v Toronto (City)* [2001] 3 SCR 158; *Pro-Sys Consultants Ld v Microsoft Corp* [2013] 3 SCR 477. The 'access to justice' lens is viewed as a way to bring non-viable claims where the amount recoverable by the individual claimant is outweighed by the cost of litigation, and provide an avenue for litigation. The 'judicial economy' lens is viewed as a way to aggregate otherwise viable claims so as to economise judicial resources rather than burden courts with large numbers of individual suits raising a common issue. The 'behavioural modification' lens is designed to address other barriers to civil redress born from a power imbalance between the litigants. It is distributive justice writ large, and is a contentious underpinning of Canada's class action regime. See J Berryman, 'Nudge, Nudge, Wink, Wink: Behavioural Modification, Cy-Près Distributions and Class Actions' (2011) 53 *Supreme Court Law Review* 133.

[67] *Evans v Bank of Nova Scotia* 2014 ONSC 2135. On very similar facts, also see the certification in British Columbia in *Tucci v Peoples Trust Company* 2015 BCSC 987.

[68] The test for vicarious liability in Canada has been laid out in *Bazley v Curry* [1999] 2 SCR 534. What is key is to determine the sufficiency of the connection between the employer's creation or enhancement of risk and the wrong complained of. In an intentional tort setting, the following factors may be used for guidance (ibid [41]): (i) the opportunity that the enterprise affords to the employee to abuse his or her powers; (ii) the extent to which the wrongful act may have furthered the employer's aims; (iii) the extent to which the wrongful act was related to friction, confrontation or intimacy inherent in the employer's enterprise; (iv) the extent of the power conferred on the employee in relation to the victim; and (v) the vulnerability of potential victims to wrongful exercise of the employee's power.

Smith J certified the class action on all causes of action. The defendant could not demonstrate that it was plain or obvious that the plaintiff could not succeed at trial. On the issue of damages for intrusion upon seclusion, the plaintiff did not have to prove that the level of harm rose above the level of emotional distress, inconvenience and upset,[69] and it was not settled law that moral or symbolic damages were analogous to punitive damages.

A similar class action has been certified in the Federal Court concerning the loss of an external hard drive, which contained personal information of 583,000 student names, from the Ministry of Human Resources and Skills Development, a department that administers Canada's student loans program.[70] The Ministry had opposed certification, claiming that the privacy tort could not be engaged because the intrusion had not been without justification, nor had it been sufficiently intrusive. In addition, the level of harm was minor – inconvenience, frustration and anxiety – rather than dire – distress, humiliation or anguish. The court accepted the plaintiff's contention that the information went beyond basic names and addresses as it included financial indebtedness, and that a reasonable person could find the intrusion highly offensive, causing distress, humiliation or anguish.

In a different context, where a hospital employee wrongfully accessed patient health records, the Newfoundland Supreme Court also certified a class action.[71] The representative plaintiff argued breach of privacy under both the Newfoundland statutory provision and the common law. The defendant objected to the certification, raising both the vicarious liability and threshold level of non-pecuniary damages issues. Both were similarly rejected by the court on the same basis, that it was not plain and obvious that the plaintiff could not establish these claims at trial.[72]

In Ontario, the interplay between the *Personal Health Information Protection Act 2004* and the common law tort of intrusion upon seclusion was explored in the context of contemplated class action proceedings by the Court of Appeal in *Hopkins v Kay*.[73] The plaintiff was one of 280 patients affected by a breach of privacy when a nurse improperly accessed patient records and disclosed their contents. The defendant hospital argued that the legislation provided a comprehensive code, including the potential for recovery of provable damages for any harm actually

[69] The argument made by the defendant was based upon a ruling that in a suit for negligence, absent physical injury, a plaintiff would have to demonstrate that the harm was a recognised psychiatric illness, or serious prolonged psychological injury. Now see *Mustapha v Culligan of Canada Ltd* [2008] 2 SCR 114, [9]; *Saadati v Moorhead* 2017 SCC 28.

[70] *Condon v Canada* 2014 FC 250. On appeal, the Federal Court of Appeal reinstated two other causes of action, negligence and breach of contract, as part of the common issues that had initially been argued by the plaintiff but disallowed by the trial court: 2015 FCA 159. This action also brought about an attempt in Saskatchewan by a competing plaintiff to have carriage of the class action within Saskatchewan. The motion was denied: *R v Horstman* [2014] SKQB 114.

[71] *Hynes v Western Regional Integrated Health Authority* 2014 CanLII 67125 (NL SC).

[72] See also *Hemeon v South West Nova District Health Authority* 2015 NSSC 287.

[73] *Hopkins v Kay* (2015) 380 DLR (4th) 506 (ONCA).

incurred to a maximum of $10,000.[74] Sharpe J, for the Court, rejected this analysis, pointing out that there were significant differences in the forms of proof between the two actions to recover damages. In the privacy tort the claim was actionable without proof of actual harm, whereas, in contrast, the legislation required proof of actual harm the claimant had suffered as a result of a contravention of the Act. There was also a difference in the application of limitation periods, the common law claim requiring commencement within two years and the legislation claim bound to a one-year limitation period. The representative plaintiff was allowed class action certification.

In *Lozanski v The Home Depot Inc*,[75] the court approved a class action settlement arising from a data breach experienced by customers who used their credit cards at a Home Depot store during a period when hackers had compromised the defendant's computer systems. Because the action was settled, the alleged privacy and breach of contract claims were never litigated, and Home Depot denied any wrongdoing. The claim settlement reflects a modest award, $250,000 being set aside to meet documented claims of loss from a class of 500,000 customers who could potentially be effected; and $250,000 being set aside to pay for free credit-monitoring services for the class.[76]

Another recently launched class action involves photos taken of students by an instructor of the Winnipeg Royal Ballet and then posted online. The instructor and photographer of the ballet school had coaxed students to partially undress during unsupervised photo sessions. The class action is still being assembled, but it will no doubt raise both intrusion upon seclusion and, possibly, the public disclosure of private facts. One suspects that much will turn on whether there was a lawful justification for the invasion, and whether a reasonable person would regard it as highly offensive.[77]

The class actions just described have all been based on the intrusion upon seclusion privacy tort. There is one case that raises public disclosure of private facts, and in rather peculiar circumstances. In *Canada v John Doe*,[78] the representative plaintiff brought a class certification action against Health Canada, the Federal Government's health ministry. Health Canada has as one of its responsibilities the administration of the *Marihuana for Medical Purposes Regulations*.

[74] *Personal Health Information Protection Act 2004* SO 2004, c 3, s 65(1) ('a person affected by the order may commence a proceeding in the Superior Court of Justice for damages for actual harm that the person has suffered as a result of the contravention of this Act'), (3) ('If … the Superior Court of Justice determines that the harm suffered by the plaintiff was caused by contravention or offence, as the case may be, that the defendants engaged in wilfully or recklessly, the court may include in its award of damages, an award, not exceeding $10,000, for mental anguish').

[75] *Lozanski v The Home Depot Inc* 2016 ONSC 5447.

[76] For a similar case of identity theft from the loss of health records on a USB stick, see *Rowlands v Durham Regional Health* 2011 ONSC 719.

[77] See J Van Rhijn, 'Winnipeg Royal Ballet Class Action Underway' (2017) 28(27) *Law Times* 10, at http://www.lawtimesnews.com/author/judy-van-rhijn/winnipeg-royal-ballet-class-action-underway-13633.

[78] *Canada v John Doe* (n 61).

Under the regulations, individuals could register and be given a licence to take marihuana for a variety of prescribed medical treatments. At the time of this action, 40,000 people were registered with the Ministry. The regulations also posted a privacy policy adhered to by the Ministry. In normal correspondence to registered users from the Ministry, an envelope was used with the title 'Health Canada' on the outside. Regrettably, to inform registered users about changes in the program, Health Canada sent out 40,000 oversize envelopes visibly marked with a return address to the Marihuana for Medical Purposes Program. Somewhat ironically, inside the envelope was a letter informing registrants that marihuana had a high value on the illegal market, which created a risk of home invasion for registrants. The representative plaintiff argued that by revealing to the world at large that he was a registrant in the program, Health Canada had infringed upon his privacy and exposed him to a variety of risks.[79] The plaintiff commenced an action arguing breach of confidence, breach of contract, negligence, intrusion upon seclusion and public disclosure of private facts. The Court of Appeal held that the trial judge had erred in allowing certification for either alleged breach of privacy, although it ultimately allowed the certification to proceed on the other grounds. The plaintiff failed on the privacy torts because he could not identify a factual basis to support the claims. On the intrusion of seclusion, there was no evidence to support that the intrusion was intentional or without justification. On the publicity to private life, the action failed on the ground that there was not the requisite publicity to the disclosure. Being seen by a postal employee, who was also bound to confidentiality, or a family member where the mail was received, did not satisfy the publicity element of the tort.

B. Discussion

Coupling an invasion of privacy with class actions will expose complex issues for resolution. An initial argument in favour of such a movement is that it will encourage access to justice by overcoming the impediment of litigation costs where 'conventional awards' effectively curb the action from being brought. By creating a class, the impact of many smaller awards to class members creates economies of scale that make it attractive to class plaintiff lawyers to incur the burden of litigation. Interestingly, the actual litigation burden on class counsel is likely to be less burdensome than in other class action proceedings. If the breach of privacy flows from a government or administrative agency, or some other commercially regulated industry player, then the reporting and investigating structure of the respective government privacy commissioners may be used to secure substantive

[79] ibid [8]. The plaintiff claimed that he had suffered the following damages: costs incurred to prevent home invasion, theft, robbery, damage to property, costs incurred for personal security, damage to reputation, loss of employment, reduced capacity for employment, mental distress, inconvenience, frustration and anxiety.

evidence of infringement with little difficulty, although, as pointed out in *Hopkins v Kay*,[80] some of the elements of proof differ. Resort to a 'conventional range' for assessment will actually help proof of the damages claim, because it minimises the need for individual proof of loss and allows the class to be differentiated according to the gradations of privacy infringement, something the assessment process in class actions has been designed to allow.[81] As already mentioned, access to justice is one of the lenses through which certification of class action proceedings is to be evaluated.

Another lens through which to evaluate a class action is behavioural modification. Currently, the privacy actions that have been brought for certification have, with few exceptions, been against government actors, particularly in the health sector. In Ontario, the Information and Privacy Commissioner of Ontario has commented that approximately 300–350 complaints are brought each year, complaining of breaches in the Ontario health sector. Half of those are self-reported, and while most of the breaches are due to carelessness – loss or theft of portable devices or incorrectly sent e-mails – two to three each month are of the snooping variety.[82] For the reasons given above about investigation, and the fact that the class members can readily be identified, these actions will be regarded as 'low-hanging fruit' by the class action plaintiff bar. If the actual damages per individual member are small, this may trigger the cy-près approach to damage distribution.[83] One of the accepted grounds justifying a cy-près distribution is where the cost of administering the funds to the class will outweigh the sums to be received by individual class members.[84] In these circumstances, the claim of behavioural modification is usually the chief driver used to support the class action suit, all the while the plaintiff's lawyer receiving its 'fair' share of the claim for bringing the action.[85] Is it appropriate, or is it even desirable, to burden the health sector with defending or settling these claims? Is this in fact an efficient way

[80] *Hopkins v Kay* (n 73).

[81] *Class Proceedings Act* 1992, SO 1992, c 6, s 24.

[82] Data given by the Privacy Commissioner speaking at the Canadian Bar Association conference, 'Access to Information and Privacy Law Symposium', Ottawa, 28–29 October 2016. Powerpoints on file with author.

[83] Cy-près is a doctrine applied in the administration of charitable trusts, which allows a trustee to seek court validation to alter the terms of the trust where the trust would otherwise fail for want of certainty of objects (the intended beneficiaries of the trust) or purpose (the intended charitable goal to be achieved). The court may authorise the trustee to apply the trust property to the 'next best thing' consistent with the settlor's charitable intentions. The doctrine, as applied in the class action regime, allows the court to distribute the damages amongst persons or organisations that are not themselves claimants but are parties that could benefit from the funds distributed, and whose activities would further the deterrence goals to prevent the activity that justified the initial class action suit.

[84] R Mulheron, *The Modern Cy-Près Doctrine* (London, UCL Press, 2006) 259.

[85] I have written elsewhere expressing my skepticism of cy-près distribution schemes in class action proceedings: J Berryman, 'Class Actions (Representative Proceedings) and the Exercise of the Cy-Près Doctrine: Time for Improved Scrutiny' in Berryman and Bigwood (eds) (n 18); J Berryman and R Carroll, 'Cy-Près as a Class Action Remedy – Justly Maligned or Just Misunderstood?' in K Barker and D Jensen (eds), *Private Law: Key Encounters with Public Law* (Cambridge, Cambridge UP, 2013) 320.

to encourage the health sector to protect client privacy better, or is it a mad grab at ostensibly deep pockets (the taxpayer) by the class action plaintiffs' bar? The sums involved are quite astronomical. In one class action that is winding its way through the system, the Rouge Valley Hospital System has been hit by a $412 million claim. Two employees of the hospital allegedly unlawfully sold the names and contact details of 8,300 patients, mainly mothers who gave birth between 2009 and 2013, to private companies that marketed registered educational savings investment plans to the patients.[86] One wonders how the class members can claim to have been harmed by these activities. One of the perversities of the class action suit against a government entity is that the burden of the award is borne by the same group, although a larger constituency of it, as the beneficiaries, namely, taxpayers. The actual perpetrators of the invasion of privacy do not bear the costs of the award. While the hospital may have contributed to the wrongdoing, its calpability should be judged against what alternative systems it could have put in place to prevent the employees from infringing patient privacy. However, this goal is one of the primary reasons that underscores the legislation and the administrative structure put in place to balance patient privacy and the efficiencies gained in the health system through digitised record keeping. The only true beneficiaries of this 'virtuous' class action circle are both class action lawyers.

Courts will need to determine whether the provisions of the respective health privacy acts should be regarded as the better way to achieve behavioural modification.[87] While this will not bar the private civil action, it may be a way to circumscribe the damage awards by shifting the line of an award to next to nothing on the 'conventional range'. The goal of behavioural modification would be removed from the class action suit and the quantification of damages left to the guidance provided by cases such as *Jones v Tsige*. I suggest that to be contacted, even hectored, by a company attempting to sell its educational savings plans seems a fairly low level of patient annoyance given the amount of unsolicited marketing that happens in our modern world, and that it is a long way from the $49,000 compensation per patient suggested by the plaintiff in its claim. Nor should the class action claim be fuelled by an argument to add punitive damages, which are allowable as part of a claim.[88] Recently, in Ontario, the legislature has lifted the penalty provisions in the *Personal Health Information Protection Act*.[89] While this does not preclude bringing a private suit, any award of punitive damages must

[86] J Eastwood, 'Rouge Valley Faces $400M Class-action Lawsuit over Privacy Breach' *The Star* (14 June 2014), at https://www.thestar.com/news/gta/2014/06/25/rouge_valley_faces_400m_classaction_lawsuit_over_privacy_breach.html.

[87] For example, two healthcare workers who snooped on the late Rob Ford's, Toronto's infamous mayor, health records were fined $2,505 each, the first individual convictions under the Ontario Act: M Warren, 'Hospital Workers Convicted for Snooping into Rob Ford's Personal Health Files' *The Star* (6 Mary 2016), at https://www.thestar.com/news/gta/2016/05/06/hospital-workers-convicted-for-snooping-into-rob-fords-personal-health-files.html.

[88] *Bank of Montreal v Marcotte* [2014] 2 SCR 725.

[89] *Personal Health Information Protection Act*, SO 2004, c 3, s 72 ($100,000 for individual and $500,000 for an organisation for wilful breach).

take cognisance of any criminal punishment as part of the proportionality analysis and whether extra deterrence is actually justified. Prosecutions under the *Privacy Act* also lead to victim surcharges,[90] which may also be resorted to by victims to compensate for the harm caused by disclosure.

IV. Elements of Injunctive Relief and Privacy

Another remedial issue raised by public disclosure of private facts is resort to injunctive relief, or orders aimed at third-party Internet service providers to take down, or otherwise alter the hierarchical order of search responses for, the offending material. In *Jane Doe 464533 v ND*, the court exercised no hesitation in granting an injunction requiring the defendant to destroy any copies of intimate images and video in his possession, and prohibiting further disclosure and dissemination. Similarly, where the tort in issue is an intrusion upon seclusion, but the injunction is required to prevent the publicising of the private information sourced from the intrusion, courts have been willing to entertain such suits unless there is a clear public interest element justifying publicising the information. So, for example, interlocutory injunctions have been granted to prevent the publication of confidential hospital records identifying doctors who have contracted HIV/AIDS yet who are still practising in the hospital,[91] to protect solicitor–client documents from being disclosed on a local television show,[92] and to prevent the publication of details associated with matrimonial proceedings where the applicant was seeking to divorce her husband, a person who had been convicted of murder and sexual assault in a high-profile case.[93] However, in the last-mentioned case, the Ontario Court of Appeal reversed the trial judge on the ground that the effect of the court's order would be to violate the 'open court' principle.[94]

In both actions, intrusion upon seclusion and public disclosure of private facts, but more so in the latter, the issue of injunctive relief has challenged courts in other jurisdictions because it raises the competing pressures of the right to freedom of expression, the principle of open courts and the hesitancy towards ordering prior restraint, particularly in alleged defamation actions. I have discussed the use of injunctions in privacy and defamation actions in an earlier article,[95] where I concluded:

> The granting of an injunction *contra mundum* should be drawn where the threat of publication is sufficiently serious as to cause a serious risk to physical or psychological

[90] *Provincial Offences Act 1990*, RSO, c P33; O Reg 161/00 Victim Fine Surcharges.
[91] *X v Y* [1988] 2 All ER 648 (QB).
[92] *Amherst (Town) v Canadian Broadcasting Corp* (1993) 126 NSR (2d) 221 (SCTD), interlocutory proceedings. Final injunction upheld: (1994) 133 NSR (2d) 277 (SCAD).
[93] *MEH v Williams* 2011 ONSC 2022.
[94] *MEH v Williams* 2012 ONCA 35.
[95] J Berryman, 'Injunctions *contra mundum*: The Ultimate Weapon in Containment' (2014) 26 *Intellectual Property Journal* 289.

> harm, or to seriously jeopardize the fairness of a criminal trial or national security. In all other cases, courts should defer to a damages remedy. Even where granting such an injunction is justified, we should be under no illusions as to its efficacy. In a globalized Internet World, there is most likely to be leakage and thus the injunction may only achieve a limited containment or prevent widespread infringement. Finally, the enforcement of any injunction is, ultimately, dependent upon effective notice being given to potential infringers.

In the first part of my conclusion, I was alluding to a decision of the Supreme Court in Canada, *AB v Bragg Communications Inc*,[96] where the plaintiff, a child, had commenced defamation proceedings against the defendant, who had created a fake digital profile of the plaintiff and circulated it amongst her friends on the Internet. The plaintiff feared that if her name was revealed she would be further victimised by cyber-bullying attacks, which were the subject matter of the alleged defamation. Although no evidence of emotional harm was specifically adduced by the plaintiff, the court accepted evidence from a variety of reports that demonstrated a link between bullying and cyber-bulling adversely affecting self-esteem and invoking fear and anxiety and an increased risk of suicide, sufficient to justify overriding any claim to the open-court principle or freedom of expression. The result was for the court to anonymise the record, thus concealing the plaintiff's identity, so as to minimally impair the right of freedom of expression and the open-court principle.[97]

In the second part of my conclusion in the article I was alluding to the difficulty involved in removing material from the Internet, particularly where the server, and thus the content, is in another jurisdiction. While commercial search engines such as Google[98] and Facebook[99] contain voluntary policies to remove URLs and web images, and indicate that they will respond to court orders, the test of whether, and the extent to which, these orders can be enforceable across jurisdictions has

[96] *AB v Bragg Communications Inc* [2012] 2 SCR 567.

[97] These issues have recently been discussed by the UK Supreme Court in *PNM v Times Newspapers Ltd* [2017] UKSC 49. The Court was asked to rule on whether an injunction that had been granted to the applicant, and which suppressed information that would reveal his identity, should be lifted. The applicant had been arrested, bailed, had his passport impounded and then been released without charge following a police investigation involving a number of persons, who were in fact convicted of crimes relating to child sex grooming and prostitution. The defendant newspapers strenuously argued their right to publish, based primarily upon the open-court principle. A majority of the Court agreed with the defendants and lifted the injunction. Discussions of rights to privacy and freedom of the press take a different direction in the UK because of the specific provisions in the European Convention on Human Rights, Art 8 (right to respect for private and family life) and Art 10 (freedom of expression). What is particularly distinctive about the construct of these rights and the open-court principle is the positive weight accorded to the newspapers' desire to identify an applicant in person so as to make a more popular story and thus sell more newspapers. Anonymised reporting is not seen as a proportionate response, because it is likely to be of less interest to the public and thus provoke less discussion of the issues at stake, which is the underpinning of the open-court principle.

[98] See, eg, Google's legal removal requests policy at https://support.google.com/legal/answer/3110420?hl=en.

[99] See Facebook's image privacy rights policy at https://www.facebook.com/help/428478523862899?helpref=faq_content.

recently been the subject of a case before the Supreme Court of Canada: *Google Inc v Equustek Solutions Inc.*[100] The case does not raise personal privacy rights[101] but is an attempt by a commercial plaintiff to bring an interlocutory injunction application to have Google remove URLs of a defendant company, which is infringing upon the plaintiff's trade secrets and confidential information by advertising and selling a competing product online. The defendant operates in a 'virtual' world. Customers are directed to its website through the Google search engine. While Google was willing to remove, or de-index, 345 URLs from its search engine, it was not willing to go further into subdirectories and subpages. The defendant, by changing the objectionable content to new pages within its websites, was able to get around the de-indexing in a manoeuvre the trial judge described as akin to the game 'Whack-a-Mole'. In addition, Google only de-indexed from its Canadian operations, Google.ca, and not its other operations, particularly Google.com.

By a majority, the Court held that the plaintiff had met the criteria for an interlocutory injunction.[102] It had demonstrated a serious issue to be tried, a fact not disputed by Google. It had provided proof of irreparable harm if the injunction were not granted, namely, loss of ongoing sales where there was little prospect of recovering from the infringing defendant company. Again, a point not disputed by Google. Lastly, the plaintiff had demonstrated that the balance of convenience lay with it. Here, Google did mount opposing argument, claiming that the court should be loath to grant an interlocutory injunction having extra-territorial reach where it possibly raises freedom of expression concerns. In addition, Google argued that it should not be subject to a court order where it was not a named party in the substantive infringement dispute.

On the latter argument, the Supreme Court rightly followed its earlier jurisprudence,[103] to the effect that even non-named parties are bound to observe a court order of which they have notice, so as to maintain the rule of law and to prevent an obstruction of justice and where it is just and convenient that the order should be granted. The majority likened the order sought by the plaintiff to *Mareva* and *Norwich* orders. On the extra-territorial issue, the court observed that it was exercising an *in personam* jurisdiction over Google, which had a significant business presence in British Columbia. While the order did have extra-territorial or global effect, it actually only required of Google that it take steps where it controlled its search engine, a matter with which Google admitted it was easy for it to comply. Google also admitted that most jurisdictions recognised some level of

[100] *Google Inc v Equustek Solutions Inc* 2017 SCC 34.

[101] But see *Vertolli v YouTube LLC* 2012 CanLII 99832 (Ont Small Claims Ct), which concerned a police person who claimed intrusion upon seclusion in respect of a recording made by an arrested suspect, which was displayed on YouTube. Motion to dismiss by YouTube on the ground that it did not disclose a reasonable cause of action rejected.

[102] The Supreme Court of Canada laid out that criteria in *RJR–MacDonald Inc v Canada (Attorney-General)* [1994] 1 SCR 311.

[103] *MacMillan Bloedel Ltd v Simpson* [1992] 2 SCR 1048.

intellectual property rights, according to which the selling of pirated goods would be unlawful. Nor should arguments about potential infringement of freedom of expression be over-extended in this context. All that was required of Google was to de-index websites that had been found in violation of several court orders, so as to prevent the causing of irreparable harm to the plaintiff.

This case will be closely watched, and will likely address some of the issues on whether the 'right to be forgotten' will translate to Canadian shores. In the right-to-be-forgotten cases, the claims to protection of freedom of expression may be stronger than in *Google Inc v Equustek Solutions*, in that the matter the claimant is seeking to de-index by the injunction is the very subject of the dispute, rather than merely to prevent the sale of an infringing good. In the right-to-be-forgotten cases, the analogy is closer to defamation, because the applicant is seeking to de-index material that, although true, does not present the person in the way he or she wishes to be represented to the world. In defamation cases, there is a practice of long standing to resist injunctions that amount to prior restraint. In contrast, in intellectual property infringement, the injunction remedy is more readily granted where the claim of irreparable harm is framed in terms of loss of a pecuniary nature as against the violation of a fundamental human or constitutional right.

V. Conclusion

In one sense, the decision in *Jones v Tsige* was clearly representative of an 'idea whose time has come',[104] a sentiment shared by the New Zealand Court of Appeal. Its quiet entry into Canadian law has not prompted a large number of reported cases, and the adoption of a conventional range to quantify damages is as unremarkable as it is eminently pragmatic. The evolution of a right of privacy to embrace a tort of public disclosure of private facts has gone in a slightly different direction than in other jurisdictions. As in other jurisdictions, Canadian courts struggle with the appropriateness of giving injunctive relief, recognising its efficacy, particularly for the tort of public disclosure of private facts, but ever mindful of the potential for violation of the open-court principle. The spectre of class actions married to privacy torts has a disruptive potential. Hang on for a wild ride.

[104] Victor Hugo.

14

Damages for Interference with Privacy Under Statute: The New Zealand Privacy Act 1993

RODGER HAINES*

I. Introduction

Under the Privacy Act 1993, the Human Rights Review Tribunal of New Zealand has jurisdiction to grant remedies, including damages, where there has been an interference with the privacy of an individual. Subject to certain exceptions relating to access to personal information, an interference with privacy requires proof of an action that breaches an information privacy principle, as well as one of the consequential forms of harm specified by the Act.[1] Presently the monetary limit for such damages is NZ$350,000, being the limit to the civil jurisdiction of the District Court.[2] Claims in excess of this amount must be referred to the High Court.[3]

* Chairperson of the Human Rights Review Tribunal since July 2011. The opinions expressed in this chapter are the personal views of the author.

[1] As explained later in this chapter, the information privacy principles are set out in the Privacy Act 1993, s 6. The term 'interference with privacy' is defined in s 66 of the Act. That section is appended at the end of this chapter. It provides that where there has been a breach of an information privacy principle (other than an information privacy request under principle 6(1) or principle 7(1)), the forms of consequential harm required to be proved by s 66(1)(b) are loss, detriment, damage or injury to the aggrieved individual, or an adverse effect on the rights, benefits, privileges, obligations or interests of the individual or significant humiliation, significant loss of dignity or significant injury to feelings. Please note that as this book was going to press a Privacy Bill was introduced into the New Zealand Parliament on 20 March 2018, receiving its first reading on 11 April 2018. It is currently awaiting examination by a select committee, which has a reporting date of 11 October 2018. If passed the Bill would repeal and replace the Privacy Act 1993. However, as presently drafted, the Bill would nonetheless continue (with minor amendments) the information privacy principles in their present form, as well as the jurisdiction of the Human Rights Review Tribunal to award the remedies currently provided for in the 1993 Act, including damages.

[2] See District Court Act 2016, s 74 and the Human Rights Act 1993, s 92Q(2). The latter provision applies in respect of proceedings under the Privacy Act 1993 by virtue of s 89 of the latter Act. Prior to 1 March 2017 the monetary limit was NZ$200,000. All dollar references in this chapter are references to the New Zealand dollar.

[3] See Human Rights Act 1993, s 92R, which is also applied to proceedings under the Privacy Act by s 89 of the latter Act.

The Tribunal also has jurisdiction to award damages under two additional statutes: the Human Rights Act 1993 for certain breaches of that Act; and the Health and Disability Commissioner Act 1994 for breaches of the Code of Health and Disability Services Consumers' Rights. While these additional jurisdictions are not the subject of this chapter, it is necessary that they be mentioned, albeit briefly, as the circumstances in which damages can be awarded under all three statutes is largely, but not entirely, the same. In so far as the terms of the different statutes are the same, the Tribunal's interpretation and application of these common provisions should be consistent in terms of principle. There are, of course, important differences between the three statutes, and recognition of this fact must be given if for no other reason than that the nature of the right infringed will shape the approach to damages. It should also be noted that only under the Health and Disability Commissioner Act does the Tribunal have jurisdiction to award exemplary damages, that is for an action 'in flagrant disregard of the rights of the aggrieved person'.[4]

The Tribunal consists of a Chairperson and two other persons appointed by the Chairperson for the purposes of each hearing from a Panel maintained by the Minister of Justice under section 101 of the Human Rights Act.[5] The Panel has a ceiling of 20 persons, only three of whom must be barristers or solicitors of not less than five years' practice.[6] In considering the suitability of persons for inclusion on the Panel, the Minister is required to have regard to the need for persons included on the Panel to have between them knowledge of, or experience in, different aspects of matters likely to come before the Tribunal; New Zealand law or the law of another country or international law on human rights; public administration or the law relating to public administration; current economic, employment or social issues; cultural issues and the needs and aspirations (including life experiences) of different communities of interest and population groups in New Zealand society.[7]

The experiences and knowledge listed are appropriately broad given that matters of human rights are to be considered.[8] A collective diversity of experience among Panel members is accordingly a requisite consideration for the Minister when making appointments. There are currently 12 members of the Panel, of whom five are lawyers. Historically only one Chairperson of the Tribunal has held office at any time, but the legislation allows for two Chairpersons to be appointed and a second Chairperson was appointed on 3 August 2017 for a term of 12 months to assist with an unprecedented increase in caseload.[9] A Chairperson

[4] Health and Disability Commissioner Act 1994, s 57(1)(d).

[5] Human Rights Act 1993, s 98.

[6] Human Rights Act 1993, s 101(1) and (2A).

[7] Human Rights Act 1993, s 101(2).

[8] S Bell et al, *Brookers Human Rights Law*, vol 1 (Wellington, Thomson Reuters, 2008) [HR101.01].

[9] Curiously, while the Human Rights Act 1993, s 99(2) makes provision for the appointment of two persons to the office of Chairperson of the Tribunal, a deputy chairperson cannot be appointed to assist with the hearing and determination of cases. On the question of the consequential delay caused by this anomaly, see *Wall v Fairfax New Zealand Ltd (Delay)* [2017] NZHRRT 8.

sitting alone has limited powers to deal with interim order applications and to give case management directions.[10] Outside these limited circumstances, the Tribunal sitting as a panel of three must make all decisions and a Chairperson must preside at all sittings. Each member of a Tribunal has an equal vote and the decision of the majority is the decision of the Tribunal.[11] The clear intention is that decisions of the Tribunal in all three of its jurisdictions be made by a panel which reflects community values and a wide range of life experiences. Sittings of the Tribunal are required to be held in public, unless the Tribunal is satisfied it is desirable to make an order prohibiting publication of any report or account of the evidence.[12]

The importance of community values and a wide range of life experiences to the Tribunal's three jurisdictions is also reflected in the fact that on any appeal to the High Court in which a question of fact is involved, two members of the Panel must be appointed 'additional members' of the High Court.[13] Two additional members must also be appointed where the grant of a remedy is referred by the Tribunal to the High Court.[14]

II. The Privacy Act 1993 – Overview

A. Purpose

The Privacy Act 1993 came into force on 1 July 1993. The Long Title to the Act describes it as:

> An Act to promote and protect individual privacy in general accordance with the Recommendation of the Council of the Organisation for Economic Co-operation and Development Concerning Guidelines Governing the Protection of Privacy and Transborder Flows of Personal Data, and, in particular,—
>
> (a) to establish certain principles with respect to—
>
> (i) the collection, use, and disclosure, by public and private sector agencies, of information relating to individuals; and
>
> (ii) access by each individual to information relating to that individual and held by public and private sector agencies; and
>
> (b) to provide for the appointment of a Privacy Commissioner to investigate complaints about interferences with individual privacy; and
>
> (c) to provide for matters incidental thereto

[10] Human Rights Act 1993, s 95; Human Rights Review Tribunal Regulations 2002, regs 16–18.

[11] Human Rights Act 1993, s 104(3), (4).

[12] Human Rights Act 1993, s 107(1), which is discussed in *Waxman v Pal (Application for Non-Publication Orders)* [2017] NZHRRT 4, [34].

[13] Human Rights Act 1993, s 126(1)(b).

[14] Human Rights Act 1993, s 126(1)(a). Apparently there has been only one such referral. See *Spencer v Ministry of Health* [2016] NZHC 1650, [2016] 3 NZLR 513, [10].

As observed by the New Zealand Law Commission in *Review of the Privacy Act 1993: Review of the Law of Privacy Stage 4*, the Act is principally concerned with the protection of personal information about individuals (human beings, not companies). The Act provides a framework for regulating the collection, storage, use and disclosure of personal information. It is mainly a data protection statute. It is principally concerned with information privacy, that is, control over access to private information or facts about individuals.[15]

While the Act protects only certain aspects of individual privacy, its human rights purpose is nonetheless unmistakable. As noted by Thomas J (dissenting) in *Brooker v Police*:[16]

> [252] Privacy can be more or less extensive, involving a broad range of matters bearing on an individual's personal life. It creates a zone embodying a basic respect for persons. This zone of privacy is imperative if our personal identity and integrity is to remain intact. Recognising and asserting this personal and private domain is essential to sustain a civil and civilised society. It is, as I have mentioned, closely allied to the fundamental value underlying and supporting all other rights: the dignity and worth of the human person.

Although information privacy is properly referred to as a human right, it would be a mistake to see the Act as purely a human rights statute and a freedom of information statute. It also has, in its insistence on conformity with the OECD Guidelines, the purpose of facilitating data flows, thereby enhancing both government and business efficiency.[17] In the performance of his functions and in the exercise of his powers, the Privacy Commissioner is required by the Act to have due regard for the protection of important human rights and social interests that compete with privacy, including the general desirability of a free flow of information and the recognition of the right of government and business to achieve their objectives in an efficient way; to take account of international obligations accepted by New Zealand, including those concerning the international technology of communications and to consider any developing general international guidelines relevant to the better protection of individual privacy.[18] No such obligations are expressly imposed on the Tribunal.

It is not possible within the confines of a short chapter such as this to give either a full or an accurate account of the Act. What is essential to understand, however, is that it applies only to 'personal information', that is to 'information about an identifiable individual'.[19] The term 'information' is not defined in the Act, an omission which appears to be deliberate. Speaking of the forerunner to the

[15] Law Commission, *Review of the Privacy Act 1993: Review of the Law of Privacy Stage 4*, NZLC IP17 (2010) [1.18].

[16] *Brooker v Police* [2007] NZSC 30, [2007] 3 NZLR 91, [252]. See further Bell et al (n 8) [PR1.05].

[17] S Penk, 'The Privacy Act 1993' in R Tobin and S Penk (eds), *Privacy Law in New Zealand*, 2nd edn (Wellington, Thomson Reuters, 2016) 53, 59.

[18] Privacy Act 1993, s 14, discussed in *Harder v Proceedings Commissioner* [2000] 3 NZLR 80, [23] (CA).

[19] Privacy Act 1993, s 2(1) definition of 'personal information'.

present provisions, McMullin J in *Commissioner of Police v Ombudsman* held that the word denotes 'that which informs, instructs, tells or makes aware'.[20] 'Personal information' includes opinion. Overall, the definition is very broad and is not limited to information that is particularly sensitive, intimate or private.

At the heart of the Act are the 12 information privacy principles. They set out when and how agencies may collect, store, use and disclose personal information. A legal obligation to comply with the information privacy principles is attached to both public and private 'agencies'.[21] The Act also sets out how those obligations are to be enforced, that is by the Privacy Commissioner at first instance by way of complaint and then by civil proceedings before the Human Rights Review Tribunal.[22] There is a right of appeal from the Tribunal to the High Court.[23]

It is to be noted that Part 6 of the Act gives to the Privacy Commissioner power to issue a code of practice, which may apply in relation to, for example, any specified information or class of information.[24] Failure to comply with such code is deemed to be a breach of an information privacy principle.[25] Codes can modify the operation of the Act for specific industries, agencies, activities or types of personal information. They often modify one or more of the information privacy principles to take account of special circumstances that affect a class of agencies (eg credit reporters) or a class of information (eg health information). The rules established by a code may be more stringent or less stringent than the principles they replace. Codes are published on the Privacy Commissioner's website. There are currently six such codes, the most notable being the Health Information Privacy Code 1994, the Telecommunications Information Privacy Code 2003 and the Credit Reporting Privacy Code 2004.

B. The Privacy Principles

Information privacy principles 1 to 4 cover the collection of personal information, principle 5 is concerned with the storage and security of personal information, and principles 6 and 7 are concerned with access to personal information by the person to whom that information relates and with correction of that information.

[20] *Commissioner of Police v Ombudsman* [1988] 1 NZLR 385, 402 (CA), cited most recently by the Tribunal in *Watson v Capital & Coast District Health Board* [2015] NZHRRT 27, [70].

[21] Privacy Act 1993, s 2(1) defines 'agency' in wide terms. It includes both public and private sector persons and bodies. An individual can be an agency for the purposes of the Act. But there are certain exclusions, a key exclusion being that of the news media in relation to their news activities. Also excluded is personal information collected or held by an individual solely or principally for the purpose of, or in connection with, that individual's personal, family or household affairs – unless its collection, disclosure or use would be highly offensive to an ordinary reasonable person. See Privacy Act 1993, s 56(1).

[22] The complaint procedure and enforcement proceedings before the Tribunal are described in section III.

[23] Human Rights Act 1993, s 123; Privacy Act, s 89.

[24] Privacy Act 1993, s 46.

[25] Privacy Act 1993, s 53(b).

Principles 8 to 11 cover the use, retention and disclosure of personal information, while Principle 12 relates to unique identifiers such as customer numbers. With one exception the information privacy principles do not confer on any person any legal right that is enforceable in a court of law. The exception applies to the entitlements conferred by information privacy principle 6(1).[26]

As it is not practical to reproduce the text of the information privacy principles here, a brief summary follows:[27]

- *Principle 1*: An agency must not collect personal information unless it is for a lawful purpose connected with a function or activity of that agency, and the collection is necessary for that purpose.
- *Principle 2*: Personal information must be collected from the individual to whom the information relates, unless certain exceptions apply.
- *Principle 3*: Where an agency collects information directly from an individual, it must generally take reasonable steps to ensure that the individual is aware of:
  - the fact that the information is being collected and why it is being collected;
  - who will receive the information;
  - the identity of the agency that is collecting and will hold the information;
  - the specific law (if any) governing the collection of the information and whether or not providing the information is voluntary or mandatory;
  - the consequences (if any) if all or any of the information is not provided;
  - the individual's rights of access to the information and to have it corrected.
- *Principle 4*: An agency must not collect personal information by unlawful means, or by means that are unfair or intrude to an unreasonable extent on the personal affairs of the individual concerned.
- *Principle 5*: An agency that holds personal information must take steps to safeguard the information against loss, unauthorised access, use, modification, or disclosure and other misuse.
- *Principle 6*: If an agency holds personal information in such a way that it can readily be retrieved, the person to whom the information relates is entitled to have confirmation of whether or not the agency holds the information, to have access to the information and, if given access, to be told that he or she may request correction of the information. Agencies may refuse to give access to the information for a variety of reasons. Those reasons are stated (exhaustively) in sections 27 to 29. Refusal is not permitted for any other reason.[28]
- *Principle 7*: Individuals are entitled to request that personal information about them is corrected and, if the information is not corrected, to request that there is attached to the information a statement of the correction sought but not made.

[26] Privacy Act 1993, s 11.
[27] The full text of the 12 information privacy principles is to be found in the Privacy Act 1993, s 6.
[28] Privacy Act 1993, s 30.

- *Principle 8*: An agency must not use personal information without taking reasonable steps to ensure that the information is accurate, up to date, complete, relevant and not misleading.
- *Principle 9*: An agency must not keep personal information for longer than is required for the purpose for which the information may lawfully be used.
- *Principle 10*: An agency that holds personal information obtained in connection with one purpose must not use it for another purpose. There are a number of situations in which this prohibition does not apply.
- *Principle 11*: An agency must not disclose personal information except in certain specified circumstances.
- *Principle 12*: An agency must not assign a unique identifier to an individual unless this is necessary to enable the agency to carry out its functions efficiently, the identifier must be truly unique and the identity of the individual must be clearly established. Unique identifiers assigned for one purpose do not have to be disclosed for another, unrelated purpose.

It is beyond the scope of a chapter on damages as a remedy to address the meaning and application of the information privacy principles. An index to the jurisprudence of the Human Rights Review Tribunal dating from 2012 can be found on the Tribunal's website.[29]

III. Complaints under the Privacy Act

A complaint by an aggrieved individual that an agency has breached an information privacy principle is required to be dealt with in accordance with the two-tier procedure prescribed by Part 8 of the Privacy Act. In the first instance the complaint must be investigated by the Privacy Commissioner. Proceedings before the Tribunal are permitted only where an investigation has been conducted under Part 8, or where conciliation under section 74 has not resulted in settlement.[30] The lodging of a complaint with the Privacy Commissioner is more than a merely formal step. An important aim of the Privacy Act is to secure voluntary compliance with its principles, and on receiving a complaint the Privacy Commissioner must attempt to reach a settlement between the parties.[31] Only if

[29] The Tribunal's home page is at www.justice.govt.nz/tribunals/human-rights/. For earlier decisions of the Tribunal dating back to 2002, see the New Zealand Legal Information Institute (NZLii) website at www.nzlii.org/nz/cases/NZHRRT/. Commentaries include P Roth (ed), *Privacy Law and Practice* (online edn, LexisNexis); P Roth and GDS Taylor, *Access to Information*, 2nd edn (Wellington, LexisNexis, 2016); Bell et al (n 8); Tobin and Penk (n 17).

[30] Privacy Act 1993, s 82.

[31] For a summary of the statutory provisions that apply to an investigation by the Privacy Commissioner, see *Director of Human Rights Proceedings [NKR] v Accident Compensation Corporation* [2014] NZHRRT 1, (2014) 10 HRNZ 279, [25] and *Gray v Ministry for Children (Strike-Out Application)* [2018] NZHRRT 13.

those efforts fail can the matter proceed to the Tribunal by way of civil proceedings. Following an adversarial hearing the Tribunal can award a wide range of remedies and substantial damages.

It is clear from the annual reports released by the Privacy Commissioner that the alternative dispute resolution scheme as facilitated by the Commissioner is an effective one, providing speedy, low-cost, informal and non-adversarial resolution of complaints where possible. The *Annual Report 2016*, for example, confirms the effectiveness of the Commissioner's informal investigation and resolution processes.[32] In the year to 30 June 2016, nearly 50 per cent of cases were settled. When cases cannot be settled, the Commissioner has the option of referring the matter to the Director of Human Rights Proceedings, who may choose to take the case to the Tribunal.[33] If no such case is taken, the person aggrieved can file his or her own proceedings in the Tribunal.

IV. Interference with Privacy

In the context of the present chapter the process by which complaints are dealt with is less important than what can be complained about. The only complaint permitted by the Privacy Act is a complaint that there has been 'an interference with the privacy of an individual', a term defined in two different ways by section 66 of the Act.[34] The first definition is contained in section 66(1), while the second is contained in section 66(2).

Under the first limb (ie section 66(1)) the individual must:

(a) prove an action by the agency which has breached an information privacy principle or a code of practice; *and*

(b) satisfy the Tribunal that that action:

 (i) has caused or may cause him or her loss, detriment, damage or injury; *or*

 (ii) has adversely affected, or may adversely affect, his or her rights, benefits, privileges, obligations, or interests; *or*

 (iii) has resulted in, or may result in, significant humiliation, significant loss of dignity, or significant injury to his or her feelings.

It can be seen that it is not sufficient for the person aggrieved to prove only a breach of an information privacy principle or a code of practice. The individual must additionally have suffered a stipulated negative consequence as a result of such breach, or there must at least be the possibility of such consequence. Only if these

[32] Privacy Commissioner, *Privacy Commissioner Annual Report 2016* (Wellington, November 2016) 16–19. See also *Gray* (n 31) [12]–[29].

[33] Privacy Act 1993, s 82(2), (4). The Director of Human Rights Proceedings is appointed under the Human Rights Act 1993, s 20A.

[34] The text of the Privacy Act 1993, s 66 is appended at the end of this chapter.

conditions are satisfied is there 'an interference with the privacy' of the individual for which the Tribunal can award one or more of the remedies listed in section 85 of the Act, including damages of the kind allowed by section 88 of the Act.[35]

While the stipulated negative consequences required in the liability context overlap to a degree with the forms of harm for which damages may be awarded, the overlap is not complete, as shown in Table 14.1.

Table 14.1 Specified negative consequences: liability and damages

Liability **Section 66(1)**	**Damages** **Section 88(1)**
(b) in the opinion of the Commissioner or, as the case may be, the Tribunal, the action—	(1) In any proceedings under section 82 or section 83, the Tribunal may award damages against the defendant for an interference with the privacy of an individual in respect of any 1 or more of the following:
(i) has caused, or may cause, loss, detriment, damage, or injury to that individual; or	(a) pecuniary loss suffered as a result of, and expenses reasonably incurred by the aggrieved individual for the purpose of, the transaction or activity out of which the interference arose:
(ii) has adversely affected, or may adversely affect, the rights, benefits, privileges, obligations, or interests of that individual; or	(b) loss of any benefit, whether or not of a monetary kind, which the aggrieved individual might reasonably have been expected to obtain but for the interference:
(iii) has resulted in, or may result in, significant humiliation, significant loss of dignity, or significant injury to the feelings of that individual.	(c) humiliation, loss of dignity, and injury to the feelings of the aggrieved individual.

Under the second limb of section 66 (ie section 66(2)), a refusal of a principle 6 request for access to personal information or a refusal of a principle 7 request that personal information be corrected does not require proof of a consequential actual or potential negative outcome. It is only necessary that the Commissioner or Tribunal (as the case may be) be persuaded there was no proper basis for the

[35] The definitional requirement of a breach plus harm confines liability to the person aggrieved. However, a wide range of persons has standing to be heard on the matters to be taken into account by the Tribunal in determining the particular proceedings. See Human Rights Act 1993, s 108, which, by virtue of s 89 of the Privacy Act 1993, applies to the latter Act. For a striking example of the application of this provision in the context of the Privacy Act, see *Director of Human Rights Proceedings v Sensible Sentencing Group Trust (Application by Victims to be Heard)* [2013] NZHRRT 26, where two victims of sexual offending by the person aggrieved were recognised as having standing to appear and to call evidence.

decision to refuse. Failure to comply with the statutory time limits attaching to requests under principles 6 and 7 is 'deemed' to be a refusal to make the information available.[36] The reason why breaches of principles 6 and 7 are treated differently from the other information privacy principles is that, alone among the principles, principle 6 confers a right enforceable in a court of law.[37] The right to request correction of personal information is the necessary and logical extension of the right of an individual to have access to personal information held by an agency. It is through principle 7 that the individual is able to request correction of the information, or to request that there be attached to the information a statement of the correction sought but not made.[38]

V. Causation

In proceedings under the Privacy Act, causation falls to be considered in two separate contexts:[39]

(a) Liability. In the context of the first limb of section 66 (ie section 66(1)), a causal link must be established between the action of the agency and one of the specified negative consequences listed in section 66(1)(b)(i) to (iii). Causation is not, however, an element of the second limb of section 66 (ie section 66(2)), particularly in those instances where the deeming provisions of section 66(3) and (4) operate.

(b) Remedy. Before damages can be awarded for an interference with the privacy of an individual, there must be a causal connection between that interference and one of the forms of loss or harm listed in section 88(1)(a), (b) or (c).[40] This causation requirement applies to both section 66(1) and section 66(2) cases.

In both contexts the causation standard is the same. The plaintiff must show that the defendant's act or omission was a contributing cause to the loss or harm in the sense that it constituted a material cause:[41]

> [59] While it has been accepted causation may in appropriate circumstances be assumed or inferred (see *Winter v Jans* HC Hamilton CIV-2003-419-8154, 6 April 2004 at [33]), it would appear no clear causation standard has yet been established in relation to s 66(1).
>
> [60] As pointed out by Gaudron J in *Chappel v Hart* (1998) 195 CLR 232, 238 (HCA), questions of causation are not answered in a legal vacuum. Rather, they are answered in

[36] Privacy Act 1993, s 66(3). The timeframe for making a decision on an information privacy request is prescribed by s 40.

[37] Privacy Act 1993, s 11.

[38] *Heta v Ministry of Social Development* [2013] NZHRRT 8, [53].

[39] *Sansom v Department of Internal Affairs* [2016] NZHRRT 17, [42].

[40] *Winter v Jans* (HC Hamilton, 6 April 2004) CIV-2003-419-854, [33].

[41] *Taylor v Orcon Ltd* [2015] NZHRRT 15, (2015) 10 HRNZ 458, [59]–[61].

> the legal framework in which they arise. In the present context that framework includes the purpose of the Privacy Act which is to 'promote and protect individual privacy' and second, the fact that s 66(1) does not require proof that harm has actually occurred, merely that it may occur. Given the difficulties involved in making a forecast about the course of future events and the factors (and interplay of factors) which might bring about or affect that course, the causation standard cannot be set at a level unattainable otherwise than in the most exceptional of cases. Even where harm has occurred it is seldom the outcome of a single cause. Often two or more factors cause the harm and sometimes the amount of their respective contributions cannot be quantified. It would be contrary to the purpose of the Privacy Act were such circumstance to fall outside the s 66(1) definition of interference with privacy. The more so given multiple causes present no difficulty in tort law. See Stephen Todd 'Causation and Remoteness of Damage' in Stephen Todd (ed) *The Law of Torts in New Zealand* (6th ed, Thomson Reuters, Wellington, 2013) at [20.2.02]:
>
>> Provided we can say that the totality of two or more sources caused an injury, it does not matter that the amount of their respective contributions cannot be quantified. The plaintiff need prove only that a particular source is more than minimal and is a cause in fact.
>
> [61] Given these factors a plaintiff claiming an interference with privacy must show the defendant's act or omission was a contributing cause in the sense that it constituted a material cause. The concept of materiality denotes that the act or omission must have had (or may have) a real influence on the occurrence (or possible occurrence) of the particular form of harm. The act or omission must make (or may make) more than a de minimis or trivial contribution to the occurrence (or possible occurrence) of the loss. It is not necessary for the cause to be the sole cause, main cause, direct cause, indirect cause or 'but for' cause. No form of words will ultimately provide an automatic answer to what is essentially a broad judgment.

In *Winter v Jans* it was accepted that causation may in appropriate circumstances be assumed or inferred from the nature of the breach.[42]

VI. Remedies

Once the Tribunal is satisfied on the balance of probabilities that any action of the defendant was an interference with the privacy of an individual, it may grant one or more of the following remedies:[43]

(a) a declaration that the action of the defendant was an interference with the privacy of an individual;

(b) an order restraining the defendant from continuing or repeating the interference, or from engaging in, or causing or permitting others to engage in,

[42] *Winter* (n 40) [33]–[34].

[43] Privacy Act 1993, ss 84, 85.

conduct of the same kind as that constituting the interference, or conduct of any similar kind specified in the order;

(c) damages in accordance with section 88;

(d) an order that the defendant perform any acts specified in the order with a view to remedying the interference, or redressing any loss or damage suffered by the aggrieved individual as a result of the interference, or both;

(e) such other relief as the Tribunal thinks fit.

In a chapter focused on damages as a remedy the other forms of relief permitted by section 85 of the Act will receive only limited attention. In the brief discussion that follows the cases cited are mentioned for the purpose of illustration only.

A. Declaration

While the granting of a declaration under section 85(1)(a) of the Act is discretionary in nature, declaratory relief should not ordinarily be denied where a clear breach of statutory obligation by an agency has been found. Only where an equally clear, but exceptionally egregious, breach of the standards to be expected of a litigant exists should declaratory relief be denied.[44] Relevant conduct includes whether the plaintiff has acted with clean hands, whether he or she has acted 'fairly and appropriately', and whether there has been delay.[45]

B. Restraining and Remedial Orders

In *Hammond v Credit Union Baywide* (*Hammond*), NZCU Baywide (Ms Hammond's former employer), in breach of information privacy principle 11, disseminated a warning about Ms Hammond to employment agencies in the Hawke's Bay geographical area, with the specific intent that Ms Hammond be unable to find employment in that area either generally or in the finance field specifically.[46] Through members of its senior management team it had simultaneously brought extreme pressure on Ms Hammond's new employer to terminate her employment. In these circumstances the Tribunal made an order restraining NZCU Baywide from continuing or repeating the interference with Ms Hammond's privacy, and further ordered under section 85(1)(d) that a retraction of the 'warning' be sent to the employment agencies.[47]

[44] *Geary v New Zealand Psychologists Board* [2012] NZHC 384, [2012] 2 NZLR 414, [107]–[108]. This principle was relied on by the Tribunal when denying declaratory relief in *Steele v Board of Trustees of Salisbury School* [2012] NZHRRT 20; *Rafiq v Commissioner of Inland Revenue* [2012] NZHRRT 12.

[45] *Geary* (n 44) [108]; *Te Wini v Askelund* [2015] NZHRRT 21, [50]; *Deeming v Whangarei District Council* [2015] NZHRRT 55, [76].

[46] *Hammond v Credit Union Baywide* [2015] NZHRRT 6, (2015) 10 HRNZ 66.

[47] ibid [184], [189.6].

In a case concerning the collection of information by CCTV surveillance, two neighbouring households (one of which operated a bed and breakfast business) fell out after the owner of the bed and breakfast installed three surveillance cameras pointing directly on to the plaintiffs' property and into their home. The Tribunal, having found breaches of privacy principles 1, 3, 4 and 6, ordered that the surveillance system be reset to comply with the information privacy principles, that the defendant cease immediately the unlawful collection of personal information, that he provide the plaintiffs with the notification required under principle 3, and that he also erase or otherwise destroy any personal information held about the plaintiffs and their family.[48]

The decisions in *Director of Human Rights Proceedings v Schubach* and in *Watson v Capital and Coast District Health Board* are examples where the Tribunal made orders under section 85(1)(d) that the withheld information be made available to the plaintiff.[49]

VII. Damages

The forms of loss and harm for which damages may be awarded for an interference with privacy are prescribed by section 88 of the Privacy Act. Only section 88(1) is relevant in the present context:

> **88 Damages**
>
> (1) In any proceedings under section 82 or section 83, the Tribunal may award damages against the defendant for an interference with the privacy of an individual in respect of any 1 or more of the following:
>
> (a) pecuniary loss suffered as a result of, and expenses reasonably incurred by the aggrieved individual for the purpose of, the transaction or activity out of which the interference arose:
>
> (b) loss of any benefit, whether or not of a monetary kind, which the aggrieved individual might reasonably have been expected to obtain but for the interference:
>
> (c) humiliation, loss of dignity, and injury to the feelings of the aggrieved individual.

Being entirely statute-based, the remedies regime in the Privacy Act is not handicapped by the challenges faced in the context of the New Zealand Bill of Rights Act 1990, where the absence of an explicit remedies provision has resulted in a sometimes controversial development of a remedies regime by the senior courts.[50]

[48] *Armfield v Naughton* [2014] NZHRRT 48, (2014) 9 HRNZ 808.

[49] *Director of Human Rights Proceedings v Schubach* [2015] NZHRRT 4; *Watson v Capital and Coast District Health Board* [2015] NZHRRT 27.

[50] A Butler and P Butler, *The New Zealand Bill of Rights Act: A Commentary*, 2nd edn (Wellington, LexisNexis, 2015) [1.3.12], chs 26–28. See also in particular JNE Varuhas, 'The Development of the Damages Remedy under the New Zealand Bill of Rights Act 1990: From Torts to Administrative Law' [2016] *New Zealand Law Review* 213.

A. Damages as a Remedy under the Privacy Act and the Development of Principle

The language used in section 88(1)(a), (b) and (c) of the Privacy Act is not materially different from that first used in the context of the civil proceedings regime in the Race Relations Act 1971.[51] It has not been possible to find any reported decision under that legislation in which the terms 'pecuniary loss', 'loss of any benefit' and 'humiliation, loss of dignity and injury to feelings' were considered.[52] The Act was repealed by the Human Rights Act.[53]

In the case of the now section 88 of the Privacy Act and its equivalent in the Human Rights Act (section 92M), there is similarly a surprising absence of detailed consideration by senior courts of the meaning and application of key terms. There is also little guidance as to the assessment of the quantum of damages for humiliation, loss of dignity and injury to feelings. In the case of the Health and Disability Commissioner Act the position is different, in that the 2000 decision of the High Court in *Director of Proceedings v O'Neil* addressed both the meaning of the common terms and the assessment of quantum.[54] That decision is discussed further in section IX.A of this chapter.

In 2004, a Full Court of the High Court was convened for the purpose of giving general guidance as to the proper quantum of awards in cases under section 92M of the Human Rights Act.[55] However, it transpired that the particular case was unsuitable for the intended purpose, the decision of the Tribunal in that case being found to be deficient in several respects. For example, in a case about sexual harassment it had failed (inter alia) to identify the conduct of the defendant on which the finding of liability was based and how it had resulted in the damages award. In addition, the Director of Human Rights Proceedings (the appellant) conceded at the hearing that there was no proper basis for challenging the award.

In dismissing the appeal, the Full Court observed (obiter) that it was the responsibility of the Human Rights Commission, the Tribunal and, on appeal, the High Court to give full effect to what Thorp J in *Coburn v Human Rights Commission* called 'the special nature and purpose of human rights legislation'.[56] The Full Court observed that it was 'special' because 'it bears on the very essence of human identity'. It was also special because it presented to the Commission,

[51] Race Relations Act 1971, s 22. Damages could be awarded for racial discrimination in such fields as access to public places, vehicles and facilities, the provision of goods and services, employment and housing.

[52] In *Race Relations Conciliator v Inglis Enterprises Ltd* [1993] NZAR 314, the then Equal Opportunities Tribunal made an award for emotional harm without discussing the ambit and application of the statutory terms.

[53] See Human Rights Act, s 146.

[54] *Director of Proceedings v O'Neil* [2001] NZAR 59, (2000) 6 HRNZ 311, [23]–[35] (HC).

[55] *Director of Human Rights Proceedings v Cropp* (HC Auckland, 12 May 2004) AP7 – SW03, *per* Baragwanath and Harrison JJ.

[56] *Coburn v Human Rights Commission* [1994] 3 NZLR 323, 334.

to the Tribunal and to the Court on appeal the challenge of doing justice to each of the complainant, the defendant and the values of the legislation.[57] In describing the outcome of the case as unsatisfactory, the Full Court referred to the fact that six years previously, Gallen ACJ had agreed with the contention that the amounts awarded in New Zealand for sexual harassment appeared to be lower than and out of step with those awarded in comparable jurisdictions.[58] The Full Court agreed that in the circumstances there should be in New Zealand the same kind of guidance in this area as was provided in England to employment tribunals by *Vento v Chief Constable of West Yorkshire Police*, where three broad bands of compensation for injury to feelings, as distinct from compensation for psychiatric or similar personal injury, were set out.[59] The Full Court concluded its judgment by recording its expectation that in a suitable case the Commission would put before the Tribunal sufficient comparative material to allow it, as the expert decision-maker, to make, in the light of the (then) $200,000 ceiling on its jurisdiction, a determination unfettered by past authority. Such decision would either itself give the necessary guidance, or provide a suitable platform for another Full Court to perform the task for which the present Full Court had been convened.[60]

It was not until the March 2015 decision in *Hammond* that the Tribunal attempted a detailed statement of the general principles to be applied when awarding damages for humiliation, loss of dignity and injury to feelings. The Tribunal identified three descriptive bands into which awards for emotional harm will generally fall.[61] In so doing it endeavoured to bring some consistency to awards, while recognising that awards are both fact-specific and inherently subjective in nature.[62]

That does not mean to say that no guidance at all is to be found in decisions of the High Court on appeal from the Tribunal under the Human Rights Act and Privacy Act. But where awards by the Tribunal have been lowered by the High Court, this has not been justified by reference to principle.[63] Rather, the High Court has simply reached a different view on the facts as to what an appropriate award should be. So, for example, in *Winter v Jans*, an award for loss of benefit under section 88(1)(b) of $4,000 to each of Mr and Mrs Jans was reduced to

[57] *Cropp* (n 55) [17]–[19].

[58] *Laursen v Proceedings Commissioner* (1998) 5 HRNZ 18, 28. See also the discussion in G Hammond, 'Beyond Dignity?' in J Berryman and R Bigwood (eds), *The Law of Remedies: New Directions in the Common Law* (Toronto, Irwin Law Inc, 2010) 188–89.

[59] *Vento v Chief Constable of West Yorkshire Police* [2002] EWCA Civ 1871.

[60] *Cropp* (n 55) [22]–[23].

[61] The *Hammond* (n 46) decision is discussed in greater detail in sections VII.A and VII.B, and in section IX.B.

[62] *Hammond* (n 46) [172]–[177].

[63] In *Chief Executive of the Ministry of Social Development v Holmes* [2013] NZHC 672, [2013] NZAR 760, [10], the High Court accepted that an appeal as to liability is a general appeal to which *Austin, Nichols & Co Inc v Stichting Lodestar* [2008] NZSC 103, [2008] 2 NZLR 141, [4]–[5] applies, but left open the question whether in respect of the exercise by the Tribunal of its discretion to award damages (and to fix quantum) it was necessary that it be demonstrated the Tribunal has made an error of principle, considered irrelevant matters, failed to consider relevant matters or was plainly wrong.

$3,500 each.[64] In *Chief Executive of the Ministry of Social Development v Holmes* (*Holmes*), an award of $7,000 for emotional harm was reduced to $2,000, largely because the High Court took a view of the facts different from that taken by the Tribunal.[65] Nevertheless, in that case the High Court, noting that the Tribunal under a new chair had lifted its award of damages, observed that to some extent this was inevitable, as earlier decisions needed to be adjusted for inflation over the years. Nor was it wrong that consistency in awards be pursued.[66] The Court rejected a submission that the Tribunal always had to take its lead from the High Court, noting that the High Court sits as an appeal court while the Tribunal deals with a much higher number of cases. The Court saw no reason why the Tribunal, at first instance, cannot come to the conclusion that it was necessary to recalibrate the level of awards against which there should be some consistency. That view would be informed by the much larger number of cases coming before the Tribunal. It could then be taken on appeal to the High Court.[67]

Because the award of damages for pecuniary loss (section 88(1)(a)) and for loss of benefit (section 88(1)(b)) does not present challenges of a substantive kind, it is intended to provide only a brief overview of the kinds of loss recognised by the Tribunal under those provisions. Thereafter the issue of emotional harm will be addressed, particularly with regard to the interpretation of the terms 'humiliation', 'loss of dignity' and 'injury to feelings', as well as the assessment of quantum.

First it is necessary to address the question of exemplary damages, the conduct of the defendant and the award of damages in excess of those sought.

B. The Question of Exemplary Damages and the Conduct of the Defendant

The three heads of damages allowed by section 88(1) are, on their face, compensatory in nature. The Privacy Act makes no provision for the award of exemplary damages. An early decision of the Tribunal given in 2003 did leave open the question, but jurisdiction to award exemplary damages was doubted on appeal. In declining to make an express determination the High Court indicated that 'aggravating' conduct of the defendant was best taken into account in the context of assessing the seriousness of the impact of the information privacy breach on the complainant.[68]

On one view it is difficult to see how jurisdiction to award exemplary damages could be found. Exemplary damages are anomalous. Civil remedies are not

[64] *Winter* (n 40) [60].
[65] *Holmes* (n 63) [115], [155].
[66] ibid [126]–[128].
[67] ibid [129].
[68] *Jans v Winter* [2003] NZHRRT 21, [152]–[154]; *Winter* (n 40) [53]–[54]. See also *C v Director of Human Rights Proceedings* (HC Auckland, 6 September 2010) CIV-2010-404-001662.

generally designed to punish. The reach of exemplary damages should therefore be confined rather than expanded.[69] The Tribunal's power to award damages is entirely statute-conferred. Each of the three permitted categories of damages is overtly compensatory in nature. No express provision is made for the award of exemplary damages. Nor is provision made for the award of damages for a wrongful interference with privacy where no loss or harm of the kind recognised in section 88(1) has occurred. On conventional principles of statutory interpretation it would be difficult to infer jurisdiction to award exemplary damages, particularly when of the three statutes under which the Tribunal has jurisdiction to award damages, only the Health and Disability Commissioner Act makes provision for the award of such damages.[70]

The view foreshadowed by the High Court in *Winter v Jans* and adopted by the New Zealand Law Commission is that a distinct punitive element is not required because the motives and conduct of the defendant are to be taken into account in the context of section 85(4), which provides that while it is not a defence that the interference with privacy was unintentional or without negligence on the part of the defendant, the Tribunal must take the conduct of the defendant into account in deciding what, if any, remedy to grant.[71] The High Court in *Winter v Jans* and in *Holmes* distinguished the fact that the breach was unintentional or without negligence from the obligation to take the conduct of the defendant into account. In both cases the High Court held the Tribunal must take into account both aggravating and mitigating conduct.[72]

While it is understandable that the conduct of a defendant might increase (or decrease) or prolong (or shorten) a plaintiff's pecuniary loss, loss of benefit or humiliation, loss of dignity or injury to feelings, there is a danger that unless properly confined, section 85(4) could draw the Tribunal into the impermissible consideration of such issues as punishment of the defendant (or of the plaintiff) or the 'equitable' apportionment of responsibility or blame for the loss or harm in fact suffered.[73]

In *Hammond* the Tribunal awarded the plaintiff $98,000 in damages for humiliation, loss of dignity and injury to feelings, because the interference with

[69] *Couch v Attorney-General (No 2)* [2010] NZSC 27, [2010] 3 NZLR 149, [178] *per* Tipping J.

[70] Health and Disability Commissioner Act 1994, s 57(1)(d). The application of this provision was considered in *O'Neil* (n 54).

[71] *Winter* (n 40) [54]; *Holmes* (n 63) [140], [143]; Law Commission, *Review of the Privacy Act 1993: Review of the Law of Privacy Stage 4*, NZLC R123 (2011) [6.61]. In *Holmes* ((n 63) [143]) it was held that in assessing the conduct of the defendant, account could be taken of the fact that the misreading of a letter sent by Mr Holmes to the Ministry of Social Development was explicable on the basis that the terms of the letter had not been clear. As to this, the Tribunal had reached the opposite conclusion, finding that the relevant paragraph had been clear.

[72] *Winter* (n 40) [52]–[54]; *Holmes* (n 63) [140].

[73] For a possible example of how such irrelevant matters can impermissibly affect a decision on remedy and damages, see *Proceedings Commissioner v Health Waikato Ltd* (2000) 6 HRNZ 274, [74]–[81].

her privacy had occurred against a background of hostility to Mrs Hammond and there had been a sustained campaign by the defendant to inflict on her as much harm and humiliation as possible, first by ensuring she could not find employment in the Hawke's Bay area (if not further afield) and then to secure her dismissal by her current employer.[74] The emotional harm caused had been substantial. The Tribunal stressed that the award of damages was to compensate for humiliation, loss of dignity and injury to feelings actually suffered, not to punish the defendant.[75]

When the *Hammond* decision was delivered on 2 March 2015, the damages award was the highest ever made by the Tribunal for emotional harm. It has since been superseded by *MacGregor v Craig*, a decision given on 2 March 2016 under the provisions of the Human Rights Act similar to section 88 of the Privacy Act.[76] In that case the Tribunal found that the defendant had flouted the terms of a confidential settlement reached under the Human Rights Act, and in so doing had relentlessly exposed Ms MacGregor to adverse media attention on a nationwide basis, and caused her to be stigmatised as having engaged in sexually inappropriate behaviour and as a person who could not manage or control her own finances. The award for humiliation, loss of dignity and injury to feelings was $120,000, to reflect the degree of emotional harm that had in fact been caused. Neither that award nor that in *Hammond* was appealed.

C. Apology

An appropriate and timely apology can be taken into account when assessing whether the defendant's conduct has ameliorated the harm caused by the privacy breach.[77] The apology cannot 'erase' the humiliation, loss of dignity or injury to feelings caused by the interference with privacy. Nor is it a 'get out of jail free' card. In most cases where damages are sought for emotional harm, the question is likely to be whether and to what degree the emotional harm experienced by the particular plaintiff has been ameliorated. While this is a fact-specific inquiry, it can be said that ordinarily an apology must be timely, effective and sincere before weight can be given to it. It is not inevitable that an apology, even if sincerely and promptly offered, will ameliorate the emotional harm experienced by the plaintiff. Much will depend on the sensitivities of the particular plaintiff and the particular circumstances of the case.[78]

[74] *Hammond* (n 46) [179]–[183].
[75] ibid [170.3].
[76] *MacGregor v Craig* [2016] NZHRRT 6, [146]–[148].
[77] *AB v Chief Executive, Ministry of Social Development* [2011] NZHRRT 16, [37]. In that case the defendant took one year to acknowledge the breach and another year to apologise for it. The Tribunal considered the apology had no mitigating effect, describing it as having been provided at the 'eleventh hour', after proceedings had been commenced, and considered it to be motivated by litigation concerns. Contrast *Williams v Accident Compensation Corporation* [2017] NZHRRT 26, where the apology was offered with alacrity and was sincerely made.
[78] *Williams* (n 77) [41].

D. Damages in Excess of those Sought

In *Holmes*, the Tribunal awarded damages higher than those sought by the self-represented plaintiff in his statement of claim. The High Court rejected a submission (based on the civil law principle that a court does not have jurisdiction to make an award higher than that claimed) that the Tribunal does not have jurisdiction to award damages in excess of those sought.[79] The Court pointed out that the Tribunal's jurisdiction under the Privacy Act is a special statutory jurisdiction, and there is nothing in the Act that requires the applicant to specify the amount of damages sought. The High Court agreed with the Tribunal's reasoning that the Privacy Act should be interpreted and applied in a manner that is not legalistic and which does not place barriers, especially of a technical nature, between the claimant and a just outcome.[80] It would accordingly be 'quite wrong' for the Tribunal or the Court to be bound by a figure nominated by a self-represented litigant.

VIII. Pecuniary Loss and Loss of a Benefit

The most commonly encountered form of pecuniary loss is that of legal expenses. Expenses of such kind, which are compensable under section 88(1)(a), are to be distinguished from costs in the proceedings before the Tribunal. In *Proceedings Commissioner v Health Waikato Ltd*, an employer withheld two items of personal information, being two letters that could have been of some help to the complainant in the context of his employment dispute with that employer. Once the existence of the letters had come to light, application had been made to the Employment Tribunal for the late introduction of this fresh evidence. The High Court (on appeal from the Tribunal) awarded legal costs of $1,000 in relation to the making of that application, and for the time and responsibility involved in making the difficult decision in the weeks before the hearing as to whether the fixture for the appeal or the application to introduce the letters should be abandoned.[81]

Other awards for legal costs have been more substantial. In *Meulenbroek v Vision Antenna Systems Ltd* the award was $6,929.00 for legal advice in the period leading to the plaintiff's dismissal for practising his religion,[82] while in *Hammond*

[79] *Holmes* (n 63) [104]–[108].

[80] In approximately 75% of cases presently before the Tribunal, one or more of the parties is self-represented: *Wall v Fairfax New Zealand Ltd (Delay)* (n 9) [5]. In addition, the Tribunal has a mandatory statutory duty to act according to the substantial merits of the case, without regard to technicalities. In exercising its powers and functions it must act in accordance with the principles of natural justice, in a manner that is fair and reasonable and according to equity and good conscience. See Human Rights Act 1993, s 105, which is incorporated into the Privacy Act 1993 by s 89 of that latter Act.

[81] *Health Waikato* (n 73) [83].

[82] *Meulenbroek v Vision Antenna Systems Ltd* [2014] NZHRRT 51, (2015) 10 HRNZ 113.

the award was $15,543.10. In another case in which a lawyer had unjustifiably withheld documents from a client, the client was awarded $1,374.25 for legal expenses incurred in hiring a second lawyer to pursue the request for the release of the file.[83]

Conventional litigation costs incurred by the successful party in the proceedings before the Tribunal can be awarded under section 85(2). However, as presently constituted, the Tribunal does not apply the civil litigation rule that costs follow the event. The High Court has agreed.[84]

As to damages under section 88(1)(b) for loss of benefit, it is to be noted that the benefit can be of a monetary kind but is not required to be, and in a series of cases the High Court has given an expansive reading to 'benefit'. It includes circumstances where the personal information was either required for, or could have been deployed in, court or tribunal proceedings. Loss of peace of mind is also a provable damage under this heading.

In *Proceedings Commissioner v Health Waikato Ltd*, the High Court held that the denial of the opportunity to use the two letters in the course of cross-examination before the Employment Tribunal and to make submissions on the letters was a loss of a benefit of a non-monetary kind. That disadvantage had been exacerbated by the need to make a contested application to use the letters as fresh evidence on the appeal.[85] In awarding $5,000 for loss of benefit, the Court placed considerable significance on the fact that the complainant had lost the benefit of being able to utilise the two letters in the cross-examination of a witness and in submissions before the Employment Tribunal so that the complainant could feel satisfied that his case had had the best presentation possible and that he had had 'a fair crack of the whip'.

In *Winter v Jans*, Mr and Mrs Jans defaulted in their obligations under a mortgage, with the result their property was sold in a mortgagee sale by public auction. Mr Winter was the real estate agent instructed by the mortgagee to sell the property. Mr and Mrs Jans being dissatisfied with the course of events, they asked Mr Winter to provide them with all their personal information held on his file. Mr Winter refused and eventually the file was 'lost'. The High Court held that Mr and Mrs Jans had lost the benefit of certainty.[86] They did not know whether there might have been documents on the file that would have assisted them in a claim against either the mortgagee bank or the real estate agency which employed Mr Winter. While the Tribunal's award was reduced to $3,500, the *Health Waikato* case was followed.

In *Grupen v Director of Human Rights Proceedings*, the claimant had been represented by Ms Grupen (a lawyer) in two civil proceedings.[87] A dispute developed over Ms Grupen's fees. That dispute went to cost revision, in which it became

[83] *Schubach* (n 49) [93].

[84] *Commissioner of Police v Andrews* [2015] NZHC 745, [2015] 3 NZLR 515, [61]–[71].

[85] *Health Waikato* (n 73) [71]–[84]. In *Dotcom v Crown Law Office* [2018] NZHRRT 7, [223]–[242], the Tribunal reviewed the relevant High Court decisions and concluded it was time for the level of awards for loss of benefit to be increased.

[86] *Winter* (n 40) [48].

[87] *Grupen v Director of Human Rights Proceedings* [2012] NZHC 580.

necessary for Ms Grupen to establish each of her attendances for which a fee had been charged. This she did by reference to handwritten entries in her diary recording the time spent and the nature of the attendance. However, Ms Grupen did not want to allow inspection of the diary entries by the complainant or his solicitor. Instead she prepared what she said was a transcript of the relevant information. The complainant's solicitor made a formal request for access to the diary entries from which the transcript had been taken. Ms Grupen refused. The Tribunal accepted that the complainant had thereby lost a benefit, namely the certainty that would have come from comparing the transcript with the actual diary entries. The complainant had been left believing that he might not have had a fair hearing in the cost revision. Damages of $5,000 were awarded under section 88(1)(b). That award and the reasoning process were upheld by the High Court on appeal.

In *Director of Human Rights Proceedings v Hamilton*, an accountant repeatedly failed to comply with a request by a client that she be given access to her personal information in the form of her tax returns, accounts and associated papers. On the question whether damages should be awarded under section 88(1)(b), the Tribunal emphasised that while the loss of benefit need not be of a monetary kind, the benefit must be one the aggrieved individual might reasonably have expected to have obtained but for the interference. In this regard the submission for the plaintiff was that the refusal by Mr Hamilton to release the personal information meant that the complainant lost the benefit of providing information and tax returns to the Inland Revenue Department in a timely fashion. The situation was said to be analogous to those circumstances in which the personal information was either required for, or could have been deployed in, court or tribunal proceedings, as in *Health Waikato* and *Winter v Jans*. The complainant had been seeking peace of mind in relation to her obligations to Inland Revenue, a benefit she had clearly lost. This loss of peace of mind was a provable damage under this limb of section 88.[88] While not disagreeing with this formulation, the Tribunal preferred to say that were it not for Mr Hamilton's sustained and obdurate refusal to provide the requested personal information, the complainant would have had the benefit of being able to obtain advice and assistance from a competent accountant able to provide effective representation.[89] Damages of $5,000 were awarded. In another case, $5,000 was similarly awarded by the Tribunal where a legal representative failed to make available to the former client a letter from the mother of the client's child, which could potentially have been deployed either in Family Court proceedings or in settlement negotiations.[90]

Damages have been awarded by the Tribunal where the loss of benefit was the loss of a good credit rating.[91] In that case, after a review of the awards made in

[88] *Director of Human Rights Proceedings v Hamilton* [2012] NZHRRT 24, [84].
[89] ibid [85].
[90] *Schubach* (n 49) [94]–[97].
[91] *Taylor* (n 41) [76].

Health Waikato and *Winter v Jans*, an award of $10,000 was made.[92] It has also been common for awards to be made for lost income.[93] Such form of loss should be readily recoverable.

IX. Damages for Emotional Harm

The third and final category of harm for which damages may be awarded is 'humiliation, loss of dignity and injury to the feelings' of the aggrieved individual. For convenience, such harm will on occasion be referred to collectively as 'emotional harm', though there is a question whether loss of dignity is an emotional harm.

Apart from the current statutory monetary ceiling of $350,000, the jurisdiction to award damages for emotional harm is not limited by a requirement that in determining whether to make an award and in determining the amount of damages, the emotional harm experienced by the person aggrieved is to be balanced against other countervailing public interests, such as the economic cost of compliance and the preservation of public funds.[94] All that the Privacy Act prescribes is a duty to take the conduct of the defendant into account in deciding what, if any, remedy to grant.[95] The Act does, however, require that the decision on remedy is made by a Tribunal that includes at least two members drawn from the Panel.

It is proposed to address next the meaning of the terms 'humiliation, loss of dignity and injury to feelings', and thereafter the assessment of quantum.

A. Humiliation, Loss of Dignity and Injury to Feelings

As mentioned, 'humiliation, loss of dignity and injury to feelings' is a category of damages common to all three of the Tribunal's jurisdictions. The Tribunal has held that an aggrieved individual is not required to establish all three of the heads of damages.[96] Those heads are to be read disjunctively, and it is not to be assumed that because one head of damage is established, the others are as well.[97]

A useful starting point is the decision in *Director of Proceedings v O'Neil*, a decision given under the Health and Disability Commissioner Act.[98] In that case

[92] ibid [77]–[80].

[93] See, eg, *Nakarawa v AFFCO NZ Ltd* [2014] NZHRRT 9; *Meulenbroek* (n 82); *Hammond* (n 46); *McClelland v Schindler Lifts NZ Ltd* [2015] NZHRRT 45; *MacGregor* (n 76).

[94] Contrast s 92P of the Human Rights Act 1993, which prescribes the matters to be taken into account when the Tribunal exercises its powers under s 92O of that Act. For the recent application of these provisions, see *Spencer* (n 14) [99]–[169].

[95] Privacy Act 1993, s 85(4), and see the earlier discussion of this provision in the context of exemplary damages.

[96] *Geary v Accident Compensation Corporation* [2013] NZHRRT 34, [148].

[97] *Schubach* (n 49) [98].

[98] *O'Neil* (n 54) [27]–[35].

the Tribunal awarded $20,000 for humiliation, loss of dignity and injury to feelings. The award was upheld by the High Court. In its decision the Court rejected a submission that the meaning of the phrase 'injury to feelings' should be restricted to humiliation or loss of dignity. The Court emphasised that semantic analysis of the phrase is inappropriate, and that the provision must be looked at and interpreted in the context of the Act as a whole and its clear purpose. The purpose of this category of damages is to provide compensation for injury to the mind, emotion or soul of a person, other than to his or her body. There is no reason why the words 'injury to the feelings' should be read or interpreted *ejusdem generis*. The 'feelings' of a person which are capable of being injured encompass a much wider range than the feeling of 'dignity', which, if harmed, may give rise to a state of humiliation. This category of damages is designed to compensate aggrieved persons, who may suffer mental, emotional or spiritual injuries (to feelings) in an infinite variety of ways. Although the High Court in this decision does not expressly address loss of dignity, it would appear the loss of dignity was conceived of as a form of emotional harm rather than as the concept of not being treated with dignity.[99]

The Court went on to say that the feelings of human beings are not intangible things. They are real and felt, but often not identified until the person stands back and looks inwards. They can encompass pleasant feelings (such as contentment, happiness, peacefulness and tranquillity) or be unpleasant (feelings such as fear, anger and anxiety). However a feeling can be described, it is clear that some feelings, such as fear, grief, sense of loss, anxiety, anger, despair, alarm and so on, can be categorised as injured feelings. They are feelings of a negative kind arising out of some outward event. To that extent they are injured feelings. It is necessary to look at the totality of the injury and the emotional state of the complainant. Injury to feelings often comprises a complex mix of feelings and emotions, which are often hard to compartmentalise and overlap. The task of fixing quantum of general damages is that of the original Tribunal that sees, hears and assesses the parties and the evidence. The High Court made approving reference to the decision in *Brickell v Attorney-General*, in which McGechan J stated that when assessing damages, the test is essentially one of fairness and community expectations.[100]

In *Winter v Jans* it was accepted that anxiety and stress come within 'injury to feelings', but not within humiliation and loss of dignity.[101] It was also accepted that not having the benefit of certainty as to whether a file lost by the real estate agent contained documents that could have assisted in a claim against the mortgagee or the real estate agent, caused an injury to feelings within the remedy provisions of

[99] ibid [28] ('Humiliation may involve loss of dignity and certainly will involve injury to feelings of self-worth and self-esteem. Humiliation, we would have thought, would always involve a loss of dignity. A loss of dignity would always have involved in injury to feelings. That would include a feeling of pride in oneself and general contentment').

[100] *Brickell v Attorney-General* (HC Wellington, 9 June 2000) CP267/97, [143]–[144].

[101] *Winter* (n 40) [36].

the Privacy Act. It was also loss of a benefit. But the Court cautioned that where the categories of emotional harm overlap, the total damages awarded should have regard to the totality of the situation.[102] The Tribunal should also endeavour to maintain some consistency in awards.[103]

The Tribunal has not to date attempted to define the three forms of emotional harm because, as observed by the Court of Appeal in the context of the almost identically worded Employment Relations Act 2000, section 123(1)(c)(i), claims for what amounts to damage for dignitary interests are 'complex and very important':[104]

> [73] … Remedies scholars (and increasingly courts) rightly see this as a particularly important and developing area of the law, which invokes a recognition of the fundamental importance of human dignity as perhaps *the* legal value in the twenty-first century. (See Hammond 'Beyond Dignity' in Berryman and Bigwood (eds) *The Law of Remedies: New Directions in the Common Law* (2009).) One of the problems identified with attempts to rigidly 'cap' awards in the developing dignity context is that the levels can ossify. At the same time, there has to be a sound basis for such awards, and there are very real conceptual and practical difficulties in establishing a spectrum as to where lines are to be drawn.

Regarding loss of dignity, the Tribunal's decision in *Hammond* made reference to the following description in *Law v Canada (Minister of Employment and Immigration)*, a case about discrimination based on age:[105]

> [53] … Human dignity means that an individual or group feels self-respect and self-worth. It is concerned with physical and psychological integrity and empowerment. Human dignity is harmed by unfair treatment premised upon personal traits or circumstances which do not relate to individual needs, capacities, or merits … Human dignity is harmed when individuals and groups are marginalized, ignored, or devalued …

This passage suggests that the loss follows from certain treatment, not necessarily emotional suffering. Contrast injury to feelings.

As to what is included in 'injury to feelings', the Tribunal in *Hammond* made reference to the relevant passages in *Winter v Jans* and in *O'Neil* already referred to.[106] In emphasising the substantial subjective element to the assessment of damages for emotional harm, the Tribunal was guided by the following description in *Vento v Chief Constable of West Yorkshire Police*:[107]

[102] ibid [49].
[103] ibid [59].
[104] *Commissioner of Police v Hawkins* [2009] NZCA 209, [2009] 3 NZLR 381, [73]. Note, however, that the Privacy Act 1993 does not contain any counterpart to the Employment Relations Act 2000, s 124, which provides that the extent to which an employee contributed to the situation that gave rise to the personal grievance may be taken into account when deciding the nature and extent of remedies to be provided.
[105] *Hammond* (n 46) [152], [170.6]; *Law v Canada (Minister of Employment and Immigration)* [1999] 1 SCR 497, [53].
[106] *Hammond* (n 46) [153], [170.7].
[107] ibid [170.5].

> [50] It is self evident that the assessment of compensation for an injury or loss, which is neither physical nor financial, presents special problems for the judicial process, which aims to produce results objectively justified by evidence, reason and precedent. Subjective feelings of upset, frustration, worry, anxiety, mental distress, fear, grief, anguish, humiliation, unhappiness, stress, depression and so on and the degree of their intensity are incapable of objective proof or of measurement in monetary terms. Translating hurt feelings into hard currency is bound to be an artificial exercise. As Dickson J said in *Andrews v Grand & Toy Alberta Ltd* (1978) 83 DLR (3d) 452 at 475–476, (cited by this Court in *Heil v Rankin* [2001] QB 272 at 292, paragraph 16) there is no medium of exchange or market for non-pecuniary losses and their monetary evaluation
>
>> '… is a philosophical and policy exercise more than a legal or logical one. The award must be fair and reasonable, fairness being gauged by earlier decisions; but the award must also of necessity be arbitrary or conventional. No money can provide true restitution.'
>
> [51] Although they are incapable of objective proof or measurement in monetary terms, hurt feelings are none the less real in human terms. The courts and tribunals have to do the best they can on the available material to make a sensible assessment, accepting that it is impossible to justify or explain a particular sum with the same kind of solid evidential foundation and persuasive practical reasoning available in the calculation of financial loss or compensation for bodily injury.

As to the evidence required to establish humiliation, loss of dignity or injury to feelings, a plaintiff would ordinarily be expected to give direct evidence, but, as recognised in *Winter v Jans*, while the normal rule is that a plaintiff must establish a causal connection between the breach and the damage, in appropriate cases the Tribunal may assume from the nature of the breach that such damages will follow.[108] In *Marks v Director of Health and Disability Proceedings*, there was an apprehended difficulty in establishing a claim on behalf of the deceased person.[109] But the Court did not consider that humiliation, loss of dignity or injury to feelings are wholly subjective, and once a breach of the Code of Health and Disability Services Consumers' Rights was established, the relevant humiliation, injury to feelings and loss of dignity could be inferred from the circumstances of the breach.

B. Quantum

In *Holmes*, the High Court accepted it was appropriate for the Tribunal to recalibrate the level of awards from time to time.[110] It is in this context that *Hammond* is a decision of some importance. After surveying awards made in previous cases,

[108] *Winter* (n 40) [34].

[109] *Marks v Director of Health and Disability Proceedings* [2009] NZCA 151, [2009] 3 NZLR 108, [67]. That was a claim under the Health and Disability Commissioner Act, s 57(1)(a)–(c).

[110] *Holmes* (n 63) [129].

the Tribunal identified three broad bands into which awards should fall. At the less serious end of the scale awards can presently range upwards to $10,000. For more serious cases awards can fall between $10,000 to about (say) $50,000. For the most serious category of cases it is contemplated that awards can be in excess of $50,000. The Tribunal emphasised that these bands are descriptive, not prescriptive. It was not intended they be a bed of Procrustes on which all future awards must be fitted. At most they were a 'rough guide'.[111] However, while acknowledging the desirability of maintaining some consistency in awards, the Tribunal noted five countervailing observations:[112]

(a) As recognised in *Winter v Jans* itself, each case is different.

(b) There is an inherently subjective element to the assessment of humiliation, loss of dignity and injury to feelings. The maintenance of consistency cannot be permitted to thwart the intention of the provision that the award be specific to the particular aggrieved individual in his or her unique circumstances.[113]

(c) Recognition must be given to the fact that as society's and the law's understanding of privacy develops and matures, the perception of what constitutes a 'serious' case will evolve and possibly change.

(d) Damages assessed in 2003 at $40,000 to mark a 'serious' case might, in hindsight, appear in need of adjustment up or down as other fact circumstances arise. Calibrating the spectrum of damages or determining where in a particular band a case is to be situated is not a formulaic or mathematical exercise. Variation must be allowed for, as well as recalibration, as new insights are gained and new fact circumstances are encountered.

(e) Old awards can be misleading unless updated to present-day values. For example, an award of $40,000 in 2003 may have to be adjusted by (say) allowing simple interest at 5 per cent per annum.

To ensure the remedies granted by the Tribunal are accessible to litigants, potential litigants and the public at large, the Tribunal has in recent years published on its website a table recording all remedies awarded from March 2012 in all three of its separate jurisdictions.

X. Conclusion

The Privacy Act has been in force for 24 years. As with the associated Human Rights Act, there has never been a comprehensive review at senior court level of

[111] *Hammond* (n 46) [176].
[112] ibid [177].
[113] The Employment Court has similarly rejected the fixing of a rigid range for awards. See *Grace Team Accounting Ltd v Brake* [2014] NZCA 541, [2015] 2 NZLR 494, [112]–[113].

the principles engaged when awarding damages under the common provisions that compensate for pecuniary loss, loss of benefit, humiliation, loss of dignity and injury to feelings.

It is not self-evident that there is presently a need for such review. Deploying the classic common law technique of incremental development, both the High Court and the Tribunal have, case by case, endeavoured to interpret and apply the remedies provisions of the Privacy Act according to the text and purpose of the Act. As a specialist body dealing with a higher number of cases, the Tribunal has recognised that this is a developing area of the law. Caution would suggest that an over-prescriptive interpretation of the Act or an over-enthusiastic formulation of guidelines for awards may well frustrate the intended flexibility of the statutory provisions. This danger has been explicitly recognised by the Court of Appeal in the employment context.[114] There are very real conceptual and practical difficulties in attempting a rigid 'capture' of the circumstances in which damages should be awarded as compensation for an interference with the privacy of an individual.

Appendix

Privacy Act 1993, s 66

66 Interference with privacy

(1) For the purposes of this Part, an action is an interference with the privacy of an individual if, and only if,—

(a) in relation to that individual,—

(i) the action breaches an information privacy principle; or

(ii) the action breaches a code of practice issued under section 63 (which relates to public registers); or

(iia) the action breaches an information privacy principle or a code of practice as modified by an Order in Council made under section 96J; or

(iib) the provisions of an information sharing agreement approved by an Order in Council made under section 96J have not been complied with; or

(iii) the provisions of Part 10 (which relates to information matching) have not been complied with; and

(b) in the opinion of the Commissioner or, as the case may be, the Tribunal, the action—

(i) has caused, or may cause, loss, detriment, damage, or injury to that individual; or

(ii) has adversely affected, or may adversely affect, the rights, benefits, privileges, obligations, or interests of that individual; or

[114] *Hawkins* (n 104) [73].

(iii) has resulted in, or may result in, significant humiliation, significant loss of dignity, or significant injury to the feelings of that individual.

(2) Without limiting subsection (1), an action is an interference with the privacy of an individual if, in relation to an information privacy request made by the individual,—

(a) the action consists of a decision made under Part 4 or Part 5 in relation to the request, including—

(i) a refusal to make information available in response to the request; or

(ii) a decision by which an agency decides, in accordance with section 42 or section 43, in what manner or, in accordance with section 40, for what charge the request is to be granted; or

(iii) a decision by which an agency imposes conditions on the use, communication, or publication of information made available pursuant to the request; or

(iv) a decision by which an agency gives a notice under section 32; or

(v) a decision by which an agency extends any time limit under section 41; or

(vi) a refusal to correct personal information; and

(b) the Commissioner or, as the case may be, the Tribunal is of the opinion that there is no proper basis for that decision.

(3) If, in relation to any information privacy request, any agency fails within the time limit fixed by section 40(1) (or, where that time limit has been extended under this Act, within that time limit as so extended) to comply with paragraph (a) or paragraph (b) of section 40(1), that failure shall be deemed, for the purposes of subsection (2)(a)(i) of this section, to be a refusal to make available the information to which the request relates.

(4) Undue delay in making information available in response to an information privacy request for that information shall be deemed, for the purposes of subsection (2)(a)(i), to be a refusal to make that information available.

15

Determinations under the Privacy Act 1988 (Cth) as a Privacy Remedy

NORMANN WITZLEB

I. Introduction

While Australia is a party to a number of human rights treaties guaranteeing a right to respect for one's private life,[1] it is a notorious weakness of Australian domestic law that it does not explicitly recognise a right to privacy. In *ABC v Lenah Game Meats Pty Ltd*,[2] the High Court was invited to recognise a common law right to privacy but decided to leave the question open. Since then, all law reform enquiries into the area have recommended closing this gap in the common law through the introduction of a statutory cause of action to protect privacy.[3] However, these recommendations have not been taken up by government. In the absence of an explicit right to privacy in Australian law, other causes of actions are put to service in the protection of private life and personal information. This includes actions for breach of confidence, trespass to land and to the person, defamation, nuisance, intentional infliction of psychiatric harm, and copyright infringement, provided always that the privacy interference is actionable under these wrongs.

In addition to these private law actions that incidentally protect privacy in some circumstances, limited relief is also available under the *Privacy Act 1988* (Cth) (the 'Privacy Act') and its equivalents in some Australian States and Territories.[4]

[1] Art 17 of the International Covenant on Civil and Political Rights, done at New York on 16 December 1966, [1980] ATS 23; Art 16 of the Convention on the Rights of the Child, done at New York on 20 November 1989, [1991] ATS 4.

[2] *ABC v Lenah Game Meats Pty Ltd* [2001] HCA 63, (2001) 208 CLR 199. Some lower courts have accepted such claims: see n 148.

[3] Australian Law Reform Commission, *For Your Information: Australian Privacy Law and Practice* (ALRC Report 108, 2008) Recommendations 74-1–74-7; Australian Law Reform Commission, *Serious Invasions of Privacy in the Digital Era* (ALRC Report 123, 2014); South Australian Law Reform Institute, *A statutory tort for invasion of privacy* (Final Report 4, 2016); New South Wales Parliament, Legislative Council, Standing Committee on Law and Justice, *Remedies for the serious invasion of privacy in New South Wales* (2016).

[4] In particular, the *Privacy and Personal Information Protection Act 1998* (NSW); *Information Privacy Act 2009* (Qld); *Personal Information Protection Act 2004* (Tas); *Privacy and Data Protection Act 2014* (Vic) and the *Information Act* (NT).

Despite appearances, the privacy legislation does not provide comprehensive protection to a person's private life. Its focus is on the protection of personal data and information privacy, whereas territorial or bodily privacy is outside its scope. Persons alleging breach of their privacy rights under the Privacy Act can complain to the Office of the Australian Information Commissioner (OAIC).[5] The Privacy Commissioner[6] is required to investigate a complaint if the act or practice in question may be an interference with the complainant's privacy[7] and the complainant has first complained to the respondent.[8] If an investigation by the Privacy Commissioner substantiates the complaint, the Commissioner has a number of remedial options, including the power to make a 'determination'.[9]

The Office of the Privacy Commissioner initially adopted a 'light touch' approach to regulation, which aimed to resolve most complaints through conciliation. In the first two decades of the Privacy Act's operations, determinations were exceedingly rare: over the first 20 years of the Privacy Act's operation, successive Commissioners issued only eight determinations. This led to criticism that the Office was too reluctant to use its powers and missed the opportunity to strengthen compliance with Australia's privacy laws through a more transparent and robust approach to enforcement.[10]

Privacy Commissioner Timothy Pilgrim adopted a more proactive stance on making determinations where a privacy breach is sufficiently serious, or where conciliation does not lead to an appropriate outcome.[11] During his term of office (2010–2018), the power to issue determinations was exercised with increasing frequency.[12] This development was based on the recognition that determinations not only have importance in resolving individual complaints, but also provide 'a public record of the OAIC's views on how privacy laws should be interpreted, and … assist complainants and respondents to better understand how privacy laws apply'.[13] There are now over 30 published determinations of the Privacy Commissioner, most making a finding in favour of the complainant and awarding

[5] *Privacy Act 1988* (Cth), s 36.

[6] The Privacy Commissioner has the 'privacy functions' under s 9 and s 12(1) of the *Australian Information Commissioner Act 2010* (Cth).

[7] *Privacy Act 1988* (Cth), s 40(1).

[8] *Privacy Act 1988* (Cth), s 40(2).

[9] *Privacy Act 1988* (Cth), s 52.

[10] See discussion in Office of the Privacy Commissioner, *Getting in on the Act: The Review of the Private Sector Provisions of the Privacy Act 1988* (2005), ch 5.

[11] T Pilgrim, '*Privacy law reform: challenges and opportunities*', Presentation at Emerging Challenges in Privacy Law Conference, 23 February 2012, at www.oaic.gov.au/media-and-speeches/speeches/privacy-law-reform-challenges-and-opportunities, accessed 25 September 2017.

[12] There was one determination in 2011, one in 2012, five in 2014, five in 2015, nine in 2016, and five in the first half of 2017. The determinations are published on the OAIC website at www.oaic.gov.au/privacy-law/determinations/, accessed 25 September 2017.

[13] T Pilgrim, 'Navigating privacy in the information age: the Australian perspective' in N Witzleb, D Lindsay, M Paterson and S Rodrick (eds), *Emerging Challenges in Privacy Law: Comparative Perspectives* (Oxford, Oxford UP, 2014) 31, 38.

redress against the interference with privacy. This emerging body of case law has yet to be examined in the legal literature. This chapter will provide a first assessment of the Commissioner's use of his remedial powers under section 52 of the Privacy Act.

In section II, this chapter will explain the regulatory context of the determinations power and give an overview of the determinations that can be made. It is common for complainants to seek multiple remedies, and for the Commissioner to award a combination of remedies, when an interference is established. Section III explores the legal framework that applies to monetary remedies under section 52 of the Privacy Act, in particular its relationship to common law remedies and compensation for economic losses. Section IV considers the assessment practices in relation to non-economic losses, which are often a complainant's main concern. Section V examines the availability of non-compensatory remedies, such as apologies or orders to review or change existing practices, which are also made quite regularly. The lack of a power to award exemplary damages will also be explored. Section VI provides some concluding observations. The chapter demonstrates how relief under section 52 of the Privacy Act provides an avenue for protecting informational privacy rights through regulatory mechanisms, and thereby supplements relief under general law discussed elsewhere in this volume. The principles governing statutory redress under section 52 are aligned with those from related areas such as anti-discrimination law, yet the case law and determinations of the Privacy Commissioner also show that the equivalent remedies in tort law continue to be highly influential in the development of the relevant approaches.

The chapter will not deal with statutory injunctions by the Federal Court or Federal Circuit Court that can be applied for by the Commissioner (or any other person) under section 98 of the Privacy Act. It will also not consider section 80W of the Privacy Act, which empowers the Commissioner to apply to the Federal Court or Federal Circuit Court for a civil penalty order against an entity in breach of a civil penalty provision under the Privacy Act. References to equivalent powers to resolve complaints under state privacy legislation will generally be made only where their application differs substantially from the use of powers under the federal Privacy Act.

II. The Power to Make Determinations under Section 52

The Privacy Act creates a regulatory regime for the protection of information privacy. It does not establish or recognise an individual claim right that provides comprehensive protection of a person's private life. The power to make determinations is available to the Commissioner when an investigation establishes an interference with privacy. The term 'interference with privacy' has a limited and technical meaning. It is defined in section 13 of the Privacy Act, amongst other things, as an act or practice that breaches an Australian Privacy Principle (APP) or an applicable registered APP code.[14]

The federal Privacy Act contains 13 APPs,[15] which govern how government agencies and certain private sector organisations may collect, use, disclose and store personal and sensitive information, and how individuals may access and correct records containing such information. They are the central element of Australia's privacy protection framework and embody its preference for principles-based regulation over a prescriptive approach to data protection. The APPs were introduced by the *Privacy Law (Enhancing Privacy Protection) Act 2012* (Cth) and took effect on 12 March 2014, replacing two previous sets of principles, the National Privacy Principles (NPPs) and the Australian Privacy Principles.[16] Section 15 of the Privacy Act prohibits a so-called 'APP entity' from doing an act, or engaging in a practice, that breaches an APP. These APP entities are all Commonwealth government agencies and private sector organisations that are subject to the APP regime. If an APP entity chooses to adopt a binding APP code registered by the Privacy Commissioner, it needs to comply with the code instead of the APPs.

The Privacy Act contains a number of important limitations that significantly curtail its reach and effectiveness. Under the 'small business exemption', private organisations with an annual turnover of $3 million or less do not need to comply with the Privacy Act unless an exception applies (eg because the business handles sensitive information).[17] Importantly, the Act also exempts acts done, or practices engaged in, by individuals unless they occur in the course of a business carried on by the individual.[18] Further exemptions apply to 'political acts and practices',[19] to employee records[20] and to acts or practices by media organisations in the course of journalism.[21]

When an act to which the Privacy Act applies constitutes an interference with privacy, the Commissioner has the power to make determinations under section 52. This power is not an unfettered discretion to grant the remedy that best fits the circumstances or that best redresses the harm; it is a power limited to the making of a number of specific declarations. The declaration under section 52(1)(b)(i) that

[14] A 'breach' is itself defined in *Privacy Act 1988* (Cth) as an act or practice that is 'inconsistent with, or contrary to,' an APP or a registered APP Code: s 6A and s 6B, respectively (which contain further exceptions).

[15] The APPs are contained in sch 1 to the *Privacy Act 1988* (Cth).

[16] The majority of the determinations discussed in this chapter relate to the NPPs and Information Privacy Principles (IPPs).

[17] *Privacy Act 1988* (Cth), s 6D.

[18] *Privacy Act 1988* (Cth), s 7B(1), which creates an exemption for the purposes of s 7(1)(ee). See also *Privacy Act 1988* (Cth), s 16, which provides that the APPs do not apply for the purposes of, or in connection with, an individual's personal, family or household affairs.

[19] *Privacy Act 1988* (Cth), s 7C.

[20] *Privacy Act 1988* (Cth), s 7B(3).

[21] *Privacy Act 1988* (Cth), s 7B(4), provided the media organisation has publicly committed to published privacy standards.

the agency or organisation has 'engaged in conduct constituting an interference with the privacy of an individual and must not repeat or continue such conduct' combines a conventional declaration with a prohibition. The declarations that 'the respondent must take specified steps within a specified period to ensure that such conduct is not repeated or continued' (section 52(1)(b)(ia)) or that 'the respondent must perform any reasonable act or course of conduct to redress any loss or damage suffered by the complainant' (section 52(1)(b)(ii)) require action on part of the respondent and are, to that extent, akin to mandatory injunctions under general law. However, the Privacy Act provides that a determination is 'not binding or conclusive between any of the parties to the determination'.[22] Similarly, an award of compensation under section 52(1)(b)(iii), which is a declaration that the 'complainant is entitled to a specified amount by way of compensation for any loss or damage suffered by reason of' the interference with privacy, is not as such legally enforceable.

This means that a declaration under section 52(1)(b) 'does not … confer a right of recovery'[23] on a successful applicant. This reflects the fact that Commonwealth judicial power can only be exercised by a court in accordance with Chapter III of the Australian Constitution.[24] The Commissioner is not vested with judicial power, and cannot make a binding and directly enforceable decision that a breach of the Privacy Act has occurred and must be remedied. Therefore, if the respondent fails to act in accordance with the declaration or declarations made in the determination, the applicant or the Commissioner can seek to enforce the determination in the Federal Court or the Federal Circuit Court of Australia.[25] This requires a *de novo* hearing. If the court is satisfied that the respondent to the determination engaged in conduct that constitutes an interference with the privacy of an individual, it has a broad discretion to make 'such orders (including a declaration of right) as it thinks fit'.[26]

Under section 96 of the Privacy Act, a decision under section 52(1) or (1A) to make a determination is also subject to review by the Administrative Appeals Tribunal (AAT or 'the Tribunal'). The AAT provides an independent merits review of the decision, and has the power to set aside, vary or affirm a privacy determination. The Tribunal can set aside determinations made in error,[27] including determinations that fail to declare that the complainant is entitled to redress. A person aggrieved by a decision of the Privacy Commissioner may also apply under section 5 of the *Administrative Decisions (Judicial Review) Act 1977* (Cth) to the Federal Circuit Court or the Federal Court of Australia for a review. The Court may refer the matter back to the OAIC for further consideration if it finds the

[22] *Privacy Act 1988* (Cth), s 52(1B).
[23] *Hall v A & A Sheiban Pty Ltd* (1989) 20 FCR 217, 282 *per* French J.
[24] *Brandy v Human Rights and Equal Opportunity Commission* (1995) 183 CLR 245.
[25] *Privacy Act 1988* (Cth), s 55A.
[26] *Privacy Act 1988* (Cth), s 55A(2).
[27] See *Telstra Corporation Limited and Privacy Commissioner* [2015] AATA 991.

Commissioner's decision involved an error of law or the Commissioner's powers were exercised improperly.

In its 2014 Report on serious invasions of privacy in the digital era, the Australian Law Reform Commission (ALRC) recommended that this complaints process also be made available for alleged breaches of the proposed statutory privacy tort. The ALRC recommended that the Privacy Commissioner's powers be extended so that the Commissioner could investigate complaints about serious invasions of privacy and make appropriate declarations in the form of determinations, which would then require enforcement by the Court.[28] This recommendation was intended to improve access to justice by utilising an established complaints process, and to give the Commissioner greater visibility and responsibility in addressing privacy harms.[29] Unfortunately, there is so far no indication from the Government that this recommendation will be adopted.

III. Compensation Awards under Section 52

A. The Framework for Compensation Awards

The framework for the assessment of compensation under section 52 of the Privacy Act has been shaped by decisions of the AAT on the occasion of appeals against determinations of the Privacy Commissioner. There have to date only been two Tribunal decisions on compensation under the Privacy Act, one in 2004 and the other in 2016. The earlier of these seminal cases, *Rummery v Federal Privacy Commissioner*,[30] has proved to be particularly influential on the Commissioner's approach towards remedies. Mr Rummery was an employee of an ACT government department who made a privacy complaint against his employer. Mr Rummery made a public interest disclosure to the Ombudsman[31] when he felt that a brief on under-age drinking he produced in his capacity as a department officer was not acted upon by his employer. When the department head contacted the Ombudsman's Office, he divulged personal information relating to Mr Rummery's employment in an attempt to influence the investigation by the Ombudsman's office in favour of the department. The Privacy Commissioner determined that Mr Rummery's privacy complaint was substantiated, but refused a declaration that Mr Rummery was entitled to compensation. Mr Rummery sought a review of this decision under section 61 (now repealed) of the Privacy Act.

The Full Tribunal of the AAT observed that it had not previously dealt with the entitlement to and assessment of compensation for an interference with

[28] Australian Law Reform Commission, *Serious Invasions of Privacy in the Digital Era* (ALRC Report 123, 2014) Rec 16-1.

[29] ibid [16.4].

[30] *Rummery v Federal Privacy Commissioner* [2004] AATA 1221.

[31] Under the *Public Interest Disclosure Act 1994* (ACT).

privacy. It therefore held that it could derive assistance from the case law interpreting the very similar provision of section 81 of the *Sex Discrimination Act 1984* (Cth) (SDA), in particular the decision of the Full Federal Court in *Hall v A & A Sheiban Pty Ltd*.[32]

The Tribunal extracted the following principles on compensation awards from this decision:

(a) where a complaint is substantiated and loss or damage is suffered, the legislation contemplates some form of redress in the ordinary course;

(b) awards should be restrained but not minimal;

(c) in measuring compensation the principles of damages applied in tort law will assist, although the ultimate guide is the words of the statute;

(d) in an appropriate case, aggravated damages may be awarded;

(e) compensation should be assessed having regard to the complainant's reaction and not to the perceived reaction of the majority of the community or of a reasonable person in similar circumstances.[33]

Whenever the Privacy Commissioner now makes a determination in favour of a complainant, the remedial considerations are usually prefaced with a reference to these principles. These principles have also been affirmed in *EQ and Office of the Australian Information Commissioner (Freedom of information)*,[34] which is the second, more recent decision of the AAT on remedies under the Privacy Act. They also guide decisions under the State privacy legislation.[35]

The alignment of the assessment of damages under privacy legislation and under federal anti-discrimination laws is fundamental. The Privacy Commissioner states in his determinations that he takes into account amounts awarded in Tribunal decisions in anti-discrimination cases, as they are recorded in the compendium Federal Discrimination Law Online,[36] and settlements contained in the Conciliation Register of the Australian Human Rights Commission (AHRC). It appears that the anti-discrimination cases mainly inform the general approach to and level of damages, because express references to these decisions are relatively uncommon.

This alignment of approach for remedial decisions is generally appropriate. The case load of the AHRC is a multiple of the cases determined by the Privacy

[32] *Hall* (n 23).

[33] *Rummery* (n 30) [32].

[34] *EQ and Office of the Australian Information Commissioner (Freedom of information)* [2016] AATA 785, [39].

[35] See, eg, *NZ v Director General, Department of Housing* [2006] NSWADT 173, [35]; *JL v Queensland Police Service* [2014] QCAT 623, [212]–[214].

[36] This publication sets out all damages awards in federal discrimination cases since 13 April 2000, which is the date on which jurisdiction under s 46PO(4) of the *Australian Human Rights Commission Act 1986* (Cth) was transferred to the Federal Court and the Federal Magistrates Court (now re-named the Federal Circuit Court): Australian Human Rights Commission, *Federal Discrimination Law 2016* (Australian Human Rights Commission, 2016) [7.2.2]–[7.2-6].

Commissioner, so that there will often be precedents from discrimination law to aide a decision on matters newly arising under the Privacy Act. While there are undeniably qualitative differences between interference with privacy and unlawful discrimination, both kinds of wrongs have in common that they affect dignitary interests of the complainants, and therefore primarily cause non-pecuniary losses. Seeking an alignment of both bodies of law promotes coherence and consistency in administrative decision-making. However, the reliance on anti-discrimination law also has the potential consequence of constricting the scope for developing new approaches in privacy law, or for diverging from established practices where there are differences between the two areas of law.

B. The Discretionary Nature of the Determinations

Under section 52(1)(b)(iv) of the Privacy Act, the Commissioner has the power to make a declaration that it would be inappropriate for any further action to be taken in the matter even when the privacy complaint is substantiated. While accepting that the Privacy Commissioner has discretion in relation to the award of compensation, the Tribunal in *Rummery* adopted the view of French J (as he then was) in *Hall*[37] that once a complaint is substantiated and loss or damage established, an award of compensation would ordinarily follow, unless 'good reason' to the contrary is shown.[38] Under the New South Wales (NSW) privacy legislation, it was similarly held that there may be 'exceptional cases' where no award would be made even if loss were established.[39]

Section 46PO(4)(d) of the *Australian Human Rights Commission Act 1986* (Cth) (AHRC Act) sets out the remedial powers of the Court in unlawful discrimination cases. In the context of this provision, it also has been considered whether the Court could award something less than full damages to which the complainant might otherwise be entitled. In *Qantas Airways Ltd v Gama*,[40] French and Jacobson JJ suggested obiter that the discretionary character of the award allows an award that does not fully compensate for the loss suffered. However, in the subsequent decision in *Richardson v Oracle Corporation Australia Pty Ltd*,[41] which dealt extensively with the issue of damages under the AHRC Act, Besanko and Perram JJ expressed reservations against this approach. It is submitted that the latter view should be applied to the largely equivalent regime under the Privacy Act. A reference to 'full compensation' raises, of course, the question of how the quantum of full compensation should be determined. In this context, it is important to note that while the *Privacy Act 1998* (Cth) imposes no cap on the amount of

[37] *Hall* (n 23).
[38] *Rummery* (n 30) [33]–[34].
[39] *NZ v Director General, Department of Housing* (n 35) [49].
[40] *Qantas Airways Ltd v Gama* [2008] FCAFC 69, (2006) 167 FCR 537, [94].
[41] *Richardson v Oracle Corporation Australia Pty Ltd* [2014] FCAFC 82, (2014) 223 FCR 334, [140].

compensation, the State privacy legislation imposes limits of $100,000,[42] $60,000[43] and $40,000,[44] respectively, on the respective Tribunals' power to award damages.

C. The Relevance of Tort Law Principles

In *Hall*, Lockhart J described the principles of tort law as 'the closest analogy that I can find and one that would in most foreseeable cases be a sensible and sound test'.[45] In contrast, French J considered in *Hall* that 'the measure of damages is to be governed by the statute and the rules applicable in tort can be of no avail if they conflict with it'.[46] While these different approaches do not necessarily affect the measure of damages in every case, they reveal a different understanding of the task at hand. In particular, they raise questions about the degree and form of interdependence between a statutory power to award damages and principles of tort law. In *Rummery*, the Tribunal referred to both views and then explained that there is 'no conflict between these principles [in tort law] and the provisions of s 52', and assessed compensation accordingly.[47] The more recent case of *EQ* explicitly referred to the view expressed in *Rummery* that the 'principles … in tort law will assist, although the ultimate guide is the words of the statute'.[48] However, the Tribunal then adopted a summary of the relevant law submitted by the respondent that was replete with citations of tort law cases on the assessment of damages, without making further mention of the statutory context in which the task of assessment of damages under the Privacy Act is situated. Similarly, the Privacy Commissioner has stated repeatedly that it 'has long been established that damages should be assessed on tort-based principles'.[49]

It appears that the privacy jurisprudence to this extent is not yet fully in step with judicial developments concerning the relationship between statutory powers to award damages and related principles under general law. The High Court considered the significance of tort law principles for the assessment of statutory compensation mainly in the context of section 82 of the (former) *Trade Practices Act 1974* (Cth).[50] In its more recent decisions in that area, the High Court has expressly rejected an approach that begins the enquiry into the statutory remedies

[42] *Information Privacy Act 2009* (Qld), s 178(a)(v); *Privacy and Data Protection Act 2014* (Vic), s 77(1)(a)(iii).

[43] *Information Act* (NT), s 115(4)(b).

[44] *Privacy and Personal Information Protection Act 1998* (NSW), s 55(2)(a); *Health Records and Information Privacy Act 2002* (NSW), s 54(1)(a).

[45] *Hall* (n 23), 239.

[46] ibid 281.

[47] *Rummery* (n 30) [41].

[48] ibid [32]; *'EQ'* (n 34) [39].

[49] eg, *'IX' and Business Service Brokers Pty Ltd t/a TeleChoice* [2016] AICmr 42, [52]; *'IQ' and NRMA Insurance, Insurance Australia Ltd* [2016] AICmr 36, [61]; *'S' and Veda Advantage Information Services and Solutions Ltd* [2012] AICmr 33, [87].

[50] *I & L Securities Pty Ltd v HTW Valuers* [2002] HCA 41, (2002) 210 CLR 109; *Murphy v Overton Investments Pty Ltd* [2004] HCA 3, (2004) 216 CLR 388. This is now s 236 of the *Australian Consumer Law*, contained in sch 2 to the *Competition and Consumer Act 2010* (Cth).

with attempting to identify analogies with a claim under the general law, because doing so 'distracts attention from the primary task of construing the relevant provisions of the Act'.[51] For damages under section 46PO(4)(d) of the AHRC Act, this approach of the High Court has also been endorsed by Besanko and Perram JJ in *Richardson*.[52]

Despite the express reference to tort-based principles, the statutory context in which damages are to be assessed under the Privacy Act is also recognised by the Commissioner. For example, in several determinations the Commissioner explained that he was guided by the principle that 'damages awards compensating for injured feelings should not be so low as to diminish respect for the public policy to which the legislation gives effect'.[53] While the purpose of the Privacy Act is obviously significant for setting the level of non-compensatory damages, there are potentially many other areas in which the statutory root or rationale of the power to award compensation may become relevant. In the context of other statutory damages provisions, these questions often concern the extent of liability through the application of limiting factors such as causation, mitigation, remoteness and contributory negligence.[54] It would therefore be desirable that the determinations of the Commissioner more explicitly acknowledge the more recent jurisprudence of the High Court in other areas on the primacy of the statute. This would put beyond doubt that the guiding principles for the assessment of compensation will primarily be found in the Privacy Act, in particular its statutory objects. Torts law principles of assessment may provide helpful analogies, but they are only aids in achieving these objectives and do not determine the approach that applies.

The statutory objects of the Privacy Act are defined in its section 2A. Of particular relevance for remedies are the stated objects: '(a) to promote the protection of the privacy of individuals'; '(b) to recognise that the protection of the privacy of individuals is balanced with the interests of entities in carrying out their functions or activities; '(d) to promote responsible and transparent handling of personal information by entities'; and '(h) to implement Australia's international obligation in relation to privacy'. Read together, these objects suggest that the Privacy Commissioner's determinations should advance the effective protection of individual privacy in line with international standards, while also protecting the legitimate interests of organisations handling personal information.

D. Compensation for Economic Losses

The dignitary dimension of privacy means that, in the majority of cases, the focus has been on claims for non-economic loss. However, there are also some

[51] *Murphy v Overton Investments Pty Ltd* [2004] HCA 3, (2004) 216 CLR 388, [44].

[52] *Richardson* (n 41).

[53] *'IQ' and NRMA Insurance* (n 49) [61]. The decision of *Hall* (n 23) refers to *Alexander v Home Office* [1988] 1 WLR 968, 975; [1988] 2 All ER 118, 122.

[54] See, eg, *I & L Securities Pty Ltd* (n 50).

determinations in which complainants sought compensation for economic losses. In *EQ and Office of the Australian Information Commissioner*, the Tribunal held that, in line with the general law, damages for economic loss are awarded to restore an individual to 'the same position as he would have been in if he had not sustained the wrong for which he is now getting his compensation'.[55]

Economic losses can arise directly from the alleged interference with privacy, for example where the mishandling of private information affects a person's credit[56] or employment.[57] Other compensable losses include expenses incurred by the complainant in connection with the making of the complaint and its investigation.[58] Both types of harm can be redressed through compensation awarded under the determinations power, provided they comprise a 'loss or damage suffered by reason of the act or practice the subject of the complaint'.[59] This phrase, which embodies a requirement to establish causation, is also contained in materially similar form in other provisions creating a statutory entitlement to compensation, such as section 81(1)(b)(iv) of the SDA or s 236 of the *Australian Consumer Law*, the successor of section 82 of the (former) *Trade Practices Act 1974* (Cth).

In *Richardson*,[60] the Full Federal Court was required to consider the similarly worded test under section 46PO(4)(d) of the AHRC Act, and held that this or similar legislative wording required

> determining what words such as 'because of' or 'by reason of' or 'by' mean in their particular statutory context, including the objects and purposes of the statute or statutory provision … that issues of what loss and damage may be recovered may raise questions of cause and effect, and may also raise questions of remoteness of damage and mitigation.[61]

Just as in other claims for monetary compensation, issues of causation can create a substantial hurdle for victims of privacy invasion. In *'EQ' and Great Barrier Reef Marine Park Authority*,[62] the applicant was employed on a casual basis as a marine conservation assistant. He alleged that he suffered economic loss of around $100,000 in the form of lost past and future employment income, as well as lost future career opportunities, when the press reported that he had been caught fishing illegally in a restricted marine conversation area and his employer restricted his duties. The applicant alleged that the loss was the result of the respondent's interference with his privacy. The respondent had a statutory duty to investigate the allegedly illegal fishing incident and disclosed the complainant's identity in a

[55] *'EQ'* (n 34) [41], [47].

[56] *'KB' and Veda Advantage Information Services and Solutions Ltd* [2016] AICmr 81; *'S' and Veda* (n 49).

[57] *'LB' and Comcare (Privacy)* [2017] AICmr 28, [43]. At the time of writing, the decision is under review by the AAT.

[58] *Privacy Act 1998* (Cth), s 52(3).

[59] *Privacy Act 1998* (Cth), s 52(1)(b)(iii).

[60] *Richardson* (n 41).

[61] ibid.

[62] *EQ* (n 34); *'EQ' and Great Barrier Reef Marine Park Authority* [2015] AICmr 11.

response to a journalist enquiry relating to the incident. While the confirmation of the complainant's identity to the journalist was found to be in breach of the respondent's privacy obligations, the evidence before the Commissioner (and the AAT) established that the circumstances of the incident and the identity of the complainant had been leaked to the journalist before he made the enquiry. (The complainant alleged that this was due to a further disclosure by the respondent in breach of the Privacy Act, but it could not be established how the journalist had obtained his tip off.) The Commissioner saw no basis for the conclusion that the news story would not have been published without the confirmation of the complainant's identity by the respondent. As a result, it was found that the privacy breach was not the cause of the applicant's loss of income.

The alleged loss of future career opportunities was based on the contention that the complainant lost employment opportunities with the research boat's sponsor, a major employer in his trade in a small geographical area. The Commissioner found that this loss was too remote because it was more directly attributable to the complainant's actions in committing the offence, rather than the respondent's disclosure of the complainant's identity. As a result, the Commissioner declined to award any damages for economic loss.

The Commissioner's decision was reviewed by the AAT, which dealt with the question of economic loss at some length. The Tribunal confirmed the findings of the Commissioner as to the interferences with privacy. Accordingly, it held that the only interference with privacy established against the respondent was the confirmation of the complainant's identity to the journalist in response to the enquiry. As discussed above, the AAT began its consideration of the compensable economic losses by reciting the principles on the assessment of damages under the Privacy Act, as identified in the case of *Rummary*. It then referred to principles that apply to the recovery of economic losses in the law of torts and seminal decisions on the compensatory measure of damages in tort,[63] on the assessment of damages for lost income,[64] and on causation and remoteness.[65]

There was no reference to decisions of the High Court that the assessment of statutory compensation was primarily to be undertaken 'in order to give effect to a statute with a discernible purpose; and that purpose provides a guide as to the requirements of justice and equity in the case'.[66] Instead, the Tribunal relied wholly on tortious authorities and summarised the relevant principles as follows:

(a) causation is ultimately a question of common sense and experience, determined on the facts of each case;
(b) in law, causation is a question identifying where legal responsibility should lie, rather than examine the cause of event from a scientific or philosophical viewpoint,

[63] *Livingstone v Rawyards Coal Company* (1880) 5 App Cas 35.
[64] *Graham v Baker* (1961) 106 CLR 340, 346–47.
[65] *Chapman v Hearse* (1961) 106 CLR 112; *Mount Isa Mines Ltd v Pusey* (1970) 125 CLR 383, 390, 401, 402; *Overseas Tankship (UK) Ltd v Morts Dock & Engineering Co Ltd (The Wagon Mound No 1)* [1961] AC 388.
[66] *I & L Securities Pty Ltd v HTW Valuers (Brisbane) Pty Ltd* (2002) 210 CLR 109, [26] *per* Gleeson CJ.

policy issues and value judgements have a role to play in determining whether, for legal purposes, a circumstances we found to be causative of loss [*sic*];

(c) a 'but for' analysis is not a sufficient test [of] causation, although it may be a guide; and

(d) where there are multiple elements, each one sufficient on its own to have caused the loss, the causation test may be considered satisfied by each one of them.[67]

The Tribunal emphasised also the significance of the decision of the High Court in *March v Stramare (E and MH) Pty Ltd*,[68] even though the approach of the majority in that decision, which described the causation enquiry as a question of common sense and experience, had been put in doubt by more recent authorities. In *Wallace v Kam*, for example, a unanimous High Court acknowledged that the determination of causation at common law 'inevitably involves two questions: a question of historical fact as to how particular harm occurred; and a normative question as to whether legal responsibility for that particular harm occurring in that way should be attributed to a particular person'.[69] This two-pronged test of causation, which clearly distinguishes between issues of 'factual causation' and 'scope of liability', had been recommended in the Ipp Report[70] and was adopted in the civil liability legislation.[71] It provides a clearer structure for causation decisions when compared with the 'common sense test', which gave courts and parties 'very little guidance about when negligent conduct will be considered to have caused harm'.[72] The confusion that the 'common sense test' can generate is also evident in the Tribunal decision of *EQ*, where it was stated that the loss resulting from the publicity surrounding the applicant's offence and the interference with privacy were 'too remote'[73] because the breach of privacy post-dated the first media contact. In reality, the confirmation of the applicant's identity was not a factual cause (in the sense of a necessary or 'but for' condition) of the applicant's loss of employment outcome, because the evidence suggested that the media publicity would have ensued in any event.

Questions relating to the causal link between the privacy interference and any subsequent economic loss arise with some regularity. In line with the general law, the onus of establishing these losses rests on the complainant.[74] In a number of cases, the complainants seek to demonstrate their loss by submitting documentary material evidencing a reduction in income or profits during the period of

[67] *EQ* (n 34) [47]; adopted in *'KA' and Commonwealth Bank of Australia Ltd* [2016] AICmr 80, [78].
[68] *March v Stramare (E and MH) Pty Ltd* [1991] HCA 12, (1991) 171 CLR 506.
[69] *Wallace v Kam* [2013] HCA 19, (2013) 250 CLR 375 [11].
[70] D Ipp et al, *Review of the Law of Negligence: Final Report* (2002) Rec 29.
[71] *Civil Liability Act 2002* (NSW), s 5D; *Civil Liability Act 2003* (Qld), s 11; *Civil Liability Act 1936* (SA), s 34; *Civil Liability Act 2002* (Tas), s 13; *Wrongs Act 1958* (Vic), s 51; *Civil Liability Act 2002* (WA), s 5C; *Civil Law (Wrongs) Act 2002* (ACT), s 45.
[72] Ipp et al (n 70) [7.25].
[73] *EQ* (n 34) [46].
[74] *'LB' and Comcare (Privacy)* (n 57) [49].

the privacy complaint.[75] However, where multiple factors could have played a role in causing these losses, the Commissioner seeks substantiation of a 'direct link'[76] between the complainant's losses and the respondent's privacy breach, whereas 'some indirect association'[77] tends not to be sufficient. If a sufficient causative link cannot be demonstrated, the claim for compensation of economic losses will be rejected.[78]

The determinations do not commonly explain how much substantiation or how much 'directness' is needed to establish a causative link. Determinations to date show that complainants are rarely successful in satisfying the Commissioner of a causal link between a privacy invasion, its impact on the complainant's psychological well-being and any subsequent drop in income or profit. Complainants therefore need to be advised to provide as much concrete and specific evidence as possible that not only shows a reduction of income and profits, but also how it is connected to the psychological effects of the privacy invasion. In many cases of privacy invasion, it will be extraordinarily difficult to establish with precision what impact the anxiety and distress caused by the interference had on the complainant's earning potential, in particular where complainants are self-employed or engaged in casual work. In these circumstances, it is therefore appropriate to point to the long-established practice at general law, under which courts adopt a flexible approach to the proof of losses. As McPherson J said in *Nilon v Bezzina*, 'The degree of precision with which damages are to be proved is proportionate to the proof reasonably available.'[79] Hayne J observed in an often-cited passage from *Placer (Granny Smith) Pty Ltd v Thiess Contractors Pty Ltd*,[80] that in cases where a party *cannot* adduce precise evidence of loss, 'it may be that estimation, if not guesswork, may be necessary in assessing the damages to be allowed'.[81]

Under section 52(3) of the Privacy Act, the Commissioner has the power to make a declaration that the complainant is 'entitled to a specified amount to reimburse the complainant for expenses reasonably incurred by the complainant in connection with the making of the complaint and the investigation of the complaint'. This power is discretionary[82] and exercised sparingly. The Commissioner generally expects that most complaints can be resolved without legal representation

[75] See, eg, *'KA' and Commonwealth Bank of Australia* (n 67); *'HW' v Freelancer International Pty Ltd* [2015] AICmr 86, [342]–[345] (this decision has been set aside: *Freelancer International Pty Ltd and Australian Information Commissioner* [2017] AATA 2426); *'S' and Veda* (n 49) [76]–[80]; *'D' v Wentworthville Leagues Club* [2011] AICmr 9.

[76] *'HS' and AMP Life Ltd* [2015] AICmr 81 [80].

[77] *'HW' v Freelancer International Pty Ltd* (n 75) [343].

[78] *'LB' and Comcare (Privacy)* (n 57) [43]; *'KB' and Veda* (n 56) [74]–[76]; *'KA' and Commonwealth Bank of Australia* (n 67) [81]–[83].

[79] *Nilon v Bezzina* [1988] 2 Qd R 420, 424.

[80] *Placer (Granny Smith) Pty Ltd v Thiess Contractors Pty Ltd* [2003] HCA 10, (2003) 196 ALR 257.

[81] ibid [38] *per* Hayne J, Gleeson CJ, McHugh and Kirby JJ agreeing.

[82] *'KB' and Veda* (n 56) [96].

and that parties bear their own costs.[83] However, where legal representation is 'reasonably necessary'[84] and its cost is not disproportionate to the harm suffered or the remedy awarded, a declaration for reimbursement may be made.[85] The Commissioner does not have the power to make a costs order, but can make a declaration in relation to a specific amount. In determining how much of the costs reasonably incurred should be reimbursed, the Commissioner has regard to the general principles of the determination of costs in legal proceedings.[86] Where a portion of legal expenses would not be recoverable on an indemnity or party-party basis under a cost assessment, the Commissioner may exclude this portion from a compensation claim.[87]

IV. Assessment of Non-Economic Losses

A. Identifying the Harm Caused by the Privacy Interference

Section 52(1AB) of the Privacy Act provides that the loss or damage includes '(a) injury to the feelings of the complainant or individual' and '(b) humiliation suffered by the complainant or individual'. In assessing compensation, the Commissioner has regard to amounts previously awarded in other privacy determinations, as well as to discrimination cases as outlined in Federal Discrimination Online and the Conciliation Register of the Australian Human Rights Commission.[88]

The legislation makes clear that it is not necessary for the 'injury to feelings' to reach the threshold of a recognised psychiatric illness. Emotional suffering in the form of anxiety, distress, feelings of humiliation and loss of confidence are compensable. The Commissioner takes into account the circumstances of the privacy breach, in particular the kind and severity of the interference, the sensitivity of the personal information in question and the duration of the breach. Where information has been disclosed, the identity of the recipients as well as the extent and consequences of disclosure will also be relevant.[89]

The Commissioner also considers the relationship between the respondent and the complainant,[90] and whether the privacy breach was the result of an oversight or

[83] Office of the Australian Information Commissioner, *Guide to privacy regulatory action* (OAIC, 2015) [1.13].

[84] In *'KB' and Veda* (n 56), the complainant was wrongly advised by the respondent that he needed to go to court before the erroneous credit record would be corrected: [96]–[97].

[85] ibid [96].

[86] *'LA' and Department of Defence* [2017] AICmr 25.

[87] ibid [53].

[88] *'CM' and Corporation of the Synod of the Diocese of Brisbane* [2014] AICmr 86, [96]; *'BO' and AeroCare Pty Ltd* [2014] AICmr 32, [53]; *'EQ'* (n 62).

[89] eg, *'JO' and Comcare* [2016] AICmr 64, [56]–[57]; *'IQ' and NRMA Insurance* (n 49) [70]; *'DK' and Telstra Corporation Ltd* [2014] AICmr 118, [76].

[90] eg, *'IV' and 'IW'* [2016] AICmr 41: medical practitioner and patient.

was intentional.[91] It is also relevant how the respondent dealt with the complaint and conducted itself throughout the investigation process.[92] While these last three factors are not objective circumstances that characterise the breach itself, they can affect the intensity of the injury to feelings caused by the breach.

Following the approach outlined in *Rummery*, the Commissioner assesses compensation having regard to the complainant's actual reaction and not to the hypothetical reaction of the majority of the community or of a reasonable person in similar circumstances.[93] On that basis, the Commissioner has close regard to the vulnerability of the complainant and the effect the privacy breach has had on his or her emotional well-being. In doing so, the Commissioner can take into account any evidence that assists in making the relevant assessments. In many cases, the Commissioner examines impact statements and other submissions made by the complainant.[94] In some cases, the complainant's evidence is corroborated by reports or statements from general practitioners[95] or clinical psychologists,[96] as well as from family,[97] friends[98] and others with insight into the mental state of the complainant.

In scenarios involving multiple potential causes of injury or loss, it becomes important to identify which injury or loss (if any) was suffered 'by reason of' the privacy interference. Complexities can arise in particular where the established interference with privacy was only one of a number of factors contributing to mental harm, or where it merely exacerbated an existing psychological condition. As discussed in section III.D, in *'EQ' and Great Barrier Reef Marine Park Authority*,[99] a journalist had obtained information from an undisclosed source that 'EQ' was under investigation for an alleged offence. In response to an enquiry by the journalist, the respondent confirmed – in breach of privacy principles – the accuracy of that information, and the matter was published in the media. The Commissioner held that the psychological consequences of the media exposure were more directly attributable to the prior disclosure for which the respondent agency could not be held responsible. In arriving at an award of $5,000, the Commissioner also gave weight to the fact that EQ was the primary contributor to his humiliation because he had engaged in the conduct under investigation.[100]

[91] *'IQ' and NRMA Insurance* (n 49) [70].

[92] *'JO' and Comcare* (n 89) [55].

[93] ibid [32]. This approach is similar to the 'egg shell skull' principle that applies in tort, under which the defendant must take her victim as she finds her, including her social, economic and physical circumstances: *Nader v Urban Transit Authority of NSW* (1985) 2 NSWLR 501, 537 *per* McHugh JA.

[94] *'LA' and Department of Defence* (n 86).

[95] *'LP' and The Westin Sydney (Privacy)* [2017] AICmr 53. At the time of writing, the decision is under review by the Federal Court.

[96] ibid; *'JO' v Comcare* (n 89)[53]; *'CP' and Department of Defence* [2014] AICmr 88 [34].

[97] eg, *'HW' and Freelancer International Pty Ltd* (n 75).

[98] *'LP' and The Westin Sydney (Privacy)* (n 95).

[99] *'EQ' and Great Barrier Reef Marine Park Authority* (n 62).

[100] ibid. On appeal, the Tribunal generally agreed with this approach, but increased the award to $8,000: *EQ* (n 34).

In *'CP' and Department of Defence*,[101] the Commissioner took into account that a number of workplace incidents apart from the privacy breach also impacted on the complainant and significantly contributed to the mood disorder, heightened anxiety and severe distress he experienced. Similar issues have arisen in a number of decisions under State privacy legislation.[102] While it is sufficient for causation that the privacy interference was a contributing cause,[103] the assessment of compensation should reflect the contribution of other causes for which the respondent does not bear responsibility.[104]

In a number of cases, the Commissioner takes into account the 'responsibility of [the respondent] to have a sound understanding of privacy obligations under the Act'. This consideration has been made in relation to financial institutions[105] and medical practitioners,[106] but also in relation to other organisations[107] that deal with sensitive information on a daily basis. In the case of *'EQ' and Great Barrier Reef Marine Park Authority*, the Commissioner stated that he gave 'greater weight to the breach of the right than to the psychological impact on the complainant'.[108] These considerations are reminiscent of damages awards for torts that protect a person's body, liberty, property and reputation from unlawful encroachment. A violation of these fundamental interests, which are protected in particular by the torts of trespass to the person and to land as well as defamation, is actionable per se. This means that a substantial award of general damages for these torts is available even when no actual loss can be proved. General damages are awarded for these torts on the basis that the loss is presumed because it is often difficult to prove it with precision,[109] or that a substantial award of damages is necessary for the vindication of the right in question.[110]

In recent times, courts[111] and commentators[112] have explored the utility of a vindicatory analysis of damages awards in tort and human rights law. The exact

[101] *'CP' and Department of Defence* (n 96).

[102] *ALZ v Worksafe NSW (No 4)* [2017] NSWCATAD 1, [40]; *AOZ v Rail Corporation NSW (No 2)* [2015] NSWCATAP 79, [31]; *RD v Department of Education and Training* [2005] NSWADT 195, [32]; *JL* (n 35) [214]–[221].

[103] *EQ* (n 34) [47].

[104] Similar considerations also apply in discrimination cases: *Gama v Qantas Airways Ltd (No 2)* [2006] FMCA 1767.

[105] *'HS' and AMP Life Ltd* [2015] AICmr 81, [80].

[106] *'IV' and 'IW'* [2016] AICmr 41, [65]; *'EZ' and 'EY'* [2015] AICmr 23, [93].

[107] *'BO' and AeroCare Pty Ltd* (n 88) [55].

[108] *'EQ' and Great Barrier Reef Marine Park Authority* (n 62) [78], referring also to *'BO' and AeroCare Pty Ltd* (n 88).

[109] *Williams v Morland* (1824) 2 B & C 910, (1824) 107 ER 620, 916 (622) *per* Littledale J: trespass to land; *Ratcliffe v Evans* [1892] 2 QB 524, 528 *per* Bowen LJ: defamation.

[110] See, eg, *Ruddock v Taylor* [2005] HCA 48, [141] (Kirby J): 'Damages are awarded to vindicate personal liberty, rather than as compensation for loss *per se*.' See also *Dillon v Plenty* (1991) 171 CLR 635, 645 *per* Mason CJ, Brennan and Toohey JJ; *Uren v John Fairfax & Sons Pty Ltd* (1966) 117 CLR 118, 150 *per* Windeyer J).

[111] *Attorney-General of Trinidad and Tobago v Ramanoop* [2005] UKPC 15, [2006] 1 AC 328; *Merson v Cartwright and the Attorney General of the Bahamas* [2005] UKPC 38.

[112] See, eg, J Edelman, 'Vindicatory Damages' in K Barker, K Fairweather and R Grantham (eds), *Private Law in the 21st Century* (Oxford, Hart Publishing, 2017) 343; K Barker, 'Private and Public: The

meaning given to vindication differs from context to context, and a universally accepted definition remains elusive, but it is clear that vindication is closely associated with the affirmation and reinforcement of rights. While all remedies have the function of redressing wrongs, and in this sense affirm rights, vindication comes most into focus when the usual rationales of compensation and punishment encounter conceptual difficulties. This may explain why a rights-based rationale for compensation holds particular appeal for wrongs that protect personal dignity interests and in human rights cases. Violation of these interests causes largely non-pecuniary harm that is by its very nature immeasurable in monetary terms and therefore difficult to redress through compensation. In these cases, compensation may be awarded without proof of actual damage, for the purpose of vindicating the legal entitlement.[113] Breaches of human rights statutes can also cause remedial difficulties when a strong response is called for, yet actual losses suffered are small and the statute does not allow the award of exemplary damages. In these cases, recourse to the purpose of vindication has been made to justify the award of a substantial amount of damages.

Similar concerns seem to underlie the cases in which the Privacy Commissioner focused on the importance of privacy obligations or the breach of the right in the assessment of compensation. In *'BO'*, the Commissioner considered that a significant amount of compensation was appropriate because of the specific vulnerability of the complainant, the sensitive nature of the information and the particular responsibilities of the respondent.[114] In *'EQ'*, the complainant's own conduct was a significant contributor to his non-economic loss,[115] so that an award reduced to reflect this contributory conduct may have appeared too low to signal the severity of the interference with privacy. However, just like in other fields in which a vindicatory rationale has been invoked, it may be asked whether vindication (or the affirmation of a right) is really a sufficiently distinct goal of remedies so as to provide a better basis for justifying the award than the recourse to the traditional rationales of compensation and punishment.[116]

Mixed Concept of Vindication in Torts and Private Law' in S Pitel, J Neyers and E Chamberlain (eds), *Tort Law: Challenging Orthodoxy* (Oxford, Hart Publishing, 2013) 59; Lord Scott, 'Damages' [2007] *Lloyd's Maritime and Commercial Law Quarterly* 465; JNE Varuhas, 'The Concept of "Vindication" in the Law of Torts: Rights, Interests and Damages' (2014) 34 *OJLS* 253; JNE Varuhas, *Damages and Human Rights* (Oxford, Hart Publishing, 2016) ch 2; N Witzleb and R Carroll, 'The Role of Vindication in Torts Damages' (2009) 7 *Tort Law Review* 16.

[113] See, for orders under s 46PO AHRC Act to provide redress against the prohibition of racial discrimination in *Racial Discrimination Act 1975* (Cth), s 9, *Wotton v State of Queensland (No 5)* [2016] FCA 1457, [1629] *per* Mortimer J, building on discussion by Varuhas, *Damages and Human Rights* (n 112) ch 2.

[114] *'BO' v AeroCare Pty Ltd* (n 88) [55].

[115] *'EQ' and Great Barrier Reef Marine Park Authority* (n 62) [79].

[116] The existence of vindicatory damages as a separate category was denied by a majority in *R (on the application of Lumba (Congo)) v Secretary of State for the Home Department* [2011] UKSC 12, [2012] 1 AC 245. See also discussion by Edelman (n 112); Barker (n 112).

While this complex question cannot be resolved here, the answer to it in the present context is further complicated by the uncertain legal status of entitlements under the Privacy Act. The long judicial tradition of protecting the body, liberty, property and reputation from unlawful encroachment makes it sound to identify the inviolability of these interests as common law rights. However, on the present state of Australian law, it is more difficult to identify an interference with privacy as an invasion of a 'right', because so far neither the common law nor the Privacy Act explicitly recognises a 'right to privacy'. Section 52 merely gives the Commissioner a power to make a determination about a privacy interference (defined in section 13 as a breach of an APP), and moreover makes these determinations discretionary and unenforceable. This currently creates another hurdle in Australia for a compensation award that puts significant weight on to the breach of the complainant's right itself, rather than the damage caused by this breach. However, other contributions to this volume demonstrate that once privacy is recognised as a right, interferences with this right should be actionable per se,[117] so that the violation itself provides the basis for a substantial award of damages.

B. The Range of Awards

The Commissioner seeks guidance in assessing the appropriate amounts from prior privacy cases in federal and State jurisdictions, settlement amounts in conciliated matters, as well as human rights cases.[118] Following the overarching principle that awards should be 'restrained but not minimal',[119] awards for non-pecuniary harm can reach up to $25,000, but the majority are at the middle or lower end of that range.

One of the highest awards under the Privacy Act made so far was in the recent case of *'LB' and Comcare (Privacy)*.[120] The respondent in that case, the federal government agency Comcare, published an improperly redacted report on its Freedom of Information website, thus disclosing sensitive health information about the complainant for a period of about 12 months. In addition to damages of $250,000 for loss of future employment income (which the Commissioner did not regard as substantiated), the complainant sought damages for non-economic loss in the amount of $150,000. The complainant alleged that she experienced 'severe shock', 'acute distress', humiliation and embarrassment, and provided reports from her treating psychiatrist and psychologist that confirmed her account of the effect

[117] See NA Moreham, 'Compensating for Loss of Dignity and Autonomy', in ch 5 of this book; JNE Varuhas, 'Varieties of Damages for Breach of Privacy', in ch 3 of this book.

[118] *'HW' and Freelancer International Pty Ltd* (n 75), [358].

[119] *Rummery* (n 30) [32]; *'EQ' and Great Barrier Reef Marine Park Authority* (n 62) [39].

[120] *'LB' and Comcare (Privacy)* (n 57). The highest amount in any Australian privacy jurisdiction was the award of $40,000, the statutory ceiling for awards under the NSW privacy legislation, in *NK v Northern Sydney Central Coast Area Health Service (No 2)* [2011] NSWADT 81.

of the disclosure of her sensitive information and that it aggravated pre-existing distress. The Commissioner did not accept the claim for economic loss and made an award of $20,000 for non-economic loss. While this award is at the upper end of existing awards, it appears low in relation to the significant distress suffered (and established through expert evidence), even having regard to the complainant's pre-existing health condition, which was the underlying source of her distress.

The next highest award of $18,000 was made in *'DK' and Telstra Corporation Ltd*,[121] where the complainant's personal information was published in the White Pages directory. As a family law judge, he regularly received threats to his life, and the disclosure of his home address to the public at large forced him to sell his home and move inter-State out of fear for his and his partner's personal safety. In arriving at the award, the Commissioner took into account similar cases from the area of anti-discrimination law, in which the wrongs resulted in applicants being uprooted and suffering disruption in all aspects of their life. Again, it appears that the award is quite low in light of the grave effects the disclosure had on the complainant's family and social life.

In two recent cases involving the unauthorised disclosure of medical information by a medical practitioner and a former employer, respectively, the Commissioner awarded damages of $10,000 and $12,000. The earlier case, *'IV' and 'IW'*,[122] concerned a one-time improper disclosure to a small group of email recipients who were not involved in the complainant's care, and which did not cause long-term emotional harm to him. In the more recent case of *'LA' and Department of Defence*,[123] the Department Archives disclosed the complainant's historical medical files to his son without the complainant's knowledge or consent. The files included reports and assessments relating to the complainant's former gambling addiction, of which his children had been unaware, and the disclosure had the consequence of exacerbating pre-existing mental health problems and affecting his family relationships.

There are a number of determinations where an amount of $10,000 was awarded for the non-economic losses caused by the inappropriate handling of sensitive financial information.[124] In *'KB' and Veda Advantage Information Services and Solutions Ltd*,[125] an award of $10,000 was made against a credit reporting body that disclosed an erroneous listing of a judgment to the complainant's credit providers, which in fact related to another person with a similar name. This resulted in three creditors imposing restrictions on credit facilities for a number of months until the record was corrected, causing the complainant embarrassment, loss of enjoyment during an overseas holiday, distress and humiliation. The Commissioner's

[121] *'DK' and Telstra Corporation Ltd* (n 89).
[122] *'IV' and 'IW'* [2016] AICmr 41.
[123] *'LA' and Department of Defence* (n 86) [41].
[124] In addition to the determinations discussed in the text, see also *'HS' and AMP Life Ltd* [2015] AICmr 81. [80].
[125] *'KB' and Veda* (n 56).

assessment took into account that there were multiple and serious breaches, which were not rectified within a reasonable period.

An award of $10,000 was also made in *'KA' and Commonwealth Bank of Australia Ltd*,[126] where the complainant was a customer of Commonwealth Bank and also a former employee of an agent for Commonwealth Bank who had access to the Bank's customer database. While the complainant and the Commonwealth Bank agent were in Fair Work proceedings over termination of her employment, she became aware that the agent had accessed her customer profile at Commonwealth Bank. The complainant suffered distress over concerns that her position in settlement negotiations might have been weakened because the agent had gained unauthorised knowledge of her difficult financial circumstances. The Commissioner held that the Commonwealth Bank interfered with the complainant's privacy when it failed to immediately limit the access rights of its agent despite being notified of the agent's potential conflict of interest.

In *'BO' and AeroCare Pty Ltd*,[127] the Commissioner awarded $8,500 for non-economic loss caused by the unnecessarily intrusive collection and disclosure of the complainant's sensitive medical information in an airport departure lounge in close proximity to the complainant's travel companion and other travellers, and in circumstances where the complainant's disability made him particularly vulnerable. The Commissioner took into account the significant distress and humiliation suffered by the complainant, the sensitive nature of the information in question and the 'responsibility of AeroCare, as an organisation, to have a sound understanding of its privacy obligations'.[128]

In *'D' and Wentworthville Leagues Club*,[129] the first determination issued by Commissioner Timothy Pilgrim, $7,500 was awarded for non-economic loss caused by the unauthorised disclosure of the complainant's former gambling habits, which caused the complainant to suffer humiliation as well as serious anxiety, panic attacks and physical symptoms.

In *'CP' and Department of Defence*,[130] a psychological report was disclosed to the complainant's general practitioner even though the complainant had expressly withdrawn his consent to the disclosure. The Commissioner awarded compensation of $5,000 because the improper disclosure had significant impact on the complainant's pre-existing psychological disorder and mental suffering, but also noted that the disclosure was very limited.

In two cases arising from the same facts, each of the complainants *'IX'*[131] and *'IY'*[132] was awarded $3,500 after they were made aware by journalists working for

[126] *'KA' and Commonwealth Bank of Australia Ltd* (n 67).
[127] *'BO' and AeroCare Pty Ltd* (n 88).
[128] ibid [55].
[129] *'D' and Wentworthville Leagues Club* [2011] AICmr 9.
[130] *'CP' and Department of Defence* (n 101).
[131] *'IX' and Business Service Brokers Pty Ltd t/a TeleChoice* (n 49).
[132] *'IY' and Business Service Brokers Pty Ltd t/a TeleChoice* [2016] AICmr 44.

Channel 9's 'A Current Affair' programme that customer information identifying them and belonging to the respondent had been found in a publicly accessible shipping container. The Commissioner held that the respondent had interfered with the complainants' privacy by not taking reasonable steps to protect their personal information from loss, misuse or unauthorised access, and by not destroying or de-identifying it when it was no longer needed. In each case, the complainants had experienced some anxiety and distress, but suffered no further consequences, physical, psychological, financial or otherwise. An award of $3,000 was also held to be appropriate for an improper release of health information to a very limited number of recipients, where the complainant suffered some anxiety and distress but no further consequences, and the respondent responded quickly and appropriately, including with an offer of apology.[133]

Acknowledging that compensation awards should not be minimal, minor invasions of privacy are compensated with awards of around $1,000–$1,500. In *'LP' and The Westin Sydney (Privacy)*,[134] for example, the complainant was awarded $1,500 for the recording of a phone conversation by the respondent hotel between the complainants and hotel staff at its front desk. The conversation was of a transactional nature, but – in breach of privacy principles – the complainant was not informed of the recording. The complainant suffered some anxiety and hurt, but the hotel changed its practices and made a number of unsuccessful attempts to apologise to the complainant.

C. The Relevance of Community Standards

As discussed, the Privacy Commissioner derives considerable assistance from cases decided under federal and State discrimination laws. However, it appears that the 2014 decision of the Full Court in *Richardson*[135] has not yet been considered in privacy jurisprudence. This important decision has significantly reshaped the approach to damages assessments under the SDA and other anti-discrimination statutes. In *Richardson*, the appellant was the victim of sexual harassment over some months, and suffered significant distress, anxiety and psychological injury in the form of a chronic adjustment disorder. At first instance, she was awarded $18,000 as compensation for non-economic loss under section 46PO(4)(d) of the AHRC Act.

The Full Court held that this amount, while within the previously accepted range for such cases, was manifestly inadequate as compensation for her loss and damage when judged by prevailing community standards.[136] Kenny J arrived at

[133] *'JO' and Comcare* (n 88).

[134] *'LP' and The Westin Sydney (Privacy)* (n 95).

[135] *Richardson* (n 41).

[136] ibid [81], [109], [117] *per* Kenny J, with whom Besanko and Perram JJ agreed on this issue.

this conclusion by a review of the awards made over the period of 30 years since the enactment of the SDA, noting that the cases adopted a 'cautious approach' and fixed awards at a 'conservative level', and that the damages range of between $12,000 and $20,000 had not changed much over the last 15 years.[137] Kenny J also referred to academic commentary that expressed concern that the level of damages then prevailing ran counter to the beneficial intent of the SDA.[138] Most significantly, her Honour considered evidence that community standards now accord a higher value to compensation for pain and suffering and loss of enjoyment of life, as shown in personal injury litigation,[139] where appellate courts had also recently lifted awards.[140] In light of her analysis, Kenny J held that an award for non-economic loss of $100,000 should be substituted for the award made at trial of $18,000. This landmark decision, and its reasoning, has subsequently been adopted in discrimination cases under other anti-discrimination statutes,[141] including at State level,[142] where tribunals also emphasised that no distinction should be made between the approach to damages taken in a court or a tribunal.[143]

Richardson also holds important lessons for awards in privacy cases. These include that, while regard to comparable decisions is useful to maintain consistency, the existing ranges of damages are not a 'tariff' that must be strictly observed, and that the level of damages requires regular review to take account of general inflation and, in particular, changes in community attitudes. Kenny J's judgment also appropriately emphasises that the various forms of pain and suffering and loss of enjoyment of life are essentially comparable, regardless of the circumstances and wrongs which have caused the plaintiff's suffering. This is not to suggest that there are no qualitative differences between sexual harassment and privacy cases, but the emotional distress and the debilitating effects caused by both types of wrong are not necessarily dissimilar.

Another potential area for comparison is defamation awards, where damages for non-pecuniary losses are traditionally generous.[144] In *Richardson*, Kenny J discussed the High Court decision in *Carson v John Fairfax & Sons Ltd*,[145]

[137] ibid [84], [85], [89] *per* Kenny J respectively.

[138] ibid [87] *per* Kenny J.

[139] ibid [95]–[96] *per* Kenny J.

[140] In particular following the decisions in *Amaca Pty Ltd v King* [2011] VSCA 447, (2011) 35 VR 280; *BHP Billiton Ltd v Hamilton* [2013] SASCFC 75, (2013) 117 SASR 329, [324]–[330].

[141] See, eg, the significant decision by Mortimer J in *Wotton v State of Queensland (No 5)* [2016] FCA 1457, [1598]–[1618] (representative proceedings by Palm Island residents concerning unlawful racial discrimination by Queensland police).

[142] *Chalker v Murrays Australia Pty Ltd* [2017] NSWCATAD 112; *Green v State of Queensland, Brooker and Keating* [2017] QCAT 008; *Power v Bouvy* [2015] TASADT 2; *Collins v Smith (Human Rights)* [2015] VCAT 1029; *Kovac v The Australian Croatian Club Ltd (No 2) (Discrimination)* [2016] ACAT 4.

[143] *Green v State of Queensland, Brooker and Keating* (n 142); *Collins v Smith (Human Rights)* (n 142).

[144] The uniform defamation legislation imposes a cap on damages for non-pecuniary loss, which is set at $389,500 from 1 July 2017: see, eg, *Defamation Act 2005* (NSW), s 35.

[145] *Carson v John Fairfax & Sons Ltd* (1993) 178 CLR 44.

in which the majority found no error in Kirby J's approach of drawing a general comparison with personal injury awards for the purpose of identifying whether a defamation verdict was manifestly excessive.[146] While sexual harassment and defamation damages both aim to compensate for non-pecuniary harm resulting from invasion of dignitary interests, Kenny J was not persuaded that a direct comparison of awards in sexual harassment cases with defamation damages provided useful guidance for deciding whether the former were too low. Her Honour referred to the different purposes of defamation damages, of providing consolation for distress and hurt, reparation for harm done to reputation and vindication of reputation, whereas damages for sexual harassment are primarily directed at pain and suffering and loss of enjoyment of life. There is an argument that the relationship between privacy wrongs and defamation[147] is closer than that between defamation and harrassment. At least where privacy invasion is in the form of unauthorised disclosure, both wrongs are primarily associated with wrongful speech, often involve the media and are characterised by the effect of this publication not only on the person affected, but also on their relationship with others in the community. In addition to defamation damages, a further possible comparator is the few judicial awards of damages for invasion of privacy in Australia by lower courts,[148] which would also suggest that the level of compensation under the Privacy Act may soon need to be reviewed.

It is noticeable from the overview of determinations above that the majority of the compensation awards that exceed $10,000 have been made in the last two years. However, the small number of determinations in total makes it difficult to discern an upward trend. It can be expected that the decision in *Richardson* will also affect future determinations in privacy cases. This would appropriately direct attention to ensuring a consistent approach between damages awards in courts and tribunals, as well as across comparable regimes that seek to redress to non-pecuniary losses, and to levels of awards that are in line with current community expectations and standards.

[146] *Richardson* (n 41) [112]–[114].

[147] For further discussion, see D Rolph, 'The Interaction Between Defamation and Privacy' in Barker, Fairweather and Grantham (eds) (n 112) 463; N Witzleb, 'Interim injunctions for invasions of privacy: challenging the rule in Bonnard v Perryman' in Witzleb et al (eds) (n 13) 407.

[148] *Jane Doe v ABC* [2007] VCC 281: $85,000 general damages for post-traumatic stress relating to publication by the broadcaster identifying the plaintiff as a victim of rape within marriage, and a further award for economic loss (breach of statutory duty, breach of confidence, negligence, invasion of privacy); *Grosse v Purvis* [2003] QDC 151, (2003) Aust Torts Reports 81-706: $178,000, comprised of $108,000 compensatory damages, $50,000 aggravated damages and $20,000 exemplary damages (invasion of privacy). But see also *Giller v Procopets* [2008] VSCA 236, (2008) 24 VR 1: $40,000, including $10,000 aggravated damages, for distribution and attempted distribution of video tapes (showing the plaintiff and defendant engaged in sexual conduct) to the plaintiff's family and others after the relationship between the plaintiff and defendant had broken down (breach of confidence); *Wilson v Ferguson* [2015] WASC 15: $35,000 for posting on the Internet, without authorisation, sexually explicit photographs and videos of the plaintiff, taken consensually during the relationship (breach of confidence);

D. The Availability of Aggravated Damages

While it is not uncommon for privacy complainants to seek declarations in relation to aggravated damages, they remain a highly exceptional remedy. The AAT confirmed in *Rummery* that 'in an appropriate case',[149] aggravated damages may be awarded. The Commissioner now routinely considers aggravated damages, even when they are not specifically sought.[150] However, applications for aggravated damages are rarely successful.[151] In fact, so far there has been only a single determination in which they have been awarded,[152] and this determination has subsequently been set aside by the AAT.

In *Rummery*, the Tribunal was very critical of the respondent department's conduct, which involved a senior department officer divulging employment-related information about the complainant in a private conversation to the Ombudsman's office, with the aim of derailing an ombudsman investigation sought by the complainant. The Tribunal called this conduct 'playing the man and not the ball',[153] and acknowledged the effect of this 'serious breach'[154] on the complainant's feelings. Yet, based on the fact that under section 52(1A) the loss includes 'injury to the complainant's feelings or humiliation suffered by the complainant', the Tribunal preferred not to identify a separate amount in aggravated damages in addition to general damages. Instead, it awarded compensation in a single amount of $8,000.

The determinations to date reveal that the Commissioner relies on two main principles to guide his decisions on when aggravated damages are warranted:

(a) aggravated damages may be awarded where the respondent has behaved 'high-handedly, maliciously, insultingly or oppressively';[155]

(b) the 'manner in which a defendant conducts his or her case may exacerbate the hurt and injury suffered by the plaintiff'.[156]

[149] *Rummery* (n 30) [32]. This principle was derived from the decision of the Full Federal Court in *Hall* (n 23) 282, 240–41 *per* Lockhart J, and 282 *per* French J, with Lockhart J himself referring to a statement to this effect by May LJ in *Alexander v Home Office* [1988] 2 All ER 118.

[150] eg, *'IQ' and NRMA Insurance* (n 49); *'IR' and NRMA Insurance* [2016] AICmr 37; *'IV' and 'IW'* (n 106); *'IX' and Business Service Brokers Pty Ltd t/a TeleChoice* (n 49).

[151] Examples of unsuccessful applications include: *'LP' and The Westin Sydney (Privacy)* (n 95); *'KA' and Commonwealth Bank of Australia Ltd* (n 67).

[152] *'HW' and Freelancer International Pty Ltd* (n 75).

[153] *Rummery* (n 30) [54].

[154] ibid.

[155] eg, *'D' and Wentworthville Leagues Club* (n 129) [51]; *'S' and Veda* (n 49), [93]; *'HW' and Freelancer International Pty Limited* [2015] AICmr 86, [379]; *'BO' and AeroCare Pty Ltd* (n 88) [57]; *'IQ' and NRMA Insurance* (n 49) [73]; all referring to *Hall v A & A Sheiban Pty Ltd* 1989) 20 FCR 217, 240.

[156] eg, *'D' and Wentworthville Leagues Club* (n 129) [52]; *'HW' and Freelancer International Pty Limited* (n 155) [379]; *'BO' and AeroCare Pty Ltd* (n 88) [57]; *'IQ' and NRMA Insurance* (n 49) [73]; all referring to *Elliott v Nanda & Commonwealth* (2001) 111 FCR 240, [2001] FCA 418, [180].

Both of these principles are in line with the common law[157] and the case law under anti-discrimination legislation.[158] However, the relationship between these two principles in the context of privacy determinations has not been identified. In particular, it remains unclear whether these two principles operate as alternatives, that is as two independent bases for awarding aggravated damages, or whether they are cumulative requirements that both need to be met.

The fact that a respondent misguidedly places the responsibility for the privacy dispute on the complainant[159] does not, without more, provide grounds for aggravated damages. Neither does the fact necessarily warrant aggravated damages that a respondent investigates a complaint for a prolonged period in accordance with the respondent's normal practices and procedures.[160] In two cases, the Commissioner acknowledged that the respondents' conduct of the case caused the complainant additional distress. In one case, the respondent did not respond in a timely manner to the initial complaint, which caused unnecessary delays.[161] In the other, the respondent submitted a potentially misleading document to the OAIC, causing the complainant additional work, delay and frustration.[162] On both occasions, the Commissioner denied aggravated damages because he did not consider that the respondents conducted their cases in a way that was high-handed, malicious, insulting or oppressive. This suggests that high-handed conduct or other bad motive or intention is required, even where it is established that the complainant's hurt and injury has been exacerbated through the manner in which the case has been handled. That, in turn, would suggest that the two principles identified above operate cumulatively, so that aggravated damages will generally only be awarded where the complainant can establish that the respondent has behaved high-handedly, maliciously, insultingly or oppressively *and thereby* exacerbated the hurt and injury suffered by the plaintiff.

The only determination for aggravated damages was made in the matter of *'HW' and Freelancer International Pty Ltd*,[163] which concerned a prolonged feud between the parties, during which the respondent published personal information identifying the complainant on a public website. The Commissioner awarded aggravated damages of $5,000, in addition to an award of ordinary compensatory damages of $10,000. In awarding this amount, the Commissioner was guided by decisions in anti-discrimination cases that awarded similar amounts.[164]

[157] *Rookes v Barnard* [1964] AC 1129; *Uren v John Fairfax & Sons Pty Ltd* (1966) 117 CLR 118, 149 *per* Windeyer J.

[158] Apart from the cases referred to in determinations, see also *Burns v Media Options Group Pty Ltd* [2013] FCCA 79, [1784]–[1785].

[159] *'BO' and AeroCare Pty Ltd* (n 88) [58]; *'S' and Veda* (n 49) [94]–[96].

[160] *'S' and Veda Advantage* (n 49) [94]–[96].

[161] *'IQ' and NRMA Insurance* (n 49), [74].

[162] *'KA' and Commonwealth Bank of Australia Ltd* (n 67) [94]–[95].

[163] *'HW' and Freelancer International Pty Ltd* (n 75). See further J Davidson, 'Aggravated damages for privacy breaches' (2016) *Privacy Law Bulletin* 84.

[164] *Elliott v Nanda & Commonwealth* (n 156); *Hughes v Car Buyers Pty Ltd* [2004] FMCA 526.

The Commissioner found that the respondent, Freelancer, demonstrated repeated disregard for its privacy obligations toward the complainant, including by making numerous unauthorised online disclosures of the complainant's personal information, which unnecessarily prolonged and increased the distress caused to the complainant. The Commissioner was satisfied that the 'manner in which Freelancer conducted itself highlighted its apparent contempt of, or at best, indifference' to the complainant's privacy complaints.[165] However, this determination was set aside by the AAT because Senior Member Taylor SC found that only a small number of privacy breaches related to a single episode were actually established.[166] The AAT decision was very critical of the Commissioner's determination to award damages for the continuum of events, without seeking to differentiate between the various identified breaches. In a further finding differing starkly from the Commissioner's determination, it was held that the privacy breaches did not cause the applicant any significant distress, hurt or loss. As a result, the awards of compensatory damages and aggravated damages were set aside and replaced with a declaration that the respondent should not repeat the conduct, but that it was otherwise inappropriate to take further action on the substantiated complaint.

V. Non-Compensatory Remedies

Under section 52(1)(b)(ii) of the Privacy Act, the Commissioner may declare that the 'respondent must perform any reasonable act or course of conduct to redress any loss or damage suffered by the complainant'. This power has been used to require respondents to make apologies or change their privacy practices.

A. Apologies

The Commissioner regularly relies on the power in section 52(1)(b)(ii) to require respondents to issue an apology to a successful complainant. Apologies are generally only ordered if the complainant expressly seeks this remedy.[167] However, in some cases, the Commissioner required an apology even though it appears not to have been sought.[168] Declarations of an apology have been made against

[165] *'HW' and Freelancer International Pty Ltd* (n 75) [383].

[166] *Freelancer International Pty Ltd* (n 75) [185]–[199].

[167] *'CP' and Department of Defence* (n 96); *'IR' and NRMA Insurance* (n 150); *'PB' and United Super Pty Ltd as Trustee for Cbus (Privacy)* [2018] AICmr 51. See also R Carroll, 'Apologies and Corrections as Remedies for Serious Invasions of Privacy', in ch 9 of this book.

[168] *'S' and Veda* (n 49); *'IQ' and NRMA Insurance* (n 49). Critical of ordered apologies if this remedy is not sought by the person aggrieved: R Carroll, 'Beyond Compensation: Apologies as a Private Law Remedy' in J Berryman and R Bigwood (eds), *The Law of Remedies: New Directions in the Common Law* (Toronto, Irwin Law, 2010) 342, 376.

government departments[169] and private sector organisations[170] alike. Usually, the apology must be in writing to the complainant and issued within four weeks of the determination.[171] The wording of the apology is normally not further prescribed, although in a recent determination the Commissioner required that the apology include an acknowledgement of the breaches and of the complainant's distress.[172]

The determinations do not contain any detailed consideration of how the Commissioner exercises his discretion to make a determination on an apology order. However, some guidance can be derived from a case in which the Commissioner declined a complainant's request for an apology. In *'LB' and Comcare (Privacy)*,[173] Comcare apologised to the complainant at the earliest practical opportunity after it had been made aware that it had mistakenly published the complainant's sensitive health information on its Freedom of Information website. The letter of apology included an acceptance of responsibility for the privacy invasion and acknowledged the complainant's distress. It provided an explanation for the disclosure and outlined what actions had been taken to remove the redacted Comcare report from the website and prevent such an incident from recurring.

An apology with these attributes is commonly regarded as satisfying all the hallmarks of a meaningful apology:[174] it was authentic, issued in a timely manner and made voluntarily, it accepted responsibility and acknowledged the complainant's feelings, and expressed remorse and explained how a similar mistake would be avoided in future.[175] As a result, the Commissioner considered it unnecessary to make a declaration for a further apology.[176] Conversely, where an apology lacks any or all of these components, it is likely to have less or no meaning for the complainant, and this may be reflected in the Commissioner's determination. This may also explain why in some cases respondents who had already issued a verbal apology or provided an explanation of the privacy interference[177] were required to follow up with a written apology.[178]

Apologies to the complainant before or during the investigation, in particular when they are voluntarily given and accepted, can also be relevant for the

[169] *'LU' and Department of Defence (Privacy)* [2017] AICmr 61; *'CP' and Department of Defence* (n 96).

[170] eg, *'IR' and NRMA Insurance* (n 150); *'BO' and AeroCare Pty Ltd* (n 88).

[171] Some determinations identify a different timeframe: *'DO' and Department of Veterans' Affairs* [2014] AICmr 124: two weeks; *'D' and Wentworthville Leagues Club* (n 129): three weeks; *'KA' and Commonwealth Bank of Australia Ltd* (n 67): six weeks.

[172] *'LU' and Department of Defence (Privacy)* (n 168).

[173] *'LB' and Comcare (Privacy)* (n 57) [43].

[174] See, eg, the model of an 'Authentic Apology' that consists of three components: affirmation, affect and action: A Allan, 'Apology in civil law: A psycholegal perspective' (2007) 14 *Psychiatry, Psychology and Law* 5.

[175] This is sometimes described as a 'full' (as opposed to a 'partial') apology: see R Carroll, 'Apologies as a Legal Remedy' (2013) 35 *Sydney Law Review* 317, 322–23.

[176] *'LB' and Comcare (Privacy)* (n 57) [43].

[177] *'IX' and Business Service Brokers Pty Ltd t/a TeleChoice* (n 49).

[178] *'D' and Wentworthville Leagues Club* (n 129) [58].

assessment of compensation.[179] In *'LA' and Department of Defence*,[180] the Commissioner identified as a mitigating factor that the Department accepted its error at the earliest opportunity and apologised to the complainant. While even a prompt and meaningful apology does not stand in the way of a claim for compensation,[181] an insincere and ineffective apology is unlikely to affect the measure of monetary relief. This is well illustrated by the leading decision of *Rummery*, in which the Department gave an apology 'as limited as it could be'[182] and only on direction from the Privacy Commissioner. This led the Administrative Appeals Tribunal to wholly disregard the apology in the assessment of damages.

There has been no case in which a determination required that the apology be public or in which an apology was awarded and compensation denied.[183] In the case of *'CM' and Corporation of the Synod of the Diocese of Brisbane*,[184] the complainant sought an order that the respondent apologise to a school staff member who was not a party to the proceedings. This request was made because the complainant was of the view that this party was penalised by the respondent for providing the complainant with support in raising the privacy issues with the respondent. The Commissioner considered that such an order was outside the scope of the outcomes he was able to order.[185]

B. No Power to Award Exemplary Damages

The Privacy Act does not mention the possibility of exemplary damages.[186] Based on the wording of section 52(1)(iii) of the Privacy Act, which refers to an entitlement to an 'amount by way of compensation for any loss or damage suffered', the Commissioner explained repeatedly that he does not have the power to make awards that are punitive in nature. In determinations considering the issue, the Commissioner referred to decisions under the (comparable) section 81 of the SDA, which has likewise been held not to include a power to grant exemplary damages. In *Hall*, the Full Federal Court expressed the view obiter that exemplary damages are not available under the SDA because they are punitive in character and would

[179] *'JO' and Comcare* (n 89).
[180] *'LA' and Department of Defence* (n 86).
[181] ibid; see also *'LB' and Comcare (Privacy)* (n 57).
[182] *Rummery* (n 30) [45].
[183] In *'DO' and Department of Veterans' Affairs* (n 170), only an apology, but no damages, was sought.
[184] *'CM' and Corporation of the Synod of the Diocese of Brisbane* (n 88).
[185] ibid [101].
[186] It should be noted, however, that the *Privacy Act 1998 (Cth)* contains a number of civil penalty provisions, including for a serious or repeated interference with privacy (s 13G) and for various contraventions under pt IIIA ('Credit reporting'). Civil penalties are payable to the Commonwealth: s 80W.

be awarded in addition to any compensation if the conduct of the respondent was of a particularly outrageous nature.[187]

In contrast, the possibility of a punitive award under the NSW privacy legislation was left open by the former President of the NSW Administrative Decisions Tribunal. In *RD v Department of Education and Training*,[188] O'Connor DCJ raised the possibility that 'some punitive component' could be 'incorporated into the damages award' if an 'error was not remedied at the first point at which it could reasonably have been identified'.[189] In *NZ v Director General, Department of Housing*, O'Connor DCJ reiterated that he did 'not see any difficulty in awarding aggravated or exemplary damages if the case justifies it'.[190] In neither case was an award for punitive damages actually made. In *NK v Northern Sydney Central Coast Area Health Service (No 2)*, the Tribunal identified a significant number of breaches of privacy obligations by a hospital, in which NK was both a patient and an employee, causing very serious consequences for NK's health and work. Montgomery S held that the respondent's conduct amounted to an 'oppressive disregard of NK's rights and its own privacy duties'.[191] While the availability of exemplary damages was considered, the issue was not determined because the Tribunal decided to award $40,000, the statutory maximum amount of damages available under the NSW legislation. Therefore, the questions of whether the NSW Acts do indeed contain a power to award exemplary damages, and whether it could be exercised in the wide circumstances identified by the obiter comments of O'Connor DCJ, must be regarded as untested.

C. Other Orders

Determinations may also contain other non-monetary remedies that are, often in combination, intended to bring about systemic change to privacy-invasive practices. In *'D' and Wentworthville Leagues Club*,[192] the Commissioner required the club to issue a written apology within three weeks of the determination, review how its staff handle personal information and improve staff training, and confirm within six months of the determination that the review of training had been completed. Similar requirements for a change of procedures directed at avoiding a reoccurrence of the privacy interference have also been made in a significant number of other cases against government agencies, as well as against private sector organisations.[193]

[187] *Hall* (n 23) 240–41 *per* Lockhart J; 282 *per* French J, referring to the equivalent limitation under (former) s 82 of the *Trade Practices Act 1974* (Cth).
[188] *RD v Department of Education and Training* [2005] NSWADT 195.
[189] ibid [33].
[190] *NZ v Director General, Department of Housing* (n 35) [52].
[191] *NK v Northern Sydney Central Coast Area Health Service (No 2)* [2011] NSWADT 81, [60].
[192] *'D' and Wentworthville Leagues Club* (n 129).
[193] eg, *'JO' and Comcare* (n 89); *'PB' and United Super Pty Ltd* (n 167).

The inherent limits to the power under section 52 of the Privacy Act became apparent in the determination in *'CM' and Corporation of the Synod of the Diocese of Brisbane*.[194] The complainant asked the Commissioner to order that the compensation be donated to a registered charity and that the respondent apologise to a third party, who was caught up in the dispute.[195] In relation to both issues, the Commissioner refused to make the orders requested because they were said to be outside the range of orders the Commissioner can make.

VI. Conclusion

In the absence of a general cause of action for the invasion of privacy in Australian law, the complaint process under the Privacy Act remains an important avenue for the protection of informational privacy. While the Privacy Commissioner resolves the majority of complaints through conciliation, the power to make determinations under section 52 of the Privacy Act has become more widely used in recent years.

This chapter has focused on the Commissioner's approach to the granting of remedies in his determinations. This approach has been shaped by a small number of cases in the AAT in which the Tribunal reviewed privacy determinations, and the much more expansive jurisprudence under the federal anti-discrimination laws. The Commissioner closely follows these decisions in his own determinations. As a dignitary wrong, invasions of privacy will generally cause non-economic losses in the form of anxiety, distress and embarrassment. These losses are compensated by amounts that are set in alignment with anti-discrimination case law, and the Commissioner follows the broad principle that the awards should be restrained but not minimal. As a result, awards remain relatively conservative, with amounts ranging between $1,500 and $20,000. Privacy determinations have yet to expressly engage with recent jurisprudence that significantly lifted the awards in sex discrimination and sexual harassment cases. It is desirable that privacy awards for non-economic losses follow these prompts and increase in line with current community expectation and standards, in particular where an interference has been serious or has had severe consequences for the complainant. Economic losses, in particular losses of income and expenses in the defence of privacy rights, can also be compensated. However, many complainants are unable to establish to the satisfaction of the Commissioner that a reduction in income or profit following an interference with privacy was indeed suffered by reason of that interference. It would be desirable to consider an approach that is more sympathetic to the difficulty of establishing such losses and their causal link to the privacy interference. Similar to the discrimination cases, complainants often seek an apology and

[194] *'CM' and Corporation of the Synod of the Diocese of Brisbane* (n 88).
[195] ibid [100]–[101].

a change of practice as an outcome additional to damages. The Commissioner makes both forms of order quite regularly.

In conclusion, the increasing use of the Commissioner's power to make determinations is to be welcomed. Privacy determinations are beginning to develop into a coherent body of case law that makes the enforcement of the Privacy Act more transparent, and which is likely to lead to improved compliance. However, the limited scope of the Privacy Act, with its focus on data protection and its broad exemptions, means that privacy determinations will continue to play only a supplementary role in the protection of privacy. The enactment of a general cause of action for invasion of privacy is still the missing centrepiece.

16

Invasion of Privacy: Cross-Border Implications

RICHARD GARNETT

The chapters in this volume all address various aspects of relief for breach of privacy, a cause of action that is becoming increasingly recognised in Commonwealth countries including England, New Zealand, Canada and possibly Australia.

The aim of this chapter is to explore the issues that arise when a privacy infringement action crosses international boundaries and cannot simply be subjected to the jurisdiction and law of one country. Relevant principles of private international law need to be consulted, addressing three key questions: (i) whether a Commonwealth court has jurisdiction and will exercise jurisdiction in respect of a claim; (ii) what law it will apply to the merits of the case, including both liability and remedies; and (iii) in what circumstances a court will recognise and enforce the judgment of a court in another country.

Given the greater interconnectedness between countries and the increased scope for simultaneous and multi-territorial infringement of rights, created in part by the Internet, a study of the private international law aspects of privacy is crucial.

Before embarking on an examination of the private international law issues, a brief survey of the substantive law on invasion of privacy in each of the four countries mentioned will first be provided.

I. Introduction: Substantive Law on Invasion of Privacy

In Australia, it is still accurate to say that a clearly identifiable and widely accepted tort of invasion of privacy has not yet emerged. However, the High Court has left open the possibility of the recognition of such a right, and some lower courts have allowed claims in tort to be brought for invasion of privacy based on unauthorised disclosure of information[1] and intrusion upon seclusion[2] respectively. Significantly

[1] *Doe v ABC* [2007] VCC 281.
[2] *Grosse v Purvis* [2003] QDC 151.

also, the Australian,[3] New South Wales[4] and Victorian[5] Law Reform Commissions and the South Australian Law Reform Institute[6] have all recommended the introduction of a statutory tort for invasion of privacy where there is an intrusion upon seclusion or misuse of private information by publication or disclosure.[7] Nevertheless, in two important recent decisions involving misuse of information by publication in the context of 'revenge porn', the Court of Appeal of Victoria[8] and Western Australian Supreme Court[9] both accepted that no tort of invasion of privacy existed in Australia. Instead, the existing equitable action for breach of confidence could be relied upon to give redress in such circumstances. It therefore remains an open question whether an action for breach of privacy exists in Australian law.

In New Zealand, the torts of intrusion into the seclusion of the claimant and misuse of private information by publication have both been recognised.[10] In Canada, similar versions of these torts have been found to exist at common law in Ontario[11] and (in the case of intrusion into seclusion) Nova Scotia.[12] In addition, four Canadian Provinces have legislated to create a right of privacy,[13] without precisely defining its scope or content.

In England, the tort of misuse of private information by publication is now recognised as a distinct cause of action, informed by Article 8 of the European Convention on Human Rights (ECHR). The key elements of the English tort are whether the claimant has a 'reasonable expectation of privacy' and, if that is established, whether the claimant's interest in protection of his or her private life outweighs countervailing interests, including those in freedom of expression.[14]

In the United States (US) by contrast, in addition to the two privacy torts above, two other types of privacy violation exist in various States: 'publicity which places the plaintiff in a false light in the public eye' and 'appropriation of the plaintiff's

[3] Australian Law Reform Commission, *Serious Invasions of Privacy in the Digital Era: Final Report*, ALRC 123 (2014) Recommendation 5-1.

[4] New South Wales Law Reform Commission, *Invasion* of *Privacy*, Report 120 (2009).

[5] Victorian Law Reform Commission, *Surveillance in Public Places*, Report 18 (2010).

[6] *A Statutory Tort for Invasion of Privacy*, Final Report 4 (2016).

[7] The NSW Law Reform Commission (in Draft Bill cl 74(1)) spoke of a cause of action 'where a person's conduct invades an individual's privacy', which may go beyond these two categories.

[8] *Giller v Procopets* (2008) 24 VR 1.

[9] *Wilson v Ferguson* [2015] WASC 15.

[10] *C v Holland* [2012] 3 NZLR 672 (intrusion into seclusion); *Hosking v Runting* [2005] 1 NZLR 1 (misuse of information).

[11] *Jones v Tsige* 2012 ONCA 32 (intrusion into seclusion); *Jane Doe 464533 v D(N)* [2016] ONSC 541 (misuse of information).

[12] *Trout Point Lodge Ltd v Handshoe* 2012 NSSC 245.

[13] Privacy Act 1996 (British Columbia); Privacy Act 1987 (Manitoba); Privacy Act 1978 (Saskatchewan); and Privacy Act 1990 (Newfoundland and Labrador).

[14] *Vidal-Hall v Google Inc* [2016] QB 1003, [51] (CA); *ETK v News Group Newspapers Ltd* [2011] EWCA Civ 439, [10]; *PJS v News Group Newspapers Ltd* [2016] UKSC 26.

name or likeness'.[15] While neither right is explicitly recognised under the laws of England, Australia, New Zealand and Canada in these precise terms, comparable protection may exist under other causes of action, such as passing off and defamation. Also, as discussed later in this chapter, it may be possible for a claimant to rely on a breach of a US tort of privacy in a proceeding in a Commonwealth court in certain circumstances. In this chapter, however, the primary focus will be on the torts considered in the four Commonwealth countries noted above: misuse of private information by disclosure and intrusion upon seclusion. Reference will also be made to the action for breach of confidence out of deference to the Australian position.

II. Personal Jurisdiction in Privacy Actions

The first question a court has to consider when confronted by a breach of privacy action that crosses national boundaries is whether it has personal jurisdiction over the defendant. In the four countries mentioned, personal jurisdiction has two aspects: common law and statutory. Common law jurisdiction is based on service of originating process on a defendant who is present within the territory of the adjudicating court (the forum), while statutory jurisdiction exists where a claimant can successfully serve the defendant outside the territory of the forum, which is typically permitted where the cause of action has a specified link with the forum. Once the court has decided that it has jurisdiction over the defendant and will not decline to exercise jurisdiction on discretionary grounds, the court will then apply its 'choice-of-law rules' to determine the law to be applied to the merits of the action. The chosen law may be local or foreign, but foreign law may be excluded in exceptional circumstances where it is procedural or contrary to the forum's public policy. These issues are discussed in detail in section III.B.

A. Common Law Jurisdiction

In Australian law, a court has personal jurisdiction over an individual defendant at common law where he or she is served with originating process while present within the forum, which means anywhere in Australia and New Zealand (under the Trans-Tasman regime).[16] The defendant's presence may only be transient, and there need be no other connection between the action and the forum. What this means in the privacy context is that a defendant who is resident in Ontario, Canada,

[15] American Law Institute, *Restatement (Second) of Torts* (1997) §§ 652A–652E; note, however, that the First Amendment to the US Constitution may impact upon the application of the US torts.

[16] *Trans-Tasman Proceedings Act 2010* (Cth) (TTPA), s 9(1).

but performs acts that infringe a claimant's privacy in Victoria, Australia, may be subject to the common law jurisdiction of the Victorian court if he or she travels to Australia and is served there. The same rule exists in New Zealand[17] (which extends to defendants in Australia under the Trans-Tasman system), Canada[18] and England,[19] in respect of defendants not domiciled in a European Union (EU) or European Economic Area (EEA) member state.[20]

In the case of a corporation, it is deemed to be present in the forum when carrying on business at a fixed and reasonably permanent place there. Such a principle again applies in all four countries.[21]

The existence of common law 'presence' jurisdiction has important consequences for a claimant seeking relief for invasion of privacy. If the claimant can validly perform service on the defendant within the forum, in principle he or she should be able to seek relief based on either local or foreign privacy laws. As will be discussed in more detail,[22] the choice-of-law rule adopted in all four common law jurisdictions examined requires application of the law of the place where the tort is committed (subject to some exceptions).

There would therefore seem to be no obstacle to an Australian claimant, for example, bringing an action in an Australian court for breach of English or American privacy law, subject to possible arguments about appropriate forum and public policy (discussed in sections II.B.iv and III.B). Such an outcome may operate as an 'indirect' method of enforcing privacy norms in Australia, at a time when the status of invasion of privacy under Australian law remains uncertain. The only real limitation is practical: that is, a person resident in a foreign country engaged in infringing an Australian claimant's privacy is unlikely to make himself or herself voluntarily available for service of process in Australia, and indeed would be well advised to stay away. A suit in an Australian court against an Australian resident defendant, by contrast, for breach of foreign privacy law, would have greater prospects of success. The same principles would apply in the case of a suit for breach of a foreign privacy law in the other three common law countries mentioned.

The above analysis would also apply to a breach of confidence action in an Australian court. A claim for breach of confidence is not regarded in private

[17] *Von Wyl v Engeler* [1998] 3 NZLR 416.

[18] *Club Resorts Ltd v Van Breda* [2012] 1 SCR 572, [79]; *Chevron Corp v Yaiguaje* [2015] 3 SCR 69, [84].

[19] *Colt Industries Inc v Sarlie* [1966] 1 All ER 673.

[20] In the case of EU-domiciled defendants, the EU Regulation of 12 December 2012 on jurisdiction and the recognition of judgments in civil and commercial matters (Brussels I Regulation recast) applies; for EEA-domiciled defendants the Lugano Convention of 21 December 2007 applies. Both instruments are in almost identical terms.

[21] For England, see *Adams v Cape Industries Plc* [1990] Ch 433, 530–44; for Australia, see *Commonwealth Bank of Australia v White* [1999] 2 VR 681; for Canada, see *Club Resorts Ltd v Van Breda* [2012] 1 SCR 572, [87]; and for New Zealand, see *Moldauer v Constellation Brands Inc* [2009] NZCA 324, [14]. Statutory rules may also exist providing for service on foreign corporations registered in the forum.

[22] See section III.A.

international law as a matter in tort[23] but is considered equitable in nature, and so, in the absence of a contractual relationship, is governed exclusively by the law of the forum.[24]

B. Service Outside the Jurisdiction: Privacy

By contrast, if the defendant is not present within the forum and cannot be served with originating process there, but can be found abroad, a plaintiff in each of the four common law countries examined may be able to serve the defendant outside the jurisdiction and so proceed in the forum. In the case of Australia, for defendants located in all countries except New Zealand, three things must be determined if the defendant appears to contest service or seek a stay of the proceedings: (i) that a relevant statutory 'gateway' for service out is available;[25] (ii) that the claimant's action is at least arguable on the merits; and (iii) that the Australian court is a 'clearly inappropriate forum'. In all Australian jurisdictions apart from Western Australia, it is possible to serve a defendant abroad without prior leave of the court.

An infringement of privacy would almost certainly be classified as a 'tort' under Australian principles of private international law, and the relevant gateways for service abroad would be as follows. In Victoria,[26] New South Wales,[27] South Australia[28] and the Australian Capital Territory[29] the rules have recently changed, so that the claimant must now show that the claim is 'founded on a tortious act which was done or which occurred wholly or partly in Australia'. All other Australian superior courts still require that 'a tort be committed in the jurisdiction'.[30] All Australian rules of court provide an additional basis of service in tort cases where damage has been suffered wholly or in part in the forum from a tortious act wherever occurring.[31]

The regime in both New Zealand and England (for defendants not domiciled in an EU or EEA member state) is similar, although prior leave to serve is still required in England. Under both countries' rules the claimant must establish three

[23] *Douglas v Hello! Ltd (No 3)* [2006] QB 125.

[24] *National Commercial Bank v Wimborne* (1978) 5 BPR 11,958, 11,982; compare the position in Singapore where it was said that the tort choice-of-law rules may apply to a breach of confidence suit where the 'factual matrix' of the complaint is analogous to tort: *Rickshaw Investments Ltd v Nicolai Baron von Uexkull* [2007] 1 SLR(R) 377.

[25] The statutory rules of court in all four countries provide grounds or 'gateways' that must be satisfied before service out of the jurisdiction is permitted. Typically, such grounds identify a connection between the forum and the claimant's cause of action; eg, the tort was committed in the forum or the contract was breached in the forum, etc. Such territorial links exist to prevent the forum court exercising an 'exorbitant' jurisdiction.

[26] Supreme Court (General Civil Procedure) Rules, r 7.02(a)(i).

[27] Uniform Civil Procedure Rules (UCPR), sch 6(a)(i).

[28] Supreme Court Civil Rules, r 40A(a)(i).

[29] Court Procedures Rules, r 6502(a)(i).

[30] See, eg, Federal Court Rules, r 10.42, item 4.

[31] See, eg, in New South Wales, UCPR, sch 6(a)(ii).

matters. The first is the existence of an arguable case that a tortious act in respect of which damage was sustained occurred in the jurisdiction,[32] or that damage was sustained there arising from a tortious act.[33] The second matter to be shown is that there is a serious issue to be tried on the merits.[34] The third element is that New Zealand or England is the appropriate forum for trial,[35] that is, the forum in which the case can most suitably be tried in the interests of the parties and the ends of justice.[36]

In Canada, by contrast, the claimant must show that the action has a 'real and substantial connection' with the forum,[37] which has been interpreted to exist in the case of a tort committed within the forum but not where damage has been suffered in the forum arising from a tort committed elsewhere.[38] The Supreme Court considered that recognising local damage as a basis for service abroad in a tort case 'risks sweeping into that jurisdiction claims that have only a limited relationship with the forum'.[39] In those Canadian provinces[40] that have enacted the Court Jurisdiction and Proceedings Transfer Act, service out is also only permissible where a tort has been committed in the forum.[41] No burden rests on the claimant in Canadian law, however, to show an arguable case on the merits, or that Canada is a more appropriate forum to establish jurisdiction. The defendant may nonetheless apply to the court for a dismissal of proceedings on the latter ground.[42]

i. Gateway: The Place Where the Tort is Committed/Place of the Tortious Act

Returning to the tort 'gateways', in Australian jurisdictions other than Victoria, New South Wales, South Australia and the ACT, and in Canada, a claimant, to validly serve a defendant abroad, must show that a tort has been committed in the forum. This rule also previously applied in England and New Zealand. Where is a tort committed for the purposes of jurisdiction? In *Distillers Co (Biochemicals) Ltd v Thompson*,[43] the Privy Council held that it is the place where 'the act on the

[32] For New Zealand, see New Zealand High Court Rules, rr 6.29(1)(a)(i), 6.27(2)(a)(i); for England, see Civil Procedure Rules, PD 6B, para 3.1(9).

[33] For New Zealand, New Zealand High Court Rules, rr 6.29(1)(a)(i), 6.27(2)(a)(ii). For England, Civil Procedure Rules, PD 6B, para 3.1(9).

[34] For New Zealand, New Zealand High Court Rules, rr 6.29(1)(a)(ii), 6.28(5)(b).

[35] For New Zealand, ibid, rr 6.29(1)(a)(ii), 6.28(5)(c).

[36] *Spiliada Maritime Corporation v Cansulex* [1987] AC 460; *AK Investments CJSC v Kyrgyz Mobil Tel Ltd* [2011] UKPC 7, [88].

[37] *Club Resorts Ltd v Van Breda* [2012] 1 SCR 572.

[38] ibid [88]–[89]; see also *Editions Ecosociété Inc v Banro Corp* [2012] 1 SCR 636.

[39] *Club Resorts Ltd* (n 37) [89].

[40] British Columbia, Saskatchewan and Nova Scotia.

[41] See s 10(g) (British Columbia), s 9(g) (Saskatchewan) and s 11(g) (Nova Scotia).

[42] *Club Resorts Ltd v Van Breda* [2012] 1 SCR 572; see section II.B.

[43] *Distillers Co (Biochemicals) Ltd v Thompson* [1971] AC 458.

part of the defendant gives the plaintiff his or her cause of complaint'. This test was approved by the High Court of Australia in *Voth v Manildra Flour Mills Pty Ltd*,[44] which confirmed that the primary focus should be on the place where the defendant acted. The place of the defendant's act varies with the tort pleaded. So, for example, in defamation the place of the wrong will be the location where the material that caused harm to the claimant's reputation was published by the defendant (in an online case, the place of downloading),[45] while in product liability cases it will often be the place where the defendant directed the goods and failed to warn the claimant of their defects.[46]

Such a test is consistent with the choice-of-law rules in all four common law countries, which require, in effect, application of the law of the place of the wrong to torts claims.[47] The result in the service abroad context is that where there is found to be a tort committed in the jurisdiction, forum law will always apply and there will be no scope for reliance on foreign tort laws. Hence, in the context of invasion of privacy, service out under this rule would not be permissible for breach of a foreign law because of the requirement for a locally committed tort.[48]

Nevertheless, in England, New Zealand and the Australian jurisdictions of Victoria, New South Wales, South Australia and the ACT, the relevant provision for service out no longer requires a tort committed in the jurisdiction, but only that 'an act' or a 'tortious act' was done there. While commentary on the New South Wales provision suggests that the rule still requires a claimant to show a locally committed tort,[49] the English experience shows that this analysis is likely inaccurate. In the English decisions interpreting the same provision it has been held that 'an act done or which occurred' in the forum requires only that 'substantial and efficacious acts' in relation to the tort be committed in England, even where substantial acts also occur elsewhere.[50] Consequently, the forum court does not have to conclude that *the tort* was committed in the forum, only that 'substantial acts' in relation to the tort occurred there. English courts have therefore accepted that service out is permissible in the case of a tort committed in a foreign country if there was also a substantial act in the forum in relation to the tort.[51]

[44] *Voth v Manildra Flour Mills Pty Ltd* (1990) 171 CLR 538.

[45] *Dow Jones & Co v Gutnick* (2002) 210 CLR 575.

[46] *Distillers Co (Biochemicals) Ltd v Thompson* [1971] AC 458.

[47] See section III.A.

[48] J Harris, 'Choice of Law in Tort – Blending in with the Landscape of the Conflict of Laws?' (1998) 61 *MLR* 33, 37.

[49] *Ritchie's Uniform Civil Procedure – NSW*, para 11.4.10 (online resource); compare Douglas and Bath, who suggest that the new rule should be easier to satisfy for claimants but then later state that 'the existing law surrounding this task [that is, identifying the place of the tort] will still be relevant': M Douglas and V Bath, 'A New Approach to Service Outside the Jurisdiction and Outside Australia under the Uniform Civil Procedure Rules' (2017) 44 *Australian Bar Review* 160, 171, 172.

[50] *Metall und Rohstoff AG v Donaldson Lufkin and Jennette Inc* [1990] QB 391.

[51] ibid; *Morin v Bonhams* [2003] EWHC 467, [62] (Comm) (affirmed [2003] EWCA Civ 1802); see also J Fawcett and JM Carruthers, *Cheshire, North and Fawcett Private International Law*, 14th edn (Oxford, Oxford UP, 2008) 384.

How would the above principles apply in the context of a service out application based on infringement of a foreign tort of privacy? The two principal causes of action discussed in this chapter are misuse of private information by publication – accepted in English and possibly Australian law – and intrusion upon seclusion, accepted in New Zealand and Canadian law, and potentially also in Australian law. In the case of misuse of private information by publication, English courts have consistently held, by analogy with defamation, that the tort is committed in the place of publication. In *Douglas v Hello!*,[52] a photographer based in California was sued in England for invasion of privacy in relation to the publication in England of photos originally taken at a wedding in New York. The court held that there was a good arguable case that the English law tort of misuse of private information had been committed in England, as the essential act complained about that invaded the rights of the claimant was the publication of the photos, and this occurred there. The place of publication was therefore recognised as the place of the tort, despite the fact that certain acts connected to the tort took place in America.

More recently, in *Vidal-Hall v Google Inc*,[53] English domiciled claimants sued a defendant incorporated in Delaware with its principal place of business in California for misuse of private information under English law. The breach of privacy was said to arise from the defendant's tracking and collating, without the claimants' consent or knowledge, information relating to the claimants' Internet usage on their Apple Safari Internet browser, which was published in the form of advertisements on the claimants' computer screens in England. Once again, as in the *Hello!* case, the court found that the tort was committed in England through the publication of the advertisements on the claimants' screens. The cause of action is based on the conveying of private information by way of publication to readers in the forum.[54]

If Australian law will also recognise a tort of invasion of privacy based on misuse of private information by publication, the above English decisions are likely to be highly authoritative on the question of whether a tort is committed in the jurisdiction for the purposes of the service abroad rules.

In England, New Zealand and the Australian jurisdictions of Victoria, New South Wales, South Australia and the ACT, where a 'tortious act' is required to have occurred in the jurisdiction for service out, the same result would likely be reached. Publication of infringing material in the forum is clearly a 'substantial and efficacious act' in relation to the tort. The interesting question is whether this broader test for service out could potentially capture a wider net of privacy claims, specifically those brought under *foreign* laws. The idea is that while the tort of breach of privacy may be found not to have been committed in the forum, in the case of a claim with elements occurring in different localities, a constituent act in

[52] *Douglas v Hello!* [2003] EWCA Civ 139.
[53] *Vidal-Hall v Google Inc* [2014] EWHC 13 (QB), affirmed [2016] QB 1003 (CA).
[54] ibid [77].

relation to the tort may have occurred locally. The result therefore would be that service out would be permissible in such a situation, but foreign law would apply to the claim under the choice-of-law rules of the forum.

In the context of the tort of misuse of private information by publication, there are typically two relevant acts in the online era – the uploading of the offending material by the defendant to a server (normally in his or her country of residence) and then the downloading by the claimant, which is the place of publication. Could it be argued in the context of a breach of privacy claim that the act of upload was also a 'substantial and efficacious act' sufficient to support service abroad if it happened in the forum? In principle, the answer would seem to be yes, but in practice such a conclusion would be unlikely to assist a claimant in most cases. Suppose the claimant is in England and the defendant is in Australia, and the defendant uploads the infringing material to a server in Australia, which is then downloaded and 'published' in England. If the claimant sues in England, it will be on a tort committed there and so there will be no need to rely on the broader principle for service out. If, by contrast, the defendant is in England and uploads material there with publication occurring in Australia, there will be no need for service out at all because the defendant will be amenable to common law service based on presence in the forum or, in the case of UK-domiciled defendants, jurisdiction under Article 4(1) of the Brussels I Regulation recast.

So, the difference in scope between the narrow and broad service out rules for tort is unlikely to be important in practice. What is the position in relation to the tort of intrusion upon seclusion? Such a tort may arise where a defendant engages in stalking, secret recording, photographing the claimant, or hacking into the claimant's computer from a remote location. Publication of information may not occur. In such cases the key conduct is arguably the act of intrusion by the defendant into the 'physical sphere of privacy' of the claimant.[55] While in most cases the act of intrusion will occur within a single territory, with the claimant and defendant in the same place, hacking, for example, or an international drone flight, may cross borders. A similar situation would arise where remote activation of a webcam located in country A was caused by a computer based in country B.[56]

Assistance on this point may be gained from *Ashton Investments Ltd v OJSC Russian Aluminium (Rustal)*,[57] where a Russia-based defendant hacked into an English claimant's computer system in London to obtain confidential information by planting spyware on the claimant's server. The claimant sued for (amongst other things) the tort of unlawful interference with business. The court found that while 'substantial and efficacious' acts in relation to the tort occurred in both England and Russia, the key location was England, which was the place to which the attack

[55] S Harder and N Witzleb, 'The Private International Law Implications of a Privacy Tort under State or Territory Legislation' (2016) 21 *Media and Arts Law Review* 121, 128.

[56] I am grateful to Jason Varuhas for this example.

[57] *Ashton Investments Ltd v OJSC Russian Aluminium (Rustal)* [2006] EWHC 2545.

was directed and in which it had its principal effects, in terms of the downloading and seizure of information by the defendant.[58]

Applying this view to the privacy tort of intrusion upon seclusion (which is not currently recognised in English law), this tort would most likely be found to occur in the place to which the intrusion was directed and had its impact on the claimant's solitude. Again, on this view, there would be no difference in outcome between the two tests of (i) a tort committed in the jurisdiction, and (ii) a tortious act done there. Further, if the locations of the acts were reversed in *Ashton*, such that the attack was launched from England at a server in Russia, service abroad again would not be required because the defendant could be served within the forum.

Some commentators[59] have noted the problem of multiple, connected invasions of privacy, such as where, for example, a defendant takes photographs of the claimant in country A and then publishes them in country B. According to the above view, two possible torts could have occurred in different places, which would complicate the jurisdictional inquiry if the defendant had to be served abroad. One response to this problem would be to create a single place of the wrong for both torts that focuses on the location where the claimant 'feels the effects of their loss of privacy',[60] which will normally be in the claimant's place of habitual residence. A problem with such an analysis, however, is that both the photographer and publisher in the example above may have little or no awareness of the residence of the claimant at the time of committing the offending conduct, for example where the claimant is temporarily abroad on holiday. Rather, the acts of photography of the claimant and of publication of material concerning that person normally involve a deliberate effort in both cases either to intrude upon the affairs of a person in a particular place, or to direct material concerning that person into a place. The defendant can be seen to be targeting a location by his or her conduct, and the current rules on the place of the wrong in privacy arguably more accurately reflect this perspective.

ii. Gateway: Damage Suffered in the Jurisdiction

The other basis for service abroad in tort cases in the countries examined is where damage was suffered in the forum arising from a tort wherever committed. Previously, English and Australian courts took different approaches to the meaning of 'damage', with English courts requiring that there be some 'significant damage' in the forum before service out was permissible under this ground.[61] A parallel was

[58] ibid [62]–[63].

[59] Harder and Witzlieb (n 55); J Oster, 'Breach of Confidence Claims under English and European Private International Law' in D Dörr and R Weaver (eds), *The Right to Privacy in the Light of Media Convergence* (Berlin, De Gruyter, 2012) 194, 203.

[60] ibid 130.

[61] *Metall und Rohstoff AG v Donaldson Lufkin and Jennette Inc* [1990] QB 391, 437; *ABCI v BFT* [2003] 2 Lloyd's Rep 146.

drawn with the position under EU law, specifically, Article 5(3) of the Brussels Convention (now Article 7(2) of the Brussels I Regulation recast), which confers jurisdiction on the member state in which the damage occurred. In a series of cases, the European Court of Justice (ECJ) held that the term 'damage' refers only to the place of immediate harm and injury not any place where consequential loss is suffered.[62] English courts then appear to have abandoned this view and adopted a new principle, according to which 'damage' would exist where damage was sustained that was recoverable in the context of the tort in question, which included consequential economic or other loss.[63] In *Vidal-Hall v Google Inc*,[64] this test was applied in the context of a claim for misuse of private information under English law, to recognise damage based on distress and anxiety incurred in the forum on the basis that this head of damage was recoverable for such a tort.

The effect of these decisions is to extend the scope of 'damage' beyond the immediate harm or injury suffered by the claimant. While distress or anxiety is regarded as a form of consequential loss in misuse of private information cases,[65] in *Vidal-Hall* this damage occurred in the same place as the direct harm, that is the loss of privacy. What would have been interesting in that case is if the distress or anxiety had been suffered in England but the loss of privacy (direct harm) had occurred elsewhere. Perhaps then the result in *Vidal-Hall* would have been different under the prior 'significant damage' test, since it would have been a situation of wrong and harm occurring abroad followed by consequential loss in England.

This observation is relevant because, more recently, the English Court of Appeal has signalled a return to the earlier position on damage. In *Brownlie v Four Seasons Holding Inc*,[66] the Court noted that the effect of the decisions recognising consequential loss as 'damage' was to make the gateway 'extraordinarily wide', and that consistency with the EU Brussels I Regulation supported the view that damage should refer only to direct damage, injury or harm. An appeal to the UK Supreme Court in *Brownlie* was recently allowed, but on different grounds.[67] The issue of the definition of 'damage' was considered by the Court but only in obiter dicta. Three judges[68] supported the expansive interpretation of 'damage', while two judges[69] endorsed the narrow view of the term adopted by the Court of Appeal. The 'majority' felt that any exorbitance in jurisdiction created by the wider construction could be controlled by a court using its power to stay proceedings on appropriate forum grounds (see section II.B.iv). By contrast, the 'minority'

[62] *Marinari v Lloyds Bank plc* (1995) ECR I-2719, [14]–[15].

[63] *Booth v Phillips* [2004] EWHC 1437 (Comm); *Cooley v Ramsey* [2008] EWHC 129 (QB).

[64] *Vidal-Hall* (n 53).

[65] *Gulati v MGN Ltd* [2015] EWHC 1482, [143]; see generally JNE Varuhas, *Damages and Human Rights* (Oxford, Hart Publishing, 2016) 90–92.

[66] *Brownlie v Four Seasons Holding Inc* [2016] 1 WLR 1814, [85], [91], citing *Erste Group Bank AG v JSC 'VMZ Red October'* [2015] EWCA Civ 379, [104].

[67] *Four Seasons Holdings Inc v Brownlie* [2017] UKSC 80.

[68] Lady Hale, Lords Clarke and Wilson.

[69] Lords Sumption and Hughes.

considered that the provision should be interpreted to align with the similarly worded EU rule. The question is therefore not entirely settled.[70]

As suggested above, though, adoption of the narrow interpretation of 'damage' would not likely affect the result in *Vidal-Hall*, since both direct harm and consequential damage were suffered in England. The same point can be made about the *Douglas v Hello!* case, where again the places of the tort, direct harm and consequential loss all coincided. The return to the earlier stricter approach on damage will have relevance, however, for those cases where an infringement of privacy and direct harm occur in country A but consequential loss is suffered in country B.

The same analysis would likely apply in the case of intrusion upon seclusion: wrong, direct harm and consequential loss may coincide in most cases, but consequential loss could be suffered elsewhere. The *Ashton* hacking case is also pertinent here, even though it was dealing with unlawful interference with business rather than the tort of intrusion upon seclusion. In that case, while the attack on the claimant's server in London was launched from Russia, the court found that it came to fruition in England where the server was targeted and the information stolen. England was also the place where the claimant suffered almost all its damage and harm, with no reference made to losses elsewhere. Again, there was no split between wrong, direct harm and consequential losses.

In New Zealand, the service out rules speak of 'the damage' being suffered in New Zealand as opposed to merely 'damage', which may suggest a narrower conception of the term in line with the English Court of Appeal interpretation. Yet the precise question has not arisen, since in all the decisions where damage within the forum was referred to, there was also a local tort.[71]

In Australia, the concept of damage under the service abroad rules has long been widely interpreted to include 'all the detriment, physical, financial and social which the plaintiff suffers as a result of the tortious conduct of the defendant'.[72] Also, damage is not limited to initial, immediate harm but includes consequential damage, whether by way of bodily injury, property damage or financial loss, wherever the initial immediate harm occurred.[73] Once consequential loss is shown to have been suffered in the forum, the claimant can sue for all its damage suffered.

Hence, there may be a difference between the English and Australian approaches to defining 'damage' for the purposes of service abroad (depending upon which of the views in the UK Supreme Court in *Brownlie* ultimately prevails). This difference

[70] Commentary is split on the issue. Those in favour of the wide view include A Briggs, 'The Hidden Depths of the Law of Jurisdiction' [2016] *Lloyd's Maritime and Commercial Law Quarterly* 236, 246–47; I Bergson, 'Consequential Damage and the Tort Gateway' (2016) 132 *LQR* 42, 43–44. Those supporting the narrow view include C Clarkson and J Hill, *The Conflict of Laws*, 4th edn (Oxford, OUP, 2011) 111; A Arzandeh, 'The English Court's Service-Out Jurisdiction in International Tortious Disputes' (2017) 133 *LQR* 144.

[71] See, eg, *Eight Mile Style LLC v New Zealand National Party* [2015] NZHC 2409, [29]; *MH Publications Ltd v Komori (UK) Ltd* [2008] NZHC 2570, [113].

[72] *Flaherty v Girgis* (1985) 4 NSWLR 248, 266; *Darrell Lea Chocolate Shops Pty Ltd v Spanish-Polish Shipping Co Inc* (1990) 25 NSWLR 668.

[73] *Flaherty v Girgis* (n 72) 266.

only becomes relevant, however, where an invasion of privacy occurs in, for example, England leading to consequential loss in Australia. Could a breach of privacy claim give rise to such loss? A recent libel case in Australia may provide guidance.

In *Barach v the University of New South Wales*,[74] a New South Wales resident sued a US resident for defamation in relation to email communications by the defendant to two US residents and an Israeli resident. While the place of publication in each case was outside Australia, the claimant successfully argued that he had suffered hurt, humiliation and embarrassment and financial loss in New South Wales upon his learning of the above communications.[75] The court specifically noted that the New South Wales rule refers to damage 'wholly or partly suffered' in New South Wales, to support the view that consequential or secondary loss is sufficient to support service out.

Arguably such a decision could be applied to the privacy area. Suppose an Australian resident celebrity was the victim of an unauthorised use of private information under English law by an English media entity, with publication only in England to a UK subscriber base, but after the claimant learned of the publication she suffered distress in Australia. Applying the *Barach* principle, there would seem to be a good argument for service abroad on the English party, based on the consequential loss suffered in Australia. Such a principle also again confirms the possibility of service out in an action based on a foreign tort.

Therefore, it seems possible for a claimant in an Australian court to commence a proceeding for breach of foreign privacy law relying only on consequential loss suffered in the jurisdiction. Since Australian law does not clearly recognise an action for invasion of privacy, this route may provide another 'backdoor' or indirect method for privacy claims to be adjudicated in Australian courts based on foreign law; not only for misuse of private information and intrusion upon seclusion, but also for wider rights of privacy endorsed in countries such as the US.

Lastly, it should be noted that in October 2015 the English Civil Procedure Rules were amended to add a new specific ground for breach of confidence and misuse of private information cases. The new rule[76] allows for service out where 'detriment' was suffered within the jurisdiction, or where detriment was suffered from an act committed within the jurisdiction. The new rule is unlikely to alter the preceding analysis.

iii. Arguable Case on the Merits

In England, Australia and New Zealand, but not in Canada, there is also a requirement for service abroad that the claimant show an arguable case on the merits. This element has arisen in at least two Commonwealth cases concerning privacy.

[74] *Barach v the University of New South Wales* [2011] NSWSC 431.
[75] ibid [41].
[76] Civil Procedure Rules, PD 6B, para 3.1(21).

In *Douglas v Hello!*,[77] the defendant argued that the only invasion of privacy that might have occurred was in New York and governed by New York law, under which there was a complete defence to liability. Once the court found an infringement of *English* privacy law to an arguable case standard, however, the merits requirement was satisfied. By contrast, in *Galloway v Frazer*[78] the High Court of Justice for Northern Ireland refused permission to serve process in the US for breach of Northern Ireland privacy law on the basis that there was no prospect of success in such a claim. Specifically, the claimant had no 'expectation of privacy' in respect of the particular information.[79]

The merits inquiry has also arisen in cases involving foreign torts more generally, where a defendant has asserted that there is no arguable case that a tort occurred under foreign law and so service should be set aside on this ground.[80]

The absence of a 'merits' test in the Canadian law of personal jurisdiction was glaringly apparent in an unusual breach of privacy case, *Szocik v England and Wales*.[81] There, the plaintiff sued the UK Government in British Columbia for stalking and harassment and 'interfering with his brain activity' through the use of electronic devices, with all acts alleged to have occurred in the forum. The claimant sued for breach of privacy based on intrusion upon seclusion under British Columbian law. While the action was dismissed on the ground that the defendant was entitled to foreign state immunity, the court made some obiter comments on the relevance of the merits of the claimant's case to the personal jurisdiction inquiry. Specifically, although the claim was 'of fanciful and doubtful merit' and 'bound to fail', the court could not reject jurisdiction for this reason.[82] At the stage of assessing whether jurisdiction exists, the court must assume that all facts alleged in the claim are true. Such reluctance to consider the merits at the stage of jurisdiction marks a sharp contrast with the position in the other common law countries examined. The logic underlying the Canadian approach is that it is undesirable to conduct 'mini-trials' on scant evidence at the jurisdictional stage, both to conserve resources and avoid prejudgment of the merits. In the other common law countries by contrast, it is considered appropriate for courts to have the power, at an early point in the proceedings, to set aside service in actions with little or no chance of success.

iv. Appropriate Forum

The third element in the rules governing service out of the jurisdiction is the issue of appropriate forum. In England, New Zealand and Canada a court will set aside

[77] *Douglas v Hello!* (n 52).
[78] *Galloway v Frazer* [2016] NIQB 7.
[79] ibid [74].
[80] See, eg, *Metall und Rohstoff* (n 50); *OT Africa Line Ltd v Magic Sportswear Corp* [2004] EWHC 2441, [24] (Comm); *Morin v Bonhams* [2003] EWHC 467 (Comm); *Brownlie* (n 66).
[81] *Szocik v England and Wales* 2012 BCSC 1480.
[82] ibid [85].

service or stay its proceedings where a court in the foreign country is the more appropriate forum,[83] and in Australia where the local court is 'clearly inappropriate'.[84] In theory a defendant served with process while present in the forum may also protest the court's jurisdiction on appropriate forum grounds, but in practice courts have been reluctant to stay their proceedings in such circumstances.[85]

The difference in wording between the tests is not merely semantic. Under the English/New Zealand/Canadian model, it will be enough for a defendant to obtain a stay if the natural forum is shown to be elsewhere, that is, the place with which the action and the parties have their 'most real and substantial connection'. In applying this test the court looks at all the 'connecting factors' of the case, such as where the parties are resident, the location of the evidence and witnesses, where the cause of action arose and what law would govern the merits. The claimant may only overcome this presumption by showing exceptional circumstances in the form of 'legitimate juridical and personal advantages' that would be lost if it were forced to sue abroad. The disadvantages that might ensue if forced to sue abroad include, for example, lack of a fair trial, inadequate damages or relief in the foreign court, and expired limitation periods. The Australian test, by contrast, is much more claimant-centred, requiring a defendant to show that it would suffer vexation and oppression by being sued in Australia; almost an abuse of process standard.[86] The fact that foreign law would govern the cause of action at trial is not determinative. Application of this principle has not surprisingly led to few cases in which stays have been granted by Australian courts.[87]

Given the difficulties referred to above in all four countries confronting a claimant wishing to serve out of the jurisdiction in respect of a foreign tort of privacy, most actions are likely to involve torts under forum law. Consequently, it will be generally hard for a defendant to show that a court in another country is a more appropriate forum under the English, New Zealand or Canadian test, or a clearly inappropriate forum under the Australian principle. In a clear line of authority, English,[88] Australian[89] and Canadian[90] courts have all routinely refused

[83] For England, see *Spiliada Maritime Corporation v Cansulex Ltd* [1987] 1 AC 460; *AK Investment CJSC v Kyrgyz Mobil Tel Ltd* [2011] UKPC 7; for New Zealand, *Club Mediterranée NZ v Wendell* [1989] 1 NZLR 216; and for Canada, *Club Resorts Ltd v Van Breda* [2012] 1 SCR 572. Note that in England, to obtain prior leave to serve abroad, a claimant must show that England is the more appropriate forum.

[84] *Voth v Manildra Flour Mills Pty Ltd* (1990) 171 CLR 538; note, however, that in the case of defendants seeking a stay of Australian proceedings in favour of New Zealand, the 'more appropriate forum' test applies: TTPA, s 19.

[85] For a New Zealand example where a stay was refused, see *Exportrade Corp v Irie Blue New Zealand Ltd* [2013] NZCA 675.

[86] *Regie Nationale des Usines Renault SA v Zhang* (2002) 210 CLR 491; *Puttick v Tenon Ltd* (2008) 238 CLR 265.

[87] For a criticism of the Australian test, see R Garnett, 'Stay of Proceedings in Australia: A "Clearly Inappropriate" Test?' (1999) 30 *Melbourne University Law Review* 64.

[88] *Berezovsky v Michaels* [2000] 1 WLR 1004, 1013–14.

[89] *Dow Jones & Co Inc v Gutnick* (2002) 210 CLR 575.

[90] *Black v Breeden* [2012] 1 SCR 666, [32]–[33].

applications to stay proceedings where a local tort is pleaded. Not only is the existence of such a tort a powerful connecting factor with the forum, but, as will be discussed in section III.A, forum law will almost always be applied to determine the merits of such an action. A court will therefore rightly consider that it is best placed and equipped to apply its own law.

The conclusion that a stay is rarely awarded in a case involving a locally committed tort is further strengthened where it is shown by the claimant that the alternative forum in another country would provide no right of recovery to the claimant, such as where, for example, no action for invasion of privacy existed or any such right would not apply to the facts of the particular case. So in the context of defamation involving the Internet, in *Dow Jones & Co Inc v Gutnick*[91] the High Court of Australia refused to stay an action for breach of Victorian libel law where the alternative forum was the US, under whose law no action could have been brought. In the privacy context, in the *Vidal-Hall* case,[92] an English court showed a similar unwillingness to stay proceedings where a local tort had been pleaded. Not only was England the place of the wrong and the place where all the claimants' damage had been suffered, but English law governed the tort and the claimants were all English residents for whom suing in the US would be burdensome.[93]

This position is acceptable in the majority of cases where the claimant has clear residential and social links to the forum, such as the claimant in *Gutnick*. The problem arises, however, where a claimant with few connections to the forum sues a foreign defendant in respect of only limited publication and distribution of infringing material in the forum. This problem became particularly acute in the defamation area where US celebrities with global reputations sued US publishers in England, where both parties had little or no connection with the forum and only a limited amount of publication occurred there. Such a phenomenon was known as 'libel tourism'[94] and caused considerable cross-Atlantic tensions until the UK Parliament legislated to curb the problem. Section 9 of the Defamation Act 2013 (UK) now provides that an English court has no jurisdiction to hear a libel action brought by a non-EU/EEA resident claimant against a non-EU/EEA resident defendant, unless England is shown to be 'clearly the most appropriate place in which to bring an action'.

The question for present purposes is whether a comparable form of 'privacy tourism' may emerge. It is conceivable, for example, that an Australian resident could sue an Australian online newspaper in England for material published in England in breach of her rights under English law. This situation could arise even

[91] *Gutnick* (n 89).

[92] *Vidal-Hall* (n 14).

[93] ibid [133].

[94] For analysis of this problem, see R Garnett and M Richardson, 'Libel Tourism or Just Redress? Reconciling the (English) Right to Reputation with the (American) Right to Free Speech in Cross-Border Libel Cases' (2009) 5 *Journal of Private International Law* 471; T Hartley, '"Libel Tourism" and Conflict of Laws' (2010) 59 *ICLQ* 25.

though the article was also more widely published and viewed online in Australia, concerned predominantly Australian content and references, and did not infringe Australian law. Should the English court exercise jurisdiction in such a case?

The problem was squarely confronted in *Ahuja v Politika Novine I Magazini DOO*,[95] where a claim for misuse of private information was brought in England against a foreign defendant publishing an online Serbian language newspaper in England. (The court accepted that by applications such as Google Translate, it was possible for the Serbian language to be translated into English.) The claimant was a highly mobile international businessman who held Serbian and Indian nationality but was a resident of England. He travelled frequently to Serbia, India and Austria, had lived until the age of nine in Serbia and was a member of the supervisory board of a large commercial enterprise in that country. He also owned property in Serbia and other countries.

The court held that an arguable case existed for breach of privacy under English law based on publication of material on the Internet that was accessible in England. Service abroad was therefore justified on the basis of either a tortious act in England or damage sustained there. The major question for the court was whether England or Serbia was the more appropriate forum for trial. The court found, unusually, that Serbia had the most real and substantial connection with the dispute, despite a tort having occurred in England. Ultimately the claimant's and defendant's links with Serbia outweighed those with England, both in quantity and quality. Not only did the claimant have strong connections with Serbia, but the defendant was a Serbian media company, the bulk of publication and disclosure occurred in Serbia, and the content of the publication related to the claimant's alleged banking transfers and activities in that country. All parties spoke Serbian and the cost of litigation in England would bear more heavily on the defendant than on the claimant in having to litigate in Serbia.[96] Lastly, there was no evidence that the claimant would not receive a fair trial in Serbia.[97]

While *Ahuja* is only a first instance decision, it suggests that courts may seek to be vigilant in deterring some of the excesses of libel tourism in the privacy context, even without specific legislative direction. Specifically, the court suggested that merely because the tort of invasion of privacy has occurred in the forum does not automatically make the local court a more appropriate forum. It will still be necessary to examine the connections between the action, the parties and the forum to resolve this question. Such an analysis, if followed in later cases, would assist in preventing any development of a form of privacy tourism. The position may be different in Australia, however, given that the defendant must satisfy the higher standard of 'vexation or oppression' to obtain a stay, rather than simply show that a foreign court is more appropriate. To that extent, the presence of a local tort would

[95] *Ahuja v Politika Novine I Magazini DOO* [2015] EWHC 3380 (QB).
[96] ibid [78].
[97] ibid [88].

be a harder factor to dislodge in Australia, although this conclusion again assumes the existence of a tort of privacy in Australian law.

Before leaving the question of the appropriate forum, the flipside of the above situation should be considered: would the pleading of a *foreign* tort of privacy survive a challenge by a defendant on appropriate forum grounds? As was noted, under the English 'more appropriate forum' test, which has been adopted in New Zealand and Canada, the existence of a local tort gives rise to a presumption that the local court is the more appropriate forum. It would appear to follow, therefore, that the existence of a foreign tort should equally point in favour of adjudication by the courts of the foreign country. Given the previously noted restrictions on service abroad in foreign tort cases, however, the question of appropriate forum is only likely to arise in New Zealand and Canada in the case of service on a defendant present within the jurisdiction. In Australia and England, the issue will arise in that situation[98] and (possibly, in the case of England) where service abroad is based on a foreign tort causing consequential loss in the forum. In the first category of case, involving defendants served within the jurisdiction, stays of proceeding have rarely been awarded; and in the second, defendants have often failed to satisfy the Australian 'clearly inappropriate forum' test, even where foreign torts have occurred.[99] On balance, therefore, there remains some scope for actions based on foreign privacy laws to be brought in Commonwealth courts.

v. No Gateways Required

Finally, an alternative basis for service out has recently been added in New Zealand[100] and the Australian jurisdictions of New South Wales,[101] Victoria,[102] South Australia[103] and the ACT.[104] This ground allows a claimant to serve process on a foreign defendant with leave of the court when the claim has a 'real and substantial connection' with the local court and such a court (in the case of Australia) is not a 'clearly inappropriate forum' and (in the case of New Zealand) is an appropriate forum. Under this approach, therefore, no 'gateway' must be satisfied. While the issue of appropriate forum is discussed in section II.B.iv, the concept of 'real and substantial connection' is new to Australian and New Zealand law, and may be interpreted, in the tort context, by reference to the Canadian principles (considered in section II.B). In practice, however, the requirement under

[98] For England this would be the case for defendants temporarily present there at the time of service. However, in the case of actions against defendants *domiciled* in the UK, for which jurisdiction would exist under Art 4(1) of the Brussels I Regulation (recast), jurisdiction cannot be declined on the ground of appropriate forum: Case C-281/02 *Owusu v Jackson* [2005] QB 801 (ECJ). See section II.D.

[99] See text and decisions cited at n 86.

[100] New Zealand High Court Rules, r 6.28.

[101] New South Wales UCPR, r 11.5.

[102] Supreme Court (General Civil Procedure) Rules, r 7.03.

[103] Supreme Court Civil Rules, r 40B.

[104] Civil Procedure Rules, r 6503.

this provision for a claimant to obtain prior leave of the court to serve abroad may operate as a deterrent to its use.

C. Service Outside the Jurisdiction: Confidence

Out of deference to the position in Australia, where an action for invasion of privacy has not yet been authoritatively accepted, a comment should be made about possible gateways for service out in breach of confidence cases in Australian courts. Since, as noted in section II.A, an action for breach of confidence is not regarded in private international law as a matter in tort, a claimant must find another basis for service. The options would appear to be (i) where the cause of action arises in Australia, which is accepted in almost all Australian jurisdictions,[105] and (ii) in New South Wales, Victoria, South Australia and the ACT, when the claim 'is made in restitution … and the alleged liability of the person arises out of an act that was done or occurred wholly or partly in Australia'.[106] The availability of the second of these gateways, however, may depend on the claimant's seeking the remedy of restitution as opposed to compensation, which may limit its scope in privacy-type cases.[107] In determining where a breach of confidence action 'arose', it is likely that the authorities already discussed on the place of the wrong in privacy cases[108] will be instructive. Note, however, that, unlike a breach of privacy action, service out will not be available in a claim for breach of confidence merely because damage was suffered in Australia, as this ground is limited to tort claims only.

D. Jurisdiction under EU Law

The final category of cases on jurisdiction concerns the status of defendants before English courts who are domiciled in an EU or EEA member state. Article 4(1) of the Brussels I Regulation recast requires that a defendant domiciled in an EU member state shall principally be sued in the courts of that member state. Article 7(2) then provides, as an exception, that a defendant may be sued in matters relating to tort in the courts of the state where the harmful event occurred. The ECJ held that where the place of the act causing harm and the place of damage were different, Article 7(2) embraced both concepts and allowed the claimant a choice of fora in such a case.[109] As noted, it has long been accepted in EU law that 'the place of damage' for the purposes of this rule is the place of primary harm or injury.

[105] See, eg, in New South Wales, UCPR, sch 6(n).
[106] See, eg, in New South Wales, UCPR, sch 6(l).
[107] Note that compensatory awards were sought in both *Giller v Procopets* (2008) 24 VR 1 and *Wilson v Ferguson* [2015] WASC 15.
[108] See section II.B.i.
[109] Case C-21/76 *Bier BV v Mines de Potasse d'Alsace SA* [1976] ECR 1735.

Hence jurisdiction would not exist in a member state where consequential loss was suffered from a breach of privacy occurring elsewhere. In any case, as has been noted, in most situations of breach of privacy by misuse of private information, the places of the wrong and harm will normally coincide.

The ECJ added a further gloss to the above analysis under Article 7(2) in *Shevill v Press Alliance SA*.[110] In that case, which involved defamation, the Court held that under Article 7(2), proceedings may be brought in the member state where the material is published, but only for damage suffered there, or alternatively in the member state of the defendant's domicile for all damage suffered.

More recently, the Court of Justice of the European Union (CJEU) had the opportunity to examine the jurisdictional options open to a claimant in a breach of privacy case. In *eDate Advertising GmbH v X; Martinez v MGN Ltd*, the Court considered two actions for breach of privacy joined in the one proceeding.[111] In *eDate*, an Austrian company (eDate) had posted material on its website concerning X, a German, who had been convicted of murder. X brought proceedings in the German courts for breach of privacy under German law. In *Martinez*, the English newspaper the *Sunday Mirror* published material on its website providing information about Martinez' (a French actor) romantic life, including photos. The claimant sued in the French courts for breach of privacy.

In *eDate* the CJEU confirmed the authority of *Shevill* in Internet breach of privacy cases, with the result that a claimant could sue, for example, in any country of breach (eg where the material is accessible to readers on the Internet) and recover for damage suffered there. Significantly, the Court also created a new ground of jurisdiction, arising from Article 7(2), that is unique to Internet actions. Henceforth, a claimant may sue to recover the entirety of the damage suffered, in the member state in which the centre of the claimant's interests is located. The concept of 'centre of main interests' was developed in the context of insolvency law and is similar to the concept of habitual residence, but also permits professional and commercial interests to be taken into account. Hence it would be conceivable for a person to have his or her centre of main interests in a country other than his or her place of habitual residence if he or she led a particularly mobile professional life.

This new ground of jurisdiction has the potential to expand significantly the scope for English claimants to obtain relief in English courts against EU-domiciled defendants for breach of privacy involving Internet activity. For this reason, the ground has received a mixed reception, with one commentator noting that in theory a claimant can now rely on Article 7(2) to secure jurisdiction in England over an EU/EEA-domiciled defendant where no tort occurred or damage was suffered in England.[112]

[110] Case C-68/93 *Shevill v Press Alliance SA* [1995] ECR I-415.

[111] Joined Cases C-509/09 and C-161/10 *eDate Advertising GmbH v X; Martinez v MGN Ltd* [2012] QB 654.

[112] A Dickinson, 'By Royal Appointment: No Closer to an EU Private International Law Settlement?' (24 October 2012) at Conflict of Laws.net; for supportive views of the decision, see T Hartley,

III. Choice of Law

A. The Presumptive Rule

Assuming a court in Australia, New Zealand, England or Canada has jurisdiction and agrees to exercise it on discretionary grounds in a privacy matter, the next question is what law it would apply; what private international lawyers refer to as the 'choice of law question'. In all four countries, the presumptive rule is to apply the law of the place where the tort is committed, although this is achieved by slight differences in wording in each jurisdiction. For example, the High Court of Australia[113] speaks of 'the law of the place of the wrong', the Supreme Court of Canada[114] refers to 'the law of the place where the [tortious] activity occurred', while in England and New Zealand, legislation stipulates 'the law of the country in which the events constituting the tort occur'.[115] The UK and New Zealand legislation further provide that where elements of the events constituting the tort occur in different countries, the applicable law is that of the country in which the most significant element or elements of those events occurred.[116]

If an action for invasion of privacy is not accepted in Australia and breach of confidence continues to be relied upon, the applicable law is the law of the forum, as already noted.[117]

The issue of where the tort was committed or 'the events constituting the events occur' was examined earlier in this chapter in the context of service abroad. It was there suggested, in the case of breach of privacy based on misuse of private information by publication, which forms part of English law and possibly exists in Australia, that the place of publication is the location of the wrong. This conclusion is supported by a series of English decisions: *Douglas v Hello! (No 3)*,[118] *Weller v Associated Newspapers Ltd*,[119] *Vidal-Hall v Google Inc*,[120] *KJO v XIM*[121] and *OPO v MLA*.[122] In *KJO v XIM*, a Hong Kong-based claimant sought an injunction in an English court to restrain an English defendant from making communications to

'Cross-border Privacy Injunctions: the EU Dimension' (2012) 128 *LQR* 197, 201, and B Hess, 'The Protection of Privacy in the Case Law of the CJEU' in B Hess and C Mariottini (eds), *Protecting Privacy in Private International and Procedural Law and by Data Protection* (Farnham, Ashgate, 2011) 81, 105–06, although both favour the non-application of the *Shevill* doctrine to Internet privacy cases.

[113] *Regie National Des Usines Renault SA v Zhang* (2002) 210 CLR 491.

[114] *Tolofson v Jensen* [1994] 3 SCR 1022.

[115] Private International Law (Miscellaneous Provisions) Act 1995 (UK), s 11(1) (PILMPA); Private International Law (Choice of Law in Tort) Act 2017 (NZ), s 8(1) (PILCLTA).

[116] PILMPA, s 11(2)(c); PILCLTA, s 8(2)(c); note that privacy is expressly excluded from the EU Regulation of 17 July 2007 on the law applicable to non-contractual obligations (Rome II) in Art 1(2)(g).

[117] See text at n 24.

[118] *Douglas v Hello! (No 3)* (n 23) (CA).

[119] *Weller v Associated Newspapers Ltd* [2015] EWCA Civ 1176.

[120] *Vidal-Hall* (n 14).

[121] *KJO v XIM* [2011] EWHC 1768 (QB).

[122] *OPO v MLA* [2014] EWCA Civ 1277.

Hong Kong residents that amounted to a misuse of private information by publication under English law. The court rejected the claimant's application for summary judgment, suggesting that the law to be applied to the tort would be Hong Kong, in respect of which expert evidence would have to be led.[123] The place of publication was therefore confirmed as the relevant governing law.

Where the tort is intrusion upon seclusion, it was argued in this chapter that the wrong occurs in the place where the claimant's domain was intruded upon.[124]

The above analysis is consistent with the position in the US, which has recognised privacy torts for much longer than Commonwealth countries. In the US, while there is no universally accepted choice-of-law approach to privacy, the most widely held view comes from the *Second Restatement on Conflict of Laws*. The *Restatement* provides that the law of the country where the invasion occurred determines the rights and liabilities of the parties unless, with respect to the issue of privacy, some other country has a more significant relationship to the occurrence and the parties.[125] The place of invasion in an intrusion upon seclusion case is the place where the plaintiff was at the time of the intrusion. This principle has been applied in a number of cases involving unlawful recording of telephone conversations, to select the law of the place where the plaintiff was located at the time of the recording.[126]

When the invasion involves publication of information about the plaintiff, the place of invasion is where the matter complained of was communicated to a person other than the plaintiff. In practice, this location will almost always be the place of publication.[127] The drafters of the *Restatement* acknowledged that the plaintiff's interests in a privacy suit are different from those in a defamation case, with the law of defamation aiming to protect reputation while privacy vindicates the claimant's interest in being left alone.[128] Yet both interests are served by applying a rule that focuses on the place where the fruits of the invasion were perceived and had their principal effects on the claimant, which will normally be the place of publication for the publication tort.

B. Exceptions to the Rule

The law of the place of the wrong is nonetheless only a presumptive choice-of-law rule in each Commonwealth country, and can be displaced in certain circumstances.

[123] *KJO v XIM* (n 121) [31].

[124] See section II.B.i.

[125] *Second Restatement on Conflict of Laws*, § 152.

[126] See, eg, *Heffernan v Hashampour*, 26 Mass L Rptr 541 (SC Mass 2009); *Howes v Hashampour*, WL 1565544 (Sup Ct Conn 2010); *Kearney v Salomon Smith Barnes*, 137 P 3d 914 (SC Cal 2006).

[127] *McNally v Pulitzer Publishing Co*, 532 F 2d 69, 78 (8th Cir 1976); *Sondik v Kimmel*, 131 AD 3d 1041 (SCNY 2015); *Bullard v MRA Holding LLC*, 740 SE 2d 622 (SC Ga 2013) (appropriation of likeness).

[128] *Second Restatement on Conflict of Laws*, § 152 comment d.

So, in England[129] and New Zealand[130] the 'general rule' can be displaced where connecting factors make it 'substantially more appropriate' for the law of another country to apply.[131] In addition, public policy will be available to exclude a foreign law in all four countries, the application of which affronts basic principles of justice and fairness of the forum, which include fundamental rules of human rights.[132] In such cases, the law of the forum normally applies by default.[133]

The question of whether application of a foreign privacy law would offend the public policy of the forum was much discussed in English commentary at a time when English law recognised no action for invasion of privacy. The clear opinion expressed then was that public policy would not operate to exclude a foreign privacy law simply because it was 'unfamiliar' to the forum.[134] While the subsequent recognition of a tort of invasion of privacy under English law has strengthened that argument, it would also apply in countries such as Australia, where the existence of a tort of invasion of privacy remains only arguable. Such a limited view of public policy would also assist in application of foreign privacy laws in the forum such as those from the US, which go beyond the currently recognised categories in Commonwealth countries. Exceptionally, however, in England, public policy may operate to bar admission of a foreign law on invasion of privacy where its application would deny freedom of the press under Article 10 of the ECHR.[135]

Note, as a related point on the English position, the CJEU in the *eDate* case[136] (discussed in section II.D), suggested that the EU Electronic Commerce Directive may have an impact on choice of law in EU/EEA member states in Internet privacy cases. Although it is beyond the scope of this chapter to discuss the Directive in detail, the Court noted that it established a 'country of origin' principle under which the law of the member state in which an e-commerce service provider

[129] UK PILMPA, s 12.

[130] NZ PILCLTA, s 9.

[131] In Canada, a very limited 'injustice' exception may exist to the law of the place of the wrong, but this should rarely be applied: *Wong v Lee* (2002) 58 OR (3d) 398, [12].

[132] UK PILMPA, s 14(3)(a)(i); NZ PILCLTA, s 11(2)(a)(i); *Oppenheimer v Cattermole* [1976] AC 249, 277–78, approved in *Kuwait Airways Corp v Iraqi Airways Company (Nos 4 and 5)* [2002] 2 AC 883, [18] (Lord Nicholls, Lords Hoffmann and Scott concurring), [114] (Lord Steyn), [137] (Lord Hope).

[133] R Mortensen, R Garnett and M Keyes, *Private International Law in Australia*, 3rd edn (Chatswood NSW, Lexis Nexis, 2015) 235.

[134] J Fawcett, M Ní Shúilleabháin and S Shah, *Human Rights and Private International Law* (Oxford, Oxford UP, 2016) 577, citing the oral evidence of Lawrence Collins in Special Public Bill Committee, 'Private International Law (Miscellaneous Provisions) Bill' (1994–95) HL Paper 36, 72; see also C Morse, 'Torts in Private International Law: A New Statutory Framework' (1996) 45 *ICLQ* 888, 901; A Reed, 'The Anglo-American Revolution in Tort Choice of Law Principles: Paradigm Shift or Pandora's Box?' (2001) 18 *Arizona Journal of International and Comparative Law* 867, 933.

[135] Fawcett et al (n 134), citing the oral evidence of Professor Paul Beaumont in Special Public Bill Committee (n 134), 75. Interestingly, there appears to be no evidence of a parallel development in the US, despite the existence of the First Amendment to the Constitution. United States courts have, however, famously refused to enforce English libel judgments on the ground that they offend US standards of freedom of expression: see, eg, *Telnikoff v Matusevitch*, 702 A 2d 230 (Md 1997).

[136] See n 111.

(or publisher) is established is applicable to its activities. The Court held that this principle applied to Internet privacy actions but did not displace national choice-of-law rules. Once these rules were applied and a law was chosen, however, the Directive requires that such law cannot impose stricter requirements on the publisher than apply under the law of the country in which it is established. Such a determination operates as a further type of public policy limitation on English courts in applying both local and foreign law.

In Australia, the principal exception to applying the domestic law of the place of the wrong is more elaborate. The High Court, in *Neilson v Overseas Projects Corporation of Victoria*,[137] held that when applying the law of the place of the wrong, the court must also apply the choice-of-law rules of that place (*renvoi*) and then apply the law selected by such rules. The aim is to ensure that 'no advantage' in terms of applicable law accrues to the claimant through choice of forum. In practice, however, such analysis only leads to different outcomes where the choice-of-law rules of the Australian forum and the place of the wrong differ (which is unlikely to be the case as between the four countries mentioned).

A choice-of-law analysis that pertains to the English tort of privacy has recently emerged. Normally, in the case of a tort, a single choice-of-law rule is applied to determine all issues of liability for reasons of convenience and certainty. In the context of privacy that crosses national boundaries, however, it has been suggested that a more sophisticated choice of law analysis may be required.

In *Douglas v Hello! (No 3)*,[138] a claim was brought against a US photographer who had taken unauthorised photos in New York and then sold them to *Hello!* magazine, which published them in England. The Court accepted that if the unauthorised photos had been published in New York, no actionable wrong would have occurred.[139] New York law, however, was not directly applicable to (what would be later confirmed as)[140] a tort of misuse of private information by publication that took place in England. As discussed, English law applied as the law of the place of publication. Therefore, the test of whether the information was private to attract the protection of English law must be resolved by English law.

Yet, the Court said, where the events to which the information relates occur outside England – here New York – the law of that place may nevertheless be taken into account as a type of 'datum'[141] in determining whether there is an 'expectation of privacy' in respect of the events under English law.[142] If, for example, New York law had provided that any member of the public had a right to be present at the wedding and to take and publish photos of the event, the claimants might not have had an expectation of privacy. That situation did not arise in *Hello!*, however.

[137] *Neilson v Overseas Projects Corporation of Victoria* (2005) 223 CLR 331.
[138] *Douglas v Hello! (No 3)* (n 23)(CA).
[139] ibid [99].
[140] *Vidal-Hall* (n 14) [51] (CA).
[141] A Mills, 'The Application of Multiple Laws under the Rome II Regulation' in W Binchy and J Ahern (eds), *The Rome II Regulation on the Law Applicable to Non-Contractual Obligations* (Boston, MA, Martinus Nijhoff, 2009) 133, 150–51.
[142] *Douglas v Hello! (No 3)* (n 23) [100](CA).

The law of New York clearly entitled the claimants to arrange for their wedding to take place in circumstances designed to ensure that the events at the wedding party remained private, especially concerning photos. The fact that the photos taken in violation of that privacy might have been lawfully published in New York was therefore irrelevant to the case.

The *Hello!* case therefore shows that the English courts, while primarily applying English law to the tort of misuse of private information, will nevertheless make a secondary reference to foreign law in defining the scope of the English right to privacy. Such an approach seeks to create a rule that is attuned to the cross-border context in which breaches of privacy can increasingly occur. The *Hello!* analysis is also consistent with the view that the law of the place where a person's privacy is invaded shapes that person's reasonable expectations of privacy in that place.

The *Hello!* case was considered and applied on this point in *Weller v Associated Newspapers Ltd.*[143] This case involved an action brought by children of a British celebrity musician in England for misuse of private information after photos were taken of them in California and then published in England by the *Mail Online*. The court noted that under the *Hello!* case, the principal law to be applied to a misuse of private information by publication in England was English law because the publication occurred there.[144] As mentioned above, however, the Court of Appeal in *Hello!* had suggested that the law of the place where the photos were initially taken may be relevant in determining whether the claimant had an expectation of privacy.

In this case, however, unlike *Hello!*, there was clear evidence that under the law of California, where the photos were taken, both the taking of the photos and their subsequent publication were lawful. Nevertheless, the court refused to take Californian law into account on the question of whether the claimants had a reasonable expectation of privacy. In *Weller*, unusually, the key issue was whether *children* have a reasonable expectation of privacy in relation to publication of photos of their faces.[145] Given 'the increasing appreciation of the importance of rights of children',[146] a court should be very hesitant to apply foreign law to excuse such conduct. Hence, the claimants did have a reasonable expectation of privacy[147] and the court found that their rights to privacy under English law had been infringed.

The defendant argued on appeal[148] that the trial judge had not considered the lawfulness of the conduct under Californian law on the question of whether a reasonable expectation of privacy existed. The Court of Appeal disagreed, finding that the judge did take the issue into account, despite giving it little weight, an approach that was consistent with the judge's discretion. The Court of Appeal

[143] *Weller v Associated Newspapers Ltd* [2014] EWHC 1163, affirmed [2015] EWCA Civ 1176.
[144] ibid [41]–[45].
[145] ibid [46].
[146] ibid [45].
[147] ibid [172].
[148] *Weller* [2015] EWCA Civ 1176.

further noted that the children who were the subject of the photos had only slight connections with California compared to those with England, where the photos were published and under whose law the breach of privacy occurred.[149] Such an analysis suggests that courts will be reluctant to allow defendants to rely on foreign law principles to avoid liability under English law.

There are other choice-of-law issues that may arise in the context of an action for invasion of privacy. First, even where the law of a foreign country is chosen to govern the merits of the action, where such law is classified as 'procedural' as opposed to 'substantive' then it will not be applied in the forum court. The rationale for this view is that procedural matters, often based on local practices and customs, are best resolved by forum law for reasons of convenience and efficiency.[150] In Australia, the High Court has suggested that all questions relating to damages, including the amount and heads recoverable, are 'substantive' questions and governed by the law applicable to the wrong, not the law of the forum.[151] In a later decision,[152] however, the court left open the correctness of this view in relation to foreign torts. In England, the House of Lords, in *Harding v Wealands*,[153] held that while the availability of heads of damages, such as pain and suffering and economic loss, was a matter for the law of the place of the wrong, questions of quantification of damages, including whether a statutory 'cap' or limitation on damages under foreign law applies, is a procedural matter and governed by the law of the forum, under section 14 of the PILMPA. Such an approach continues to apply to privacy cases, given their exclusion from the Rome II Regulation.[154] In New Zealand[155] and Canada[156] the same position is taken as that in *Harding*. The scope for 'forum shopping' by claimants, offered by a wide interpretation to procedure in the context of damages, will only be relevant, however, in the context of actions for breach of *foreign* privacy laws in common law courts, which, as noted above, are unlikely to be common.

The choice-of-law position in respect of injunctive relief, which is often sought in breach of privacy claims, may no longer be straightforward. While traditionally the injunction as an equitable remedy was governed exclusively by the law of the forum,[157] in recent academic commentary[158] and judicial decisions[159] it has

[149] ibid [70]–[71].

[150] R Garnett, *Substance and Procedure in Private International Law* (Oxford, Oxford UP, 2012) 10–11.

[151] *John Pfeiffer Pty Ltd v Rogerson* (2000) 203 CLR 503.

[152] *Regie Nationale Usines Renault v Zhang* (2002) 210 CLR 491, [99].

[153] *Harding v Wealands* [2007] 2 AC 1.

[154] See text to n 116.

[155] *Stewart v Franmara Inc (No 2)* [2012] NZHC 1771.

[156] *Somers v Fournier* (2002) 60 OR (3d) 225.

[157] *Baschet v London Illustrated Standard Co* [1900] 1 Ch 73; *Warner Bros Pictures Inc v Nelson* [1937] 1 KB 209.

[158] See generally Garnett (n 150) ch 10; A Briggs, 'Conflict of Laws in Commercial Remedies' in A Burrows and E Peel (eds), *Commercial Remedies: Current Issues and Problems* (Oxford, Oxford UP, 2003) 271.

[159] See, eg, *Shanghai Electric Group Co Ltd v PT Merak Energi Indonesia* [2010] SGHC 2.

been suggested that the grant of such a remedy on the facts (at least where it is final in nature) should be resolved by the law of the place of the wrong. The logic underpinning this view is that where possible, the law applicable to both right and remedy should be the same, to reflect the close connection between the two concepts and to prevent complex choice of law bifurcation.

C. Proposed Reforms

Both lawmakers and commentators have made proposals for reform in relation to the choice-of-law rules for privacy.

As noted in section III.B, privacy and personality rights were excluded from the ambit of the Rome II Regulation, yet in 2012 the European Parliament produced a proposal on choice of law which has not yet been implemented.[160] Under the resolution, the presumptive rule (1) is to apply the law of the country in which the most significant element or elements of the loss or damage occur.[161] The law of the defendant's habitual residence will apply instead, however, if that person could not reasonably have foreseen the consequences of his or her acts occurring in the country selected in (1).[162] Further, when a violation is caused by publication of printed matter or a broadcast, the law in (1) is deemed to be the country to which the publication or broadcasting service is principally directed or, if this is not apparent, the country in which editorial control is exercised.[163] Lastly, the law applicable to any injunction proceedings against a publisher or broadcaster regarding violation of privacy resulting from the handling of personal data shall be the law of the defendant's habitual residence.[164]

The above approach has some similarities to that adopted in Commonwealth countries and the US, in its focus on the place where the invasion of privacy causes its principal harm and effects. More weight appears to be given to the position of the defendant, however, at least in matters of invasion by publication.

To capture fully the diverse interests involved in a privacy action, some commentators[165] have proposed choice-of-law tests focusing on the idea of closest connection. Factors relevant to establishing the closest connection include the place of habitual residence of the claimant and, in the case where the invasion occurred by way of publication, the place of the defendant's residence or business, the extent and scope of the publication in a particular jurisdiction, whether the

[160] Resolution [2013] OJ C261/17 E.
[161] ibid Art 5(a)(1).
[162] ibid Art 5(a)(2).
[163] ibid Art 5(a)(3).
[164] ibid Art 5(a)(4).
[165] T Thiede, 'A Topless Duchess and Caricatures of the Prophet Mohammed: A Flexible Conflict of Laws Rule for Cross-Border Infringements of Privacy and Reputation' (2012–2013) 14 *Yearbook of Private International Law* 247, 266; Harder and Witzleb (n 55) 139.

publication was directed at a certain country or countries, and whether the harm in a particular country was objectively foreseeable.

While the criteria identified are undoubtedly relevant, arguably they create too much of a smorgasbord of choice, which could lead to uncertainty for advisers and inconsistency in judicial decisions.[166] Instead, a basic rule that selects the law of the place of the wrong – where the invasion occurred – subject to displacement where another country is substantially more appropriate (such as where the parties share a common habitual residence), would be clearer, better structured and simpler to apply.

Lastly, some commentators[167] have noted that within Europe, the fact that all member states of the EU are parties to the ECHR and are required to respect both the right to respect for private life (Article 8) and freedom of expression (Article 10) and the right to an effective remedy (Article 13), may operate as a force of convergence and harmonisation on the individual national laws of privacy. If such a development continues and differences between national laws fall away, then choice-of-law problems may arise less often.

IV. Recognition and Enforcement of Foreign Judgments

The third major private international law issue relevant to privacy actions is the recognition and enforcement of foreign judgments. The issue arises because occasionally the defendant (particularly if served abroad) has no assets in the forum, and the claimant, to obtain satisfaction on a judgment, must take the judgment to a foreign country and execute against property of the defendant there. The general rules for recognition and enforcement in Australia, New Zealand and England are derived from 1933 UK legislation,[168] although England has a separate regime for enforcement of judgments from EU/EEA countries under the Brussels/Lugano instruments, and Australia and New Zealand employ the Trans-Tasman system for enforcement of each other's judgments. The Canadian approach to recognition and enforcement is generally similar to the general common law approach, but it has diverged in at least two important respects.

The general approach to recognition and enforcement in Australia, New Zealand and England requires first that the claimant show that the foreign court had 'international jurisdiction' over the defendant. International jurisdiction means that the defendant must either have been present for service in the territory of the foreign court, or have submitted to the jurisdiction of that court. 'Submission' in this context refers to active participation in the merits of the proceeding as

[166] See *Neilson* (n 137) [93], where Gummow and Hayne JJ suggested that excessively open-textured choice-of-law rules that give courts too much discretion can 'generate a wilderness of single instances'.

[167] A Dickinson, 'Privacy and Personality Rights in the Rome II Regime – Not Again?' (19 July 2010) at Conflict of laws.net; Fawcett et al (n 134) 577.

[168] Foreign Judgments (Reciprocal Enforcement) Act 1933 (UK).

opposed to simply appearing to contest the jurisdiction of the foreign court.[169] In Canada, by contrast, a foreign judgment may be enforced in that country where the defendant had a 'real and substantial connection' with the foreign jurisdiction.[170] In practice, the real and substantial connection has operated to expand the range of foreign judgments capable of recognition and enforcement. Note that under the Australia–New Zealand Trans-Tasman regime, a judgment from one country will be enforceable in the other without any requirement of 'international jurisdiction'.[171] A similar approach applies in the case of recognition and enforcement of EU/EEA judgments in England.[172]

The next requirement for a foreign judgment to be enforceable in each of the common law countries mentioned is that it was final and conclusive. Finality in this context means that the judgment is not capable of being varied or amended by the court that pronounced it.[173] The practical effect of this requirement is that judgments for interim, interlocutory or provisional relief are generally not enforceable across borders, a conclusion which is particularly significant in privacy claims, where injunctive relief is often sought. The same principle applies under the Trans-Tasman regime, but not under the Brussels/Lugano regime, where interim relief granted by the court of another member state is enforceable.[174]

A further requirement for recognition and enforcement of foreign judgments under the traditional common law regime is that the judgment requires the defendant to pay a sum of money to the claimants, such as an award of damages. In situations where final non-monetary relief has been sought, such as injunctions and declarations, this principle has historically been rigidly observed. In Canada, however, it has been suggested by the Supreme Court in *Pro Swing Inc v Elta Golf Inc*[175] that the 'fixed sum' rule is outdated in a time of increased technological change and modern communications, and when national courts need to cooperate with one another in the resolution of transnational disputes. Consequently, in *Pro Swing* it was held that a foreign non-money judgment may be enforced in Canada where the foreign order (i) is clear and specific, both as to its intended territorial scope and the obligations that it imposes on the defendant, and (ii) does not impose a burden on the Canadian justice system or the rights of third parties.[176] Non-monetary judgments are also enforceable in Australia and New Zealand under the Trans-Tasman regime, and in England in respect of EU/EEA judgments under the Brussels/Lugano system.[177] The importance of injunctive relief in breach of privacy actions reinforces the significance of this decision.

[169] For an Australian example see *Wong v Jani-King Franchising Inc* [2014] QCA 76.
[170] *Morguard Invesments v De Savoye* [1990] 3 SCR 1077, 1107.
[171] TTPA, ss 66, 79(1).
[172] See eg Brussels I Regulation recast, Chapter III.
[173] *Nouvion v Freeman* (1889) 15 App Cas 1.
[174] See, eg, Brussels I Regulation recast, Arts 2(a), 42(2).
[175] *Pro Swing Inc v Elta Golf Inc* [2006] 2 SCR 612.
[176] ibid [30].
[177] See, eg, Brussels I Regulation recast, Arts 2(a), 36.

Recently, a question has arisen concerning the effect of extraterritorial injunctive relief in breach of confidence cases involving the Internet. For example, in *Google Inc v Equustek Solutions Inc*,[178] the Supreme Court of Canada issued an injunction requiring Google to de-index, on a worldwide basis, websites of a company that had been engaged in conduct in breach of the claimant's rights to confidential information under Canadian law. Similar extraterritorial relief was granted by the Supreme Court of New South Wales in *X v Twitter*.[179] In response to the Canadian decree, a US judge then granted an order[180] that prevented enforcement of the Canadian injunction in the US to the extent that it prohibited Google from publishing search result information within the US. While such extraterritorial injunctive relief carries the risk of retaliatory orders and conflicts of jurisdiction between national courts, more balanced approaches are possible. For example, issuing courts can exercise self-restraint in granting orders that may violate the laws of other countries, and courts in affected states can generally recognise such relief, at least where vital national interests are not threatened.

Lastly, once a foreign judgment satisfies the prerequisites for recognition and enforcement, the burden then shifts to the defendant to establish a ground to impeach the judgment, such as that it was procured by fraud,[181] involved a denial of natural justice,[182] is contrary to the public policy of the forum,[183] or is a penal or revenue judgment. In the area of privacy, public policy may be the most likely ground relied upon, although as discussed under exclusion of foreign law,[184] this defence will not be engaged simply because the foreign court's judgment involves application of a law that is 'unfamiliar' to the forum. The judgment must instead involve a determination that is repugnant to the fundamental values of the forum because it involves either a serious breach of procedural fairness or human rights, or other internationally unconscionable conduct. While the public policy defence also exists under the Trans-Tasman and the Brussels/Lugano regimes, it has been rarely applied to deny enforcement of foreign judgments.

V. Conclusion

This chapter has examined some key private international law issues in relation to invasion of privacy actions in Australia, England, New Zealand and Canada. It has

[178] *Google Inc v Equustek Solutions Inc* 2017 SCC 34.

[179] *X v Twitter* [2017] NSWSC 1300.

[180] *Google LLC v Equustek Solutions Inc* 2017 WL 5000834 (ND Cal Nov 2, 2017).

[181] *Owens Bank Ltd v Bracco* [1992] 2 AC 443 (HL); *Quarter Enterprises Pty ltd v Allardyce Lumber Co Ltd* (2014) 85 NSWLR 404.

[182] *Adams v Cape Industries plc* [1990] Ch 433.

[183] For Australian decisions, see *Stern v National Australia Bank* [1999] FCA 1421, [143]; *Jenting Overseas Investment Pte Ltd v Townsing* (2008) 221 FLR 398, [22].

[184] See section III.B.

focused on the torts of misuse of private information by publication and intrusion upon seclusion, which are the causes of action increasingly recognised in those countries.

The above countries' rules of personal jurisdiction generally admit claims for breaches of local privacy laws, even where committed by foreign defendants. Actions for violations of foreign privacy laws may also be brought, but in more limited circumstances. Interestingly, while the status of privacy as a tort in domestic law is most uncertain in Australia of all the four countries, Australian jurisdictional rules are the most expansive in allowing privacy suits to be adjudicated. There is, however, no evidence of any phenomenon comparable to 'libel tourism' developing in the privacy area.

In terms of choice of law, similar rules apply in all four countries, with a general trend in favour of the law of the place of the wrong. This location will be the place of seclusion in an intrusion case and the place of publication in a misuse of private information action. In the case of a foreign tort, application of local law may be justified, however, where certain issues of remedies or public policy are involved, or where the action has little connection with the place of the wrong. Lastly, the recognition and enforcement of foreign judgments rules, while containing restrictive rules on international jurisdiction and non-money judgments (apart from in Canadian law), nevertheless permit generally wide circulation of privacy judgments across borders.

INDEX